Statistical
Analysis
for Business Decisions

PRENTICE-HALL INTERNATIONAL SERIES IN MANAGEMENT

Baumol	*Economic Theory and Operations Analysis, 2nd ed.*
Boot	*Mathematical Reasoning in Economics and Management Science*
Brown	*Smoothing, Forecasting and Prediction of Discrete Time Series*
Chambers	*Accounting, Evaluation and Economic Behavior*
Churchman	*Prediction and Optimal Decision: Philosophical Issues of a Science of Values*
Clarkson	*The Theory of Consumer Demand: A Critical Appraisal*
Cohen and Cyert	*Theory of the Firm: Resource Allocation in a Market Economy*
Cyert and March	*A Behavioral Theory of the Firm*
Fabrycky and Torgersen	*Operations Economy: Industrial Applications of Operations Research*
Greenlaw, Herron, and Rawdon	*Business Simulation in Industrial and University Education*
Hadley and Whitin	*Analysis of Inventory Systems*
Holt, Modigliani, Muth, and Simon	*Planning Production, Inventories, and Work Force*
Hymans	*Probability Theory with Applications to Econometrics and Decision-Making*
Ijiri	*The Foundations of Accounting Measurement: A Mathematical, Economic, and Behavioral Inquiry*
Kaufmann	*Methods and Models of Operations Research*
Lesourne	*Economic Analysis and Industrial Management*
Mantel	*Cases in Managerial Decisions*
Massé	*Optimal Investment Decisions: Rules for Action and Criteria for Choice*
McGuire	*Theories of Business Behavior*
Miller and Starr	*Executive Decisions and Operations Research*
Muth and Thompson	*Industrial Scheduling*
Nelson (editor)	*Marginal Cost Pricing in Practice*
Nicosia	*Consumer Decision Processes: Marketing and Advertising Implications*
Peters and Summers	*Statistical Analysis for Business Decisions*
Pfiffner and Sherwood	*Administrative Organization*
Simonnard	*Linear Programming*
Singer	*Antitrust Economics: Selected Legal Cases and Economic Models*

PRENTICE-HALL, INC.
PRENTICE-HALL INTERNATIONAL, INC., UNITED KINGDOM AND EIRE
PRENTICE-HALL OF CANADA, LTD., CANADA
J. H. DE BUSSY, LTD., HOLLAND AND FLEMISH-SPEAKING BELGIUM
DUNOD PRESS, FRANCE
MARUZEN COMPANY, LTD., FAR EAST
HERRERO HERMANOS, SUCS., SPAIN AND LATIN AMERICA
R. OLDENBOURG VERLAG, GERMANY
ULRICO HOEPLI EDITORE, ITALY

Statistical
Analysis
for Business Decisions

WILLIAM S. PETERS

Professor of Business Statistics
The University of New Mexico, Albuquerque

GEORGE W. SUMMERS

Professor of Management
The University of Arizona, Tucson

PRENTICE-HALL, INC., *Englewood Cliffs, New Jersey*

PRENTICE-HALL INTERNATIONAL, INC., *London*
PRENTICE-HALL OF AUSTRALIA, PTY. LTD., *Sydney*
PRENTICE-HALL OF CANADA, LTD., *Toronto*
PRENTICE-HALL OF INDIA PRIVATE LTD., *New Delhi*
PRENTICE-HALL OF JAPAN, INC., *Tokyo*

To
Helen
and
Marion

Preface

The past ten years have witnessed an unparalleled increase in the application of quantitative methods to the solution of business problems. Applications stemming from finite mathematics, operations research, econometrics, and simulation techniques have been employed in a variety of marketing, finance, accounting, and management problems. These quantitative methods have been incorporated in the curricula of collegiate schools of business in a variety of ways. The number of hours of required statistics courses frequently has been increased; course sequences in quantitative methods have been introduced; mathematical prerequisites have been raised; offerings in operations research and management sciences have become more common and more extensive.

As the quantitative approach increasingly pervades the business scene and the collegiate curriculum, a thorough grounding in probability and statistics becomes ever more necessary. This text is designed to meet the need of upper division undergraduate and graduate students whose previous background in formal mathematics or statistics is fairly limited. The basic material in the first five chapters is included to insure a reasonably homogeneous foundation on which to build a course. If detailed coverage of the basic material is included, the entire text should prove more than sufficient for a one-semester course.

The unifying theme of this book is the role of statistical evidence in the formation of inferences and in the selection of strategies in matters affecting business operations. Chapters 1 through 4 constitute an introduction to finite probability and discrete probability distributions. They permit early exposure to the problem of inference through Bayes' theorem and the concept of information odds, or likelihood. Chapters 5 and 6 are devoted to continuous probability distributions of original events and sample statistics. Traditional significance tests of single-valued null hypotheses and the Neyman-Pearson viewpoint of statistical decision tests are introduced in Chapter 7.

Chapter 8 is a pivotal chapter. It treats confidence limits in the classical sense first and then as cut-off points on a Bayesian posterior distribution of the parameter predicated on an equi-probable or weak distribution of prior probabilities. Chapter 9 parallels for binomial and Poisson parameters the methods of inference that were presented for parameters of continuous distributions in Chapters 7 and 8. Applications of Bayesian decision methods are covered in Chapters 10 and 11. Chapter 10 introduces the fundamental concepts, including the normal loss integral, and Chapter 11 concentrates on optimal sample size determination.

The final six chapters comprise an integrated approach to multivariate analysis as applied to problems of organizations. Chapters 12 and 13 concentrate on detecting associations among classified variables. Chapter 12 presents some of the more useful nonparametric techniques, and Chapter 13 discusses analysis of variance. Definition and measurement of strengths of relationships are treated from the viewpoints of regression in Chapters 14 and 15 and of correlation in Chapter 16. Analysis of variance concepts and tests are employed in all three chapters. Throughout these chapters statistical assumptions are stated in the form of parameter models, and the illustrations employed are actual simulations from the stated models. Chapter 17 presents an introduction to discriminant analysis, a technique increasingly used in classification decisions.

The book incorporates additional features we have found useful in our own teaching. Among these are: the generous use of examples in introducing important ideas and methods; the use of model populations and simulation in the approach to sampling distributions; a sequence and distinction between classical significance tests, statistical decision making and expected value methods; an emphasis on integration of analysis of variance and regression methods; and introduction of certain concepts and techniques from matrix algebra as a basis for efficient explanation and computation in the latter portions of multivariate analysis. Finally, answers to many exercises are included as a stimulus to self-study.

We are indebted to many persons, from teachers who first challenged us to tackle a subject, to students who have challenged our latest efforts. More specifically, we are indebted to Morris Hamburg, Edward L. Wallace, and Raymond E. Willis, Jr., for reviewing our original outline and some key chapters. We express gratitude, too, to Edward C. Bryant, Paul E. Green, and Michael A. Halbert for their constructive criticisms of the original manuscript. We also are indebted to Arizona State University and to the

University of Arizona for making time available, and to members of the editorial staff of Prentice-Hall for their constant encouragement and professional expertise. Lastly, we are indebted to the literary executor of the late Sir Ronald A. Fisher, F.R.S., Cambridge, to Dr. Frank Yates, F.R.S., Rothamsted, and to Messrs. Oliver and Boyd, Ltd., Edinburgh , for permission to reprint Table III from their book, "Statistical Tables for Biological, Agricultural, and Medical Research."

WILLIAM S. PETERS

GEORGE W. SUMMERS

Contents

1

INTRODUCTION TO PROBABILITY   1

2

PROBABILITY PROCESSES   23

3

PROBABILITY AND STATISTICAL INFERENCE   46

4

PROBABILITY DISTRIBUTIONS FOR DISCRETE VARIABLES   65

5

PROBABILITY DISTRIBUTIONS FOR CONTINUOUS VARIABLES   91

6

SAMPLING DISTRIBUTIONS OF MEANS AND VARIANCES 113

7

SIGNIFICANCE TESTS AND DECISION PROCEDURES 140

8

ESTIMATION AND THE PROBABILITY DISTRIBUTION OF A PARAMETER 165

12

TESTS FOR ASSOCIATION AND GOODNESS OF FIT   268

13

ANALYSIS OF VARIANCE   297

14

LINEAR REGRESSION   329

15

MULTIPLE AND CURVILINEAR REGRESSION   348

16

CORRELATION   377

17

DISCRIMINANT ANALYSIS   401

Statistical
Analysis
for Business Decisions

1

Introduction
to Probability

Before anyone can understand the use of statistics in business decision making, he must know some of the fundamentals of probability. Probability is the cornerstone on which modern statistical decision theory rests. As is often the case with basic concepts, leading authorities have disagreed about the definition of probability. Some writers prefer not to attempt a substantive definition, being content to say only that probability is a measure having certain properties and subject to certain operating rules. We will begin by giving some of the concepts or views that have been taken of probability. These may not qualify as rigorous definitions, but they will suggest how the fundamental idea has been put to use.

1-1 Probability Concepts

The mathematicians who developed probability theory were interested in games of chance. In these games, objects such as coins, dice, or decks of cards are used to generate events whose outcomes become the subject of bets. The uncertainty of the outcomes, and the gains or losses that hinge upon them, create the interest in the game. But a player wants to know what a fair bet is, so that he can risk his stake when the odds are favorable, and withhold his winnings (if the game permits) when the odds are against him. The advantage of "knowing the odds" led wealthy gamblers in the eighteenth century to turn to mathematicians for help. Could they figure the chances of winning at craps, or evaluate different systems of betting at a roulette table?

Good answers here could be worth a considerable sum to a wealthy gambler. Let us start at the beginning.

A priori probabilities. A die has six sides. If we shake and roll a well-balanced die, we feel that any one side is as likely to show face up as another. We define the probability of an *event* (such as a "one") as the ratio of the number of ways in which the event can occur to the total number of ways that the die could fall. We then speak of the probability of an event, E, as

$$P(E) = \frac{\text{number of outcomes that yield } E}{\text{total number of equally likely outcomes}}. \qquad (1\text{--}1)$$

Probabilities of this kind are termed *a priori* probabilities because before one can construct such a probability he must either know or assume that he knows some critical facts about the mechanism or process that produces the outcomes. We must know, or be willing to assume, that we are dealing with an honest (evenly balanced) die, and that the method of rolling the die is a fair one. After ruling out the possibility that the die might come to rest on an edge, we are then led to assert that there are six *equally likely outcomes* of a die-toss. The act of throwing the die is termed a *trial* or *experiment*. A priori probabilities are then restricted to events that can be produced by experiments having equally likely outcomes.

If we are convinced that we are dealing with an experiment with equally likely outcomes, we can construct the probability of an event simply by enumerating or counting the relevant equally likely outcomes. If we desire the probability of the event snake-eyes (two "ones") on a throw of two dice, the equally likely outcomes can be enumerated as in Table 1–1.

Table 1-1

SUMS OF SPOTS FOR THIRTY-SIX EQUALLY LIKELY OUTCOMES
OF A THROW OF TWO DICE

		Die A					
		1	2	3	4	5	6
	1	2	3	4	5	6	7
	2	3	4	5	6	7	8
Die B	3	4	5	6	7	8	9
	4	5	6	7	8	9	10
	5	6	7	8	9	10	11
	6	7	8	9	10	11	12

Each cell in the table stands for a possible outcome of the experiment "throwing two dice." We started with six equally likely outcomes of a single

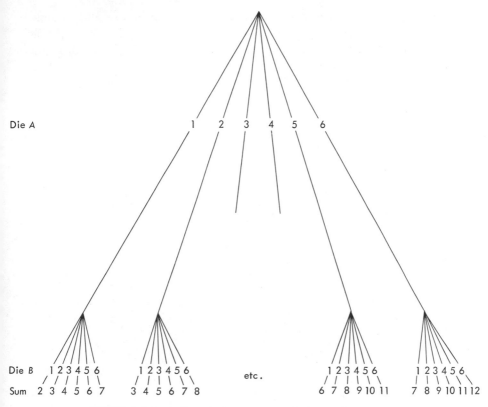

FIGURE 1-1 Tree diagram for outcomes of a toss of two dice

throw. For each of these there are six equally likely outcomes of a second throw, thus making 36 equally likely outcomes of two throws. Only one of these is snake-eyes, so the probability of snake-eyes is 1/36. Similarly, six out of the 36 equally likely outcomes are "sevens," so the probability of a seven is 6/36.

Another useful method of portraying or visualizing equally likely ways is the "tree" diagram. This is shown for the outcomes of two dice in Fig. 1–1. Die A may fall in any one of six equally likely ways, and for each of these die B has six equally likely outcomes. The resulting $6 \times 6 = 36$ equally likely outcomes of throwing two dice together are identified by the thirty-six different routes through the tree diagram.

The probabilities of different sums of the numbers occurring on two die faces can be summarized either from the table of equally likely outcomes or the tree diagram and put in the form of Table 1–2. In this table, the events that can occur are listed in the left-hand column. The list is *exhaustive* in that no event other than those listed can occur. The list is *mutually exclusive* in that no two listed events can occur at the same time. The association of such a list of events with their probabilities is a probability function, often simply called a *probability distribution*. Any rule that associates the possible events with their probabilities is a probability distribution. The rule may be stated as a table, a graph, or a mathematical formula. We will be concerned later with some general forms of probability distributions that occur again and again in statistical work. These will be stated mathematically.

Table 1-2

PROBABILITY DISTRIBUTION OF THE SUM
OF SPOTS UPON THROWING TWO DICE

Sum E	Equally likely ways of producing sum	Probability of sum $P(E)$
2	1	1/36
3	2	2/36
4	3	3/36
5	4	4/36
6	5	5/36
7	6	6/36
8	5	5/36
9	4	4/36
10	3	3/36
11	2	2/36
12	1	1/36
Total	36	36/36

Let us extend our study of a priori dice probabilities to the sums of spots on a toss of three dice. How can we count the number of equally likely ways of producing various sums? Thinking of the three dice as A, B, and C, we can imagine a box with $6 \times 6 \times 6 = 216$ cells. We could think of writing in each cell the sum of the numbers corresponding to its A, B, and C dimension. Then we could count up the number of cells having in them the sum 3, sum 4, and so on to sum 18. Most people find this hard to visualize in detail. We might construct a tree diagram with 216 final branches, but this would be a cumbersome affair.

In Table 1–3 we extend our study of the outcomes of two dice to the case of a toss of three dice.

In the body of the table are the numbers of equally likely ways of producing different sums for the first two dice *and* a particular outcome on the third die. For example, there are four ways of producing the sum 5 on the first two dice and a 1 on the third die. This yields a sum of 6 on the three dice. But the sum of 6 could also be produced by a sum of 4 together with a 2, a sum of 3 along with a 3, and sum of 2 along with a 4. These can occur in three, two, and one way, respectively. The sum 6 on a throw of three dice can then occur in $4 + 3 + 2 + 1 = 10$ equally likely ways from among the total of 216 equally likely outcomes. The event "sum of six" has a probability of 10/216.

Table 1-3

DISTRIBUTION OF 216 EQUALLY LIKELY
OUTCOMES OF A THROW OF THREE DICE

Dice A and B		Outcome of Die C						Total
Sum	Ways	1	2	3	4	5	6	outcomes
2	1	1	1	1	1	1	1	6
3	2	2	2	2	2	2	2	12
4	3	3	3	3	3	3	3	18
5	4	4	4	4	4	4	4	24
6	5	5	5	5	5	5	5	30
7	6	6	6	6	6	6	6	36
8	5	5	5	5	5	5	5	30
9	4	4	4	4	4	4	4	24
10	3	3	3	3	3	3	3	18
11	2	2	2	2	2	2	2	12
12	1	1	1	1	1	1	1	6
Total outcomes		36	36	36	36	36	36	216

We could extend the dice-throwing example to trials of four and five throws by this same method. It would illustrate that counting the numbers of equally likely outcomes to obtain probabilities of events quickly becomes quite tedious. Luckily, there are some formulas that can be used in place of these direct-enumeration methods. Still, one can use the tabular array and the tree diagram as aids in grasping the underlying structure of many probability problems.

Probability and relative frequency. I hold in my hand 50 pennies. I have examined them and found that 15 are dated prior to 1950. Blindfolded, you select a penny. The probability that it will have a date prior to 1950 is $15/50 = .30$. Note that this formulation of probability is based on complete a priori knowledge of this particular set of pennies. It seems to be simply the proportion of pennies in the collection having the characteristic we are interested in. If you continue to select pennies from the collection, the proportion with dates earlier than 1950 would be expected to approximate .30 more and more closely. In fact, you might object, if 50 pennies are selected, will not the relative frequency of pre-1950 pennies be exactly $15/50 = .30$? This depends on whether you keep each penny after being told of its date, or put it back in my hand before selecting again. In the first case you are sampling without replacement, and the relative frequency of pre-1950 pennies will be exactly .30 after you have selected 50 pennies. In the second case you are sampling with replacement, and you could make 100, 150, 200, or any number of selections. As the number of trials is increased, the relative frequency of pre-1950 pennies could be expected only to approximate .30 more and more closely. The probability of an event can be defined as the *expectation of the relative frequency* of the event. Where the number of trials can be increased without limit, the probability of an event can only be *approximated* by experience.

The idea of a priori probabilities is entirely consistent with the relative-frequency definition of probability. Although the probability of a "one" on a throw of an evenly balanced die is obtained a priori, we really do expect that with an honest die the proportion of "ones" thrown will approximate 1/6 more closely as the die is continually thrown. If we had a die of such uncertain balance that we were unwilling to entertain any a priori notions, we would estimate the probability of a "one" on that die by making some tosses and recording the proportion of "ones." How close we might be to the long-run relative frequency of a "one" for that die with any given amount of experience is a question we will tackle later. But we would surely feel that the more trials we made, the closer our estimate would be.

Subjective prior probabilities. In the forming of a priori probabilities, we found that we either had to know or be willing to assume complete knowledge about the process or mechanism that is to generate the relevant events. If they know, or are willing to assume, that a die is evenly balanced and will be tossed fairly, rational men will agree that the probability of a "one" is one-sixth. The probability "one-sixth" may be viewed either as the relative frequency of "ones" as the die is repeatedly tossed, or as the *degree of belief* in the proposition that the first toss will result in a "one." In either case, the probability established prior to experience could be termed logical; there are objective reasons for the degree of belief assigned.

Most processes that concern business decision-makers are much more complicated than coin tossing and dice throwing. Yet these decision-makers make statements about their degree of belief in propositions such as "this new venture will succeed" or "the price of this common stock will rise." They then act on the basis of these beliefs. Their understanding of the processes leading to success or failure of the venture, or a rise or fall of the stock price, may be quite imperfect. And the process may never behave in the same way again. Knowledge is incomplete, and well-informed men may disagree on what degree of belief should be attached to a particular proposition. A statement of degree of belief in an event based on personal considerations is termed a *subjective prior probability*.

Probability as degree of belief. The concept of probability that encompasses all the viewpoints already introduced is probability as a measure of belief. The several viewpoints represent different reasons for an assessment of degree of belief. One may assess degree of belief from an a priori understanding of the nature of a process producing an event, on the basis of objective empirical evidence of the relative frequency of occurrence of similar events, or he may employ prior subjective considerations. If this generalization tends to blur the distinctions previously made, it only reflects the truth that one's degree of belief in any complicated proposition at any point in time is likely to be based on a mixture of objective and subjective considerations. *The major task of statistics is to provide a method for the use of objective evidence in the formation or modification of belief.*

Probability and odds. Many persons are more familiar with the language of odds than of probability. Odds are a statement of the chances *for* an event related to the chances *against* the event. The odds for rolling a seven on a throw of two dice are 6 to 30 or 1 to 5. Of the 36 equally likely outcomes, 6 will produce a "seven" and 30 will not. Probability represents the chances *for* the event related to the *total* chances. Odds of 1 to 5 are the same as the probability 1/6. In the game of "craps" the roller wins if he rolls a seven or eleven on the first roll, and loses if he rolls two, three, or twelve. Any other number rolled is called "point," and the roller wins if he can re-roll "point" before he rolls a seven. What are the odds of winning the game if four is "point"? The odds at this stage are the chances of rolling a four against the chances of rolling a seven, or 3 to 6. The probability of winning the game, given that four is "point," is $3/(6 + 3) = 3/9$.

EXERCISES

1.1 A manufacturer operating under a list-price and trade-discount system sells to three distributors. Because of differences in services performed, A gets a discount of 30 per cent off list, B gets 35 per cent, and C gets 40 per cent. Each distributor in turn sells through three exclusive outlets which receive 10, 15, and 20 per cent off list. Assume that the business is equally divided among the distributors and among the three outlets dealing with each distributor.

(a) Draw up a table of equally likely net margins paid to distributors.

(b) Show the same information in the form of a tree diagram.

(c) Construct the probability distribution of net margins paid to distributors.

1.2 A game is played by tossing a fair coin and then cutting a card from a well-shuffled standard bridge deck. A zero is scored for tails and 1 for heads. Clubs count 1, diamonds 2, hearts 3, and spades 4.

(a) Draw up a table showing the equally likely total scores for the game.

(b) Construct the probability distribution of the total score.

1.3   Suppose the game in Exercise 1.2 has a third element, the throwing of a fair die, which is scored 1 for a "one," 2 for a "two," etc., to 6 for a "six."

(a) Draw up a table like Table 1–3 showing the 48 equally likely outcomes of the game.

(b) Construct the probability distribution of the total score.

1.4   In the game in Exercise 1.3, what are the odds against getting a score of 8? What are the odds for a score of 8 as against a score of 10?

Ans. 41 to 7; 7 to 3.

1-2   Probability Notation

In working with probabilities we must specify exactly what expected relative frequency we have in mind. To aid in this we resort to a certain amount of shorthand notation. Consider a population comprised of the labor force in a small town, as presented in Table 1–4.

Table 1-4

OCCUPATION AND EMPLOYMENT STATUS
OF THE LABOR FORCE, SMALLTOWN, U.S.A.

	Occupation		
	Skilled workers	Unskilled workers	
Employment status	B_1	B_2	Total
Employed (A_1)	172	228	400
Unemployed (A_2)	28	72	100
Total	200	300	500

Suppose we had the names of the 500 workers and were to make a drawing from the list to select a representative for a labor-management program. The table contains information on two kinds of events that could result from a drawing in which each of the 500 persons had an equal probability of selection. These are the employment status of the person selected and his skill level. As shorthand, use the symbol A for employment status and B for skill level, or occupational status. Attributes such as employment status and occupational status are often referred to as *characteristics*. If we are concerned with probabilities of only one characteristic, we use the term *marginal probability*. Such probabilities come from the margins of a typical table. The marginal probabilities of employment status are

$$P(A_1) = 400/500 = .80,$$
$$P(A_2) = 100/500 = .20,$$

and the marginal probabilities of occupational status are

$$P(B_1) = 200/500 = .40,$$
$$P(B_2) = 300/500 = .60.$$

Sometimes we are interested in the joint occurrence of two or more characteristics. The probability that the worker selected will be an unemployed skilled worker is $28/500 = .056$. We shall designate this by $P(A_2 B_1)$. Given a table of *joint probabilities*, we can obtain the marginal probabilities by adding across and down. The joint probability distribution and the two marginal probability distributions that can be derived from the original table are shown below:

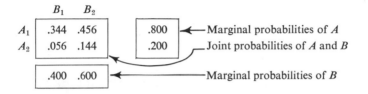

We can center our attention on a subset of the total population we are interested in and construct what are known as *conditional probabilities*. Thus we can speak of employment and unemployment among *skilled workers*. Skilled workers become a subpopulation of interest, and the probabilities refer to expected relative frequencies of employed and unemployed persons in drawing from that restricted group. The notation for this example is $P(A_2 | B_1)$. The vertical line separates the event to be predicted from the condition of restriction. The expression would read, "probability of A_2 *given* B_1." In a two-by-two table like the example here, two kinds of conditional probability tables can be drawn up.

In this case, they are:

Probabilities of $A|B$

	B_1	B_2
A_1	.86	.76
A_2	.14	.24

Probabilities of $B|A$

	B_1	B_2
A_1	.43	.57
A_2	.28	.72

These conditional probability tables simply give the decimal fraction equivalents of the percentage distribution of persons in each skill level by employment status $(A | B)$, and the percentage distribution of persons in each employment status by skill level $(B | A)$.

1-3 Rules for Combining Probabilities

The labor-force example of the previous section served only to define some terminology. We learned nothing about the labor force in Smalltown that wasn't fairly evident from the original table to begin with. Probability calculations take on greater utility when they are used to find the probabilities of complex events that represent combinations of more elemental events. This was illustrated to a degree by the probabilities we found for the results of throws of two and of three dice. We did this by directly counting the equally likely outcomes involved, and found that this could quickly become very tedious. Fortunately, there are some fundamental rules for combining probabilities that can help us here. They will be presented as theorems and illustrated.

MULTIPLICATION THEOREM. *The probability of two events is found by multiplying the probability of the first event by the conditional probability of the second event given the first.*

$$P(AB) = P(A) \cdot P(B \mid A). \tag{1-2}$$

Consider a box of cartridges containing four good cartridges and two defectives. Two cartridges are to be selected without replacement—that is, the first cartridge drawn will not be put back before we draw the second. What is the probability that two defectives will be selected? The probability of drawing a defective on the first draw is $P(D_1) = 2/6$, and the probability of drawing a defective on the second draw, given that a defective was drawn on the first draw, is $P(D_2 \mid D_1) = 1/5$. The multiplication theorem then gives the probability of drawing a defective on both the first and the second draw as

$$P(D_1 D_2) = P(D_1) \cdot P(D_2 \mid D_1) = 2/6 \cdot 1/5 = 2/30.$$

When we sample without replacement from the box of cartridges, the probability of drawing a defective cartridge on the second draw depends on whether a defective cartridge was drawn on the first draw. If we first draw a defective, then the composition of the box when we make the second draw will be one defective and four good cartridges; if we first draw a good cartridge, two defective and three good cartridges will remain. This dependence can be shown in a tree diagram for the two draws, along with the resulting joint probabilities.

First draw	Second draw	First and second jointly

The joint probability table, together with the marginal probabilities, would appear as follows:

| First draw | Second draw | | Marginal |
	D_2	G_2	(first draw)
D_1	2/30	8/30	10/30
G_1	8/30	12/30	20/30
Marginal (second draw)	10/30	20/30	30/30

If we sampled *with* replacement, the joint probability table would have the following values.

| First draw | Second draw | | Marginal |
	D_2	G_2	(first draw)
D_1	4/36	8/36	12/36
G_1	8/36	16/36	24/36
Marginal (second draw)	12/36	24/36	36/36

The composition of the box will be the same at the time of the second draw as when the first draw was made. In conditional terminology $P(D_2|D_1)$ = 2/6, and $P(D_2|G_1) = 2/6$ as well. These conditional probabilities are equal to the marginal probability of drawing a defective on either draw, shown as 12/36 in the table. Symbolically:

$$P(D_2 \mid D_1) = P(D_2 \mid G_1) = P(D_1) = P(D_2).$$

Because the conditional probabilities are equal to the marginal probabilities in the sampling-with-replacement case, we can restate $P(D_1 D_2)$ as

$$P(D_1 D_2) = P(D_1) \cdot P(D_2).$$

In sampling with replacement we have arranged the selection so that the probability of drawing a defective on the second draw does not depend on, or *is independent of*, the result of the first draw. In short, D_1 and D_2 are *independent events*. We have seen an example of an important special case of the multiplication theorem, namely:

MULTIPLICATION THEOREM FOR INDEPENDENT EVENTS: *Where A and B are independent events, their joint probability is the product of their separate marginal probabilities.*

$$P(AB) = P(A) \cdot P(B). \tag{1-3}$$

Two events are independent if the probability of the one event does not depend on whether or not the other event occurred. When this is the case, $P(B|A) = P(B)$. The marginal probability of B, $P(B)$, is also called the unconditional probability of B—the probability of B without regard to whether A occurred. For example, in sampling the cartridge box *without replacement*, the marginal probability of a defective on the second draw is 2/6. This probability is the answer to the question, "What is the probability of drawing a defective on the second draw?" asked *before we have any knowledge* about the result of the first draw. This is not equal to $P(D_2 \mid D_1) = 1/5$ or $P(D_2 \mid G_1) = 2/5$. The draws are not independent events. However, in sampling with replacement $P(D_2) = P(D_2 \mid G_1) = P(D_2 \mid D_1) = 2/6$, and the draws are independent events.

In the cartridge-sampling example we were concerned with whether the probability of an event, B, was independent of another event, A. Event B was the occurrence of a defective on the second draw, and event A the occurrence of a defective on the first draw. In other contexts, event B may stand for a particular observation on one draw, and event A for another observation on the same draw. Recall the example on skill level and employment status of workers in Smalltown.

Event B would be the observation of a worker's skill level and event A would be the observation of his employment status. We can ask whether unemployment is *independent* of skill level. If the probability of unemployment among skilled workers is different from the probability of unemployment among unskilled workers, then unemployment is said to *depend on* (be *not* independent of) occupation. This is called functional dependence. A check of the conditional probabilities in this example reveals that unemployment is functionally dependent on worker skill.

$$P(A_2 \mid B_1) = 28/200 = .14,$$
$$P(A_2 \mid B_2) = 72/300 = .24.$$

The probability that an unskilled worker will be found to be unemployed is larger than the probability of unemployment among the skilled workers. It follows, of course, that $P(A_2 \mid B_1)$ and $P(A_2 \mid B_2)$ are not equal to the marginal or unconditional probability of unemployment, $P(A_2) = 100/500 = .20$.

Extensions of the multiplication theorems. Our original statements of the multiplication theorems involved but two events. This was done for brevity and clarity. The multiplication theorems can be extended to three, four, or any number of events. The extensions to three events and "k" events are

three events: $P(ABC) = P(A) \cdot P(B \mid A) \cdot P(C \mid AB)$;

"k" events: $P(ABC \ldots K) = P(A) \cdot P(B \mid A) \cdot P(C \mid AB) \cdot$
$$P(D \mid ABC) \cdot \ldots \cdot P(K \mid ABC \ldots J).$$

For the special case of independent events, we would have

three events: $P(ABC) = P(A) \cdot P(B) \cdot P(C)$;

"k" events: $P(ABC \ldots K) = P(A) \cdot P(B) \cdot P(C) \cdot \ldots \cdot P(K)$.

For example, the probability of selecting four hearts in a row in sampling with replacement from a well-shuffled standard deck of cards is

$$P(H_1 H_2 H_3 H_4) = P(H_1) \cdot P(H_2) \cdot P(H_3) \cdot P(H_4)$$
$$= [P(H)]^4 = (1/4)^4 = 1/256.$$

This is not the same as the probability of drawing four hearts to fill a heart flush in a game of five-card stud poker. Why not?

Also, there are important "reversibilities." The general two-event statement of the multiplication theorem,

$$P(AB) = P(A) \cdot P(B \mid A),$$

could also be stated

$$P(BA) = P(B) \cdot P(A \mid B).$$

If B follows A in time, you may wonder what the conditional probability $P(A \mid B)$ means. How can A depend on B if A occurs before B? Suppose you were told that two cartridges were selected without replacement from a box that contained two defective and four good cartridges, and that the second cartridge selected was defective. Given this knowledge, can you state the probability that the first cartridge selected was defective? The probability asked for is the conditional probability of a prior event given knowledge of a subsequent event. If A precedes B, $P(B \mid A)$ says that since I have observed that A occurred, the probability that B will occur is such and such. By contrast, $P(A \mid B)$ says that since I observe that B occurred, my assessment of the probability that A also occurred is so and so. Consulting the "tree diagram" at the beginning of this section, we find that we would expect D_2 to occur in $2/30 + 8/30 = 10/30$ of a long run of trials. In $2/30$ of these trials, D_1 precedes D_2. Therefore the probability of D_1 conditional on having observed D_2 is $2/30 \div (2/30 + 8/30)$, or $1/5$.

The addition theorem. Where two or more events must occur to have a "success," we have found that the probability of a success can be obtained by applying the appropriate form of the multiplication theorem. When the occurrence of *either* A or B qualifies as a "success," a rule of combination involving addition applies. As with the multiplication theorem, there is a general and a special case of the addition theorem. We state first the general theorem for two events.

THE ADDITION THEOREM. *The probability of occurrence of at least one of two events is the sum of their marginal probabilities less the probability of their joint occurrence.*

$$P(A \text{ or } B) = P(A) + P(B) - P(AB). \tag{1-4}$$

To illustrate, ask for the probability of a head on one or the other toss of two fair coins. (The use of "or" here is inclusive—that is, it implies that "heads" on both coins qualifies as a success.) Using subscripts for the first and second coin, we know a priori that $P(H_1) = 1/2$ and $P(H_2) = 1/2$. The addition theorem then states that

$$P(H_1 \text{ or } H_2) = P(H_1) + P(H_2) - P(H_1 H_2).$$

If H_1 and H_2 are independent events, then we obtain $P(H_1 H_2)$ from $P(H_1) \cdot P(H_2)$, and the answer is

$$P(H_1 \text{ or } H_2) = 1/2 + 1/2 - (1/2 \cdot 1/2) = 3/4.$$

A look at the joint probability table for the results of two coin tosses makes evident the logic underlying the formula. In adding together the marginal probability of a head on the first toss and the marginal probability of a head on the second toss we have counted one of the equally likely elemental outcomes of the two tosses twice. The shaded cell, representing the outcome $(H_1 H_2)$, has been counted in both marginal probabilities, and must therefore be subtracted out as indicated in the formula.

	Second toss		
First toss	H_2	T_2	
H_1	1/4	1/4	1/2
T_1	1/4	1/4	1/2
	1/2	1/2	2/2

Note that if "or" is used exclusively, the probability of a success is $P(H_1 T_2) + P(T_1 H_2) = 1/2$.

When it is not possible for the two events, A and B, to occur together, they are termed mutually exclusive. In such a case the probability of their joint occurrence, $P(AB)$, is zero. This leads to a special case of the addition theorem for mutually exclusive events.

THE ADDITION THEOREM FOR MUTUALLY EXCLUSIVE EVENTS. *The probability of occurrence of one or the other of two mutually exclusive events is the sum of their separate probabilities.*

$$P(A \text{ or } B) = P(A) + P(B). \tag{1-5}$$

This form of the addition theorem was used implicitly when we simply "counted up" the number of equally likely outcomes of an experiment that satisfied a given event. The probability of a number divisible by 3 on a toss of one die, for instance, is $P(3 \text{ or } 6) = P(3) + P(6) = 1/6 + 1/6 = 2/6$. The outcomes "three" and "six" are mutually exclusive. If a "three" occurs on a toss of one die, a "six" cannot possibly occur as well, and vice versa.

The addition theorem for mutually exclusive events takes the place of the direct counting of equally likely outcomes that we employed earlier. For example, to find the probability of the sum "four" on a toss of two fair dice, first list the mutually exclusive ways of obtaining the sum "four," then find their separate probabilities, and finally employ the addition theorem for mutually exclusive events to get the probability of a "four." (The subscripts identify the two dice.)

$$P(1_1 3_2) = P(1) \cdot P(3) = 1/6 \cdot 1/6 = 1/36$$
$$P(2_1 2_2) = P(2) \cdot P(2) = 1/6 \cdot 1/6 = 1/36$$
$$P(3_1 1_2) = P(3) \cdot P(1) = 1/6 \cdot 1/6 = \underline{1/36}$$

$$\text{probability of the sum "four"} = 3/36$$

Using the table of outcomes for obtaining probability of a "four" by direct counting (Table 1–1) would produce the same result.

In finding the probability of a complex event it is important to visualize the separate mutually exclusive outcomes that can produce the complex event. Suppose three draws are to be made, with replacement, from a bin of parts containing 10 per cent defective parts. What is the probability that at least one of the draws will produce a defective part? The "answer" $.10 + .10 + .10 = .30$ is not correct because the outcome of a defective on a particular draw does not exclude the getting of a defective on another draw. There are, however, three mutually exclusive ways that the *total* draw can yield a defective. A defective part may be produced by the first draw, or *failing that*, it may occur on the second draw, or *not having been produced by either of the first two draws*, a defective could occur on the third draw. These mutually exclusive ways of drawing a defective part are detailed below and the final probability obtained:

$$P(D_1) = .100$$
$$P(G_1 D_2) = (.90)(.10) = .090$$
$$P(G_1 G_2 D_3) = (.90)(.90)(.10) = \underline{.081}$$

$$P(\text{draw of "three" producing at least one defective}) = .271$$

The final probability (.271) of producing at least one defective *includes* the outcomes of defectives on any two or all of the draws. To appreciate this, we can look at the total draw of three in terms of a *different set* of mutually exclusive outcomes. These outcomes are the number of defectives produced in the total draw. We can get 0, 1, 2, or 3 defectives. We know that the probabilities of an exhaustive list of mutually exclusive outcomes add to 1.0. The quickest way to get the probability of at least one defective is to figure the complement of the probability that the draw of three parts will produce no defectives. This is $1 - P(G_1G_2G_3) = 1 - (.90)^3 = .271$.

Asking for a different probability may require us to construct a different fundamental set of mutually exclusive outcomes. Find the probability that the draw of three will produce *exactly one* defective part. If we view the draw of three parts as a total event, the mutually exclusive ways of producing exactly one defective are

$$P(D_1G_2G_3) = (.10)(.90)(.90) = .081$$
$$P(G_1D_2G_3) = (.90)(.10)(.90) = .081$$
$$P(G_1G_2D_3) = (.90)(.90)(.10) = \underline{.081}$$

P(draw of "three" producing
exactly one defective) $= .243.$

Extensions of the addition theorem. In the preceding examples we have already extended the addition theorem to the case of three mutually exclusive events. For the sake of completeness, the extension for three and "k" mutually exclusive events can be stated:

three events: $P(A \text{ or } B \text{ or } C) = P(A) + P(B) + P(C);$

"k" events: $P(\text{at least one of } k) = P(A) + P(B) + P(C)$
$$+ \cdots + P(K).$$

We began to tackle (incorrectly) the problem of the probability of producing precisely one defective part in three draws by adding the probabilities of a defective on each of the separate draws—that is, $.10 + .10 + .10 = .30$. But we saw that the occurrences of defectives on the separate draws were not mutually exclusive events. We can use the approach of mutually exclusive events if we return to the general form of the addition theorem. Remember that this form called for subtracting the probability of the events occurring together from the sum of the marginal probabilities of the events.

$$P(A \text{ or } B) = P(A) + P(B) - P(AB).$$

The extension to three nonmutually exclusive events is shown in Fig. 1–2. Such diagrams are called Venn diagrams after the logician J. Venn (1834–1923), and also Euler diagrams, after the mathematician L. Euler, (1707–1783).

The region encompassed by each of the large circles represents the probability of a defective on the separate draws, or $P(D)$. The region encompassed by all three circles represents the probability of a defective on one or

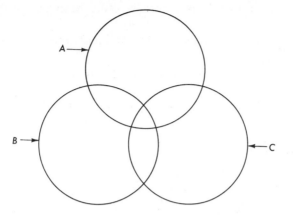

FIGURE 1-2 Venn diagram for three nonmutually exclusive events

another of the three draws, but this is obviously not equal to $P(D_1) + P(D_2)$ $+ P(D_3)$ because the regions overlap. Examine the character of the overlap. The overlap between any pair of circles represents the probability of a defective occurring on both of the indicated draws. There are three such overlapping regions, which represent $P(D_1D_2)$, $P(D_1D_3)$, and $P(D_2D_3)$. Another region in the center is contained within all three circles, and is also part of the region of overlap between each pair of circles; it represents $P(D_1D_2D_3)$. The event $D_1D_2D_3$ is not mutually exclusive with the events D_1, D_2, D_3, D_1D_2, D_1D_3, or D_2D_3. This assignment of probabilities to the regions in the diagram assists us in seeing the reasoning behind the general form of the addition theorem for three outcomes:

$$P(A \text{ or } B \text{ or } C) = P(A)+P(B)+P(C)-P(AB)-P(AC)-P(BC)+P(ABC),$$
$$P(D_1 \text{ or } D_2 \text{ or } D_3) = .10 + .10 + .10 - .01 - .01 - .01 + .001$$
$$= .300 - .029 = .271.$$

This is the same answer that we obtained previously. The reason that $P(ABC)$ must be added in at the end is that $P(AB \text{ or } AC \text{ or } BC) = P(AB) + P(AC)$ $+ P(BC) - P(ABC)$. The probability of at least two defectives is the sum of the probabilities of the several ways of getting two defectives less the probability that these events occur together. The term $P(AB \text{ or } AC \text{ or } BC)$ *is* the probability that the events A or B or C occur together—that is, the probability that at least a pair of the elemental events occur together.

EXERCISES

1.5 Arrivals of ore ships in a certain British port are known to be random with the following probabilities of various numbers of arrivals during the course of a week: No arrivals—.10; one arrival—.20; two arrivals —.30.

(a) What is the probability of more than two arrivals during a week?
Ans. .40.

(b) What is the probability of exactly one arrival in each of three successive weeks? *Ans.* .008.

(c) What is the probability of exactly two arrivals during a period of two weeks? *Ans.* .10.

(d) What is the probability that at least one ship will arrive during a period of three weeks? *Ans.* .999.

1.6 Two cards in succession are to be drawn from an ordinary playing deck, with the first card being replaced and the deck shuffled before the second card is drawn.

(a) What is the probability of drawing either the ace of spades or the queen of hearts on the first draw? *Ans.* 2/52.

(b) What is the probability of drawing first the ace of spades and then the queen of hearts? *Ans.* 1/2704.

(c) What is the probability that the ace of spades and the queen of hearts will be the two cards drawn? *Ans.* 2/2704.

(d) What is the probability that neither the ace of spades nor the queen of hearts will appear? *Ans.* 2500/2704.

(e) What is the probability that at least one of the cards drawn will be either the ace of spades or the queen of hearts? *Ans.* 204/2704.

1.7 A consumer in a blindfold taste panel, when presented with two brands of cheese in random order, is able to make four correct identifications in four tries.

(a) What is the probability of accomplishing this if the consumer really has no ability to discriminate (is merely guessing)?

(b) What is the probability of failing to make all four identifications correctly if the consumer's probability of discriminating correctly on any given choice is .90?

1.8 A group of six men and four women draw lots for three prizes by placing their names on slips of paper and having three names drawn at random from the collection of slips. The drawing is without replacement.

(a) Draw a tree diagram showing the probabilities of the prize going to a man and to a woman on the first draw, the conditional probabilities of the outcome of the second draw given the first draw, the conditional probabilities of the third draw given the first and second, and the joint probabilities of the outcomes of all three draws.

(b) What is the probability that no prize is won by a man? One prize? Two prizes? Three prizes? *Ans.* 24/720; 216/720; 360/720; 120/720.

1.9 Do Exercise 1.8 under the condition that each name is replaced before the next draw.

1-4 Permutations and Combinations

When equally likely individual outcomes are present, formulas for permutations and combinations are an aid in calculating the probabilities of complex events that are defined in terms of the individual outcomes. Consider a group of six clubwomen, A, B, C, D, E, and F. If three women are randomly selected to play bridge with a visiting speaker, what is the probability that B will be among them? We could calculate this from the multiplication theorem by finding the complement of the probability that B would remain unselected after three draws.

$$P(B \text{ included}) = 1 - (5/6)(4/5)(3/4) = 60/120 = 1/2.$$

We can also find the total number of trios that could be formed from among the six women, and then find the number of these that would include B. The number of trios that include B related to the total number of trios that could be formed gives the probability that B would be a member of the trio selected. These are examples of combinations. A combination is a set of n elements. The number of different combinations of n elements that can be formed from K elements is given by

$$_K C_n = \frac{K!}{(K-n)! n!}. \tag{1-6}$$

The factorial (!) in the expression means the product of the integer indicated and all other smaller positive integers; $K! = K(K-1)(K-2) \ldots (K - K + 1)$. The values $0!$ and $1!$ can occur in expressions for combinations and are both equal to unity or 1. In our example, $K = 6$ clubwomen and $n = 3$ to be selected.

$$_6 C_3 = \frac{6!}{(6-3)!(3!)} = \frac{6 \cdot 5 \cdot 4 \cdot 3 \cdot 2 \cdot 1}{(3 \cdot 2 \cdot 1)(3 \cdot 2 \cdot 1)} = 20.$$

There are twenty groups of three that could be selected. To find how many of these would include B, find how many pairs may join with B to form a group of three. Such pairs must be selected from among the five other women, so we want the number of combinations of 5 things 2 at a time.

$$_5 C_2 = \frac{5!}{(5-2)!(2)!} = \frac{5 \cdot 4 \cdot 3 \cdot 2 \cdot 1}{(3 \cdot 2 \cdot 1)(2 \cdot 1)} = 10.$$

The probability that B will be a member of the trio selected is then $10/20 = 1/2$.

While a combination refers to a set of n elements, a *permutation* refers to an *ordered* set of n elements. In the example of the clubwomen we might ask in how many distinct orders or sequences can three persons be drawn from among the six. The answer is the number of permutations of six things taken three at a time. The general permutation formula is

$$_KP_n = \frac{K!}{(K-n)!}.$$
                                                                                    (1–7)

In our example,

$$_6P_3 = \frac{6!}{(6-3)!} = \frac{6\cdot5\cdot4\cdot3\cdot2\cdot1}{3\cdot2\cdot1} = 120.$$

Any one of the six ladies may be the first selected, and any of the five remaining may be selected second, and any of the four then remaining may be selected third. If we then ask how many of these 120 ordered sets of three ladies include B, the following reasoning applies. There are three positions to be filled. Clubwoman B may fill any one of these—a total of $_3P_1 = 3$ ways. Given any one of these ways, the remaining five ladies may fill the two remaining positions in $_5P_2 = 20$ ways. Therefore, the number of ways that B may be included is

$$_3P_1 \cdot {_5P_2} = 60$$

Then the probability of B's being included if three ladies are randomly chosen from the six is $60/120 = 1/2$ as before.

We emphasized above that permutations are concerned with the possible orders of elements selected while combinations are not. To highlight the difference, consider a traveling basketball squad that has nine players. The coach must select a starting team for tonight's game. How many different teams can he field? As the question stands, it is ambiguous. If we want to know how many different sets of five players can be designated to start the game, the answer is the number of *combinations* of nine things taken five at a time:

$$_9C_5 = \frac{9!}{(9-5)!5!} = \frac{9\cdot8\cdot7\cdot6}{4\cdot3\cdot2\cdot1} = 126 \text{ combinations.}$$

However, if in selecting a team the coach must also designate positions (assignment, or order) on the team, then we are concerned with the number of *permutations* of nine things taken five at a time:

$$_9P_5 = \frac{9!}{(9-5)!} = 9\cdot8\cdot7\cdot6\cdot5 = 15{,}120 \text{ permutations.}$$

Note the connection between the two, however. Having picked a given set of five players to start the game, we might ask how many ways the coach could assign them to the five positions. The answer is $_5P_5 = 5\cdot4\cdot3\cdot2\cdot1 = 120$. Thus, there are 126 teams, or sets of starters, and 120 ways of assigning each team to positions, and

15,120 assignments = (126 teams) × (120 assignments per team).

The equivalent general expression is

$$_KP_n = {}_KC_n \times {}_nP_n,$$ (1–8)

$$\frac{K}{(K-n)!} = \frac{K!}{(K-n)!n!} \times \frac{n!}{(n-n)!}.$$

The coach's job seems complicated indeed in view of the number of alternatives he must weigh. It is unlikely, though, that all his players are realistic choices for all positions. Suppose he classifies his squad as two centers, four forwards, and three guards. How many different sets of starters, comprised of one center, two forwards, and two guards, are there?

$$_2C_1 \cdot {}_4C_2 \cdot {}_3C_2 = \frac{2\cdot1}{1\cdot1} \cdot \frac{4\cdot3\cdot2\cdot1}{2\cdot1\cdot2\cdot1} \cdot \frac{3\cdot2\cdot1}{1\cdot2\cdot1},$$

number of sets of starters = 2 × 6 × 3 = 36.

How many different assignments are there?

$$_2P_1 \cdot {}_4P_2 \cdot {}_3P_2 = \frac{2\cdot1}{1} \cdot \frac{4\cdot3\cdot2\cdot1}{2\cdot1} \frac{3\cdot2\cdot1}{1},$$

number of assignments = 2 × 12 × 6 = 144.

The relationship here is easy to see. The center selected can be assigned to only one position, but the two forwards selected can be assigned in two ways, and the two guards selected can each be assigned to one or the other guard position.

EXERCISES

1.10 Six offices are to be assigned to six executives—one president, two vice presidents, and three division heads.
   (a) If we distinguish among individuals, in how many ways can the six executives occupy the six offices. *Ans.* 720
   (b) The president's office is predetermined. If we distinguish between vice presidents, in how many ways can they occupy the remaining five offices? *Ans.* 20
   (c) What is the answer in part (b) if we do not distinguish between vice presidents? *Ans.* 10
   (d) If there is but one presidential office, two vice presidential offices, and three offices for division heads, how many possible assignments of the six men are there? *Ans.* 12.

1.11 A drawer contains four black, six brown, and two blue socks.
    (a) If Mr. McGoo selects two socks from the drawer at random (without replacement), what is the probability that they match?
                                                                       Ans. 1/3.
    (b) If McGoo selects three socks, what is the probability that they are all of a different color?   *Ans.* 12/55.
    (c) Check your answer to (b) by finding the number of combinations of three socks that can be selected, and then the number of these that contain at least a matching pair.

1.12 Four jobs of one kind may be filled by men only, and five jobs of another kind may be filled by either men or women.
    (a) If seven men and two women are available, in how many ways can the jobs be filled?
    (b) If seven men and four women are available, in how many ways can the jobs be filled?

REFERENCES

Goldberg, S., *Probability: An Introduction*. Englewood Cliffs, N.J.: Prentice-Hall, Inc., 1960.

Mosteller, F., R. E. K. Rourke, and G. B. Thomas, Jr., *Probability and Statistics*. Reading, Mass., and London, England: Addison-Wesley Publishing Co., Inc., 1961.

2

Probability
Processes

In Chapter 1 we saw how probabilities of complex events could be found by applying the multiplication and addition theorems or the formulas for permutations and combinations. The reason for acquiring some facility with these calculations was not to enable us to figure dice and coin-tossing probabilities, though these do serve well as introductory examples. Some of the other examples we have used involved sampling situations, and notice is called to features common to both. In each, we know the probability of an elemental event, and the theorems or formulas are employed to find the probability of a complex event made up of a specified combination of elemental events. One such complex event is that of winning at dice by rolling a "ten" and then rerolling "ten" before rolling a seven; another is that of drawing no more than one defective in twenty draws with replacement from a lot in which 15 per cent of the parts are defective. In the first instance the elemental events are the occurrence of each face on a single roll of one die, and in the second they are the occurrence of a defective and the occurrence of a good part on a single draw from the lot. These examples are no different in principle from the shorter sampling examples already introduced.

The reason for interest in the probability of a given complex sample outcome is that decisions in practical matters often must be based on sample information. An inspection scheme could call for no further inspection of a production lot if a sample of twenty yielded one or fewer defectives. The probability of a 15 per cent defective lot producing one or fewer defectives would then represent the chance of failing to submit a 15 per cent defective lot to further inspection. Knowing this probability would tell us how well or badly the decision system operates in screening out 15 per cent defective lots.

In this chapter we study sampling from discrete probability distributions. Formulas for figuring the probabilities of sample outcomes are presented, and some important features of probability distributions of sample outcomes are introduced.

2-1   Finite and Infinite Populations

A *statistical population* refers to the total collection of observations that can possibly comprise a sample, given the purpose of an investigation. A statistical population may be finite or it may be infinite. Suppose we were to sample a collection of 100 components to gain some knowledge about the proportion of the 100 components that are defective. We might sample the components with or without replacement. The components could be numbered from 00 to 99, and 100 corresponding pieces of paper put in a bowl. Selection of a sample of components for testing could then be made by selecting slips of paper from the bowl.* Selection could be *without replacement*, meaning that a number selected from the bowl would not be replaced before another number was selected. A "sample" of 100 observations then would comprise the statistical population. If sampling were *with replacement*, any number selected would be replaced before we drew again—in which case it would be possible to draw a sample of any size. Sampling a finite set of objects *with replacement* artificially creates an infinite statistical population. The principles that we will develop for this sampling situation apply, therefore, to sampling from any infinite statistical population.

Suppose the 100 components are the first 100 turned out by a new production process. Our interest might well lie in gaining some knowledge about the proportion of defective components that would be turned out by the new process if it were allowed to continue to operate under current conditions. The statistical population, or collection of observations relevant to this purpose is infinite—the long run output of the existing process. Whether we sampled the 100 components with or without replacement would not alter this fact.

---

* One should be careful to mix the slips of paper thoroughly before each draw. Unfortunately, there is no way of knowing what "thoroughly mixing" means in this context. We want to be assured that each element in the population that is present (in the bowl) on any draw really has an equal chance of selection. Use of a random number table (see Chapter 5) more truly "guarantees" this than any physical process for mixing a counterpart of the objects to be sampled; therefore, it is the preferred method. However, mixing papers or chips in a bowl will serve us temporarily as an operational definition of equal probability of selection.

2-2 Binary and Multifold Populations

Consider a finite population made up of two classes of observations, A of which are of one type and B of which are of another type. The types usually signify a qualitative distinction, such as normal and improperly functioning components, male and female students, or buyers and nonbuyers of a product. We term such a population a binary (meaning twofold) population. If there are more than two classes of observations, we use the term multifold (meaning many-class) population. The defining characteristic of binary or multifold populations could be quantitative as well as qualitative. Families classified by number of children $(0, 1, 2, 3, 4, 5$ or more) or machines classified by number of breakdowns in a day $(0, 1, 2, 3, 4$ or more) are multifold populations. So also are families classed by annual income categories, firms classed by categories of earnings per dollar of invested capital, and so on.

In short, the categorization of any characteristic into two classes creates a binary population, and division into more than two classes creates a multifold population. The binary population case will be treated first; then we will generalize to the multifold population. In each instance we want to find a method of counting the number of equally likely ways in which a sample may be drawn and the number of equally likely ways of producing a specified sample outcome so that we can construct directly

P (given sample outcome)

$$= \frac{\text{number of equally likely ways of producing outcome}}{\text{number of equally likely ways of drawing sample}}.$$

A brief example. A set of objects consists of five members, four of one class and one of another class. What is the probability that a sample of three will produce two members of the first class and one of the second if sampling is conducted (1) without replacement; (2) with replacement? We will use the following symbols:

A = number of members of first class in population ($A = 4$ above),
B = number of members of second class in population ($B = 1$ above),
K = number of members in population ($K = 5$ above),
n = sample size ($n = 3$ above),
a = number out of A in sample outcome ($a = 2$ above),
b = number out of B in sample outcome ($b = 1$ above).

The population and the sample can be visualized in the accompanying diagram. First we want to know in how many ways the K population members can be drawn into the n sample positions or spaces. Your experience with tree diagrams should permit you to verify that if sampling is with replacement there are $5 \times 5 \times 5$ different ways of drawing the five popula-

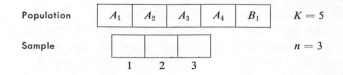

tion members into the three numbered sample positions. Any one of the five members can be drawn into the first sample position, and for each of these any one of the five may then be drawn into the second position, and for each of the resulting 25 first and second positions jointly, any of the five may be drawn into the third position. In sampling with replacement there will be K^n distinct ways of drawing the sample.

In sampling without replacement, similar reasoning will lead you to $5 \times 4 \times 3$ distinct ways of drawing the sample in this illustration. Any one of the five elements may be drawn first, but only four possibilities exist for the second draw, and three for the third. This corresponds with the number of possible *permutations* (or orders) of K things taken n at a time, which we introduced in Chapter 1.

$$_K P_n = \frac{K!}{(K-n)!}.$$

In our brief sampling example, the number of distinct ways of drawing the sample without replacement can be figured from

$$_K P_n = {}_5 P_3 = \frac{5!}{(5-3)!} = \frac{5 \cdot 4 \cdot 3 \cdot 2 \cdot 1}{2 \cdot 1} = 60.$$

With replacement the number of distinct and equally likely ways was

$$K^n = (5)^3 = 125.$$

Next, we have to determine how many of these different but equally likely ways of drawing the sample will produce the outcome that concerns us: $a = 2$, and $b = 1$. The diagram below helps us to visualize this.

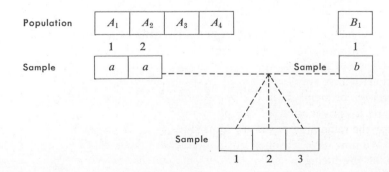

We must determine (1) in how many ways the subscripted A members can be drawn into the a ordered positions in the sample; (2) in how many ways the subscripted B members can be drawn into the b ordered positions in the sample. These questions parallel for the groups exactly what we have already done in figuring the number of ways of drawing the total sample. In our example the results are

without replacement:

$$_AP_a = \frac{A!}{(A-a)!} = \frac{4!}{(4-2)!} = \frac{4\cdot3\cdot2\cdot1}{2\cdot1} = 12,$$

$$_BP_b = \frac{B!}{(B-b)!} = \frac{1!}{(1-1)!} = \frac{1!}{0!} = \frac{1}{1} = 1;$$

with replacement:

$$A^a = 4^2 = 16,$$

$$B^b = 1^1 = 1.$$

The number of ways of ordering a out of A members *and* b out of B members will be the product $_AP_a \cdot {_BP_b}$ without replacement and $A^a \cdot B^b$ for sampling with replacement. We must account for the fact that for *each* way of ordering a of A, there can be a number of ways of ordering b of B elements.

Finally, given that a out of A members are ordered in a given manner, in how many ways can they be drawn into the n sample positions? That is, in how many ways can a members be drawn, collectively, into the three sample positions? The answer here is intuitively evident: they may occupy positions 1 and 2 in the sample sequence, positions 1 and 3, or positions 2 and 3. The number of orders in which a out of A may be drawn has already been taken into account. We are not concerned with order now, but only in how many ways a members, *however ordered*, can fit into n positions. This corresponds to the number of combinations of n things a at a time.

$$_nC_a = \frac{n!}{(n-a)!a!},$$

$$_3C_2 = \frac{3!}{(3-2)!2!} = \frac{3\cdot2\cdot1}{1\cdot2\cdot1} = 3.$$

It is not necessary to consider separately the combinations of sample positions which may be occupied by b out of B members. There are only two classes of members in the population; since we have assigned a of one class to a combination of sample positions, b of the second class must occupy the remaining positions. Note that $_nC_a = {_nC_b}$ when $a + b = n$.

We now have reasoned out how to count the number of equally likely ways of producing a given sample outcome in sampling from a binary population. Substituting the more general term, *elements*, for members, our method of counting is:

(number of ways of combining a out of n positions)
$\times$ (number of ways of ordering a out of A elements)
$\times$ (number of ways of ordering b out of B elements).

In sampling without replacement this becomes

$$_nC_a \cdot {_A}P_a \cdot {_B}P_b,$$

and in sampling with replacement we will have

$$_nC_a \cdot A^a \cdot B^b.$$

Then, the probability of drawing a out of A elements and b out of B elements in a sample of n out of K elements becomes

without replacement:

$$P(a \text{ of } A \text{ and } b \text{ of } B) = \frac{_nC_a \cdot {_A}P_a \cdot {_B}P_b}{_KP_n}; \qquad (2\text{--}1)$$

with replacement:

$$P(a \text{ of } A \text{ and } b \text{ of } B) = \frac{_nC_a \cdot A^a \cdot B^b}{K^n}. \qquad (2\text{--}2)$$

Equation (2–1) is termed the hypergeometric formula. Another formula commonly employed to give the same result is

$$P(a \text{ of } A \text{ and } b \text{ of } B) = \frac{_AC_a \cdot {_B}C_b}{_KC_n}.$$

Equation (2–2) is the formula for the binomial distribution, which we take up in more detail in Chapter 4.

Extension to sampling from multifold population. When three kinds of population elements are present (the symbols A, B, and C denoting the number of each), we will want to know the number of different ways that a of A, b of B, and c of C can be drawn. For each way of ordering a of A elements there will be a number of distinct ways of ordering b of B elements, and for each way of jointly ordering the foregoing there will be a number of ways of ordering c of C. The number of ways of jointly ordering all three will be the product of the several individual order counts. There will be $_nC_a$ different sets of sample positions that can be occupied by a elements. Then given any one of these combinations, b elements can occupy the $(n - a)$ remaining sample positions in $_{(n-a)}C_b$ ways. Once a of A and b of B are assigned to positions in the sample sequence, the positions occupied by c of C elements would be determined. This reasoning leads to the following extensions for the probability of a given sample outcome in sampling from finite sets of objects.

without replacement:

$$P(a \text{ of } A, b \text{ of } B, \text{ and } c \text{ of } C) = \frac{{}_nC_a \cdot {}_{(n-a)}C_b \cdot {}_AP_a \cdot {}_BP_b \cdot {}_CP_c}{{}_KP_n}$$

$$= \frac{{}_AC_a \cdot {}_BC_b \cdot {}_CC_c}{{}_KC_n} ;$$

(2–3)

with replacement:

$$P(a \text{ of } A, b \text{ of } B, \text{ and } c \text{ of } C) = \frac{{}_nC_a \cdot {}_{(n-a)}C_b \cdot A^a \cdot B^b \cdot C^c}{K^n}.$$

(2–4)

With this extension to a set of objects involving three kinds of elements, further extension to four, five, or any number of categories can be made by expanding the formulas according to the pattern already begun. The probability distributions obtained from the "without replacement" formula are called hypergeometric distributions; those obtained from the "with replacement" formula are called multinomial distributions.

EXERCISES

2.1 A merchant has obtained five motor scooters and three tape recorders to be available as prizes in a contest. There are three winners who agree to a drawing for their prizes. Five slips indicating "motor scooter" and three indicating "tape recorder" are placed in a bowl.

(a) If the winners draw without replacement, what is the probability that two motor scooters and one tape recorder will be given away?
Ans. 15/28.

(b) If the drawing is with replacement, what is the probability that two motor scooters and one tape recorder will be given away?
Ans. 225/512.

2.2 Suppose the merchant obtains, in addition to the motor scooters and tape recorders, two electric guitars.

(a) If three winners draw for prizes with replacement, what is the probability that the merchant will be short one electric guitar?
Ans. .008.

(b) If seven winners draw without replacement, what is the probability that the merchant will have one of each prize left?   *Ans.* 1/4.

2-3   Mean and Variance of Probability Distributions

For many purposes it is desirable to have summary measures of important properties of probability distributions. Such measures are termed *parameters* because they refer to an entire population of outcomes of a process. They are measures *over the entirety of possible* observations. When the outcomes in a probability distribution are values of a variable, the most important parameters are the mean, or expected value, and the variance. The mean measures the central location of the distribution of values, and the variance measures the spread of values over the domain of the variable. Although there are other measures of central location and variability, the mean and variance are the most versatile and consequently the most widely used measures of these basic characteristics. In statistical notation, parameters are traditionally denoted by Greek letters, μ denoting population mean and σ^2 denoting population variance. The formulas for mean and variance of the probability distribution of a random variable, X are

$$\mu = \Sigma[X \cdot P(X)], \tag{2-5}$$

$$\sigma^2 = \Sigma[(X - \mu)^2 \cdot P(X)]. \tag{2-6}$$

Thus the mean is the summation of values of the variable weighted by their respective probabilities, and the variance is the summation of squared deviations of values of the variable from the mean weighted by their respective probabilities.

Suppose that an automobile insurance company has studied its records for a certain class of insured drivers during the past year. They have tabulated the number of drivers with zero, one, and two accidents during the year (none had more than two accidents) and reduced the data to relative frequencies. Strictly speaking, such data permit only an estimate of the probability distribution of numbers of accidents to individuals under the existing accident-generation process, but we shall proceed as if we had complete knowledge of the infinite statistical population. The probability distribution would appear as

Number of accidents, X	$P(X)$
0	.20
1	.50
2	.30
Total	1.00

Computation of the mean and variance of the probability distribution of accidents per year is carried out as follows.

X	$P(X)$	$X \cdot P(X)$	$X - \mu$	$(X - \mu)^2$	$(X - \mu)^2 \cdot P(X)$
0	.2	0.0	−1.1	1.21	.242
1	.5	0.5	−0.1	.01	.005
2	.3	0.6	0.9	.81	.243
		1.1			.490

$$\mu = \Sigma[X \cdot P(X)] = 1.1; \qquad \sigma^2 = \Sigma[(X - \mu)^2 \cdot P(X)] = .490.$$

2-4 Two Probability Processes

Our insurance company might be concerned about the distribution of accidents to expect over a two-year period. They might be considering a raise in rates for drivers involved in four or more accidents in a two-year period on the grounds that such drivers are "accident-prone." Accident-proneness involves the idea of repeated accidents. To suppose that there are accident-prone drivers amounts to saying that the more accidents a driver has in one year, the more he can be expected to have in the following year.

On the other hand, if drivers are all of one kind, or *homogeneous*, with respect to susceptibility to accidents, then the number of accidents that a particular driver had in a given year would not change our expectation as to the number of accidents he would have in the succeeding year. Absence of accident-proneness corresponds, in fact, to a condition of *independence* of accident experience in any year from the experience of previous years. In probability terminology we can state

$$P(X_n \mid X_{n-1}) = P(X_n),$$

which says that the probability of a driver's having X number of accidents in the nth year, given the number he had in the preceding year, is the same as the marginal probability of his having X accidents in the nth (or any) year. When sequential events are independent, we already know from Chapter 1 that the combined or joint probabilities of the possible outcomes of the events can be obtained from the products of the marginal probabilities of outcomes. Specifically,

$$P(AB) = P(A) \cdot P(B)$$

or

$$P(X_1 X_2) = P(X_1) \cdot P(X_2).$$

Using this rule of combination, we can calculate what the distribution of accidents for a two-year period would be if there were no accident-proneness in the population, and if the yearly accident distribution remained the same. We multiply the marginal probabilities of different numbers of accidents in the first year by the marginal probabilities for the second year. The result is a joint probability distribution of first- and second-year accidents. The results are shown below. For example, the probability of one accident in the first year and two accidents in the second year is $P(X_1 = 1) \cdot P(X_2 = 2) = .5(.3) = .15$.

		Second Year			
First Year		0	1	2	X_2
X_1	$P(X_1)$	.2	.5	.3	$P(X_2)$
0	.2	.04	.10	.06	
1	.5	.10	.25	.15	
2	.3	.06	.15	.09	

The possible values of $(X_1 + X_2)$ represent the accidents per driver for a two-year period. By summation from the distribution above, we can find the following probability distribution of two-year accident experience.

$(X_1 + X_2)$	$P(X_1 + X_2)$
0	.04
1	.20
2	.37
3	.30
4	.09
Total	1.00

If there were no accident-prone group in the population, and the overall accident rate remained constant, 9 per cent of the drivers would be expected to have four accidents in two years. Under the suggested rule their rates would be unjustifiably increased.

Suppose a rule of seven or more in four years was proposed. Assuming independence of successive accident experience, what proportion of drivers would be caught by this rule? Seven accidents in four years can be produced by three in one two-year period and four in the other two-year period. Eight accidents require four in each two-year period. Using the probabilities for a two-year period above, we have

$$P(7 \text{ in four years}) = .30(.09) + .09(.30) = .0540,$$

$$P(8 \text{ in four years}) = .09(.09) = .0081,$$

$$P(7 \text{ or } 8 \text{ in four years}) = .0540 + .0081 = .0621.$$

If this question had been asked before we had gone to the trouble to get the two-year distribution, we could have used Eq. (2–4). We view the population as follows:

X	$P(X)$	Number of elements
0	.2	$2 = A$
1	.5	$5 = B$
2	.3	$3 = C$
		$10 = K$

To produce eight accidents in four years ($n = 4$) we must draw two accidents in each of four successive years—that is, four two-accident elements.

$$P(a \text{ of } A, b \text{ of } B, \text{ and } c \text{ of } C) = \frac{{}_nC_a \cdot {}_{(n-a)}C_b \cdot A^a \cdot B^b \cdot C^c}{K^n}$$

$$P(0 \text{ of } 2, 0 \text{ of } 5, \text{ and } 4 \text{ of } 3) = \frac{{}_4C_0 \cdot {}_4C_0 \cdot 2^0 \cdot 5^0 \cdot 3^4}{10^4}$$

$$= \frac{1 \cdot 1 \cdot 1 \cdot 1 \cdot 81}{10,000} = .0081.$$

To produce seven accidents in four years, we must draw, with replacement, three of the two-accident elements and one of the one-accident elements.

$$P(0 \text{ of } 2, 1 \text{ of } 5, \text{ and } 3 \text{ of } 3) = \frac{{}_4C_0 \cdot {}_4C_1 \cdot 2^0 \cdot 5^1 \cdot 3^3}{10^4}$$

$$= \frac{1 \cdot 4 \cdot 1 \cdot 5 \cdot 27}{10,000} = \frac{540}{10,000} = .0540.$$

These are the same values we just obtained.

In the accident example so far we have calculated some results for a sequence of events, or probability process, under an assumption of independence of successive observations. What about a process that does not assume such independence? Recall that year-to-year independence of accident experience prevailed when

$$P(X_n \mid X_{n-1}) = P(X_n).$$

Dependence prevails as long as the above equation is not satisfied. Although there is only one way of satisfying the independence criterion, there are a multitude of ways in which it may fail to be satisfied. This amounts to admitting that various degrees of difference can exist in accident-proneness among the driver population. To get the sharpest focus on our problem, we select the case where the conditional probabilities are as follows:

	$P(X_n \mid X_{n-1})$		
X_{n-1}	0	1	2
0	1.0	0.0	0.0
1	0.0	1.0	0.0
2	0.0	0.0	1.0

This means, for example, that the probability of a driver's having two accidents in a year, given that he had two accidents in the preceding year, is 1.0, a certainty. Applying the conditional probabilities in this table to first-year probabilities would yield the following "X_1 by X_2" probability table.

First year		Second year			
X_1	$P(X_1)$	0	1	2	X_2
0	.2	0.2	0.0	0.0	
1	.5	0.0	0.5	0.0	
2	.3	0.0	0.0	0.3	

The probability distribution of total accidents per driver for the two years combined would then be

$(X_1 + X_2)$	$P(X_1 + X_2)$
0	0.2
1	0.0
2	0.5
3	0.0
4	0.3
Total	1.0

If there is complete year-to-year dependence among numbers of accidents, the rate raise for those with four accidents in two years would apply to the entire 30 per cent of drivers having two accidents per year.

EXERCISES

2.3 A plant has a nighttime repair facility for machines breaking down during the daytime production shift. The probability distribution of daily breakdowns, or arrivals (A), and the probability distribution of service capacity (S) in the repair facility are independent of one another and are given below.

A	$P(A)$		S	$P(S)$
0	3/6		0	1/3
1	2/6		1	2/3
2	1/6			

(a) Find the probability distribution of $(A - S)$ after the first day and night of operation of this system. Rearrange this to represent the number of machines waiting for repair, W_1.

(b) Generate the probability distribution of the number of machines waiting to be repaired (1) at the end of the second day's production shift—that is, $W_1 + A_2$; (2) at the end of the second night of operation of the repair facility, or W_2.

(c) What is the expected number of machines waiting for repair after the first day and night of operation; after the second day and night?   *Ans.* .33; .57.

2.4 You can simulate the occurrence of differing numbers of arrivals and service capacities in the system of Exercise 2.3 by throwing dice, with one die representing arrivals and the other service capacity.

(a) Run twenty simulations through the second night of operation, and compare the average number of machines waiting for repair at that time with the expected number in part (c) of Exercise 2.3.

(b) Simulate twenty successive days and nights of operation of the system, recording arrivals, service, and number waiting. Calculate your average daily arrivals and your average service *capacity.* Comment on the behavior over time of the number waiting.

2.5 Note the following set of conditional (or transitional) probabilities for values of a process in any period (*n*) given the previous (*n* − 1) period.

	X_n		
X_{n-1}	0	1	2
0	1.0	0.0	0.0
1	0.1	0.9	0.0
2	0.0	0.5	0.5

Assume a starting point with all members of the population having the value "2" in the starting period. With the aid of a tree diagram, carry the process through three successive periods. Calculate the mean of the distribution of X for each period.   *Ans.* 1.5; 1.2; 1.005.

2-5 Mean and Variance of Outcomes of Probability Processes

The sets of conditional probabilities of numbers of accidents in the current period given the numbers of accidents in the preceding period, $P(X_n | X_{n-1})$, can be employed to generate any number of periods of accident experience. If $P(X_n | X_{n-1}) = P(X_n)$ as in the first example, the accident probabilities generated correspond to what we would expect under complete independence from period to period. On the other hand, in the example just concluded we generated the probability distribution of numbers of accidents for a two-year period under complete positive dependence. Both of these processes can be carried further to generate probabilities of accidents for a three-year, four-year, or any desired period under the conditions assumed.

Instead of being shown in tabular form, the entire process out to four years of cumulative experience under independence is shown in "tree diagram" form in Fig. 2-1. The numbers at the "junctions" of the tree represent cumulative numbers of accidents up to that junction, and the probability entered midway along the branch leading to any junction indicates the probability of the particular sequence of outcomes leading to that junction. Thus, the nine probabilities in the X_1 by X_2 table appear after the second branching. There would be 27 probabilities in the X_1 by X_2 by X_3 table, and they appear after the next set of branches. Finally, the 81 probabilities in the X_1 by X_2 by X_3 by X_4 table appear at the extreme right. For example $P(0_1 0_2 0_3 1_4)$ is the second entry from the top at the right: .0040. To obtain the probability distributions of numbers of accidents per worker for any period we need only add up the probabilities of the mutually exclusive sequences that lead to particular cumulative numbers of accidents.

We do not show the generation of probabilities for the case of complete dependence. There would be entries only along the branches 0, 0, 0, 0, 1, 1, 1, 1, and 2, 2, 2, 2, however. The distributions for differing numbers of periods generated by the completely dependent model differ only by a constant scale factor equal to the number of periods cumulated. The basic single-period probability distribution was $P(0) = .2$, $P(1) = .5$, and $P(2) = .3$. For two periods we had $P(0) = .2$, $P(2) = .5$, and $P(4) = .3$, and for four periods we would have $P(0) = .2$, $P(4) = .5$, and $P(8) = .3$.

The resulting probability distributions for two, three, and four years are shown in Table 2-1.

Recall, from page 30, that the mean, μ, of the probability distribution of accidents for a single period was 1.1 and the variance, σ^2, was .49. Using the basic formulas for mean and variance, you should be able to verify the figures in Table 2-2 for the mean and variance of cumulative accident experience under each of the models.

The growth of the mean and the variance under independence as the periods are lengthened summarizes quickly the obvious fact that the probability distribution of accidents as the number of periods, n, increases has a greater average and a greater variability than does the distribution of accidents for a single period. Both measures increase by a factor of n—a fact you probably find intuitively obvious in the case of the mean and vaguely reassuring in the case of the variance. We will simply state here two important theorems that have just been illustrated.

I. *The expected value (or mean) of a sum of independent random variables is equal to the sum of the expected values (or means) of the separate random variables.*

$$\mu_{(X_1+X_2+X_3+\cdots+X_n)} = \mu_{X_1} + \mu_{X_2} + \mu_{X_3} + \ldots + \mu_{X_n}. \qquad (2\text{--}7)$$

II. *The variance of a sum of independent random variables is equal to the sum of the variances of the separate random variables.*

$$\sigma^2_{(X_1+X_2+X_3+\cdots+X_n)} = \sigma^2_{X_1} + \sigma^2_{X_2} + \sigma^2_{X_3} + \ldots + \sigma^2_{X_n}. \qquad (2\text{--}8)$$

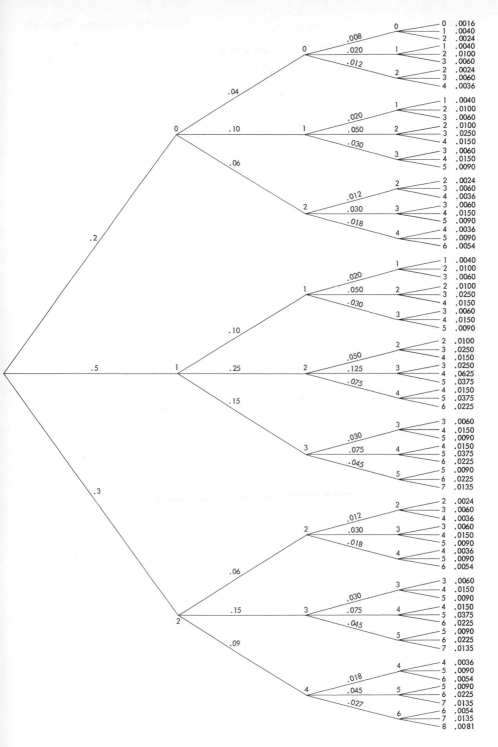

FIGURE 2-1 Probabilities of sums of a random variable

Table 2-1

PROBABILITY DISTRIBUTIONS OF CUMULATIVE NUMBERS
OF ACCIDENTS FOR DIFFERING PERIODS
UNDER INDEPENDENCE AND COMPLETE DEPENDENCE

X	P(X) Under independence			P(X) Under dependence		
	$n = 2$	$n = 3$	$n = 4$	$n = 2$	$n = 3$	$n = 4$
0	.04	.008	.0016	.2	.2	.2
1	.20	.060	.0160			
2	.37	.186	.0696	.5		\
3	.30	.305	.1720		.5	
4	.09	.279	.2641	.3		.5
5		.135	.2580			
6		.027	.1566		.3	
7			.0540			
8			.0081			.3
	1.00	1.000	1.0000	1.0	1.0	1.0

Table 2-2

MEAN AND VARIANCE OF CUMULATIVE ACCIDENTS
UNDER TWO PROBABILITY PROCESS MODELS

Period	Mean		Variance	
	Independence	Complete dependence	Independence	Complete dependence
$n = 1$	1.1	1.1	.49	.49
$n = 2$	2.2	2.2	.98	1.96
$n = 3$	3.3	3.3	1.47	4.41
$n = 4$	4.4	4.4	1.96	7.84

In the case of the dependent model, the mean increases by the same factor, n, but the variance increases by a factor of n^2. The relationship that holds here and in general is

I. *If each of the values of a random variable is multiplied by a constant, c, the mean of the resulting random variable will be c times the mean of the original random variable.*

$$\mu_{cX} = c\mu_X. \tag{2-9}$$

II. *The variance of a random variable, each of whose values is multiplied by a constant, c, will be equal to the variance of the original variable multiplied by the square of c.*

$$\sigma_{cX}^2 = c^2 \cdot \sigma_X^2. \tag{2-10}$$

In our example,

$$\sigma_{3x}^2 = 3^2\sigma_x^2 = 3^2(.49) = 4.41.$$

2-6 Independence, Dependence, and Covariance

The two models we have presented represent the extremes of complete (positive) dependence and complete lack of dependence of individual accident experience on the preceding period's experience. What about partial dependence? To develop an understanding of a measure of dependence, we will first introduce a symbol for the differences, $X - \mu$, involved in the computation of the variance.

$$x = X - \mu. \tag{2-11}$$

The lower case x is a single symbol standing for the deviation of the value of a variable, X, from the mean of the probability distribution of X. The mean of x (that is, μ_x as opposed to μ_X) is zero, as can be seen from the following.

$$\mu_x = \Sigma[(X - \mu) \cdot P(X)] = \Sigma[X \cdot P(X)] - \mu\Sigma[P(X)] = \mu - \mu = 0.$$

Adding or subtracting a constant from each of the values of a variable does not affect the variance. This means that the variance of X is the same as the variance of x. That is

$$\sigma_X^2 = \sigma_x^2$$
$$\Sigma[(X - \mu)^2 \cdot P(X)] = \Sigma[x^2 \cdot P(x)].$$

With these new terms, we can now state the variance of the sum of two random variables, whether independent or dependent, as

$$\sigma_{X_1+X_2}^2 = \sigma_{x_1+x_2}^2 = \Sigma[(x_1 + x_2)^2 \cdot P(x_1 + x_2)].$$

Expanding, we obtain

$$\sigma_{X_1+X_2}^2 = \Sigma[(x_1^2 + 2x_1x_2 + x_2^2) \cdot P(x_1 + x_2)].$$

And summing by parts yields

$$\sigma_{X_1+X_2}^2 = \Sigma[x_1^2 \cdot P(x_1)] + 2\Sigma[x_1x_2 \cdot P(x_1x_2)] + \Sigma[x_2^2 \cdot P(x_2)].$$

The first and last terms are $\sigma_{X_1}^2$ and $\sigma_{X_2}^2$ respectively. The expression $\Sigma[x_1x_2 \cdot P(x_1x_2)]$ is known as the covariance of (or between) X_1 and X_2. The standard symbol for this covariance is $\sigma_{X_1X_2}$. We can then write

$$\sigma^2_{X_1+X_2} = \sigma^2_{X_1} + 2\sigma_{X_1X_2} + \sigma^2_{X_2}. \qquad (2\text{-}12)$$

The covariance is intimately connected with the ideas of independence and dependence that were introduced in the data-generation models. To gain a familiarity with the covariance term, consider the table constructed previously for the combined outcomes of first- and second-year accident experience under the assumption of independence.

		Second year			
First year		0	1	2	(X_2)
X_1	$P(X_1)$	.2	.5	.3	$P(X_2)$
0	.2	.04	.10	.06	
1	.5	.10	.25	.15	
2	.3	.06	.15	.09	

The joint probabilities in the table are the probabilities of different combinations of first- and second-year accident experience. They are also the probabilities of different values of x_1x_2, as the following array emphasizes. Remember that $\mu_{X_1} = \mu_{X_2} = 1.1$.

		x_2			
		−1.1	−.1	.9	
	−1.1	1.21	.11	−.99	
x_1	−.1	.11	.01	−.09	Values of x_1x_2
	.9	−.99	−.09	.81	

The covariance is, then, the sum of the values of x_1x_2 weighted by their respective probabilities:

$$\sigma_{X_1X_2} = (1.21)(.04) + (.11)(.10) + (-.99)(.06) + \cdots$$
$$+ (.11)(.10) + (.01)(.25) + (-.09)(.15) + \cdots$$
$$+ (-.99)(.06) + (-.09)(.15) + (.81)(.09),$$
$$\sigma_{X_1X_2} = 0.$$

This result is general for two independent random variables, and the expression

$$\sigma^2_{X_1+X_2} = \sigma^2_{X_1} + 2\sigma_{X_1X_2} + \sigma^2_{X_2}$$

becomes

$$\sigma^2_{X_1+X_2} = \sigma^2_{X_1} + \sigma^2_{X_2}. \qquad (2\text{-}13)$$

As indicated previously, this leads to a variance of two years of accident experience under the independence model of

$$\sigma^2_{X_1+X_2} = \sigma^2_{X_1} + \sigma^2_{X_2} = .49 + .49 = .98.$$

The covariance of first- and second-year experience under the "complete dependence" model involves the same table of x_1x_2 values but uses the set of probability weights exhibited on page 34 and reproduced below:

			X_2	
		0	1	2
	0	.2	—	—
X_1	1	—	.5	—
	2	—	—	.3

$$\sigma_{X_1X_2} = .2(1.21) + .5(.01) + .3(.81) = .490.$$

This results in a variance of cumulative experience of

$$\sigma^2_{X_1+X_2} = \sigma^2_{X_1} + 2\sigma_{X_1X_2} + \sigma^2_{X_2}$$
$$= .49 + 2(.49) + .49 = 1.96.$$

Under complete dependence, $\sigma^2_{X_1+X_2} = \sigma^2_{2X}$ where, as in the current case, the marginal probability distributions of X_1 and X_2 are the same and can be indicated simply by X without any subscript. When we apply the rule already introduced for the variance of a random variable multiplied by a constant, the above result is duplicated.

$$\sigma^2_{cX} = c^2\sigma^2_X,$$
$$\sigma^2_{2X} = 2^2(.49) = 1.96.$$

The results that we have seen for the covariance in the extreme cases of independence and complete dependence suggest that the covariance term in our accident example can take values ranging from zero to .49. This is in fact correct,* and the general limits of positive covariance between two random variables are

$$\text{Cov}_{\text{min}} = 0, \qquad \text{Cov}_{\text{max}} = \sigma_{X_1}\sigma_{X_2}.$$

A measure of degree of dependence can then be constructed by comparing the actual value of the covariance to the value it would take under complete dependence. This ratio is termed the *correlation coefficient*, and is indicated by the Greek letter ρ (rho).

$$\rho = \frac{\sigma_{X_1X_2}}{\sigma_{X_1}\sigma_{X_2}} \qquad (2\text{--}14)$$

---

* As long as the dependence is positive. Negative dependence is covered later in this section.

A set of conditional probabilities of X_2 given X_1 is shown below. Considered in terms of yearly accident experience, these probabilities show a slight tendency for individual accident experience to be repeated. The means of X_1 and X_2 are both 1.1, as with our previous examples. The calculation of the covariance is shown, along with the resulting correlation coefficient of .245.

$P(X_1)$	X_1	$P(X_2 \mid X_1)$ X_2 0	1	2	X_1	$P(X_1X_2)$ X_2 0	1	2
.2	0	.5	.2	.3	0	.10	.04	.06
.5	1	.2	.5	.3	1	.10	.25	.15
.3	2	.0	.7	.3	2	.00	.21	.09
					$P(X_2)$	.20	.50	.30

X_1, X_2	x_1x_2	$P(x_1x_2)$	$x_1x_2 \cdot P(x_1x_2)$
0, 0	1.21	.10	.1210
0, 1	.11	.04	.0044
0, 2	$-.99$	.06	$-.0594$
1, 0	.11	.10	.0110
1, 1	.01	.25	.0025
1, 2	$-.09$	.15	$-.0135$
2, 0	$-.99$	.00	.0000
2, 1	$-.09$	.21	$-.0189$
2, 2	.81	.09	.0729
		1.00	$.1200 = \sigma_{X_1X_2}$

$$\rho = \frac{\sigma_{X_1X_2}}{\sigma_{X_1}\sigma_{X_2}} = \frac{.1200}{\sqrt{.49}\cdot\sqrt{.49}} = \frac{.1200}{.4900} = .245.$$

Negative dependence. To round out our discussion of dependence we present, in the context of the accident-experience example, a case of negative dependence. The conditional probabilities below on the left will produce the joint probabilities on the right. Note that the conditional probabilities

X_1	$P(X_2 \mid X_1)$ X_2 0	1	2	$P(X_1)$	$P(X_1X_2)$ X_2 0	1	2
0	.1	.5	.4	.2	.02	.10	.08
1	.0	.8	.2	.5	.00	.40	.10
2	.6	.0	.4	.3	.18	.00	.12
				$P(X_2)$:	.20	.50	.30

imply that those with no accidents in the first year are very likely to have one or two accidents in the second year, and those with two first-year accidents are quite likely to have no second-year accidents. This is not just lack of accident-proneness but its opposite, a sort of temporary "immunity" followed by "reinfection." As cumulative experience is generated here, substantial segments of the population will shift back and forth between no accidents and two accidents per year. Complete negative dependence would involve conditional probabilities of 1.0 along the "northeast to southwest" diagonal of the conditional probability table, in which case this back-and-forth shifting would be complete. We leave it as an exercise for the student to show that the correlation coefficient, ρ, is $-.265$ in this example.

With negative dependence, the variance of the sum of two random variables is reduced from what would prevail under independence, because the covariance term is negative. Under complete negative dependence the sum of two identical random variables will be a constant, and the variance of the sum will be reduced to zero. The covariance will equal $-\sigma_{X_1}\sigma_{X_2}$. Therefore, the degree of dependence can still be indicated by the measure

$$\rho = \frac{\sigma_{X_1 X_2}}{\sigma_{X_1}\sigma_{X_2}}.$$

The limits of this measure under negative dependence are zero (no dependence) and -1.0 (complete negative dependence).

In general, then, the correlation coefficient, ρ, indicates extent of dependence, with the algebraic sign indicating whether the dependence is positive or negative.

The variance of the difference between two random variables. Occasions will arise later where we will be concerned with the possible differences between two random variables. For example, cash income and cash outlay connected with a prospective investment are not a matter of certainty, but the expectation of income and outflow might be expressible as probability distributions. The difference between income and outlay is, of course, net cash inflow, a quantity critical to the firm's financial planning. Therefore, the parameters of the probability distribution of $(X_1 - X_2)$, or income minus outflow, would be of considerable interest. Paralleling the development of the formula for the variance of the sum in Eq. (2–12), the variance of the difference between two random variables is

$$\sigma^2_{X_1-X_2} = \sigma^2_{X_1} - 2\sigma_{X_1 X_2} + \sigma^2_{X_2} \tag{2-15}$$

Thus, if X_1 and X_2 are independent, the variance of $(X_1 - X_2)$ is the same as the variance of $(X_1 + X_2)$—namely, the sum of the separate variances of X_1 and X_2. However, the sign attached to the covariance term is negative for the difference case; it was positive for the case of the sum. Therefore the effect of dependence on the variance of the difference is just the reverse of what it was for the variance of the sum. Positive dependence will reduce the variance of a difference, and negative dependence will increase the variance of a difference. This can be seen intuitively, for if outlay tends to rise when income rises, and fall when income falls, then the variability of *net* income expected over time will be limited. However, if the reverse is true (negative dependence), then the net income generated will be highly variable.

Covariance and correlation are important measures of association among variables. Association among variables is the central concern of Chapters 12 through 17 in this text.

EXERCISES

2.6   In order to release oceanographic recording devices from beneath the sea, a release mechanism is used in which a steel knife edge corrodes a series of magnesium pins. When the last pin is broken, a ballast weight is released and the buoyant assembly rises to the surface. Suppose the mean corrosion time per pin is sixty hours with a standard deviation of ten hours.

(a) What will be the mean and variance of the total corrosion time for sets of four pins in series if corrosion times of the pins are independent of one another?   *Ans.* 240; 400.

(b) What will be the mean and variance of the total corrosion time for sets of four pins in series if the corrosion time of each pin is completely dependent on that of the preceding pin in the series?
Ans. 240; 1600.

(c) Suppose that batches of pins received at any given time are apt to be cut from the same material, and that the properties of the material vary over time. What does the above suggest about the manner of assigning pins to a series?

2.7   Consider a population made up of an equal number of each of the values 1, 4, and 7.

(a) Find the probability distribution of one-half of the sum resulting from two random draws from the population.

(b) Calculate the variance of the probability distribution found in part (a).

(c) Derive the same variance from the variance of the underlying population.

2.8   Utilizing the distribution found in Exercise 2.7:

(a) Find the joint distribution of such values in a pair of draws of two each.

(b) List the probability distribution of differences in a pair of such draws, and calculate the variance of this distribution.

(c) Show analytically how the same variance can be derived from the variance of the underlying population in Exercise 2.7.

2.9   (a) Show that the correlation coefficient, ρ, between X_1 and X_2 in the example given on negative dependence in Sec. 2–6 is $-.265$.

      (b) Using the same example, find the probability distribution of accidents for a two-year period.

      (c) Combine two two-year periods to obtain the probability distribution of accidents for a four-year period.

REFERENCES

Kemeny, J. G., A. Schleifer, Jr., J. L. Snell, and G. L. Thompson, *Finite Mathematics With Business Applications*. Englewood Cliffs, N.J.: Prentice-Hall, Inc., 1962.

Kemeny, J. G., H. Mirkil, J. L. Snell, and G. L. Thompson, *Finite Mathematical Structures*. Englewood Cliffs, N.J.: Prentice-Hall, Inc., 1958.

3

Probability
and Statistical
Inference

In Chapters 1 and 2 we have not said anything about making inferences about parameters (measures of numerical characteristics of populations) from data contained in a sample from the population. Rather we have supposed that we knew the value of a parameter in a population; then we have gone ahead to work out some consequences that flow from this knowledge. If we know the probability of each die face to be 1/6, we can figure the probability of the roller's winning a dice game by throwing "seven" or "eleven" on the first throw of two dice. If we know the mean and variance of a population of X, we can figure the expected value and the variance of the sum of X on independent draws of n observations from the population. The character of the results in both of these examples is deductive. Given the parameter(s) involved and the addition and multiplication theorems, or the theorems on sums of independent random numbers, the deductions follow.

The inductive problem in statistics is how to draw conclusions about parameters, or true states of affairs, from the partial information contained in a sample. Although deductive arguments will be found to play a critical role in this problem of statistical inference, our emphasis shifts now to the problem of saying something about a population based on the data of a sample. Since the word *statistic* stands for a numerical characteristic of a sample, we could say that the problem of inference is the problem of *making a statement about a parameter on the basis of a statistic.*

3-1   Point Estimates of Population Parameters

The reason we draw a sample is because we want information, however imperfect, about the state of affairs in the population from which it is drawn. An important method of inference is the estimation of the value, or state, of a population characteristic from data present in a sample. Estimation is the principal concern of Chapter 8, but we can now introduce two important estimates and one important criterion for estimation methods. The two estimates are those for the mean and variance of a population; the criterion is that of an unbiased estimate.

Let us consider an example. Below is a small finite population of the three values $X = 1$, $X = 3$, and $X = 11$, together with the calculation of the mean and variance of the population. The number of elements in the population is $N = 3$.

X	$X - \mu$	$(X - \mu)^2$
1	-4	16
3	-2	4
11	$+6$	36
$\overline{\overline{15}}$		$\overline{\overline{56}}$

$$\mu = \frac{\Sigma X}{N} = \frac{15}{3} = 5, \qquad \sigma^2 = \frac{\Sigma (X - \mu)^2}{N} = \frac{56}{3} = 18\tfrac{2}{3}.$$

Expressing the formulas for the mean and variance in terms of N rather than summations of values weighted by probabilities should cause no problems. Previously we used the symbol $P(X)$ for probability; $P(X)$ is equal to f/N, where f is the absolute frequency of a given value in the population. It follows then that

$$\mu = \Sigma [X \cdot P(X)] = \Sigma \left[X \cdot \frac{f}{N} \right] = \frac{\Sigma (fX)}{N}.$$

Where each equally likely X element is separately listed, all of the f's are equal to unity, and

$$\mu = \frac{\Sigma X}{N}. \tag{3-1}$$

By the same reasoning for the variance:

$$\sigma^2 = \Sigma [X - \mu)^2 \cdot P(X)] = \frac{\Sigma [f(X - \mu)^2]}{N},$$

$$\sigma^2 = \frac{\Sigma [(X - \mu)^2]}{N}. \tag{3-2}$$

Estimating the population mean. Using the mean of a sample as an estimate of the population mean might occur to you as a reasonable procedure. Let us examine this a little more closely with the advantage we have of complete knowledge about our population. We will consider the results from all possible samples of size 2 that our population can generate. The symbol for number of observations in a sample is n. In our case $n = 2$. Below are shown the $N^n = 3^2 = 9$ possible results in sampling *with replacement*.

Sample	Sample mean	Sample	Sample mean
1, 1	1	3, 3	3
1, 3	2	3, 11	7
1, 11	6	11, 1	6
3, 1	2	11, 3	7
		11, 11	11

The symbol for sample mean is $\bar{X}$, and

$$\bar{X} = \frac{\Sigma X}{n}. \tag{3-3}$$

The mean of the possible sample means is denoted by $\mu_{\bar{x}}$, and in sampling with replacement

$$\mu_{\bar{x}} = \frac{\Sigma \bar{X}}{N^n} = \frac{1 + 2 + 6 + 2 + 3 + 7 + 6 + 7 + 11}{9} = \frac{45}{9} = 5.$$

While this result may not surprise you, it is of considerable importance. It is an example of the generalization:

$$\mu_{\bar{x}} = \mu. \tag{3-4}$$

This says that the average or expected value of all possible estimates of the population mean made by employing the sample mean is equal to the parameter we seek to estimate. If an estimating procedure has this feature, any estimate it produces is termed an *unbiased estimate*.

If sampling is without replacement, the sample mean is still an unbiased estimate of the population mean. There are now $_N P_n$ possible samples, and the results for our example are shown below for the $_3P_2 = 6$ possible samples.

Sample	Sample mean	Sample	Sample mean
1, 3	2	3, 11	7
1, 11	6	11, 1	6
3, 1	2	11, 3	7

$$\mu_{\bar{x}} = \frac{\Sigma \bar{X}}{_N P_n} = \frac{2 + 6 + 2 + 7 + 6 + 7}{6} = \frac{30}{6} = 5.$$

Estimating the population variance. We have seen that the mean of a random sample is an unbiased estimate of the mean of its parent population, because the expectation of the sample mean is exactly equal to the mean of the population. In dealing with variances, however, we encounter a problem. The variance of a population is the expected value, or mean, of the squared deviations of the population values from the mean of the population. We might be inclined to use the analogous calculation from the sample values in order to estimate the population variance. However, the sample mean squared deviation $\Sigma[(X - \bar{X})^2]/n$, is not an unbiased estimate of the population variance. Table 3–1 illustrates this fact for our example population.

Table 3-1

AVERAGE OF SAMPLE MEAN SQUARED DEVIATIONS
FOR NINE EQUALLY LIKELY SAMPLES FROM A POPULATION
WITH $\sigma^2 = 18\frac{2}{3}$

Sample	$\bar{X}$	$\Sigma[(X - \bar{X})^2]/n$
1, 1	1	0/2 = 0
1, 3	2	2/2 = 1
1, 11	6	50/2 = 25
3, 1	2	2/2 = 1
3, 3	3	0/2 = 0
3, 11	7	32/2 = 16
11, 1	6	50/2 = 25
11, 3	7	32/2 = 16
11, 11	11	0/2 = 0
		84

Mean of nine variance estimates $= 84/9 = 9\frac{1}{3}$.

We find that the average of the sample mean squared deviations is not equal to the population variance. The "trouble" that we have run upon here can be appreciated if we recast the problem in the light of our complete knowledge of this example population. Try working the example above, but use the fact that we know the population mean to be 5.0. Compute the squared deviations of the values in each sample from 5.0 before dividing by 2. The average value of this calculation, $\Sigma[(X - \mu)^2]/n$, for the nine possible samples will be equal to $18\frac{2}{3}$, the population variance. It then becomes fairly evident why the average of the sample mean squared deviations underestimates the population variance. The trouble lies in the variation of the sample means from the population mean. For a sample whose mean is not equal to the population mean, use of the sample mean in computing squared deviations results in a smaller mean squared deviation than would use of the population mean.

Although it is not proved here, the adjustment factor necessary to transform a sample mean squared deviation into an unbiased estimate of the variance of the parent population is exactly $n/(n-1)$. This is a large relative adjustment for small sample sizes and a small relative adjustment for large sample sizes, as we would expect. If this adjustment factor is applied to each of the equally likely sample mean squared deviations previously enumerated, it will raise them all by a factor of $2/(2-1) = 2$. The average estimated variance will then be equal to the population variance.

We will define the statistic, s^2, to be the unbiased estimate of the population variance derived wholly from the sample observations. It is most easily thought of as the sum of squared deviations from the sample mean divided by $(n-1)$. When we use the term sample variance, or variance of the sample, we will mean the statistic s^2.

$$s^2 = \frac{\Sigma\,[(X-\bar{X})^2]}{n}\left(\frac{n}{n-1}\right),$$

$$s^2 = \frac{\Sigma\,[(X-\bar{X})^2]}{n-1}. \tag{3-5}$$

The divisor $(n-1)$ is known as the *degrees of freedom* present in the estimate of the variance. Had we taken samples of size one from our example population, there would have been no way to estimate the population variance solely on the basis of one sample. After all, there is no variability present in a sample of one, so that it could hardly be used to estimate the variability of the parent population. There is one degree of freedom for estimating a population variance from a sample of size two, two degrees of freedom are present for this purpose in a sample of size three, and so on. In general, in a sample of size n there are $n-1$ independent deviations from the sample mean on which to base an estimate of the variance. Another way to put this is to say that the degrees of freedom, $n-1$, represent the number of independent pieces of information present about the variability of the population. Two observations must be drawn before there is any information about the population variance, and each observation added to the sample adds one additional independent piece of information about the population variance.

EXERCISES

3.1 Let the letters A, B, C, and D stand for large but equally numerous subgroups of the populations indicated. Let the members of the subgroups have the values shown in the table.

Subgroup	Population			
	I	II	III	IV
A	2	0	2	1
B	3	2	2	1
C	3	4	2	5
D	4	6	6	5

For each population find:
(a) The variance.   *Ans.* 0.5; 5.0; 3.0; 4.0.
(b) The probability distribution of the mean resulting from two independent random draws from the population. Draw a graph of the distribution.
(c) The variance of the distribution in part (b), as calculated from the distribution.   *Ans.* 0.25; 2.5; 1.5; 2.0.

3.2 (a) Find the probability distribution of the mean resulting from three random draws from each population of Exercise 3.1. Draw a graph of the distribution.
(b) Find the variance of each distribution in part (a), as calculated from the distribution.   *Ans.* 0.167; 1.67; 1.0; 1.333.

3.3 Consider an infinite population with an equal number of the values 1, 4, and 7. List the 27 possible samples of size three. Calculate $s^2 = \Sigma[(X - \bar{X})^2]/(n - 1)$ for each sample, and find the mean of the 27 estimates of the variance. Does this equal the population variance?

3-2 Bayes' Theorem and Statistical Inference

A very important application of conditional probabilities is known as Bayes' theorem after the Reverend Thomas Bayes (1702–1761), who pointed out its significance as a basis for statistical inference. It can be illustrated by the following problem.

> PROBLEM. *There are ten urns, three (U_I) containing nine red balls and one white ball each, and seven (U_{II}) containing two red balls and eight white balls each. In exterior appearance the urns are indistinguishable. An observer selects an urn at random and from the urn selected draws a red ball. What is the probability that the urn selected was of type U_I?*

We can solve the problem in a direct manner. After all, there are 41 red balls in the ten urns [(9 per type I urn) × (3 type I urns) + (2 per type II urn) × (7 type II urns)] and 27 of them are in the type I urns. Therefore, if a red ball is selected, the probability that it came from a Type I urn is 27/41. This direct solution actually masks the significance of the question we have answered. Now that we know the answer to the question we can examine the significance of the problem.

The probability problems we have encountered so far have all called for the probability of an outcome of an experiment given a particular true state of affairs in some underlying population. We developed a number of probability problems concerning the outcomes of sample draws from a box of cartridges that we knew contained four normal cartridges and two bad ones. We found the probability of observing certain sample evidence given a true state of affairs. Using E for evidence or event, and S for true state, we can shorten this to $P(E \mid S)$. In the urn problem, we asked for the probability that a particular true state of affairs prevailed given a sample event.

We observed that a red ball was drawn and then asked for the probability that it was drawn from urn I. Urn I and urn II represent two possible populations, or states of affairs, that could have produced the observation "one red ball." The probability that the red ball came from urn I represents an *inference about a true state made in the light of particular sample evidence.* Previously in calculating $P(E|S)$ we predicted (or made inferences about) sample events given a true state. In calling instead for $P(S|E)$, the probability of a state given the evidence, we have reversed the "direction" of the inference desired.

The formal solution to the problem can be visualized with the aid of the accompanying tree diagram.

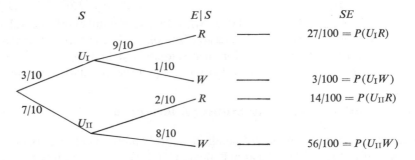

Now recall the basic form of the multiplication theorem. Where the events are designated S and E, it is

$$P(SE) = P(S) \cdot P(E|S).$$

But $P(SE)$ can also be stated as

$$P(SE) = P(E) \cdot P(S|E).$$

Then we have an equation for $P(S|E)$:

$$P(S|E) = \frac{P(SE)}{P(E)}.$$

And substituting the first expression for $P(SE)$ yields

$$P(S|E) = \frac{P(S) \cdot P(E|S)}{P(E)}. \qquad (3\text{--}6)$$

Equation (3–6) is known as Bayes' theorem. Bayes' theorem provides a way of combining or weighing objective statistical evidence, $P(E|S)$, against prior probabilities of states, $P(S)$, to arrive at a current inference about the true state of affairs. The current inference, $P(S|E)$, is sometimes called the revised or posterior probability of the true state.

Let us apply Bayes' Theorem to the urn problem.

$$P(U_I | R) = \frac{P(U_I) \cdot P(R | U_I)}{P(U_I) \cdot P(R | U_I) + P(U_{II}) \cdot P(R | U_{II})}$$

$$= \frac{(3/10)(9/10)}{(3/10)(9/10) + (7/10)(2/10)} = 27/41$$

The prior probability has been revised in the light of the objective evidence. Prior to observing the color of the ball drawn, the chances of selecting a type I urn were three in ten. But the evidence of a red ball causes us to revise our belief that a type I urn was sampled—from a probability of 3/10 to a probability of 27/41. The assertion that the urn was selected on a random basis made the prior probability an objective one. But the principle of Bayes' Theorem applies with equal force even when the prior probabilities are subjective.

3-3 Bayes' Theorem, Prior Odds, and Information Odds

Consider the following problem. An industrial research department has received five experimental components from a supplier. Past experience has led the department to believe that either two or three of the five components will function properly. They have assigned probability .4 to the state two effective components and probability .6 to the state three effective components. Three of the five components are then sampled and two are found to function properly. What probabilities should now be established for each of the above states?

This is a Bayes'-theorem problem. We have prior probabilities of states, $P(S)$, and some statistical evidence, and we wish to compute the probabilities of states given the evidence, $P(S | E)$. This requires

$$P(S | E) = \frac{P(S) \cdot P(E | S)}{P(E)}.$$

The $P(E | S)$ can be computed from Eq. (2–1) because we are involved in sampling without replacement from a finite binary population. This equation was

$$P(a \text{ of } A \text{ and } b \text{ of } B) = \frac{_nC_a \cdot _AP_a \cdot _BP_b}{_KP_n}.$$

Let A stand for effective and B for defective components. If $A = 2$, and $B = 3$ is the true state, the probability of $a = 2$ and $b = 1$ is

$$P(2 \text{ of } 2 \text{ and } 1 \text{ of } 3) = \frac{_3C_2 \cdot _2P_2 \cdot _3P_1}{_5P_3} = \frac{3(2)(3)}{60} = .3,$$

$$P(a = 2 | A = 2) = .3.$$

If $A = 3$ and $B = 2$, then the probability of observing $a = 2$ and $b = 1$ is

$$P(2 \text{ of } 3 \text{ and } 1 \text{ of } 2) = \frac{{}_3C_2 \cdot {}_3P_2 \cdot {}_2P_1}{{}_5P_3} = \frac{3(6)(2)}{60} = .6,$$

$$P(a = 2 | A = 3) = .6.$$

Then, applying Bayes' theorem yields

State (S)	P(S)	$P(E\|S)$ $P(a = 2\|A)$	P(SE)	$P(S\|E)$ $P(A\|a = 2)$
$A = 2$	.4	.3	.12	.25
$A = 3$	.6	.6	.36	.75
			$P(E) = .48$	1.00

When we are concerned only with two states, we can form our inference in terms of odds on the states of concern. For instance, the odds on the state $A = 3$ against the state $A = 2$ are .75 to .25 or 3 to 1. Given the sample evidence in conjunction with the prior assessment, the state $A = 3$ is three times as likely as the state $A = 2$. To reach this inference we need not carry our calculations to the $P(S|E)$ column, for this column is always proportional to the $P(SE)$ column. The odds of 3 to 1 could just as well have been obtained from .36 to .12 in the $P(SE)$ column. Backing up still further, these odds could have been obtained as the product of prior odds and the odds that would be established solely from the sample evidence.

$$\frac{.6}{.4} \times \frac{.6}{.3} = \frac{.36}{.12} = \frac{3}{1}.$$

We will call the odds established from $P(E|S)$ the "information odds" and the odds established from the prior probabilities simply the "prior odds." The odds on two states are then *the product of the prior odds and the information odds.*

Information odds can be computed quite handily from the combinatorial formulas for the probabilities of sample events that were presented in Chapter 2. In the binary population case we will be concerned with the information odds on the true states (A and B out of K) as against the true state (A' and B' out of K). A sample of size n has yielded a particular a and b. The information odds, or ratio of $P(E|S)$ to $P(E|S')$, condense to the following:

sampling without replacement:

$$\frac{P(a \text{ of } A \text{ and } b \text{ of } B)}{P(a \text{ of } A' \text{ and } b \text{ of } B')} = \frac{{}_nC_a \cdot {}_AP_a \cdot {}_BP_b / {}_KP_n}{{}_nC_a \cdot {}_{A'}P_a \cdot {}_{B'}P_b / {}_KP_n} = \frac{{}_AP_a \cdot {}_BP_b}{{}_{A'}P_a \cdot {}_{B'}P_b}, \qquad (3\text{-}7)$$

sampling with replacement:

$$\frac{P(a \text{ of } A \text{ and } b \text{ of } B)}{P(a \text{ of } A' \text{ and } b \text{ of } B')} = \frac{{}_nC_a \cdot A^a \cdot B^b / K^n}{{}_nC_a \cdot A'^a \cdot B'^b / K^n} = \frac{A^a B^b}{A'^a B'^b}. \tag{3-8}$$

To illustrate this calculation of information odds on true states, consider the following problem.

PROBLEM. *A national company has twenty sales territories. The market research director believes that the current year's sales performance in ten of these is below standard. The sales manager believes that only five are below standard. They agree on a method of testing performance compared to standard, and apply this to four territories selected at random, without replacement. Two of the four are found below standard, and two above. What are the odds that the sales manager's belief will prevail over that of the market research director after the remaining sixteen territories are tested?*

$A = 5, B = 15$ Sales manager's belief

$A' = 10, B' = 10$ Market research director's belief

$a = 2, b = 2$ Sample evidence

$$\text{Odds } (A = 5 : A' = 10) = \frac{{}_AP_a \cdot {}_BP_b}{{}_{A'}P_a \cdot {}_{B'}P_b} = \frac{{}_5P_2 \cdot {}_{15}P_2}{{}_{10}P_2 \cdot {}_{10}P_2}$$

$$= \frac{(5)(4)(15)(14)}{(10)(9)(10)(9)} = \frac{4200}{8100} = \frac{14}{27}.$$

Of course the evidence favors the view of the market research director. After all, he maintains that half of the twenty territories are below standard, and half of the territories studied were found below standard. But only four territories were studied and it should not surprise you that the evidence is far from conclusive. The sales manager's view is still more than half as credible as the market research director's. Of course, they could both be wrong, but that is not our question.

Suppose now that having recognized the inconclusiveness of the four-territory study, our parties agree to expand the study to eight territories. This is done, and two more substandard territories are found. The total situation now is:

$A = 5, B = 15$ Sales manager's belief

$A' = 10, B' = 10$ Market research director's belief

$a = 4, b = 4$ Sample evidence

$$\text{Odds } (A = 5 : A' = 10) = \frac{{}_AP_a \cdot {}_BP_b}{{}_{A'}P_a \cdot {}_{B'}P_b} = \frac{{}_5P_4 \cdot {}_{15}P_4}{{}_{10}P_4 \cdot {}_{10}P_4}$$

$$= \frac{(5)(4)(3)(2)(15)(14)(13)(12)}{(10)(9)(8)(7)(10)(9)(8)(7)} = \frac{13}{84}.$$

The odds favoring the sales manager's belief are now slimmer.

If the sample outcomes in the study of four and eight territories were the result of sampling with replacement, the odds on true states would be different. Sampling with replacement would mean that the sampling mechanism could select any given territory more than once, and the results for a territory would be counted as many times as the territory appeared in the sample.

The odds in this situation would be

Outcome: $a = 2, b = 2$.

$$\text{Odds } (A = 5 : A' = 10) = \frac{A^a B^b}{A'^a B'^b} = \frac{(5)^2(15)^2}{(10)^2(10)^2}$$

$$= \left(\frac{1}{2} \cdot \frac{3}{2}\right)^2 = \left(\frac{3}{4}\right)^2 = \frac{9}{16}.$$

Outcome: $a = 4, b = 4$.

$$\text{Odds } (A = 5 : A' = 10) = \frac{A^a B^b}{A'^a B'^b} = \frac{(5)^4(15)^4}{(10)^4(10)^4}$$

$$= \left(\frac{1}{2} \cdot \frac{3}{2}\right)^4 = \left(\frac{3}{4}\right)^4 = \frac{81}{256}.$$

Compare the odds achieved by the two sampling methods. After the first sample of four, sampling without replacement yields the more disparate odds—14 to 27 as against 9 to 16. After the results of the expanded sample the comparison becomes 13 to 84 as against 81 to 256, a much more marked difference. The reason goes back to the fact that sampling with replacement creates an infinite statistical population about which the truth can never be known. In sampling without replacement, however, the truth can be known because the statistical population is finite. In fact with a sample of 4 out of 20 sales territories we know the truth about 20 per cent of the population. Common sense tells us that we would learn more by sampling a small finite population without replacement than with replacement. Comparison of the odds shows the effect in our particular example.

EXERCISES

3.4   Two identical urns each contain five poker chips. Urn 1 contains two red and three black chips, and urn 2 contains four red and one black chip. An observer is to identify the urns by sampling. A coin is flipped to determine whether to sample the urn on the left or the one on the right, and one chip is drawn from the urn selected.
      (a) Draw a tree diagram showing the marginal probabilities of selecting

each urn, the conditional probabilities of the sample outcome given the urn selected, and the joint probabilities of selecting each urn and observing each outcome.

(b) What is the probability that urn 1 was sampled if a black chip was drawn?   *Ans.* 3/4.

(c) What is the probability that urn 2 was sampled given that a red chip was observed?   *Ans.* 2/3.

3.5 Consider the urns of Exercise 3.4 except that there are now five type 2 urns and one type 1 urn. The urns are numbered from one to six and selection of an urn is made by rolling a die. Two chips are drawn, with replacement, from the urn selected. Using Bayes' theorem, find the probability that the type 1 urn was selected:

(a) If two black chips are observed.

(b) If one red and one black chip are observed.

(c) If two red chips are observed.

3.6 Refer to the populations of Exercise 3.1.

(a) If a sample of five produces two "2's," what are the odds that it came from population III as against population II?   *Ans.* 1 to 3.

(b) If a sample of ten produces four "2's," what are the odds on population III as against II as the source of the sample?   *Ans.* 1 to 9.

(c) A sample of four is to be taken from a population whose characteristics are unknown. What odds for population III as against population II would be established by the occurrence of one "2"? Of no "2's"?   *Ans.* 1 to 9; 1 to 81.

3.7 Refer to the populations of Exercise 3.1. Using combinatorial formulas, find:

(a) The number of possible sample sequences of size three that will produce one "6" and two "2's" from population III.

(b) The number of possible sample sequences of size three that will produce a sum of "10" from population I.

(c) The odds that a sample of three with a sum exceeding 10 came from population III as against population II.

3.8 A plant has been receiving periodic shipments of ten units each of an expensive component for a pilot production project. In the past, 75 per cent of these shipments had but one defective component in the ten, and 25 per cent of the shipments had two defectives.

(a) A current shipment of ten components is received and the first unit tried is found to be defective. Combine the prior experience and the current information to establish the odds that the current shipment has nine good components as against eight good components.
                                                                                   Ans. 3 to 2.

(b) The next two components tried are found satisfactory. At this point what are the odds in part (a)?   *Ans.* 27 to 14.

3-4 Probability and Decision-Making Systems

Consider a personnel department faced with the task of screening applicants for a particular job classification in a large organization. A test containing skill and aptitude items related to performance on the job is available. A cut-off score is determined, and applicants whose score equals or exceeds this level are referred to the department concerned. Applicants scoring below the cut-off point are screened out.

The foregoing is a description of a decision system. The decision system involves (1) the test instrument, and (2) the decision rule. Application of the rule to the results of the test instrument should be related to whether an applicant is really suited, or would perform satisfactorily on the job. Suppose that, prior to instituting the decision system, the company tried out the aptitude test on two groups of employees—one group known to have performed satisfactorily in the job in question, and another group who had not performed satisfactorily. Based on the suggested cut-off point for referring candidates, they constructed the following table.

	True state	
	Suited	Not suited
Decision	(S_1)	(S_2)
Refer (D_1)	.90	.20
Not refer (D_2)	.10	.80
Total	1.00	1.00

Here we find that 90 per cent of the group who were really suited for the job would have been referred by the decision system, and 80 per cent of those not really suited would not have been recommended. Apparently the decision system is related to the true state of affairs, but not perfectly related. Indeed, this is the type of result we would expect, for few if any such tests predict performance perfectly.

Let us skip an important step, and consider that the study of the validity of the aptitude-skill test was made on groups large enough and similar enough to current applicants for the job so that we can accept the proportions above as probabilities for future applications of the decision system. Under this consideration, the table presents conditional probabilities of decisions given the true state of affairs. That $P(D_1 | S_1)$ is quite different from $P(D_1 | S_2)$ means that the decisions are not independent of, but are quite highly related to the true state of affairs. The set of conditional probabilities reveals an important feature of the decision system—namely, its error characteristics. We know that, if an applicant is truly suited for the job, we stand a .10 chance of not referring him. If an employee is not suited for the job, we stand a .20 chance of making the mistake of referring him.

Note that changing the severity of the decision rule will only result in trading off one of these conditional error probabilities against the other. To cut down the proportion of unsuited applicants who would be recommended we could raise the cut-off score, but this would increase the proportion of really suitable employees whom we fail to recommend. Similarly, lowering the cut-off score would reduce the probability of not referring a suitable applicant, but raise the probability of referring unsuitable applicants.

The only way to reduce both of the conditional error probabilities is to improve the test used in the decision system. This amounts to developing a test instrument that bears a closer relationship to the true state of affairs. To do this would involve further effort and expense, which might or might not be justified by decreased error conditions.

Our discussion of the features of a decision system has so far centered on the question of how the decision system will operate if a particular state of affairs prevails. "What is the probability that the decision system will recommend an applicant who is really suited to the job?" is a question of this kind. While the answer to such a question is extremely useful, many persons would have asked a quite different question: "What is the probability that an applicant recommended by the decision system is really suited to the job?" After all, the quality of performance on the job will depend directly on the quality of applicants recommended. The answer to this question requires a probability of the type $P(S|D)$, as opposed to the $P(D|S)$ probabilities that were discussed above. Rather than the probability of a particular decision given a state of affairs, we want the probability of a particular state of affairs given a decision. The study of validity of the aptitude-skill test yielded $P(D|S)$ directly. If $P(SD)$, the joint probability table, can be obtained, $P(S|D)$ can be calculated directly from it. But $P(SD) = P(S) \cdot P(D|S)$. Evidently, to answer the kind of question posed, we need to know the proportions of applicants who are really suited and not suited for the job.

The proportion of applicants who are really suited for the job is a characteristic that the company might be able to investigate through a sample survey. At some cost, a sample of current applicants could be tried out on the job for whatever period needed to determine their suitability. The proportion of this group who were found suitable could be used as an estimate of the quality of applicants that will be encountered in the future. Detailed problems of estimation are dealt with in Chapter 8. Suppose this to have been done, and the proportion of suitable applicants found to be .30—that is, $P(S_1) = .30$ and $P(S_2) = .70$. The joint probability table can then be constructed:

Decision	True state		$P(D)$	
	S_1	S_2		
D_1	.27	.14	.41	$P(S_1 D_1) = .30(.90) = .27$
D_2	.03	.56	.59	$P(S_1 D_2) = .30(.10) = .03$
$P(S)$	.30	.70	1.00	$P(S_2 D_1) = .70(.20) = .14$
				$P(S_2 D_2) = .70(.80) = .56$

Then, the conditional probabilities of states, given one or the other decision, are

Decision	True state		Total	
	S_1	S_2		
D_1	.66	.34	1.00	$P(S_1|D_1) = .27/.41 = .66$
D_2	.05	.95	1.00	$P(S_2|D_1) = .14/.41 = .34$
				$P(S_1|D_2) = .03/.59 = .05$
				$P(S_2|D_2) = .56/.59 = .95$

Based on our estimate of the state of suitability of applicants, fully 34 per cent of all applicants referred by the decision system will be unsuited to the job. From this point of view the decision system does not seem to be a very satisfactory one. Before accepting this conclusion, however, we should investigate another point.

Expected value. Most persons have some familiarity with the idea of the expected value of a gamble. Suppose you are fortunate enough to find someone who will pay you $8 if you roll a "one" on a throw of a die in return for your promise to pay him $1 if you roll any other number. In a long run of throws you would expect to win $8 one-sixth of the time and lose $1 five-sixths of the time. The expected value of the gamble to you is

$$\tfrac{1}{6}(\$8) + \tfrac{5}{6}(-\$1) = \$1.33 - \$.83 = \$.50.$$

In a long run of throws you expect to win $.50 per throw on the average. This is the expected value of any given number of throws, including one. Formalizing the terms involved, we have

$$V = \text{the value associated with an outcome, } X,$$
$$\bar{V} = \text{expected value,}$$
$$\bar{V} = \Sigma\,[P(X)\cdot V].$$

In the personnel referral problem, each combination of state and decision has certain value consequences. Referring a suitable employee creates an opportunity for gains through higher labor productivity; referring an unsuitable employee involves negative values of possible spoiled work and costs of subsequent separation; failing to refer a suitable employee involves certain implicit costs represented by a lost opportunity. Assessment of these values could be a difficult matter. If the joint probability distribution of states and decisions is available, and the value of each state and decision combination has been assessed, then we can find the expected value of the decision system.

Suppose values have been determined as shown in the right-hand panel below. The units could be monetary or might represent some other index of value.

	JOINT PROBABILITIES				CONDITIONAL VALUE	
	True state				True state	
Decision	S_1	S_2	$P(D)$	Decision	S_1	S_2
D_1	.27	.14	.41	D_1	50	−10
D_2	.03	.56	.59	D_2	−20	0
$P(S)$	.30	.70	1.00			

Letting X stand for the combination of states and decisions, we have

$$\bar{V} = \Sigma\,[V \cdot P(X)]$$
$$= (50)(.27) + (-20)(.03) + (-10)(.14) + (0)(.56)$$
$$= 11.5 \text{ per decision.}$$

We pointed out before that the probability of referring unsuitable employees could be decreased by raising the cut-off score separating the "refer" from the "do not refer" groups. However, it might "pay" now to lower the cut-off score, since the loss of value from referring an unsuitable employee is less than that of not referring a suitable employee—that is, $-10 > -20$. Whether such a change should be made under the current value conditions depends on how the two error probabilities change as the cut-off point is lowered. In short, we would have to know the error probabilities under the new decision rule so that the expected value under the new rule could be calculated.

We also pointed out that the company could search for a test that would lead to a decision system in which the decisions depended more closely on the true state of affairs. Such a decision system would have a joint probability distribution of states and decisions closer to the following:

	S_1	S_2	$P(D)$
D_1	.30	.00	.30
D_2	.00	.70	.70
$P(S)$	.30	.70	1.00

This table presents a perfect decision system. The system refers all suitable employees and fails to refer all unsuitable employees. The expected value of this perfect decision system is $(50)(.30) + (0)(.70) = 15$ per decision. The perfect decision system would raise our expected value by 3.5 per decision. This is the expected value to the decision-maker of completely removing decision error. In other words, it is the *expected value of perfect information*.

A preview of decision-system analysis. The personnel example just completed provides a sampling of the "flavor" of statistical decision making. It also emphasizes the role of probability in a decision system based on sample information. Some aspects of this role are:

1. Probability theory can be employed to find the conditional probabilities of alternative decisions given alternative states, $P(D|S)$.

2. To find the conditional probabilities of states given decisions, $P(S \mid D)$, unconditional probabilities of states, $P(S)$, are required. Objective estimates of these probabilities can be made from samples, as for example the survey to determine the proportion of qualified persons in the applicant population.

3. When probabilities of states are available we can find the joint probability distribution of states and decisions.

4. Given the joint probability and conditional value of each combination of state and decision, we can calculate the expected value of a decision system.

5. Where the expected value of a decision system can be found, the decision rule can be altered to find the optimal rule for a given test instrument.

6. When probabilities of states are available and values are assessed, the expected value of one decision system can be evaluated against another, or compared with the value of a perfect decision system.

EXERCISES

3.9 The probabilities that effective and defective assemblies of a particular system will operate without breakdown for a preliminary period are given below.

Probability of :	Effective assemblies	Defective assemblies
Successful operation	.80	.40
Breakdown	.20	.60

(a) Suppose that 60 per cent of all assemblies on hand are effective, and construct the joint probability table.

(b) What is the probability that an assembly is effective given that it has broken down?   *Ans.* 1/3.

(c) What is the probability of an assembly's operating successfully given that it is defective?   *Ans.* 2/5.

3.10 Suppose the result of a lower cut-off score in the employee referral problem in Sec. 3–4 is that 95 per cent of the suitable and 40 per cent of the unsuitable employees would be referred. Find the expected value of this decision rule.   *Ans.* 11.15.

3.11 Ninety per cent of persons applying to a firm for credit are "good credit risks." The probability of a good credit risk's owning his own home is .70, and for bad risks the same probability is .40. Seventy per cent of the good credit risks within each ownership class have checking accounts in local banks, while this percentage is 50 for bad risks.

(a) Draw a tree diagram showing, from left to right, the probabilities of the states of credit risk, the conditional probabilities relating to home ownership, and the joint probabilities of credit-risk and home-ownership status.

(b) What is the probability that a home owner is a poor credit risk?
Ans. .06.

(c) What is the probability that an applicant who does not own his home is a good credit risk? *Ans.* .82.

3.12 Extend the tree diagram of Exercise 3.11 to show the conditional probabilities relating to checking accounts given credit status and home ownership, and the joint probabilities of all three characteristics. Suppose the firm adopts a decision rule to grant credit automatically to applicants verified to own their home and possess a local checking account, and to refuse credit to applicants having neither of these properties. In all other instances decision is to be delayed pending further investigation.

(a) What is the probability that an applicant to whom credit is automatically granted is a poor credit risk?

(b) What is the probability that an applicant who is automatically refused credit is a good credit risk?

(c) How would the answers above have compared with parts (b) and (c) of Exercise 3.11 if all home owners had local checking accounts and no one without a local checking account was a home owner? What does this suggest about the use of multiple criteria for decision making?

3.13 The World Series may require four, five, six, or seven baseball games. Assuming two evenly matched teams:

(a) In how many different ways (won and lost sequences) can a given team win the series? (Remember that the winning team cannot lose the last game!) *Ans.* 35.

(b) If teams are in the fourth game, what are the odds that they stand two games to one as opposed to three games to none? *Ans.* 3 to 1.

(c) If the teams are in the fifth game, what are the odds that they stand two games to two as opposed to three games to one? *Ans.* 3 to 2.

3.14 Between evenly matched teams in a World Series, find the following:

(a) The probability that the series will last only four games. *Ans.* 1/8.

(b) Given that the series goes to five games, find the probability that the team winning the fifth game won three of the previous four games. *Ans.* 2/7.

(c) Find the probability that the series lasts only five games. *Ans.* 1/4.

3.15 A carnival concessionaire operates a game in which the player throws three balls onto a board containing thirty white slots and ten red slots. The slots are arranged in such a manner that it makes no difference whether the player aims the balls or not.

(a) Find the probability of two of the three balls landing on red; all three balls landing on red. *Ans.* 9/64; 1/64.

(b) If the player bets that two of the three balls will land on red and wins, the operator pays off $6 for each dollar bet; on a winning bet of all three on red the operator pays $50 for each dollar bet. Which is the wiser bet for the player?

3.16 The rules of craps are given at the end of Sec. 1–1.

(a) What is the probability that the roller wins by rolling a point and subsequently rerolling "point" before a seven?　　　*Ans.* .2707.

(b) What is the probability that the roller wins a game of craps?
　　　　　　　　　　　　　　　　　　　　　　Ans. .4929.

(c) "Side bets" are frequently made on rerolling "point" before "seven." Which is the better bet for the roller—one paying off $9 for $5 bet when "four" is point, or one paying off $7 for $5 bet when "five" is point?

REFERENCES

Chernoff, H., and L. E. Moses, *Elementary Decision Theory.* New York: John Wiley & Sons, Inc., 1959.

Goldberg, S., *Probability: An Introduction.* Englewood Cliffs, N.J.: Prentice-Hall, Inc., 1960.

4

Probability
Distributions
for Discrete Variables

In Chapter 1, we learned some basic rules for combining the probabilities of elemental events to find the probabilities of more complex events. We also learned that a probability distribution is simply an exhaustive listing of the possible outcomes of an experiment or trial together with their associated probabilities. In mathematical language, it is a functional statement or rule of transformation between the outcomes and the probabilities of the outcomes. The rule may be in the form of a table, graph, or mathematical formula; for the types of probability distributions continually encountered in statistical applications it is helpful to have a mathematical formulation. The computation of the probabilities involved is reduced to a routine operation, and mathematical analysis can be used in the development of statistical methods involving these distributions.

In this chapter we will study some applications of two probability distributions for discrete variables: the binomial distribution and the Poisson distribution. We will also see how a continuous distribution, the so-called normal curve, may be used to approximate certain binomial and Poisson probability distributions.

The Binomial Distribution

A mailing service states that 90 per cent of the addresses in a list it maintains are current. If four names are selected independently from the list, what is the probability that none is current? One? Two? Three? Four? You should already be able to work this problem. The probability of a current address on a single draw is 9/10. For four draws to produce no current addresses, each of four independent trials must produce an outcome whose individual probability is 1/10. Therefore, $P(\text{zero current}) = (\frac{1}{10})^4 = 1/10,000$.

There are a number of mutually exclusive ways of finding one current address in four. We can list these ways (employing subscripts for the sequence of draws), calculate their individual probabilities by the multiplication theorem for independent events, and sum the probabilities of the mutually exclusive sequences that represent but one current address. Using the symbol S for a current address, and F for a noncurrent address,

$$P(S_1F_2F_3F_4) = \tfrac{9}{10}\cdot\tfrac{1}{10}\cdot\tfrac{1}{10}\cdot\tfrac{1}{10} = 9/10,000$$

$$P(F_1S_2F_3F_4) = \tfrac{1}{10}\cdot\tfrac{9}{10}\cdot\tfrac{1}{10}\cdot\tfrac{1}{10} = 9/10,000$$

$$P(F_1F_2S_3F_4) = \tfrac{1}{10}\cdot\tfrac{1}{10}\cdot\tfrac{9}{10}\cdot\tfrac{1}{10} = 9/10,000$$

$$P(F_1F_2F_3S_4) = \tfrac{1}{10}\cdot\tfrac{1}{10}\cdot\tfrac{1}{10}\cdot\tfrac{9}{10} = \underline{9/10,000}$$

$$P \text{ (one current)} = \qquad\qquad\qquad 36/10,000$$

By this point, the reader may have observed that each individual way of producing exactly one success in four trials has a probability of $(9/10)^1 \cdot (1/10)^3$, and that the four ways of producing one success are the number of ways of assigning one success (S) to the sequence of four draws—that is, $_4C_1$. Thus, the probability of one success could have been obtained by

$$_4C_1(\tfrac{9}{10})^1(\tfrac{1}{10})^3 = 4(9/10,000) = 36/10,000.$$

Similar reasoning would lead us to state the probability of two successes as

$$_4C_2(\tfrac{9}{10})^2(\tfrac{1}{10})^2 = 6(81/10,000) = 486/10,000,$$

the probability of three successes as

$$_4C_3(\tfrac{9}{10})^3(\tfrac{1}{10})^1 = 4(729/10,000) = 2916/10,000,$$

and of four successes as

$$_4C_4(\tfrac{9}{10})^4(\tfrac{1}{10})^0 = 1(6561/10,000) = 6561/10,000.$$

Notice that the product of the terms involving 9/10 and 1/10 raised to different powers represents the probability of any *one* of the sequences that will result in the designated number of successes, and that the combination term represents the number of such sequences that exist.

The type of problem illustrated above can now be stated in general terms that define a *binomial probability process*.

A trial can give rise to but two mutually exclusive outcomes, S and F. The probabilities of a success, P(S), and a failure, P(F), are known. Find the probability that n independent trials will result in r successes.

Letting $P(S) = p$, and $P(F) = q$, then the formula for the probability of r successes in n independent trials is given by

$$P(r) = {}_nC_r \cdot p^r \cdot q^{n-r}. \tag{4-1}$$

4-2 The Binomial Distribution and Errors of Decision

A neighborhood baker has a considerable reputation for his apple pie. Having an experimental turn of mind, however, he has developed a new recipe. He is fond of the new pie, but has no idea whether his customers will prefer it to the old. He decides to bake up five of the experimental pies and give them to a sample of his customers along with his regular apple pie. They are to compare the pies, reporting back their preference.

The baker is concerned, of course, with the state of preference of all of his apple pie customers. As a businessman, he has decided that he ought to change over to the new recipe if more than 60 per cent of his customers prefer it to the old. He knows intuitively, though, that a sample of five will not provide a definitive account of the state of preference in his customer population. Being a good forward planner, he wonders what decision he should reach about his pie recipes depending on how his survey of customer preference comes out. After all, there is no sense in making the survey unless it gives him some idea what action to take! Considering the possible sample outcomes, he arrives tentatively at the following rule for decision.

1. If less than a majority in the sample prefer the new recipe, continue with the old apple pie.
2. If all five customers in the sample prefer the new recipe, adopt it in place of the old apple pie.
3. If three or four of the five customers prefer the new recipe, postpone any final decision. (The baker feels he would not know how to act in this event, and might bake up another five pies to try out on a further sample of customers.)

With the aid of the binomial distribution we can trace the consequences of the baker's decision rule. *Given any specified proportion of his clientele preferring the new recipe*, the appearance of preference in a random sample of five is a binomial process, if sampling is with replacement. (If sampling is without replacement it is a hypergeometric process, which can be approximated by the binomial when the ratio of sample to population size, n/N, is small.) We want to find the probability of r out of 5 preferences for the new pie in a group of 5 independently occurring preferences, where r stands, in turn, for the integers $0, 1, 2, 3, 4,$ and 5.

But, the student may well object: "The true measure of preference in the population must be known before the binomial distribution can be employed. This is what the baker is trying to find out—it is the end of the survey and not the beginning." While this is correct, we can reason as follows. We want to evaluate the consequences of any proposed decision rule *before* we finally adopt the rule, spend money on gathering the information called for, and make the decision. The consequences of a decision rule are the chances of correct and incorrect decisions that would flow from adopting the rule. Since we do not *know* the true state of affairs, we would prefer a rule that has a considerable assurance of leading to a correct decision over a wide range of true states. We want to protect ourselves against errors no matter what the true state of affairs is—to hedge all bets, so to speak. To find what these errors are, we ask: How would our decision rule work if state S_1 existed? If state S_2 were the case? S_3? S_4? S_5?...S_n? In short, we answer a series of "if-then" questions by finding in each instance a conditional probability—the probability of a particular decision *given* a particular state. We can then see if the decision rule provides the wide range of protection we seek. If not, we can consider changing the decision rule.

Now we can proceed to find the probabilities of sample outcomes given a variety of true states. We are going to consider true states from zero per cent preferring the new apple pie ($p = 0.0$) to 100 per cent preferring the new apple pie ($p = 1.0$) at intervals .10 apart. Many more true states could be considered, but these will be enough to outline the consequences of the baker's proposed decision rule. Table 4–1 presents the sample outcomes and their probabilities given each true state. Keeping in mind that the sample size is five ($n = 5$), you should be able to verify the probabilities in Table 4–1 through the binomial formula:

$$P(r \mid p) = {}_nC_r \cdot p^r \cdot q^{n-r}.$$

Table 4-1

PROBABILITIES OF SAMPLE OUTCOMES GIVEN VARIOUS TRUE STATES

True state (p)

Sample outcome (r)	0.0	.10	.20	.30	.40	.50	.60	.70	.80	.90	1.00
0	1.000	.5905	.3277	.1681	.0778	.0312	.0102	.0024	.0003	—	—
1	—	.3280	.4096	.3601	.2592	.1563	.0768	.0284	.0064	.0005	—
2	—	.0729	.2048	.3087	.3456	.3125	.2304	.1323	.0512	.0081	—
3	—	.0081	.0512	.1323	.2304	.3125	.3456	.3087	.2048	.0729	—
4	—	.0005	.0064	.0284	.0768	.1563	.2592	.3601	.4096	.3280	—
5	—	—	.0003	.0024	.0102	.0312	.0778	.1681	.3277	.5905	1.000
Total	1.000	1.0000	1.0000	1.0000	1.0000	1.0000	1.0000	1.0000	1.0000	1.0000	1.000

For example,

$$P(r = 2 \mid p = .30) = {}_5C_2(.30)^2(.70)^3 = 10(.09)(.343) = .3087,$$
$$P(r = 4 \mid p = .90) = {}_5C_4(.90)^4(.10)^1 = 5(.6561)(.01) = .3280.$$

Note that the binomial formula produces probability distributions of differing "shape" depending on the value of p. When $p = .50$ the probabilities are symmetrical about np, or 2.5 for the example of Table 4–1. For values of p below .50 the probabilities are concentrated at lower values of r but are skewed, or "tail off" toward the higher values.

In order to relate these probabilities to the baker's proposed decision rule, one should have the rule clearly in mind. In briefest form, it was

$D_1 = $ Continue with old recipe. Adopt D_1 if $r = 0, 1,$ or 2.

$D_2 = $ Change to new recipe. Adopt D_2 if $r = 5.$

$D_0 = $ Refuse to decide between D_1 and D_2. Adopt D_0 if $r = 3$ or 4.

By summing the appropriate entries in Table 4–1, we can find the probabilities of D_1, D_2, and D_0 for each of the true states of preference, p. These probabilities are shown in the first three columns of Table 4–2. For example, if the true proportion of customers preferring the new recipe is .30, the probability of continuing with the old recipe, D_1, is .8369, the probability of changing to the new recipe, D_2, is .0024, and the probability of refusing to decide, D_0, is .1607. These probabilities add to 1.0, since all possible sample outcomes are associated with one of the three decisions.

Table 4-2

PROBABILITIES OF DECISIONS AND CHARACTERISTICS OF DECISION RULE FOR
BAKER'S APPLE PIE PROBLEM

True state	Probability of D_1	Probability of D_2	Probability of D_0	Probability of a terminal decision $1 - P(D_0)$	Error condition D_e	Probabliity of decision error $P(D_e)$
0.00	1.0000	.0000	.0000	1.0000	D_2	—
.10	.9914	.0000	.0086	.9914	D_2	—
.20	.9421	.0003	.0576	.9424	D_2	.0003
.30	.8369	.0024	.1607	.8393	D_2	.0024
.40	.6826	.0102	.3072	.6928	D_2	.0102
.50	.5000	.0312	.4688	.5312	D_2	.0312
.60	.3174	.0778	.6048	.3952	D_2	.0778
.70	.1631	.1681	.6668	.3332	D_1	.1631
.80	.0579	.3277	.6144	.3854	D_1	.0579
.90	.0086	.5905	.4009	.5991	D_1	.0086
1.00	.0000	1.0000	.0000	1.0000	D_1	—

Characteristics of the decision rule. The last three columns of Table 4–2 summarize the consequences of the decision rule. Remember that the baker stated, in effect, that if he knew that the true proportion preferring the new recipe was more than .60, his business decision would be to switch to the new recipe; otherwise, he would stick with the old recipe. Therefore, to adopt D_2 (change to new recipe) would be a decision *error* for any true state equal to or less than $p = .60$. Similarly, to adopt D_1 if the value of p were greater than .60 would constitute a decision *error*. These facts are noted under the column headed "error condition." The entries are the decisions that, if adopted, would constitute an error under the state given. The term D_e, or decision error, is applied to these error conditions.

Note that D_0, refusing to make a decision, is never an error condition. It is not a *terminal*, or a final decision. The action involved in a D_0 decision is suspension of judgment and seeking of further information to enable a terminal decision to be made. It follows that $1 - P(D_0)$ is the probability of reaching a terminal decision, which we will call *terminal decision capacity*. Other things being equal, we would like a decision system that has a high terminal decision capacity. However, other things are not equal. The decision-maker seeks to avoid incorrect terminal decisions—that is, to minimize the probability of terminal decision error. The probability of *terminal decision error* is shown in the final column of Table 4–2.

High terminal decision capacity and low terminal decision error, while both desirable in a decision rule, are partially in conflict. One way to insure accuracy, or lack of terminal error, is to adopt a decision rule that inhibits terminal decision capacity. At the extreme we can insure that we will never make an error by never making a decision. This extreme is forestalled by paying attention to terminal decision capacity.

Raising terminal decision capacity, with a constant sample size, tends to increase terminal decision error. One raises decision capacity by being willing to discriminate more closely between the alternate terminal decisions D_1 and D_2. For example, a decision rule calling for continuing the old recipe if 0, 1, 2, or 3 customers in the sample preferred the new, and adopting the new recipe if 4 or 5 preferred the new would have a terminal decision capacity of 1.0 whatever the true state. The possibility of delaying the terminal decision has been ruled out entirely. But our baker was unwilling to discriminate this finely from a sample of five. In effect, he made an intuitive judgment that such a procedure would have high probabilities of terminal decision error.

To develop the basis for this judgment, we can consider changes in the baker's decision rule. Figure 4–1 shows the terminal decision capacity and error curves for the original rule together with the curves for two other rules for the sample size $n = 5$. The three rules can be summarized as follows:

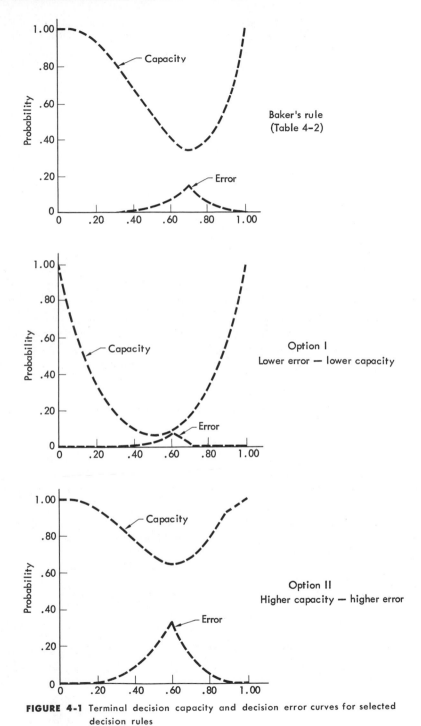

FIGURE 4-1 Terminal decision capacity and decision error curves for selected decision rules

Sample outcome	Decision under original rule	Decision under Option I	Decision under Option II
0	D_1	D_1	D_1
1	D_1	D_0	D_1
2	D_1	D_0	D_1
3	D_0	D_0	D_0
4	D_0	D_0	D_2
5	D_2	D_2	D_2

Optional Rule I provides less error, but at a sacrifice of terminal decision capacity. Optional Rule II moves in the other direction, providing increased terminal decision capacity at the expense of higher decision error. By working with Table 4–1 you should be able to verify the points on the curves for these optional rules.

The most extreme positions that the two curves could take represent extreme sorts of decision behavior. The refusal to make any positive decisions at all leaves one entirely uncommitted and "error-free." Insistence on the making of positive decisions with no evidence at all maintains terminal decision capacity at 1.0 but leaves decision accuracy a matter of the chance concurrence of the true state of affairs and the appropriate decision. After looking at the curves our baker may decide, after all, that he prefers his original decision rule. But he has now made the choice on the basis of the consequences of this rule compared to alternatives available.

4-3   The Mean and Variance of the Binomial Distribution

The mean and variance of a binomial distribution can be derived directly from the mean and variance of the underlying binary population. The underlying population is completely defined by $P(S) = p$, the probability of a success, and $P(F) = q$, the probability of a failure on a single trial or draw from the population.

If we let an occurrence of a success take the value 1, and an occurrence of a failure the value zero, the population has the following distribution:

X	$P(X)$
0	$q = 1 - p$
1	p

The mean of the binary population is

$$\mu = \Sigma[X \cdot P(X)]$$
$$= 0(q) + 1(p) = p.$$

The variance of the binary population is

$$\sigma^2 = \Sigma[(X - \mu)^2 \cdot P(X)]$$
$$= (0 - p)^2 q + (1 - p)^2 p$$
$$= p^2 q + q^2 p$$
$$= pq(p + q) = pq,$$
$$\text{since} \quad p + q = 1.$$

Thus a binary population of X has the parameters

$$\mu_X = p, \tag{4-2}$$
$$\sigma_X^2 = pq. \tag{4-3}$$

The binomial formula in Eq. (4–1) provides the probability distribution of r successes in n independent trials or draws from the binary population. The number of successes, or r, where a success has the value 1 and a failure the value zero, is simply $r = \Sigma X$. The binomial distribution then can be viewed as the probability distribution of ΣX. Remembering the rules for the mean and variance of a sum, we have

$$\mu_r = p_1 + p_2 + p_3 + \ldots + p_n = np, \tag{4-4}$$
$$\sigma_r^2 = p_1 q_1 + p_2 q_2 + p_3 q_3 + \ldots + p_n q_n = npq. \tag{4-5}$$

The mean and variance of the binomial distribution depend, then, only on the parameters of the underlying binary population and the number of independent trials, or sample size. Summarizing, we have

	Mean	Variance
Binary population	p	pq
Binomial distribution	np	npq

EXERCISES

4.1 A store with a one-price policy is attempting to keep its price for a given item to different people in line with a competitor who sells at varying discounts. The store sends out four shoppers each week who buy the competitor's item at the best price they can get. If the store manager knew that half or more of the competitor's sales were at lower prices, he would lower his price, and if less than half were at lower prices he would raise his price.

(a) Assuming random selection, find the probabilities of 0, 1, 2, 3, and 4 sales at lower prices if the true proportion of the competitor's sales at lower prices were 0.0; 0.1; 0.3; 0.5; 0.7; 0.9; 1.0.

    (b) Plot the curves for terminal decision capacity and decision error for a rule of raising the price if none of four shoppers buys lower, lowering price if all four buy lower, and doing nothing if one, two, or three of the four buy lower.

    (c) Plot the curves for terminal decision capacity and decision error for a rule of raising the price of an item if none or one out of four buys lower, lowering price if three or four buy lower, and doing nothing if two buy lower.

4.2   Find the mean and variance of the seven binary populations mentioned in Exercise 4.1(a) and the mean and variance of each of the seven binomial probability distributions.

4-4 The Poisson Distribution

Many events of concern in business are counted in a context of time or space. Examples are the number of surface defects in 4×8 sheets of plywood, the number of calls per minute to a central telephone exchange, the number of requests per week to supply a spare part from a central supply facility, or the number of errors per page of typed manuscript. The events actually occur at "points" in a continuum of time or space, but for convenience or necessity in studying the pattern of occurrence of the events, time or space is divided into intervals or units.

    The Poisson formula, attributed to the French mathematician Simeon Poisson (1781–1840), provides a probability distribution for the number of occurrences in the selected unit of time or space which depends only on the mean number of occurrences per stated unit. That is, given only the mean number of defects per 4×8 plywood sheet, the probability of 0, 1, 2, etc., defects per sheet can be determined; or given the mean number of requests per week for the spare part, the formula will supply the probability that 0, 1, 2, etc., requests will be received in a randomly selected week.

    Such a formula can be nothing more than the result of a set of assumptions about an underlying process that produces numerical observations. We saw that the binomial formula can be arrived at employing only the fundamental probability theorems once we assume that the observations are produced by independent trials from an underlying population with constant probability of a success. The underlying process that will produce a Poisson distribution of occurrences per observed unit is as follows:

    1. The number of occurrences is independent from unit to unit.

    2. The probability of a single occurrence in an infinitessimal unit is proportional to the size of the unit.

    3. The probability of more than one occurrence in an infinitessimal unit is negligible in comparison to the probability of a single occurrence.

These conditions can be illustrated in terms of the occurrence of defects at points along a spool of copper wire. Condition 1 means that finding any number of defects in a given segment of the wire tells us nothing (beyond what we already know from the average number of defects per segment) about how many defects to expect in the next segment of wire. Condition 2 says that for very small segments, the probability of a defect is proportional to the size of the segment. Condition 3 means that we can find a segment so small that the probability of more than one defect is negligible compared to the probability of one defect in that segment. In common terms these conditions mean that there is no tendency for the events to "cluster" in time or space. The events occur individually and collectively at random over the time or space continuum. These characteristics are likely to be reasonably approximated in a variety of "traffic" situations, such as passage of vehicles along an open highway, calls to a telephone exchange, and demands on a supply facility, or in the production of accidents by a system in a steady state of operation. If one is in doubt as to whether the Poisson distribution is applicable to a particular situation of interest, the solution is to gather some data from the process to compare with the probability distribution calculated from the Poisson formula. Then he can check whether the Poisson "model" provides a reasonable prediction of the actual pattern of occurrences. This comparison involves methods covered in later chapters, but the first step would be to find the Poisson probabilities in the manner to be discussed here.

The only parameter we must know in order to apply the Poisson formula is μ—the mean frequency of occurrence per observed unit of time or space. The Poisson formula for r, the number of occurrences per observed unit, is

$$P(r) = e^{-\mu}\left(\frac{\mu^r}{r!}\right), \tag{4-6}$$

where e is the constant (to four decimals) 2.7183.

Given the value of μ for any particular problem, $e^{-\mu} = 1/e^{\mu}$ will be a constant. The computation of probabilities is carried out by substituting the desired values of r in the expression $(\mu^r/r!)$. For example, consider the Poisson distribution of demand per week for a certain spare part, the average demand per week having been determined to be 0.1 parts.

We know that $\mu = .1$. Then,

$$e^{-\mu} = 2.7183^{-.1} = 1/2.7183^{.1}.$$

Then

$$\log e^{-\mu} = \log 1 - .1 \log. 2.7183$$
$$= -.1(.4343) = -.0434$$
$$= 9.9566 - 10,$$

and

$$e^{-\mu} = .905$$

$$P(r) = e^{-\mu}\left(\frac{\mu^r}{r!}\right) = .905\left(\frac{\mu^r}{r!}\right)$$

$$P(0) = .905\left(\frac{.1^0}{0!}\right) = .905\left(\frac{1}{1}\right) \quad = .905$$

$$P(1) = .905\left(\frac{.1^1}{1!}\right) = .905(.1) \quad = .090$$

$$P(2) = .905\left(\frac{.1^2}{2!}\right) = .905(.005) \quad = .005$$

$$P(3) = .905\left(\frac{.1^3}{3!}\right) = 1.905(.00017) = .000$$

$$P(r \leq 3) = \overline{1.000}$$

By the time we have carried the Poisson probabilities out to $r = 3$, we have cumulated very nearly all of the distribution, though of course there is some very small probability of any number of demands, however large.

Poisson distributions with increasing means. Not surprisingly when you think of the small average demand per week, the Poisson distribution above is highly skewed to the right. The most common demand in a week is zero, and the distribution tails off rapidly for 1, 2, and 3 demands. To see what happens for other values of the mean, consider the Poisson probabilities of demand for four-week intervals, for thirteen-week intervals, and for yearly intervals. With an average demand of .10 per week, the average demand for a four-week interval would be .4, for a thirteen-week interval $\mu = 1.3$, and for a yearly interval $\mu = 5.2$. The results are shown in Table 4–3.

Table 4-3

POISSON PROBABILITIES OF DEMAND DURING VARIOUS
TIME INTERVALS FOR A PART WITH MEAN DEMAND
OF .10 PER WEEK

Demand per period	Length of period		
r	4 weeks	13 weeks	52 weeks
0	.670	.273	.006
1	.268	.354	.028
2	.054	.230	.075
3	.007	.100	.129
4	.001	.032	.168
5		.009	.175
6		.002	.151
7			.113
8			.073
9			.042
10			.022
11			.011
12			.004
13			.002
14			.001
Total	1.000	1.000	1.000

Note that as the mean, μ, increases, or in this example as longer time intervals are considered, the skewness of the Poisson distribution diminishes. This tendency continues, and the Poisson distribution becomes very nearly symmetrical by the time a mean of ten is reached. A mean of 10.4 corresponds to average demand per two-year period in our example.

The Poisson distribution in inventory control. One important use of the Poisson distribution is suggested by the example of the distribution of demand for a spare part. If inventories are to be checked and replenished at periodic fixed intervals, one must set an inventory quantity to which stocks will be built up. This quantity, once established, will be drawn down by demands until the next check and replenishment time. But how large should this inventory level be? This depends on how sure one wants to be that stocks will not run out and a request come in after stocks are depleted. The latter event is known as a "stock-out."

The level of assurance against stock-outs should be set in accordance with an economic analysis of relevant cost elements that cannot be detailed at this point. Suppose, on the basis of such an analysis, that we want assurance against a stock-out of .95. This means we are willing to run a 5 per cent risk of a stock-out, a level that would work out over time to an average of one stock-out condition in twenty time intervals. From the Poisson distribution, we want to find the lowest level of demand, r, for which the probability of demand *exceeding r* is less than .05. If stocks are checked and replenished weekly, we can see from our original computation of Poisson probabilities that this inventory level is 1. From Table 4–3 we can see that if the interval is every four weeks the level is 2, since $P(r > 2) = .008$ and $P(r > 1) = .062$. For quarterly restocking it is 3, and for annual restocking the inventory quantity is 9. Note how the ratio of this minimum stock to the average level of demand, μ, changes as longer periods between replenishment are considered. This ratio moves from $1/.1 = 10$ to $2/.4 = 5$ to $3/1.3 = 2.3$ to $9/5.2 = 1.7$. This example only begins to suggest the usefulness of the Poisson distribution in the economic analysis and operation of inventory control systems.

The Poisson approximation to the positively skewed binomial. We saw that binomial probability distributions for small values of n become increasingly skewed as p departs from .50. For values of p less than .50 this skewness is to the right. We have also seen that the Poisson distribution has a greater degree of right skewness the smaller the mean number of occurrences per unit of time or space. While this point of similarity is a significant one, the differences between the binomial and Poisson data situations should first be noted. In the binomial sampling situation the unit of experience is a certain number of trials of an elemental event. We observe the number of successes and the number of failures. In the Poisson situation the unit of experience is a selected interval of time or space, and we count the occurrences of a given phenomenon within each interval. There is nothing in the Poisson situation comparable to the number of trials, n, or to the number of failures. We can count the number of occurrences but we cannot count the number of nonoccurrences.

Consider random samples of size ten taken from a large lot of bearings of which 5 per cent are defective. Our concern is with the probabilities of 0, 1, 2, . . ., 10 defective bearings in the sample. The binomial probability distribution with $p = .05$, $q = .95$, and $n = 10$ would apply. However, suppose we conceive the lot of bearings to be thoroughly mixed and placed in small boxes each containing ten bearings. Now if we think of counting the number of defective bearings per box, we are counting the occurrence of a phenomenon in an arbitrarily defined spatial unit. The average number of defective bearings per box would be 5 per cent of 10, or .5. Now from the Poisson formula we can find the probabilities of 0, 1, 2, . . ., 10 occurrences per unit given a mean occurrence per unit of .50. These are compared in Table 4–4 with the probabilities of 0, 1, 2, . . . , 10 from the binomial expansion with $p = .05, q = .95$, and $n = 10$.

Table 4-4

POISSON PROBABILITY DISTRIBUTION WITH
$\mu = .5$ AS AN APPROXIMATION TO THE BINOMIAL
PROBABILITY DISTRIBUTION WITH $p = .05$ and $n = 10$

r	$P(r)$ Binomial	$P(r)$ Poisson
0	.5987	.607
1	.3152	.303
2	.0746	.076
3	.0105	.012
4	.0009	.002
5	.0001	—
—	—	—
—	—	—
—	—	—
10	—	—
Total	1.0000	1.000

The agreement of the two sets of probabilities, although not exact, is relatively close unless one is concerned with estimating the very small binomial probabilities at $r = 4$ and $r = 5$ on the tail of the distribution. Remember—the binomial probabilities are the "correct" values we are seeking to estimate by using the Poisson. In general, the Poisson probabilities will be closer to the binomial probabilities the smaller the value of p and the larger the value of n in the binomial situation.

Whether to use the Poisson approximation to the binomial is a question of how close is "close," which can only be answered in terms of the requirements of an applied problem. In general, users seem to have no reservations when p is less than .10 and np is less than 5. The Poisson is often the only practical alternative when dealing with binomial sampling situations in which p is small and n exceeds the values commonly covered in tables of binomial probabilities.

The variance of the Poisson distribution. The variance, σ^2, of a Poisson distribution is exactly equal to its mean, μ. This fact is of very practical significance in connection with the normal approximation to the Poisson, discussed later in this chapter.

4-5 Tables of Cumulative Binomial and Poisson Probabilities

Probabilities are given in Appendix A for the binomial distribution and in Appendix B for the Poisson distribution. These are "cumulative" tables. For the binomial distribution, the table gives the probability of obtaining a specified number of successes, r_o, *or greater* given n and p:

$$P(r \geq r_o \mid n, p).$$

The Poisson table gives the probability of r_0 occurrences *or fewer* given μ, the expected number of occurrences for an interval:

$$P(r \leq r_o \mid \mu).$$

The cumulative forms are the most convenient for general-purpose tables. The probability of any discrete number of occurrences can be obtained by subtracting adjacent entries, and "more than," "equal to or more than," and "less than" probabilities can be obtained fairly directly. For example, consider ten observations ($n = 10$) of a binomial process in which $p = .35$. We will find the probabilities that r is

    (a) equal to or greater than 3,
    (b) less than 3,
    (c) exactly 3,
    (d) more than 3,
    (e) equal to or less than 3
    (f) equal to 2, 3, or 4.

The values in boldface are read from the table.

    (a) $P(r \geq 3) = \mathbf{.7384}$
    (b) $P(r < 3) = 1 - P(r \geq 3) = 1 - .7384 = .2616$
    (c) $P(r = 3) = P(r \geq 3) - P(r \geq 4) = \mathbf{.7384} - \mathbf{.4862} = .2522$
    (d) $P(r > 3) = P(r \geq 4) = \mathbf{.4862}$
    (e) $P(r \leq 3) = 1 - P(r \geq 4) = 1 - .4862 = .5138$
    (f) $P(2 \leq r \leq 4) = P(r \geq 2) - P(r \geq 5) = \mathbf{.9140} - \mathbf{.2485} = .6655$

The mechanics of working with an "equal to or less than" table such as the Poisson table of Appendix B can be carried out in a similar manner.

EXERCISES

4.3   A purchasing department is considering an acceptance sampling scheme for incoming lots of a manufactured item that can be classified as either good or bad. The plan calls for taking a random sample of 20 items from each lot. If there are no defectives in the sample, the lot is accepted; otherwise the lot is rejected.

(a) Find from the binomial distribution the probability of rejecting a 1 per cent defective lot, and the probability of accepting a 10 per cent defective lot.   *Ans.* .1821; .1216.

(b) Find from the Poisson distribution the approximations to the probabilities above.   *Ans.* .181; .135.

(c) Suppose the sample size is increased to 50, and lots are rejected only if two or more defectives are observed in the sample. What are the Poisson approximations to the probabilities in (a)?

Ans. .090; .040.

4.4   Demand for a certain replacement part was estimated to be distributed according to the Poisson with an expected demand of 3.0 per month.

(a) What is the probability that no demands will be experienced in a month?   *Ans.* .050.

(b) If stocks are to be replenished monthly, what is the minimum stock level that will limit the probability of demand exceeding the stock within a month to five in a hundred? One in a hundred?

Ans. 6; 8.

4.5   One thousand feet of wire from a production run are examined and two defects are found. Find the odds that the long-run process quality was one defect per thousand feet as against 1.5 defects per thousand feet.

Ans. Approx. 37 to 50.

4.6   If two thousand feet of wire were to produce four defects, what would the odds in Exercise 4.5 become?

4.7   Given the demand distribution of Exercise 4.4:

(a) Find the probability of experiencing a demand of 11 in a period of three months.

(b) If 11 demands are experienced, what are the odds that the process mean is 9.0 as against 7.0?

4.8   Suppose that "rejection" in Exercise 4.3 means that the lot is subjected to 100 per cent inspection with any defectives found being replaced by acceptable items. What will be the long-run percentage of defective items finally accepted in lots whose proportion defective is .01? .03? .05? .07? .09?   *Ans.* .82%; 1.63%; 1.79%; 1.64%; 1.36%.

4.9   In Exercise 4.3, assume an acceptable lot is one with $p \leq .10$, and that the decision rule is revised to call for accepting the lot if no defectives are found, taking a further sample if one or two defectives are found, and rejecting the lot if three or more defectives are found.

(a) Plot the curves for terminal decision capacity and terminal decision error at values of p from .01 to .41 at intervals of .05.

(b) Using a sample of 50 calling for accepting the lot if zero or one defective is found, further sampling if two, three, or four defectives are found, and rejecting the lot if five or more defectives are found, plot the curves for terminal decision capacity and terminal decision error.

4.10 During a period of 50 weeks demand for two spare parts was distributed as follows:

Weekly demands	Number of weeks Part A	Part B
0	34	21
1	12	21
2	4	7
3	—	1
Total	50	50

(a) Estimate the mean and variance of weekly demand for part A.

(b) Find the Poisson probabilities for distributions having the same mean demand per week as the sample of 50 weeks for part A; for part B.

4-6 A Sequential Decision Rule

In the baker's decision problem we were concerned with the decision errors that could follow upon the adoption of a rule for decision making. We also said that there might be some sample outcomes which would lead to no decision; if this happened the baker would seek more evidence in the form of a further sample before reaching a final decision. A procedure of this kind can be formalized in a sequential decision rule.

In acceptance sampling, sequential decision rules are frequently employed. For example, a sample of 30 is taken from an incoming lot of a manufactured item. If no defectives are found, the lot is accepted; if two or more defectives are found, it is rejected (or held for 100 per cent inspection); if one defective is found, a further sample of 30 is taken. If the cumulative number of defectives out of 60 is three or more, the lot is rejected. Otherwise 30 more items are selected. If the cumulative number of defectives is three or more the lot is rejected, and if less than three the lot is accepted.

This sequential plan can be summarized cumulatively as follows.

n	Accept if :	Continue sampling if :	Reject if :
30	$r = 0$	$r = 1$	$r \geq 2$
60	n.a.	$r = 1$ or 2	$r \geq 3$
90	$r = 1$ or 2	n.a.	$r \geq 3$

The tree diagram in Fig. 4–2 shows the different routes that can lead to accepting the lot and the routes that lead to rejecting the lot. Here, the numbers entered on the branches represent outcomes of the first, second, and third samples separately rather than in combination. The mutually exclusive ways of rejecting a lot can now be listed and the probability of rejecting a lot of any specified quality then found. Using subscripts for the successive samples, the probability of rejection is

$$P(r_1 \geq 2) + P(r_1 = 1) \cdot P(r_2 \geq 2) + P(r_1 = 1) \cdot P(r_2 = 0) \cdot P(r_3 \geq 2)$$
$$+ P(r_1 = 1) \cdot P(r_2 = 1) \cdot P(r_3 \geq 1).$$

Using the Poisson approximation to the binomial with $\mu = np = 30(.01) = .3$, let us figure the probability of rejecting a 1 per cent defective lot. Using Appendix B to determine the individual probabilities, we find

$$P(\text{reject}) = .037 + .222(.037) + .222(.741)(.037) + .222(.222)(.259)$$
$$= .037 + .008 + .006 + .001,$$
$$P(\text{reject}) = .052.$$

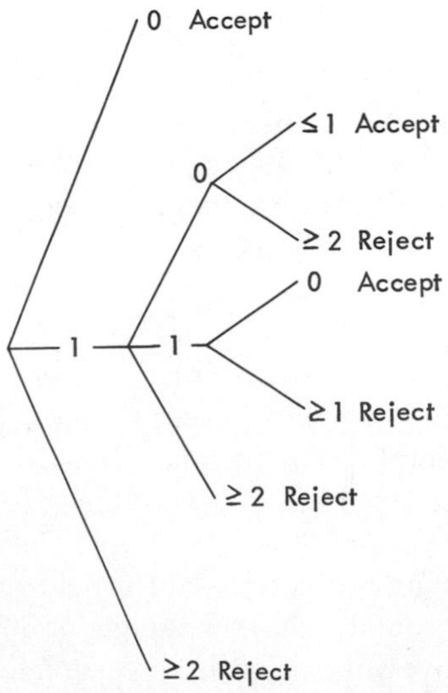

FIGURE 4-2 Decision procedure based on number of defectives observed in sequential samples of size thirty each

Suppose an 8 per cent defective lot is presented for inspection. What is the probability of rejecting it? With $p = .08$, $\mu = np = .08(30) = 2.4$, and we find

$$P(\text{reject}) = .692 + .217(.692) + .217(.091)(.692) + .217(.217)(.909)$$
$$= .692 + .150 + .014 + .043,$$
$$P(\text{reject}) = .899.$$

4-7 The Normal Distribution

The normal probability distribution is the most widely known and important distribution in the field of statistics. One of its early uses was in describing the behavior of errors ascribable to repeated measurements of the same physical, biological, or astronomical quantity or property. From this context the term "normal law of error" is drawn. The normal law of error is a model in which the frequency of error is inversely proportional to a function of the size of error, and errors of overestimate of a given size are just as likely as errors of underestimate of the same size. The true measure of the length of a steel bar tends to give rise to observed measurements at that value; however, a large number of factors operating independently of one another tend to produce errors in the measured lengths. The errors are produced by variation in such things as the exact positioning of the measuring instrument, the physical properties of the gauge, the manner of operation or reading of the gauge, and a host of other factors.

It is obvious that the expected size of the errors of measurement will depend on the inherent precision of the measuring device. An ordinary yardstick will produce relatively large errors, a set of industrial calipers smaller errors, and an electronic measuring device perhaps still smaller errors. The distribution formed by errors of measurement, however, often conforms to the normal curve. The equation of the normal distribution is

$$f(X) = \left(\frac{1}{\sigma\sqrt{2\pi}}\right) e^{-(1/2)[(X-\mu)/\sigma]^2} \tag{4-7}$$

The terms in the equation are as follows:

$X =$ value of the variable, or observed measure;
$\mu =$ population mean of X, or true measure;
$\sigma =$ standard deviation of X;
$\pi =$ the mathematical constant (to four decimals) 3.1416;
$e =$ the mathematical constant (to four decimals) 2.7183.

Note that one of the terms in the equation is σ, the standard deviation. This is the first time we have encountered this term. *The standard deviation is a measure of variation defined as the square root of the variance.*

The terms π and e always have the values indicated, and μ and σ are the parameters describing a particular normal curve. For example, with $\mu = 20$ and $\sigma = 3$ the equation will describe one normal curve, and for $\mu = 0$ and $\sigma = 5$ it will describe another normal curve. With μ and σ given, the variable element in the normal distribution function is X in the expression $(X - \mu)/\sigma$ appearing as part of the exponent on the right-hand side. With this in mind let us examine the equation.

When the value of X considered is μ, the mean of X, then $(X - \mu)/\sigma = 0$. The entire exponent becomes zero and $e^0 = 1$, a maximum. The normal distribution function will yield its maximum value at this point, which will be equal to $1/\sigma\sqrt{2\pi}$. As we consider X values at increasing deviations from μ, the exponent will take on smaller and smaller fractional values. Further, these values will be the same for X at any deviation below the mean as for X at the same deviation above the mean. Thus, the normal distribution function is symmetrical with its maximum at the mean. It diminishes as we move away from the mean in either direction, and approaches but never reaches zero.

If we use $(X - \mu)/\sigma$ rather than X as the variable in the equation for the normal curve, all normal distributions are transformed into a *standard normal distribution*. The expression $(X - \mu)/\sigma$ is called the *standard normal deviate, z*.

$$z = \frac{X - \mu}{\sigma}. \qquad (4\text{--}8)$$

When transformed into the variable z, all normal distributions have a mean of zero and a standard deviation of one (unity). Using the standard normal deviate, z, the normal distribution function becomes

$$f(z) = \frac{1}{\sqrt{2\pi}} e^{-(1/2)z^2}. \qquad (4\text{--}9)$$

This function is graphed in Fig. 4–3.

A table of ordinates of the standard normal curve gives values of the ordinate, $f(z)$, at different values of z. The function $f(z)$ is called the standard normal density function. The density at $z = 0$ is $1/\sqrt{2\pi} = .3989$. This and other values of $f(z)$ may be found in Appendix C.

In Fig. 4.3 the area under the standard normal density function is 1.0. The area to the left of any value of z, that is, z_o, will give the probability of z equal to or less than z_o. The table of $P(z \leq z_o)$ is called the table of areas of the standard normal distribution. Appendix D presents these probabilities. As indicated in Fig. 4–3, these probabilities can be visualized as areas under the standard normal density function or as points on the *cumulative* standard normal distribution.

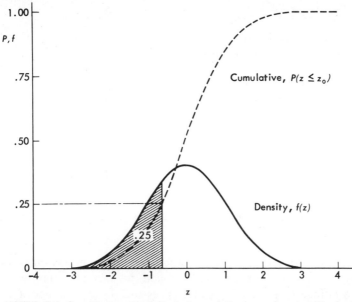

FIGURE 4-3 Graphic representation of cumulative normal probability function and normal probability density function

Employing the table of areas. To use the table of areas to find probabilities pertaining to a particular normal distribution, the values of the particular X variable must be converted to values of the standard normal deviate, z. For example, suppose that a machine turns out parts with a mean breaking strength of 220 pounds pressure and a standard deviation of 2.0 pounds. In the following examples the figures in boldface come directly from Appendix D. The specified values of X are to be interpreted *exactly*. That is, 219 pounds means exactly 219, not 219 after rounding to the nearest pound, or to any other fraction thereof. Thus $P(X \leq 219) = P(X < 219)$.

To find $P(X \leq 219)$:

$$z = \frac{X - \mu}{\sigma} = \frac{219 - 220}{2.0} = -0.5,$$

$$P(X \leq 219) = P(z \leq -0.5) = \mathbf{.3085}.$$

To find $P(219 \leq X \leq 223)$:

$$z = \frac{X - \mu}{\sigma} = \frac{223 - 220}{2.0} = 1.5,$$

$$P(219 \leq X \leq 223) = P(z \leq 1.5) - P(z \leq -0.5)$$

$$= \mathbf{.93319} - \mathbf{.3085} = .62469.$$

To find $P(X > 223)$:

$$P(X > 223) = 1 - P(X \leq 223) = 1 - P(z \leq 1.5)$$
$$= 1 - .93319 = .06681.$$

Let us find the probability that X *rounded to the nearest pound* will equal 221—that is, $P(220.5 \leq X \leq 221.5)$.

$$P(220.5 \leq X \leq 221.5) = P(.25 \leq z \leq .75)$$
$$= P(z \leq .75) - P(z \leq .25)$$
$$= .7734 - .5987 = .1747.$$

4-8 The Normal as an Approximation to Binomial and Poisson Distributions

The two distributions that we have studied in this chapter are discrete probability distributions. They were applied to variables that were the result of counting or enumerating occurrences such as the number of defects in a length of wire, or the number preferring one product over another in a sample of n consumers. While the normal probability model is a continuous distribution, it can be used to approximate discrete probabilities. One forms an interval about the discrete value. The probability of 18 defects in a length of wire becomes, if a normal approximation is applied, the probability of 17.5–18.5 defects.

Approximation to Poisson. We saw in the preceding section that Poisson distributions became increasingly symmetrical as the mean, μ, was increased. In fact, the Poisson distribution approaches a normal distribution whose variance is equal to the mean ($\sigma^2 = \mu$) as the mean increases.

To illustrate this, and also the use of the normal table of areas, the normal estimates of Poisson probabilities for a distribution with $\mu = 9.0$ are shown in Table 4–5. In the first column we reduce the values of X to values of z. For example, z at $X = 17.5$ is $(17.5 - 9.0)/3.0 = 2.83$. The second column gives the probability from the table of areas. $P(z \leq 2.83)$ $= .997673$. In the third column, successive probabilities from the second column are subtracted to obtain the probabilities within intervals of 1.0. At $X = 18.5$, $z = 3.17$, and $P(z \leq 3.17) = .9992378$. Then, $P(17.5 \leq X \leq 18.5) = .9992378 - .997673 = .0015648$. This compares with the Poisson probability for $P(r = 18)$ of .0029 in the final column.

The results of the normal approximation agree reasonably well with the Poisson probabilities. The largest relative discrepancies are in the "tails" of the distribution where the probabilities are small. In general, as μ increases such discrepancies diminish and the normal approximation to the Poisson distribution improves.

Table 4-5

PROBABILITIES FROM THE NORMAL CURVE WITH $\mu = 9.0$ AND $\sigma = 3.0$
COMPARED WITH POISSON PROBABILITIES AT INTEGER VALUES OF r FOR $\mu = 9.0$

r	X interval	z_0 (upper limit)	Normal probability $P(z \leq z_0)$	In interval	Poisson probability $P(r)$
0	≤ 0.5	-2.83	.002327	.002327	.0001
1	0.5– 1.5	-2.50	.006210	.003883	.0011
2	1.5– 2.5	-2.17	.01500	.008790	.0050
3	2.5– 3.5	-1.83	.03362	.01862	.0149
4	3.5– 4.5	-1.50	.06681	.03319	.0337
5	4.5– 5.5	-1.17	.1210	.05419	.0607
6	5.5– 6.5	$-.83$	.2033	.0823	.0910
7	6.5– 7.5	$-.50$	.3085	.1052	.1171
8	7.5– 8.5	$-.17$	.4325	.1240	.1318
9	8.5– 9.5	.17	.5675	.1350	.1318
10	9.5–10.5	.50	.6915	.1240	.1186
11	10.5–11.5	.83	.7967	.1052	.0970
12	11.5–12.5	1.17	.8790	.0823	.0727
13	12.5–13.5	1.50	.93319	.05419	.0504
14	13.5–14.5	1.83	.96638	.03319	.0324
15	14.5–15.5	2.17	.98500	.01862	.0194
16	15.5–16.5	2.50	.993790	.008790	.0109
17	16.5–17.5	2.83	.997673	.003883	.0058
18	17.5–18.5	3.17	.9992378	.0015648	.0029
19	18.5–19.5	3.50	.9997674	.0005296	.0014
20	19.5–20.5	3.83	.99993593	.00016853	.0006
21	20.5–21.5	4.17	.99998477	.00004884	.0003
≥ 22	≥ 21.5	4.50	1.000000	.00001523	.0004
				1.00000000	1.0000

Approximation to the binomial. We saw that the binomial formula yielded skewed distributions for values of p and q departing from .50, especially for small values of n. In general, with increasing n the binomial distribution will become more symmetrical through a great part of its range. Probabilities from the normal distribution approximate binomial probabilities when $p = .50$ quite closely even for modest values of n. Larger values of n are required before the normal distribution provides a reasonable approximation to binomial probabilities when p and q depart from .50.

Table 4–6 shows the binomial probabilities for $p = .10$, $n = 100$, along with the approximations provided by employing the normal distribution. Since $\mu = np$ and $\sigma = \sqrt{npq}$ in the binomial distribution, the normal probabilities found are for a distribution with a mean of $10 = .10(100)$ and a standard deviation of $3 = \sqrt{100(.10)(.90)}$. This normal distribution is the same, except for the increase in the mean from $\mu = 9$ to $\mu = 10$, as the normal distribution in Table 4–5. Also shown is the normal approximation to the binomial with $p = .50$ and $n = 16$. This is a normal distribution with a mean of $16(.50) = 8$ and a standard deviation of $\sqrt{16(.50)(.50)} = 2.0$. The normal distribution seems to provide fairly good estimates of the binomial probabilities in both cases.

A rule of thumb is that the normal approximation to the binomial may be used when both np and nq equal or exceed 10. Thus, the minimum n for a normal approximation would be 20 if $p = .50$, 100 if $p = .10$, and 1000 if $p = .01$. Remember that in binomial situations where $p \leq .10$ and $np \leq 5.0$, the Poisson distribution provides a good approximation.

Table 4-6

NORMAL APPROXIMATION TO BINOMIAL
PROBABILITIES IN TWO SITUATION

r	X interval	$p=.10$, $n=100$ Binomial $P(r)$	Normal $P(X)$	$p=.50$, $n=16$ Binomial $P(r)$	Normal $P(X)$
0	≤ -0.5	(a)	.00007622	(a)	.00008842
1	0.5– 1.5	.0003	.0015648	.0003	.00048858
2	1.5– 2.5	.0016	.003883	.0018	.002403
3	2.5– 3.5	.0059	.008790	.0085	.00924
4	3.5– 4.5	.0159	.01862	.0278	.02784
5	4.5– 5.5	.0339	.03319	.0667	.06554
6	5.5– 6.5	.0596	.05419	.1221	.1210
7	6.5– 7.5	.0889	.0823	.1746	.1747
8	7.5– 8.5	.1148	.1052	.1964	.1974
9	8.5– 9.5	.1304	.1240	.1746	.1747
10	9.5–10.5	.1319	.1350	.1221	.1210
11	10.5–11.5	.1198	.1240	.0667	.06554
12	11.5–12.5	.0988	.1052	.0278	.02784
13	12.5–13.5	.0743	.0823	.0085	.00924
14	13.5–14.5	.0513	.05419	.0018	.002403
15	14.5–15.5	.0327	.03319	.0003	.00048858
16	15.5–16.5	.0193	.01862	(a)	.00008842(b)
17	16.5–17.5	.0106	.008790		
18	17.5–18.5	.0054	.003833		
19	18.5–19.5	.0026	.0015648		
20	19.5–20.5	.0012	.0005296		
21	20.5–21.5	.0005	.00016853		
22	21.5–22.5	.0002	.00004884		
≥ 23	≥ 22.5	.0001	.00001523		
	Total	1.0000	1.00000000	1.0000	1.00000000

(a) less than .00005; (b) $P(X \geq 15.5)$.

4-9 A Summary of Distribution Situations and Available Approximations

Table 4–7 provides a cross-classification of the two discrete distribution situations with the three probability distribution formulas we have studied.

The formulas pertaining to the underlying situation occupy the boxes where the formula descriptor is the same as the situation descriptor. In the remaining boxes are the three approximations that have been discussed in this chapter. The vacant box indicates that the binomial formula cannot be applied in a Poisson distribution situation.

Table 4-7

SUMMARY OF FORMULAS AND APPROXIMATIONS
FOR BINOMIAL AND POISSON PROBABILITY DISTRIBUTIONS

Available formula	Distribution situation	
	Binomial	Poisson
Binomial	$P(r) = {}_nC_r p^r q^{n-r}$	
Poisson	When $p \leq .10$ and $np \leq 5$, $\mu = np$	$P(r) = e^{-\mu}\left(\dfrac{\mu^r}{r!}\right)$
Normal	When np and $nq \geq 10$, $\mu = np$, $\sigma = \sqrt{npq}$	When $\mu \geq 10$, $\sigma = \sqrt{\mu}$

EXERCISES

4.11 In a standard normal distribution find
   (a) $P(z \leq 1.35)$.   *Ans.* .91149.
   (b) $P(z \leq -2.58)$.   *Ans.* .004940.
   (c) $P(z \geq 2.33)$.   *Ans.* .009903
   (d) $P(-1.96 \leq z \leq 1.96)$.   *Ans.* .950.
   (e) $P(z > 1.64)$.   *Ans.* .05050.
   (f) $P(z > -1.28)$.   *Ans.* .8997.

4.12 A machine is designed to produce parts having a mean diameter of 2.000 centimeters and a standard deviation of .030 centimeters. If the distribution of diameters is normal,
   (a) What is the probability that a randomly selected part will have a diameter exceeding 2.050 cm? 2.060 cm?
   (b) What is the probability that a randomly selected part will measure 2.05 to the nearest .01 cm?
   (c) The parts are designed to fit into a machined slot in a certain assembly. A machine cuts the slots to a mean diameter of 2.050 cm with a standard deviation of .040 cm. What is the mean and standard deviation (assuming independence) of the difference between the diameter of the slot and the diameter of the part?   *Ans.* .05; .05.
   (d) What is the probability that a randomly selected part will not fit into the slot in a randomly selected assembly?   *Ans.* .1587.

4.13 A machine produces bolts which are 10 per cent defective. Using the normal (area) approximation, find the probability of the following outcomes in a random sample of 400 bolts.

(a) No more than 32 defectives. *Ans.* .1056.

(b) Thirty-six to 44 (inclusive) defectives. *Ans.* .5468.

(c) Fifty-four or more defectives. *Ans.* .01222.

4.14 A manufacturer ships an electronic component in packages of 100. If 5 per cent of the components are defective, find the probability (using the normal and the Poisson approximations) of a package containing

(a) More than 10 defectives. *Ans.* .005868; .014.

(b) Two or fewer defectives. *Ans.* .1251; .125.

4.15 Demand for a replacement part has a Poisson distribution with a mean demand per month of 3.0. Find the normal approximation to

(a) The probability of experiencing more than 40 demands in a year.

(b) The probability of experiencing more than 18 demands in a four-month period.

(c) Check your approximation in (b) with the Poisson probability.

4.16 A firm submits large incoming lots of manufactured items to the following acceptance sampling scheme. A sample of 50 is taken and the lot accepted if no defectives are found. If three or more defectives are found, the lot is rejected. If one or two defectives are found, a further sample of 100 is taken. If the total number of defectives *in the cumulative sample* is two or less, the lot is accepted; otherwise the lot is rejected.

(a) Show this decision procedure in a tree diagram.

(b) Using Poisson approximations to the required probabilities, calculate the probability of rejecting a 1 per cent defective lot.
Ans. .142.

(c) Using the binomial, calculate the probability of rejecting a 5 per cent defective lot. *Ans.* .9141.

REFERENCES

Duncan, A. J., *Quality Control and Industrial Statistics* (rev. ed.). Homewood, Ill: Richard D. Irwin, Inc., 1959.

Lindgren, B. W., and G. W. McElrath, *Introduction to Probability and Statistics*. New York: The Macmillan Company, 1959.

Wolf, F. L., *Elements of Probability and Statistics*. New York: McGraw-Hill Book Company, 1962.

5

Probability
Distributions
for Continuous Variables

The situations to which we applied the binomial and Poisson distributions in Chapter 4 all involved discrete variables. The variables were the result of counting or enumerating phenomena such as the number of defects in a length of wire, or the number preferring a certain brand of product in a sample of n consumers. While the normal curve is a continuous function, we learned how to employ the table of areas of the normal curve to estimate probabilities for the discrete values that are encountered in the binomial and Poisson situations.

This chapter is concerned with probability distributions for continuous variables. Continuous variables arise from the process of measurement, as opposed to counting or enumerating. A truly continuous variable is one which, subject only to the accuracy inherent in the measurement instruments used, can take on *any* value over the range of the variable measure employed. We will consider two general forms or model distributions of continuous variables that are commonly employed in statistical work—the normal and the chi-square distributions. We shall see how these forms are used as models for describing the distribution of single observations in a population. The same distribution models will be found later to apply to problems of inference about parameters, particularly the population mean and variance.

5-1 Percentiles of a Normal Probability Distribution

In previous examples we worked with a specified value of X in a normal distribution and found from the table of areas the probability of X's failing to exceed the value specified. On many occasions we will want to reverse this procedure, and find the value of X in a normal distribution that has a specified probability of not being exceeded. For example, we dealt with a normal distribution of breaking strengths with $\mu = 220$ and $\sigma = 2.0$. Can we find the breaking strength exceeded by but 10 per cent of the products?

We work with "z" expression, but the problem requires a solution in terms of a value of the variable, X. The expression

$$z = \frac{X - \mu}{\sigma},$$

rewritten in terms of X, is

$$X = \mu + z\sigma. \tag{5-1}$$

Consulting the standard cumulative normal distribution, we find that the value of z corresponding to the probability .90 is 1.28—that is, $P(z \leq 1.28) = .90$, approximately.

Knowing the mean and standard deviation, we have

$$X_{.90} = 220 + 1.28(2.0),$$
$$X_{.90} = 220 + 2.56 = 222.56 \text{ pounds.}$$

The value $X_{.90}$ pounds is called the 90th percentile of the distribution. The term "percentile" relates directly to the cumulative "equal to or less than" distribution. The 5th percentile of X, which is abbreviated as $X_{.05}$, is the value of X that has a probability of .05 of failing to be exceeded—that is, $P(X \leq X_{.05}) = .05$. To find $X_{.05}$ if X is normally distributed, we find $z_{.05}$ and then apply the standard normal expression as we did above. That is,

$$X_{.05} = \mu + z_{.05}\sigma.$$

In similar fashion other percentiles of any normally distributed variable may be found. The terms decile and quartile are also employed frequently. There are nine deciles: $X_{.10}, X_{.20}, X_{.30}, \ldots, X_{.90}$; and three quartiles: $X_{.25}, X_{.50},$ and $X_{.75}$. The 50th percentile, fifth decile, and second quartile are all the same value, which is more commonly termed the *median*.

5-2   Fitting a Normal Distribution to Observed Data

The process of comparing an observed distribution to the normal distribution model has long been termed "fitting" a normal distribution. The reason for comparing the distribution form of an observed continuous variable with the normal model is to see whether the normal model "fits," or describes the observed data reasonably well. Although discussion of the criterion for a "reasonable" fit must be delayed until Chapter 12, we can see some of the advantages to be gained if a model distribution is judged to be satisfactory. The advantages are economy and flexibility. If a model distribution form fits the data, it is an economical description. Knowing only the mean and standard deviation of a normal distribution, we know the probability of values within any specified interval or can locate any desired percentile of the distribution. We will also see later that certain generalized statistical and decision-making techniques have been worked out for normally distributed variables.

Table 5-1 contains data on speeds of 365 passenger automobiles observed in passing a highway check station. The equipment employed permitted observations of speeds only to the nearest even two miles per hour. The observed data are thus approximate, as is the case for any truly continuous variable. The data represent all vehicles passing the checkpoint in a westbound direction between 3:40 and 4:40 P.M. on a particular weekday; our interest is in what they can tell us about speeds at this location and time, and about total traffic load in general. That is, the data are a *sample* of observations produced by a particular underlying traffic process.

Table 5-1

DISTRIBUTION OF SPEEDS OF 365 PASSENGER
AUTOMOBILES PASSING A HIGHWAY CHECK POINT[a]

Speed (mph)	Number of vehicles
29.0–31.0	4
31.0–33.0	6
33.0–35.0	9
35.0–37.0	21
37.0–39.0	19
39.0–41.0	59
41.0–43.0	59
43.0–45.0	66
45.0–47.0	62
47.0–49.0	25
49.0–51.0	22
51.0–53.0	3
53.0–55.0	8
55.0–57.0	1
57.0–59.0	—
59.0–61.0	1
Total	365

[a] Courtesy of Arizona State Highway Department.

The fitting procedure consists in describing in some detail the probabilities under a normal distribution having the same mean and variance as the observed distribution. First, we must estimate the mean and variance of the traffic distribution. This is conveniently done through formulas containing f, the numbers or frequencies of observations in intervals of X along the variable scale. For example, there were 21 automobiles observed at approximately 36 mph, or between 35.0 and 37.0 mph in terms of the continuous variable. The expression 35.0–37.0 is termed the *interval*, the *midpoint* of the interval is $36.0 = X$, and the *frequency* of observations in the interval is $21 = f$. The boundaries of the interval are the values 35.0 and 37.0 exactly. In these "frequency" terms, the expressions for estimated mean and variance become

$$\bar{X} = \frac{\Sigma(fX)}{n}, \tag{5-2}$$

$$s^2 = \frac{\Sigma[f(X - \bar{X})^2]}{n - 1}, \tag{5-3}$$

where n is the size of the sample.

The numerator of the formula for s^2 will be recognized as the total squared deviations of the sample observations from their own mean. In general, it is easier and more accurate to compute s^2 from an equivalent expression,

$$s^2 = \frac{\Sigma(fX^2) - [\Sigma(fX)]^2/n}{n - 1}. * \tag{5-4}$$

Table 5-2 contains the calculations leading to the totals required in Eqs. (5–2) and (5–3) or (5–4). Our estimate of the mean speed is

$$\bar{X} = \frac{\Sigma(fX)}{n} = \frac{15,694}{365} = 43.00 \text{ mph.}$$

If Eq. (5–3) is used for the variance, we have

$$s^2 = \frac{\Sigma[f(X - \bar{X})^2]}{n - 1} = \frac{8221}{364} = 22.585.$$

Using Eq. (5–4), we obtain the estimated variance from

$$s^2 = \frac{\Sigma(fX^2) - [\Sigma(fX)]^2/n}{n - 1} = \frac{683,020 - (15,694)^2/365}{364}$$

$$= \frac{683,020 - 674,799}{364} = \frac{8221}{364} = 22.585.$$

---

* It is even more accurate, in terms of reducing the effect of rounding errors, to compute the variance from

$$s^2 = \frac{n[\Sigma(fX^2)] - [\Sigma(fX)]^2}{n(n - 1)}.$$

However, to emphasize the character of the estimated variance as the sample sum of squared deviations divided by degrees of freedom, we will continue to use Eq. (5–4) for expository purposes.

The second alternative is the more efficient calculation procedure since only the fX and fX^2 products are required in addition to the original distribution. The fX products are needed for the calculation of the mean anyway, so only one further set is required for the variance. If one writes down a column of X, X^2, and f values, $\Sigma(fX)$ and $\Sigma(fX^2)$ can be obtained on a rotary calculator without writing down the individual fX and fX^2 products.

Table 5-2

CALCULATION OF MEAN AND VARIANCE FROM A FREQUENCY DISTRIBUTION

| X | f | Employing Eq. (5-4) | | Employing Eq. (5-3) | |
		fX	fX^2	$(X - \bar{X})^2$	$f(X - \bar{X})^2$
30	4	120	3,600	169	676
32	6	192	6,144	121	726
34	9	306	10,404	81	729
36	21	756	27,216	49	1,029
38	19	722	27,436	25	475
40	59	2,360	94,400	9	531
42	59	2,478	104,076	1	59
44	66	2,904	127,776	1	66
46	62	2,852	131,192	9	558
48	25	1,200	57,600	25	625
50	22	1,100	55,000	49	1,078
52	3	156	8,112	81	243
54	8	432	23,328	121	968
56	1	56	3,136	169	169
58	—	—	—	225	—
60	1	60	3,600	289	289
Total	365	15,694	683,020		8,221

The standard deviation is the square root of the variance, and we obtain

$$s = \sqrt{22.585} = 4.752 \text{ mph.}$$

Having estimated the mean and standard deviation of the speed distribution as 43.00 and 4.752 respectively, we can now describe the normal distribution having these parameters, and compare it in detail with the actual distribution of automobile speeds. The normal probabilities for the intervals in the actual data are found, and compared with the relative frequencies in the same intervals from the actual data. This procedure is shown in Table 5-3. The z values for the upper boundaries, X_u, of the intervals are consulted in the normal "area" table, and successive differences between these "cumulative" normal probabilities lead to the normal probabilities of X in the intervals listed.

For example, consider the interval 45.0–47.0. The standard normal deviate for $X = 45.0$ is $(45.0 - 43.0)/4.752 = .42$, and, for $X = 47.0$, $z = (47.0 - 43.0)/4.752 = .84$. The cumulative probabilities $P(z \le .42)$

Table 5-3

FITTING A NORMAL DISTRIBUTION WITH PARAMETERS
$\mu = 43.00$ AND $\sigma = 4.752$ AND COMPARING
THE FITTED WITH THE ACTUAL DISTRIBUTION

Interval X_L to X_U	z for X_U $(X_U - \mu)/\sigma$	Normal probability $P(X \leq X_U)$	In interval	Observed relative frequency in interval
below 29.0	−2.95	.0016	.0016	—
29.0–31.0	−2.53	.0057	.0041	.011
31.0–33.0	−2.10	.0179	.0122	.016
33.0–35.0	−1.68	.0465	.0286	.025
35.0–37.0	−1.26	.1038	.0573	.057
37.0–39.0	−0.84	.2005	.0967	.052
39.0–41.0	−0.42	.3372	.1367	.162
41.0–43.0	0.00	.5000	.1628	.162
43.0–45.0	.42	.6628	.1628	.181
45.0–47.0	.84	.7995	.1367	.170
47.0–49.0	1.26	.8962	.0967	.068
49.0–51.0	1.68	.9535	.0573	.060
51.0–53.0	2.10	.9821	.0286	.008
53.0–55.0	2.53	.9943	.0122	.022
55.0–57.0	2.95	.9984	.0041	.003
57.0–59.0	3.37	.9996	.0012	—
59.0–61.0	3.79	.9999	.0003	.003
61.0 and over		1.0000	.0001	—
Total			1.0000	1.000

$= .6628$ and $P(z \leq .84) = .7995$ are given in the next column. The probability of X within the interval 45.0–47.0—that is, $.7995 - .6628 = .1367$—
is then shown. The final column contains, for this interval, $f/n = 62/365 =$
.170 from the observed distribution of automobile speeds.

The actual distribution appears slightly more "peaked" in the center
than the normal distribution. Note the central four intervals from 39.0 to
47.0 mph. The probability of speeds from 39.0 to 47.0 according to the normal
distribution is .5990, while the same probability *estimated* from the actual
distribution is .675. The presence of a 45-mph speed limit probably ex-
plains this "peaking" tendency. Figure 5–1 affords a graphic comparison of
the actual with the fitted normal distribution.

EXERCISES

5.1   A manufacturer stated that a particular variety of fertilizer marketed
      in 50-lb bags contained an average of 13.0 lb of inert matter, and that
      the amounts per 50-lb bag were normally distributed with a standard
      deviation of 2.0 lb.

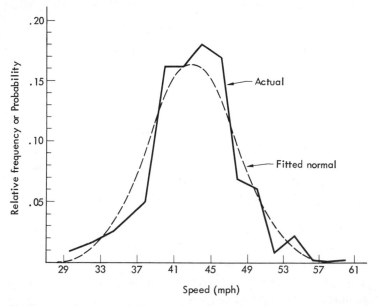

FIGURE 5-1 Actual and fitted normal distribution of 365 automobile speeds

(a) What is the probability that a randomly selected bag will contain less than 10 lb? 10–15 lb? 15–17.5 lb? over 18 lb of inert matter?
    Ans. .06681; .77449; .14648; .00621.

(b) Designating X_P as any given percentile of the probability distribution of pounds of inert matter in 50-lb bags, find $X_{.01}$; $X_{.05}$; $X_{.10}$; $X_{.60}$; $X_{.75}$; $X_{.90}$.   *Ans.* 8.34; 9.72; 10.44; 13.50; 14.34; 15.56.

(c) If he wanted to offer customers 99.5% assurance that the inert matter did not exceed 15 lb, what mean would he have to achieve if the standard deviation were not changed? What standard deviation if the mean were unchanged?   *Ans.* 9.84; 0.775.

5.2 In a test of 100 measured weights of certain cuts of meat offered for sale in a supermarket, the following distribution of errors, in ounces, was observed.

Interval	f	d
−3.5 to −2.5	1	−3
−2.5 to −1.5	4	−2
−1.5 to −0.5	15	−1
−0.5 to +0.5	26	0
+0.5 to 1.5	19	1
1.5 to 2.5	16	2
2.5 to 3.5	14	3
3.5 to 4.5	5	4
Total	100	

(a) Using the formulas,

$$\bar{X} = 0 + [\Sigma\,(fd)]/n$$

and

$$s^2 = \frac{\Sigma\,(fd^2) - [\Sigma\,(fd)]^2/n}{n - 1}$$

estimate the mean and variance of the population of errors.

Ans. 0.87; 2.56.

(b) Operating standards called for a normal distribution of errors with a mean of zero and a standard deviation of 1.5 ounces. Using the table of areas, find the probabilities of errors in the above intervals under the operating standards.

(c) Using the midpoints of the intervals, plot a line graph of the relative frequencies from the actual distribution and a line graph of the probabilities in (b) on the same chart.

(d) Using the boundaries of the intervals, show the two cumulative distributions in (c) on the same chart.

5.3 The following are data on leakage currents (in microamps) of a random sample of 50 integrated circuits.

17.1	8.1	12.5	8.2	10.8
18.6	4.3	8.0	9.3	5.3
14.8	14.0	10.4	15.2	12.8
7.2	5.3	17.4	9.2	11.8
12.8	8.4	26.3	6.0	9.6
10.6	9.1	7.1	5.5	9.9
13.3	17.1	10.1	6.6	23.3
5.9	7.5	15.5	5.3	9.8
7.7	15.2	14.4	15.7	9.0
10.1	8.5	11.1	8.8	7.0

(a) Construct a frequency distribution of the leakage currents, using a convenient interval of 2.0 microamps.

(b) Estimate the mean and variance of the population from the original data (if a calculator is available) and from the frequency distribution. For the variance from the original data, use the formula,

$$s^2 = \frac{\Sigma\,(X^2) - (\Sigma\,X)^2/n}{n - 1}$$

Ans. 10.95; 21.66 (original data).

5.4 Plot $X_{.01}$, $X_{.05}$, $X_{.10}$, $X_{.30}$, $X_{.50}$, $X_{.70}$, $X_{.90}$, $X_{.95}$, and $X_{.99}$ for a normal distribution with the same mean and standard deviation as the distribution in Exercise 5.2. On the same graph, plot the cumulative relative frequencies from the observed distribution.

5-3   Further Descriptive Measures of Variable Characteristics

In addition to the mean and variance, other descriptive measures of variable characteristics are commonly encountered. One set of measures is based on the values of certain percentiles illustrated previously in connection with normal distributions.

The median is a positional measure often used as an indication of central location. We have defined the median of a population as $X_{.50}$, the 50th percentile of a probability distribution. The range between the first and third quartiles, $X_{.75} - X_{.25}$, is sometimes used as an indication of variability in a distribution. It is the range within which the middle 50 per cent of the values in a population fall. When we have only a sample of the population to work with, we can only *estimate* these or any other percentiles.

Positional measures can be approximated from a frequency distribution of sample data by a process of linear interpolation within the appropriate class interval. The cumulation of the frequency distribution on an "equal to or less than" basis is needed for these approximations. One may cumulate either the actual frequencies, f, or the relative frequencies, f/n. In Table 5-4 we show the relative frequencies from the automobile speed data. When the cumulative frequencies in either absolute or relative terms are stated on an *equal to* or *less than upper limit* basis, the positional values can be estimated on the basis of an assumption of an even distribution of the observations within the class containing the position.

Table 5-4

RELATIVE FREQUENCY DISTRIBUTION AND CUMULATIVE
RELATIVE FREQUENCY DISTRIBUTION OF AUTOMOBILE SPEEDS

Speed (mph)	Relative frequency	
	In interval	Cumulative[a]
29.0–31.0	.011	.011
31.0–33.0	.016	.027
33.0–35.0	.025	.052
35.0–37.0	.057	.109
37.0–39.0	.052	.161
39.0–41.0	.162	.323
41.0–43.0	.162	.485
43.0–45.0	.181	.666
45.0–47.0	.170	.836
47.0–49.0	.068	.904
49.0–51.0	.060	.964
51.0–53.0	.008	.972
53.0–55.0	.022	.994
55.0–57.0	.003	.997
57.0–59.0	—	.997
59.0–61.0	.003	1.000

[a] Proportion of speeds equal to or less than upper limit of interval stated.

For example, let us estimate $X_{.25}$ on this basis. We know that .161 of the frequencies are cumulated to 39.0 mph and .323 are cumulated to 41.0 mph. Using a linear interpolation, we then estimate that .250 of the frequencies would be cumulated at $(.250 - .161)/(.323 - .161)$ of the distance from 39.0 to 41.0. Where $\hat{X}_P$ stands for an estimated percentile of X, this may be expressed as

$$\hat{X}_{.25} = 39.0 + \left(\frac{.250 - .161}{.323 - .161}\right) 2.0$$

$$= 39.0 + 1.099 = 40.099 \text{ mph.}$$

Similarly, we can estimate the second quartile, $\hat{X}_{.50}$, as

$$\hat{X}_{.50} = 43.0 + \left(\frac{.500 - .485}{.666 - .485}\right) 2.0 = 43.166 \text{ mph,}$$

and the third quartile can be estimated as

$$\hat{X}_{.75} = 45.00 + \left(\frac{.750 - .666}{.836 - .666}\right) 2.0 = 45.988 \text{ mph.}$$

The estimate of the range encompassing the middle 50 per cent of the population of automobile speeds sampled at the particular location, data, and hour is then

$$\hat{X}_{.75} - \hat{X}_{.25} = 45.988 - 40.099 = 5.889 \text{ mph.}$$

If the normal model is applied to the data, this same range would be

$$(\mu + z_{.75}\sigma) - (\mu + z_{.25}\sigma) = \sigma(z_{.75} - z_{.25}).$$

Using our estimate of the standard deviation, we obtain

$$4.752[.677 - (-.677)] = 4.752(1.354) = 6.434 \text{ mph.}$$

This reflects in another way what we have already noted—that the middle portion of the actual distribution of speeds is more concentrated than the fitted normal distribution. This is a feature of peakedness rather than of overall dispersion, for the fitted normal distribution has the same standard deviation as the actual speed data.

Skewness. We are familiar with skewness, or lack of symmetry in a distribution, from our discussion of the binomial expansion for different values of p, and our work with the Poisson distribution for small values of μ. The mean of a set of values is like a balance point in that the sum of the moments about it, $\Sigma(X - \bar{X})$, or $\Sigma[f(X - \bar{X})]$ for a frequency distribution, is equal to zero. The median, on the other hand, divides the area under a frequency curve into two equal parts. The effect of lack of symmetry in a distribution on the relative locations of these two averages can be appreciated in these terms from Fig. 5–2.

When a frequency distribution is symmetrical the mean, or balance point, will correspond to the median, $X_{.50}$. However, with a long tail to the left, the balance point will be below the 50th percentile. This is called *negative skewness*. With *positive skewness*, the longer tail of the distribution is on the right and the balance point will be above the 50th percentile. In our

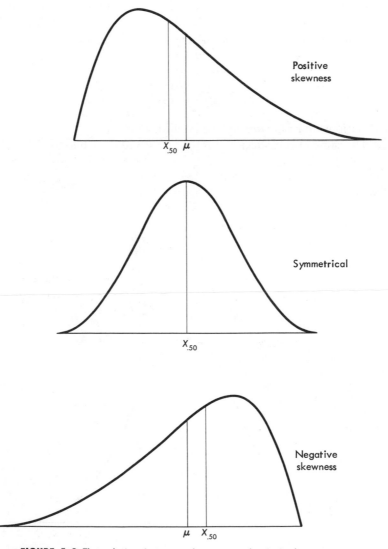

FIGURE 5-2 The relation between skewness and principal averages

speed distribution, $\bar{X} = 43.00$ and $\hat{X}_{.50} = 43.166$, indicating a slight skewness to the left, or negative skewness.

Kurtosis. Two distributions having the same dispersion and skewness can differ in how flat the distribution is in relation to its dispersion. This feature is termed *kurtosis*, and is usually measured with the normal distribution as a point of reference. The ratio of a range of central values compared to a range that encompasses a large proportion of the distribution will serve to measure this feature. In a normal distribution the range that encompasses, for example, the middle 32 per cent of the values is $z_{.66}-z_{.34}$. Consulting the standard normal area table, we find these z values to be $+.41$ and $-.41$. The range encompassing the middle 90 per cent of a normal distribution is $z_{.95}-z_{.05}$, and these values are $+1.64$ and -1.64. The kurtosis for a normal distribution could then be measured as

$$Ku = \frac{z_{.66} - z_{.34}}{z_{.95} - z_{.05}} = \frac{.41 - (-.41)}{1.64 - (-1.64)} = \frac{.82}{3.28} = 0.25$$

This relationship is shown graphically in Fig. 5-3.

The same kurtosis measure for an observed distribution is found from

$$Ku = \frac{\hat{X}_{.66} - \hat{X}_{.34}}{\hat{X}_{.95} - \hat{X}_{.05}}.$$

For the speed data,

$$Ku = \frac{44.934 - 41.235}{50.533 - 34.840} = \frac{3.699}{15.693} = 0.236$$

The relation of the central range to the base range in the speed distribution is seen as somewhat smaller than the ratio for a normal distribution,

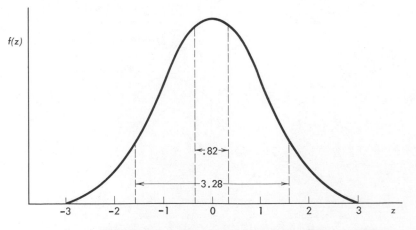

FIGURE 5-3 Kurtosis of a normal distribution

reflecting a distribution curve that is higher in relation to its spread than the normal curve. Such a curve is termed "leptokurtic," while a relatively flat distribution is termed "platykurtic." For a platykurtic distribution, *Ku* as defined above would be more than 0.25.

   Relative variability and skewness. The kurtosis measure, *Ku*, just presented, is an index or coefficient independent of the units used to measure any particular variable, such as speeds in miles per hour. It can be used to compare any two distributions regardless of the units in which the variables are expressed. Comparisons of variability and skewness among distributions are also facilitated by the use of dimensionless coefficients of these properties. Coefficients of variability are constructed by relating a measure of dispersion to a measure of central location in a distribution. For example, the standard deviation is related to the mean to form the *coefficient* of *variation*.

$$C.V. = \frac{\sigma}{\mu} \qquad \text{(for a population)}, \qquad (5\text{--}5)$$

$$C.V. = \frac{s}{\bar{X}} \qquad \text{(for a sample)}. \qquad (5\text{--}6)$$

   This is a useful way to think about variability. Suppose 50 persons estimated both the weight and length of a particular steel bar. The mean of the weight estimates was found to be 60 lb and the standard deviation 6 lb, while the mean and standard deviation of the estimated lengths were 20 in. and 1 in., respectively. The relative variability of the weight estimates is $6/60 = .10$, and that of the length estimates is $1/20 = .05$. The group is about twice as efficient in estimating the length as it is in estimating the weight of the bar. If the estimates are normally distributed, about two-thirds of the estimates of length are within 5 per cent of the mean estimate. The coefficient of variability is often given in percentage terms—that is, $(s/\bar{X}) \times 100$.

   Skewness coefficients are constructed by relating an absolute indication of skewness to a measure of dispersion. One form is called the Pearsonian skewness coefficient after the famous statistician Karl Pearson (1857–1936). It is based on the relationship between the mean and median in skewed distributions.

$$\text{Sk} = \frac{3(\mu - X_{.50})}{\sigma}. \qquad (5\text{--}7)$$

   A symmetrical distribution will have a Pearsonian skewness coefficient of zero, and positive and negative coefficients will indicate right and left skewness, respectively.

   Other distribution measures. There are other measures of central location, variability, skewness, and kurtosis of frequency distributions. One system is based on moments. The first moment about the mean is zero, as we indicated in discussing the mean as a balance point. The second moment, or average *squared deviation* about the mean is the variance. The third moment, or average *cubed deviation* about the mean, is an absolute measure of skewness, and the fourth moment is a measure of kurtosis. The moment *coefficient* of skewness is the third moment divided by σ^3, and the moment *coefficient* of kurtosis is the fourth moment divided by σ^4. These moment coefficients are not used now as extensively as they once were as descriptive measures.

Measures of relative variability and skewness employing the quartiles are often useful if one is working with published frequency distributions in which the uppermost class interval is left open—for example, $25,000 annual income and over. When this is done, the standard deviation cannot be estimated. A coefficient of variability based on the quartiles is

$$\frac{(\hat{X}_{.75} - \hat{X}_{.25})/2}{(\hat{X}_{.75} + \hat{X}_{.25})/2}.$$

A coefficient of relative skewness based on the quartiles is

$$\frac{(\hat{X}_{.75} - \hat{X}_{.50}) - (\hat{X}_{.50} - \hat{X}_{.25})}{\hat{X}_{.75} - \hat{X}_{.25}}.$$

The coefficient of variability can be seen to be half of the interquartile range divided by the midpoint of the same range. The numerator of the skewness coefficient depends on the difference in the concentration of frequencies in the third quarter compared with the concentration in the second quarter of the distribution. The denominator depends on the concentration of frequencies in the middle half, or the average concentration in the second and third quarters of the distribution.

EXERCISES

5.5   Below are the earnings as a per cent of capital funds for the 50 largest commercial banks in the United States and the net profit as a per cent of invested capital for the 50 largest merchandising firms in 1964.

Commercial banks

11.7	9.5	8.7	8.9	10.6
10.4	11.4	11.1	9.4	9.6
9.9	9.2	10.5	12.2	9.8
9.5	10.0	12.2	11.1	11.4
10.2	9.3	10.2	10.2	14.3
8.7	10.2	10.2	11.4	16.7
10.3	9.8	10.7	12.1	11.1
10.2	8.2	10.2	12.7	9.1
9.9	9.8	13.1	11.4	11.9
9.5	11.0	10.2	10.1	10.4

Merchandising firms

15.1	10.4	11.5	12.3	3.5
9.0	7.9	8.4	11.8	15.1
14.7	21.3	7.6	16.6	19.5
11.9	8.5	7.7	12.1	13.5
17.0	12.1	10.7	15.4	10.6
3.4	13.4	4.2	13.3	10.2
9.9	13.8	11.0	11.7	8.2
15.4	10.7	17.5	14.6	10.7
8.4	6.6	11.6	19.5	18.6
8.9	8.1	14.4	3.1	8.5

(a) Using about ten classes, construct frequency tables of the ratios for commercial banks and for merchandising firms.

(b) Plot a cumulative frequency chart showing the two distributions.

(c) Estimate $X_{.25}$, $X_{.50}$, and $X_{.75}$ from each frequency table, and calculate a coefficient of variability and a coefficient of skewness for each of the distributions.

5.6 The data in Exercise 5.5 come from *The Fortune Directory* (August, 1965), published by Time, Inc., New York. Consult *The Fortune Directory* for the latest year available, and make a comparison as in (a), (b), and (c) for the 50 largest commercial banks in that year with those in 1964. Do the same for the 50 largest merchandising firms.

5.7 From the frequency distribution constructed in Exercise 5.3, estimate $X_{.50}$ and calculate the Pearsonian coefficient of skewness.

5.8 Estimate the mean and standard deviation from the frequency distributions in Exercise 5.5, and calculate the Pearsonian skewness coefficients for the two distributions.

5-4 The Chi-Square (χ^2) Distributions

We said earlier in this chapter that the normal distribution was only one of several continuous probability distributions which statisticians find useful. Many variables in business and economics are not symmetrically distributed. Family income, assets of business establishments, dollar value of individual sales slips in a retail store, consumption of a product by individuals, and a host of other economic variables are commonly found to have some positive skewness. Such variables are effectively restricted on the low end of the scale; no sale can be for less than zero dollars. But the variable is not so restricted on the upper end. The typical sales amount will usually be fairly small—that is, the maximum frequency density will occur toward the low end of the range of sales amounts. There will be a "tailing off" of frequency density toward the upper end of the scale where the larger but less frequently occurring sales amounts are located.

A mathematical function which frequently is useful as a model for distributions which are skewed to the right is the "gamma" function. One subclass of this family of distributions which has wide applicability in statistics is known as chi-square distributions. In this section we shall illustrate the use of such a distribution as a *model* for a relative frequency (probability) distribution of an event occurring in a firm—the distribution of dollar value of sales made to individual customers.

Before we go on to illustrate the use of a chi-square distribution as a model of a particular observed frequency distribution, we will examine some of the general properties of chi-square distributions. In Fig. 5-4 are shown three of the many shapes which chi-square distributions can assume.

The first thing to notice in the figure is that m controls the amount of skewness. The larger the value of m, the more nearly symmetrical the distribution becomes. In fact, for very large values of m the chi-square distribution becomes essentially normal in shape. The chi-square distribution is a flexible type of model that may be capable of fitting actual distributions exhibiting large differences in skewness.

There is a different chi-square distribution for each value of the parameter m. The mean and variance of any chi-square distribution depend entirely on m. The mean of a chi-square distribution is equal to m, and the variance of a chi-square distribution is equal to twice the value of m.

The parameter m is called the *degrees of freedom*. This is the same degrees of freedom that we encountered in Chapter 3 in estimating a population variance. Chi-square distributions play a critical part in statistical inferences about variances, and we will meet them in Chapters 6 and 7 in this connection; however, this use need not detain us here.

Appendix E contains the percentiles of chi-square distributions for

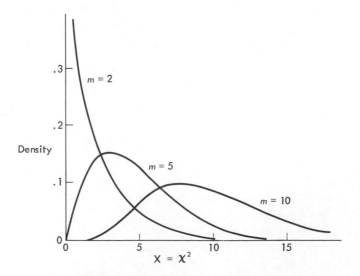

FIGURE 5-4 Three chi-square distributions

differing values of the parameter m. For example, we find that if X follows the chi-square distribution with $m = 5$, $X_{.05} = 1.15$, $X_{.50} = 4.35$, and $X_{.95} = 11.1$. Many writers use the symbol, χ^2, in referring to a variable distributed according to the chi-square distribution, and we will follow this practice. If you locate the above values of X (or χ^2) on the horizontal axis of Fig. 5–4, you will see where these percentiles cut the distribution for $m = 5$. The right skewness in this chi-square distribution is reflected by comparing the median χ^2 of 4.35 with the mean χ^2 of 5 (the degrees of freedom, m).

Earlier we introduced the Pearsonian measure of relative skewness. We can use it now to illustrate the decrease in positive skewness of chi-square distributions as m increases. The Pearsonian coefficient employs the mean, median, and standard deviation of a distribution. Given m for a chi-square distribution, we know that

$$\mu_{\chi^2} = m, \tag{5-8}$$

$$\sigma^2_{\chi^2} = 2m. \tag{5-9}$$

The formula for the Pearsonian skewness coefficient employs the mean, standard deviation, and median of a distribution. For a chi-square distribution we have

$$\text{Sk}_{\chi^2} = \frac{3(\mu_{\chi^2} - \chi^2_{.50})}{\sigma_{\chi^2}},$$

$$\text{Sk}_{\chi^2} = \frac{3(m - \chi^2_{.50})}{\sqrt{2m}}.$$

For $m = 2$, the skewness coefficient is

$$\text{Sk}_{\chi^2} = \frac{3(2.0 - 1.39)}{\sqrt{2(2)}} = \frac{1.83}{2} = .915.$$

For $m = 18$, we have

$$\text{Sk}_{\chi^2} = \frac{3(18 - 17.3)}{\sqrt{2(18)}} = \frac{2.1}{6} = .35.$$

For $m = 50$, the relative skewness becomes

$$\text{Sk}_{\chi^2} = \frac{3(50 - 49.3)}{\sqrt{2(50)}} = \frac{2.1}{10} = .21.$$

As m grows increasingly large, chi-square distributions not only become less skewed, but approach the normal distribution form. The standard normal deviate for such a chi-square distribution is

$$z = \frac{\chi^2 - \mu_{\chi^2}}{\sigma_{\chi^2}} = \frac{\chi^2 - m}{\sqrt{2m}}. \tag{5-10}$$

5-5   Fitting a Chi-Square Distribution to Observed Data

Table 5–5 presents a distribution of a random sample of dollar sales checks in a retail chain store. The positive skewness in the distribution is apparent, and should suggest to us that a chi-square distribution might provide a reasonable fit.

      The advantage of finding a suitable model is principally one of economy. If we can really trust the model to apply to stores in this chain, then we need much less information on each store to know its entire sales distribution. If we find that chi-square distributions have been applicable for many stores in the chain, then from that point on we need only know the mean size of sales checks for a given shop in order to describe the entire probability distribution of sales amounts.

Table 5-5

SALES CHECKS FOR STORE A

Sales class	Number of checks	Relative frequency	Cumulative relative frequency
X	f	est. $P(X)$	est. $P(X \leq X_u)$
0–and under 10.00	0	.00	.00
10–15.00	18	.09	.09
15–20.00	49	.25	.34
20–25.00	49	.25	.59
25–30.00	45	.23	.82
30–35.00	22	.11	.93
35–and over	14	.07	1.00
Total	197	1.00	

$$\bar{X} = \$24, \qquad s^2 = \$47$$

      The first step is to select the proper chi-square distribution. This is simple. Table 5–5 tells us that the sample mean is $24 and the sample variance is $47, almost twice the mean. These certainly would not be unusual sample results from a population with a chi-square distribution in which μ is 24. So we'll select the chi-square distribution for which $\mu = m = 24$ as our trial model.

      The next step is to see how well this trial model fits the observed sales distribution. The technique consists in plotting the cumulative probability curve for the chi-square model selected and comparing this with the cumulative relative frequencies from the observed distribution. This exactly parallels what we did earlier in comparing the normal distribution model to an actual distribution.

      By using the percentiles of chi-square for $m = 24$ we can get well over ten points on the cumulative frequency curve for our distribution model. For instance, we see that .01 of the model distribution lies below a chi-square

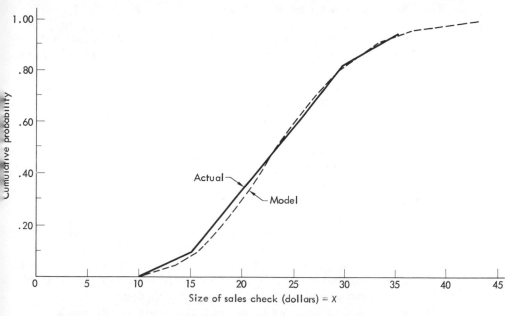

FIGURE 5-5 Cumulative distribution of sales amounts and chi-square model with $m = 24$

value of 10.9. Other percentiles of chi-square for $m = 24$ have been similarly read off and plotted in cumulative distribution form in Fig. 5–5. To check our actual sales distribution against the model we plot the "less than or equal to" curve from Table 5–5 of the actual distribution. The fit appears close enough for practical purposes. Of course, chi-square distributions for $m = 23$ or $m = 25$ might actually be a better fit without our being able to detect it on our graph. In a later chapter we shall study an analytical goodness-of-fit test which will help us to make such fine distinctions.

In this case, a straightforward procedure paid off. But what if the plot of the points in Fig. 5–5 had *not* fallen so nicely along our chi-square curve for $m = 24$? Would this mean we would have to abandon all hope of *any* chi-square distribution serving as an adequate model? Suppose that the sales distribution has much greater positive skewness than the particular model curve that we chose. If the positive skewness were appreciably greater, the variance would be considerably more than double the mean. In such a case, we might have to fit a more general gamma distribution. This type of distribution allows us freedom to select both the mean and variance of a positively skewed model. By contrast, the chi-square distribution allows us freedom to select either the mean or the variance, but not both. We shall not take up the fitting of a generalized gamma distribution because suitable tables are not widely available. However, the same basic approach making use of the cumulative distribution plots would be employed.

5-6   Transformation of Variables

Often when a distribution model, such as the normal or chi-square, will not fit the data in their original form, it will fit the data after a relatively simple transformation has been made. A common transformation is to take the logarithms of the original variable. Log X is sometimes found to be normally distributed for data whose original values are quite positively skewed. The procedure for fitting a normal curve to log X is exactly the same as for X once the logarithms of the original data have been taken.

Transformations can be employed in order to permit the fitting of a chi-square distribution to observed data. If the mean and variance of a distribution can be brought into a one-to-two ratio by a transformation of the X variable, then a chi-square distribution may be found to fit the data so transformed. Suppose we had a sales check distribution with a mean of 20 and variance of 160. Multiplying all of the values by 1/4 will result in a distribution with a mean of 20/4 = 5 and a variance of $160/(4)^2 = 10$. Since the ratio of the mean to the variance of the transformed distribution is one to two, a chi-square distribution with $m = 5$ would be a reasonable model to try. There is no guarantee of a good fit, but without an approximate 1:2 ratio of the mean to the variance, we know that a chi-square distribution would be inappropriate.

EXERCISES

5.9   Plot a cumulative distribution of the leakage data of Exercise 5.3 and compare this with a chi-square distribution with 11 degrees of freedom.

(a) Estimate $X_{.50}$ from your frequency distribution and compute the Pearsonian skewness coefficient for the leakage data.

(b) Find the Pearsonian skewness coefficient for a chi-square distribution with 11 degrees of freedom.

5.10 Using the leakage data of Exercise 5.3,

(a) Set up intervals of log microamps of 0.1000 starting with .5500. Find the antilogs of these class limits and tally a frequency distribution.

(b) From the frequency distribution in (a), calculate the logarithmic mean and variance, and the median.   *Ans.* 1.002; .03285; .996.

(c) Find the probability of log leakages between .85 and 1.15, and between .75 and 1.25 for a normal distribution of log leakages having the same mean and variance as the observed distribution. Compare these probabilities with the relative frequencies from your log leakage distribution.   *Ans.* .5934 vs. 29/50; .8324 vs. 42/50.

5.11 Given the following data on reported incomes of a random sample of 100 families:

Income ($ thousands)	Number of families
0– 2	1
2– 4	10
4– 8	35
8–12	30
12–16	15
16–20	5
20–24	2
24–28	1
28–32	1
Total	100

(a) Estimate the mean and the variance of the population.
(b) Plot a cumulative curve for the income data. On the same graph plot the cumulative distribution of X, where $X = \chi^2 - 3.6$, where χ^2 has 13 degrees of freedom. Comment on the fit of the chi-square distribution.
(c) Compute the Pearsonian skewness coefficient for the income distribution, and for a chi-square distribution with 13 degrees of freedom.

5.12 In studies of tourism in an area, a common survey method is to take a random sample of parties found at places of overnight accommodation, such as hotels, motels, campsites, etc. In one such survey, the reported lengths of stay in the area were as follows:

Length of stay (nights)	Number of parties
1	40
2	64
3	36
4	40
5	20
	200

(a) Compute the mean length of stay for the parties surveyed.
(b) Note that the probability of a party's inclusion in the sample is directly proportional to its length of stay in the area. Weight the frequencies by the reciprocal of the length of stay and compute the mean of this adjusted distribution.
(c) The harmonic mean, H, of a set of observations, X, is defined as

$$H = \frac{n}{\dfrac{f_1}{X_1} + \dfrac{f_2}{X_2} + \cdots + \dfrac{f_n}{X_n}}.$$

Compute the harmonic mean of the original frequency distribution.

Note that this agrees with the result in (b), and that the harmonic mean of a sample will give an unbiased estimate of the arithmetic mean of a population when the sampling method gives equal probability of inclusion to each element of ΣX rather than N in the population.

5.13 Members of the class will work in pairs on this assignment. The project is a frequency distribution analysis of traffic characteristics related to signalized intersections. Find a location where traffic enters a four-way intersection with a fixed-phase stoplight (that does not have a pedestrian operated push-button for changing the signal) from a direction in which there is not another stoplight for a distance of four blocks (about one-half mile). Observe fifty red cycles, recording the number of vehicles *stopped by the light* during each cycle. When you have done this, add up the number of vehicles stopped during all fifty cycles and divide by fifty. Round this figure to the nearest whole number, and call the result K. Take up a position two-thirds of a block from the signal in the direction from which the traffic you have been counting comes. Starting with the passage of any vehicle, record the amount of time elapsed for the next K vehicles to pass your observation post. Do this for fifty samples of K vehicles, recording the elapsed times.

(a) Compute the mean and variance of the number of vehicles stopped during red cycles.

(b) Using your mean as an estimate of μ, find the Poisson probabilities for the distribution of vehicles stopped during red cycles.

(c) Construct a frequency distribution of elapsed times for K vehicles to pass, using seven to ten classes.

(d) Using the mean and standard deviation from your observed distribution, fit a normal distribution to the same class intervals.

(e) Compare your observed and model distributions graphically, commenting on the fit or lack of fit.

REFERENCES

Croxton, F. E., and D. J. Cowden, *Applied General Statistics*, 3rd ed. Englewood Cliffs, N.J.: Prentice-Hall, Inc., 1967.

Ehrenfeld, S., and S. Littauer, *Introduction to Statistical Method*. New York: McGraw-Hill Book Company, 1964.

Yule, G. U., and M. G. Kendall, *An Introduction to the Theory of Statistics*. New York: Hafner Publishing Co., 1950.

6

Sampling
Distributions
of Means and Variances

In Chapter 5 we saw how the normal and the chi-square distributions could be employed as models for probability distributions of elemental events occurring in business. The events were the occurrence of individual values of a continuous variable characteristic. Before using a probability model for individual values, we would have to be satisfied that the model fits a sample of actual data reasonably well; to this end we made graphic comparisons of a sample distribution with the fitted model in the examples of the automobile speeds and the sales check data.

In this chapter we will study a much more potent application of mathematical probability distributions for continuous variables. This is the use of these model distributions as sampling distributions. Here we are concerned not with the elemental events or single values, but with a statistic made up of all the values in a sample. Such statistics, like the mean and the variance, describe the collection of elemental events drawn in a sample.

In Chapter 3 we encountered the basic idea of a sampling distribution. There we dealt with populations which could take on only a limited number of discrete values. In these cases we made an exhaustive listing of the equally likely outcomes of samples of a small size, e.g., $n = 2$. From this we constructed the probability distribution of a statistic, e.g., the sample mean in samples of size $n = 2$. The probability distribution of the sample mean is also called the *sampling distribution of the mean*.

In the case of continuous variables we cannot construct a sampling distribution by listing or enumerating possible sample sequences. We cannot conceive of a list of equally likely sample sequences, because individual values of the variable can occur anywhere along the continuous range of the variable. However, through experiments we can approximate a sampling distribution of a statistic from such a continuous population. In this chapter we will conduct several such experiments, or *simulations*, to illustrate important properties of the sampling distributions of means and variances. The method of generating the samples is useful in any kind of study employing simulation. After the general properties of each sampling distribution have been discussed, its uses are illustrated in problems of the control of industrial processes.

6-1 A Monte Carlo Experiment

The procedure that we will use to simulate the drawing of samples from a parent population is called *the Monte Carlo method.* Our objective is to study the behavior of certain statistics (means and variances) in repeated samples from a parent population. First of all, then, we need a parent population. In our previous chapter the usefulness of population models was discussed, so rather than select any particular population distribution, we will select one of the "model" forms. The earliest developments in sampling theory dealt with sampling from normal populations, so we will follow history in this regard. We know from Chapter 5 that any particular normal distribution can be transformed to the standard normal distribution with zero mean and unit standard deviation. Therefore we will deal directly with samples derived from the standard normal population.

The table of random numbers. Now that we have selected a population, we need a method of drawing random samples from it. One of the most useful general techniques begins with a table of random numbers. Appendix N presents a portion of an entire book full of random numbers. The random numbers in this table are *random rectangular numbers*; that is, they represent successive draws from a population of numbers in which each digit, zero through nine, appears with equal frequency. These numbers are generated in such a manner that no pattern or order is discernible in their sequence.

The numbers in Appendix N were generated by a special routine on an electronic computer. Such routines approximate the outcomes of successive throws of a very carefully balanced ten-sided die. You could think of generating a table of random rectangular numbers yourself through such a physical process. If you constructed such a table in this manner and then read through it in any systematic fashion, no pattern should be evident in the numbers selected. For instance, if you had selected enough numbers to minimize accidents, you would find nearly equal quantities of the digits 0 through 9 in your results. Further, you could examine the sequence, or order, in your results. Suppose you made a frequency distribution of the digits that followed a "1" in your results. You should find, once again, about equal numbers of the ten digits. The same thing should be found for the digits following the sequence "1, 2," or any other.

The above tests and a host of similar additional tests have been performed on the master table from which Appendix N was taken. No significant patterns or sequences have been found in the table. Because of these tests we presume that there is no bias either in favor of or against any digit in our Appendix N. All digits are presumed to occur with equal probability for any given path through the table. Thus the digits represent individual draws from a rectangular statistical population.

How can we use the table of random numbers to select samples? If our population consisted of a finite number of observations, we could assign serial numbers to them. Then we would pick an arbitrary starting point and an arbitrary path through the table of random numbers. As an item's serial number came up in the table, the item would go into the sample. Our model population, however, is a continuous variable, and we cannot list such a population. We can visualize it as a graph of the standard normal curve, or density function. How can we use the table of random numbers to select values from this sort of statistical population?

Transforming the random numbers. In Chapter 5 we described how to plot a cumulative probability distribution. The curve shown in Fig. 6–1 is the cumulative distribution for a normally distributed population with $\mu = 0$ and $\sigma = 1.0$. Suppose we think of the vertical axis in Fig. 6–1 as being divided into 100 equal intervals. The first interval begins at .00 and ends at .01 on the F scale. The last interval runs from .99 through 1.00.

Next, we go to the table of random rectangular numbers. We reason that, if we take the digits in pairs, there are exactly 100 such pairs. The first is 00 and the last is 99. If we start at an arbitrary point and proceed through the table in a systematic manner, we should get random draws of all possible numbers from 00 through 99. We can then match each of our two-digit random numbers to its counterpart on the vertical scale of Fig. 6–1. From this point we can proceed horizontally to the right until we reach the cumulative curve. Then we can drop vertically to the horizontal axis, where we can read a counterpart z value for a normal population. This z value will be one value in our sample from the normal population.

Again consult Fig. 6–1. About 10 per cent of the numbers we will select from the random number table will fall between .10 and .20 on the F scale. The same will be true for any such interval on the F scale. Consider the 10 per cent of the rectangular random numbers which can be expected to fall between .40 and .50 on the F scale. When we move horizontally to the cumulative normal curve and then vertically down to the horizontal axis, we see that these random numbers will be transformed into z values. Their z values will lie between $-.255$ and $.000$, an interval which has a probability

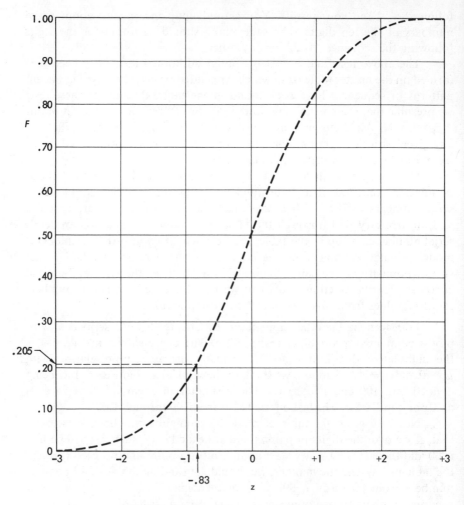

FIGURE 6-1 Cumulative normal distribution

of .10—that is, $P(-.255 \leq z \leq 0) = .10$. This use of Fig. 6–1 will transform a set of random rectangular numbers into a set of *random normal numbers*. The cumulative probability distribution for any other continuous population will transform random rectangular numbers into random numbers distributed in accordance with that population.

We now select a sample of ten rectangular random numbers to continue our numerical example. Appendix N has 25 double columns of numbers and 50 rows. A starting point of the thirtieth row and the seventh double column was chosen arbitrarily. Here you can read the digits "20." Thus we take .20 as our first rectangular random number. Arbitrarily now take the next two digits to the left of the pair we just used; this pair is 73 or .73 for the *F* scale. Then go on and take the next pair to the left of 73 as the next two-digit random number. Continue this way all the way to the left end of the row, then move up to the left end of the row above and go right by pairs in that row. Continuing to move across and up the rows in serpentine fashion produces the random rectangular numbers in the leftmost column of Table 6–1.

Table 6-1

TWO RANDOM SAMPLES OF SIZE TEN FROM
A STANDARD NORMAL POPULATION

	Sample a		Sample b
Rectangular	Normal	Rectangular	Normal
.20	−.83	.10	−1.25
.73	.63	.48	−.04
.17	−.93	.19	−.86
.83	.97	.49	−.01
.37	−.32	.85	1.06
.52	.06	.15	−1.02
.23	−.72	.74	.66
.42	−.19	.79	.82
.48	−.04	.54	.11
.11	−1.20	.58	.21

The first number drawn, "20," stands for the twenty-first of 100 equal intervals from .00 to 1.00 (the random number "00" is the first interval— that is, .00 to .01). The "*F*" value given to the random number "20" is, however, .205, the midpoint of the interval .20 to .21. In Fig. 6–1 go horizontally to the cumulative normal curve and drop vertically to the *z* axis. Here read a *z* value of −.83. Next perform this same transformation on all the ten rectangular random numbers in the sample. The result is the set of random normal numbers in the second column of Table 6–1. Further draws produce the second sample of ten.*

Let us summarize the results so far. In Table 6–2 we show the two samples of $n = 10$ that we drew from the standard normal population. For each of these samples we have computed the sample mean, $\bar{X}$, and the estimated variance, s^2. For the first sample, the mean, $\bar{X}_a$, is −.26. For the second sample, $\bar{X}_b = -.03$. Recall that, for the parent population, $\mu = 0$.

---

* There are tables of random normal deviates from which we could directly have obtained our samples. See, for example, *Handbook of Tables for Probability and Statistics*, published by the Chemical Rubber Co., Cleveland, Ohio, 1966, Table XII. However, the graphic method is a general one, applicable to any form of population distribution.

Here we see that neither of the sample means is equal to the other, nor is either equal to the mean of the parent population. Similarly, the variance for the first sample is found to be .4815 and the variance of the second sample is .6246. We recall that $\sigma^2 = 1$. Both of our sample estimates fall below the value they are meant to estimate ($\sigma^2 = 1$).

Table 6-2

LISTING OF SAMPLES FROM A NORMAL POPULATION
($n = 10$, $\mu = 0$, $\sigma = 1$)

Sample a		Sample b		Sample c		Sample d	Sample e
X_{a0}	−.83	X_{b0}	−1.25	X_{c0}	.43	·	·
X_{a1}	.63	X_{b1}	−.04	X_{c1}		·	·
X_{a2}	−.93	X_{b2}	−.86			·	·
X_{a3}	.97	X_{b3}	−.01			·	·
X_{a4}	−.32	X_{b4}	1.06			·	·
X_{a5}	.06	X_{b5}	−1.02			·	·
X_{a6}	−.72	X_{b6}	.66			·	·
X_{a7}	−.19	X_{b7}	.82			·	·
X_{a8}	−.04	X_{b8}	.11			·	·
X_{a9}	−1.20	X_{b9}	.21			·	·
$\bar{X}_a$	−.26	$\bar{X}_b$	−.03	·		·	·
s_a^2	.4815	s_b^2	.6246	·		·	·

Frequency distributions of the sample statistics. Although it is logically impossible to collect all the samples of size $n = 10$ that our normal parent population can yield, we can certainly collect enough to gain some insights about sampling distributions. For each subsequent sample we shall calculate the mean, $\bar{X}$, and the estimated variance, s^2. After we have taken a number of samples of size 10, we can group the corresponding sample means into a frequency distribution. We can also group our collection of sample variances into another frequency distribution.

In Table 6–2 we showed the first two samples of $n = 10$ from a normal parent population with $\mu = 0$ and $\sigma = 1$. We also showed the sample mean, $\bar{X}$, and the sample variance, s^2, for each sample. In Table 6–3 we show a frequency distribution of the means of 200 samples each of size $n = 10$ from the same normal parent population. Also shown in Table 6–3 is the distribution of variances of the 200 samples.

In Fig. 6–2 we have graphed the relative frequencies for the 200 sample means and the 200 sample variances given in Table 6–3. Each of these is an approximation to the probability distribution of a statistic in the sampling situation we have created. On the one hand we have approximated the sampling distribution of means, and on the other the sampling distribution of variances, *in samples of size ten taken at random from a normally distributed population with a mean of zero and a variance of 1.0.*

Table 6-3

OBSERVED VALUES OF $\bar{X}$ AND s^2 FROM A NORMAL POPULATION
WITH $\mu = 0$ AND $\sigma^2 = 1$
(n = 10 FOR EACH OF THE 200 SAMPLES)

Sample mean ($\bar{X}$)		Sample variance (s^2)	
Class midpoint	Frequency	Class midpoint	Frequency
−.75	2	.10	3
−.65	3	.30	18
−.55	7	.50	33
−.45	13	.70	28
−.35	13	.90	29
−.25	19	1.10	26
−.15	22	1.30	20
−.05	24	1.50	18
.05	26	1.70	10
.15	19	1.90	6
.25	17	2.10	3
.35	12	2.30	1
.45	11	2.50	2
.55	5	2.70	1
.65	4	2.90	1
.75	3	3.10	1
	200		200

	Distribution of $\bar{X}$	Distribution of s^2
Mean	−.009	1.001
Variance	.1035	.2983
Standard deviation	.322	.546

6-2 Sampling Distributions of the Mean and Variance

Consider the concept of the sampling distribution in the following way. A sampling distribution is a special type of probability distribution. It is a distribution of the population of *values of a given statistic that could be generated in random samples of a given size taken from a specified parent population.* We have been talking about the sample mean, random samples of size $n = 10$, and a normal parent population with $\mu = 0$ and $\sigma = 1$. If we change any single one of these specifications, we are talking about an entirely different sampling distribution—an entirely different derived population of statistics.

Since a sampling distribution is a special kind of population, it must also have parameters. The probability distribution of the sample mean itself has a mean, and it has a variance. Since both are calculated for a population, albeit a special type, both values are parameters. The grand mean of all the

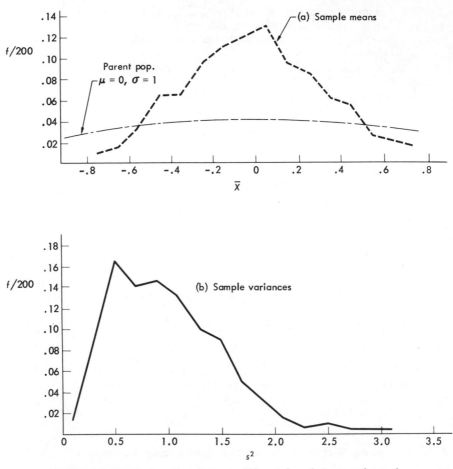

FIGURE 6-2 Distribution of statistics in 200 samples of size ten drawn from the standard normal population

sample means is denoted by the symbol $\mu_{\bar{X}}$ and the variance of all the sample means by the symbol $\sigma^2_{\bar{X}}$.

In Fig. 6–2 we showed the distribution of the 200 sample s^2 values obtained in as many samples of size ten taken from the standard normal parent population. This distribution is an approximation of the sampling distribution of the variance in samples of size $n = 10$ from a standard normal population. This sampling distribution has parameters. The mean of the probability distribution of sample variances is designated by μ_{s^2}. The variance of this sampling distribution is given the symbol $\sigma^2_{s^2}$.

Notice the values given at the bottom of Table 6–3. First, we have taken the grand mean of the 200 sample means. This is an approximation to $\mu_{\bar{X}}$. The estimate of $\mu_{\bar{X}}$ from our 200 means is $-.009$. No amount of experimental sampling would produce enough means to allow us to compute $\mu_{\bar{x}}$, since there are an infinite number of possible samples of size ten. The second calculation we have made is the variance of the 200 sample means. As we see in the table, this has a value of .1035. This value is an estimate of $\sigma_{\bar{x}}^2$.

Properties of the sampling distribution of means. In Chapter 2 we reviewed the rules for finding the mean and variance of sums of random variables and random variables multiplied by a constant factor. The values obtained for the mean and variance of our experimental sampling distribution should then come as no surprise. We learned, first, that the expected value of the sum of n independently drawn values of a random variable was the sum of the expected values upon each draw, or

$$\mu_{\Sigma x} = \Sigma \left(\mu_1 + \mu_2 + \mu_3 + \ldots + \mu_n \right) = n\mu_x.$$

Therefore, the expected value of the mean of a sample n independent observations is

$$\mu_{\Sigma x/n} = \frac{n\mu_x}{n},$$

$$\mu_{\bar{x}} = \mu_x. \tag{6-1}$$

Drawing a sample with the aid of a table of random numbers insures that the sequential draws are independent. The mean of the 200 sample means from samples of size ten does seem to be fairly close to the population mean of zero. (See Exercise 6.2.)

Second, we learned that the variance of the sum of n independently drawn values was equal to n times the underlying population variance, and that the variance of a random variable multiplied by a constant was always equal to the variance of the random variable multiplied by the square of the constant. Combining these rules, the variance of the probability distribution of the mean of n values independently drawn from a specified population is

$$\sigma_{\Sigma x}^2 = n\sigma_x^2,$$

$$\sigma_{\Sigma x/n}^2 = n\sigma_x^2 \left(\frac{1}{n^2} \right),$$

$$\sigma_{\bar{x}}^2 = \frac{\sigma_x^2}{n}. \tag{6-2}$$

For the expected value of the variance among the means of samples of size ten from a population with a variance of 1.0 we would then have

$$\sigma_{\bar{x}}^2 = \frac{\sigma_x^2}{n} = \frac{1.0}{10} = .1000.$$

The value obtained in our limited simulation of this infinite process again seems quite close at .1035.

The third important characteristic of the sampling distribution of means is its shape. The distribution in Fig. 6–2 appears roughly bell-shaped, and one can imagine a smoothed "normal" curve being drawn through it.

To summarize, if a parent population has a specified mean and variance, then the sampling distribution of means from random samples of size n will

(1) *have a mean equal to the mean of the parent population;*
(2) *have a variance equal to $1/n$ times the variance of the parent population.*

If, in addition, the parent population has a normal distribution, then

(3) *the sampling distribution of means will be normally distributed.*

The central limit theorem. We have stated the theorem that when the parent population is normal, the sampling distribution of means will be normal for *any* value of n. But what happens to the shape of sampling distributions of means when the parent population is not normal? If we are limited to dealing with normal parent populations, we are indeed quite restricted. Fortunately, mathematical statisticians have been able to prove what is perhaps the most important theorem in all of modern statistical inference. This theorem is called the *central limit theorem.* It assures us that, as n grows large, the associated sampling distribution of means approaches normality. The only restriction is that the parent population must have a finite variance, a condition that is fulfilled in the vast majority of practical situations. Furthermore, much investigation has shown that the sampling distribution of means approaches normality quite rapidly as n increases. For instance, only a very severely skewed parent distribution would produce a noticeably skewed sampling distribution of means if n were larger than 20 or so.

The sampling distribution and errors of estimate. We have seen that $\mu_{\bar{X}}$, a parameter of the sampling distribution of means, is precisely and exactly equal to μ_X, a parameter of the parent distribution, and that this is true regardless of the form of the parent distribution. We used this equality in Chapter 3 to define the meaning of the statement that $\bar{X}$, the mean of any one random sample from a population of X, is an unbiased estimate of μ_X, the mean of the parent population.

The second property of the sampling distribution of means dealt with $\sigma_{\bar{X}}^2$. This is the variance of the distribution of sample means. Its square root is a standard deviation, specifically the standard deviation of the probability distribution of the sample mean. Subtracting a constant from a set of values does not change the variance, so that $\sigma_{\bar{X}}^2$ is the variance of $\bar{X} - \mu$ as well as the variance of $\bar{X}$. The distribution of $\bar{X} - \mu$ is the distribution of errors of estimate. The standard deviation of the sampling distribution of means is thus traditionally termed the *standard error of the mean*. The standard error of the mean, symbolically, is

$$\sigma_{\bar{x}} = \frac{\sigma_x}{\sqrt{n}} . \tag{6–3}$$

Once again, it is important to remember that this statement is true for the sampling distribution of the mean from *any* infinite parent population. The only requirement is that the samples be collected at random. It makes no difference whether the parent distribution is normal, U-shaped, heavily skewed, or any other shape. So long as it has a finite variance, Eq. (6–3) is true.

The relationship between the standard error of the mean and the sample size, n, is critically important to our later work. It says that increasing the size of a sample will reduce the errors of estimate in using the sample mean to estimate the population mean. But this reduction, measured by the change in the standard error of the mean, is not directly proportional to the increase in sample size. The size of sampling error is inversely proportional to the *square root* of sample size. For example, to cut the standard error of the mean in half, we would have to quadruple the sample size.

The finite population multiplier. All we have said above applies to sampling from infinite populations. Notice that the standard error of the mean depends only on the sample size. No mention has been made of the size of the population because it is presumed to be infinitely large.

The standard error formula can be modified to apply to sampling from a finite population. Where N signifies the size of the parent population, the formula is

$$\sigma_{\bar{x}} = \frac{\sigma}{\sqrt{n}} \sqrt{\frac{N - n}{N - 1}} . \tag{6–4}$$

The factor on the right is termed the finite population multiplier. When N is large, it approaches the square root of the complement of the proportion of the population sampled. Thus, if we sampled 10 per cent of a large finite population, the proper standard error is $\sqrt{.90}$, or approximately .95 times $\sigma/\sqrt{n}$. The correct standard error is but 5 per cent smaller than the figure given by the formula appropriate to an infinite population. In sample surveys of large finite populations the sampling fractions are often much smaller than 10 per cent, and the effect of the finite multiplier is therefore quite small. However, it is important to use the multiplier when a sample exceeds a substantial fraction of a finite population. We suggest 10 per cent as a rule of thumb.

6-3 Employing the Sampling Distribution of Means

A certain soft drink manufacturer advertises on his bottles that the contents are 12 fluid ounces. The law requires that no more than 1 per cent of the bottles have contents below advertised weight. The proprietor of our soft drink business has a machine which fills the bottles automatically. This machine stops filling when the combined weight of the bottle and its contents is enough to push the filling switch down. There is an adjustable setting for this cut-off point, which we will assume is accurately calibrated to select the mean weight of the filled bottles. We shall also assume that all empty bottles weigh *exactly* the same. From the manufacturer of the filling machine and our own previous experience with it we know that the machine has $\sigma = .2$ fluid ounces for content weight. In other words, the standard deviation of the content weight distribution is .2 fluid ounces.

The first problem facing the bottler (which does not involve a sampling distribution) is to determine the value to which he should set the filling machine's adjustment screw so that at least 99 per cent of the bottles will contain 12 ounces or more. If the distribution of content weights is normal, we can find this setting. An assumption of normality is fairly reasonable in connection with such a physical process, and in any event could be checked empirically.

We can now restate our problem. The value we set on the adjustment screw is the mean of a normal distribution with $\sigma = .2$ such that only 1 per cent of its area is below 12. We can find the value of μ by working the z transformation backwards.

$$\mu = X - z\sigma_x, \qquad z_{.01} = -2.33,$$
$$\mu = 12.0 - (-2.33)\,(.2)$$
$$= 12.47 \text{ fluid ounces.}$$

So far we have made no use of the properties of the sampling distribution of the mean. These come into play when we ask the next question. How can the bottler be reasonably sure that the filling machine is maintaining the proper mean content weight (12.5 fl. oz. for convenience)? How can we have reasonable assurance that no parts of the machine have come loose?

Suppose the bottler has set the machine to fill to a mean weight of 12.5 ounces. We can think of this as μ for a parent population with $\sigma = .2$ fluid ounces. Let's suppose he decides to take samples, each composed of ten bottles, at random times. He computes the mean content weight per bottle in each sample. His history of successive sample means might appear as the graph plotted in Fig. 6–3. Each point is the mean of a random sample of the content weights of ten bottles selected from a normal population with $\sigma = .2$ fluid ounces. For the first nine of the 18 $\bar{X}$'s shown, the mean of the

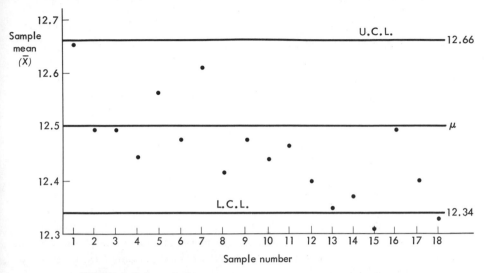

FIGURE 6-3 Control chart on mean content weight of ten bottles

parent population was 12.5 ($\mu = 12.5$). The second nine, however, were deliberately drawn from a parent population in which $\mu = 12.4$. We have in this manner simulated an adjustment slippage on the machine that caused the mean fill weight to fall off .1 ounces. Our problem as industrial statisticians would be to detect such shifts when we do not know they have occurred.

From the assumption of a normal parent population we know that the sampling distribution of the arithmetic mean will be normal. The standard normal deviate now takes the form

$$z = \frac{\bar{X} - \mu}{\sigma_{\bar{X}}}, \qquad \text{where} \quad \sigma_{\bar{X}}^2 = \frac{\sigma_X^2}{n}. \qquad (6\text{--}5)$$

From our parent population parameters and sample size we know that

$$\sigma_{\bar{X}}^2 = \frac{(.2)^2}{10} = .004,$$

$$\sigma_{\bar{X}} = \sqrt{.004} = .0632 \text{ fl. oz.}$$

Equation (6–5) can be restated as an expression for $\bar{X}$, the sample mean:

$$\bar{X} = \mu + z\sigma_{\bar{X}}. \qquad (6\text{--}6)$$

If μ remains at 12.5 fluid ounces, then 99 per cent of a long run of sample means should fall between $\mu + z_{.005}\sigma_{\bar{X}}$ and $\mu + z_{.995}\sigma_{\bar{X}}$. The sample means corresponding to these limits are

$$\bar{X}_{.005} = 12.5 + (-2.58)(.0632) = 12.34 \text{ fl. oz.,}$$
$$\bar{X}_{.995} = 12.5 + (2.58)(.0632) = 12.66 \text{ fl. oz.}$$

These boundaries are the solid horizontal lines we have drawn equidistant from $\mu = 12.5$ in Fig. 6–3. The first, $\bar{X}_{.005}$, is called the *Lower Control Limit* and $\bar{X}_{.995}$ is the *Upper Control Limit*.

If the mean filling weight actually remains at 12.5 fluid ounces, if σ remains at .2 fluid ounces, and if we continue to sample at random, we know what should happen. All but 1 per cent of our $\bar{X}$'s should fall within the control limits. If a sample falls outside the control limits, we know that an event with but a .01 probability of occurring *when $\mu = 12.5$ and $\sigma = .2$* has in fact occurred. It is customary in such cases to look for an *assignable cause* of the variation of $\bar{X}$ from the process mean, μ. The rarity of the event if the process parameters are being met leads us to suspect that they are in fact not being met. On the other hand, as long as individual sample means are within the control limits, no search for assignable causes of variation is made. This means the bottler acts as if the process parameters were in fact $\mu = 12.5$ and $\sigma = .2$.

We know that the second nine samples were actually picked from a parent population in which the mean had shifted to $\mu = 12.4$ fluid ounces. Yet the sample means continue to stay within the control limits up through sample number 14. The failure of our technique to detect this shift in μ is the price we have to pay for setting our control limits so wide and for taking samples of only ten each. Yet we may not want to set narrower control limits. If we narrowed the control limits for means of samples of size ten, we would increase the likelihood of our looking for an assignable cause when there really was nothing wrong. Larger samples would increase the expenses of sampling.

In our present example, because we deliberately changed μ, we know that there is something wrong after sample number 9 is taken. The parent population mean, μ, has shifted from 12.5 fluid ounces to 12.4 fluid ounces. Since $\sigma_{\bar{X}}$ is still .0632 fluid ounces, the shift in μ amounts to slightly more than 1.58 standard errors of the mean.

We can look at the situation another way.

$$z = \frac{\bar{X} - \mu}{\sigma_{\bar{X}}} = \frac{12.34 - 12.40}{.0632} = -.95.$$

This says that our established lower control limit is .95 standard errors below our new population mean (12.4). This implies that 17 per cent instead of .5 per cent of our $\bar{X}$'s can now be expected to fall below the lower control limit. Figure 6–3 shows that it took five samples before we happened to hit one such sample mean. Nonetheless, this procedure did detect a relatively small shift in the mean filling weight fairly soon (see Exercise 6.3).

You may have noticed another rather strange pattern in Fig. 6–3. The means of samples number 8 through number 15 all lie below 12.5. Now 12.5 is the median, as well as the mean, of the distribution of sample means when the filling machine is working properly. The probability is one-half that a sample mean will fall below the median of the sampling distribution. The probability of seven successive sample means below 12.5 when the machine is working properly is, therefore, only $(1/2)^7 = 1/128$. By setting up a rule about sequences in advance, just as we set up the control limits for means of individual samples, we can put probability to work for us in an additional way.

EXERCISES

6.1 A manufacturing process, when properly adjusted, is known to produce parts with a mean diameter of 2.00 inches and a tolerance (standard deviation) of .05 inches. Assuming the distribution of diameters to be normally distributed, find the following for samples of size 25.
(a) $P(\bar{X} > 2.02)$.   *Ans.* .02275.
(b) $P(1.975 < \bar{X} < 2.025)$.   *Ans.* .98758.
(c) $\bar{X}_{.01}$; $\bar{X}_{.99}$.   *Ans.* 1.9767; 2.0233.
(d) $\bar{X}_{.10}$; $\bar{X}_{.90}$.   *Ans.* 1.9872; 2.0128.

6.2 Refer to Table 6–3.
(a) What is the probability that $\bar{X}$ will exceed $-.009$ in a random sample of 2000 taken from the population specified?   *Ans.* .6554.
(b) Using Eq. (6–3) and the properties of the sampling distribution of means, find and compare with the observed relative frequency:
$$P(-.20 < \bar{X} < .20). \quad \textit{Ans. .4714 vs. 91/200.}$$
$$P(\bar{X} > .60). \quad \textit{Ans. .02872 vs. 7/200.}$$
(c) Using appropriate approximations to the binomial distribution, find the probability of getting more means than actually observed in the ranges indicated in (b).   *Ans.* .6331; .229.

6.3 Refer to Sec. 6–3 and Fig. 6–3.
(a) What is the probability that five successive sample means will fail to fall outside the lower control limit when the mean is in fact 12.4 ounces?
(b) If the mean shifts to 12.34, what is the probability that the change will be undetected after five samples are taken?
(c) What shift in the mean has a fifty-fifty chance of remaining un-detected after two successive samples?

6.4 Prepare a graph comparing the cumulative distribution of the means of the 200 samples (Table 6–3) with a normal distribution with a mean of zero and a standard deviation of 1.0.

6-4 The Sampling Distribution of Variances

In Table 6–2 we showed the variances of the first two random samples of $n = 10$ from our parent normal population with $\mu = 0$ and $\sigma = 1$. In Fig. 6–2(b) and in Table 6–3 we showed the distribution of 200 such sample variances.

In Table 6–3 the grand mean of the s^2 values from the 200 samples was given as 1.001. This is very close to the value of σ^2 for the parent population ($\sigma^2 = 1.000$). Figure 6–2(b) should remind you of the shape of a distribution we studied in Chapter 5. The frequency distribution of variances is skewed to the right and is unimodal. These are characteristics of chi-square distributions.

Our distribution of 200 sample variances is an approximation of the sampling distribution of variances from samples of size ten taken at random from a normal population with $\mu = 0$ and $\sigma^2 = 1$. The properties of the probability distribution of a sample variance from a normal parent population, supportable by mathematical proofs, are several. First, the expected value of the sample variance is equal to the variance of the population. We encountered this feature of s^2 as an unbiased estimate of σ^2 in Chapter 3.

$$\mu_{s^2} = \sigma^2. \tag{6–7}$$

Second, the probability distribution of the sample variance, s^2, of a random sample from *any normal population* can be obtained from the transformation:

$$s^2 = \chi^2\left(\frac{\sigma^2}{m}\right), \tag{6–8}$$

where χ^2 is the random variable, $m = n - 1$, and where the particular chi-square distribution employed has m degrees of freedom.

In our example the parent population was the standard normal distribution whose variance, σ^2, is 1.0, so that $\sigma^2/m = 1/9$. Equation (6–8) says that the statistic, s^2, in samples of size ten from a normal population with $\sigma^2 = 1.0$ follows the same probability distribution as does $\chi^2(1/9)$ with nine degrees of freedom. Note that the mean of this distribution is $m(1/9) = 1.0 = \sigma^2$. Let us see if our 200 sample s^2 values follow this distribution.

Figure 6–4 shows the cumulative distribution of the 200 sample s^2 values from Table 6–3 compared with the cumulative percentiles of $\chi^2(1/9)$ for nine degrees of freedom. The latter are the percentiles from the $m = 9$ row of Appendix E multiplied by 1/9. The dots in Fig. 6–4 are the cumulative distribution points for our 200 sample variances. The fit is not quite as close as seemed to be the case for the sampling distribution of means, but it is still close enough to illustrate the point.

The sample statistic which is distributed according to chi-square

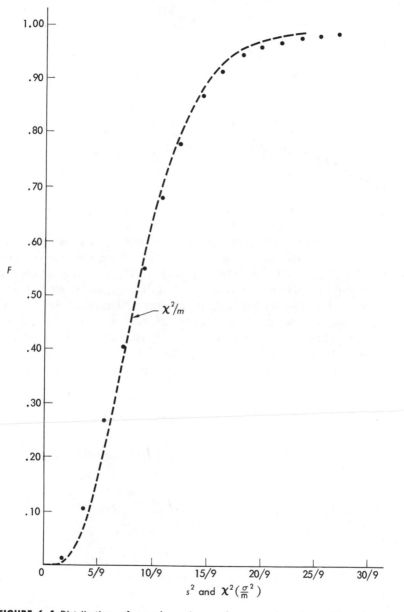

FIGURE 6-4 Distribution of sample variances from samples of $n = 10$ and χ^2/m distribution for $m = n - 1 = 9$

without any multiplicative factor attached is $(ms^2)/\sigma^2$. Transposition of Eq. (6–8) produces

$$\chi^2 = \frac{ms^2}{\sigma^2}. \tag{6–9}$$

The statistic $(ms^2)/\sigma^2$ is the ratio of the sample sum of squared deviations to the population variance, since $ms^2 = (n-1)s^2 = \Sigma\,[(X - \bar{X})^2]$. At different times Eq. (6–8) or Eq. (6–9) may be the more convenient to use. These two equations parallel for variances the more familiar ones involving sample means. The comparisons are given below.

	Means	Variances
Tabled statistic	$z = \dfrac{\bar{X} - \mu}{\sigma_{\bar{X}}}$	$\chi^2 = \dfrac{ms^2}{\sigma^2}$
Sample statistic distributed as	$\bar{X} = \mu + z\sigma_{\bar{X}}$	$s^2 = \dfrac{\chi^2\sigma^2}{m}$

The normal approximations to the sampling distribution of variances. We have said that the sampling distribution of the variance is a chi-square distribution no matter what the sample size. The only requirements are that the parent population be normal and that the samples be selected at random. We learned in Chapter 5 that as the number of degrees of freedom increases, the chi-square distribution approaches the normal distribution form. Correspondingly, as sample size grows large, the sampling distribution of variances from a normal parent population approaches normality. For large n, then, the sampling distribution of s^2 can be approximated by the standard normal deviate, z, where

$$z = \frac{s^2 - \sigma^2}{\sigma_{s^2}}.$$

But $\sigma_{s^2}^2 = \sigma_{\chi^2}^2(\sigma^2/m)^2$ since $s^2 = \chi^2(\sigma^2/m)$. Further, since $\sigma_{\chi^2}^2 = 2m$, we can obtain

$$\sigma_{s^2}^2 = 2m\left(\frac{\sigma^2}{m}\right)^2 = (\sigma^2)^2\frac{2}{m}$$

$$\sigma_{s^2} = \sigma^2\sqrt{\frac{2}{m}}.$$

Then the standard normal deviate becomes

$$z = \frac{s^2 - \sigma^2}{\sigma^2\sqrt{2/m}}. \tag{6–10}$$

This means that in dealing with sufficiently large samples taken from a normal population whose variance is known, one may find the probability that s^2 will fail to exceed any given value by finding the probability that z fails to exceed the value given by Eq. (6–10). Some examples are included in the next set of exercises.

6-5 Employing the Sampling Distribution of the Variance

Let us return to the bottle-filling example used earlier in this chapter. Modern industrial processes are monitored with an eye to keeping them in control. A process in control is a process operating as it was designed to operate. One of the first steps in maintaining control was illustrated in our earlier discussion: we prepared a control chart with predetermined control limits for the sample mean, and we sought to correct the process if a sample mean fell above the upper limit or below the lower control limit.

These control limits were determined on the basis of our knowledge of the sampling distribution of the mean. At that time we had to assume that the standard deviation for the filling machine was equal to and remained equal to .2 fluid ounces. But, in fact, not only can the mean filling weight slip out of adjustment, but also the variability inherent in the machine can change because of shaft wear or other mechanical malfunctions.

With our knowledge about the sampling distribution of the variance we can also set up a control chart for the variability of the bottle-filling operation. We know that s^2 will be distributed as $\chi^2(\sigma^2/m)$, where σ^2 is the specification variance of .04 and m is the sample size less one, or $n - 1 = 9$. The mean of the sampling distribution of s^2 will be .04, the specification variance. Percentiles of the sampling distribution of s^2 can be obtained by substituting the corresponding percentiles of χ^2 with nine degrees of freedom in the expression, $s^2 = \chi^2(\sigma^2/m)$.

Suppose that we were willing to run a 10 per cent risk of investigating the variance of the process when nothing was really wrong with it. We would then set an upper control limit at $s^2_{.95}$ and a lower control limit at $s^2_{.05}$.

$$s^2_{.95} = \chi^2_{.95}\left(\frac{\sigma^2}{m}\right) = 16.9\left(\frac{.04}{9}\right) = .0751,$$

$$s^2_{.05} = \chi^2_{.05}\left(\frac{\sigma^2}{m}\right) = 3.33\left(\frac{.04}{9}\right) = .0148.$$

These values are plotted as the upper and lower control limits for s^2 in Fig. 6–5. In this same figure we have also plotted the median s^2, or $s^2_{.50} = .0371$, obtained in the same manner as the foregoing percentiles. We can use this line to check sequences of s^2 values from successive samples that fall on one side of the median line, just as we suggested for sample means in the earlier control chart. Notice that the upper and lower control limits for the variance are not equidistant from $s^2_{.50}$. This reflects the skewness of the chi-square distribution for nine degrees of freedom.

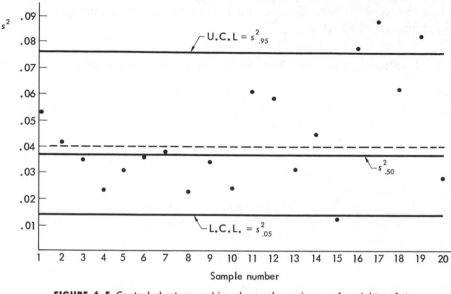

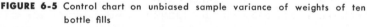

FIGURE 6-5 Control chart on unbiased sample variance of weights of ten bottle fills

To illustrate the operation of this control chart, we have selected 20 samples of ten each. Samples 1 through 10 were drawn from a normal population with variance equal to .04, the specification value. For samples 11 through 20 we have simulated a failure of the process by drawing the samples from a normal population with $\sigma^2 = .09$. The results are shown in control chart form in Fig. 6–5. The first sample variance beyond the control limits is sample 15. An analyst reading the control chart at that point would suspect that the variability is unusually small rather than unusually large. Any control chart reflects a process of generating data that involves more than the production operation alone. The assignable cause here may well lie in some element of the process wholly aside from the machine. Perhaps a man on the production line or one of the quality control inspectors was selecting only bottles he thought were "typical," or reading weight measurements with an inadvertent bias toward what he knew to be the specification mean weight.

When the sample variances begin to jump out of control on the high side as in samples 16, 17, and 19, we would shut down. We would suspect the machine. We would look for wear in bearings or on shafts or cams. Partially loosened cams or shafts might slip part of the time and stick part of the time to introduce additional variation.

In actual quality control practice, control charts are seldom established for s^2 to check for variability. Rather the charts are built using the range of the sample observations—for two reasons: (1) the range is easier to compute and can readily be taught to regular foremen on the production line; (2) for the small samples generally used in quality control, an estimate of the population variance based on the range of sample values is nearly as efficient as an estimate based on s^2.

EXERCISES

6.5 The data below are the results from 20 samples of ten each taken at successive intervals from a process designed to produce normally distributed pressures averaging 110 pounds with a standard deviation of 10 pounds.

Sample	$\bar{X}$	s^2	Sample	$\bar{X}$	s^2
1	112.0	72.7	11	107.9	72.9
2	110.8	153.2	12	116.7	111.5
3	106.8	213.0	13	113.8	80.0
4	106.1	108.0	14	105.2	55.8
5	108.2	66.5	15	116.0	52.5
6	111.5	167.1	16	110.3	87.3
7	111.1	116.9	17	109.4	62.6
8	107.5	28.4	18	117.0	61.4
9	107.8	158.6	19	113.4	54.9
10	114.2	35.7	20	111.7	115.2

(a) Determine the 95 per cent control limits for means of samples of size ten, and plot the sequence of 20 means in control chart fashion.
Ans. 103.80; 116.20.

(b) What is the probability of as many or more sample means than actually observed beyond the upper control limit if the process was in fact in control when the 20 samples were taken? (Use the Poisson.)
Ans. .090.

(c) Determine the 95 per cent control limits for the sample variance. Is there any evidence that the variance is out of control?
Ans. 30; 211.1; no.

(d) Considering the entire set of data as one sample of $n = 200$, find the probability of the sample mean's exceeding the observed mean if the process was in fact in control.
Ans. .1093.

6.6 Compute the means of samples 1–5, 6–10, 11–15, and 16–20 from the data of Exercise 6.5.

(a) For each of the four samples of 50 observations, find the probability of a larger sample mean than actually observed, given that the process was in control.

(b) Calculate the mean of samples 1–10 and the mean of samples 11–20. Given each of these means, find the probability that the process when under control would produce a larger mean in a sample of $n = 100$.

6.7 Average the sample variances for samples 1–10, and for samples 11–20 of Exercise 6.5. Each of these yields an estimated variance with 90 degrees of freedom.

(a) Using the chi-square table, find the probability of an estimated variance exceeding each of the two you have computed if the process variance was in fact 100.   *Ans.* Approx. .20; .95 < P < .975.

(b) Using Eq. (6–10), find the normal approximation to the probabilities in (a).   *Ans.* .2090; .95053.

6.8 Plot the cumulative distribution of the 20 sample variances against the cumulative distribution of $\chi^2(100/9)$, where χ^2 has nine degrees of freedom.

6-6   The Student "t" Distribution

Control charts for sample means such as shown in Fig. 6–3 have been found to be highly useful in industry. In addition to controlling manufacturing processes, they have been applied in clerical, accounting, and auditing operations to control magnitudes of error.* But these control charts require advance knowledge of the value of the variance before they can be employed. After a large number of sample variances are available we might be willing to use the average sample variance as if it were equal to the population variance. But how many samples would this require, and what do we do in the meantime? At the beginning of a new operation no one may have a reasonable estimate of the variance.

After a process is installed, often the only information about its operation that we can depend upon is contained in our first sample. Think of the bottle-filling example. Suppose we have just installed the machinery, and are concerned with whether the setting at 12.5 ounces really controls the average fill at that figure. We have made this setting, have started operations, and have just selected our first sample of ten bottles (n has been picked arbitrarily). We have calculated $\bar{X}$ and s^2 for this sample. How do we know whether the setting is accurate? We cannot set control limits from $12.5 + z\sigma_{\bar{X}}$, since we do not know the value of σ in the expression $\sigma_{\bar{X}} = \sigma/\sqrt{n}$. Is there some way that we can fill in the gap in our information? Yes, there is. We have calculated s^2 for our first sample. We know that this number is an unbiased estimate of σ^2. We might be tempted to substitute s for σ in the expression, $\bar{X} = \mu + z(\sigma/\sqrt{n})$.

This substitution would, in effect, amount to

$$z' = \frac{\bar{X} - \mu}{s_{\bar{X}}}, \quad \text{where} \quad s_{\bar{X}} = \frac{s}{\sqrt{n}}.$$

* See, for example, R. M. Cyert and H. Justin Davidson, *Statistical Sampling for Accounting Information* (Englewood Cliffs, N.J.: Prentice-Hall, Inc., 1962).

What we have done is to manufacture *one* new statistic out of *two* that are already familiar to us. We have combined both $\bar{X}$ and s from the same sample into one new statistic, which for the moment we are calling z'. This new statistic has a sampling distribution. Let us compare it with the sampling distribution for the statistic.

$$z = \frac{\bar{X} - \mu}{\sigma_{\bar{X}}}, \qquad \text{where} \qquad \sigma_{\bar{X}} = \frac{\sigma}{\sqrt{n}}.$$

What might be the appearance of the sampling distribution of our new statistic based only upon sample information? If, in fact, the machine is producing a mean fill weight of $\mu = 12.5$ ounces, the numerator of the equation for z' will be distributed normally about 0 as was the numerator of z. On the other hand, the denominator of z was fixed at a single value, whereas the denominator of our new statistic fluctuates from sample to sample. This fluctuation, when combined with that already in the numerator, should tend to make our new statistic's sampling distribution more variable than was the sampling distribution of $(\bar{X} - \mu)/\sigma_{\bar{X}}$. On the basis of these considerations we might expect the distribution to be roughly bell-shaped and symmetrical, but with greater dispersion than a normal distribution.

The continuous probability distribution which is appropriate to the situation just described is known as "Student's t distribution." It was developed by W. S. Gossett (1876–1937).* The derivation of Student's t distribution allowed modern statistics to get under way, for it provided the theory that made possible the drawing of statistical inferences wholly from sample data.

The graph of a t distribution is shown in Fig. 6–6 as a dotted curve. The solid curve is the standard normal curve for comparative purposes.

We saw earlier that we must specify two numbers before we can isolate a specific normal curve for consideration. We must designate both μ and σ, which are zero and one respectively in the standard normal distribution. The t distribution is a function of the degrees of freedom, m. That is, there is a different t distribution for each value of the parameter, m. The mean of any t distribution is zero, and the variance of a t distribution for values of m exceeding 2 is

$$\sigma_t^2 = \frac{m}{m - 2} \qquad \text{for} \quad m \geq 3.$$

For smaller values of m, the variance cannot be expressed simply and will not be presented here. The particular t distribution shown in Fig. 6–6 has $\mu = 0$ and $m = 2$ as shown on the label. We cannot find the variance from the above equation, but it is greater than 1.

---

* Gossett was employed by the Guiness Brewery of Dublin and London, who insisted that he use a pseudonym in signing professional articles. Gossett's articles were simply signed "Student."

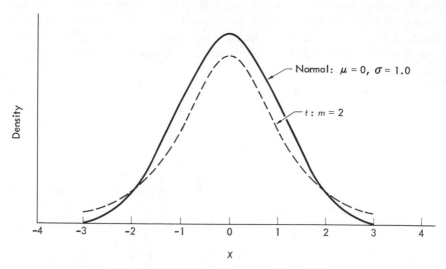

FIGURE 6-6 The *t* and the normal distributions

From Fig. 6–6 we can see that this *t* distribution, like the normal, is symmetrical. Indeed, all *t* distributions are symmetrical, bell-shaped curves. But a difference is readily apparent. Relative to the normal distribution, the *t* distribution for $m = 2$ has had a portion of its area shifted from the middle to each of the tails. This shift in area gives the *t* distribution more variance than the standard normal distribution. The *t* distributions for small values of *m* have variances appreciably greater than unity. But, as the value of *m* increases, the difference between the *t* distribution and the standard normal curve decreases. Note what happens to the variance, $m/(m - 2)$, as *m* increases. In fact, as *m* grows large without limit, the *t* distribution approaches the normal distribution. For most practical purposes, the normal distribution can be used in place of the *t* distribution if $m \geq 30$.

The table of selected percentiles of *t* for differing degrees of freedom is given in Appendix F. The arguments for the table are *m* and *P*. The argument *m* is the number of degrees of freedom for the *t* distribution of interest. The argument *P* is the probability that *t* is equal to or less than the indicated value. Thus the table corresponds graphically to the proportionate area in the lower tail of the probability density function of *t*.

Formally, the *t* distribution can be defined in terms of its square, t^2. The square of *t* is the ratio between the square of a standard normal variable and a variable distributed as chi-square. In the current example, the ratio

$$m \left(\frac{\bar{X} - \mu}{\sigma / \sqrt{n}} \right)^2 \div \frac{ms^2}{\sigma^2}$$

is of this form. The numerator is normally distributed, and the denominator is distributed as chi-square. In reducing this ratio, σ^2 and m cancel out and one obtains

$$\frac{(\bar{X} - \mu)^2}{s^2/n}$$

The square root of this expression amounts to our "z-type" expression with an estimated standard error rather than a known standard error. It is distributed according to Student's t.

$$t = \frac{\bar{X} - \mu}{s_{\bar{X}}}, \qquad \text{where} \quad s_{\bar{X}} = \frac{s}{\sqrt{n}}. \qquad (6\text{--}11)$$

Equation (6–11) applies only if the data are derived by random sampling from a normally distributed population. In applications where particular nonnormal parent distributions appear to recur, it may be possible to find a suitable transformation which will lead to normal parent distributions.

6-7 Employing the Student *t* Distribution

From our first sample in the bottle-filling operation we have values of $\bar{X}$ and s. We have established the setting at 12.5 ounces, and have taken a random sample of $n = 10$ fills from the resulting process output. Suppose s^2 from the sample is .064. Now we can determine any desired percentile of *the sampling distribution of means of samples of size ten from a normally distributed population with* $\mu = 12.5$ *but* σ^2 *unknown.*

Written as an expression for the sample mean, Eq. (6–11) becomes

$$\bar{X} = 12.5 + ts_{\bar{X}}$$
$$= 12.5 + t(.08).$$

We go to Appendix F and look up, say, the .005 and .995 percentiles of t for nine degrees of freedom. These are -3.250 and $+3.250$, respectively. We then have

$$\bar{X}_{.005} = 12.5 + (-3.250)(.08) = 12.5 - .26 = 12.24 \text{ oz.,}$$
$$\bar{X}_{.995} = 12.5 + 3.250(.08) = 12.5 + .26 = 12.76 \text{ oz.}$$

Should our sample mean lie outside these limits, we would doubt that our setting was operating to produce an average fill of 12.5 ounces, and we would have to further calibrate the machine. For a subsequent check we would have a new set of limits based on the best estimate of the variance available at that time.

By the time the settings for mean fill have been established we may feel that we have a close and stable estimate of σ^2. At this point we can establish the control charts on mean and variability introduced previously. As long as the process is in control with respect to variability, the mean can be checked through the control chart for means from a normal population with known variance (Fig. 6–3). However, should the variability go out of control, we would have to revert to checking the mean through limits established by the t distribution—because we would no longer "know" the variance of the population.

Our example has illustrated the fundamental importance of the t distribution in modern statistics. Without this distribution we would not be able to begin a quality control operation on sound theoretical grounds with a sample of ten. Instead we would have to wait for a much larger sample size—one from which the variance could be regarded for all practical purposes as known.

Quality control operations afford a good example of how valuable it is to be able to work with small samples. In testing "pilot" processes we may need a check after a few experimental pieces have been produced. One hundred per cent inspection of routine output is very expensive and often not especially accurate because relatively unskilled inspectors must be used. In many cases testing a product destroys the item tested. Here, clearly, the usefulness of working with small samples is evident.

EXERCISES

6.9   Assume in Exercise 6.5 that there is no prior knowledge or specification about the variance of the population.

    (a) Assuming that the process variance remains constant, the best estimate of it after sample number 2 is taken is the average of the two sample s^2 values. There are $2 \times 9 = 18$ degrees of freedom in this estimate. Using this estimate, establish the 95 per cent control limits for the mean of a sample of size ten. *Ans.* $102.94 - 117.06$.

    (b) Using the best estimate of σ^2 available after the second sample is taken, establish the 95 per cent control limits for the mean of a sample of size 20.   *Ans.* $105.01 - 114.99$.

    (c) Using the best estimate of the variance available after three samples are taken, establish the 95 per cent control limits for the mean of a sample of size ten; of size 30.

                                Ans. $102.16 - 117.84$; $105.46 - 114.54$.

6.10 Refer to Exercise 5.2, and assume an underlying normal distribution.

    (a) Suppose a sample of 16 produced a mean of $+.66$ ounces and an estimated standard deviation of 2.4 ounces. If $\mu = 0$ and $\sigma = 1.5$, what is the probability of a sample mean exceeding that observed?

    (b) Making no assumption about the population variance, find approximately the probability in (a).

(c) What is the probability of a variance exceeding 5.76 in a random sample of size 16 if the population variance is 2.25?

6.11 Samples 1–10 in Exercise 6.5 actually were taken from a population in which $\mu = 110$ and $\sigma = 10$, while the parent population of samples 11–20 was $\mu = 113$ and $\sigma = 10$.

(a) What is the probability that the mean of a sample of ten will fall beyond the upper control limit of Exercise 6.5(a) when $\mu = 113$?

Ans. .1562.

(b) What is the probability that five successive means will all fail to exceed the upper control limit? Ten successive means?

Ans. .4785; .183.

6.12 Use the normal approximation to find the probability that a population with a mean of 35 and an estimated variance of 45 will produce a sample mean of less than 34.65 in a sample of size 180:

(a) Assuming an infinite population. *Ans.* .2420

(b) If the population numbered 500. *Ans.* .1894

6.13 Using the Monte Carlo technique of Sec. 6–2, take 100 samples of size two from the following distributions as assigned: (1) χ^2 with $m = 2$; (2) χ^2 with $m = 8$; (3) χ^2 with $m = 20$; (4) χ^2 with $m = 50$.

(a) Plot the cumulative distribution of the means of your 100 samples along with the cumulative normal distribution with a mean of m and standard deviation of $\sqrt{2m/n}$.

(b) Reduce your 100 means of samples of size two to 50 means of samples of size four and 25 means of samples of eight by averaging the means of successive pairs of samples. Plot the cumulative distributions of these sample means along with the cumulative normal distributions with a mean of m and a standard deviation of $\sqrt{2m/n}$.

(c) Do your results agree with what the central limit theorem would lead you to expect? Explain.

REFERENCES

Anderson, R. L., and T. A. Bancroft, *Statistical Theory in Research*. New York: McGraw-Hill Book Company, 1952.

Dixon, W., and F. J. Massey, Jr., *Introduction to Statistical Analysis*, 2nd ed. New York: McGraw-Hill Book Company, 1957.

Griffin, J. I., *Statistics: Methods and Application*. New York: Holt, Rinehart & Winston, Inc., 1962.

Mood, A., and F. A. Graybill, *Introduction to the Theory of Statistics*, 2nd ed. New York: McGraw-Hill Book Company, 1963.

7

Significance
Tests
and Decision Procedures

The most widespread tool of statistical analysis based on the probability distribution of a statistic given a parameter is the *significance test*. For the first three decades of the twentieth century the development and application of tests of significance were of major importance in the spread of statistical methods into a variety of applied fields in both the natural and the social sciences. We have already, in effect, applied the idea of a test of significance in developing control charts in Chapter 6. In that example, a test run on the outcome of the mean in a single sample would be identified as a test of the *null hypothesis* that the population mean was equal to the specification mean of 12.5 ounces of fill per bottle. If the sample mean turned out to be beyond the 99 per cent control limits, this result would be said to be *significant at the 1 per cent level*. This phrase means that, if the null hypothesis were true, greater differences between the sample mean and the hypothesized population mean would occur but 1 per cent of the time—that is, with probability .01. This could be taken as grounds for looking for an *assignable cause* of the variation between the sample mean and the hypothesized population mean. In many applications, differences significant at the .05 level have been used as grounds for doubting the truth of the null hypothesis.

7-1   Significance Tests and Decision Tests

Acceptance sampling for the quality of shipments of manufactured products illustrates the demands placed on a decision test. Upon receiving a shipment of goods, a company samples the shipment to determine its quality. In the case of a measured indicator of quality, the shipment must be accepted or rejected on the basis of the sample mean, for example. Rejection may mean the return of the goods to the supplier, or the assessment of some penalty in terms of the price to be paid.

The alternative hypotheses are that the shipment does or does not conform to some minimum quality specification. Acceptance of the one hypothesis is tantamount to rejection of the alternative. The user of a decision test is relying on the test to make an unequivocal choice between alternative states as the sole basis for selection of a course of action.

The theory of statistical decision tests was developed in the 1930's by E. S. Pearson and J. Neyman. The most important concept is that of *errors of the first and second kind*. Errors of the first kind, also called Type I and alpha errors, are those that lead to rejection of the null hypothesis when it is true. Errors of the second kind, also called Type II and beta errors, are those that lead to acceptance of the null hypothesis when an alternative hypothesis is true. We will use the process control example of the last chapter to review these decision errors rather fully. This development will lead us to the very important idea of *the power of a statistical test*. The power of a test is the probability, conditional on a true state or parameter, that the test will lead to rejection of the null hypothesis. A *statistical decision test* is designed to permit a choice between alternative hypotheses based solely on the sample data. The test requires specification of allowable probabilities of errors of the first and second kind. In the *significance test*, only errors of the first kind are controlled. Frequently this leads to the collection of additional information before a decision is made.

Let us view a null hypothesis test for the means of the bottle-filling process as a decision test. We assume that the parent population is normal and that the variance is in control, and we plan to take a sample of size ten at periodic intervals. On the basis of each sample mean, we will make one of the following decisions.

D_1: Conclude $\mu < 12.5$ and investigate the process;
D_0: Conclude $\mu = 12.5$ and do nothing;
D_2: Conclude $\mu > 12.5$ and investigate the process.

The null hypothesis is that $\mu = 12.5$ ounces, and acceptance of the null hypothesis will lead to the decision to do nothing. A specification of the allowable risk of rejecting the null hypothesis when it is true (the error of the first kind) will lead to a set of decision limits which are the upper and lower control limits that we encountered before. As long as the sample mean falls within the decision limits, we accept the null hypothesis and implicitly reject the alternatives.

We have restated the process control problem in the language of decision theory. When we viewed the problem in the context of a significance test we talked about suspecting an assignable cause of variation rather than a rule for decision. The foreman was to regard a significant difference as something to be investigated *before* concluding that μ does not equal 12.5, rather than as a *rule for concluding* that μ does not equal 12.5. This is the essence of the historical difference between decision tests and significance tests.

7-2   Alpha and Beta Errors for a Test of a Null Hypothesis

The allowable risk of rejecting the null hypothesis when it is true is called the alpha risk, or alpha error. In the current example rejection of the hypothesis that $\mu = 12.5$ in favor of either alternative, $\mu > 12.5$ or $\mu < 12.5$, would lead to an action different from what would be taken if $\mu = 12.5$ were accepted. Suppose we specify .05 as the allowable alpha error. The alpha risk of .05 is split between the two tails of the sampling distribution. Letting μ_o stand for the value of the mean when the null hypothesis is true, we have

$$z_L = z_{\alpha/2} = z_{.025} = -1.96,$$

$$z_u = z_{1-(\alpha/2)} = z_{.975} = +1.96,$$

$$\bar{X}_L = \mu_o + z_L \sigma_{\bar{X}}$$

$$= 12.5 + (-1.96)(.0632) = 12.376,$$

$$\bar{X}_u = \mu_o + z_u \sigma_{\bar{X}}$$

$$= 12.5 + (1.96)(.0632) = 12.624.$$

The subscripts refer to the lower decision limit and the upper decision limit. Thus $\bar{X}_L$ and $\bar{X}_u$ are the decision limits in terms of the sample mean. In order to limit the alpha error to .05, we will reject the hypothesis that $\mu = 12.5$ only if the sample mean turns out to be below $\bar{X}_L$ or above $\bar{X}_u$ (less than 12.376 or more than 12.624). If the mean is below $\bar{X}_L$ we adopt D_1, and if the mean is above $\bar{X}_u$ we adopt D_2; otherwise, we adopt D_0.

Limiting the alpha error to .05 is a procedure that gives us high assurance—probability .95—of accepting the null hypothesis when it is really true. In the control example, this means a high assurance of leaving the process alone when we would want to do just that. This is shown graphically in Fig. 7–1.

So far we have only considered the possibility of error in adopting D_1 or D_2 when we should have adopted D_0 (when $\mu = 12.5$). This was the alpha error. But what about the error of adopting D_0 when we should have adopted D_1 or D_2? This is called the beta error. In general, the beta error is the probability of accepting the null hypothesis when it is false.

We would ideally like to take action D_1 or D_2 if the population mean were at all different from 12.5 ounces. The hypotheses $\mu < 12.5$ and $\mu > 12.5$ represent the alternatives to the null hypothesis, $\mu = 12.5$. Unlike the null

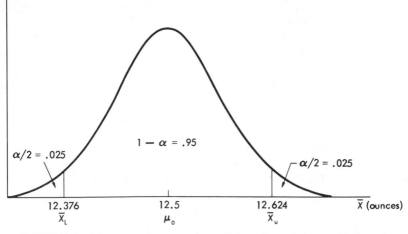

FIGURE 7-1 Alpha errors for test of a null hypothesis that $\mu = 12.5$ ($\sigma = .2$, $n = 10$)

hypothesis, the alternative hypotheses may be true in infinitely many ways. In order to study the behavior of beta errors we have to consider a number of these in turn. Let us start with the case where $\mu = 12.45$ and consider the beta error under this condition.

In Fig. 7–2 we have shown what the sampling distribution of $\bar{X}$ would look like for $n = 10$ and $\mu = 12.45$.* Our decision procedure will lead us to reject the null hypothesis if a sample mean of less than 12.376 or greater

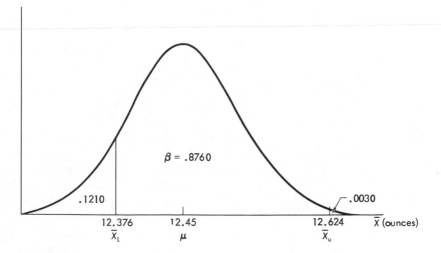

FIGURE 7-2 Example of a beta error for test of a null hypothesis that $\mu = 12.5$ (when $\mu = 12.45$ with $\sigma = .2$ and $n = 10$)

* We assume that σ does not change as μ changes from $\mu = 12.5$.

than 12.624 is observed. Now, calculating the z value for $\bar{X} = 12.376$ on the condition that $\mu = 12.45$, we find that $z = -1.17$, and that $P(z \leq -1.17) = .1210$. This is the probability of concluding $\mu < 12.5$ when $\mu = 12.45$. The probability of concluding $\mu > 12.5$ when $\mu = 12.45$ is $P(\bar{X} > 12.624 \,|\, \mu = 12.45)$. For this upper decision limit the z value is 2.75 and the above probability is .0030. The probability of accepting the null hypothesis when $\mu = 12.45$ is then $1 - (.1210 + .0030) = .8760$. This is the beta error conditional on the true state $\mu = 12.45$. Using conditional notation, we would write $(\beta \,|\, \mu = 12.45) = .8760$. This beta error is shown graphically in Fig. 7–2.

Notice that if we were to conclude $\mu > 12.5$ when $\mu = 12.45$ it would be a wrong inference about the parameter, just as would the conclusion that $\mu = 12.5$. The beta error is the probability of erroneously accepting the null hypothesis, or 1.0 less the probability of rejecting it in favor of *either* alternative. We will see that this detail about the more distant decision limit becomes trivial as we consider beta errors for larger departures of the process mean from 12.5.

7-3 The Power Curve for a Null Hypothesis Test

The value of $1 - \beta$ gives the power of the decision rule to reject the null hypothesis when it is false. Given $\mu = 12.45$, our decision rule has very low power: $1 - .8760 = .1240$. But this is a direct consequence of our setting the alpha level at .05 so as to have high assurance of accepting the null hypothesis when it is true. This meant, in the bottle-filling process, that we wanted to be reasonably sure of "letting well enough alone."

Since beta errors are conditional on the true mean, we can calculate them for a myriad of different states. The plotting of the complements of a series of beta values against the corresponding values of the parameter is called the *power curve* for a statistical test. In Table 7–1 we show the calculation of points on the power curve for our decision test regarding the bottle-filling operation. The first column of Table 7–1 contains the values of μ which we have selected. In the second column the lower decision limit, $\bar{X}_L = 12.376$, is converted to z, given the stated values of μ. In the next column we show the z value for the upper decision limit. Then we obtain beta, the probability of erroneously accepting the null hypothesis, by finding the probability of a sample mean within the decision limits. The power of rejection, $1 - \beta$, is then given. Note that when $\mu = 12.20$ the *lower* decision limit is far out on the right tail of the sampling distribution, and $1 - \beta$ is virtually equivalent to $P(\bar{X} \leq 12.376)$. The value $\bar{X}_L = 12.376$ is 2.78 standard errors above 12.20, and the probability of a sample mean equal to or less than 12.376, given $\mu = 12.20$, is .9973. This is the power of the test to reject the null hypothesis at that value of the true state. Our test has high power when $\mu = 12.20$, but the power steadily declines as parameter values closer to 12.50 are considered.

A little thought convinces us that as we consider values of μ exceeding

12.5, the pattern will be symmetrical to the one we have already traced. We would be concerned primarily with the upper decision limit $\bar{X}_u = 12.624$. At values of μ exceeding 12.624 the probability of accepting the null hypothesis will be, effectively, the entire lower tail probability below 12.624. The power of the test to reject the null hypothesis will be the complement of this. At values of μ close to 12.5, we will have to take account of the probability that a sample mean will fall below the lower decision limit.

Table 7-1

CALCULATION OF BETA ERRORS, β, AND THE POWER, $1 - \beta$, OF
A TEST FOR SELECTED VALUES OF μ

μ	z_L $(\bar{X}_L - \mu)/\sigma_{\bar{X}}$	z_u $(\bar{X}_u - \mu)/\sigma_{\bar{X}}$	$P(\bar{X} \le \bar{X}_L)$	$P(\bar{X} \le \bar{X}_u)$	Beta Error $P(\bar{X}_L \le \bar{X} \le \bar{X}_u)$	$1 - \beta$
12.20	2.78	6.70	.9973	1.0000	.0027	.9973
12.25	1.99	5.91	.9767	1.0000	.0233	.9767
12.30	1.20	5.12	.8849	1.0000	.1151	.8849
12.35	.41	4.33	.6591	1.0000	.3409	.6591
12.40	−.38	3.54	.3520	.9998	.6478	.3522
12.45	−1.17	2.75	.1210	.9970	.8760	.1240

Figure 7–3 shows two additional power curves. These are for samples of 25 and 100 observations each, with decision limits for the sample mean determined from the same alpha criterion of .05. The decision limits for the test when $n = 25$ are 12.422 and 12.578, and the limits when $n = 100$ are 12.461 and 12.539. When the true mean is equal to a decision limit, the power curve will be at a height of .50. By following across the graph at a .50 probability of rejecting the null hypothesis, one will intercept the power curves at values that reveal the decision limits.

The height of a particular power curve is a measure of the ability of a given test procedure to reject the null hypothesis when it is false. The higher the curve at a given point, the greater the power of the test. We can also see from Fig. 7–3 that a region of low power is inherent in any test that has a low alpha risk level. Between any decision limit and the mean stated in the null hypothesis, the probability of rejecting the null hypothesis will drop from .50 to the alpha level at the value of the parameter specified by the hypothesis. However, given any alpha error limitation, by increasing the sample size we can achieve a test that has greater power to reject the null hypothesis when it is false.

The lessons to be drawn from the consideration of beta errors are two. First, in designing a decision test we must consider beta as well as alpha errors. If one does not like the beta errors that result from a particular sample size in conjunction with a specified alpha error, he will have to consider a larger sample. In a business problem the real determinants here are the costs of decision error versus the costs of increased information. This is treated in

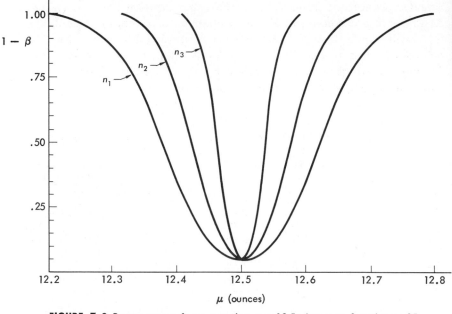

FIGURE 7-3 Power curves for a test that $\mu = 12.5$ when $\sigma = .2$ and $\alpha = .05$ with $n_1 = 10$, $n_2 = 25$, $n_3 = 100$

the approach to decision theory in Chapters 10 and 11, but should otherwise be considered informally. Second, a test of significance using an alpha criterion *only* cannot be treated as an unequivocal decision test. Acceptance of the null hypothesis may well entail substantial beta errors at parameter values that represent material departures from the null hypothesis value. The only way to guard against accepting a null hypothesis that is materially false is to consider beta errors—preferably when determining sample size in the first place. A method for doing this that does not directly incorporate the cost factors is included in Sec. 7–8; an economic basis for sample size determination is presented in Chapter 11.

EXERCISES

7.1   Specifications for the manufacture of a certain antibiotic tablet called for 25.0 milligrams per tablet of a compound called "Z." Long experience with the manufacturing process had shown that the distribution of the weights of "Z" in the tablets was normal with a standard deviation of 2.0 milligrams regardless of the mean weight. The manufacturer is contemplating a sample inspection of each lot prior to shipment in order to make a decision between shipping the lot and holding the lot for reprocessing. Reprocessing is desired for both overweight and underweight lots.

   (a) For a sample size of 16, what should be the decision limits if the probability of incorrectly holding a shipment that meets specifications is to be limited to .05?   *Ans.* 24.02; 25.98.

   (b) Plot the power curve for the decision rule in (a) at intervals of .40 milligrams from $\mu = 23.0$ to $\mu = 27.0$.

7.2   Given the situation in Exercise 7.1:

   (a) Plot the power curve for samples of size 16 with alpha at .20.

   (b) Plot the power curve for samples of size 36 with alpha at .05.

   (c) Plot the power curve for samples of size 16 with alpha at .01.

7.3   If the mean shifts to 26.0 milligrams, what is the probability of erroneously shipping the lot under the rule in Exercise

   (a) 7.1(a)?

   (b) 7.2(a)?

   (c) 7.2(b)?

   (d) 7.2(c)?

7-4 Generalized Significance Tests for Variables

We now proceed to a collection of common significance tests involving means and variances. These employ the standard normal, Student t, and chi-square distributions that we have already encountered, and another important distribution known as the F distribution.

   In applications in business and industry the null hypothesis usually represents the condition that the results of an innovation would be *no better or no worse* than an existing procedure. The significance test should be taken as guide to further action. If the observed statistic is significant, we should assume there is a real difference worth further investigation as to its magnitude and economic importance. If the observed result is insignificant, we have no firm basis for concluding that a real difference exists.

   To make the various tests easier to follow we will use a four-step general format. We will use lambda, λ, to denote a parameter and, l to denote the corresponding sample statistic. The steps are:

   1. State the null hypothesis, H_0, and the alpha error limitation.

$$H_0: \quad \lambda = \lambda_o \quad \text{with } \alpha \text{ specified}$$

   2. Identify the appropriate standard test statistic.

$$f(l \mid \lambda).$$

   3. Define the boundaries of the region for accepting H_0—in accordance with the alpha criterion. The acceptance region always lies between these boundaries.

   4. Accept or reject the null hypothesis, H_0, in accordance with the observed statistic, l_o, and the region defined in step (3).

Example: Test for means, variance known. To illustrate the steps, consider the test for means that we have already covered. The null hypothesis, H_0, was that $\mu = 12.5$, and the alpha error was set at .05. Under the condition that σ was known to be .2 and assuming the parent population to be normally distributed, the appropriate test statistic was the normal z. Suppose an actual sample of size ten yielded a mean of 12.6. Following the four steps, we would have

1. $H_0: \mu = 12.5$ with $\alpha = .05$.

2. $z = \dfrac{\bar{X} - \mu}{\sigma_{\bar{X}}}$.

3. $z_{\alpha/2} = -1.96$; $z_{1-(\alpha/2)} = 1.96$.

4. $z_0 = \dfrac{\bar{X} - \mu}{\sigma_{\bar{X}}} = \dfrac{12.6 - 12.5}{0.2/\sqrt{10}} = 1.58$. Accept H_0.

This seems at first glance to be a rather cumbersome way of indicating that the sample mean is within the decision limits for $\bar{X}$ that we set up previously. Indeed, one way of doing the calculations is as good as another. Once one gets used to the standardized form, however, it proves to be the handier one to carry through.

Example: Test for means, variance unknown. A class of 16 trainees accomplishes a given task in an average of 27.5 minutes with an estimated standard deviation of 5.2 minutes. At $\alpha = .05$, test the hypothesis that this performance is a random sample from a population with a mean time of 25.0 minutes.

1. $H_0: \mu = 25.0$ with $\alpha = .05$.

2. $t = \dfrac{\bar{X} - \mu}{s/\sqrt{n}}$ with $m = n - 1 = 16 - 1 = 15$. Assumptions: Random sample from normally distributed parent population.

3. $t_{\alpha/2} = t_{.025} = -2.131$; $t_{1-(\alpha/2)} = t_{.975} = 2.131$.

4. $t_0 = \dfrac{\bar{X} - \mu}{s/\sqrt{n}} = \dfrac{27.5 - 25.0}{5.2/\sqrt{16}} = 1.92$. Accept H_0.

Example: Test for a single variance. An employee selection test has been given for many years. The variance of the scores has remained stable at 9.0. Twenty-five persons were tested last month with a resulting variance, s^2, of 1.98. Has the population variance remained the same, subject to $\alpha = .05$?

1. $H_0: \sigma^2 = 9.0$ with $\alpha = .05$.

2. $\chi^2 = \dfrac{ms^2}{\sigma^2}$ with $m = n - 1 = 24$. Assumptions: Random sample from normally distributed population.

3. $\chi^2_{\alpha/2} = \chi^2_{.025} = 12.40$; $\chi^2_{1-(\alpha/2)} = \chi^2_{.975} = 39.36$.

4. $\chi^2_0 = \dfrac{ms^2}{\sigma^2} = \dfrac{24(1.98)}{9.0} = 5.28$. Reject H_0.

7-5 Test for Equality of Variances—The F Distribution

We have seen that we use the chi-square distribution when we are testing a single population variance. But suppose now that we have two samples, which may have come from populations with different variances. We can test a null hypothesis that the two samples came from the same population (with respect to variance) by means of the F distribution.

Formally, the F distribution is the ratio of two independent random variables, each of which is distributed as χ^2/m. The two distributions may or may not be based upon the same number of degrees of freedom—that is, the m's may be different.

As we have already learned, s^2/σ^2 based upon random samples from a normal population is a random variable distributed as χ^2/m. Suppose we compute s_1^2/σ^2 and s_2^2/σ^2, where s_1^2 and s_2^2 represent sample variances in independent random samples from the same normal population.

Next, suppose that from these two ratios we make a single ratio

$$\frac{s_1^2/\sigma^2}{s_2^2/\sigma^2}.$$

Both numerator and denominator of this ratio will be distributed as χ^2/m, and therefore the ratio will follow an F distribution. We can state

$$F = \frac{s_1^2}{s_2^2}, \tag{7-1}$$

because the variance, σ^2, cancels out in the previous ratio. In this application F represents the sampling distribution of ratios of two independent estimates of the variance of a normal parent population. There is a different F distribution for each possible combination of degrees of freedom in the numerator and the denominator.

The F distributions were developed by R. A. Fisher around 1924 and later designated by George Snedecor, an American agricultural statistician, as the F distribution(s) in Fisher's honor. Appendix G contains selected percentiles of F for various numerator and denominator degrees of freedom. Assuming normal parent populations, the F distribution enables us to test the null hypothesis that two sample variances came from parent populations with the same variance. Empirical studies have shown that moderate departures from the normality assumption will not produce noticeable departures from the F distributions. Sample ratios of variances at the low* or high end of the appropriate F distribution will cast doubt on the null hypothesis of equal population variances.

Example: Two clerical training programs have been used in a large insurance firm. Twenty-one clerks trained in the old program have a variance in their error rates on their jobs of 146. Thirteen clerks from the new program

*See footnote to Appendix G, p. 477.

have an error rate variance of 200. Subject to $\alpha = .05$, can it be concluded that the variance is different for those trained in the two programs?

1. $H_0: \sigma_1^2 = \sigma_2^2$ with $\alpha = .05$.
2. $F = s_1^2/s_2^2$ with $m_1 = n_1 - 1 = 20$ and $m_2 = n_2 - 1 = 12$. Assumptions: Independent random samples from normally distributed populations.
3. $F_{\alpha/2} = F_{.025} = .374$, $F_{1-(\alpha/2)} = F_{.975} = 3.07$.
4. $F_o = s_1^2/s_2^2 = \dfrac{146}{200} = 0.73$. Accept H_0.

7-6 Test for the Equality of Two Means

We saw in Chapter 2 that the expectation of the sum of two random variables was the sum of their individual expected values, and that the variance of the sum of two independent random variables was the sum of their individual variances. Using X_1 and X_2 for the random variables,

$$\mu_{X_1+X_2} = \mu_{X_1} + \mu_{X_2},$$
$$\sigma_{X_1+X_2}^2 = \sigma_{X_1}^2 + \sigma_{X_2}^2.$$

Relations for the differences between independent random variables were also shown to be

$$\mu_{X_1-X_2} = \mu_{X_1} - \mu_{X_2},$$
$$\sigma_{X_1-X_2}^2 = \sigma_{X_1}^2 + \sigma_{X_2}^2.$$

If the variables involved are means of independent random samples, then the statements involving differences become

$$\mu_{\bar{X}_1-\bar{X}_2} = \mu_{\bar{X}_1} - \mu_{\bar{X}_2},$$
$$\sigma_{\bar{X}_1-\bar{X}_2}^2 = \sigma_{\bar{X}_1}^2 + \sigma_{\bar{X}_2}^2.$$

If $\bar{X}_1$ and $\bar{X}_2$ have normal sampling distributions, then $\bar{X}_1 - \bar{X}_2$ will also be normally distributed, and can be written in terms of the standard normal deviate as

$$z = \frac{(\bar{X}_1 - \bar{X}_2) - (\mu_1 - \mu_2)}{\sigma_{\bar{X}_1-\bar{X}_2}}, \tag{7-2}$$

where

$$\sigma_{\bar{X}_1-\bar{X}_2}^2 = \frac{\sigma_{\bar{X}_1}^2}{n_1} + \frac{\sigma_{\bar{X}_2}^2}{n_2}. \tag{7-3}$$

Example with variance known. A tire manufacturer makes two types of tires. For type A, $\sigma = 2500$ miles, and for type B, $\sigma = 3000$ miles. A taxi fleet has tested 50 type A tires and found they have a mean life of 24,000 miles. In a similar test, 40 type B tires had a mean life of 26,000 miles. Subject to an alpha risk of .01, test the null hypothesis that the mean life of the two types of tires is the same.

1. $H_0: \mu_A - \mu_B = 0; \alpha = .01.$

2. $z = \dfrac{\bar{X}_A - \bar{X}_B}{\sigma_{\bar{X}_A - \bar{X}_B}}.$ Assumptions: Normal $\bar{X}_A$ and $\bar{X}_B$ from central limit theorem. Sample A is drawn independently from sample B.

3. $z_{\alpha/2} = z_{.005} = -2.58, z_{1-\alpha/2} = z_{.995} = 2.58.$

4. $\sigma^2_{\bar{X}_A - \bar{X}_B} = \dfrac{\sigma^2_A}{n_A} + \dfrac{\sigma^2_B}{n_B},$

$$= \frac{(2500)^2}{50} + \frac{(3000)^2}{40} = 350{,}000$$

$$z_0 = \frac{\bar{X}_A - \bar{X}_B}{\sigma_{\bar{X}_A - \bar{X}_B}} = \frac{24{,}000 - 26{,}000}{\sqrt{350{,}000}} = \frac{-2000}{592}$$

$$= -3.38. \text{ Reject } H_0.$$

As is more frequently the case, we do not know the standard deviations of the populations and must use the sample information to estimate the standard error. To estimate $\sigma^2_{\bar{X}_1 - \bar{X}_2}$ our job is to estimate $\sigma^2_1/n_1 + \sigma^2_2/n_2$. The best unbiased estimate of this quantity is $s^2_1/n_1 + s^2_2/n_2$. However, this estimate is not distributed as chi-square, and thus substitution of its square root in the denominator of Eq. (7–2) does not lead to a statistic distributed as Student's t. However, an estimate of $\sigma^2_{\bar{X}_1 - \bar{X}_2}$ that does have a chi-square distribution can be made if one assumes that the variances of the two populations are equal. Under this assumption,

$$\sigma^2_{\bar{X}_1 - \bar{X}_2} = \frac{\sigma^2}{n_1} + \frac{\sigma^2}{n_2} = \sigma^2 \left(\frac{n_1 + n_2}{n_1 n_2} \right).$$

The best unbiased estimate of the common variance, σ^2, is a weighted average of the individual sample variances, where each variance is weighted by its associated degrees of freedom. This weighted, or pooled, estimate is

$$\bar{s}^2 = \frac{m_1 s^2_1 + m_2 s^2_2}{m_1 + m_2}. \tag{7-4}$$

Having this estimate, we can then make a corresponding estimate of $\sigma^2_{\bar{X}_1 - \bar{X}_2}$ as

$$s^2_{\bar{X}_1 - \bar{X}_2} = \bar{s}^2 \left(\frac{n_1 + n_2}{n_1 n_2} \right). \tag{7-5}$$

The standard test statistic is then Student t, with degrees of freedom equal to $m_1 + m_2$.

$$t = \frac{(\bar{X}_1 - \bar{X}_2) - (\mu_1 - \mu_2)}{s_{\bar{X}_1 - \bar{X}_2}}. \tag{7-6}$$

The assumptions necessary to the test are that the data are independent random samples from normally distributed populations having the same variance. The equality-of-variance assumption can be subjected to a null hypothesis test employing the F distribution.*

Example with variance estimated. Two types of paint have been tested for six months by exposure to the same weather conditions. Inspectors score several patches of each type. Type A received a mean score of 85.25 with a variance of 25 on four patches, and Type B a mean score of 88.00 with a variance of 5.5 on five patches. Subject to an alpha risk of .10, can we conclude that there is a difference in the wearing qualities of the two paints?

1. $H_0: \mu_A - \mu_B = 0; \ \alpha = .10.$

2. $t = \dfrac{\bar{X}_A - \bar{X}_B}{s_{\bar{X}_A - \bar{X}_B}}$ with $m_1 + m_2$ degrees of freedom. Assumptions: Independent samples from normally distributed populations with equal variances.

3. $t_{\alpha/2} = t_{.05} = -1.895; \ t_{1-(\alpha/2)} = t_{.95} = 1.895.$

4. $\bar{s}^2 = \dfrac{m_1 s_1^2 + m_2 s_2^2}{m_1 + m_2} = \dfrac{3(25) + 4(5.5)}{3 + 4} = \dfrac{97}{7} = 13.86;$

   $s_{\bar{X}_A - \bar{X}_B}^2 = \bar{s}^2 \left(\dfrac{n_1 + n_2}{n_1 n_2} \right) = 13.86 \left(\dfrac{4 + 5}{4 \cdot 5} \right) = 6.24;$

   $s_{\bar{X}_A - \bar{X}_B} = \sqrt{6.24} = 2.50;$

   $t_o = \dfrac{85.25 - 88.00}{2.50} = -1.1. \ \text{Accept } H_0.$

7-7   Test for Mean Difference

Many occasions arise in which we are interested in the *mean difference* between pairs of observations in two sets of data. In these cases, there is a basis for matching each observation in the one set with a particular observation in the second set. Consider, for example, a check on the speed of a dozen typists six weeks after they had completed a formal training course. We have two samples of speeds—those achieved at the end of the course and those measured six weeks later. Call the first X_1 and the second X_2. We are concerned with whether there is a change in average speed under these training and post-training conditions between the termination of the course and six weeks later. The t test for difference between the means presented earlier is not proper

---

* If a preliminary F test is run, then of a large number of tests run when $\sigma_1^2 = \sigma_2^2$ and $\mu_1 = \mu_2$, α of them will lead erroneously to concluding that $\sigma_1^2 \neq \sigma_2^2$. Of the remaining $1 - \alpha$ subjected to the test for means, α of them will lead erroneously to concluding that $\mu_1 \neq \mu_2$. Thus, the proportion of cases which will lead to the erroneous conclusion that the population variances or the population means (but not both) are not equal will be $1 - (1 - \alpha)^2$.

here because the samples are not independent. Rather, we would expect that the typists who were above the average speed at the end of the course would still be the relatively fast typists six weeks later.

The proper test to run is a test of the mean difference between speeds. Here the values of $X_1 - X_2$ are the individual observations ($d = X_1 - X_2$) and a test is made of the significance of the sample mean, $\bar{d}$, from a hypothesized population mean difference, Δ, of zero. Except for $\bar{d}$ and Δ as opposed to the symbols $\bar{X}$ and μ, this is exactly the same as any other test involving means. Generally the variance of d must be estimated from the sample, and we are involved in a Student t test for means. We will illustrate a significance test for mean difference among matched or paired observations.

Example: Given the data of Table 7-2, test the null hypothesis that the post-training period of six weeks results in no change in mean typing speeds.

Table 7-2

DATA FOR TESTING THE SIGNIFICANCE OF A MEAN DIFFERENCE

Trainee	Typing speed		$d = X_1 - X_2$	d^2
	End of training X_1	Six weeks later X_2		
1	67	63	4	16
2	65	63	2	4
3	66	65	1	1
4	59	63	-4	16
5	68	66	2	4
6	71	71	0	0
7	63	64	-1	1
8	66	70	-4	16
9	63	59	4	16
10	66	65	1	1
11	65	62	3	9
12	64	60	4	16
			12	100

1. $H_0: \Delta = 0$; $\alpha = .05$.

2. $t = \dfrac{\bar{d} - \Delta}{s_{\bar{d}}}$ with $m = n - 1 = 11$. Assumptions: Random sample from a normal population of d.

3. $t_{\alpha/2} = t_{.025} = -2.201$; $t_{1-(\alpha/2)} = t_{.975} = 2.201$.

4. $\bar{d}_o = \dfrac{\Sigma d}{n} = \dfrac{12}{12} = 1.0$;

$$s_d^2 = \frac{\Sigma d^2 - (\Sigma d)^2/n}{n - 1} = \frac{100 - (12)(12)/12}{11} = 8.0;$$

$$s_{\bar{d}}^2 = \frac{s_d^2}{n} = \frac{8}{12} = .667;$$

$$t_o = \frac{\bar{d} - \Delta}{s_{\bar{d}}} = \frac{1.0}{.817} = 1.22. \text{ Accept } H_0.$$

Purposive pairing of observations. The test of mean difference can be viewed as a way of dealing properly with positive dependence between the observations in two samples. When X_1 and X_2 are correlated, we saw in Chapter 2 that the variance of the difference is

$$\sigma_{X_1 - X_2}^2 = \sigma_{X_1}^2 + \sigma_{X_2}^2 - 2\sigma_{X_1 X_2}.$$

If the observations are positively dependent, the covariance will be positive and the variance of $X_1 - X_2$ will be smaller than it would be if X_1 and X_2 were independent. In our construction of power curves for a significance test for means, we saw that decreasing $\sigma_{\bar{X}}$ by increasing n would increase the power of the test to detect real departures from the null hypothesis parameter. Any other method of decreasing the standard error that enters into a significance test will have the same effect. Decreasing the variability of differences through deliberate pairing of observations is a case in point.

Deliberate pairing is done when one wants to study the effect of varying a particular factor between two populations. The object is to form pairs in which an individual from one population is matched with an individual from the other population. The basis of matching is similarity of factors, other than the one under test, which are believed to influence the criterion variable. For example, a course for teaching touch typing is available. A company wants to compare the effectiveness of the new course with the one it now uses. From a new group of trainees matched pairs might be chosen, one member of the pair being assigned to the existing course and the other to the new course. It is unlikely that any two persons will match on all relevant factors; however, some that might be used are typing skill before training, manual dexterity, and general intelligence. A possible criterion of "matching" might be that each member of a pair has test scores in the same stanine, or ninth of the distribution, on each characteristic employed. Once the pairs are selected, the test for mean difference is made in the manner already indicated.

EXERCISES

7.4 From past experience a certain auditing operation averaged 90 audits per day. A new routine was introduced, and the following numbers of audits were completed on six successive days:

115   144   91   165   242   131

(a) At $\alpha = .05$, test the null hypothesis that there has been no change in the process mean.   *Ans. $t = 2.71$; reject.*

(b) What assumptions have you made in the test in (a)?

7.5 Scheduled flight time between two cities was 135 minutes. On nine flights the run was made in the following times:

135	121	155
157	130	135
138	144	130

(a) At $\alpha = .05$, is the sample evidence sufficient to conclude that the scheduled time is not being met?   *Ans. $t = .85$; no.*

(b) A standard deviation of 5 minutes or less in flight times was considered acceptable. At $\alpha = .05$, can we conclude that this standard is being exceeded?   *Ans. $\chi^2 = 44.8$; yes.*

7.6 A laboratory made five determinations of the amount of impurities in batches of a certain compound. The values were 12.4, 12.6, 12.0, 12.1, and 12.7 milligrams.

(a) Estimate the variance in impurities among batches.   *Ans. .093.*

(b) Given the estimate in (a), what sample means would permit the company to establish at $\alpha = .01$ that the mean impurities per batch yielded by the process was different from 12.4 milligrams?

Ans. 11.77, 13.03.

7.7 During a "cents-off" deal for Brand A soap in a certain city, its daily sales rate and that of competing Brand B were checked in five stores selected at random. The results to the nearest carton were:

Store	Brand A	Brand B
1	4	14
2	28	2
3	16	20
4	31	5
5	9	11

At $\alpha = .10$, test the hypothesis that the variability of sales rates among stores was the same for both brands. What assumption about the population distribution did you make?   *Ans. $F = 2.68$; accept.*

7.8 A survey of the use of a common health facility among two Indian tribes living in a community produced the following data on visits per family during the past year.

	Sample size	Mean	Variance
Mohave	61	5.71	43.7
Chemchuevi	35	4.12	28.0

(a) At $\alpha = .05$, test the hypothesis that there is no difference in the variance of the usage rates between the two tribes.

(b) Test the hypothesis that there is no difference in the mean usage rate between the two tribes, using $\alpha = .05$.

7.9 The time taken to process nine randomly selected data decks with a particular computer program was determined. After modification of the program the decks were run again with the following results.

Deck	First run (minutes)	Second run (minutes)
1	5.0	5.5
2	5.1	3.7
3	4.0	3.8
4	5.2	4.0
5	4.7	3.7
6	7.3	6.4
7	5.5	6.5
8	7.3	5.6
9	6.7	6.4

(a) Estimate the variance of the differences between running times on the first run and the second run.   *Ans.* .809.

(b) Estimate the standard error of the *mean difference* between the running times.   *Ans.* .30.

(c) Test the hypothesis that the mean difference between running times for the population of data decks is zero, employing $\alpha = .10$.
                                    Ans. $t = 1.93$; reject.

7.10 At $\alpha = .05$, test the hypothesis that the mean difference in sales rates between brands in Exercise 7.7 was zero. What assumption about the populations is necessary to make this test?

7-8 Rules for Terminal Decisions

In order to use a test of a null hypothesis as a rule for decision, we must set up the decision limits in advance by specifying allowable levels of both alpha and beta errors. Otherwise the test is nothing more than a rule of prudence for forestalling premature rejection of the null hypothesis. A test based on an alpha criterion alone cannot provide a rule for deciding between alternative hypotheses.

In discussing the power of a test we pointed out the inevitability of a region of low power between the decision limits and the null hypothesis parameter. Such a region is not necessarily fatal, because the consequences of ignoring small departures of the true state from the state represented by the null hypothesis are often immaterial. Would the bottler in our example be greatly concerned if he acted as if the process mean were 12.5 ounces when it was in fact 12.501 ounces? 12.505 ounces? The critical question is: Just when would he be concerned? The questions he would have to answer before

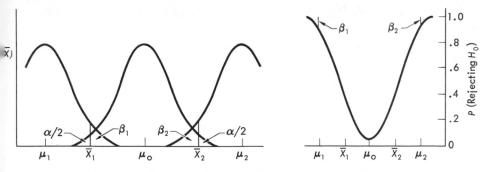

FIGURE 7-4 Determination of decision limits to limit alpha and beta errors

a decision rule could be determined are: (1) How sure do you want to be of taking the correct action when $\mu = 12.5$? and (2) By how much can μ vary from 12.5 before you want to be, say, 95 per cent sure of taking action to correct the process? Suppose the answer to the first question is also 95 per cent sure and the answer to the second is no more than .1 ounces. The situation is portrayed in Fig. 7-4. Here, μ_o represents the null hypothesis mean; $\mu_o = 12.5$. The lower parameter, μ_1, is a mean of 12.4 ounces and the higher parameter, μ_2, is a mean of 12.6 ounces. These represent the real deviations from μ_o that we are concerned with detecting.

Consider the lower decision limit, $\bar{X}_1$. It must be located at a high enough percentile of the sampling distribution that prevails when μ_1 is true ($\mu_1 = 12.4$) so that $P(\bar{X} > \bar{X}_1) = \beta_1$ or .05. It must also be low enough on the sampling distribution that prevails when μ_o is true ($\mu_o = 12.5$) so that $P(\bar{X} < \bar{X}_1) = \alpha/2$, or .025 in this case. Two equations for $\bar{X}_1$ can be written embodying these requirements.

$$\bar{X}_1 = \mu_1 + z_{1-\beta}\frac{\sigma}{\sqrt{n}},$$

$$\bar{X}_1 = \mu_o + z_{\alpha/2}\frac{\sigma}{\sqrt{n}}.$$

Setting the right-hand members equal to each other and solving for n will give an equation for the required sample size. It is

$$n = \left[\frac{\sigma(z_{1-\beta} - z_{\alpha/2})}{\mu_o - \mu_1}\right]^2. \tag{7-7}$$

Substituting the required sample size in either equation for $\bar{X}_1$ will then yield the lower decision limit. The upper decision limit will be equidistant from μ_o. In the current example

$$\beta_1 = .05, \qquad z_{1-\beta} = 1.64,$$
$$\alpha = .05, \qquad z_{\alpha/2} = -1.96;$$

$$n = \left[\frac{.2(1.64 + 1.96)}{12.5 - 12.4}\right]^2 = (7.2)^2 = 51.84,$$

$$\bar{X}_1 = 12.50 + (-1.96)\left(\frac{.2}{7.2}\right) = 12.50 - .054 = 12.446 \text{ ounces},$$

$$\bar{X}_2 = 12.50 + (1.96)\left(\frac{.2}{7.2}\right) = 12.50 + .054 = 12.554 \text{ ounces}.$$

A sample size of 52 will meet the requirements. The power curve for this resulting test is shown in the right-hand panel of Fig. 7–4. It will lie between the curves for $n = 25$ and $n = 100$ shown in Fig. 7–3.

Two-action tests with beta criteria. Two-action decision problems are common in business and industry. Whenever two methods are under consideration for accomplishing a clerical, manufacturing, selling, or promotional task, the question arises as to which method is better. The choice may be between an existing method about which much is known and a new method for which sample evidence can be gathered, or it may be between two methods where experimental evidence must be gathered on each. To design a test which will yield a rule for a *final decision* between the two alternative actions we consider two alternative hypotheses separated by a region of relative indifference. Neither of these hypotheses is considered a null hypothesis in the sense of a test of significance. The method will yield a sample size, n, and a critical value, $\bar{X}_c$, for the decision test. *The decision rule will be to accept one hypothesis if the sample mean falls below the critical value and the other hypothesis if the sample mean falls above the critical value.*

As an example of a two-action case consider the following. Using its present method of routine work, a clerical office averages 123 units of output per day. A new routine has been suggested which involves virtually no learning time on the part of personnel. It would be worthwhile to shift to the new routine if the output rate under it were greater than 123. Past experience has indicated that a standard deviation of 15 units in daily output can be expected regardless of the particular routine employed. It is agreed to run a trial test of the new routine, but the question is: How many days should the trial last? The statistician must now ask the office manager, "How high must the true (long-run) mean under the new procedure be before you want to be, say, 95 per cent sure that your trial test will lead you to adopt it? And how low must the true mean under the new procedure be before you want to be 95 per cent sure that your final decision will be to abandon it and return to the old routine?" Suppose the answers to these questions are 128 and 118 units per day, respectively. Then we have the following:

Given:

$$\mu_1 = 118, \qquad \beta_1 = .05;$$
$$\mu_2 = 128, \qquad \beta_2 = .05.$$

Assume: Normally distributed population with $\sigma = 15$.
Required: Sample size, n, and critical value, $\bar{X}_c$.

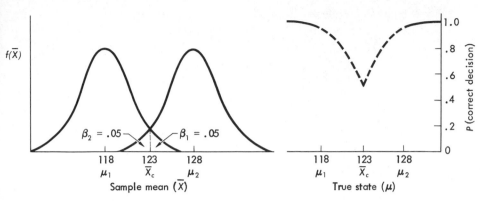

FIGURE 7-5 Sampling distributions and power curve for two-action test with equal beta criteria

The required sampling distributions are shown in the left panel of Fig. 7–5.

Since the beta risks are the same, the critical value will be found midway between μ_1 and μ_2 at $\bar{X}_c = 123$. The distance from $\bar{X}_c$ to either μ_1 or μ_2 is $1.64\sigma_{\bar{x}}$ because of the beta levels implied by the question phrasing "95 per cent sure." Setting up the equation, we solve for sample size n.

$$1.64\sigma_{\bar{x}} = \frac{1.64\sigma}{\sqrt{n}} = \frac{128 - 118}{2} = 5,$$

$$n = \left(\frac{1.64\sigma}{5}\right)^2 = \left(\frac{1.64 \cdot 15}{5}\right)^2 = (4.92)^2 = 24.2.$$

The sample size required is 25 days, the critical value is $\bar{X}_c = 123$, and the resulting beta risks will actually be a shade below .05. The power curve in Fig. 7–5 shows the probability of a correct choice between the alternative decisions. The dashed portion of the curve shows this probability over the region of relative indifference. It drops to .50 at a value of μ equal to the decision limit but never falls below .50. More important, the probability of a correct decision for true states below μ_1 and above μ_2 is at least .95, as required.

The formulas for the critical value and sample size in the "equal-beta" two-action situation reduce to

$$\bar{X}_c = \mu_1 + \frac{\mu_2 - \mu_1}{2},$$

$$n = \left(\frac{2z_{1-\beta}\sigma}{\mu_2 - \mu_1}\right)^2. \tag{7-8}$$

The specification need not be made in terms of equal beta risks. The manager might not be willing to accept much risk of adopting the new routine if it is really no better than the old. Suppose he insists on 99 per cent assurance that the old routine will be adopted if the true mean under the new routine is 123 or less, and again 95 per cent assurance that the new routine will be adopted if its long-run mean exceeds 128.

This problem then reduces to

$$\mu_1 = 123; \qquad \beta_1 = 1 - .99 = .01, \qquad z_{1-\beta} = +2.33;$$
$$\mu_2 = 128; \qquad \beta_2 = 1 - .95 = .05, \qquad z_{\beta_2} = -1.64;$$
$$\sigma = 15.$$

For the critical value, $\bar{X}_c$, we then have the two equations

$$\bar{X}_c = \mu_1 + z_{1-\beta}\frac{\sigma}{\sqrt{n}},$$

$$\bar{X}_c = \mu_2 + z_{\beta_2}\frac{\sigma}{\sqrt{n}}.$$

Equating the two right-hand expressions and solving the resulting expression for n yields

$$n = \left[\frac{\sigma(z_{1-\beta} - z_{\beta_2})}{\mu_2 - \mu_1}\right]^2. \tag{7-9}$$

Having found n, we may now substitute in either expression for $\bar{X}_c$ to obtain the two-action critical value. The procedure here is, incidentally, a general one that will work for the "equal-beta" case as well. The solution is

$$n = \left[\frac{15(2.33 + 1.64)}{128 - 123}\right]^2 = (11.9)^2 = 142 \text{ days (approximately)},$$

$$\bar{X}_c = \mu_1 + z_{1-\beta}\frac{\sigma}{\sqrt{n}}$$

$$= 123 + 2.33\left(\frac{15}{11.9}\right) = 123 + 2.94 = 125.94 \text{ units per day.}$$

The requirements here are much more demanding than previously. An experiment lasting 142 days would be needed, with the final decision based on the sample mean at the end of that time. Any sample mean below 125.94 will dictate a terminal act in favor of the old routine, and any value above 125.94 will dictate final adoption of the new routine.

Sequential procedures. The two-action decision test illustrated above is an example of a *single-sample procedure*. Single-sample procedures result in a specification of sample size and critical value(s) for making a final, or terminal, decision. Once the decision rule is set up, the sample must be collected in its entirety. Since the sample size in the above example is so large, a sequential decision method would have some appeal. Under such a procedure the office manager might analyze 25 days experience under the proposed new routine and then have a decision rule calling for either

1. a terminal decision to adopt the old routine,
2. a terminal decision to adopt the new routine,
3. continue sampling for another 25 days.

If course 3 is adopted, then the same three alternatives will be evaluated after another 25 days, and so on until a terminal decision is reached. The 25-day period is just illustrative; the period could be ten days at a time, or even a day at a time.

Such a plan is called a sequential sampling or sequential decision procedure. Methods for establishing the rules for sequential decision tests were developed by Abraham Wald* in the United States during World War II when he was a consultant to the Statistical Research Group of Columbia University. Within the framework of classical decision tests, sequential analysis is the only way to deal rigorously with a decision problem in which one of the alternatives is to delay a terminal decision in favor of gathering further evidence. The great contribution of sequential procedures is that a terminal decision often can be reached with a smaller total sample size than with a single-sample procedure.

7-9   The Use of Approximations to Test Statistics

In using a particular sampling distribution in a test of a null hypothesis about a parameter, we must be aware of the restrictions that are involved. For example, the t distribution test for means is strictly correct only if the sample is drawn from an underlying normal population, and the normal distribution test for means is correct when the underlying population is normal and its variance is known. When some of the conditions for exactly correct application are not met, certain approximations can sometimes be used. In other instances, approximate methods are employed because they are more convenient. In this section we discuss some of these approximate procedures and the situations in which their use is reasonable.

Normal distribution is an approximation to student t. The t distribution approaches the normal distribution as the degrees of freedom, which depend on sample size, increase. Therefore, the normal is often used as an approxi-

---

* The definitive publication is Abraham Wald, *Sequential Analysis* (New York: John Wiley & Sons, Inc., 1947).

mation to the t distribution in a test of a null hypothesis about the mean of a normally distributed population when the population variance is estimated from a relatively large sample. A sample size exceeding 30 is often given as a minimal size in this connection. The .05 significance level from t with $m = 30$ is ± 2.042, and the normal would approximate this as ± 1.96. The test statistic for the normal as an approximation to t in this situation would be

$$z = \frac{\bar{X} - \mu}{s/\sqrt{n}}. \qquad (7\text{--}10)$$

The normality assumption regarding the parent population. Note that, in using the normal curve as an approximation to the t distribution above, we did not drop the restriction regarding a normally distributed population. This is another matter entirely, one that depends on the central limit theorem. The central limit theorem says that as sample size increases, the z statistic $(\bar{X} - \mu)/\sigma_{\bar{X}}$ approaches the standard normal distribution regardless of the shape of the parent distribution of X. Thus, where we know the variance of the population but are unwilling to assume the population to be normally distributed, we may rely on the central limit theorem to "validate" the use of the normal distribution as a test statistic. How rapidly the sampling distribution approaches normality depends on what shape the population distribution does have, but authorities appear willing to use this approximation with quite modest sample sizes of around 20. Remember here that we are talking about the "known variance" situation, so this rule of thumb on sample size is a different one from the $n > 30$ suggested in connection with the normal as an approximation to Student's t distribution.

Unknown population distribution and variance. The use of the normal distribution as a test statistic for means when both the *shape and variance* of the underlying population are unknown rests on invoking the central limit theorem *and* ignoring as inconsequential any difference between the standard deviation estimated from the sample, s, and the population standard deviation, σ. The test statistic would be the same as Eq. 7–10, but the standard normal test statistic is not being used as an approximation to Student t in this case. Student t applies only to samples from normally distributed populations. The rule of thumb of $n > 30$ does not apply. What concerns us, given that the sample size is large enough to invoke the central limit theorem safely, is the error that could arise in using s in place of σ in the equation for the normal test statistic—that is,

$$\frac{\bar{X} - \mu}{s/\sqrt{n}} \simeq \frac{\bar{X} - \mu}{\sigma/\sqrt{n}}.$$

This approximation should only be used for large samples from populations which are not highly skewed. "Large" here means of the order of 100 or more.

EXERCISES

7.11 Refer to Exercise 7.1. How large a sample must be taken if, in addition to the requirement in (a), the manufacturer wants to limit the probability of erroneously shipping out a lot varying from the specification by .5 milligrams or more to .05? *Ans.* 208.

7.12 A desirable feature of a certain plastic piece turned out in large quantities by a manufacturing process is tensile strength. The process is to be controlled by taking samples at periodic intervals and adjusting the process if the average tensile strength in the sample falls below a specified figure; otherwise no adjustment is made. Assume a normally distributed population with a standard deviation of .6 pounds tensile strength.

(a) Draw the curve for the probability of adjusting the process given a sample size of nine with a critical value of 19.0 pounds, using values of μ from 18.5 to 19.5 at intervals of .10.

(b) Using the same values, show the curve for a sample size of 25 with the critical value at 19.0 pounds.

(c) How large a sample size is needed to give .99 assurance that the process will be investigated if the mean tensile strength is below 18.6, and to give .99 assurance that no adjustment will be sought if the mean is above 19.4? *Ans.* 13.

7.13 A random sample of 196 subscribers to a magazine yielded a mean annual recreational expenditure of $272, and a sample standard deviation of $70. Using the normal approximation,

(a) Plot the power curve for the test of the null hypothesis that $\mu = \$260$, using an alpha level of .05.

(b) Using the sample data, test the hypothesis that $\mu = \$260$, at $\alpha = .05$.

7.14 A firm marketing fashion and novelty items for teen-agers has decided that active promotion to the teen-age market should be discontinued when the average age of buyers drops below 14.0 years. From experience, the firm has accepted 1.2 years as the standard deviation of the age distribution of purchasers of its products at any time.

(a) Find the critical value, and the size of a random sample of buyers that would be required to limit β_1 for $\mu = 13.5$ to .01 and β_2 for $\mu = 14.0$ to .05. *Ans.* 13.79; 91.

(b) How large a sample would be required to limit the standard error of the mean to .05 years? *Ans.* 576.

(c) If a sample of the size dictated by (b) is used, how far could μ depart from any critical value before beta falls to .05? .02? .01?

Ans. .082; .1025; .1165.

REFERENCES

Bryant, E. C., *Statistical Analysis*, 2nd ed. New York: McGraw-Hill Book Company, 1965.

Hogben, L., *Statistical Theory*. London: George Allen & Unwin, Ltd., 1957.

Quenouille, M. H., *Introductory Statistics*. London: Pergamon Press, Ltd., 1950.

8

Estimation
and the
Probability Distribution
of a Parameter

In the preceding chapters we have been concerned with the statistical evidence that could be generated in specified sampling situations. The sampling situations consisted of a specification of relevant population parameters and assumptions about the process giving rise to statistical observations. Knowing mean demand per time period for a product and assuming individual demands to occur independently at random, we used the Poisson distribution to predict the distribution of demands per time period. Such a prediction can be extremely useful in controlling inventories. Similarly, knowing the mean and variance of a quality measure for a production process in a state of statistical control and assuming the population of measures to be normally distributed, we can use prediction of the means of random samples in the form of a control chart to check whether the process continues in control.

Notice in both examples that what is predicted is the behavior of sample observations *given* the parameter, or true state. A statistical prediction is a statement about an occurrence phrased in terms of a probability. We estimate or predict the occurrence of sample means within certain limits by stating their probability based on the appropriate sampling distribution. While the effective inference made when a sample mean falls beyond an upper control limit is that the population mean has increased, we made no probability statement to that effect in Chapter 6. Nor were probability statements about the parameter made in the significance tests of Chapter 7. We now turn our attention to the problem of estimating or predicting the true state given some sample evidence. This is the traditional meaning of *estimation* in statistics, though—as we have emphasized—prediction can "run" from parameter to statistic as well as from statistic to parameter.

In this chapter we first discuss the nature of the problem of estimating parameters from statistics. Second, we present the traditional approach in which the key concept is the confidence interval. Third, we examine two methods, Bayesian inference and fiducial inference, for stating the probability distribution of a parameter based on a statistic.

8-1   Point Estimation

Suppose we want to know the mean age of heads of household in a large new suburban development. The data are not available from the developer's realtor, and we do not have the resources to call on every household in the community. This means we must use some sort of sampling. The realtor agrees to provide a listing of households currently living in the development, from which we can take a random sample. We might decide to ask the head of each household drawn to give us his date of birth. On the assumption that we have truthful answers to this question, we will have a collection of accurate observations of age—one for each household in our sample.

The problem of estimation amounts to deciding what to do with the collection of ages in order to estimate the mean age of heads of household in the entire development. A beginning student might find the arithmetic mean, $\bar{X}$, of the sample, and think no more about it. But why not take the highest and lowest age in the sample and divide by two? Or why not take the central, or median age? Either of these measures of central tendency, and others as well, could be employed as estimates of the population mean, μ. Before the statistician can determine which of these is the best estimate, he must have a very clear definition of what "best" means.

A number of criteria have been employed by mathematical statisticians for deciding the merits of different estimators. Among these are the criteria that an estimator should be *unbiased, consistent*, and *efficient*.

We have already discussed the meaning of an unbiased estimator in Chapters 3 and 6. We said that $\bar{X}$ is an unbiased estimator of μ because the mean of the sampling distribution of $\bar{X}$ equals μ; in symbols, $\mu_{\bar{X}} = \mu$. That is, the mean of the probability distribution of the estimate equals the parameter we seek to estimate.

Take another example from Chapter 3. There, σ^2 was defined as the variance of a parent population. Then we defined s^2 as

$$s^2 = \frac{\Sigma\,[(X - \bar{X})^2]}{n - 1}.$$

The mean of the sampling distribution of s^2 is precisely equal to σ^2, the variance of the parent population. The sample s^2 is, then, an *unbiased* estimator of population variance.

An example of a biased estimator is s, the sample standard deviation, as an estimator of σ, the parent population standard deviation. The reason that s is a biased estimator of σ is that the mean of the sampling distribution of s values is generally not equal to σ, the standard deviation of the parent population.

As n increases, a *consistent* estimator more closely approximates the parameter for which it is an estimate. The sample mean, $\bar{X}$, is a consistent estimator of μ. We have seen in our study of the sampling distribution of $\bar{X}$ that the standard error of this sampling distribution is $\sigma/\sqrt{n}$. What happens to this ratio as n (sample size) increases? If we are discussing an infinite population, then the denominator of the ratio grows large without limit, which means that the standard error of the sample mean approaches zero. The sample mean, $\bar{X}$, and variance, s^2, are consistent estimators of μ and σ^2, respectively.

The sample mean, $\bar{X}$, is the most *efficient* unbiased estimator of the mean of a normal population. The most efficient among a given class of estimators is the estimator whose sampling distribution has the smallest variance *for a given n*. As an illustration, assume that we have a sample of ten numbers from a normal population. We want to estimate μ. Suppose that we compute $\bar{X}$, and suppose that we also find the median of the sample values. Both can be used as estimates of the population mean. One way to choose between them is to examine their sampling distributions for samples of size ten. If we do so, we will find that the variance of the sampling distribution of the mean is less than the variance of the sampling distribution of the median.* Thus the sample mean is a more *reliable*, or *efficient*, estimator than is the median.

We have discussed the concepts of lack-of-bias, consistency, and efficiency in estimators. The sample mean as an estimate of the population mean usually satisfies all the criteria. It is the most efficient among consistent unbiased estimators of the population mean. But, as we saw in Chapter 3, the average squared deviation in a sample is a biased estimator of σ^2, the population variance. Consequently, in practice we usually use the unbiased estimator, s^2, as our estimate of the population variance. The sample s^2 is the most efficient among all consistent unbiased estimators of the population variance. In this sense, $\bar{X}$ and s^2 may be described as "best unbiased estimates" of μ and σ^2, respectively.

We have seen that the process of point estimation involves finding that statistic from a given sample which constitutes our best single-number guess as to the value of a specified parameter. The best single-number or point estimator has been defined as the most efficient among the class of consistent unbiased estimators. But while it may be comforting to be assured that we have made the best unbiased estimate possible in a given situation,

---

* The standard error of the median in sampling from a normally distributed population is equal to $\sqrt{\pi/2}\,\sigma_{\bar{X}}$, or $1.25331\sigma_{\bar{X}}$.

we would like to know *how good* the estimate is. No absolute measure of the goodness of an estimate is possible if the estimate is confined to a point on the scale of a continuous variable. For this reason we turn now to interval estimates.

8-2 Interval Estimation

We have seen that statistics fluctuate about population parameters in accordance with their sampling distributions. One consequence of this fluctuation is that any point estimate of a parameter is virtually certain to be in error, however little, from the parameter. But when we allow our estimate to take up an interval of values, a measure of confidence in the estimate can be developed. Common sense suggests that there should be a higher probability of making correct estimates the wider we set this range, provided that each larger range considered includes all the values in each lesser range.

Mean—variance known. To explain the process of interval estimation we shall use some examples. In the initial example we know the standard deviation of the population but are uncertain about the mean of the population. At first glance this seems impractical, but recall the process control examples in Chapter 6. Here we dealt with separate control charts for mean and variance. It could easily develop that a process long in control with respect to the variance could go out of control with respect to the mean. Here we would know the variance, yet might want to make an interval estimate of μ.

The population in question is a water-softening process. Hardness of water is measured in parts per million (ppm) of calcium carbonate. The variability in observed hardness from one sampling to another depends chiefly on the method of measurement, but is quite well known for commonly used methods. For a particular method in use, the standard deviation, σ, is known to be .6, and the distribution of observed hardness measures for uniform water quality is assumed to be normally distributed. Nine independent tests are made of the hardness of the output of the softening process, and the mean hardness of the sample of nine tests is found to be 20.13 parts of calcium carbonate per million. The procedure for calculating the 99 per cent (symmetrical) confidence limits for the mean hardness will be given first, followed by the classical explanation of the procedure. The development is as follows:

$$\sigma_{\bar{X}} = \frac{\sigma}{\sqrt{n}} = \frac{.6}{\sqrt{9}} = .2 \, \text{ppm.}$$

Now note the z expression and its transposition.

$$z = \frac{\bar{X} - \mu}{\sigma_{\bar{X}}},$$

$$\mu = \bar{X} - z\sigma_{\bar{X}}. \tag{8-1}$$

If we assume that our sample mean of 20.13 represents a value at the 99.5 percentile of the sampling distribution of means of samples of size nine from the population, we will obtain a lower-limit estimate of the population mean as follows:

$$L = \bar{X} - z_{.995}\sigma_{\bar{X}}$$
$$= 20.13 - (2.58)(.2) = 20.13 - .516,$$
$$L = 19.614 \text{ ppm}.$$

If we assume that our sample mean of 20.13 is at the lower end of the sampling distribution at the .5 percentile of $\bar{X}$'s, we will obtain an upper-limit estimate of the population mean.

$$U = \bar{X} - z_{.005}\sigma_{\bar{X}}$$
$$= 20.13 - (-2.58)(.2) = 20.13 + .516,$$
$$U = 20.646 \text{ ppm}.$$

The interval from 19.614 to 20.646 ppm is called a *99 per cent confidence interval* (or .99 confidence interval). Note that we selected two values which would leave .5 per cent of the area in the opposite tails of two different normal sampling distributions. The sketch in Fig. 8–1 illustrates the procedure.

If we wished to construct the 95 rather than the 99 per cent confidence interval, we would replace $z_{.995}$ and $z_{.005}$ above with $z_{.975}$ and $z_{.025}$. These two quantities are equal to $+1.96$ and -1.96 instead of $+2.58$ and -2.58. Thus the .95 confidence interval is 19.738 through 20.522 parts per million. By finding the appropriate z values we can construct the confidence interval corresponding to any desired confidence coefficient.

We will now interpret the confidence interval in the manner of Neyman-Pearson, who based their view on an objective relative frequency definition of probability. Earlier, in Chapter 6, we knew μ and examined the distribution of $\bar{X}$. Now we have one single value of $\bar{X}$ and we want an interval estimate of μ. The only thing we have at our disposal is some knowledge about the sampling distribution of $\bar{X}$ relative to μ. We do not know μ.

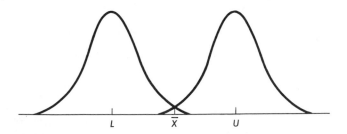

FIGURE 8-1 Sampling distributions and the confidence interval

Yet we do know that μ is *some* fixed value, whereas $\bar{X}$ fluctuates from one sample to the next.

Imagine taking many different samples of nine each from our water-softening process. We would calculate $\bar{X}$ for each sample and then carry out the steps already outlined to calculate the .99 confidence interval for μ on the basis of each sample of nine tests. The sample mean would lie at varying distances from the population mean, μ. Some sample means would lie at $\mu + 1.0\sigma_{\bar{X}}$, some at $\mu - .5\sigma_{\bar{X}}$, some at $\mu + 2.8\sigma_{\bar{X}}$, and so on. Adding and subtracting $2.58\sigma_{\bar{X}}$ from any sample mean establishes the interval estimate we are concerned with. We would have a series of interval estimates as below:

Sample no.	Sample mean $(\bar{X})$	$L = \bar{X} - 2.58\sigma_{\bar{X}}$	$U = \bar{X} + 2.58\sigma_{\bar{X}}$
1	$\mu + 1.00\sigma_{\bar{X}}$	$\mu - 1.58\sigma_{\bar{X}}$	$\mu + 3.58\sigma_{\bar{X}}$
2	$\mu - .50\sigma_{\bar{X}}$	$\mu - 3.08\sigma_{\bar{X}}$	$\mu + 2.08\sigma_{\bar{X}}$
3	$\mu + 2.80\sigma_{\bar{X}}$	$\mu + .22\sigma_{\bar{X}}$	$\mu + 5.38\sigma_{\bar{X}}$
$\vdots$	$\vdots$	$\vdots$	$\vdots$

The situation is shown graphically in Fig. 8–2. The first two interval estimates are correct—their limits bracket the population mean. The interval estimate from the third sample is, however, incorrect because the interval constructed does not include the population mean. It fails to do so simply because the sample mean happened to be at $\mu + 2.8\sigma_{\bar{X}}$, or 2.8 standard errors above the population mean. The process of adding and subtracting $2.58\sigma_{\bar{X}}$ to and from the sample mean will fail to yield an interval that includes the population mean whenever the sample mean lies more than $2.58\sigma_{\bar{X}}$ from the population mean. But the probability that a sample mean deviates from

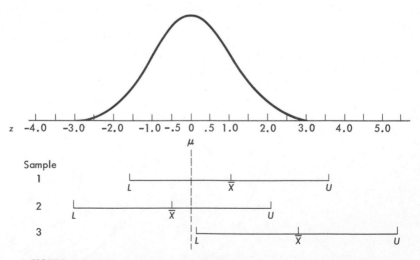

FIGURE 8-2 Ninety-nine per cent confidence intervals from three samples (normal population with σ known)

the population mean by more than $2.58\sigma_{\bar{x}}$ is known from the properties of the sampling distribution. It is .01. By this reasoning we can say that the *process of setting an interval estimate* by $\bar{X} \pm 2.58\sigma_{\bar{x}}$ has a .99 probability of producing a correct estimate. It is 99 per cent reliable, meaning that in the long run, 99 per cent of interval estimates made in this manner will be correct. In this view the probability .99 does not refer to any particular interval set up by the procedure, but to the long-run relative frequency with which such intervals are bound to bracket the parameter being estimated.

We have seen that we can employ the sample mean to construct confidence intervals for the mean of a normal population when σ is known. We simply apply the appropriate percentiles of the standardized form of the sampling distribution, in this case the standard cumulative normal distribution. This can be generalized as follows:

Let the confidence coefficient be $(1 - \alpha)$. Then:

$$
\begin{aligned}
L &= \bar{X} - z_{1-(\alpha/2)}\sigma_{\bar{x}}, \\
U &= \bar{X} - z_{\alpha/2}\sigma_{\bar{x}}.
\end{aligned}
\tag{8-2}
$$

In this context α is the allowable risk or probability of making an incorrect estimate. For example, the .90 confidence interval would be obtained as

$$
\begin{aligned}
L &= \bar{X} - z_{.95}\sigma_{\bar{x}} = \bar{X} - 1.64\sigma_{\bar{x}}, \\
U &= \bar{X} - z_{.05}\sigma_{\bar{x}} = \bar{X} + 1.64\sigma_{\bar{x}}.
\end{aligned}
$$

Mean—variance estimated. Having formulated the interval estimation problem in this way, we can see more easily what must be done if the underlying sampling distribution is not normal. We know that the sampling distribution of means from a normally distributed population with unknown variance is the Student t with $m = n - 1$ degrees of freedom. More specifically,

$$
t = \frac{\bar{X} - \mu}{s_{\bar{x}}}, \qquad \text{where} \quad s_{\bar{x}} = \frac{s}{\sqrt{n}},
$$

and

$$
s^2 = \frac{\Sigma[(X - \bar{X})^2]}{n - 1}.
$$

Then, the expression for the population mean is

$$
\mu = \bar{X} - ts_{\bar{x}}.
$$

Again, assuming the sample mean to be on the one hand at the $\alpha/2$ percentile of a "high" sampling distribution, and on the other hand at the $1 - (\alpha/2)$ percentile of a "low" sampling distribution, we get the $1 - \alpha$ symmetrical confidence interval from

$$L = \bar{X} - t_{1-(\alpha/2)} s_{\bar{X}},$$
$$U = \bar{X} - t_{\alpha/2} s_{\bar{X}}. \tag{8-3}$$

Suppose six breaking-strength tests on a particular type of fishing line yield a mean breaking strength of 71.00 ounces and a variance of 20.0 ounces. The .95 confidence interval for the population mean would be found as

$$s_{\bar{X}} = \frac{s}{\sqrt{n}} = \frac{\sqrt{20}}{\sqrt{6}} = 1.825;$$

$$t_{.025, m=5} = -2.571, \qquad t_{.975, m=5} = 2.571;$$

$$L = 71.00 - (2.571)(1.825) = 66.31 \text{ ounces},$$

$$U = 71.00 - (-2.571)(1.825) = 75.69 \text{ ounces}.$$

Variance. Confidence limits for the variance, σ^2, may be found in an analogous fashion by substituting the appropriate percentiles of chi-square, the standard form of the appropriate sampling distribution, in the expression

$$\sigma^2 = \frac{ms^2}{\chi^2}.$$

Where $(1 - \alpha)$ is the confidence coefficient, the general expressions will be

$$L = \frac{ms^2}{\chi^2_{1-(\alpha/2)}},$$
$$U = \frac{ms^2}{\chi^2_{\alpha/2}}. \tag{8-4}$$

For the .98 confidence limits for the variance of breaking strength of fishing line based on the preceding sample results, we first find $\chi^2_{.01}$ and $\chi^2_{.99}$ for five degrees of freedom $(m = n - 1 = 6 - 1 = 5)$. Substituting in the above expressions,

$$L = \frac{5(20)}{15.1} = 6.62,$$

$$U = \frac{5(20)}{.554} = 180.5.$$

The statement that $6.62 < \sigma^2 < 180.5$ was established by a procedure which is 98 per cent reliable. Remember that both the t distribution for setting confidence limits on the population mean and the chi-square distribution for setting confidence limits on the population variance assume that the parent population is normally distributed.

You have just seen the process of setting a confidence interval for a population variance. Let's interpret this in terms of the sampling distribution of variances. Our symbols indicate that L is a low estimated value of population variance. For our example, we got a value of 6.62 when we solved for L. This means that the variance of the population will have to be 6.62 in order to produce a sample result ($s^2 = 20$) so large that only 1 per cent of sample s^2 values could be expected to exceed this number. Similarly, the upper estimated value of 180.5 is a value of σ^2 so large that our given sample results ($s^2 = 20$) will mark the boundary for the smallest 1 per cent of sample s^2's. In other words, if $\sigma^2 = 180.5$, we would expect a sample result of $s^2 = 20$ or smaller only 1 per cent of the time.

We have placed confidence intervals on the population mean when the population variance is known. We have placed confidence intervals on the population mean when the population variance is unknown. Finally, we have illustrated how to place confidence intervals on the population variance. The process of constructing confidence intervals is a perfectly general one. Confidence intervals can be constructed from any statistic whose sampling distribution is known.

8-3 The Confidence Interval and Significance Tests

In Chapter 7 we studied a number of tests of statistical significance. We emphasized that a significance test based only on an alpha error limitation should not be regarded as a basis for choosing among alternative hypotheses. However, when a difference reaches a significance level such as .05 we begin to suspect that the parameter represented by the null hypothesis is not true. This is nothing more than statistical prudence, for the larger the difference represented by the evidence, the more doubt is cast on the null hypothesis. When the sample mean does not achieve a prescribed level of significance, it has been customary to say that we accept the null hypothesis. But keep in mind that this is the only hypothesis we have tested. In the bottle-filling example of Chapter 7 we could have used the sample mean to test the hypothesis that the process mean was 12.51, 12.52, 12.55, or any other value rather than $\mu = 12.5$ ounces. Imagine testing a multitude of such values, employing a .05 significance level, on the basis of a particular sample mean. We would soon find that all values of the parameter that fall within the 95 per cent confidence limits are acceptable hypotheses using a .05 significance criterion. This can be appreciated by noting that since all such parameters are within $1.96\sigma_{\bar{x}}$ of the sample mean, the sample mean is within $1.96\sigma_{\bar{x}}$ of any one of the same parameters. The same relationship between significance tests and confidence limits holds in applications based on t, χ^2, or any other sampling distribution.

From the above argument we have another interpretation of the confidence interval. The $1 - \alpha$ central confidence interval based on a given statistic contains all the values of the parameter that would be accepted employing an α significance criterion. If we are interested in only one hypothesized parameter, a significance test is called for. If we are interested in all of the values of the parameter that the evidence will support as credible, the confidence interval should be employed.

EXERCISES

8.1   Refer to Exercise 6.5. Given the mean of samples 16–20 combined and assuming the standard deviation of the population to be 10,
(a) Find the 90 and the 95 per cent central confidence intervals for the population mean.   *Ans.* 110.04–114.68; 109.59–115.13.
(b) Is the hypothesis that the population mean is 110 acceptable at the .10 significance level? At the .05 significance level?   *Ans.* No; yes.

8.2   Weekday traffic past a certain business location on five randomly selected days was 235, 215, 220, 241, and 253. Assuming a normal distribution of daily traffic, place 90 and 99 per cent confidence limits on the mean daily traffic at the location.
Ans. 218.03–247.57; 200.89–264.71.

8.3   A random sample of the percentage of space devoted to nonfood items in 21 randomly selected independent supermarkets in a large city produced a mean of 25.6 per cent and an estimated standard deviation of 4.8 per cent. Assuming normality of the underlying distribution, place 95 and 99 per cent confidence limits on the population mean.

8.4   Find the 95 per cent confidence interval for the mean and the 95 per cent confidence interval for the variance of the population in Exercise 5.3.   *Ans.* 9.63–12.27; 15.12–33.59.

8.5   Find the 90 per cent confidence interval for the variance of the population in Exercise 7.6.

8.6   Find the 95 per cent confidence interval for the population mean difference in running times in Exercise 7.9.

8-4   Bayes' Theorem and Posterior Probabilities

In our early study of probability in Chapter 3 we computed "odds on true states" in a binomial sampling situation after having observed a particular outcome in the sample. To review this concept briefly, suppose a random sample of $n = 6$ from a large voter population yields three Democrats. What are the odds that the population contains 40 per cent as against 50 per cent Democrats? We would find from the binomial the probability of observing 3 out of 6 Democrats given a population proportion, p, of .40 and then relate this to the probability of observing 3 out of 6 Democrats given a population proportion, p, of .50. The computation is

$$\frac{P(r = 3 \,|\, p = .40)}{P(r = 3 \,|\, p = .50)} = \frac{{}_6C_3(.40)^3(.60)^3}{{}_6C_3(.50)^3(.50)^3} = (.8)^3(1.2)^3 = .885.$$

The sample outcome of three Democrats is .885 as likely to have been produced by a 40 per cent Democratic population as by a 50 per cent Democratic population. We could then say that the odds on the state $p = .40$ relative to the state $p = .50$ are 885 to 1000. If one uses the statistical evidence as the sole basis for a bet on $p = .40$ and against $p = .50$, a fair bet should then have a payoff of $10.00 for each $8.85 placed on the proposition that $p = .40$. Put another way, one who would bet on $p = .40$ should be willing to pay up to $8.85 for a payoff of $10.00 should he win.

Bayes theorem was stated in Chapter 3 as

$$P(S \,|\, E) = \frac{P(S) \cdot P(E \,|\, S)}{P(E)}.$$

The symbol S referred to a state and E referred to an observed statistic. $P(S)$ is the prior probability of a state, $P(E \,|\, S)$ the probability of a statistic given the state, and $P(E)$ is the marginal probability of the statistic—that is, $P(E \,|\, S)$ summed over the alternative states. In the example on party affiliation, suppose the prior probability of the state $p = .40$ to be 1/3 and that of the state $p = .50$ to be 2/3. We would then have from Bayes' theorem:

$$P(p = .40 \,|\, r = 3) = \frac{\frac{1}{3}P(r = 3 \,|\, p = .40)}{\frac{1}{3}P(r = 3 \,|\, p = .40) + \frac{2}{3}P(r = 3 \,|\, p = .50)}$$

$$= \frac{\frac{1}{3}(.2765)}{\frac{1}{3}(.2765) + \frac{2}{3}(.3125)},$$

$$P(p = .40 \,|\, r = 3) = \frac{.2765}{.9015} = .307,$$

$$P(p = .50 \,|\, r = 3) = 1 - P(p = .40 \,|\, r = 3) = .693.$$

So far we have just reviewed the arithmetic of Bayes' theorem. What about the meaning of the prior probabilities and the final probabilities, often called *posterior probabilities*, that we obtained? First, our example is somewhat artificial in that there are but two discrete states, $p = .40$ and $p = .50$. This is done just for convenience and is not a point at issue.

The prior probabilities are a requisite for applying Bayes' theorem, and two interpretations have been given them. In the first interpretation, the prior probabilities are viewed as relative frequencies of occurrence of a set of parameters. This set is sometimes called a superpopulation. In our example, the superpopulation might stand for cities with differing proportions of

Democrats. The investigator knows that in the superpopulation of cities one-third have 40 per cent Democrats and two-thirds have 50 per cent Democrats. He has taken a sample of six from one of the cities and observed three Democrats. But for some reason he doesn't know from which class of city the sample came and wants to make a probability statement about it. The posterior probabilities from Bayes' theorem provide such statements, and in this case, they can be given a relative frequency interpretation. Assume one were to select cities repeatedly with probabilities of selection of the two classes according to the prior probabilities, and from the city selected he were to draw a random sample of six voters. Then consider all those occasions when three of the six voters were Democrats. In 30.7 per cent of such occasions, a subsequent census would reveal the city to be a member of the class of city with 40 per cent Democrats.

This is the urn model of the original example in Chapter 3. The urns are the members of a superpopulation, as are the cities in the current example. The question is which urn, or city, produced the sample, and Bayes' theorem provides a relevant probability statement.

While Bayes' theorem is not objectionable, statisticians concerned with applications questioned its relevance because prior probabilities would seldom be known in the sense of the preceding example. One area of application in which we might recognize a counterpart to the superpopulation of urns is in acceptance sampling. From long experience with a supplier a purchaser might be able to construct a prior probability distribution of the quality of shipments. When a new shipment arrives and a sample is drawn, the question is: Which quality class of shipment did the sample come from? It must be assumed that the current shipment is a random sample from the superpopulation of past shipments. Even if an objective probability distribution of past shipment quality is available, one might not wish to make this assumption.

Statisticians who adopt a subjective view of probability have thought of the prior probabilities as subjective measures of belief in the alternative values of the parameter. In this case we need not conceive of a superpopulation whose members occur with the relative frequencies of the prior probabilities. The investigator knows what city he sampled in the physical sense, but he does not know the proportion of Democrats in that city. But *prior to taking the sample* he would have given 2-to-1 odds on 50 per cent Democrats as against 40 per cent. His subjective prior probability is $P(p = .40) = 1/3$, assuming again that $p = .40$ and $p = .50$ are the only possibilities in our abbreviated example. As long as the investigator's "priors" represent his considered feelings, the subjectivist will not argue with them.

If one admits the idea of subjective prior probability, then the posterior probabilities produced by Bayes' theorem represent the degree of belief in the alternative states that should be held after the objective evidence bearing on the states has been collected. The posterior probabilities are personal to the individual who formed the subjective prior probabilities. This means that another investigator with different priors will have different posterior probabilities after looking at the same evidence.

The use of Bayes' theorem to weigh objective evidence against subjective prior probabilities of states has not been without its critics. These critics worry about "how good" an investigator's priors are. The parameter, after all, has a particular (true) value, and one man may be better at guessing it a priori than another. One man's prior belief about the parameter may be closer to the truth than another's. From the subjective viewpoint, however, this objection is a logical trap. Once having admitted subjective measures of belief as prior probabilities, we have to admit that posterior probabilities are also personal, no matter how much we may worry about it.

In the absence of objective prior probabilities it has been suggested that equal prior probabilities of states be employed. This position stems from Laplace (1749–1827), who adopted Bayes' theorem as the fundamental method of statistical inference. Use of equal prior probabilities has been criticized as unrealistic because it seems to say that the state of belief prior to taking a sample is one of complete ignorance, a condition never really met in practice. On the other hand, use of equal prior probabilities results in final inferences that are not affected by the subjective elements of belief to which many statisticians object. When the results of a study are likely to be used by persons or firms other than the immediate investigator, it would seem especially important to avoid the introduction of subjective personal beliefs.

The resurgence of Bayesian inference owes much to interest on the part of applied statisticians working in collegiate schools of business. As we saw in our introduction to decision systems in Chapter 3, probabilities of states are a necessary prerequisite for finding the expected value of a decision system. The use of a probability distribution of a parameter to express the degree of belief in alternative states has great attractiveness in business decision making, where available strategies are weighed on the scales of monetary gain. One who adopts this viewpoint may or may not admit subjective probabilities into his calculations.

Bayes' theorem, stated in terms of odds on two alternative states, rather than probabilities, is

$$\frac{P(A\,|\,E)}{P(B\,|\,E)} = \frac{P(A)}{P(B)} \cdot \frac{P(E\,|\,A)}{P(E\,|\,B)}. \tag{8-5}$$

In Chapter 3 we called $P(E\,|\,A)/P(E\,|\,B)$ the information odds. In the language used in connection with Bayes' theorem we can summarize the above as

posterior odds = prior odds × information odds.

As more objective information about the true state becomes available through increased sampling, the information odds come to overwhelm the prior odds in the determination of the posterior odds. This happens with even fairly modest sample sizes, and it will not matter much what the prior odds were. To show this effect, consider prior odds of 50:50 versus 1: 2 on the state $p = .40$ and $p = .50$ in our example, and the statistical results of 3 Democrats out of 6, 25 out of 50, and 50 out of 100. The probabilities of r given $p = .40$ and $p = .50$ for the larger samples can be looked up in Appendix A.

For the sample of 6 with $r = 3$ we would have:

50 : 50 priors:

$$\text{posterior odds} = \frac{1}{1} \cdot \frac{.2765}{.3125} = \frac{.885}{1.000};$$

1 : 2 priors:

$$\text{posterior odds} = \frac{1}{2} \cdot \frac{.2765}{.3125} = \frac{.442}{1.000}.$$

For $r = 25$ out of 50:

50 : 50 priors:

$$\text{posterior odds} = \frac{1}{1} \cdot \frac{.0405}{.1122} = \frac{.361}{1.000};$$

1 : 2 priors:

$$\text{posterior odds} = \frac{1}{2} \cdot \frac{.0405}{.1122} = \frac{.180}{1.000}.$$

For $r = 50$ out of 100:

50 : 50 priors:

$$\text{posterior odds} = \frac{1}{1} \cdot \frac{.0103}{.0796} = \frac{.129}{1.000};$$

1 : 2 priors:

$$\text{posterior odds} = \frac{1}{2} \cdot \frac{.0103}{.0796} = \frac{.065}{1.000}.$$

While the posterior odds in favor of $p = .40$ as against $p = .50$ with 1 : 2 priors are always one-half of what they would be with 50 : 50 priors, increasing the objective information makes us more and more confident in either case that $p = .40$ is *not* the true state. This is because the information odds become more disparate as the amount of information increases. Now presuming that $p = .50$ was the true state, actual samples would not yield exactly one-half Democrats as in our figures. But given the decrease in the variance of the sampling distributions of r given $p = .40$ and r given $p = .50$ as n increases, greater disparity in the information odds is to be expected.

8-5 Fiducial Probability and Likelihood

In dealing with normal sampling distributions of $\bar{X}$ given μ, we have become familiar with probabilities of the following kind when μ is known.

$$P[\bar{X} \leq (\mu + z_\alpha \sigma_{\bar{X}})] = \alpha.$$

Here, α represents an area in the *lower* tail of the sampling distribution of $\bar{X}$ given μ and σ. It defines percentiles of the cumulative probability distribution of the sample mean. The positions of $\bar{X}$ and μ in such an expression can be algebraically reversed. This leads to the statement

$$P[\mu \geq (\bar{X} - z_\alpha \sigma_{\bar{X}})] = \alpha. \tag{8-6}$$

This can be read as a statement about the probability of the population means' exceeding a certain value, $\bar{X} - z_\alpha \sigma_{\bar{X}}$. The same α is an area in the upper tail of a probability distribution of μ. In this interpretation the sample mean is regarded as fixed, and the term $z\sigma_{\bar{X}}$ represents the normal distribution of sampling errors. Now, however, the population mean, μ, is regarded as a random variable. Probability statements about the population mean derived from this reversal of the positions of $\bar{X}$ and μ are known as *fiducial* probability statements. The method was proposed by Sir Ronald Fisher who used the adjective "fiducial" to call attention to the fact that such statements are not statements of long-run relative frequency: they are statements of degree of belief. The method proposed by Fisher does not involve Bayes' theorem. Thus, writers speak of fiducial inference on the one hand and Bayesian inference on the other.

The fiducial method has dispensed with the prior distribution of the parameter, and an inference has been constructed by employing only what is termed the *likelihood function*. The likelihood function is the empirical, or second, element in Bayes' theorem. It corresponds to the function we have used to construct information odds in the discrete examples introduced previously.

To illustrate the *likelihood function*, consider the evidence $\bar{X} = 150$ in a random sample of size 64 from a normally distributed population with the known variance, $\sigma^2 = 256$. The standard error of the mean $\sigma_{\bar{X}}$, is $\sigma/\sqrt{n} = 16/8 = 2$. In this situation we know that $z = (\bar{X} - \mu)/\sigma_{\bar{X}}$ is normally distributed, given any specified value of μ. Let us consider various values of μ and the resulting function $f(\bar{X} \mid \mu)$ for the known $\bar{X} = 150$. This can be done by reading ordinates of the normal curve at values of z corresponding to the specified values of μ. Some of these ordinates are reproduced below.

μ	$z = (150 - \mu)/2$	$f(z \mid \mu) = f(\bar{X} \mid \mu)$
145	+2.5	.01753
146	+2.0	.05399
147	+1.5	.1295
148	+1.0	.2420
149	+0.5	.3521
150	0.0	.3989
151	−0.5	.3521
152	−1.0	.2420
153	−1.5	.1295
154	−2.0	.05399
155	−2.5	.01753

The function $f(\bar{X} \mid \mu)$ for various μ is termed the likelihood function, and values of this function are called likelihoods. We find that 150 is the most likely value for μ given $\bar{X} = 150$. The likelihoods diminish as we consider values of μ departing from the sample mean. In fact the likelihood function can be described by a normal distribution with a mean of $\bar{X} = 150$ and a standard deviation of $\sigma_{\bar{X}} = 2.0$ The standard normal deviate for such a distribution is

$$\hat{z} = \frac{\mu - \bar{X}}{\sigma_{\bar{X}}}. \tag{8-7}$$

We use $\hat{z}$ in order to distinguish this standard normal deviate from the more familiar $z = (\bar{X} - \mu)/\sigma_{\bar{X}}$. Note that $\hat{z} = -z$ and Eq. (8–6) becomes

$$P[\mu \leq (\bar{X} + \hat{z}\sigma_{\bar{X}})] = \alpha. \tag{8-8}$$

Now we have a probability statement in which α is again a percentile of a cumulative normal probability distribution. The normal area curve corresponding to this distribution is shown in Fig. 8–3. This distribution portrays the state of our belief about μ, the true mean of the population

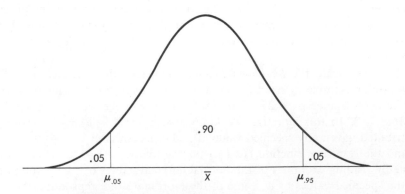

FIGURE 8-3 Normal fiducial probability distribution of μ

of X, given $\bar{X}$. The maximum-likelihood estimate, $\bar{X}$, could be termed $\hat{\mu}$, the "hat" signifying estimated mean. The standard error of the sample mean, $\sigma_{\bar{X}}$, measures also the spread of our belief about the population mean, μ, and therefore may be referred to as σ_μ. A normal fiducial probability distribution of the population mean may be indicated by either

$$\mu = \bar{X} + \hat{z}\sigma_{\bar{X}},$$

or

$$\mu = \hat{\mu} + \hat{z}\sigma_\mu. \tag{8-9}$$

Employing the probability distribution of μ, we can make probability statements such as

$$P[(\bar{X} - 1.64\sigma_{\bar{X}}) < \mu < (\bar{X} + 1.64\sigma_{\bar{X}})] = .90.$$

This says that, on the basis of a given sample mean, the probability that the population mean lies in the interval $\bar{X} \pm 1.64\sigma_{\bar{X}}$ is .90. While the same calculation yields a 90 per cent confidence interval for μ based on the particular sample mean, no probability statement of this kind was made in connection with the traditional confidence interval. Probability statements about confidence intervals are confined to the probability that repeated applications of the confidence interval *procedure* will lead to correct estimates—that is, intervals that include the unknown but unique population mean. They were statements of long-run relative frequency, as opposed to a degree of belief based on the evidence.

Fiducial intervals for the mean and variance. The $1 - \alpha$ central fiducial interval for μ is obtained from

$$\mu_{\alpha/2} = \bar{X} + \hat{z}_{\alpha/2}\sigma_{\bar{X}},$$

$$\mu_{1-(\alpha/2)} = \bar{X} + \hat{z}_{1-(\alpha/2)}\sigma_{\bar{X}}. \tag{8-10}$$

When the variance, and consequently the standard error of the mean, had to be estimated from the sample observations, we found that sampling distributions of the mean from normally distributed populations followed Student's t distribution. We could state a lower-tail probability regarding the sample mean as

$$P[\bar{X} \leq (\mu + t_\alpha s_{\bar{X}})] = \alpha,$$

where $t = (\bar{X} - \mu)/s_{\bar{X}}$ with $m = n - 1$.

Defining $\hat{t} = -t$, a reversal of the positions of $\bar{X}$ and μ similar to what has already been shown for the normal expression produces

$$P[\mu \leq (\bar{X} + \hat{t}_\alpha s_{\bar{X}})] = \alpha, \tag{8-11}$$

where $\hat{t} = (\mu - \bar{X})/s_{\bar{X}}$ with $m = n - 1$.

Because the t distribution is symmetrical, the regular table of t can be read as a table of $\hat{t}$. For the $1 - \alpha$ central fiducial interval we have then

$$\mu_{\alpha/2} = \bar{X} + \hat{t}_{\alpha/2}s_{\bar{X}},$$
$$\mu_{1-(\alpha/2)} = \bar{X} + \hat{t}_{1-(\alpha/2)}s_{\bar{X}}. \tag{8-12}$$

The fiducial intervals for the mean discussed above correspond numerically to central confidence intervals of the traditional kind. This happens because the variance and shape of the sampling distribution of means do not depend on the true population mean. When the sampling distribution of means is normal or Student t, $\sigma_{\bar{X}}$ or $s_{\bar{X}}$ does not depend on μ.

In dealing with the variance of a normally distributed population, the expression involving χ^2 can be arranged as

$$\sigma^2 = ms^2\left(\frac{1}{\chi^2}\right).$$

Given particular sample evidence, ms^2 is fixed. The variable element, $1/\chi^2$, depends only on the degrees of freedom, which are also known. Therefore, if we substitute the .025 and .975 levels of $1/\chi^2$, we will obtain the .025 and .975 levels of the probability distribution of the population variance, σ^2. In general, the $1 - \alpha$ central fiducial limits for the variance are

$$\sigma^2_{\alpha/2} = \frac{ms^2}{\chi^2_{1-(\alpha/2)}},$$
$$\sigma^2_{1-(\alpha/2)} = \frac{ms^2}{\chi^2_{\alpha/2}}. \tag{8-13}$$

This produces the same numerical result as the $1 - \alpha$ central confidence interval. The difference lies in interpretation. According to the fiducial argument we are allowed to say that the probability is .95 that the population variance lies within the interval.

Fiducial probability offers a way of assessing probabilities of states directly on the basis of objective sample information. Fisher proposed the fiducial method as a means of avoiding Bayes' theorem, which he considered objectionable because of problems raised by the use of prior probabilities. The fiducial approach is compatible with the view of probability as degree of belief, yet avoids the subjective elements that can be introduced through prior probabilities.

Fiducial probabilities and two-action decision problems. The two-action decision problem was discussed in Sec. 7–8. It is usually a situation where the question is whether to adopt a new procedure in preference to an existing procedure, or which of two new procedures to adopt. Where the criterion of effectiveness of the procedures is a mean, we are concerned with whether the population mean exceeds some predetermined figure. The predetermined figure typically is the level of effectiveness at which it pays to switch from the old to the new procedure—an economic break-even point. In the case of alternative methods of accomplishing a new task, the predetermined figure might be the *true difference* in effectiveness at which the two methods are considered equal economically. When the evidence on comparative effectiveness is based on a sample, we can then form the fiducial probability:

$$P(\mu > \mu_b) \qquad \text{for experimental vs. existing procedure,}$$

or

$$P(\Delta > \Delta_b) \qquad \text{for two experimental procedures,}$$

where $\Delta = \mu_1 - \mu_2$.

Here μ_b and Δ_b stand for predetermined levels based on economic factors. The probability $P(\mu > \mu_b)$ relative to $P(\mu < \mu_b)$ expresses the odds, based on the evidence, that the new method is in fact better than the old, or $P(\Delta < \Delta_b)$ relative to $P(\Delta > \Delta_b)$ would assess the odds that one experimental procedure is better than another. The odds required for a final decision might depend on factors not taken into account in the calculation of the economic break-even point. Otherwise, any odds in favor of $P(\mu > \mu_b)$ would dictate adopting the new technique, and any odds favoring $P(\mu < \mu_b)$ would dictate staying with the old. The factors affecting the choice of critical odds levels apart from 50–50 would be the behavior of cost and return relationships apart from the break-even point, and the attitude of the decision-maker towards economic and noneconomic risks. It is conceivable that a decision-maker might insist on 10:1 odds that a new method is better before adopting it because errors of commission are more noticeable to his supervisor than errors of omission. Unless 10:1 odds are achieved, he will either decide in favor of the existing method or collect further evidence. In a decision involving alternative methods for a new task, he might insist on 2:1 odds either way before making a decision, and conducting further experimentation otherwise. No generalization can be made in the absence of a value or cost criterion.

A correspondence prevails between tests of the null hypothesis that $\lambda = \lambda_o$ and fiducial probabilities that $\lambda < \lambda_o$ and $\lambda > \lambda_o$ when normal z, Student t, or chi-square sampling distributions apply. A difference between the statistic, l_o, and the parameter λ_o significant at an α risk level corresponds to odds of at least $1 - \alpha/2$ to $\alpha/2$ in favor of one or the other of the states $\lambda < \lambda_o$ and $\lambda > \lambda_o$. A principle that holds is that the odds for a statistic's exceeding the observed value given a parameter are equal to the odds against a parameter greater than the one specified given the statistic. This principle allows immediate conversion of a probability statement about a statistic based on normal z, Student t, or chi-square to an equivalent fiducial probability statement about the parameter based on the sample evidence. In general, given a hypothesis, λ_o, and corresponding sample evidence l_o,

$$\frac{P(l > l_o)}{P(l < l_o)} = \frac{P(\lambda < \lambda_o)}{P(\lambda > \lambda_o)}. \tag{8-14}$$

8-6   Revising the Probability Distribution of the Mean

A fundamental theorem of Bayesian statistics states that, if an infinite population of X is normally distributed and if

1. the prior probability distribution of μ_X is normal, and if
2. the likelihood distribution, $f(\bar{X} \mid \mu)$, based on the result of an un-biased sampling procedure is normal,

then the revised, or posterior distribution of the mean, $P(\mu \mid \bar{X})$, will be normal with mean and variance equal to

$$\hat{\mu} = \frac{\left(\frac{1}{\sigma^2_{\mu_1}}\right)\hat{\mu}_1 + \left(\frac{1}{\sigma^2_{\mu_2}}\right)\hat{\mu}_2}{\frac{1}{\sigma^2_{\mu_1}} + \frac{1}{\sigma^2_{\mu_2}}}, \tag{8-15}$$

$$\sigma^2_\mu = \frac{1}{\frac{1}{\sigma^2_{\mu_1}} + \frac{1}{\sigma^2_{\mu_2}}}, \tag{8-16}$$

where $\hat{\mu}_1$ and $\sigma^2_{\mu_1}$ refer to the prior distribution, and $\hat{\mu}_2$ and $\sigma^2_{\mu_2}$ refer to the likelihood distribution. Note that the revised mean of the probability distribution of μ is a weighted average of the mean of the prior distribution and the mean of the likelihood distribution. The weights are the reciprocals of the variances of the respective distributions, and are sometimes referred to as the precision or information content of the respective estimates. Note that Eq. (8–16) implies that the information content of the revised distribution is the sum of the information content of the prior distribution and the likelihood, for

$$\frac{1}{\sigma^2_\mu} = \frac{1}{\sigma^2_{\mu_1}} + \frac{1}{\sigma^2_{\mu_2}}.$$

Equations (8–15) and (8–16) can be rearranged to produce the following formulas, which are more convenient for calculation purposes.

$$\hat{\mu} = \frac{\hat{\mu}_1\sigma^2_{\mu_2} + \hat{\mu}_2\sigma^2_{\mu_1}}{\sigma^2_{\mu_1} + \sigma^2_{\mu_2}}, \tag{8-17}$$

$$\sigma^2_\mu = \frac{\sigma^2_{\mu_1}\sigma^2_{\mu_2}}{\sigma^2_{\mu_1} + \sigma^2_{\mu_2}}. \tag{8-18}$$

When the variance of the prior distribution is large in relation to the variance of the likelihood distribution, $\hat{\mu}$ and σ_μ^2 will approach $\hat{\mu}_2$ and $\sigma_{\mu_2}^2$ respectively.

When one has evidence from two separate samples, the fiducial distribution of the mean from the first sample stands in the logical position of a Bayesian prior distribution. One might think of applying Eqs. (8–15) and (8–16) with the subscripts representing the parameters of the fiducial distributions from the separate samples. This would amount to

$$\hat{\mu} = \frac{\left(\frac{1}{\sigma_{\bar{X}_1}^2}\right)\bar{X}_1 + \left(\frac{1}{\sigma_{\bar{X}_2}^2}\right)\bar{X}_2}{\frac{1}{\sigma_{\bar{X}_1}^2} + \frac{1}{\sigma_{\bar{X}_2}^2}},$$

$$\sigma_\mu^2 = \frac{1}{\frac{1}{\sigma_{\bar{X}_1}^2} + \frac{1}{\sigma_{\bar{X}_2}^2}}.$$

But, since $1/\sigma_{\bar{X}}^2 = n/\sigma_X^2$, these expressions reduce to

$$\hat{\mu} = \frac{n_1\bar{X}_1 + n_2\bar{X}_2}{n_1 + n_2}, \tag{8–19}$$

$$\sigma_\mu^2 = \frac{\sigma_X^2}{n_1 + n_2}. \tag{8–20}$$

If the variance of X is not known, we would make the best estimate of it available from the two samples. Equation (8–19) would be unaffected, but Eq. (8–20) would become

$$\sigma_\mu^2 = \frac{\bar{s}^2}{n_1 + n_2}, \tag{8–21}$$

where

$$\bar{s}^2 = \frac{(n_1 - 1)s_1^2 + (n_2 - 1)s_2^2}{n_1 + n_2 - 2}.$$

For large samples

$$\bar{s}^2 \simeq \frac{n_1 s_1^2 + n_2 s_2^2}{n_1 + n_2}.$$

Suppose an initial sample of 50 from a large population of wage earners yielded a mean take-home pay of $450 per month and a standard deviation, s, of $35. A further sample of 100 wage earners produces a mean of $460 and a standard deviation of $40. The total sample size is large enough to apply a normal fiducial distribution. The distribution would have the parameters

$$\hat{\mu} = \frac{n_1 \bar{X}_1 + n_2 \bar{X}_2}{n_1 + n_2}$$

$$= \frac{50(450) + 100(460)}{50 + 100} = \$456.67,$$

$$\sigma_\mu^2 = \frac{\bar{s}^2}{n_1 + n_2} = \frac{n_1 s_1^2 + n_2 s_2^2}{(n_1 + n_2)^2}$$

$$= \frac{50(35)^2 + 100(40)^2}{(100 + 50)^2} = 9.83,$$

$$\sigma_\mu = \sqrt{9.83} = \$3.14.$$

This method for combining sample evidence involves the pooling of the evidence from two samples before a probability distribution of the parameter is constructed. It is not the equivalent of taking a prior distribution based on the first sample and revising it through Bayes' theorem in the light of the evidence of the second sample. The effective difference is in using a pooled estimate of the population variance of single observations. Consider the case of the mean. A normal subjective prior distribution would be combined with large-sample evidence, where the subscript "1" represents the prior distribution, by

$$\hat{\mu} = \frac{\left(\frac{1}{\sigma_{\mu_1}^2}\right)\hat{\mu}_1 + \left(\frac{1}{s_{\bar{X}}^2}\right)\bar{X}}{\frac{1}{\sigma_{\mu_1}^2} + \frac{1}{s_{\bar{X}}^2}},$$

$$\sigma_\mu^2 = \frac{1}{\frac{1}{\sigma_{\mu_1}^2} + \frac{1}{s_{\bar{X}}^2}}.$$

In the case of two samples, however, we use Eq. (8–21), which involves a pooled estimate of the variance. We do not weight the means of two separate probability distributions of μ by the information content of these separate distributions. Rather, the sample evidence is combined to obtain on the one hand the mean of the probability distribution of μ and on the other hand the variance of the probability distribution of μ conditional on the total evidence. The question of pooling evidence concerning the variance of single observations does not arise when the prior probability is subjective, for then $\sigma_{\mu_1}^2$ carries no implication whatever for σ_X^2.

EXERCISES

8.7   A marketing research agency conducted a survey to determine the average time shoppers spend in a certain metropolitan department

store. For a random sample of 169 customers, $\bar{X} = 47.4$ minutes and $s = 18.2$. Using the normal approximation,
(a) Find the fiducial interval $\mu_{.10}-\mu_{.90}$. *Ans.* 45.61–49.19.
(b) Find the fiducial interval $\mu_{.30}-\mu_{.70}$. *Ans.* 46.67–48.13.
(c) What odds would you give that the mean time spent by all shoppers is less than 50 minutes? *Ans.* About 31 to 1.

8.8 In four trial readings of a "30-second" commercial, an announcer averaged 29.2 seconds with an s^2 of 5.76 seconds. Assuming his reading times to be normally distributed, what are the approximate odds, if he continued to read the commercial in the same manner, that his average reading time would be less than 30 seconds? *Ans.* About 7 to 3.

8.9 A random sample of 16 electronic tubes from a large shipment was submitted to a life test. The sample mean was 750 hours and the sample standard deviation was 40 hours. Assuming a normal distribution of lengths of life,
(a) Find $\sigma^2_{.10}$ and $\sigma^2_{.90}$. *Ans.* 1076, 2807.
(b) Find $\mu_{.01}$ and $\mu_{.99}$. *Ans.* 724.0, 776.0.

8.10 To estimate the total number of vacant single-family housing units in an area, a planning commission took a random sample of 100 of the 5000 city blocks comprising the area. The numbers of vacant single-family housing units were

Number of vacancies	Number of blocks
0	10
1	20
2	35
3	22
4	8
5	5
	100

Using the normal approximations,
(a) Find the 95 per cent confidence limits for the total number of vacant single-family housing units in the area. *Ans.* 9,415–11,885.
(b) What is the fiducial probability that there are over 10,000 vacant single family units in the area? *Ans.* .8485.

8.11 To determine whether there was an increase in audience viewing with the inauguration of a new program schedule, a local TV station arranged for records to be kept by a random sample of 64 families owning sets. The sample mean increase in viewing hours for the station's programs was 1.2 hours per week, and the standard deviation was 6.0 hours. Using the normal approximation,
(a) Plot the power curve from $\mu = -2.0$ to $\mu = 5.0$ at intervals of

.50 for a test of the alternatives $\mu < 0$ and $\mu > 0$ with the critical value at $\bar{X} = +2.5$.

(b) Draw the power curve for the test in (a) with the critical value at $\bar{X} = 0.0$.

(c) What is the probability of $\bar{X} \geq 1.2$ if $\mu = 0.0$?   *Ans.* .05480.

(d) What is the probability that $\mu < 0$ given $\bar{X} = 1.2$?   *Ans.* .05480.

8.12 A random sample of 49 observations on the time taken by workers to perform a certain task yielded a mean of 50.2 minutes and a standard deviation of 7.0 minutes. Subsequently, 176 additional observations produced a mean of 51.1 minutes and a standard deviation of 8.0 minutes. Using large-sample normal approximations,

(a) Find the 90 per cent fiducial limits based on the first sample.
Ans. 48.56–51.84.

(b) Combine the sample evidence to construct the 90 per cent fiducial limits based on the total evidence.   *Ans.* 50.051–51.757.

REFERENCES:

Fisher, R. A., *Statistical Methods and Scientific Inference*, 2nd ed. New York: Hafner Publishing Co., Inc., 1959.

Good, I. J., *Probability and the Weighing of Evidence*. New York: Hafner Publishing Co., Inc., 1950.

Jeffreys, H., *Theory of Probability*, 3rd ed. Oxford: The Clarendon Press, 1961.

Lindley, D. V., *Introduction to Probability and Statistics from a Bayesian Viewpoint*, Part 2, *Inference*. New York: Cambridge University Press, 1965.

Savage, L. J., *The Foundations of Statistical Inference*. London: Methuen & Co., Ltd.; New York: John Wiley & Sons, Inc., 1962.

9

Statistical Inference
for Binomial
and Poisson Parameters

Chapters 7 and 8 on significance tests, decision procedures, and estimation have been concerned with continuous variable characteristics. The variables involved have been the result of a measuring process. The exact values of individual observations could thus fall anywhere along a continuous variable scale, though in any given situation observations can be made only to the degree of precision of a particular measuring instrument.

In Chapter 4 we discussed probability distributions of discrete variables resulting from a process of counting as opposed to measuring. In the present chapter we review this material, and then present methods for making tests of significance, determining decision rules, and estimating the parameters of the populations giving rise to such enumerative data.

9-1   Review of the Binomial and Poisson Distributions

An attribute is one class of either a twofold or manifold classification. For example, we can classify manufactured parts as defective or not defective, families as having incomes of $10,000 or more or below $10,000, or advertisements as appealing or not appealing as rated by housewives.

Parameters of binary populations. The mean and variance of a binary population were introduced in Chapter 4. Belonging to the class (defectiveness, high income, subjective appeal) is given a value of one, and not belonging to the class (not defective, low income, lack of subjective appeal) is given a value of zero. A binary population is then a population of zeros and ones, and its distribution is simply the proportion, or probability, of zeros and of ones.

In Table 9–1 are three different binary populations. For each population the mean, μ, and variance, σ^2, are calculated by familiar methods. The results illustrate what was demonstrated algebraically in Chapter 4: that in a binary population where p is defined as the probability of encountering a specified characteristic,

$$\mu_X = p, \tag{9-1}$$

$$\sigma_X^2 = pq \quad \text{where } q = 1 - p. \tag{9-2}$$

Table 9-1

MEAN AND VARIANCE OF SEVERAL BINARY POPULATIONS

Population I $p = .20$				Population II $p = .60$				Population III $p = .90$		
X	$P(X)$	$X \cdot P(X)$	$X^2 \cdot P(X)$	X	$P(X)$	$X \cdot P(X)$	$X^2 \cdot P(X)$	X	$P(X)$	$X \cdot P(X)$	$X^2 \cdot P(X)$
0	.80	—	—	0	.40	—	—	0	.10	—	—
1	.20	.20	.20	1	.60	.60	.60	1	.90	.90	.90
	1.00	.20	.20		1.00	.60	.60		1.00	.90	.90

$\mu = \Sigma [X \cdot P(X)] = .20,$
$\sigma^2 = \Sigma [X^2 \cdot P(X)] - \mu^2$
$= .20 - .04 = .16.$

$\mu = \Sigma [X \cdot P(X)] = .60,$
$\sigma^2 = .60 - (.60)^2$
$= .60 - .36 = .24.$

$\mu = \Sigma [X \cdot P(X)] = .90,$
$\sigma^2 = .90 - (.90)^2$
$= .90 - .81 = .09.$

Note the relationship between the variance and the mean. There is really only one independent parameter in a binary population, namely p. It happens that the mean is equal to this one parameter, p, and the variance is equal to $p(1 - p)$. All binary populations with $p = .50$ have a variance of $pq = (.50)(.50) = .25$; all binary populations with $p = .10$ or $p = .90$ have a variance of .09; and so on.

The binomial probability distribution. The sampling distribution of the *number* of observations having a given characteristic in a random sample of specified size from an infinite binary population* is given by the succesive terms of the formula $_nC_rp^rq^{n-r}$, where n is the size of sample. We are familiar with the binomial formula from Chapter 4. When the underlying population values are designated as X and can take on only the values zero and one, the binomial formula gives the probabilities of the possible values of the sum of X, or the total number of "successes" in n trials.

---

* If the sampling is from a finite binary population, it must be conducted with replacement.

$$P(r) = P(\Sigma\, X) = {_nC_r}p^r q^{n-r}. \qquad (9\text{-}3)$$

That the mean of the sampling distribution of the *number* of successes in a random sample of size n is np and its variance is npq follow directly from the fundamental theorems for the mean and variance of sums of identical independent random variables.

$$\mu_r = \mu_{\Sigma X} = n\mu_X = np, \qquad (9\text{-}4)$$

$$\sigma_r^2 = \sigma_{\Sigma X}^2 = n\sigma_X^2 = npq. \qquad (9\text{-}5)$$

In some situations we will want to talk about the *proportion* rather than the *number* of successes in a sample of n observations. We will use the designation p', since p already stands for the true proportion in the population. The sample proportion, p', is the mean of the X's in the sample.

$$p' = \frac{\Sigma\, X}{n}.$$

The mean and variance of the sampling distribution of *proportions* are related to those of *numbers* simply through the division by the sample size, n.

$$\mu_{p'} = \mu_{\Sigma X/n} = np\left(\frac{1}{n}\right),$$

$$\mu_{p'} = p. \qquad (9\text{-}6)$$

This is what we would expect. As with means, the mean of the sampling distribution of the statistic is equal to the underlying parameter. For the variance,

$$\sigma_{p'}^2 = \sigma_{\Sigma X/n}^2 = npq\left(\frac{1}{n^2}\right),$$

$$\sigma_{p'}^2 = \frac{pq}{n}. \qquad (9\text{-}7)$$

The sampling distribution of the number of successes is given in Eq. 9-3. The same expression produces the sampling distribution of r/n, or p'. Appendix A gives cumulative probabilities of $r \geq r_o$ for various p values up to $n = 20$. This table gives cumulative probabilities for p values at intervals of .01 up to .50. For p values above .50 the table can be read as giving the probability of r equal to *or less* than $n - r_o$, given p equal to the complement of the indicated value. For example, one can read directly in the table that

$$p(r \geq 3 \,|\, n = 10, p = .20) = .3222.$$

The rule cited tells us that

$$p(r \leq 7 \,|\, n = 10, p = .80) = .3222.$$

The Poisson probability distribution. We learned in Chapter 4 that the Poisson distribution can be used as a probability distribution for the number of occurrences of an event per *unit* of a time or space continuum. In this situation the units are arbitrary divisions of a continuum of time or space, and can be made smaller and smaller. The Poisson formula is derived from the limiting condition as the divisions become smaller, which is to say that the number of units or intervals become more and more numerous.

When r is used for the number of occurrences in an interval of size i, the Poisson formula is

$$P(r) = e^{-\mu}\left(\frac{\mu^r}{r!}\right). \tag{9–8}$$

The parameter, μ, is the mean number of occurrences of the event in intervals of size i. *The variance of a Poisson distribution equals its mean.* Tables of Poisson probabilities give $P(r \leq r_0 \,|\, \mu)$.

9-2 Significance Tests for Binomial and Poisson Parameters

In Chapter 7 we used a four-step format for tests of a single-valued null hypothesis. The steps were (1) state the null hypothesis and the alpha error limitation, (2) identify the appropriate sampling distribution, (3) define the boundaries of the acceptance region for the null hypothesis in accordance with the alpha criterion, and (4) accept or reject the null hypothesis in accordance with the observed sample statistic. In testing a hypothesis about a binomial or a Poisson parameter steps 3 and 4 can be accomplished by computing a probability level based on the statistic given that the null hypothesis is true and comparing this level directly with $\alpha/2$.

For example, a random sample of 16 recent purchasers of an article revealed that 5 had major complaints requiring adjustment. Test the null hypothesis, at an alpha level of .05, that the true proportion having complaints in the population was .10. The steps are

1. $H_0: p = .10$.
2. Binomial distribution, $n = 16$, $p = .10$.
3. Reject H_0 if $P(r \leq 5 \,|\, n, p) \leq .025$ or if $P(r \geq 5 \,|\, n, p) \leq .025$.
4. $P(r \geq 5 \,|\, n = 16, p = .10) = .0170$; reject H_0.

We find that the sample result is in the rejection region of the sampling distribution that prevails when H_0 is true, and thus the risk of rejecting a true hypothesis at the level of significance represented by this sample is less than the specified alpha level.

The test for a Poisson parameter is made in a similar fashion. The tests for binomial and Poisson parameters can be summarized as follows:

Hypothesis	Distribution	Reject hypothesis if
$p = p_0$	Binomial	$P(r \geq r_0 \mid p_0)$ or $P(r \leq r_0 \mid p_0) \leq \alpha/2$
$\mu = \mu_0$	Poisson	$P(r \geq r_0 \mid \mu_0)$ or $P(r \leq r_0 \mid \mu_0) \leq \alpha/2$

In Chapter 4 we learned that in certain circumstances various approximations to the binomial or Poisson distributions are suitable. The situations were summarized in Table 4–7. When the Poisson approximation to a binomial probability is suitable, we use $\mu = np_0$, and find the probability

$$P(r \geq r_0 \mid \mu = np_0) \qquad \text{or} \qquad P(r \leq r_0 \mid \mu = np_0)$$

depending on whether the sample number, r_0, is greater than or less than the expected number under the null hypothesis, np_0. If either of these probabilities is less than $\alpha/2$, the null hypothesis must be rejected.

When the normal approximation to a binomial probability is appropriate, we can find

$$P\left(z \geq \frac{r_0 - .5 - np_0}{\sqrt{np_0 q_0}}\right) \qquad \text{if } r_0 > np_0,$$

or

$$P\left(z \leq \frac{r_0 + .5 - np_0}{\sqrt{np_0 q_0}}\right) \qquad \text{if } r_0 < np_0.$$

When the normal approximation to the Poisson distribution is appropriate, we can find

$$P\left(z \geq \frac{r_0 - .5 - \mu_0}{\sqrt{\mu_0}}\right) \qquad \text{if } r_0 > \mu_0,$$

or

$$P\left(z \leq \frac{r_0 + .5 - \mu_0}{\sqrt{\mu_0}}\right) \qquad \text{if } r_0 < \mu_0.$$

Again, if either member of the pair of probabilities is less than $\alpha/2$, we are in the region of the sampling distribution that calls for rejection of the null hypothesis. A convenient way to remember the continuity correction of half a unit in the numerator of the z expressions is to recall that the adjustment always *reduces* the absolute difference between r_0 and np_0 or μ_0 by half an observation.

EXERCISES

9.1   In an acceptance inspection agreement, a supplier agreed to a procedure in which a satisfactory lot was defined as one with 10 per cent
or fewer defectives. A sample of 100 was to be taken from each lot,
and the lot rejected if the sample yielded 15 or more defectives. Using
the normal approximation, find
(a) The risk to the supplier of having a 10 per cent defective lot rejected.
Ans. .06681.
(b) The risk to the purchaser of accepting a 20 per cent defective lot.
Ans. .08379.

9.2   A bag contains one red and seven white marbles. Eight draws are made
from the bag, with replacement. Using (1) the binomial formula, and
(2) the Poisson approximation, find the probability that in eight such
drawings a red ball is selected exactly three times.   *Ans.* .0561; .0614.

9.3   Find the Poisson approximations to the probabilities in Exercise 9.1.
Does the situation conform to the guidelines for using the Poisson?
Ans. .083; .105; no.

9.4   In the past, 65 per cent of the parties entering a store made no purchases. A recent random sample of 900 parties contained 635 who
made no purchases. At an alpha level of .05, test the hypothesis that
there has been no change in the proportion making no purchases.

9.5   A random sample of 200 contracts of sale revealed ten to be in violation of state statutes. Is this evidence sufficient to conclude that the
true proportion is different from 2.5 per cent?
(a) At an alpha risk level of .05?
(b) At an alpha risk level of .10?

9.6   During a particular week a retailer received 25 requests for discontinued items. Assuming a Poisson process, test the hypothesis, at
alpha = .05, that the mean weekly rate is 16.
(a) Use the Poisson distribution.
(b) Use the normal approximation to the Poisson distribution.

9-3   Determining a Decision Rule in Two-Action Problems

In Chapter 7 we discussed two-action problems in which a decision was
made depending on the value of the statistic, $\bar{X}$, in a sample of size n.
Acceptance sampling based on the number of defectives observed in a specified
sample from each incoming lot is a prime example of a two-action problem
involving a binomial parameter.

   Binomial parameter. Suppose a purchaser has an acceptance sampling
scheme for incoming lots in which a sample of 15 items is taken from each

incoming lot and the lot accepted only if no defectives are found in the sample. Otherwise the lot is held for 100 per cent inspection. The probability of accepting lots of specified true proportions defective is read at $P(r \leq 0)$ in Appendix A for corresponding values of p. Some of these are reproduced in Table 9-2.

Table 9-2

PROBABILITIES OF ACCEPTANCE IN AN ACCEPTANCE SAMPLING SCHEME
WITH $n = 15$ AND ZERO DEFECTIVES TO ACCEPT

Lot proportion defective	Probability of accepting lot
(p)	$P(r \leq 0 \mid p)$
.01	.8601
.02	.7386
.03	.6333
.04	.5421
.05	.4633
.10	.2059
.15	.0874
.20	.0352
.25	.0134

The decision rule provides fairly good assurance against accepting a lot as bad as 25 per cent defective, but not very high assurance that a lot as good as 1 per cent defective will be accepted. Shifting the "rejection number" from one or more defectives to two or more defectives will simply trade off one assurance against the other. If zero or one defective out of 15 permits the lot to "pass" inspection, we get

p	P (accepting lot)
.01	.9904
.25	.0802

There is now good assurance that a 1 per cent defective lot will be accepted, but not very high assurance that a 25 per cent defective lot will be rejected. As was the case before, we can cut down on both kinds of decision error simultaneously only by increasing sample size.

Binomial parameter—Poisson approximation. Suppose the materials management department in the preceding inspection problem decided they should have .99 assurance that a lot as good as 1 per cent defective would be accepted, and .99 assurance that a lot as bad as 10 per cent defective would be rejected. What sample size and decision limit would provide this assurance? Such a problem can be solved only through a trial-and-error procedure by working with the tabled binomial probabilities, and may easily require sample sizes not in readily available tables. However, the Poisson approximation can be conveniently employed. The procedure is detailed in Table 9-3.

Table 9-3

SAMPLE SIZE REQUIRED TO LIMIT BETA ERRORS
DETERMINED FROM POISSON APPROXIMATION

Maximum acceptance number	Rejection error (β_1)			Acceptance error (β_2)		
	μ	np/p	n_{max}	μ	np/p	n_{min}
0				4.6	4.6/.10 =	46
1	.15	.15/.01 =	15	6.6	6.6/.10 =	66
2	.40	.40/.01 =	40	8.5	8.5/.10 =	85
3	.80	.80/.01 =	80	10.0	10.0/.10 =	100
4	1.20	1.20/.01 =	120	12.0	12.0/.10 =	120

The first column lists the maximum acceptance number—that is, the largest number of defects in the sample that will lead to acceptance of the lot. Given each maximum acceptance number, we will then determine a sample size that will limit the rejection error probability to β_1, in this case .01, and also a sample size that will limit the specified acceptance error probability to β_2, also in this case .01. Consider the rejection error entries for a maximum acceptance number of 1. We scan down the column in the Poisson probability table under $r = 1$. We are reading $P(r \leq 1 \,|\, \mu)$. We look for the last, or lowest, μ for which this probability equals or exceeds .99, the acceptance assurance desired. We find this quickly at $\mu = .15$. Since in the Poisson approximation to the binomial distribution $\mu = np$, then $\mu/p = np/p = n$. The β_1 limitation refers to a lot for which $p = .01$, so the n that will secure the β_1 error limitation if a maximum acceptance number of one is employed is $np/p = .15/.01 = 15$. Note that this is a *maximum* sample size because if we increase the sample size beyond this, the probability of rejecting the good lot will exceed β_1.

The entries under acceptance error, or β_2, represent the first, or highest, values of μ for which $P(r \leq$ maximum acceptance number) fails to exceed β_2. We find this occurs for a maximum acceptance number of zero at $\mu = 4.6$, where $P(r \leq 0 \,|\, \mu = 4.6) = .01$, and for a maximum acceptance number of one it occurs at $\mu = 6.6$, where $P(r \leq 1 \,|\, \mu = 6.6) = .01$. You should verify quickly the remaining entries. Here the calculation of np/p yields a *minimum* sample size, because if we decrease the sample size below this, the probability of accepting the (bad) lot will exceed β_2.

Note that if the maximum acceptance number is one, the sample size cannot exceed 15 if β_1 is to be limited to .01, and must equal or exceed 66 if β_2 is to be limited to .01. There is no sample size with this maximum acceptance number that will provide the assurances desired. But as the maximum acceptance numbers are increased, the sample sizes converge, and indeed eventually "cross over." In this case, n_{max} for β_1 and n_{min} for β_2 fortuitously work out to be equal at a maximum acceptance number of four. This is the minimum sample size which, with its associated decision limit, will provide the required limitations on beta errors.

To check the technique through again, try to verify that if the two beta errors in the example are relaxed to .05, any sample size between 64 and 80 with a maximum acceptance number of two will be suitable. Of course, one would then recommend a sample size of 64.

A caution to be observed in applying this technique relates to the goodness of the Poisson approximation to the binomial. The Poisson approximation is good for low values of p, and Chapter 4 suggested a rule of thumb of $p \leq .10$ and $np \leq 5$. In getting a Poisson solution for sample size of $n = 120$ to limit the beta error at $p = .10$, the value of np of 12 exceeds this rule-of-thumb value. The error in the Poisson approximation to the binomial will be on the conservative side for the β_2 calculation, however. That is, the true beta error as calculated from the binomial distribution would be somewhat less than the beta error implied by the Poisson approximation. This results from the fact that the Poisson approximation is less highly skewed to the right than the applicable binomial distribution. The probability density is thus greater in the lower tail of the binomial distribution than in the Poisson approximation, which means that the distance from a low percentile set by β_2 to the mean in the binomial distribution will be less than we allowed by applying the Poisson. The decision limit figured from the Poisson to limit β_2 to .05, for example, actually limits β_2 to some risk less than .05.

Binomial parameter—normal approximation. A normal distribution approximation can be applied to find the decision rule required in a binomial sampling situation provided that the final solution for sample size meets certain requirements. To illustrate, suppose a local marketer of coffee wishes to evaluate his advertising methods. He decides that if 60 per cent or more of the housewives in the local market have heard of his brand, his advertising has been "successful," while if 50 per cent or fewer have heard of his brand, his advertising has been "unsuccessful." He further wants to limit the probability of concluding his advertising has been successful when it was really unsuccessful to .025, and desires a .05 limitation on the probability of concluding that his advertising was unsuccessful when it was in fact successful. How large should a random sample of housewives be and how many should be required to have heard of his brand to consider the advertising a success?

We let n be the sample size and r_c the critical decision number. The values in the problem are

$$p_1 = .50, \quad \beta_1 = .025, \quad p_2 = .60, \quad \beta_2 = .05.$$

The probability, β_1, is an upper-tail limitation and $z_{1-\beta} = 1.96$; β_2 is a lower-tail limitation and $z_{\beta_2} = -1.64$. We have two equations for r_c which derive from separate sampling distributions:

$$r_c = np_1 + z_{1-\beta}\sqrt{np_1q_1},$$

$$r_c = np_2 + z_{\beta_2}\sqrt{np_2q_2}.$$

Solving these equations simultaneously for n yields

$$n = \left(\frac{z_{1-\beta}\sqrt{p_1q_1} - z_{\beta_2}\sqrt{p_2q_2}}{p_2 - p_1}\right)^2. \qquad (9\text{--}9)$$

This can be seen as a special case of Eq. (7–9), since p_1q_1 and p_2q_2 are the standard deviations of the binary populations. With $p_1 = .5$ and $p_2 = .6$, the solution for our example is

$$n = \left[\frac{(1.96)(.50) - (-1.64)(.49)}{.60 - .50}\right]^2 = 17.836^2 = 318.12.$$

The decision limit, r_c, is then

$$r_c = np_1 + z_{1-\beta}\sqrt{np_1q_1}$$
$$= 318.12(.5) + 1.96\sqrt{318.12(.50)(.50)}$$
$$= 159.06 + 1.96(8.820) = 176.3.$$

A sample of 319 housewives should be taken, and the advertising considered a success if 177 or more have heard of the marketer's brand.

This normal approximation method is limited to situations where the resulting sample size is such that np_1 and nq_1 exceed ten and np_2 and nq_2 exceed ten as well. That is, the sample size has to be large enough for the normal approximation to the beta levels to be reasonable. In many cases where this is not so, the Poisson approximation illustrated previously will apply.

Poisson parameter. The Poisson method introduced as an approximation in the case of a binomial parameter can be applied as the exact method for determining sample size when we are sampling a Poisson process. We will reillustrate the numerical example of Table 9–3 in the context of a Poisson process. A manufacturer is concerned with quality of cloth as determined by the number of defects per square yard. A process mean of .1 defects per square yard is considered "good" quality, while 1 defect per square yard is considered "poor" quality. The manufacturer wants a decision rule for sampling large production runs of cloth that will give him .99 assurance of rejecting (reprocessing) poor-quality runs and .99 assurance of accepting (shipping out) good-quality runs. The determination of the number of yards of cloth to inspect and the maximum acceptance number is given in Table 9–4. Compare this with the development of Table 9–3 earlier.

Table 9-4

SAMPLE SIZE REQUIRED TO LIMIT BETA ERRORS—POISSON PARAMETER

Maximum acceptance number	Rejection error (β_1)			Acceptance error (β_2)		
	μ	μ/μ_1	units$_{max}$	μ	μ/μ_2	units$_{min}$
0	—	—	—	4.6	$4.6/1.0 =$	4.6 yd
1	.15	$.15/.1 =$	1.5 yd	6.6	$6.6/1.0 =$	6.6
2	.40	$.40/.1 =$	4.0	8.5	$8.5/1.0 =$	8.5
3	.80	$.80/.1 =$	8.0	10.0	$10.0/1.0 =$	10.0
4	1.20	$1.20/.1 =$	12.0	12.0	$12.0/1.0 =$	12.0

The manufacturer can meet the requirements by sampling 12 yards of cloth from each run and accepting the run oniy if 4 or fewer defects are found.

Poisson parameter—normal approximation. A normal approximation can be applied to determining the decision rule that will meet specified beta errors in reaching a decision about the mean of a Poisson process.

The z expression for the normal approximation to the Poisson, restated as an equation for r_c, the critical decision number, is $r_c = \mu + z\sqrt{\mu}$. Let us define "sample size" in the Poisson situation as a multiple of the units in which the mean expectancy, μ, is expressed. Then, given μ_1 and μ_2 with corresponding β_1 and β_2 limitations, the expressions for the critical decision number in a sample of n become

$$r_c = n\mu_1 + z_{1-\beta}\sqrt{n\mu_1},$$
$$r_c = n\mu_2 + z_{\beta_2}\sqrt{n\mu_2}.$$

Solution for n produces the expression, of a familiar type,

$$n = \left(\frac{z_{1-\beta}\sqrt{\mu_1} - z_{\beta_2}\sqrt{\mu_2}}{\mu_2 - \mu_1}\right)^2 \tag{9–10}$$

Returning to the cloth example, let μ_1 be 9.0 flaws per 100 yards and μ_2 be 16.0 flaws per 100 yards, and suppose the manufacturer wants 95.0 per cent assurance that he will reject quality at or above $\mu_2 = 16.0$, and the same assurance that he will accept quality at or below $\mu_1 = 9.0$. Note here that there is not quite a twofold difference between good and poor quality, while in the previous example there was a tenfold difference. The assurance levels yield $z_{1-\beta} = +1.64$ and $z_{\beta_2} = -1.64$, and the solution is

$$n = \left(\frac{1.64\sqrt{9} - (-1.64)\sqrt{16}}{16 - 9}\right)^2 = \left(\frac{11.48}{7}\right)^2 = 2.69 \text{ hundred yards.}$$

The sample required will be 269 yards of cloth, and the decision point will be

$$r_c = n\mu_1 + z_{1-\beta}\sqrt{n\mu_1}$$
$$= 2.69(9) + 1.64\sqrt{2.69(9)}$$
$$= 24.21 + 1.64\sqrt{24.21} = 24.21 + 8.07 = 32.28.$$

If 32 flaws are found, the lot will be accepted, and 33 flaws will lead to rejection. The limitation on the normal approximation is that $n\mu_1$ and $n\mu_2$ both exceed ten because the beta errors apply to these mean expectancies. This requirement is met in the current example, so we would use the approximation that we have carried through.

EXERCISES

9.7 As a result of a large-scale survey a local brewer was convinced that one-third of the consumers in his area compared his beer favorably with the most popular beer. He decided to take a random sample of 200 consumers each succeeding month to check on changes in preference.

(a) If he is willing to run a 10 per cent risk of erroneously concluding a change has occurred, what sample numbers should lead him to conclude there has been a change in preference? Use the normal approximation.   *Ans.* $r \geq 79; r \leq 55$.

(b) Plot the power curve for the above test at p values from .20 to .50 at intervals of .05.

9.8 Suppose the brewer in Exercise 9.7 is resigned to the fact that changes will occur and is concerned only with deciding whether current preference is less than one-third or greater than one-third.

(a) Find the sample size and decision point that will give him 95 per cent assurance against concluding that preference exceeds one-third when it is really 25 per cent or less, and 95 per cent assurance against concluding that preference is less than one-third when it is really 40 per cent or more.   *Ans.* 102; 32.7.

(b) Find the sample size and decision point for a .05 limitation on the risk of concluding $p > 1/3$ when $p \leq .30$ and a .10 limitation on the risk of concluding $p < 1/3$ when $p \geq .35$.   *Partial Ans.* 743.

9.9 In a clerical operation of transcribing data onto punched cards one incorrect card per hundred is considered satisfactory but four incorrect cards per hundred are considered substandard. Given large batches of cards, what sample size and maximum acceptance number should be employed to give at least .95 assurance against errors of misclassification of either kind?   *Ans.* 300; 6.

9.10 A service facility was designed to handle 50 persons per hour. If demand is more than 60 per hour, management wishes to augment the facility. When persons arrive and cannot be served, they often do not wait, but go elsewhere. Assuming a Poisson process, how many hours must arrivals at the facility be observed

(a) If management wants to distinguish between demand of 50 or less and 60 or more with .10 maximum risk of either kind of misidentification? *Ans. 3.6.*

(b) If the risks in (a) are to be cut to .01? *Ans. 11.9*

(c) What decision point should be established in (a) and in (b)? *Ans. 197.2; 651.9.*

9.11 To test the suitability of selling a new product door-to-door a company considered an experiment. If a salesman could sell as many as 1.0 products per hour they wished to adopt door-to-door selling. If sales were as few as .25 per hour they would abandon the idea completely, and if sales were between these limits they would seek to improve the selling approach. Assuming random selection, find the decision rule required to limit the risk of either kind of terminal decision error to .10.

9.12 Solve for the decision rule in Exercise 9.11 using the normal approximation. Would the resulting decision errors exceed the requirements?

9-4 The Probability Distribution of a Binomial Parameter

In our previous study of the behavior of sample means from normally distributed populations we found that the likelihood of the observed mean given various values for the population mean followed the same distribution function as the sampling distributions. The likelihood function for the observed sample mean given various values for the population mean followed the normal distribution curve if the population variance was known and the Student t if the population variance had to be estimated from the sample. This was because the shape of the sampling distribution in these situations does not depend on the population mean.

We know that the shape of the binomial distribution varies from skewness to the right at low values of p to symmetry at $p = .50$ to skewness to the left at values of p above .50, and that the variance changes with different values of p. Table 9-5 illustrates how the binomial sampling distribution changes in the case of $n = 4$ for selected values of p. The table is arranged so that the sampling distributions for various p values read horizontally.

Reading Table 9-5 vertically gives us for a given observed number of successes, r_o, the values of $P(r_o|p)$ for different values of p. These are the *likelihoods* that form the empirical content of Bayes' theorem. They are the

Table 9-5

BINOMIAL PROBABILITIES FOR EXACT NUMBERS OF
SUCCESSES FOR SELECTED VALUES OF p WITH $n = 4$

p	\multicolumn{5}{c}{r = number of successes}	Total
	0	1	2	3	4	Total
.2	.4096	.4096	.1536	.0256	.0016	1.0000
.4	.1296	.3456	.3456	.1536	.0256	1.0000
.5	.0625	.2500	.3750	.2500	.0625	1.0000
.6	.0256	.1536	.3456	.3456	.1296	1.0000
.8	.0016	.0256	.1536	.4096	.4096	1.0000

equivalent of the probabilities of the sample event given alternative states, $P(E|S)$, in the statement of Bayes' theorem,

$$\frac{P(S) \cdot P(E|S)}{P(E)} = P(S|E).$$

Values of the likelihood function could be determined for many more values of p than are shown in Table 9–5. For example, given $r_o = 1$, the following values could be read from the binomial table:

p	$P(r = 1 \mid n = 4)$
.23	.4200
.24	.4214
.25	.4219
.26	.4214
.27	.4201

This series of likelihoods suggests what is true in the case of binomial sampling: that the sample proportion is the *maximum-likelihood* estimate of the population proportion. The probability of the sample outcome, given $p = .25$, is greater than for any other value of p. Our principal concern, however, is to explore how the evidence, which can be summarized by the likelihood function, can be converted into a probability distribution of the binomial parameter conditional on the evidence.

Bayesian solution. The Bayesian solution to the construction of a probability distribution of the parameter, p, conditional on the evidence, r_o, is to invoke prior probabilities which can be combined with the likelihood to produce a posterior distribution of p in the light of the evidence. This solution is the beta distribution, which has the density

$$f(p \mid \alpha, \beta) = \frac{(\alpha + \beta + 1)!}{\alpha! \, \beta!} p^\alpha (1 - p)^\beta.$$

In this distribution, α and β are the conventional symbols for the parameters. They should not be confused with other uses of these same symbols.

In applications involving a binomial parameter, $\alpha = a + r_o$ and $\beta = b + (n - r_o)$, where a and b represent parameters of a prior beta distribution of p, and r_o and $n - r_o$ are the observed number of successes and failures in a sequence of n draws from the population.

The beta distribution with parameters a and b (the prior distribution) or with α and β (the posterior distribution) has an integral, or total area, of 1.0. The mean and variance of the beta distribution of p are

$$\mu_p = \frac{\alpha + 1}{\alpha + \beta + 2}, \tag{9-11}$$

$$\sigma_p^2 = \frac{(\alpha + 1)(\beta + 1)}{(\alpha + \beta + 2)^2(\alpha + \beta + 3)}. \tag{9-12}$$

The values of the parameters of the beta distribution must both exceed -1.0. When both are equal to zero, the distribution of p is uniform (equal likelihood) over the interval from zero to 1.0. The mean and variance of p from Eqs. (9–11) and (9–12) will then be

$$\mu_p = \frac{0 + 1}{0 + 0 + 2} = \frac{1}{2},$$

$$\sigma_p^2 = \frac{(0 + 1)(0 + 1)}{(0 + 0 + 2)^2(0 + 0 + 3)} = \frac{1}{12}.$$

In the formulation given here for the beta distribution, the parameters can take on integer values only, because they are involved in the factorials in the expression of the beta distribution function. A more general definition of the beta distribution function can be given in which the parameters can take on any real numbers exceeding -1.0. However, for the construction of a posterior distribution based on the evidence in combination with equal priors, this more complete formulation is unnecessary. With the parameters (a and b) of the prior distribution at zero, α and β will always be integers because r_o and $n - r_o$, the observed numbers of successes and failures, are always integers.

It is clear that with uniform priors, the probability distribution of p conditional on the evidence observed will be determined by the likelihood of the observed number of successes as a function of p. The posterior distribution of p will then have a beta distribution with $\alpha = r_o$ and $\beta = n - r_o$. From Eqs. (9–11) and (9–12) it can be seen that μ_p approaches $r_o/n = p'$, as n increases. In addition, σ_p^2 approaches $p'q'/n$ as the information, r_o and $n - r_o$, increases, for

$$\sigma_p^2 \simeq \frac{\alpha \cdot \beta}{(\alpha + \beta)^2(\alpha + \beta)} = \frac{r_0(n - r_0)}{n^2 \cdot n}$$

$$= \frac{r_0}{n} \cdot \frac{n - r_0}{n} \cdot \frac{1}{n} = \frac{p'q'}{n}.$$

Finally, the beta distribution approaches the normal distribution as α and β increase. A large sample approximation to the posterior distribution of the binomial parameter when the prior distribution embodies equal likelihood is, then, a normal distribution with

$$\mu_p = p', \tag{9-13}$$

$$\sigma_p^2 = \frac{p'q'}{n}. \tag{9-14}$$

This can be summed up by the statement that, for large-sample evidence, $P(p \leq p_0) = P(\hat{z} \leq z_0)$, where $\hat{z}$ is normally distributed, and

$$\hat{z}_0 = \frac{p_0 - p'}{\sqrt{p'q'/n}}. \tag{9-15}$$

Table 9–6 gives a guide to the sample size required for this approximation to be reasonable. Note that as p' departs from .50, the required sample size increases fairly rapidly.

Table 9-6

RECOMMENDED MINIMUM SAMPLE SIZES FOR USE OF THE NORMAL
APPROXIMATION TO THE DISTRIBUTION OF THE TRUE PROPORTION

Sample result (p')	Minimum sample size
.50	30
.40	60
.30	150
.20	300
.10	900
.05	2,000
.02	5,000
.01	10,000

Fiducial method. A fiducial method is available that reduces considerably the size of the sample required. Recall that the fiducial argument depends upon the sampling distribution's having constant shape and variance regardless of the value of the parameter considered. Although this is not true for the natural form of binomial sampling distributions, there is a transformation of p' that yields normal sampling distributions with variance independent of p down to fairly modest sample sizes. This is the trigonometric function 2 arcsine $\sqrt{p'}$, where the angle is measured in radians (1 radian = $180/\pi$ degrees). We will designate the transformation as g, the transformed binomial parameter as H, and the transformed sample proportion as h. That is, $H = g(p)$ and $h = g(p')$. A table accomplishing the transformation is available in Appendix M.

The transformed variable h is normally distributed with mean and variance

$$\mu_h = H, \tag{9-16}$$

$$\sigma_h^2 = \frac{1}{n}. \tag{9-17}$$

The standard normal deviate is then

$$z = \frac{h - H}{1/\sqrt{n}}, \tag{9-18}$$

and application of the fiducial argument will yield

$$\hat{z} = \frac{H - h}{1/\sqrt{n}} \quad \text{and} \quad H = h + \frac{\hat{z}}{\sqrt{n}}. \tag{9-19}$$

Suppose a sample of 64 yields 16 successes. We then have $p' = .25$, and we can establish, for example, the 95 per cent fiducial limits for p. This involves setting fiducial limits on H and then converting back to obtain the limits for p.

$$h = g(p') = 1.0472,$$

$$H_{.025} = h + \frac{\hat{z}_{.025}}{\sqrt{n}} = 1.0472 - .245 = .8022,$$

$$H_{.975} = h + \frac{\hat{z}_{.975}}{\sqrt{n}} = 1.0472 + .245 = 1.2922.$$

To transform the fiducial limits for H to fiducial limits for p we read out from Appendix M that $p = .152$ corresponds to the limit .8022 and $p = .362$ corresponds to the limit 1.2922. Thus, $.152 - .362$ is the 95 per cent fiducial interval for p.

The arcsine transformation can be used as long as $np'q'$ exceeds 10. In the above example $np'q' = 12$. With $p' = .25$, Table 9-6 indicates that the sample-size requirement for a normal approximation with variance $p'q'/n$ would be in excess of $n = 200$.

For an example where either the large-sample normal approximation or the arcsine transformation may be employed, consider the probability that p equals or exceeds .225 given sample evidence of $r = 80$ in a sample of 400. In the large-sample approximation we would have $p' = 80/400 = .200$ and

$$\hat{z}_0 = \frac{p_o - p'}{\sqrt{p'q'/n}} = \frac{.225 - .200}{\sqrt{(.20)(.80)/400}} = 1.25,$$

$$P(p \geq .225) = P(\hat{z} \geq 1.25) = .1056.$$

The arcsine transformation would presumably yield the more accurate answer:

$$\hat{z}_0 = \frac{H_o - h}{1/\sqrt{n}} = \frac{g(p_o) - g(p')}{1/\sqrt{n}} = \frac{.9884 - .9273}{.05} = 1.22,$$

$$P(p \geq .225) = P(\hat{z} \geq 1.22) = .1112.$$

9-5 The Probability Distribution of a Poisson Parameter

A theorem of Bayesian statistics states that if a Poisson parameter is characterized by vague prior knowledge, and r occurrences are observed in an interval of length i, then the posterior distribution of the mean rate of occurrence in intervals of length i is distributed as $\chi^2/2$ with $2r$ degrees of freedom.* For example, suppose in a five-week period 12 requests are received for a certain technical document. Assuming the process to generate a Poisson distribution with constant mean, μ, the probability distribution of 2μ, conditional on the evidence, follows the chi-square distribution with 24 degrees of freedom. The .05 and .95 levels of 2μ, for example, can then be read from the tabled chi-square distribution. They are 13.8 and 36.4, respectively. Taking one-half of these values yields 6.9 and 18.2, which are the 5th and 95th percentiles of the posterior probability distribution of the Poisson mean, μ.

A direct fiducial approach is not available because the variance of the sampling distribution of r depends on μ through $\sigma_r = \sqrt{\mu}$. However, as with the binomial, a transformation is available that results in a very nearly normal sampling distribution with variance independent of the relevant parameter. Specifically, $\sqrt{r}$ is approximately normally distributed with mean $\sqrt{\mu}$ and variance $1/4$ for any μ as long as $\mu \geq 10$. This means that a fiducial distribution of $\sqrt{\mu}$ can safely be constructed when $r \geq 16$ by taking

$$\sqrt{\mu} = \sqrt{r} + \frac{\hat{z}}{2}.$$

In the example of 12 requests for a technical paper, 90 per cent fiducial limits for μ can be obtained by

---

* D. V. Lindley, *Introduction to Probability and Statistics from a Bayesian Viewpoint*, Part 2, *Inference* (New York: Cambridge University Press, 1965), p. 155.

$$\mu_{.05} = \left(\sqrt{12} - \frac{1.64}{2}\right)^2 = (3.464 - .82)^2 = 2.644^2 = 6.99,$$

$$\mu_{.95} = \left(\sqrt{12} + \frac{1.64}{2}\right)^2 = (3.464 + .82)^2 = 4.284^2 = 18.35.$$

These are very close to the 5th and 95th percentiles of the posterior probability distribution of μ obtained earlier. The standard normal deviate for the fiducial distribution is

$$\hat{z} = \frac{\sqrt{\mu} - \sqrt{r}}{\frac{1}{2}} = 2(\sqrt{\mu} - \sqrt{r}). \tag{9–20}$$

If the observed number of occurrences is large enough, a normal fiducial distribution of μ can be constructed directly. This approximation is through the standard normal deviate

$$\hat{z} = \frac{\mu - r}{\sqrt{r}}. \tag{9–21}$$

This approximation relies on the central limit theorem to assure normality plus the practical effect that the range of sampling error will be so restricted that $\sqrt{r}$ will not vary much from $\sqrt{\mu}$ over the effective range of error. Let us try this technique in comparison with the square root transformation for constructing the 95 per cent fiducial limits for the Poisson parameter conditional on observing 25 occurrences. The normal $\hat{z}$ approximation would produce

$$r \pm 1.96\sqrt{r} = 25 \pm 1.96\sqrt{25}$$
$$= 15.2 - 34.8.$$

The square root transformation would have given

$$\left[\sqrt{r} \pm \frac{1.96}{2}\right]^2 = (5 \pm 0.98)^2,$$

$$4.02^2 \text{ to } 5.98^2 \qquad \text{or} \qquad 16.16\text{–}35.76.$$

The square root transformation is to be preferred, but the two methods give very nearly the same result when the number of occurrences exceeds 50.

9-6 Some Exact Methods

Probabilities from the beta distribution of a binomial parameter given uniform priors and sample evidence can be read from a table of binomial probabilities as follows:

$$P(p \leq p_o) = P(r \geq r_o + 1 \mid n + 1, p_o), \tag{9-22}$$
$$P(p \geq p_o) = P(r \leq r_o \mid n + 1, p_o). \tag{9-23}$$

If we read across the row for $r_o + 1$ out of $n + 1$ in the binomial probability table, Eq. (9–22) will yield cumulative lower-tail probabilities for the posterior distribution of p. Suppose two successes are observed in six observations from a binomial process when the investigator has virtually no prior knowledge about p. What is the probability that p does not exceed .50? We read

$$P(p \leq .50) = P(r \geq 3 \mid n = n_o + 1 = 7, p = .50) = .7734.$$

Suppose, in this same situation, that we want to find $p_{.10}$ and $p_{.90}$. Here, we read across the $r = 3$ row for $n = 7$ looking for the binomial probability equal to .10. We find the tabled probability .1005 at $p = .17$, telling us that

$$P(p \leq .17) = P(r \geq 3 \mid n = 7, p = .17) = .1005.$$

This is as close as we can read for $p_{.10}$ given the make-up of the table. For $p_{.90}$, continue reading across the same row looking for the tabled probability .90. We do not find it because, having read out to the $p = .50$ column, we have only cumulated the lower-tail beta probability up to .7734. At this point, drop down to the row giving the complement of .7734, namely .2266, which is the $r \geq 5$ row in this case. Now read back along this row looking for the tabled probability .10. At $p = .40$ we find .0963. This is the binomial probability,

$$P(r \geq 5 \mid n = 7, p = .40) = .0963.$$

From this probability we know that

$$P(r \leq 2 \mid n = 7, p = .60) = .0963$$

and, therefore, in accordance with Eq. (9–23),

$$P(p \geq .60) = P(r \leq 2 \mid n = 7, p = .60) = .0963$$

and

$$P(p \leq .60) = 1 - .0963 = .9037.$$

Thus, $p_{.1005} = .17$ and $p_{.9037} = .60$, as close as can be conveniently read in the table for $p_{.10}$ and $p_{.90}$.

Suppose the process is observed further and that by the time 49 observations have been made 16 successes have been observed. What is the probability that p is less than .45?

$$P(p \leq .45) = P(r = 17 \mid n = 50, p = .45) = .9573.$$

Since $np'q' = 49(16/49)(33/49)$ exceeds 10 in the situation above, let us see how the arcsine transformation approximates the above probability.

$$\hat{z}_o = \frac{H_o - h}{1/\sqrt{n}} = \frac{g(p_o) - g(p')}{1/\sqrt{n}} = \frac{1.4706 - 1.2175}{1/\sqrt{49}} = 1.77,$$

$$P(p \le .45) = P(\hat{z} \le 1.77) = .9616.$$

Probabilities relevant to a Poisson parameter can be read from Poisson tables in the following manner when prior knowledge is vague or absent.

$$P(\mu \le \mu_o) = P(r \ge r_o | \mu_o), \tag{9-24}$$

$$P(\mu \ge \mu_o) = P(r < r_o | \mu_o). \tag{9-25}$$

Recall the example in which 12 requests were received over a five-week period for a certain technical document. What is the probability that the long-run average demand per five-week period is 10 or less?

$$P(\mu \le 10) = P(r \ge 12 | \mu = 10) = 1 - P(r \le 11 | \mu = 10)$$
$$= 1 - .697 = .303.$$

What is the probability that $\mu \ge 15$?

$$P(\mu \ge 15) = P(r < 12 | \mu = 15) = P(r \le 11 | \mu = 15) = .185.$$

If one wants to read a cumulative probability distribution of μ from the Poisson table of Appendix B, the most convenient method is to read down the column for *one less than* the observed number of occurrences to obtain the *upper*-tail probabilities for the distribution of μ. This follows from Eq. (9–25). In the current example, $r_o - 1 = 12 - 1 = 11$, and we can read, for example, that

$$P(r \le 11 | \mu = 7.0) = .947 = P(\mu \ge 7.0).$$

Therefore, $\mu_{.053} = 7.0$. Continuing, we find that $\mu_{.945} = 18$ because

$$P(r \le 11 | \mu = 18) = .055 = P(\mu \ge 18).$$

These results are exact, and in agreement with the chi-square technique discussed in Sec. 9–6. The same example discussed there produced $\mu_{.05} = 6.9$ and $\mu_{.95} = 18.2$. In the chi-square tables we are restricted to convenient percentiles, while in the Poisson table we are restricted to convenient values of μ.

9-7 Combining Sample Evidence

In Sec. 8–6 we saw that an inference based upon two samples could be accomplished by pooling the evidence of the two samples. The same method is applicable to two (or more) samples from binomial or Poisson processes. In the binomial situation we have for two samples:

$$\hat{\mu} = \frac{r_1 + r_2}{n_1 + n_2} = \bar{p}. \tag{9-26}$$

If $n_1 + n_2$ is small, probability statements about p can be made by consulting the appropriate tabled binomial probability as in Eqs. (9–22) and (9–23). If $(n_1 + n_2)\bar{p}\bar{q}$ exceeds 10, a fiducial distribution for p can be constructed using the arcsine transformation as in Eq. (9–19). Where

$$h = g(\bar{p}) \qquad \text{and} \qquad H = g(p),$$

$$\hat{z} = \frac{H - h}{1/\sqrt{n_1 + n_2}}. \tag{9-27}$$

Finally, if $n_1 + n_2$ meets the sample size requirements of Table 9–6, a normal fiducial distribution p can be constructed. In this case

$$\hat{z} = \frac{p_0 - \bar{p}}{\sqrt{\bar{p}\bar{q}/(n_1 + n_2)}} \tag{9-28}$$

For a Poisson parameter, if r_1 occurrences are observed in an interval of length i_1, and r_2 occurrences in an interval of length i_2, then the probability distribution 2μ in intervals of length $i_1 + i_2$ will be distributed as chi-square with $2(r_1 + r_2)$ degrees of freedom. This simply amounts to treating the combined sample just as we treated a single sample previously.

If $r_1 + r_2$ exceeds 16 or so, a fiducial distribution employing the total evidence can be constructed through the square root transformation. The mean rate will be in terms of an interval of length $i_1 + i_2$ in the expression

$$\hat{z} = \frac{\sqrt{\mu} - \sqrt{r_1 + r_2}}{\frac{1}{2}}. \tag{9-29}$$

Finally, if $r_1 + r_2$ exceeds 50 or so, a normal fiducial distribution of μ in intervals of length $i_1 + i_2$ can be constructed through

$$\hat{z} = \frac{\mu - (r_1 + r_2)}{\sqrt{r_1 + r_2}}. \tag{9-30}$$

As is true for a single sample, if one desires to express the mean rate in terms of intervals of some other length, this is easily done. If the evidence consisted of eight days of observation, and we were concerned with the mean rate per day, fiducial limits for the mean rate in periods of eight days would be established, and then simply divided by eight. If a summary is to be made by giving the mean and standard deviation of the fiducial distribution of the daily rate, the mean *and* standard of the eight-day rate would both be divided by eight.

EXERCISES

9.13 A random sample of 79 accounts receivable revealed 17 to be over six months delinquent. Eleven of the delinquent accounts proved to be uncollectable.

(a) Use the arcsine transformation to find the probability that the proportion of delinquent accounts exceeds .15; .25; .35.
$$Ans. .9332; .2297; .0037.$$

(b) Use the binomial table to find the probability that the proportion of delinquent accounts that are uncollectable is greater than .20; .40; .60; .80. *Ans.* 1.0000; .9797; .6257; .0513.

9.14 Find the 95 per cent fiducial interval for the true proportion in 9.13(a). Approximate $p_{.025}$ and $p_{.975}$ from the binomial table for the proportion in 9.13(b). *Ans.* .132–.312; .41, .83.

9.15 Refer to Exercise 9.5. Using the Poisson approximation to the binomial process, find

(a) The 5th and 95th percentiles of the probability distribution of the mean number in samples of 100. *Ans.* 2.725; 7.85.

(b) The probability that the true proportion exceeds 2.5 per cent.
$$Ans. .968.$$

9.16 In a random sample of 300 subscribers to a magazine, 138 had heard of a new product advertised in the magazine and 69 had tried the product. Using (1) the arcsine transformation and (2) the large-sample normal approximation, find

(a) The probability that more than 50 per cent of the subscribers had heard of the product. *Ans.* .08226; .08226.

(b) The probability that more than 20 per cent of the subscribers had tried the product. *Ans.* .8980; .8907.

(c) The 95 per cent fiducial intervals for the proportion of subscribers who had heard of the product and the proportion of subscribers who had tried the product.
Ans. .404–.517 and .4036–.5164; .184–.279 and .1824–.2776.

9.17 A merchandiser kept an account of the requests for a particular style of floor covering that he could obtain on special order. During the first month he had 7 requests, after two months he had 16 requests, and after five months he had 32 requests. Assuming a Poisson process, employ the table of Poisson probabilities to find the probability that the true demand level is less than 5 per month.

(a) Given the evidence of the first month. *Ans.* .238.

(b) Given the evidence after two months. *Ans.* .049.

9.18 For the data of Exercise 9.17 estimate the probability that the mean demand level is less than 5 per month given the evidence of all five months using (1) the square root transformation and (2) the large-sample normal approximation.   *Ans.* .09510; .1075.

9.19 Refer to Exercise 9.4.

   (a) Find the 90 and 95 per cent fiducial intervals for the proportion of parties making no purchase.   *Ans.* .681–.731; .676–.736.

   (b) What are the odds that there has been an increase in the proportion of parties making a purchase?   *Ans.* 9999 to 1.

9.20 An inspection sampling scheme called for a sample of size 10 with the lot to be rejected if one or more defectives were found.

   (a) If exactly one defective is found, what are the odds that the lot contains more than 20 per cent defectives?   *Ans.* 32 to 68.

   (b) If no defectives are found, what are the odds that the lot contains less than 10 per cent defectives?   *Ans.* 69 to 31.

REFERENCES

Bierman, H., C. P. Bonini, L. E. Fouraker, and R. K. Jaedicke, *Quantitative Analysis for Business Decisions*, rev. ed. Homewood, Ill.: Richard D. Irwin, Inc., 1965.

Lindley, D. V., *Introduction to Probability and Statistics from a Bayesian Viewpoint*, Part 2, *Inference*. New York: Cambridge University Press, 1965.

Schlaifer, R., *Probability and Statistics for Business Decisions*. New York: McGraw-Hill Book Company, 1959.

10

The
Economics
of Decision Theory

Previous chapters in this book have been devoted to statistical tests of significance and statistical decision tests. We learned how to set a rule for a decision test that would keep decision errors within prescribed limits. The error limitations were strictly of a statistical nature—that is, they were limits to the probability of a prescribed decision error given a specified value (or values) of the parameter, or true state. If such limitations were based on the *economic* consequences of decision errors, these consequences were not explicit in the methods employed.

In this chapter we turn to methods for decision making under uncertainty that take explicit account of the economic consequences of alternative acts given different states of affairs that may prevail. Decisions made employing these methods take account of both the probabilities of error and the costs of error. Chapter 10 is devoted to an explanation of the basic procedures and Chapter 11 to methods for determining the optimal amount of information to gather in order to make terminal decisions employing these procedures.

10-1 The Payoff Table

A sales agent is considering whether he should take on a new product which can be sold to his existing customers during the coming selling season. The product is such that it would be sold only one to a customer. The salesman is considering three strategies. First, he could operate as always, trying to sell the new item along with his regular line. Second, he could add a secretary in his office to distribute literature and handle inquiries about the product, thereby increasing his effectiveness and his costs as well. Third, he could hire an assistant to make calls to promote the new item. This would be more productive than the second alternative but more costly as well, since a larger fixed salary and traveling expenses would be involved.

The payoff from each of the three strategies depends upon a state of nature. In this problem we shall assume that the sales agent has determined (correctly) that the payoff depends on whether the initial acceptability of the product to his customers is high or low. Given the two possible states of nature (high or low acceptability), and the three strategies, we might find the payoff table to be of the type given in Table 10–1(a). If initial acceptance is low (state A), the cost of the office-based strategy 2 is greater than the revenue it creates. The net payoff is −40, a loss. Strategy 1 produces a small net return, and strategy 3 produces the best net return because of the face-to-face contact between customers and the assistant salesman. If initial acceptance is high (state B), the more attention devoted to the product the higher the payoff.

The sales agent does not know in advance which of the two states will prove to be true. If Table 10–1(a) describes the possible payoffs, he should nevertheless always choose strategy 3. Strategy 3 will produce the best payoff

Table 10-1

EXAMPLES OF TYPES OF PAYOFF TABLES

(a) A Dominant Strategy

State	Strategy 1	2	3
A	20	−40	40
B	140	170	210

(b) Dominated Strategy

State	Strategy 1	2	3
A	20	40	−40
B	140	170	210

(c) No Dominant or Dominated Strategy

The Salesman's Payoff Table

State	Strategy 1	2	3
A: Low acceptance	40	20	−40
B: High acceptance	140	170	210

(d) No Dominant State

State	Strategy 1	2	3
A	20	40	80
B	70	30	−80

regardless of which state of nature proves to be true. Strategy 3 is *dominant* over the other two. When a payoff table contains a strategy that is dominant over all other strategies, there is no decision problem.

A second possible form of payoff table appears in Table 10–1(b). We can eliminate strategy 1 from consideration because it is dominated by strategy 2. When we compare strategies 2 and 3 we see that 2 is best if state A occurs, but 3 is best if state B occurs.

In Table 10–1(c), which we shall assume represents the actual situation in the decision problem, we have a third type of payoff table. No strategy is dominant over one or both of the other two. Consequently, none of the strategies can be disregarded at this point in the discussion.

We have seen that, given n states, strategy a dominates strategy b if the payoff V_{ia} exceeds V_{ib} for any given state, i. One may speak also of dominant states. State a dominates state b if for any strategy j the payoff V_{aj} exceeds V_{bj}. In the payoff table 10–1(c) state B dominates state A. High initial acceptance produces a higher payoff than low initial acceptance regardless of which strategy is selected. This is true of all the payoff tables thus far illustrated. It is not, however, true in payoff Table 10–1(d). Here, if the agent operates as usual (strategy 1), he will be better off if initial acceptance is high. However, if he elects to operate with the office-based helper or the field assistant (strategies 2 or 3), he will do better if initial acceptance is low. Increasing sales assistance under low initial product acceptance produces increasing payoffs, while under high initial acceptance, increasing effort yields smaller payoffs. This might reflect a situation where increasing sales effort was largely wasted if customers were already "sold" on the product. We will concentrate our discussion on payoff tables with *no dominant or dominated strategies but with dominant states throughout*. Such a table is exemplified by 10–1(c), which we will assume is *the* payoff table for the agent's decision problem.

10-2 Decision Rules Under Uncertainty

A number of rules for selecting a strategy under complete uncertainty have been suggested. Complete uncertainty means that nothing is known about the likelihood of any state of nature. The first decision rule is the *maximin gain* (or minimax loss) rule. In this rule you consider the worst payoff under each strategy and select the strategy whose poorest payoff is best. You maximize the minimum gain that might occur, or in the case of losses you minimize the maximum loss that could occur. In the salesman's payoff table—10–1(c)— strategy 1 has a minimum gain of 40—higher than the minimum gain under any other strategy. The maximin rule dictates strategy 1.

Another rule that has been suggested is the *maximax gain* (or minimin loss) rule. Under this rule you select the strategy whose maximum gain is the highest. If the payoff table is comprised wholly of losses, or costs, the rule

dictates adopting the strategy whose minimum loss is lowest. In the salesman's problem the payoff 210 under strategy 3 is the maximum of the maximal
gains under the various strategies. The maximax rule would dictate strategy 3.

In the salesman's decision problem, the maximin strategy protects
against a state of low product acceptance, and the maximax strategy prepares
for a state of high acceptance. The payoff table has a dominant state throughout. In such a situation, the maximin strategy will be associated with the
state that is least favorable *under all strategies*, and the maximax strategy will
be associated with the state that is most favorable *under all strategies*. In
other words, with a dominant state the maximax strategy is the one that
yields the best payoff under the generally most favorable state, and the
maximin strategy yields the best payoff under the generally least favorable
state. Under these conditions we might say that the adopter of the maximax
strategy *acts as* one would act if he were certain that the most favorable state
(in this case B) would occur, and the maximin strategist *acts as* one would act
who was certain that the least favorable state (in this case A) would occur.
An optimist would be a "maximaxer" and a pessimist would be a "mini-
maxer."

A third decision rule under uncertainty is often called the *minimax
regret* rule. Under this rule the decision-maker considers each strategy and
state combination and asks himself how much payoff is sacrificed by selecting
a given strategy compared to the strategy that would be best if the state
involved were to come to pass. Thus each payoff in a row corresponding to a
particular state is compared to the highest payoff in that row. These differences
are called *regrets*, and in the salesman's problem the regrets are as shown
below.

	Original Payoffs				Regrets		
	Strategy				Strategy		
State	1	2	3	State	1	2	3
A	40	20	−40	A	0	20	80
B	140	170	210	B	70	40	0

If strategy 2 is selected and product acceptance turns out to be low
(state A), the decision-maker will regret his choice of strategy. The measure
of his regret will be the additional payoff he lost by not selecting the best
strategy given state A. Regrets correspond to the concept of opportunity
costs in economics. The opportunity cost of one course of action is the return
foregone by not selecting an optimal alternative course. The opportunity
costs, also termed *opportunity losses*, in the "Regrets" table are *conditional*
opportunity losses. As with the underlying payoffs, the opportunity losses of
any strategy are conditional on the occurrence of a particular state.

The minimax regret rule calls for selecting the strategy whose maximum regret is a minimum—that is, minimizing the maximum regret. This

rule would dictate strategy 2. Its maximum regret is 40, while the maximum regrets for strategies 1 and 3 are 70 and 80, respectively.

At this point our salesman has three recommended rules for selecting a strategy under a condition of complete uncertainty about the true state. Each of these rules selects a different one of his three available strategies. But we will ask him to consider another idea—namely, the concept of Bayesian strategies. With this consideration, however, the assumption of complete uncertainty about states is abandoned.

10-3 Bayesian Strategies Under Partial Uncertainty

We have seen in the salesman's problem that adopting the maximin gain rule is equivalent to acting as if the probability that the generally least favorable state (A) will occur is 1.0, and adopting the maximax gain rule is equivalent to acting as if the probability that the generally most favorable state (B) will occur is 1.0. So far, the minimax regret rule just seems to effect some kind of "hedge" between the consequences that can occur under the two states. But these three rules are rules for decision making under complete uncertainty. This means that no information is available about the probabilities of the various states. Suppose we could get such information. We know that were the probability for high acceptance (state B) 1.0, we would select strategy 3, and were the probability of low acceptance (state A) 1.0, we would select strategy 1.

A Bayesian strategy is a strategy that is optimal under some set of probabilities of the true states. The criterion of optimality is maximum expected gain or minimum expected loss if payoffs are expressed as losses. Defining V_{ij} as the payoff under the ith state of nature given the jth strategy, we find the expected value of the jth strategy to be

$$\bar{V}_j = V_{1j}{\cdot}P(S_1) + V_{2j}{\cdot}P(S_2) + \ldots + V_{rj}{\cdot}P(S_r),$$

$$\bar{V}_j = \sum_{i=1}^{r} V_{ij}{\cdot}P(S_i). \tag{10-1}$$

Strategy 1 is the Bayesian strategy for $P(A) = 1.0$, and strategy 3 is the Bayesian strategy for $P(A) = 0$. Strategy 1 has the highest return if low acceptance is a certainty, and strategy 3 has the highest return if high acceptance is a certainty. But what about other probabilities? Using P for the probability of state A in our example, we find the expected value of each strategy to be

$$\bar{V}_1 = 40P + 140(1 - P) = 140 - 100P,$$
$$\bar{V}_2 = 20P + 170(1 - P) = 170 - 150P,$$
$$\bar{V}_3 = -40P + 210(1 - P) = 210 - 250P.$$

These equations are graphed in Fig. 10–1. The expected values of strategies 2 and 3 are equal at $P = .40$, and the expected values of strategies 1 and 2 are equal at $P = .60$. Within the range of $P(A)$ from .40 to .60 strategy 2 has the highest expected value.

We find, then, that strategy 3 is the Bayesian strategy if the probability of low product acceptance is below .40. Strategy 2 is the Bayesian strategy from .40 to .60, and strategy 1 is the Bayesian strategy if the probability of low product acceptance exceeds .60.

Subjective and objective probabilities. We can now view the salesman's problem in a different light. Under complete uncertainty, he could choose among maximin gain, maximax gain, and minimax regret as rules for selecting a strategy. If, however, he can come up with a statement about the probability that the product will have a low initial acceptance level, the Bayesian criterion of maximum expected gain will determine his strategy. If he is

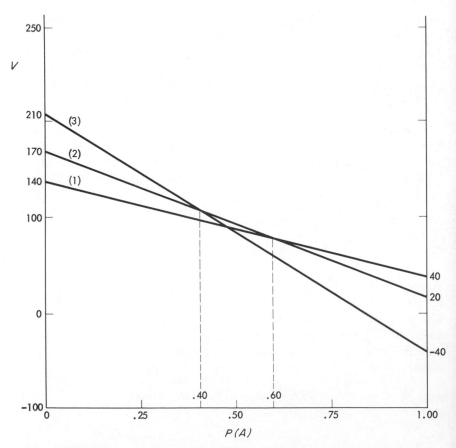

FIGURE 10-1 Bayesian strategies for the salesman's decision problem

prepared to state that this probability is less than .40, then his optimal strategy is the third alternative: to hire an assistant to do "missionary" promotion. Once we have a probability statement about the possible states, selection of the optimal terminal decision is straightforward.

To be useful, "low initial acceptance level" should have been defined in some way when the salesman calculated the payoff figures for the different strategies. The point has not been a critical one up to now. Suppose our salesman tells us that initial acceptance means expressing an interest in the product, and that low initial acceptance means that 33 per cent or less of his customers are interested. His decision problem is now reduced to assessing the probability that the proportion of interested customers in the population is .33 or less. Defining p as the population proportion interested in the product, we can say that the salesman will

adopt strategy 1 if $P(p \leq .33) > .60$,

adopt strategy 2 if $.40 \leq P(p \leq .33) \leq .60$,

adopt strategy 3 if $P(p \leq .33) < .40$.

As stated above, the salesman might assess this probability subjectively. If he does not feel that he can do this, one recourse is to take a sample. Suppose he decides to interview sixteen customers selected at random and observe the number who are interested. We know then that the probability distribution of the true proportion interested will be given by either

$$P(p \leq p_o) = P(r \geq r_o + 1 \mid n + 1, p_o)$$

or

$$P(p > p_o) = P(r \leq r_o \mid n + 1, p_o).$$

Consulting the binomial probability tables, we find that

if $r_o = 4$, $P(p \leq .33) = .7087$;

if $r_o = 5$, $P(p \leq .33) = .5105$;

if $r_o = 6$, $P(p \leq .33) = .3153$.

Thus, if the salesman finds four (or fewer) of the sixteen customers interested, he should adopt strategy 1, if five are interested he should adopt strategy 2, and if six (or more) are interested, he should follow strategy 3. If a terminal decision must be made on the basis of the sample of sixteen, the decision problem is solved. All that remains is to take the sample and make the decision as indicated. But a sample of sixteen might seem to some to be scanty evidence for a terminal decision. Let us examine the economics of this question.

10-4 The Expected Value of Perfect Information

To investigate the question of delaying a terminal decision imagine that the salesman is in the situation depicted below.

		Payoffs under strategy		
State (S)	P(S)	1	2	3
A: $p \leq .33$	.36	40	20	−40
B: $p > .33$	.64	140	170	210
	1.00			

Such probabilities of states could have been established from the objective evidence of a sample or they could have been assessed subjectively. The above set agrees with what would be established from observing $r = 4$ in a sample of $n = 11$. Since $P(A) < .40$, we know that the best decision is strategy 3, but let us figure the expected values for each strategy.

$$\bar{V}_1 = .36(40) + .64(140) = 14.4 + 89.6 = 104.0,$$
$$\bar{V}_2 = .36(20) + .64(170) = 7.2 + 108.8 = 116.0,$$
$$\bar{V}_3 = .36(-40) + .64(210) = -14.4 + 134.4 = 120.0.$$

The expected value of the optimal strategy is $\bar{V}_3 = 120$. Hiring the missionary salesman is the best terminal decision that can be made, *if one must be made*, on the basis of the existing information about the state of initial customer interest. Symbolically, we let $\bar{V}_{\text{opt}}$ stand for the expected value of the optimal strategy.

The expected value of perfect information depends on a quantity called the *expected value of perfect prediction*, or *expected value under certainty*. The expected value under certainty is predicated on three conditions. First, we imagine a long run of independent occurrences of states with relative frequencies corresponding to the salesman's assessment of probabilities of .36 for state A and .64 for state B. Second, we imagine that our salesman is free to choose strategy 1, 2, or 3 at each point in the sequence of occurrences. Third, we assume that the salesman knows in advance of each trial in the sequence whether state A or state B will occur. When the decision-maker knows that the next occurrence will be state A, he will choose strategy 1 in advance, and gain 40. When state B is to occur he will choose strategy 3 in advance, and gain 210. Our current evidence entitles us to believe that, in a long series of such trials, state A will occur 36 per cent of the time and state B 64 per cent of the time. The expected value of operating with a perfect predictor of each trial is, therefore, $.36(40) + .64(210) = 148.8$. This is the expected value under certainty.

The expected value under certainty will be given the symbol $\bar{V}_m$. As we have seen, it is the sum of the products of the probabilities of states, $P(S_i)$, and the maximum conditional payoffs attached to those states, V_{m_i}.

$$\bar{V}_m = \sum_i V_{m_i} \cdot P(S_i). \tag{10-2}$$

With a perfect predictor in the salesman's new-product example, we would expect to gain 148.8. Without this predictor the salesman would adopt the optimal strategy (strategy 3) which has an expected value of 120. The expected value of a perfect predictor (or perfect information) in this decision situation is, therefore, $148.8 - 120.0 = 28.8$. It will be convenient from here on to treat these payoffs as hundreds of dollars. If the salesman could obtain a perfect prediction for less than \$2880, he should do so if his objective is to maximize expected gain. Rather than adopt strategy 3, he would delay terminal action until the prediction was available. The difference between the expected value under certainty and the expected value of the optimal decision under uncertainty is called the *expected value of perfect (or complete) information*. Symbolically,

$$\bar{V}_c = \bar{V}_m - \bar{V}_{\text{opt}}. \tag{10-3}$$

The expected values $\bar{V}_c$, $\bar{V}_m$, and $\bar{V}_{\text{opt}}$ are expectancies based on the currently *available information about the true state*. Perfect information is information with no sampling error. If we are dealing with an infinite population, perfect information is a limit approached by best unbiased estimates from samples of increasing size. If we are dealing with a finite population, perfect information can be achieved by a *complete* census, if we assume that the individual observations are accurate. If our salesman could completely and accurately canvass his customers for \$2000 to determine the level of initial acceptance of the new product before deciding which way to promote it, our current expectation is that it would pay him to do so.

The expected value of perfect information can be found by dealing directly with opportunity losses, or "regrets." It is the *expected opportunity loss of the optimal strategy*. The optimal decision in the salesman's problem is strategy 3. We can find $\bar{V}_c$ from the table of opportunity losses as follows:

$$\bar{V}_c = .36(80) + .64(0) = 28.8.$$

In general,

$$\bar{V}_c = \sum_i L_i \cdot P(S_i) = \bar{L}_{\text{opt}}, \tag{10-4}$$

where L_i are the opportunity losses under the optimal strategy given each state.

The equivalence of $\bar{V}_c$ and $\bar{L}_{\text{opt}}$ emphasizes that the expected value of perfect information (at no cost) is the cost of uncertainty. By making a decision in favor of strategy 3 now as against obtaining perfect information and then deciding, we are incurring an expected opportunity loss of $.36[40 - (-40)] = 28.8$.

10-5 Combining Information About States

Suppose that the probabilities of states that we worked with in the previous section were based on a random sample of 11 that yielded 4 interested customers. Suppose now that the salesman is impressed by our arguments about the value of perfect information to the extent that he agrees to take a further sample of 38 customers before making his decision. He does this, and 15 of the 38 indicate a genuine interest in the product. In the previous sample 4 out of 11 customers indicated interest, so the total evidence is now 19 interested customers out of 49. Based on this total evidence, the probability that initial acceptance is low, $P(p \leq .33)$, is now

$$P(p \leq .33) = P(r \geq 20 \,|\, n = 50, p = .33) = .1826.$$

The decision problem, given the combined information to date, is

		Payoffs Under Strategy		
State (S)	P(S)	1	2	3
A: $p \leq .33$	.18	40	20	−40
B: $p > .33$	.82	140	170	210

The probability is now .82 that *more than 33 per cent* of the customers have a real interest in the product. The expected value of the optimal decision, to hire the promotional assistant, is now $.18(-40) + .82(210) = 165.0$. The expected value under certainty is now $.18(40) + .82(210) = 179.4$, and the expected value of perfect information is now $179.4 - 165.0 = 14.4$. The expected opportunity cost of acting now is only $.18(80) = 14.4$, a much lower cost of uncertainty than before.

In the above example, the additional information has increased the expected value of the optimal strategy. The additional evidence has confirmed our original belief that state B, high initial product acceptance, prevails. However, this will not always be the case. Consider what the situation would be had the sample of 38 yielded 11 rather than 15 interested customers. The total evidence would be 15 interested customers out of 49, and would have produced the following probabilities of states:

$$P(p \leq .33) = P(r \geq 16 \,|\, n = 50, p = .33) = .6120,$$
$$P(p > .33) = 1 - .6120 = .3880.$$

The situation would then be as in the following table:

		Payoffs under strategy		
State (S)	$P(S_i)$	1	2	3
A: $p \leq .33$	.61	40	20	-40
B: $p > .33$	.39	140	170	210

The optimal decision would now be strategy 1 with expected value

$$\bar{V}_{opt} = \bar{V}_1 = .61(40) + .39(140) = 24.4 + 54.6 = 79.0.$$

The expected value under certainty would now be

$$\bar{V}_m = .61(40) + .39(210) = 24.4 + 81.9 = 106.3.$$

The expected value of complete information would now be

$$\bar{V}_c = \bar{V}_m - \bar{V}_{opt} = 106.3 - 79.0 = 27.3.$$

Here the additional information would have changed the optimal decision, reduced the expected value of the optimal decision, and very slightly lowered the expected value of perfect information. The cost of uncertainty would now be $2730 rather than $2880. This does not mean that we would have been wrong to collect the additional information, however. The current and the previous assessment of $\bar{V}_c$ cannot be put on an equal footing. The current assessment has incorporated the previous as well as the additional evidence, and stands by itself as the appraisal of the situation in view of our total knowledge to date. Once the current appraisal is made, the previous assessment is no longer relevant.

EXERCISES

10.1 An investor was considering stock purchases in two competing companies. He determined the following payoff table contingent upon whether company A or company B wins out in a competition for share of the market.

State	Invest in A	Invest in B
A wins out	30	0
B wins out	40	80

(a) What is the maximin strategy? the maximax strategy? the minimax regret strategy?

(b) At what probability of A's winning out is the expected value of the two strategies the same?   *Ans.* 4/7.

10.2 The investor in Exercise 10.1 wonders about a strategy of putting half his money in each of the two stocks. Consider the three strategies: invest in A, invest in B, and the "mixed" strategy.
  (a) Which strategy is best according to the maximin criterion? the maximax criterion? the minimax regret criterion?
  (b) At what probability of A's winning out is the expected value of investing in A the same as for the mixed strategy?   *Ans.* 4/7.
  (c) Is the mixed strategy a Bayesian strategy?   *Ans.* No.

10.3 A company has an opportunity to computerize its records department. However, existing personnel have job security under a union agreement. The costs of the three alternative programs for the changeover depend on the attitude of the union toward retraining, and have been estimated as follows:

	Cost of Changeover ($ thousands)		
Attitude of the union	General retraining	Selective retraining	Hire new employees
Antagonistic	940	920	900
Passive	810	800	820
Enthusiastic	700	710	860

  (a) What is the minimax strategy? the minimin strategy?
  (b) Construct the opportunity loss table and determine the minimax regret strategy.
  (c) The probabilities of the states are assessed at .5, .3, and .2, respectively. Find the expected cost of each act, the expected opportunity loss of each act, and the expected cost under certainty.
  (d) Given the above probabilities, what is the expected value of perfect information?   *Ans.* $12 thousand.

10.4 Faced with a new market opportunity, management evaluated three courses of action against sales level in the new market as follows:

Sales	Probability of sales	Operate as always	Expand current operation	Build new capacity
Under 30,000	.10	20	−20	−40
30,000–50,000	.50	30	40	0
Over 50,000	.40	40	60	80

Find the expected value of perfect information.   *Ans.* 12.

10.5 A merchant receives an ungraded product which he can sell for $6.00 a thousand. However, he can grade the individual items at a cost of $.50 a thousand. The grading will separate the items into grade A and grade B. Grade A items can be sold for $12.00 a thousand and grade B items for $4.00 a thousand.

(a) At what quality (proportion of grade A items) does it pay to grade the product?   *Ans.* .312.
(b) A lot of 1000 is received. A sample of ten items produces four grade A items. What is the expected value of grading the lot?
                                                                                                    Ans. $6.70.
(c) Given the data of part (b), what is the probability that the quality of the lot is below the level specified in (a)?   *Ans.* .23.

10-6   Linear Payoffs and Break-Even Analysis

Up to this point we have assumed that the payoffs under each strategy were constant below a boundary of $p = .33$ and constant at another value above the boundary. For example, under strategy 1 the return was 40 for any $p \leq .33$ and 140 for any $p > .33$. In many instances it is more reasonable to expect that the return will be a linear function of p than that it will take two discrete values for different ranges of p. Suppose the salesman has 2000 customers and his experience is that he can ultimately sell 80 per cent of those who express an initial interest in a product, and that his net margin per item sold is $12.50. Then for each 1 per cent, or 20 customers, expressing an interest, he expects to sell 16. This will add 16 ($12.50) = $200 to his net return. The value or net return under strategy 1 is then

$$V_1 = 200p,$$

where $V =$ income in $ hundreds and $p =$ proportion of customers with initial interest.

This is a linear payoff function, in contrast to the "step" function which we used throughout our discussion of the salesman's decision problem. Linear payoff functions are quite common in business and are typically assumed in the traditional technique known as break-even analysis. The following situation represents a typical break-even problem.

A machine costing $5000 turns out a product that can be sold at $2 each. The variable costs of manufacturing and marketing the product are $1.50 per item. The traditional break-even chart for this example is shown in Fig. 10–2. The income (I) line follows the linear function, $I = 2\mu$, where μ is the number of units sold. The fixed cost of the machine is represented by the horizontal line at $5000. This line emphasizes that fixed costs (by definition) do not vary with or depend on sales. Total costs are shown by the equation, $TC = 5000 + 1.5\mu$. They are the sum of fixed costs, 5000, and variable costs, 1.5μ.

The break-even level of sales occurs when total income (I) equals total costs (TC). Graphically, this is the point on the μ axis where the income and the total-cost lines cross. Algebraically, this point is found by setting income equal to total costs and solving for μ.

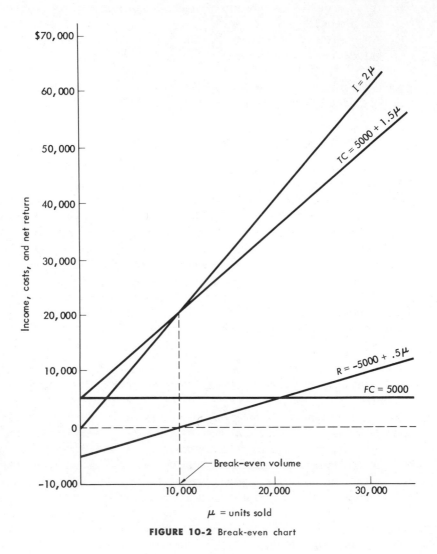

FIGURE 10-2 Break-even chart

$$I = TC,$$
$$2\mu = 5000 + 1.5\mu,$$
$$.5\mu = 5000,$$
$$\mu = 10,000 = \text{break-even sales in units.}$$

The break-even analysis can be condensed by developing an equation for *net* return, R, which is simply income less costs, or $R = I - TC$. The break-even sales volume occurs when net return is zero. This equation for R is also shown in Fig. 10–2, having been obtained as follows:

$$R = I - TC,$$
$$R = 2\mu - (5000 + 1.5\mu)$$
$$= -5000 + .5\mu.$$

The break-even volume can be found from this equation. It is the volume, μ, at which net return, R, is zero. Solving:

$$.5\mu = 5000.$$

$$\mu = \frac{5000}{.5} = 10,000 \text{ units.}$$

In this context .5 is the variable return per unit less the variable costs per unit; in our example, $\$.5 = \$2.00 - \$1.50$. In break-even terminology this divisor is often called the *variable contribution rate*. Thus the break-even volume can be found by (fixed costs) ÷ (variable contribution rate).

The net return function represents the payoffs under the decision to undertake the venture conditional on the state of sales volume, μ. The problem is to determine which of the following decisions (or strategies) is preferable.

1. Do not undertake the venture and accept payoff $V_1 = 0$.
2. Undertake the venture and accept payoff $V_2 = -5000 + .5\mu$.

In obtaining the break-even volume of sales above, we have determined a critical volume of sales which would cause us to be indifferent as between the two strategies. If we knew that sales volume was going to be 10,000 units, we would not care whether we undertook the venture or not. We must assume that the facts as presented include all relevant costs and that the alternative decisions exhaust the choices available.

If the true state of sales (μ) is known in advance, the decision problem is trivial, and can be summarized as follows:

True state	Optimal decision	Consequences
$\mu \le 10,000$	1	$V = V_1 = 0$
$\mu > 10,000$	2	$V = V_2 = -5000 + .5\mu$

We are to undertake the venture if the sales volume exceeds the break-even point, otherwise not. This is the decision rule under certainty.

10-7 Linear Payoffs and a Normal Probability Distribution of States

We have solved the decision problem under certainty. We must now consider the problem when only partial information is available. Suppose our information comes from a market survey of a large random sample of potential customers. From the survey data we have estimated total sales to the market (all potential customers) at 16,000 units with a standard error of 4000 units. This is equivalent to a fiducial probability distribution of total sales, μ, with a mean, $\hat{\mu}$, of 16,000 and a standard deviation, σ_μ, of 4000. Let us

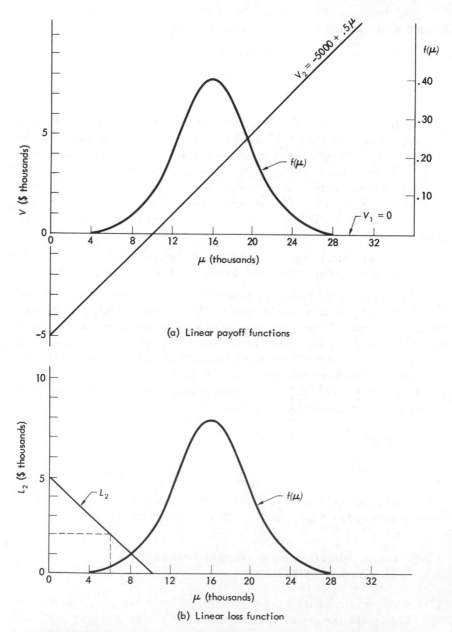

(a) Linear payoff functions

(b) Linear loss function

FIGURE 10-3 Normal loss integral problem with fiducial distribution of μ

assume that the sample size was large enough for a normal fiducial distribution to be employed.

In Fig. 10–3(a) we show three functions. The first is the normal fiducial distribution of sales volume. Its ordinates are read on the right vertical scale. The second function is the payoff function should we decide to go ahead with the venture, $V_2 = -5000 + 0.5\mu$. The third function is $V_1 = 0$, the payoff function should we decide not to undertake the venture. The lines for V_1 and V_2 cross at $\mu = 10{,}000$, the break-even point.

From a visual inspection it is evident that V_2 has a positive expected value, while the return should we not undertake the venture is zero. The expected value of V_2 is

$$\bar{V}_2 = -5000 + .5\hat{\mu}$$
$$= -5000 + .5(16{,}000)$$
$$= \$3000.$$

This follows from the theorem on expected values in Eq. (2–8), as applied to the term $.5\hat{\mu}$.

The optimal strategy is to purchase the machine and market the product. Our next task is to find the expected value of perfect information. Recall that this value is the expected opportunity loss of the optimal strategy. Let us examine the opportunity losses of strategy 2. As long as the total demand, μ, exceeds the break-even point, μ_b, there will be no opportunity loss. We would not regret our decision to undertake the venture. For $\mu < \mu_b$, however, strategy 1 would have resulted in zero return while strategy 2 would have resulted in a return of $-5000 + .5\mu$, a negative amount. For example, if demand were really only 6000 units, the return from strategy 2 would be $-5000 + .5(6000) = -2000$ dollars. The opportunity loss relative to strategy 1 would be $V_1 - V_2$, or $5000 - .5\mu$, in this case 2000 dollars. The opportunity loss function is termed $L(\mu)$. The expression for $L(\mu)$ in our problem is

$$L_2(\mu) = \begin{cases} a - b\mu, & \mu < \mu_b, \\ 0, & \mu \geq \mu_b, \end{cases}$$

where a is the fixed cost and b is the unit variable cost or variable contribution rate. The graph of $L_2(\mu)$ with the fiducial distribution superimposed appears in Fig. 10–3(b). The opportunity loss of 2000 dollars at $\mu = 6000$ is shown on the graph. The slope of the L_2 line is $-b$, while the slope of the V_2 line was $+b$. Opportunity loss increases by .5 dollars for each additional unit of deficiency of demand below the break-even point. The loss function can be stated as

$$L_2(\mu) = \begin{cases} b(\mu_b - \mu), & \mu < \mu_b, \\ 0, & \mu \geq \mu_b. \end{cases}$$

The normal loss integral. The variable, μ, in the loss function just illustrated can be shifted to units of σ_μ, as follows:

$$b(\mu_b - \mu) = b\sigma_\mu \left(\frac{\mu_b - \mu}{\sigma_\mu} \right)$$

$$= b\sigma_\mu \left[\left(\frac{\mu_b - \hat{\mu}}{\sigma_\mu} \right) - \left(\frac{\mu - \hat{\mu}}{\sigma_\mu} \right) \right]$$

$$= b\sigma_\mu (\hat{z}_b - \hat{z}), \qquad \hat{z} < \hat{z}_b.$$

Then,

$$L_2(\mu) = \begin{cases} b\sigma_\mu(\hat{z}_b - \hat{z}), & \hat{z} < \hat{z}_b, \\ 0, & \hat{z} \geq \hat{z}_b. \end{cases}$$

The quantity $b\sigma_\mu$ is the increment in the loss function per standard-deviation change in μ. In our problem $b\sigma_\mu = \$.5\,(4000) = \$2000$. The opportunity loss of the optimal act increases by \$2000 per standard deviation, or 4000 units, deficiency in demand below the break-even demand of 10,000 units. The break-even demand, expressed in standard deviation units, is

$$\hat{z}_b = \frac{\mu_b - \hat{\mu}}{\sigma_\mu}. \tag{10-5}$$

Recall that the break-even demand can be found from

$$\mu_b = \frac{a}{b}, \tag{10-6}$$

where a is the fixed cost outlay.

The graph of the loss function, $L_2(\mu)$, with the variable scale shifted to $\hat{z} = (\mu - \hat{\mu})/\sigma_\mu$ is shown in Fig. 10-4(a). The opportunity loss at $\mu = 6000$ now appears at $\hat{z} = (6000 - 16,000)/4000 = -2.5$. The break-even point, $\hat{z}_b$, is $(10,000 - 16,000)/4000 = -1.5$. The opportunity loss at $\mu = 6000$ can be expressed as

$$b\sigma_\mu(\hat{z}_b - \hat{z}) = \$0.5(4000)[-1.5 - (-2.5)] = \$2000.$$

In our previous examples in which payoffs were fixed values for discrete states or for states representing an interval of a parameter we found the expected value of complete information by summing the products of opportunity losses, L_i, and the probabilities of incurring these losses, $P(S_i)$. This was expressed in Eq. (10-4).

$$\bar{V}_c = \sum_i L_i \cdot P(S_i).$$

Now, however, the opportunity losses of the optimal act depend on the true value of μ, a continuous variable. We have transformed μ to $\hat{z}$ by relating μ to the parameters of the normal fiducial distribution of μ. Each value on our loss function is $b\sigma_\mu(\hat{z}_b - \hat{z})$. The technique for summing the products of these losses and their probabilities in the case of a continuous function is integration. However, the integration need not be carried out because we can make use of a standard table of the normal loss integral.

A rough appreciation of the argument for the applicability of the nor-

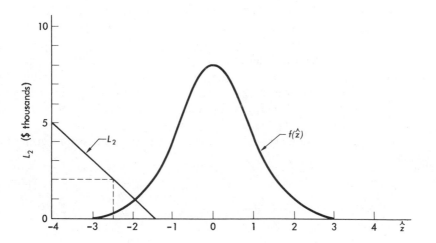

(a) Standard normal fiducial distribution and the loss function

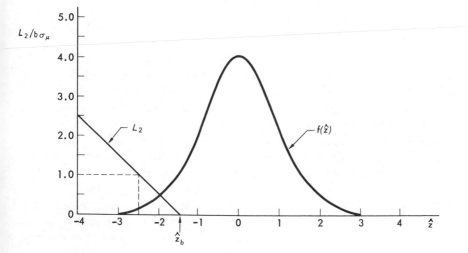

(b) Standard normal fiducial distribution and standard loss function

FIGURE 10-4 Transformations of normal loss integral problem

mal loss integral in obtaining the expected value of perfect information will be given here. Since each value on the loss function in our problem is $b\sigma_\mu(\hat{z}_b - \hat{z})$, the integral of this loss function will be $b\sigma_\mu$ times the integral of $\hat{z}_b - \hat{z}$ for all $\hat{z} < \hat{z}_b$. If we agree to treat $\hat{z}_b$ as the origin and the direction toward the nearer tail of the distribution as positive, the integral of $\hat{z} - \hat{z}_b$ is, in effect, the continuous summation of the products of probabilities under the standard normal distribution and a loss line with a slope of 1.0. This is called the normal loss integral. The standard loss function for our problem is shown in Fig. 10–4(b). Its nonzero portion originates at $\hat{z} = -1.5$ and rises toward the lower tail of the normal $\hat{z}$ distribution. The difference between Fig. 10–4(a) and Fig. 10–4(b) is the factor $b\sigma_\mu$ in the vertical scale of the former.

Values of the unit normal loss integral are tabled in Appendix H. The table is entered with a value of $\hat{z}_b$, and one obtains the integral represented by a standard loss function rising toward the near tail of the standard normal distribution. Since the normal distribution is symmetrical, the loss integral originating at $\hat{z}$ is the same as at $-\hat{z}$.

For the continuous case, the expected value of perfect information then, is,

$$\bar{V}_c = b\sigma_\mu \mathscr{L}, \qquad (10\text{–}7)$$

where $\mathscr{L}$ is the normal loss integral for $\hat{z}_b$.

In our machine-purchase problem,

$$\hat{z}_b = \frac{\mu_b - \hat{\mu}}{\sigma_\mu} = \frac{10{,}000 - 16{,}000}{4000} = -1.5,$$

$$\mathscr{L} = .02931,$$

$$\bar{V}_c = b\sigma_\mu \mathscr{L} = \$.5(4000)(.02931) = \$58.62.$$

Since the expected value of perfect information is only $58.62, we would make the decision now to buy the machine (strategy 2), unless further information was extremely cheap.

One will encounter situations in which $\hat{\mu} < \mu_b$, and the optimal act will be not to undertake the venture represented. In this case the opportunity loss function will be just the reverse of the type shown in Fig. 10–3(b). The opportunity losses are zero for all $\mu < \mu_b$, and rise with a slope of $b\sigma_\mu$ to the right of μ_b. The procedure for using Eq. (10–7) is exactly the same, however.

The use of a normal fiducial distribution of μ assumes that μ has no upper or lower bounds. There is some probability of opportunity losses, however large. If, in practice, there is an effective limit to opportunity losses, we need not be much concerned if this limit is at least $3\sigma_\mu$ from the mean of the fiducial distribution. In our example we cannot lose more than the $5000 fixed costs, which would occur if demand, μ, were zero. However, this lower boundary is at $\hat{z} = -4.0$, or four standard deviations below the mean of the fiducial distribution of μ.

Conversion to a binary gamble. The salesman's problem at the beginning of the chapter involved fixed payoffs under each decision for each of two states rather than linear payoffs. The two states were $p \leq .33$ and $p > .33$. In the break-even problem there are similarly two states that concern us. These are (1) the probability that demand is below the break-even point, in which case we lose by buying the machine, and (2) the probability that demand exceeds the break-even level, in which case we make a profit. The probabilities are easily found.

$$P(\mu \leq \mu_b) = P(\hat{z} \leq \hat{z}_b),$$
$$P(\mu \leq \mu_b) = P(\hat{z} \leq -1.5) = .06681,$$
$$P(\mu > \mu_b) = 1 - .06681 = .93319.$$

We also learned in the salesman example that the expected value of perfect information was the difference between the expected value under certainty and the expected value of the optimal strategy. Restating this relationship for the expected value under certainty yields

$$\bar{V}_m = \bar{V}_{opt} + \bar{V}_c.$$

In the machine-purchase problem we know both $\bar{V}_{opt}$ and $\bar{V}_c$, and so find the expected value under certainty to be

$$\bar{V}_m = \$3000 + \$58.62 = \$3058.62.$$

We saw in our discussion of Eq. 10–4 that $\bar{L}_{opt}$ and $\bar{V}_c$ were equivalent in the discrete case. This is also true in the continuous case. In the current example, the expected value of the optimal act ($\$3000$) is the integral of the payoffs under strategy 2 to buy the machine. This is the integral of $V_2 = -5000 + .5(\mu)$, where μ is the normal fiducial probability distribution of demand. The expected value under certainty is then the integral of the probability distribution of V_{opt}.

Knowing the expected opportunity loss of the optimal act to be $\$58.62$, and knowing the probability of a loss to be .06881, we can compute a conditional expectancy, namely the expected loss *given* that a loss occurs. It is

$$\bar{V}_{opt} \mid V < 0 = \frac{-\bar{L}_{opt}}{P(V < 0)}$$

$$= \frac{-\$58.62}{.06681} = -\$877.41.$$

In like manner we can figure the expected profit or gain if a gain occurs:

$$\bar{V}_{opt} \mid V > 0 = \frac{\bar{V}_{opt} + \bar{L}_{opt}}{P(V > 0)} = \frac{\$3058.62}{.93319} = \$3277.60.$$

Now the decision to purchase the machine can be interpreted as a twofold, or binary, gamble just as we interpreted the salesman's optimal strategy. It may be looked upon as a gamble involving a .06681 probability of losing $877.41 and a .93319 probability of gaining $3227.60. Computing the expected value of this gamble "reverses" the calculations we have just made. It would be

$$\bar{V}_{opt} = .06681(-\$877.41) + .93319(\$3277.60)$$
$$= -\$58.62 + \$3058.62 = \$3000.$$

Using L and G for loss and gain, we can summarize this as

$$\bar{V}_{opt} = P(L)\cdot\frac{-\bar{L}_{opt}}{P(L)} + P(G)\cdot\frac{\bar{V}_m}{P(G)}. \tag{10-8}$$

Stating this conversion in tabular form emphasizes its similarity to the salesman's fixed conditional return problem discussed earlier. The table is shown below.

		Expected payoffs under strategy	
State (S)	P(S)	1	2
A: $X \le 10,000$	.06681	0	−877.41
B: $X > 10,000$	.93319	0	3277.60

$$\bar{V}_{opt} = .06681(-877.41) + .93319(3277.60) = \$3000,$$
$$\bar{V}_m = .06681(0) + .93319(3277.60) = \$3058.62,$$
$$\bar{V}_c = 3058.62 - 3000 = \$58.62.$$

Conversion to value scale. The result of a linear payoff function of μ and a normal probability distribution of μ is a normal probability distribution of payoff, or net return, from the venture under consideration. In the current problem, demand for the machine's output can be expressed as

$$\mu = \hat{\mu} + \hat{z}\sigma_\mu$$
$$= 16,000 + 4000\hat{z},$$

and the linear payoff function was

$$V = -5000 + .5\mu.$$

Then

$$V = -5000 + .5(16,000 + \hat{z}\sigma_\mu)$$
$$= 3000 + .5\sigma_\mu\hat{z}$$
$$= 3000 + 2000\hat{z}.$$

The last statement is the equation for net return. Net return has a normal probability distribution with a mean of $3000 and a standard deviation of $2000. This is often a useful way to formulate the problem. In general terms, where $V = -a + b\mu$ and μ has a normal fiducial distribution,

$$\bar{V} = -a + b\hat{\mu},$$
$$\sigma_V = b\sigma_\mu, \tag{10-9}$$
$$V = \bar{V} + \hat{z}\sigma_V,$$
$$\hat{z}_b = \frac{-\bar{V}}{\sigma_V}, \tag{10-10}$$
$$\bar{V}_c = \sigma_V \mathscr{L}. \tag{10-11}$$

In the machine-purchase problem,

$$\hat{z}_b = \frac{-\bar{V}}{\sigma_V} = \frac{-3000}{2000} = -1.5,$$
$$\mathscr{L} = .02931,$$
$$\bar{V}_c = \sigma_V \mathscr{L} = \$2000(.02931) = \$58.62.$$

These are the same values as we obtained previously. It is often convenient, however, to work with the fiducial distribution of net return, V, from the outset.

10-8   Combining Evidence About Payoffs

In the salesman's problem we found that additional information required us to revise our conclusions about the probabilities of states, and thus could affect the expected values of the several strategies available. This is also true in decision problems with linear opportunity losses and a normal probability distribution of the decision parameter. Suppose a marketing strategy involves solicitation of 20,000 firms. Fixed costs of the marketing program will be $500,000. The variable return is twenty cents per dollar of sales. A test marketing experiment involving solicitation of sixty randomly selected firms is carried out with a result of mean sales per firm, $\bar{X}$, of $124 with a sample standard deviation, s, of $25. At this point we have

$$\hat{\mu}_X = \$124, \quad \sigma_\mu = s_{\bar{X}} = s/\sqrt{n} = \$25/\sqrt{60} = \$3.23$$

Each dollar increase in mean sales per firm amounts to an increase of 20,000 ($.20), or $4,000 in net return from the marketing program. Therefore,

$$\bar{V} = a + b\hat{\mu}_X$$
$$= -\$500,000 + 4000(\$124) = -\$4000.$$
$$\sigma_V = b\sigma_\mu = 4000(\$3.23) = \$12,920.$$

The decision to go ahead with the marketing program has negative expected value, and the optimal strategy is not to go ahead. The opportunity losses of the optimal strategy not to go ahead are the gains possible from the decision to adopt the marketing program. The expected value of these opportunity losses is the expected value of perfect information

$$\hat{z}_b = \frac{-\bar{V}}{\sigma_V} = \frac{(\$4000)}{\$12,920} = .31$$

$$\bar{V}_c = \sigma_V \mathcal{L} = \$12,920(.2630) = \$3398.$$

Suppose the test marketing is extended to 100 more randomly selected firms with the result of a sample mean sales of $128 and a standard deviation of $22. We now have

$$\bar{X}_1 = \$124, \; s_1 = \$25, \; n_1 = 60$$

$$\bar{X}_2 = \$128, \; s_2 = \$22, \; n_2 = 100$$

The best unbiased estimates of μ_X and σ_X^2 are now made by pooling the evidence.

$$\hat{\mu}_X = \frac{n_1 \bar{X}_1 + n_2 \bar{X}_2}{n_1 + n_2} = \frac{60(124) + 100(128)}{60 + 100} = \$126.50$$

$$\hat{\sigma}_X^2 = \bar{s}_X^2 \simeq \frac{n_1 s_1^2 + n_2 s_2^2}{n_1 + n_2} = \frac{60(25^2) + 100(22^2)}{60 + 100} = 536.87$$

From $\bar{s}_X^2$ we then obtain σ_μ^2, as in Eq. (8–21).

$$\sigma_\mu^2 = \frac{\bar{s}_X^2}{n_1 + n_2} = \frac{536.87}{160} = 3.36$$

$$\sigma_\mu = \sqrt{3.36} = \$1.83$$

The decision to go ahead with the marketing program can now be evaluated in the light of the cumulative evidence.

$$\bar{V} = -\$500,000 + 4000(\$126.50) = \$6,000.$$

$$\sigma_V = b\sigma_\mu = 4000(\$1.83) = \$7,320.$$

$$\hat{z}_b = \frac{-\bar{V}}{\sigma_V} = \frac{-\$6,000}{\$7,320} = -.82$$

$$\bar{V}_c = \sigma_V \mathcal{L} = \$7,320(.1160) = \$849.12$$

A further sample would be combined with the current evidence in the same manner. In Chapter 11 we consider the cost of further evidence in relation to its expected value as the determinant of whether to continue sampling.

10-9 Extensions of Two-Action Problems

In the example just discussed, the problem was whether or not to invest in a specified venture. That is, the possible strategies were (1) go ahead with the marketing program, and (2) abandon the program. Situations can be encountered in which there are several possible programs for investment; they can be analyzed by extending the methods already developed.

Suppose that there are two machines available for fabricating a product. The finished product can be sold for \$400, but the machines differ in their cost characteristics. Machine 1 cost \$100,000, and the variable costs of manufacture and sale if this machine is bought will be \$350 per unit. Machine 2 cost \$400,000, but variable costs can be held to \$290. Demand is established at 4000 units subject to a normal error distribution with standard deviation equal to 1000 units. The strategies can be stated (in dollars) as follows:

$$\text{Strategy 1: Buy machine 1}$$
$$V_1 = -100,000 + (400 - 350)\mu$$
$$= -100,000 + 50\mu.$$

$$\text{Strategy 2: Buy machine 2}$$
$$V_2 = -400,000 + (400 - 290)\mu$$
$$= -400,000 + 110\mu.$$

The expected values of the strategies are

$$\bar{V}_1 = -100,000 + 50(4000) = \$100,000,$$
$$\bar{V}_2 = -400,000 + 110(4000) = \$40,000.$$

Purchase of machine 1 is the optimal strategy under uncertainty. The opportunity losses associated with this strategy are the outcomes for which $V_2 - V_1$ is positive. If this were the case, strategy 2 would be preferred to strategy 1, and we would have regretted our decision to purchase machine 1. The equation for $V_2 - V_1$ is

$$V_2 - V_1 = -400,000 + 110\mu - (-100,000 + 50\mu)$$
$$= -300,000 + 60\mu.$$

The nonzero segment of the loss function commences at the break-even point, or level of demand, μ, for which $V_2 = V_1$.

$$0 = -300,000 + 60\mu_b,$$
$$\mu_b = \frac{a}{b} = \frac{300,000}{60} = 5000.$$

The expected value of this loss function is the expected value of perfect information.

$$\bar{V}_c = \bar{L}_{V_2 - V_1} = b\sigma_\mu \mathscr{L}.$$

We then obtain the expected value of perfect information from

$$\hat{z}_b = \frac{\mu_b - \hat{\mu}}{\sigma_\mu} = \frac{5000 - 4000}{1000} = 1.0$$

$$\mathscr{L} = .08332,$$

$$\bar{V}_c = b\sigma_\mu \mathscr{L} = \$60(1000)(.08332) = \$4999.$$

If the alternative existed to purchase neither machine, we would have a third strategy with payoff $V_3 = 0$. In this case the expected opportunity loss of the optimal strategy can be found by summing the expected opportunity losses of the optimal strategy relative to each of the other strategies. In the current problem,

$$V_1 = \$100,000,$$

$$V_2 = 40,000,$$

$$V_3 = 0.$$

We already have the expected opportunity loss of strategy 1 compared with strategy 2. The opportunity loss of strategy 1 compared with strategy 3 can be found in the usual manner.

$$V_1 = -a + b\mu = -100,000 + 50\mu,$$

$$\mu_b = \frac{a}{b} = \frac{100,000}{50} = 2000,$$

$$\hat{z}_b = \frac{\mu_b - \hat{\mu}}{\sigma_\mu} = \frac{2000 - 4000}{1000} = -2.0,$$

$$\bar{V}_c = b\sigma_\mu \mathscr{L} = \$50(1000)(.00849) = \$424.$$

The expected opportunity loss of buying machine 1 now compared to the alternative of waiting for perfect information and then deciding accordingly on machine 1, machine 2, or no machine (strategy 3) is $\$4999 + \$424 = \$5423$. This would seem large enough to consider gathering further information about demand before making a terminal decision.

The graphics of this three-action problem can be seen in Fig. 10–5. The b factor for $V_2 - V_1$ is the angle of intersection of the $V_2 - V_1$ return lines, and is redrawn directly below as the $V_2 - V_1$ line rising to the right. The $V_3 - V_1$ line rises in the left tail of the normal distribution with a slope of $\$50$. These are the nonzero segments of the opportunity loss function for strategy 1. Between the points where these segments of the loss function originate, strategy 1 is the preferred act under certainty.

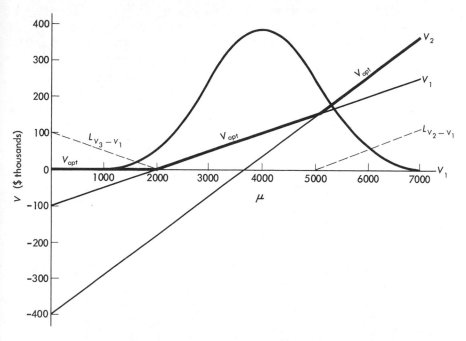

FIGURE 10-5 Three-action normal loss integral decision problem

The extension to three strategies indicates the manner in which the two-action technique can be extended to analyze a decision problem with any number of alternative acts or strategies. Given a linear payoff function for each strategy and a normal fiducial distribution of the parameter that determines the payoffs, we first find the expected values of each strategy. Then, we find the expected opportunity loss of the optimal strategy under uncertainty compared to each of the other strategies in turn. Summing these, we obtain the expected opportunity loss of the optimal strategy. This is the expected value of perfect information.

One caution to observe is that there are no dominated strategies. Such a situation can be spotted easily when dealing with linear payoff functions: a dominated strategy will be one with a payoff function having the same slope but a lower intercept than the payoff function for an alternative strategy. This corresponds to an alternative with greater fixed costs but no larger variable contribution rate than some other strategy available.

EXERCISES

10.6 With a $200,000 investment in his distribution system, a marketer can reduce his direct distribution cost per unit by $5.00. He has a normal subjective probability distribution of demand with a mean of 50,000 units over the life of the investment, and a standard error of 8000 units.

    (a) Find the expected return from the investment.   *Ans.* $50,000.

    (b) Find the expected value of perfect information and the expected value under certainty.   *Ans.* $2024; $52,024.

    (c) Reduce the decision to invest to a binary gamble.

10.7 A manufacturer must decide whether to manufacture and market a new seasonal novelty which has been developed to sell for $1.50 a unit. If he proceeds with the venture he will have to purchase special machinery at a cost of $5000, which will be scrapped at the end of the season. The variable cost of manufacture and sale is $.50 per unit. It is possible to manufacture in small batches over the season as demand occurs so that there is no risk of left-over merchandise. The manufacturer's subjective probability distribution of demand is normal with a mean of 5300 units and a standard deviation of 2000 units.

    (a) What is the probability that demand will be less than 5000 units? more than 10,000 units?

    (b) What is the expected value of perfect information?

10.8 The manufacturer in Exercise 10–7 conducts a survey from which a normal fiducial distribution of demand is established with a mean of 6000 units and a standard deviation of 1000 units.

    (a) Use Eqs. (8–17) and (8–18) to find the mean and variance of the posterior probability distribution of demand.

                                           Ans. 5860; 800,000.

    (b) Find the expected value of perfect information in view of part (a).

                                              Ans. $80.37.

10.9 In connection with the development of a new property a mining company knew it would have to spend $3 million. The probability distribution of revenues was normally distributed with a mean of $9 million and a standard deviation of $1.6 million. Other costs, unconnected with revenue, were estimated at $4 million with a normally distributed error of $1.2 million.

    (a) What is the expected value of perfect information?   *Ans.* $166,640.

    (b) Translate the proposal to develop the property into a binary gamble.

10.10 Parameters of the probability distributions of the present value of net cash flows from an investment are given below. The distributions for each year are normal and independent of one another.

Year	Mean	Standard deviation
1	$20 thousand	$3 thousand
2	$30 thousand	$6 thousand
3	$50 thousand	$6 thousand

    (a) The investment involves a certain current cost of $94 thousand. Find the expected value of perfect information.   *Ans.* $1353.

    (b) The probability distribution of net present value from an alternative investment is normal with a mean of $6000 and a standard deviation of $18,000. Compare the two investments as binary gambles.

10.11 Assume in Exericse 10.10 that second-and third-year returns are completely dependent (correlated) and that the correlation coefficient, ρ, between first-year returns and second- and third-year returns is .50. Find the expected value of perfect information.   *Ans.* $2982.

10.12 A port authority had just opened a new tollbridge. The annual interest and amortization charges of $3,942,000 are to be met by a toll charge of 20 cents per vehicle, with any operating deficits made up by a charge against the authority's general account. Only 36 days of records are available for estimating annual traffic. During this period mean daily traffic was 54,800 vehicles with a standard deviation among the 36 daily rates of 7,200 vehicles.

(a) Assuming random sampling from a normally distributed population, how much reserve should be set up in the coming year's budget against the contingency of an operating deficit?

Ans. $13,166.

(b) A subsequent 64 days of observation yields a mean and standard deviation of daily traffic rates of 54,300 and 7,600 respectively. Given the total evidence, should any increase be made in the budgeted reserve?   *Ans.* No.

10.13 A processor receives a lot of 10,000 items. His processing costs are $54,000, plus $10,000 extra for each thousand that fail to meet a prescribed quality standard. When processed in this manner he can sell the output for $94,000. A random sample of 225 items from the lot has revealed 81 that fail to meet the quality standard.

(a) What is the expected return from processing?   *Ans.* $4000.

(b) What is the standard deviation of the probability distribution of return from processing?   *Ans.* $3200.

(c) What is the expected value of perfect information?   *Ans.* $161.89.

10.14 An additional sample of 99 items from the lot in Exercise 10.13 produced 27 that failed to meet the quality standard. In view of this further evidence, what is the expected value of perfect information?

Ans. $4.49.

REFERENCES

Bierman, H., C. P. Bonini, L. E. Fouraker, and R. K. Jaedicke, *Quantitative Analysis for Business Decisions*, rev. ed. Homewood, Ill. Richard D. Irwin, Inc., 1965.

Chernoff, H., and L. E. Moses, *Elementary Decision Theory*. New York: John Wiley & Sons, Inc., 1959.

Schlaifer, R., *Probability and Statistics for Business Decisions*. New York: McGraw-Hill Book Company, 1959.

11

Optimal
Information
Gathering

Chapter 10 gave an introduction to decision procedures based on expected values. Of particular importance was the "normal linear loss" class of problem. This was illustrated first by a decision problem involving two strategies, and we then found that extensions could be made to handle problems with three or more strategies. In these problems the optimal strategy is simply the one carrying the highest expected return. In the simplest problem, finding the optimal strategy is only a matter of finding whether the expected value of the positive action (make the investment, establish the branch store, or whatever) exceeds the certain value of zero from adopting the alternative to do nothing.

The important contribution of statistical analysis to decision making under partial uncertainty lies in the concept of the expected value of perfect information. With the aid of the table of the normal loss integral, we were able to find this quantity in "normal linear loss" problems. We emphasized that the expected value of perfect information is the expected opportunity cost of adopting the optimal strategy under present conditions of uncertainty as opposed to waiting for perfect information before making a decision. It is the expected additional return from the decision to delay a final decision pending the receipt of perfect information.

11-1 The Expected Value of Sample Information

In most cases we will have to be satisfied with the receipt of additional but not complete information. The expected value of complete information is the limiting case of the expected return from gathering further sample information. Estimating the value of further sample information is, then, critical to the decision-making process.

To illustrate, suppose a break-even analysis involving commercialization of potential demand for a new product has established the break-even gross revenue at $1,985,000. A sample survey of 100 potential customers out of a total identified market of 50,000 customers has yielded an estimated mean revenue per customer of $40 and an estimated standard deviation of revenues per customer of $12. That is,

$$\bar{X} = \$40, \qquad s_X = \$12, \qquad n = 100.$$

We need to find the mean and standard deviation of the probability distribution of total revenue. We designate total revenue as R. First, it is clear that the expected total revenue is found from the product of the estimated mean per customer and the number of customers in the population:

$$\hat{\mu}_R = N \cdot \bar{X} = 50,000 \, (\$40) = \$2,000,000.$$

The equation for the variance of a random variable times a constant is employed to find the variance of R as the variance of $(N\bar{X})$:

$$\sigma_R^2 = \sigma_{N\bar{X}}^2 = N^2 \sigma_{\bar{X}}^2,$$

or equivalently,

$$\sigma_R = N\sigma_{\bar{X}}.$$

Our estimate of $\sigma_{\bar{X}}$ is $s_X/\sqrt{n}$, so that

$$\sigma_R = \frac{Ns_X}{\sqrt{n}} = \frac{50,000(\$12)}{\sqrt{100}} = \$60,000.$$

Since the expected value exceeds the break-even revenue, the optimal act is to commercialize the product, and the expected net return is

$$\bar{V} = -\$1,985,000 + \hat{\mu}_R = -\$1,985,000 + \$2,000,000 = \$15,000.$$

In an example where only revenues are subject to uncertainty, the uncertainty in *net* returns is the same as the uncertainty in gross returns, and therefore

$$\sigma_V = \frac{Ns_X}{\sqrt{n}}. \tag{11-1}$$

The break-even point can now be expressed, as before, in standard deviation units and the expected value of perfect information found.

$$\hat{z}_b = \frac{-\bar{V}}{\sigma_V} = \frac{-\$15,000}{\$60,000} = -.25,$$

$$\bar{V}_c = \sigma_V \mathscr{L} = \$60,000(.2863) = \$17,178.$$

Now let's consider the situation we would be in if we wanted to increase the sample by, say, 125 customers. Our expectation of the sample mean and estimated standard deviation would be the same, namely $40 and $12. With a total sample of 225, however, the uncertainty in net return would be expected to be

$$\sigma_{V'} = \frac{N s_x}{\sqrt{n'}}. \tag{11-2}$$

In this expression the "primes" are used to specify the *cumulative* sample size and the resulting expected uncertainty of net value. These should be clearly distinguished from the values derived from the sample originally taken. We are dealing with a conditional expectation in that we are studying before the fact (of taking an incremental sample) where we expect to be after the fact. Substituting in Eq. (11-2), we find that a total cumulated sample of 225 would be expected to yield a fiducial distribution of net return with a standard deviation of

$$\sigma_{V'} = \frac{N s_x}{\sqrt{n'}} = \frac{50,000}{\sqrt{225}}(\$12) = \$40,000.$$

We now define $\mathscr{L}'$ as the normal loss integral that we would expect to obtain on the basis of cumulative evidence of a total sample of n'.

$$\mathscr{L}' = \mathscr{L}\left(\hat{z} = -\frac{\bar{V}'}{\sigma_{V'}}\right). \tag{11-3}$$

Verbally, $\mathscr{L}'$ is the normal loss integral, $\mathscr{L}$, for the $\hat{z}$ value at the break-even point on the basis of the anticipated total evidence.

Because $\sigma_{V'}$ will be smaller than σ_V with an increase in sample size, the conditional expectation is that the point of zero net return will lie more standard deviation units from the expected return, $\bar{V} = \bar{V}' = \$15,000$. In the current case,

$$\mathscr{L}' = \mathscr{L}\left(\hat{z} = \frac{-\$15,000}{\$40,000}\right),$$

$$\mathscr{L}' = \mathscr{L}(\hat{z} = -.38) = .2374.$$

The conditional expected value of perfect information then follows as

$$\bar{V}'_c = \sigma_{V'}\mathcal{L}' \qquad (11\text{-}4)$$

$$= \$40,000(.2374) = \$9496.$$

We anticipate, then, that the increase in sample size will reduce the opportunity loss of the optimal strategy from \$17,178 to \$9496. This reduction in the opportunity loss of acting under uncertainty is the anticipated value of the increase in information afforded by the larger sample. It is the expected value of (further) sample information, which we indicate by $\bar{V}_s$.

$$\bar{V}_s = \bar{V}_c - \bar{V}'_c. \qquad (11\text{-}5)$$

In our example,

$$\bar{V}_s = \$17,178 - \$9496 = \$7682.$$

The expected value of further sample information as here defined is a contingent value based on expectations about the mean and variance of the probability distribution of the parameter should the additional sample be taken. In the first reference at the end of the chapter, the student will find a Bayesian approach that takes account of the entire "preposterior" distribution of the mean of the revised distribution of the parameter.

11-2 Determination of Optimal Sample Size

Suppose we know that the cost per sample observation is \$27 and that there is no fixed cost element. Then the expected net economic value of the further sample of 125 is $\$7682 - \$27(125) = \$7682 - \$3375 = \$4307$. However, it is possible that an increase in sample size of less than 125 or more than 125 would have a still higher expected net economic value. Ideally, we would like to increase the sample size until the increment in expected value of further sample information just equaled the increment in cost of additional observations. This would be the sample size (n'_{opt}) at which the expected increment in net economic value over acting now would be at a maximum. The increment in the cost of information is

$$C_s = k(n' - n), \qquad (11\text{-}6)$$

where C_s = cost of further sample information,

   k = cost per sample observation,

   n' = total cumulative sample size,

   n = size of sample already observed.

In our example $k = \$27$. Let us work out the expected net value of different increase in sample size. The results are shown in Table 11–1. Suppose we consider a further sample of 300, which would mean a total contemplated sample of $n' = 400$. The calculations would be

$$\sigma_{V'} = \frac{Ns_x}{\sqrt{n'}} = \frac{50,000(\$12)}{\sqrt{400}} = \$30,000,$$

$$\hat{z}_b' = \frac{-\bar{V}'}{\sigma_{V'}} = \frac{-\$15,000}{30,000} = -.50,$$

$$\bar{V}_c' = \sigma_{V'}\mathscr{L}' = (\$30,000)(.1978) = \$5930,$$

$$\bar{V}_s = \bar{V}_c - \bar{V}_c' = \$17,180 - \$5930 = \$11,250.$$

Table 11-1

APPROXIMATION TO OPTIMAL SAMPLE SIZE

($\bar{V} = \$15,000$, $\sigma_V = \$60,000$, $n = 100$, $\bar{V}_c = \$17,180$)

n'	$\sigma_{V'}$	$\hat{z}_b'$	$\bar{V}_c'$	$\bar{V}_s$ $(\bar{V}_c - \bar{V}_c')$	Value of last 100 observations
200	$42,430	−.35	$10,530	$6,650	$6,650
300	34,640	−.43	7,630	9,550	2,900
400	30,000	−.50	5,930	11,250	1,700
500	26,830	−.56	4,830	12,350	1,100
600	24,490	−.61	4,060	13,120	770
700	22,680	−.66	3,470	13,710	590
800	21,210	−.71	2,980	14,190	480
900	20,000	−.75	2,620	14,560	370

These values appear in Table 11-1 in the row for n', or total sample size of 400. The expected net value of the *additional* sample of 300 is $11,250. In the final column of Table 11-1 we show the increment to the expected value of further sample information for each increase of 100 in the size of sample. Each additional group of 100 sample observations costs us 100($27), or $2700. Here we see that the increase in total sample size from $n' = 200$ to $n' = 300$ would increase the expected value of further sample information by $2900, and would have an expected *net* value of $2900 − $2700 = $200. The next increase from $n' = 300$ to $n' = 400$, however, produces an increase in $\bar{V}_s$ of only $1700 compared to $2700 incremental sampling cost. More detailed calculations with smaller increments of n' would be required to locate more precisely the value of n'_{opt}, but it would appear to be around 300.

A graphic approximation to determining optimal sample size is shown in Fig. 11-1. Here we have plotted the expected value of sample information, $\bar{V}_s$, against sample size, n'. Since we have already taken a sample of 100, the n' scale for cumulative sample size starts at 100. The values for the $\bar{V}_s$ line come directly from Table 11-1. Also plotted is the cost of further sampling, $C_s = k(n' - n)$—in our example $27(n' - 100)$. The maximum expected

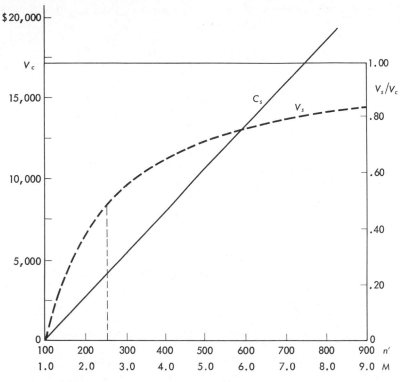

FIGURE 11-1 Graphic approximation of optimal sample size

net value of further information occurs when $\bar{V}_s - C_s$, the distance between the two lines, is largest. This occurs when the slope of the $\bar{V}_s$ line is equal to k, the slope of the C_s line. As close as can be determined graphically, this occurs at $n' = 300$.

11-3 A Nomograph for Optimal Sample Size

The supplementary scales $\bar{V}_s/\bar{V}_c$ and M in Fig. 11-1 suggest a way of generalizing the graphic approximation to determining optimal sample size. Both the ratio of the expected value of sample information to the expected value of perfect information, $\bar{V}_s/\bar{V}_c$, and the sample-size multiple, $M = n'/n$, are independent of the dimensions in any particular problem. The behavior of $\bar{V}_s/\bar{V}_c$ with increasing sample-size multiple, M, is a function of $\hat{z}_b$ for the original sample. For example, our original sample of $n = 100$ yielded $\hat{z}_b = -.25$. The normal loss integral at $\hat{z}_b$ in conjunction with σ_V determines $\bar{V}_c$ through the equation $\bar{V}_c = \sigma_V \mathscr{L}$. A sample-size multiple of 4, or $n' = 400$, would be expected to cut the standard deviation in half, thus doubling $\hat{z}_b$—that is, $\sigma_{V'} = \sigma_V/\sqrt{M}$ and $\hat{z}_b' = -\bar{V}/\sigma_{V'} = \hat{z}_b\sqrt{M} = -.25\sqrt{4} = -.50$. Then $\hat{z}_b'$ determines $\mathscr{L}'$ in the equation $\bar{V}_c' = \sigma_{V'}\mathscr{L}'$, which in turn determines $\bar{V}_s$ through $\bar{V}_s = \bar{V}_c - \bar{V}'_c$. The ratio $\bar{V}_s/\bar{V}_c$, then, is a function only of $\hat{z}_b$ and M. The general equation is

$$\frac{\bar{V}_s}{\bar{V}_c} = \frac{\mathscr{L} - (\mathscr{L}'/\sqrt{M})}{\mathscr{L}},\qquad (11\text{-}7)$$

where $\mathscr{L}$ is the normal loss integral for $\hat{z}_b$ and $\mathscr{L}'$ is the normal loss integral for $\hat{z}'_b = \hat{z}_b\sqrt{M}$.

The ratio $\bar{V}_s/\bar{V}_c$ for different sample-size multiples given various initial $\hat{z}_b$ values is plotted in Fig. 11–2. To use the nomograph, first compute $\hat{z}_b$ from the original sample to determine which line to consult.

In our problem we had

$$\hat{z}_b = \frac{-\bar{V}}{\sigma_V} = -\frac{\$15,000}{\$60,000} = -.25.$$

Next, reduce the sampling costs to a fraction of $\bar{V}_c$. A convenient method is to deal with the cost of doubling the sample as a fraction of $\bar{V}_c$. In our example

$$\frac{nk}{\bar{V}_c} = \frac{100(\$27)}{\$17,180} = .157.$$

Draw a line (or lay a straight edge) from the origin through $nk/\bar{V}_c$ at the sample-size multiple, $M = 2$ (this can be seen to be the intercept of the C_s line in Fig. 11–1 at $M = 2$ read against the $\bar{V}_s/\bar{V}_c$ scale at the right). Then approximate the sample-size multiple by comparing this slope with the slope of the appropriate $\hat{z}_b$ line. The $\hat{z}_b = .25$ line does not appear on the nomograph, so we must interpolate visually between the $\hat{z}_b = .20$ and $\hat{z}_b = .30$ lines. As near as can be determined the optimal sample-size multiple is about 2.5, and we then have

$$n'_{\text{opt}} = nM_{\text{opt}},$$
$$n'_{\text{opt}} = 100(2.5) = 250 \text{ (approx.)}.$$

To provide for reasonable discrimination between lines and slopes, the graphs have been drawn out only to a sample-size multiple of $M = 4$. With this arrangement it is possible to run off the graph in searching for an optimal multiple. A process of "doubling back" can be used in these situations, however. Suppose the cost per observation in our market-potential problem were $6.00 rather than $27.00. The cost of doubling the sample as a fraction of $\bar{V}_c$ would be $nk/\bar{V}_c = 100(\$ 6.00)/\$17,180 = .035$. When we lay a straight edge down at this slope, it becomes evident that the $\hat{z}_b = .25$ line has a greater slope all the way out to $M = 4.0$, but that at this point the slopes are approaching equality.

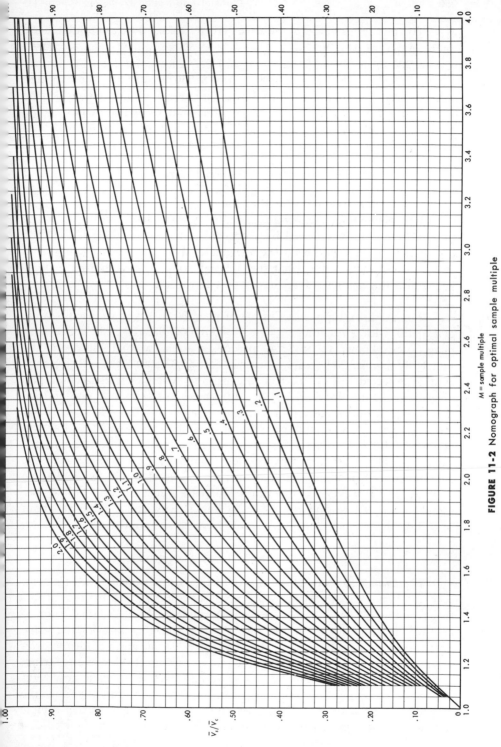

M = sample multiple

FIGURE 11-2 Nomograph for optimal sample multiple

To consider sample-size multiples greater than 4.0 we can double back in the graph. At $M = 4$, $\hat{z}_b' = -.25\sqrt{4} = -.50$, and $\sigma_{V'}\mathscr{L}' = (\sigma_V/\sqrt{M})\mathscr{L}' = (\$60,000/2)(.1978) = \$5930$. *From this reference point* $(M = 4)$ *further* doubling the sample size costs $400(\$6.00)/\$5930 = .40$ times the expected value of perfect information. Thus, beyond a multiple of 4.0 we consider the value line at $\hat{z}_b = .50$ in relation to a cost line with a slope of $.40$ per sample multiple. These two slopes appear to be equal at a multiple of about 1.6, which would then reduce to an optimal sample size of

$$n'_{\text{opt}} = 100(4)(1.6) = 640 \text{ (approx.)}.$$

This is an additional sample of 540.

It is possible for the sample size already taken to be greater than optimal. This would be revealed by a cost line whose slope exceeds even the initial slope of the value line at the relevant level of $\hat{z}_b$. It is possible in such a case to work back to find what the optimal sample size would have been, and hence the amount of resources that have been wasted by "oversampling."

For example, suppose a sample of size 500 to have produced a value of $\hat{z}_b = 1.0$, with a resulting $\bar{V}_c = \sigma_V \mathscr{L} = \$10,000(.08332) = \$833$. The sampling cost is known to be $3.40 per observation, so that increasing the sample by another 500 observations will cost $\$3.33(500)/\$833 = 2$ times the existing expected value of perfect information. At all sample-size multiples exceeding 1.0, the slope of the $\hat{z}_b = 1.0$ line is less than 2.0. The optimal sample size is thus smaller than the sample already taken. However, if we think of *reducing* the sample by a factor of 4, the applicable value line will be the one for $\hat{z}_b = .50$, and σ_V would be raised to $20,000. The expected value of perfect information at this level would be $(\$20,000)(.1978) = \$3956$, and the cost of doubling the sample from this level would be $\$3.33(125) = \$416$, or $\$416/\$3956 = .105$ times $\bar{V}_c$. With a cost slope of $.105\bar{V}_c$ per sample multiple, we find the $\hat{z}_b = .50$ line has an equal slope at about $M = 3.4$. The optimal sample size would have been, in retrospect,

$$n'_{\text{opt}} = 500(1/4)(3.4) = 425 \text{ (approx.)}.$$

Fixed sampling costs. If the cost of further sampling has a fixed element, d, in addition to an incremental cost per observation, k, then the cost of further sampling will be $d + k(n' - n)$. This cost line can be placed on the nomograph by locating the origin, $d/\bar{V}_c$, at $M = 1.0$, and then locating the value $(d + kn)/\bar{V}_c$ at $M = 2.0$. If no segment of the value line given $\hat{z}_b$ for the original sample lies above this cost line, then the expected net value of any further sample is negative. A terminal decision would therefore be made now without further sampling. If a segment of the appropriate $\hat{z}_b$ line lies above the cost line, then the optimal sample-size multiple and optimal further sample size can be determined. These will be the same as if there were no fixed cost element. Only the incremental cost element, k, affects the optimal amount of further sampling if any further sampling is justified.

If further sampling costs are entirely fixed, $k = 0$ and the cost line is horizontal at $d/\bar{V}_c$. If the fixed cost is in excess of the value of perfect information, we take no further sample. If $d < \bar{V}_c$, the optimal amount of further sampling is not reached short of complete information. In practice a large sample short of this will be taken. The nomograph can be used here to insure that the further sample is *large enough* so that its expected net value is not negative. We want a total sample sufficiently large so that the fixed cost line lies below the value line, and beyond this we might pick a sample-size multiple at which the value line has become quite flat.

11-4 Optimal Sample Size with Subjective Priors

So far we have proceeded as if the initial probability distribution of net return were produced from sample evidence. In such instances the initial sample size must be large enough so that the normal distribution is a reasonable approximation to the shape of the probability distribution of the parameter, V, because we use the normal loss integral to evaluate $\bar{V}_c$ initially. There are situations in which no direct sample evidence has yet been gathered. The decision-maker is convinced, however, that the current decision environment is closely analogous to some prior experience. In such cases an initial subjective probability distribution of net return can be based on the best judgment of the individual responsible for the decision. Consider a machine replacement problem in which the alternative to operating with 15 machines currently in use is to replace them with 15 new improved machines. The anticipated life of the new machines is 2000 operating days, and an incremental analysis has been made indicating that the net saving by adopting the new machines would be zero if average output per day under the new machines were 12.30 production units. Further, for any change of one unit in average production per day from this level, the cost analyst has determined that the change in net saving by adopting the new machines would be $284,000 over the 2000-day planning period. No direct evidence is available on the performance of the new machines in the exact manufacturing process under consideration. However, after examining the design specifications and performance data in other applications, the chief engineer states that he expects the mean output per day for the new machines will be 12.10. Note that at this output it would not pay to buy the new machines.

We take 12.10 as the mean, $\hat{\mu}$, of the chief engineer's subjective probability distribution of μ, the average output per day under the new machines. Then we must find out more about his beliefs concerning μ. We ask him to give us a range within which he would give 50–50 odds that the mean will fall. Suppose he responds with the interval 11.80 to 12.40 units per machine per day. On the assumption that his subjective distribution of μ is normal (which might be checked by sketching the results that follow and asking the chief engineer whether they represent his feelings adequately), we then have

$$\hat{z}_{.25} = -.67, \qquad \hat{z}_{.75} = .67,$$

$$\hat{z} = \frac{\mu - \hat{\mu}}{\sigma_\mu},$$

$$\sigma_\mu = \frac{\mu - \hat{\mu}}{\hat{z}} = \frac{12.40 - 12.10}{.67} = \frac{.30}{.67} = .45.$$

The subjective normal probability distribution of μ with a mean of 12.10 and a standard deviation of .45 takes the place of the normal fiducial distribution of μ that we would use if we had objective sample evidence (of sufficient size). We then have

$$\hat{z}_b = \frac{\mu_b - \hat{\mu}}{\sigma_\mu} = \frac{12.30 - 12.10}{.45} = .44,$$

$$\bar{V}_c = b\sigma_\mu \mathscr{L} = \$284,000(.45)(.2169) = \$27,720.*$$

In order to evaluate whether it is desirable to obtain further information from an objective sample we are going to need an estimate of the variability of the daily output rates of the 15 new machines. If the chief engineer is willing to specify a range within which he will give (or take) specified odds that these output rates will fall, an estimate can be made. Suppose he states that he would give 95-to-5 odds that a daily output rate randomly selected from the 15 machines would be between 7.3 and 16.9. Assuming a normal distribution of output rates, X, then

$$\hat{z}_{.025} = -1.96, \qquad \hat{z}_{.975} = 1.96,$$

$$\hat{z} = \frac{X - \hat{\mu}}{\sigma_X},$$

$$\sigma_X = \frac{X - \hat{\mu}}{\hat{z}} = \frac{16.9 - 12.10}{1.96} = 2.45.$$

We now have subjective values for σ_μ and σ_X. Now, from the usual

---

* The alternate solution using V throughout is

$$\bar{V} = \$284,000(12.10 - 12.30) = -\$56,800,$$

$$\sigma_{\hat{V}} = b\sigma_\mu = \$284,000(.45) = \$127,800,$$

$$\hat{z}_b = \frac{-\bar{V}}{\sigma_V} = \frac{-(-\$56,800)}{\$127,800} = .44,$$

$$\bar{V}_c = \sigma_V \mathscr{L} = \$127,800(.2169) = \$27,720.$$

formula for $\sigma_{\bar{x}}$ restated to solve for sample size, we can estimate the *objective sample equivalent* of the chief engineer's subjective knowledge.

$$n = \frac{\sigma_X^2}{\sigma_{\bar{X}}^2} = \frac{\sigma_X^2}{\sigma_\mu^2} = \frac{(2.45)^2}{(.45)^2} = 29.6.$$

The chief engineer's subjective knowledge is the equivalent of a random sample of 29.6 operating days selected from the 15 new machines. Suppose the cost of such an experiment is $200 per machine day. Then the engineer's expertise is worth $200(29.6) = $5920 in this decision situation. The cost to double this evidence is $5920/$27,720 = .214 times the existing expected value of perfect information. We are now in a position to consult the optimal sample-size nomograph. With an initial $\hat{z}_b = .44$ and a cost slope of .214 the optimal sample-size multiple appears to be about 2.1. Thus, total evidence equivalent to 2.1(29.6) = 62.2 randomly selected operating days from the 15 machines should be gathered. This means that 62.2 − 29.6 = 32.6 machine operating days should be observed before making a final decision.

It should be borne in mind that we have relied on the judgment of an expert at two critical points: (1) in the formation of the initial subjective probability distribution of μ_x, and (2) in estimating the underlying standard deviation of single observations. We have also assumed that both of these distributions are normal. If a normal initial subjective probability distribution is inappropriate, then the procedure indicated here would have to be abandoned. If we are not willing to use a judgment on the effective range of single observations together with a normal distribution assumption to estimate the standard deviation of single observations, then the alternative would be to take a pilot sample to assess the standard deviation. In this case, the pilot sample would be used, in the manner previously illustrated, to establish the initial fiducial distribution of the decision parameter.

11-5 Optimal Sample Size—Binomial Parameters

In Chapter 9 we discussed the normal approximation to the fiducial distributions of binomial process parameters. Subject to sample size limitations suggested in Table 9–6, this distribution was given as

$$\hat{z} = \frac{p - p'}{\sqrt{p'q'/n}},$$

p = proportion (population),

p' = proportion in sample of size n,

$q' = 1 - p'$.

The procedures for normal loss integral problems involving proportions exactly parallel those already illustrated for means. Consider an investment of $60,000 to market a product sold on a "one-to-a-customer" basis. The market is defined as 80,000 names on a mailing list. The margin of selling price over variable costs would normally be $2.50 per customer sold. Solicitation is by mail, and a pilot test is designed for a random sample of 200 names from the mailing list. The cost of the market test is $.75 per mailing. The test is carried out, and 56 orders are received, which are filled on a custom basis at no profit or loss. Should an expanded sample test be made, and if so how large should the additional test be?

The terms employed are

N = size of market or population = 80,000,

p = true proportion who would purchase,

n = sample size = 200,

b = variable return coefficient = $2.50(80,000) = $200,000,

p' = sample proportion purchasing = 56/200 = .28,

k = cost per sample observation = $.75.

The problem reduces to

$$V = -\$60,000 + \$200,000p,$$
$$\bar{V} = -\$60,000 + \$200,000p',$$
$$= -\$60,000 + \$200,000(.28) = -\$4000.$$

The optimal strategy is to forego the investment if a terminal decision must be made on the basis of the evidence in hand. However, the expected value of perfect information is

$$b = \$200,000,$$

$$p_b = \frac{a}{b} = \frac{\$60,000}{\$200,000} = .30,$$

$$\sigma_p = \sqrt{\frac{p'q'}{n}} = \sqrt{\frac{.28(.72)}{200}} = .032,$$

$$\hat{z}_b = \frac{p_b - p'}{\sigma_p} = \frac{.30 - .28}{.032} = .62,$$

$$\bar{V}_c = b\sigma_p \mathscr{L} = \$200,000(.032)(.1633) = \$1045.$$

The alternate solution method, using V throughout, is

$$\bar{V} = -\$4000,$$

$$\sigma_V = b\sigma_p = \$200,000(.032) = \$6400,$$

$$\hat{z}_b = \frac{-\bar{V}}{\sigma_V} = \frac{(-\$4000)}{\$6400} = .62,$$

$$\bar{V}_c = \sigma_V \mathscr{L} = \$6400(.1633) = \$1045.$$

To find the optimal further sample size we proceed as before. The cost increment per sample multiple for the sample-size nomograph is $kn/\bar{V}_c$ = \$.75(200)/\$1045 = .144 in this problem.

Consulting the $\hat{z}_b = .62$ line and a cost slope of .144 we find the slopes equalized at about $M = 2.8$. Therefore, the optimal total sample size is

$$n' = 200(2.8) = 560 \text{ (approx.).}$$

A further market test of about 360 mailings should be conducted. The total sample size of 560 is not so large a proportion of the total population of 80,000 that we should be much concerned about applying the finite population multiplier to refine the solution. This can become a significant element in sample-size estimation when an initial—or, as is more likely, a proposed—sample size exceeds around 10 per cent of a finite population. In such cases one might find the optimal sample size using the methods already outlined as a first approximation. Then, applying the finite multipliers to the relevant standard error formulas, we could rework the problem on a trial-and-error basis with somewhat smaller sample sizes to find the optimal sample size.

If the initial belief about a binomial parameter is in the form of a normal *subjective* probability distribution, the determination of sample size is made in essentially the same manner as when the existing belief is in the form of an *objective* normal probability distribution. The only additional step required is to reduce the subjective distribution to an equivalent objective sample size in order to form the critical cost ratio $kn/\bar{V}_c$. Suppose an expert estimates a proportion as .62, giving 70–30 odds that he is within .05 of the true value. Further interrogation indicates that the normal distribution is a reasonable model of the shape of his subjective "priors." Then

$$\hat{z}_{.15} = -1.04, \qquad \hat{z}_{.85} = 1.04,$$

$$\sigma_p = \frac{p - \hat{p}}{\hat{z}} = \frac{.67 - .62}{1.04} = .048,$$

Employing the relationship between the standard deviation of the probability distribution of p and sample size then yields

$$\sigma_p = \sqrt{\frac{\hat{p}\hat{q}}{n}},$$

$$n = \frac{\hat{p}\hat{q}}{\sigma_p^2} = \frac{.62(.38)}{(.048)^2} = 102.$$

The subjective evidence is equivalent to 102 sample observations. The cost of 102 observations would be related to the expected value of perfect information in a decision situation in order to find the cost slope to consult in determining optimal further sample size.

EXERCISES

11.1 In a market comprised of 40,000 potential customers a service facility
is capable of handling up to 500,000 customer visits during a planning
period. However, a larger number of visits can be handled at a net
return to the facility of $2 per visit if they are forecast and planned for
in advance. Prior to a planning period a sample of 400 potential customers produced an estimated mean demand of 12.40 visits with a sample standard deviation of 4.0 visits.
(a) What is the expected value of perfect information?   *Ans.* $3165.
(b) What is the expected value of an additional sample of 400?
                                                            Ans. $1575.
(c) If the cost of sampling is $3 per observation, what is the optimal
    further sample size?   *Ans.* 320 approx.

11.2 A real estate developer was considering an investment of $1,400,000.
The firm's analyst estimated revenues at $1,530,000, and stated that this
figure was the mean of a normal probability distribution of revenues
with a standard deviation of $100,000. An outside consultant claimed
that he could cut this error in half with a further survey costing $3000.
If this claim is accepted, and both the analyst and the outside consultant
are assumed to produce unbiased estimates,
(a) What is the expectation of the value of perfect information *after* the
    outside consultant completes his survey?   *Ans.* $73.20.
(b) Should a decision on the investment be made now, or should the
    outside consultant be engaged?   *Ans.* Engage consultant.

11.3 A fabricator performs a polishing operation on lots of rough-cut steel
pins, selling each lot for $1500. His costs are $1000 if the pins are free
of certain defects, but increase by $12.50 for each percentage of the pins
which contain these defects. If he concludes he would lose money, he
does not undertake the polishing operation. He can sample each lot of
steel pins at a cost of 80 cents for each 100 pins examined.
(a) If a sample of 100 from a lot reveals 36 defective pins, what is the
    expected value of perfect information?   *Ans.* $6.84.
(b) Given the above result, is it economical to continue sampling? If
    so, what is the expected optimal *total* sample size?
                                                    Ans. Yes; 300 approx.

11.4 Suppose a prior distribution of past lot quality in Exercise 11.3 is normally distributed with a mean of 32 per cent defective and a standard
deviation of 10 percentage points.
(a) Without sampling, what is the expected return per lot? *Ans.* $100.
(b) With perfect information what is the expected return per lot?
                                                            Ans. $115.02.
(c) Given the sample outcome of Exercise 11.3(a), find the revised
    parameters of the probability distribution of the proportion defec-
    tive.   *Ans.* .3525, .0432.

(d) Find the expected value of perfect information given the sample outcome of 36 defectives out of 100.   *Ans*. $3.71.

11.5 A used-car salesman claims he can sell 16 cars a week off a certain used-car lot, and is willing to lay 5-to-1 odds that he will average at least 15 a week. How long must a trial test go on before his claim can be disputed on the basis of evidence? (Assume a Poisson distribution.)
                                                                     Ans. 16 weeks.

11-6   Estimation with Linear Loss Functions

In our work in decision making up to this point we have been faced with a limited number of alternative strategies. We select the strategy that has the highest expected value among the alternatives available. Estimation may be viewed as a limiting case of decision making in that there is a continuum of possible strategies. Each value that may be adopted for an estimate represents a possible strategy, and selection of the best estimate is equivalent to selecting an optimal strategy. In previous chapters we have adopted the criterion of the most efficient in the class of consistent, unbiased estimates. This criterion seemed more or less reasonable in the absence of information about the cost consequences of errors of estimate. However, because our current task is to take explicit account of economic consequences, we need to reconsider the problem of estimation.

Estimation of single occurrence, parameter(s) known. In Chapter 8 we emphasized that prediction may run from parameter to sample, or from sample to parameter. To introduce economic considerations into estimation we select initially a problem of predicting (or estimating) a sample occurrence when the parameter of the parent population is known. It is a common inventory problem.

Consider a merchandiser who restocks a given item weekly. His market has been quite stable for some time, so that weekly demands on this stock are well known; in fact, an empirical probability distribution of weekly demands can be drawn up. The merchandiser's problem is to set the beginning-of-week stock level for such an item. This amounts to estimating or predicting individual values of weekly demand, X, given virtually complete knowledge of the probability distribution of X. What value, $\hat{X}$, should the merchandiser adopt as his estimate of X for any given week?

Suppose the merchandiser's gross margin for each item sold is $50, and his costs of holding the item over into the next week are $10. The latter costs could include storage, insurance charges, and deterioration of the product. The probability distribution of weekly demand is given in Table 11–2. This distribution has a mean of 2.09, so we might try $\hat{X} = 2$ for our estimate of demand (stock level). The column labeled C under $\hat{X} = 2$ contains the costs of error in using $\hat{X} = 2$. If demand, X, actually is zero, we will have to carry the two unsold items over into the following week at a cost of $10 each, or

Table 11-2

EXPECTED COSTS OF ERRORS OF ESTIMATE UNDER
ALTERNATIVE ESTIMATES OF DEMAND

Demand	Probability	$\hat{X}=2$		$\hat{X}=3$		$\hat{X}=4$		$\hat{X}=5$	
X	P(X)	C	P(X)·C	C	P(X)·C	C	P(X)·C	C	P(X)·C
0	.08	$20	1.6	$30	2.4	$40	3.2	$50	4.0
1	.32	10	3.2	20	6.4	30	9.6	40	12.8
2	.25	0	0.0	10	2.5	20	5.0	30	7.5
3	.18	50	9.0	0	0.0	10	1.8	20	3.6
4	.12	100	12.0	50	6.0	0	0.0	10	1.2
5	.05	150	7.5	100	5.0	50	2.5	0	0.0
	1.00		$23.3		$22.3		$22.1		$29.1

$20. If, on the other hand, X turns out to be 5, we have lost the opportunity to sell the 3 extra items at a gross margin of $50 each, or $150. In the next column these conditional losses are multiplied by their probabilities and summed to obtain the expected opportunity loss of stocking 2, or using $\hat{X}=2$ as the estimate of demand. In the remaining columns this same computation is carried out for other estimates of demand, or strategies for stock level. We see that $\hat{X}=4$ is the optimal strategy because it has the minimal expected opportunity loss.

In the problem above the probability distribution of X was discrete. Let us look at the same kind of problem in the environment of a continuous probability distribution of X. If the costs of overestimation and underestimation are linear functions of the amount of overestimate and underestimate, respectively, then we have the following situation:

$$C_u = b_u(X - \hat{X}) \qquad \text{for } \hat{X} < X,$$
$$C_o = b_o(\hat{X} - X) \qquad \text{for } \hat{X} > X,$$

where C_u = total cost of an underestimate,

b_u = cost per unit of underestimate,

C_o = total cost of an overestimate,

b_o = cost per unit of overestimate.

Now consider the behavior of the expected cost of errors of estimate as $\hat{X}$ is increased by one unit. (The units of measure can be made arbitrarily small.) The expected cost of underestimates, C_u, decreases by $b_u \cdot P(X > \hat{X})$, and the expected cost of overestimates increases by $b_o \cdot P(X < \hat{X})$. The expected total cost of error from underestimates and overestimates will increase by $b_o \cdot P(X < \hat{X}) - b_u \cdot P(X > \hat{X})$. If we consider first a very low value of $\hat{X}$, a marginal increase in $\hat{X}$ will *lower* the expected total cost of error because $P(X > \hat{X})$ is close to 1.0. We will want to increase $\hat{X}$ as long as the expected cost of underestimates that we avoid by so doing exceeds the expected cost of overestimates that we add. By the familiar marginal principle from economics, the optimal $\hat{X}$ will be reached when the marginal loss from increasing $\hat{X}$ equals the marginal gain from increasing $\hat{X}$. This point occurs when

$$b_o \cdot P(X < \hat{X}) = b_u \cdot P(X > \hat{X}).$$

The above expression can be solved for P_c, the percentile of X at which the total expected cost of error is minimized.

$$b_o P_c = b_u(1 - P_c),$$

$$P_c = \frac{b_u}{b_o + b_u}. \tag{11-8}$$

The optimal estimate is then the value of $\hat{X}$ for which $P(X \leq \hat{X}) = P_c$. We can call this $\hat{X}_{opt}$. With costs of underestimate per unit of $50 and costs of overestimate per unit of $10, for example, P_c would be $5/(5+1) = .833$. The optimal stock level would be at $X_{.833}$. At this level the odds of being overstocked ($\hat{X}_{opt} > X$) as against being understocked ($\hat{X}_{opt} < X$) are 5 to 1. Note that this is the ratio between what the merchandiser stands to gain by stocking an additional unit and what he stands to lose by so doing.

Once P_c is determined, finding $\hat{X}_{opt}$ is routine. If X is normally distributed, we find $\hat{X}_{opt} = \mu_X + z_{P_c}\sigma_X$. If X is a discrete variable, we find the highest level of X_o for which $P(X \leq X_o) < P_c$ and the lowest level for which $P(X \leq X_o) > P_c$. In the discrete example carried out earlier, $P_c = .833$. Cumulating the probability distribution of demand, we find $P(X \leq 3) = .83$ and $P(X \leq 4) = .95$. These values of X bracket P_c, and one of them will be $\hat{X}_{opt}$. The expected opportunity loss for each of the values can be calculated as we did in Table 11-1, or one can calculate the increment in expected opportunity loss between the two values.

Calling X_L the lower of the two candidate values for $\hat{X}_{opt}$, the change in expected opportunity *loss* between them will be

$$b_o \cdot P(X \leq X_L) - b_u \cdot P(X > X_L). \tag{11-9}$$

In our example this is

$$\$10(.83) - 50(.17) = 8.3 - 8.5 = -\$.20$$

Thus we know that $\hat{X} = 4$ is optimal rather than $\hat{X} = 3$.

This result has a straightforward interpretation. The probability $P(X > X_L)$ is the probability of selling the next unit (the fourth in our example) if we should stock it, and $P(X \leq X_L)$ is the probability of failing to sell the next unit. The payoffs involved are $+\$50$ should we sell the $(X_L + 1)$st unit and $-\$10$ should we fail to sell it. Therefore, the expected *gain* from stocking the fourth unit is $.17(\$50) + .83(-\$10) = \$.20$, and we should stock it.

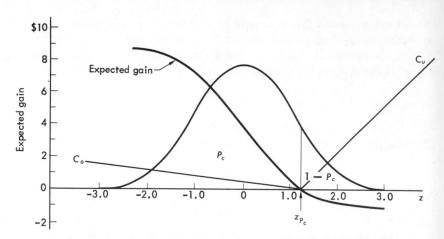

FIGURE 11-3 Expected gain from increases in estimate and optimal estimate

Figure 11–3 shows an example in the case of a normal distribution of demand with unit costs of underestimate, b_u, of \$9, and of overestimate, b_o, of \$1. The expected gain from increasing the estimate is shown. For example, at $z = -.253$ it is $.60(\$9) - .40(\$1) = \$5$. At this level there is a .60 probability that an additional unit stocked will be sold, thereby decreasing the conditional loss from failure to have inventory when demanded by \$9, and a .40 chance that an additional unit will be unsold and result in increased inventory costs of \$1. We will increase the estimate—that is, the stock level—as long as the expected gain from further increases is positive. At $z = 1.28$ the marginal value of further increases becomes $.10(\$9) - .90(\$1) = 0$.

Estimation of a parameter given the sample. The second case of optimal estimation is estimating a parameter from sample evidence. The method is similar to that already given, except that we are dealing now with the probability distribution of the parameter given the sample data. Suppose an ethical drug firm estimates its yearly volume for a new product on the basis of a test sampling among a random sample of physicians. The physicians are given a supply of the product with the request that they prescribe it where appropriate. After a suitable time the firm obtains reports on quantities prescribed. From these results the yearly volume for the product is projected. The projection method is accepted as unbiased, and is

$$\bar{X} \cdot G = \text{estimated yearly volume.}$$

The first term, $\bar{X}$, is the mean quantity prescribed per physician in the sample. The term G is a factor which takes account of the proportion of practicing physicians sampled, the length of the time period of the sample study, and the difference in test marketing versus normal marketing operations. The last element is based on the experience of the company in test marketing a number of new products. Thus, the estimate of yearly volume is a linear function of the mean usage in the market test.

Because of commitments of company resources to existing products, management has made the judgment that overestimating demand for a new product is twice as costly, per unit of error, as underestimating its demand. The cost of underestimating μ is

$$C_u = b_u(\mu - \hat{\mu}), \qquad \hat{\mu} < \mu,$$

and the cost of overestimating is

$$C_o = b_o(\hat{\mu} - \mu), \qquad \hat{\mu} > \mu.$$

Previously $\hat{\mu}$ has been used interchangeably with $\bar{X}$, but now $\hat{\mu}$ stands for any estimate of μ. Suppose the mean usage among 400 physicians is $\bar{X} = 1450$ grams and $s = 960$ grams. Then the fiducial distribution of μ has a mean of 1450 and a standard deviation equal to $960/\sqrt{400} = 48$ and is approximately normal owing to the large sample size. The optimal estimate of μ to use in estimating yearly volume is

$$\hat{\mu}_{\text{opt}} = \bar{X} + \hat{z}_{P_c}\sigma_\mu, \tag{11-10}$$

where $P_c = \dfrac{b_u}{b_o + b_u}$ and $\sigma_\mu = s_{\bar{X}} = s/\sqrt{n}$.

In our problem $b_o = 2b_u$, and

$$P_c = \frac{b_u}{2b_u + b_u} = \frac{1}{3}.$$

Then

$$\hat{\mu}_{\text{opt}} = \bar{X} + \hat{z}_{P_c}\sigma_\mu = 1450 + (-.43)(48)$$
$$= 1450 - 20.6 = 1429.4.$$

If the probability distribution of the parameter given the sample evidence is not normal the same principles hold. If the evidence comes from a small sample from a population assumed to be normally distributed, $\hat{t}$ would apply. The critical percentile, P_c for $\hat{t}$ is substituted in the expression,

$$\hat{\mu}_{\text{opt}} = \bar{X} + \hat{t}_{P_c}s_{\bar{X}}.$$

If the underlying process generating the sample observations is binomial, and $np'q'$ exceeds .10 or so, then the arcsine square root transformation can be employed to find the optimal estimate of the parameter, p. Applying Eq. (9-19), the expression would be

$$\hat{H}_{\text{opt}} = h + \hat{z}_{P_c}(1/\sqrt{n})$$

The optimal estimate of the binomial parameter is then read from Appendix Table M as the value of p corresponding to the tabled value $\hat{H}_{\text{opt}}$.

If the process is Poisson the square root tranformation can be employed with modest sample sizes. The optimal estimate of mean number of occurrences in intervals corresponding to the exposure of the sample is

$$\sqrt{\hat{\mu}_{\text{opt}}} = \sqrt{r} + \hat{z}_{P_e}(1/2)$$

Optimal estimates from suitably large samples can be obtained from the normal approximations given in Chapter 9 for binomial and Poisson parameters. The expressions for these will be, respectively,

$$\hat{p}_{\text{opt}} = p' + \hat{z}_{P_e}\sqrt{\frac{p'q'}{n}}$$

$$\hat{\mu}_{\text{opt}} = r + \hat{z}_{P_e}\sqrt{r}$$

11-7 Optimal Sample Size for Estimation

When (1) costs of underestimating and of overestimating a parameter are linear, and (2) the cost per unit of underestimate (b_u) equals the cost per unit of overestimate (b_o), and (3) the cost of sampling is a linear function of the size of sample, the optimal sample size can be obtained directly. The following problem is illustrative.

Shipments of 500 components are received periodically by a buyer. The purchase contract calls for a fixed price plus a premium for extra quality. Extra quality is determined by a rating scale, and the agreed price is $4000 + 80μ, where μ is the mean quality rating of the shipment. The sample mean quality rating of 25 components from a shipment just received is 180 points and the sample standard deviation is 20 points. The cost of testing one component is $2. Should the price for the current shipment be based on this evidence, or should more components be tested? If further sampling is called for, how large a total sample should be tested?

If the buyer wants to pay no less than is fair and the seller receive no more than is fair, then one party's loss is not the other's gain. The buyer incurs opportunity losses to the extent of any overestimate of the true quality of the current shipment, while the seller incurs opportunity losses to the extent of any underestimate in quality. The mean quality of the current shipment, μ, is unknown. Because $b_o = b_u$, the optimal estimate of μ is the existing sample mean, $\bar{X}$. The probability distribution of errors of estimate is then established by the fiducial distribution of μ given $\bar{X}$. If $\bar{X} > \mu$, the buyer will have paid $80 per unit of overestimate too much, and if $\bar{X} < \mu$, the seller will have received $80 per unit of underestimate too little. The opportunity losses from overestimating are $b_o(\bar{X} - \mu)$ for $\mu < \bar{X}$, and the opportunity losses from underestimating are $b_u (\mu - \bar{X})$ for $\mu > \bar{X}$. Both of these linear loss functions have nonzero segments originating at $\bar{X}$—that is at $\hat{z} = 0$. The evaluation of acting now on the basis of the current sample mean is

$$\hat{\mu}_{\text{opt}} = \bar{X} = 180,$$

$$\sigma_\mu = \frac{s_X}{\sqrt{n}} = \frac{20}{\sqrt{25}} = 4.0,$$

$$\bar{V}_c = \frac{b_o s_X \mathscr{L}}{\sqrt{n}} + \frac{b_u s_X \mathscr{L}}{\sqrt{n}},$$

$$\bar{V}_c = \$80(4.0)(.3989) + \$80(4.0)(.3989) = \$255.30.$$

We have assumed a normal distribution of the population of quality point ratings for individual components in the shipment, and have used a normal approximation to $\hat{t}$. The sample of 25 is a little below the rule-of-thumb level of 30 for the normal approximation to t.

Now we can consider further sampling of the current lot. As we think of increasing the total sample from n to n', our expectation of the mean quality rating is unchanged. We expect, however, that the standard error of the mean will be $s_X/\sqrt{n'}$. Since the opportunity losses originate at $\bar{X} = \bar{X}'$, the normal loss integral constant will continue to be the value of $\mathscr{L}$ at $\hat{z} = 0$, which is .3989, or approximately .40. With loss lines of equal slope rising in either direction from the mean of a normal probability distribution of μ, the expected value of perfect information becomes

$$\bar{V}_c = \frac{.80bs_X}{\sqrt{n}}. \tag{11-11}$$

The value of incremental sample information is, as before, the expected decrease in $\bar{V}_c$ as we contemplate increases in sample size.

$$\bar{V}_s = \bar{V}_c - \bar{V}'_c = \frac{.80bs_X}{\sqrt{n}} - \frac{.80bs_X}{\sqrt{n'}}.$$

As n' increases, $\bar{V}_s$ increases, and the optimal total sample size will be the n' at which the change in $\bar{V}_s$ per observation is equal to the cost per observation, k. This optimal total sample can be shown to be

$$n'_{\text{opt}} = \sqrt[3]{\left(\frac{.4bs_X}{k}\right)^2}. \tag{11-12}$$

With the cost per sample observation of \$2, the optimal sample size in the testing problem is

$$n'_{\text{opt}} = \sqrt[3]{\left(\frac{.4 \cdot 80 \cdot 20}{2}\right)^2} = \sqrt[3]{(320)^2} = 47 \text{ (approx.).}$$

Therefore, we should sample $47 - 25 = 22$ additional components before using the mean (of all 47) to determine the price to be paid for the shipment.

If a normal subjective probability distribution of the mean has been formed, Eq. (11–11) becomes $\bar{V}_c = .80b\sigma_\mu$. If an estimate can be made (either subjectively or from past samples) of the standard deviation of single observations, then Eq. (11–12) can be employed using σ_x. Since n'_{opt} refers to the optimal *total* evidence we will have to subtract from n'_{opt} the sample-size equivalent of the subjective evidence. The optimal sample evidence to collect will be

$$n'_{\text{opt}} - \left(\frac{\sigma_x}{\sigma_\mu}\right)^2.$$

Binomial parameters. If the parameter involved is a population proportion, p, and an initial sample has yielded a sample proportion, p', then s_x in Eqs. (11–11) and (11–12) become $\sqrt{p'q'}$. The initial sample must be large enough for a normal probability distribution of p to be reasonable.

If the original estimate of the binomial parameter is a normal subjective probability distribution, then Eq. (11–11) becomes $\bar{V}_c = .80b\sigma_p$, and s_x in Eq. (11–12) becomes $\hat{p}\hat{q}$, where $\hat{p}$ is the mean of the subjective distribution. The optimal sample evidence to supplement the subjective evidence will be from a sample size of

$$n'_{\text{opt}} - \frac{\hat{p}\hat{q}}{\sigma_p^2}.$$

This further sample size must be large enough for a normal fiducial distribution of p to be constructed.

11-8 A Note on Utility

Throughout our discussion of decision making based on expected values we have not questioned the appropriateness of the dollar measure of value or desirability. Use of expected monetary value as a criterion for evaluating alternative decisions implicitly assumes at least

1. that the desirability of an incremental dollar of net proceeds is independent of the number of dollars already earned or held.
2. that the desirability of a given expected dollar amount does not depend on the particular probability-payoff combination that produced the expected value. The decision-maker is assumed to be indifferent as among all alternatives with equal expected value. For example, a .01 chance of gaining $100,000 is regarded as an alternative no more and no less desirable than a .10 chance of gaining $10,000 or a .80 chance of gaining $1250, and so on.

That these two assumptions do not necessarily describe the way decision-makers feel about different alternatives under uncertainty has long been recognized by mathematicians and others.*

If one does not wish to assume that a decision-maker's marginal utility for money gain is constant, he could consider setting out to find and employ a money-utility transformation curve for the individual or business corporation. This is a problem with many theoretical and practical difficulties. An entire literature has grown up around utility measurement and related issues.†
If utility measurements could be routinely obtained, they would be used in place of the dollar values that have been employed throughout our treatment. The statistician who employs the expected-money-value criterion should be aware of the utility problem. This means using some common-sense precautions when the effective range of payoffs from alternative strategies is so wide that an assumption of constant marginal utility of money gain over the range is questionable.

EXERCISES

11.6 A baker located in a commuter terminal sells a fancy chocolate cake on weekdays. The cake sells for $6 and the ingredients cost the baker $3. If the cakes are not sold on the day they are baked, they are sold to a local hotel at a price of $2. Demand at the terminal is known to be Poisson distributed with a mean of 5 per day.
   (a) Find the expected incremental return from stocking the fourth cake; the seventh cake.   *Ans.* $1.94; −$.048
   (b) What is the optimal number of cakes to stock?   *Ans.* 6.
   (c) If the baker attaches a good-will loss of $5 to failure to have a cake when demanded, what is the optimal number of cakes to stock?
   Ans. 8.

11.7 A cab company agreed to purchase tires from a manufacturer at a price of $.50 per thousand miles of guaranteed tread life. However, if the average tread life in a lot was less than the guarantee, the manufacturer was to make a downward adjustment in price of $1.25 per thousand miles deficiency. The manufacturer had run a sample test of 64 of the tires, resulting in a sample mean of 22,267 miles and a sample standard deviation of 2104 miles.
   (a) What is the optimal tread life for the manufacturer to guarantee?
   Ans. 22,114.

---

* Daniel Bernoulli, "Exposition of a New Theory on the Measurement of Risk," reprinted (in translation) in George A. Miller, ed., *Mathematics and Psychology* (New York: John Wiley & Sons, Inc., 1964), pp. 36–52.
   † See, for example, William J. Baumol, *Economic Theory and Operations Analysis*, 2nd ed. (Englewood Cliffs, N.J.: Prentice-Hall, Inc., 1965), chap. 22, "Neumann-Morgenstern Cardinal Utility," and the references provided therein.

(b) Suppose the guarantee arrangement applied to individual tires rather than to the tread life per tire for a lot. Assuming a normal distribution, use the sample data to estimate the optimal guarantee.

Ans. 21,047.

11.8 A company allocated extra advertising allowances for its premium-grade products to shops in major suburban markets on the basis of average income in those markets. In one market a pilot sample of 50 families yielded an average income of $12,500 and a standard deviation among incomes of $5000. The cost of errors of misallocation of advertising moneys was determined to be $50 per dollar error in average income. Preparation of sampling lists to draw the pilot sample had cost $5000 and could be used for subsequent sampling. The direct costs of further sampling were $15 per family.

(a) What is the expected value of perfect information?   *Ans.* $28,283.

(b) Find the expected net economic value of an additional 150 observations.   *Ans.* $11,892.

(c) What is the optimal total sample size?   *Ans.* 354.

11.9 A prospective client, concerned with determining the proportion of consumers in various markets who had tried his product, stated that he would pay $10,000 to know this proportion in a market, but that for every .01 (one percentage point) error in a survey the information would be worth $2000 less to him. A research firm can sample the client's markets at a cost of $5 per observation.

(a) What is the optimal size sample in a market in which the true proportion is .50?   *Ans.* 400.

(b) What is the optimal size sample in a market in which the true proportion is .10?   *Ans.* 363.

(c) If a sample is taken and 144 out of 400 consumers interviewed have tried the product, what is this information worth to the client?

Ans. $6160.

11.10 A supplier estimated that monthly demand for his product was normally distributed with a mean of 50 thousand and a standard deviation of 8 thousand gallons. The cost of carrying excess stock is $.20 per gallon and the profit loss of an out-of-stock condition is $1 per gallon.

(a) What is the optimal quantity to stock monthly?

Ans. 57.76 thousand.

(b) What is the marginal return at a stock quantity of 60 thousand?

Ans. −$.0733 per gallon.

11.11 What is the optimal *further* sample size to take in Exercise 10.13 if:

(a) the cost per sample observation is $.10?   *Ans.* 360 (approx.).

(b) the cost per sample observation is $.40?   *Ans.* 135 (approx.).

11.12 Fourteen calls during a month are made for a certain spare part. Assuming a Poisson process, what is the optimal estimate of mean monthly demand if the cost per unit of underestimation is assessed at nine times the cost per unit of overestimation?

(a) Use the square root transformation.   *Ans.* 19.2.

(b) Use the tabled Poisson distribution.   *Ans.* 19 (approx.).

11.13 An opportunity is offered at a cost of $22 to participate in a venture with a .10 probability of gaining $100 and a .90 probability of gaining $10. Jones has a utility function for money amounts given by $U(M) = M + .01M^2$, where M is the money amount.

(a) Would you expect Jones to participate in the venture?

Ans. yes.

(b) Smith has a utility function, $U(M) = \log M$. How much would he be willing to pay to buy into this venture?   *Ans.* $12.59.

REFERENCES

Schlaifer, R., *Probability and Statistics for Business Decisions*. New York: McGraw-Hill Book Company, 1959.

Baumol, W. J., *Economic Theory and Operations Analysis*, 2nd ed. Englewood Cliffs, N. J.: Prentice-Hall, Inc., 1965.

12

Tests
for Association
and Goodness of Fit

So far all our work has been in one-variable analysis. We have dealt with probability distributions for original variables and sampling distributions for statistics. We have examined the theory of estimation and seen a number of applications of fiducial distributions. Finally, we have seen how economic loss functions can be employed in connection with these tools of statistical inference to develop decision systems that maximize expected monetary gain. Through all this the object of our concern has been the true value of a single parameter. We have been dealing with *univariate* analysis.

12-1 Identification and Measurement of Relationships

There is another problem at least as important for statistical inference as those just discussed. This is the problem posed by multivariate analysis. In this type of analysis we are searching for relationships among variables. We want to find factors that produce variation in some variable of interest to us.

An example of a problem in multivariate analysis is the relationship between advertising and sales. Practically everyone suspects that the more a merchandiser advertises the greater will be his sales. But two very important questions arise. First, how can we gain some assurance that changes in the amount of advertising do in fact produce changes in the amount of sales? Second, assuming that there is a relationship between advertising and sales, how do we discover what the relationship is?

Many businessmen believe there is a positive relationship between advertising and sales—that is, an increase in advertising will produce some increase in sales. Yet one cannot make a decision on the basis of this knowledge, however certain it is. How different the situation would be if an additional $100 of advertising produced only an additional $90 of sales instead of an additional $200 of sales. Both relationships are positive, but only the second has a chance of being profitable after other incremental costs are subtracted. And even then we would want to know if this relationship prevailed at all levels of advertising expenditure or if, as further increases in expenditure were made, the increments in sales slackened off.

Each of us attempts to bring about results that conform to his wants and desires. Frequently, however, we do not control the factors that directly produce a desired result; we can only affect a result indirectly. Such is the case with a businessman and his sales. He does not buy his own goods. He must bring about sales indirectly by influencing customers through such means as price, location, and advertising. Yet the relationships between his manipulation of any one of these factors, such as advertising, and the resulting changes in sales are by no means obvious. What sort of advertising copy should he use? In which media should he advertise? Are there interrelationships between the type of copy and the type of advertising medium chosen? Are his sales results affected by the day of the week on which he advertises? Is there a different relationship for each type of copy, each type of medium, and each day of the week? What are the effects of differences in consumer income? How about differences in background of potential customers? Do customer ages and occupations have an influence? What, if any, are the effects of competition on the relationships between advertising and sales? We could enumerate several hundred possible factors that might reasonably affect the relationship between advertising and sales for a given business firm. Clearly, not even large firms can afford to investigate at one and the same time several hundred factors that may affect a given desired result.

Two major types of technique are called for. First, we need a series of search techniques. These techniques are needed to establish the simple fact that a relationship does or does not exist among variables. We need "quick-screening" techniques for rapidly eliminating irrelevant factors, but we want to retain factors that have a strong influence on results; thus the job for search techniques is to separate strong factors from weak ones. We shall call such techniques *tests for association*. We shall study them in this chapter and the next.

A second type of tool we need is a set of techniques to describe the specific relationship among two or more variables. For example, it would be helpful to know whether successive absolute increases in a specific type of advertising expense produce sales increases at a constant absolute rate, a constant relative rate, a decreasing absolute rate, or some other possibility. If we had the true relationship, another fact could be brought to light. Within the permissible limits of our advertising budget we could find out whether an additional \$100 spent in this sort of advertising always produced more than \$100 of additional sales. Unfortunately we practically never have the entire statistical population available to develop multivariate relationships; usually we must do the job from samples. As we learned earlier, this means we can never be certain we have the correct relationship. Along with our techniques for estimating underlying relationships on the basis of samples, we need techniques to estimate the error in our predictions based on such sample relationships. In summary, this second class of techniques estimates underlying relationships among variables. It also gives us the sampling errors to be expected from these estimates. Either *regression* or *correlation analysis* is called for here. We shall study these in Chapters 14, 15, and 16.

12-2 Differences Among Proportions

A firm has experienced 60 per cent brand preference for one of its products in a particular market. The marketing manager wants a decision technique that will signal any change in this preference level as time passes so that he can make changes in his promotional program. He is considering a periodic random sampling of 400 consumers in the market area. For what sample outcomes should he conclude a change in preference level has taken place? This is a control problem that we already know how to solve. Since p is .6 and n is 400, both np and $n(1 - p)$ are greater than 5 which we shall assume is large enough to employ the normal approximation to the binomial distribution. Suppose an alpha risk of .10 is selected; then we can find control limits from

$$U = np + z_{.95}\sqrt{np(1 - p)},$$
$$L = np + z_{.05}\sqrt{np(1 - p)}.$$

For our example,

$$U = 240 + 1.64\sqrt{400(.24)} = 256$$

and

$$L = 240 - 16 = 224.$$

The marketing manager would conclude no change had occurred as long as a sample of 400 produced between 224 and 256 consumers favoring his brand. Usually, a more accurate approximation to the normal distribution is obtained if .5 is added to U and subtracted from L to compensate for using the continuous normal distribution as a representation of the discrete binomial. We shall ignore this refinement during the course of the explanation but include it at the end. We shall call it "the continuity correction."

We can look at the above problem in a different way. We shall assume that the true population preference proportion is p. We shall consider that

r consumers in a random sample of n prefer the brand of interest. As was implied above, if np and $n(1 - p)$ are both 5 or more, the statistic

$$z = \frac{r - np}{\sqrt{np(1 - p)}}$$

will be distributed approximately as the unit normal distribution. Futhermore, the square of a random variable that is distributed as a unit normal statistic is distributed as chi-square with one degree of freedom. This means that

$$\frac{(r - np)^2}{np(1 - p)}$$

will be distributed approximately as chi-square with one degree of freedom.

Suppose we have taken a random sample of 400 and have found that 256 prefer brand A, the brand of interest in our example. Using the symbols just defined, we can say the sample size is $n = 400$, the observed number who prefer brand A is $r = 256$, and the observed number who do not prefer brand A is $n - r = 144$. Next, we see that the expected number who prefer brand A (if $p = .6$) is $np = 400(.6) = 240$ and the expected number who do not is $n(1 - p) = 160$. If we use f to denote observed frequencies and g to denote expected frequencies, we can construct the following table:

	General case		Example	
	f	g	f	g
Prefer brand A	r	np	256	240
Do not prefer A	$n - r$	$n(1 - p)$	144	160
Total	n	n	400	400

We compare observed and expected frequencies by finding the statistic

$$\sum_i \left[\frac{(f_i - g_i)^2}{g_i} \right]. \tag{12-1}$$

For our example, the result is

$$\frac{(256 - 240)^2}{240} + \frac{(144 - 160)^2}{160} = 2.67.$$

In the general case discussed above and illustrated in the table,

$$\sum \left[\frac{(f - g)^2}{g} \right] = \frac{(r - np)^2}{np} + \frac{(n - r - n + np)^2}{n(1 - p)}$$

$$= \frac{(1 - p)(r - np)^2 + p(-r + np)^2}{np(1 - p)}$$

$$= \frac{(r - np)^2}{np(1 - p)},$$

which we learned earlier is distributed approximately as chi-square with one degree of freedom. From the chi-square table we see that $\chi^2(.90, 1) = 2.71$ —that is, $\chi^2_{.90} = 2.71$ with one degree of freedom. Except for an error attributable primarily to rounding, the value we found for

$$\chi^2 = \sum_i \left[\frac{(f_i - g_i)^2}{g_i} \right]$$

is $\chi^2(.90, 1)$.

If we had used 224 for r and 176 for $n - r$, we would also have obtained $\chi^2(.90, 1)$, except for a slight rounding error. When we found L and U by means of the normal approximation, we used $z_{\alpha/2}$ and $z_{1-(\alpha/2)}$ with $\alpha = .10$. We have just seen that use of L (or U) in Eq. (12–1) will give us very nearly $\chi^2(\alpha, m)$. The two tests on a sample proportion are equivalent. If a sample were to yield a number less than L or greater than U who prefer brand A, then that number used in conjunction with Eq. (12–1) would yield a value of chi-square greater than 2.71.

The chi-square technique described above can be extended to form a comprehensive test for observations from several samples from a binary population. Suppose that the marketing manager in the above example had taken four samples, each with 400 consumers, and suppose that the results were as shown in the following table:

	Sample			
	1	2	3	4
Prefer brand A	248	260	252	258
Do not prefer A	152	140	148	142
Total	400	400	400	400

The marketing manager wonders whether this composite evidence is consistent with expected frequencies of 240 who prefer brand A and 160 who do not for each sample.

We know that Eq. (12–1) applied to any one of the samples can be treated as belonging to a chi-square distribution with one degree of freedom. It can also be shown that the *sum* of k random variables each distributed as chi-square with one degree of freedom is a random variable distributed as chi-square with k degrees of freedom. For our example we find that

$$\sum_i \sum_j \left[\frac{(f_{ij} - g_{ij})^2}{g_{ij}} \right] = \left[\frac{(248 - 240)^2}{240} + \frac{(152 - 160)^2}{160} \right]$$

$$+ \cdots + \left[\frac{(258 - 240)^2}{240} + \frac{(142 - 160)^2}{160} \right]$$

$$= 9.708.$$

This can be interpreted by referring to a table for chi-square with four degrees of freedom. We see that $\chi^2(.95, 4) = 9.49$. If we select an alpha risk level of .05, the composite evidence from the four samples would lead us to reject the hypothesis that p is .6 for all four samples. At least one of them is likely to have come from a population with a different proportion preferring brand A.

We used expected frequencies of 240 and 160 for each of the four samples in the above example. We were testing the hypothesis that each sample came from only one binary population with $p = .6$. Even if our hypothesis had been that each sample came from a different binary population, the test would still apply. For some reason we might expect that $p_1 = .3$, $p_2 = .4$, $p_3 = .5$, and $p_4 = .6$, for instance. We would use expected frequencies of 120 and 280 to compare with 248 and 152 in the first sample, and so on for the others. Then we would find

$$\chi^2 = \sum_i \sum_j \left[\frac{(f_{ij} - g_{ij})^2}{g_{ij}} \right] \tag{12-2}$$

and interpret it as a chi-square variable with four degrees of freedom.

In all the preceding examples in this section we had prior information, independent of the sample data, as to the value for p. Many times we do not have such information and we must use the sample data to get it. To illustrate the procedure for this case, we shall work with data on three salesmen. The first has made 30 calls during the past month and 15 of these calls resulted in sales orders. The other two salesmen got orders from 22 out of 35 calls and 13 out of 29 calls, respectively. The data can be arranged as follows:

	Salesman			
	1	2	3	Total
Sales order	15	22	13	50
No sales order	15	13	16	44
Total calls	30	35	29	94

The sales manager wants to know whether the salesmen can be considered of equal effectiveness with respect to their ratio of sales orders to calls. This is equivalent to testing the hypothesis that $p_1 = p_2 = p_3$ for the three populations from which the samples came.

We have no given information on the value of p_i. Instead we substitute the consolidated estimate $\bar{p} = 50/94$. The expected frequencies for the first and second salesman's sales orders are

$$g_{11} = \frac{50(30)}{94} = 16.0 \quad \text{and} \quad g_{12} = \frac{50(35)}{94} = 18.6.$$

In general, $g_{1j} = n_j \bar{p}$ and $g_{2j} = n_j(1 - \bar{p})$. Rather than using the general formulas, we can get the remaining expected frequencies by subtraction from marginal totals. Thus $g_{21} = 30 - 16.0 = 14.0$, $g_{22} = 35 - 18.6 = 16.4$, $g_{13} = 50 - g_{11} - g_{12} = 15.4$, and $g_{23} = 29 - 15.4 = 13.6$. This way of obtaining g_{13} is equivalent to $50(29)/94$, but the use of marginal totals emphasizes that there are only two degrees of freedom rather than the three we might expect from earlier examples in this section. We have lost a degree of freedom from using sample information to form an estimate against which a test can be run.

Since all values of g_{ij} are greater than 5, we know that $n_j \bar{p}$ and $n_j(1 - \bar{p})$ are greater than 5 for all n_j. We can calculate

$$\chi^2 = \sum_i \sum_j \frac{(|f_{ij} - g_{ij}| - .5)^2}{g_{ij}} \tag{12-3}$$

$$= \frac{(|15 - 16| - .5)^2}{16} + \frac{(|15 - 14| - .5)^2}{14} + \cdots + \frac{(|16 - 13.6| - .5)^2}{13.6}$$

$$= \frac{(1 - .5)^2}{16} + \frac{(1 - .5)^2}{14} + \cdots + \frac{(2.4 - .5)^2}{13.6}$$

$$= 1.4983.$$

It can be shown that, even when $\bar{p}$ is used in place of p, the above statistic is still distributed as chi-square. The degrees of freedom, however, must be reduced as described above. The value 1.50 is approximately $\chi^2(.52, 2)$. The three samples could very well have come from the same binary population. Note that we have included the continuity correction in Eq. (12–3). In actual practice this correction may also be included in Eqs. (12–1) and (12–2).

12-3 Contingency Table Tests

The techniques of the previous section are not restricted to tests on binary populations. We need not have each sample restricted to only two categories. We can use the same approach to analyze data from multifold populations.

To qualify for treatment by contingency table tests, data must fulfill two requirements. First, the random variable must be a frequency count. Second, at least one of the descriptive variables should be qualitative. If all descriptive variables are quantitative, the closely related quantile test in Sec. 12–4 is appropriate. For instance, suppose we have conducted a market survey on consumers' opinions concerning a new brand of cereal, LIFO. Suppose we have classified those interviewed on two variables: age and opinion about the new cereal.

For this example we count the number of respondents. The number of respondents is the random variable. There are two descriptive variables. One is the age of the respondent; this is quantitative continuous. The second is the opinion the respondent holds about LIFO: LIFO better than currrent preferred brand, LIFO worse than current preferred brand, or no choice between the two brands. This variable is qualitative.

The data that came from our hypothetical market survey appear in Table 12–1. We assign frequencies to classes based on the descriptive variables. Each consumer is assigned to an age-opinion class. We want to see whether a consumer's opinion about our new brand tends to be contingent upon or associated with his age.

Table 12-1

HYPOTHETICAL MARKET SURVEY: CONSUMERS' OPINIONS
ABOUT "LIFO" CLASSIFIED BY AGE GROUPS

Age	LIFO better	LIFO worse	No choice	Total
(a) DATA FROM HYPOTHETICAL MARKET SURVEY				
20–29.99	175	263	51	489
30–39.99	193	290	22	505
40–49.99	75	63	8	146
50 and over	41	15	15	71
Total	484	631	96	1211
Per cent	40	52	8	100
(b) EXPECTED RESPONSES UNDER HYPOTHESIS OF INDEPENDENCE*				
20–29.99	195.4	254.8	38.8	489.0
30–39.99	201.8	263.1	40.0	505.0
40–49.99	58.4	76.1	11.6	146.0
50 and over	28.4	37.0	5.6	71.0
Total	484.0	631.0	96.0	1211.0
(c) CONTRIBUTIONS TO TOTAL CHI-SQUARE				
20–29.99	2.03	.23	3.53	5.79
30–39.99	.34	2.65	7.66	10.65
40–49.99	4.44	2.09	.83	7.36
50 and over	5.16	12.49	14.14	31.79
Total	11.97	17.46	26.16	55.59

* Figures may not add to marginal totals because of rounding.

Given a contingency table such as Table 12–1(a), our rationale is straightforward. We compute theoretical frequencies for each of the cells on the assumption that consumers' opinions are independent of age. Then we compare the observed frequency (f) in each cell with the expected frequency (g) for that same cell by means of the chi-square measure of discrepancy, and sum these measures over all cells.

Refer to the bottom row in Table 12–1(a). If opinion is independent of age, we would expect 40 per cent of each age group to think LIFO better,

52 per cent to think LIFO worse, and 8 per cent to be undecided. When we apply these percentages to 489, we get the results shown in the first row of Table 12–1(b). Thus $(484/1211)(489) = 195.4$, and so on. The same procedure is carried out for the 505 respondents who are in their thirties, the 146 respondents in their forties, and the 71 respondents who are fifty years of age and over. This procedure gives us the 12 expected values shown in the cells in Table 12–1(b).

Table 12–1(c) shows the individual components of the chi-square statistic as well as the statistic itself. These come from Tables 12–1(a) and (b) in the following manner:

$$\sum_i \sum_j \frac{(|f_{ij} - g_{ij}| - .5)^2}{g_{ij}} = \frac{(|175 - 195.4| - .5)^2}{195.4} + \cdots + \frac{(|15 - 5.6| - .5)^2}{5.6}$$
$$= 2.03 + \cdots + 14.14 = 55.59.$$

When we use the marginal totals to compute the expected frequencies as we have done here, the degrees of freedom for a two-way contingency table with r rows and c columns are $(r - 1)(c - 1)$. This will only be true, of course, if $g_{ij} \geq 5$ for each cell so that a contribution is calculated for all rc cells. Otherwise a cell with an expected frequency of less than 5 would be combined with an adjacent cell. For our example, chi-square is 55.59 with $(4 - 1)(3 - 1) = 6$ degrees of freedom. $\chi^2(.999, 6)$ is only 22.5. Our result is so far beyond 22.5 that we must reject the hypothesis that age and opinion are independent.

Since we have established the strong likelihood that consumers' opinion about our new cereal differs by age group, we are justified in making separate estimates of preference for each age group. We can construct separate fiducial distributions for the true proportion preferring "LIFO" in each age group. The sample proportions for each age group are shown in Table 12–2 along with the sample sizes. These are given the symbols p' and n, respectively. Since np' and $n(1 - p')$ are relatively large for each of the four samples,

Table 12-2

SAMPLE SIZE, POINT AND INTERVAL ESTIMATES OF PROPORTIONS
PREFERRING LIFE BY AGE CLASS

		Point estimates		
Age class	n	Mean (p')	Standard deviation	Interval estimate*
20–29	489	.36	.02	.32–.40
30–39	505	.38	.02	.34–.42
40–49	146	.51	.04	.43–.59
50 and over	71	.58	.06	.46–.70

*$\alpha = .05$.

we can use the normal approximation with variances $[p'(1 - p')]/n$. Standard deviations are shown. The table thus contains the mean and standard deviation of the fiducial distribution of preference for each age class. From this information the .95 interval estimates have been formed.

An examination of the interval estimates would lead us to suspect that there is a distinct break in preference pattern at about age 40. The heavy overlap in intervals for the age groups under 40 suggests these two groups may have very nearly the same preference pattern. We might also suspect that age groups over 40 have the same preference pattern.

Our sequence here illustrates on a small scale the relation between search and measurement techniques in dealing with association. Having found a highly significant result in the chi-square test for association, we went on to specify more closely the quantitative character of the relationship involved. This involves estimating the parameters that will tell us not only that preference varies with age but also how preference varies with age. In the present case, we may feel that the differential in preference is so sharp between groups under age 40 and those over 40 that our promotional campaign will have to be age-specific.

We have illustrated the contingency table test by showing two descriptive factors (age and opinion) operating upon a random variable (consumer preference frequency). It is possible to extend the technique to any number of descriptive variables. At least one of these descriptive variables must be qualitative in order for us to call it a contingency table test.

EXERCISES

12.1 The marketing manager in a food manufacturing firm obtained the following data from four independent consumer preference studies on a cereal product. Perform a chi-square test of the hypothesis that the proportion of consumers who prefer brand A is .6. Be sure to include the continuity correction in your calculations.

	Sample			
	1	2	3	4
Prefer brand A	248	260	252	258
Do not prefer A	152	140	148	142
	400	400	400	400

Note that these are the same data used in the text example. The continuity correction was not made in the text. Does its use alter the conclusion?

12.2 In a large insurance firm one department consists of three sections all of which have the same functions. Each section supervisor has evaluated the performance of the people in her section. The results are shown below.

| | Supervisor | | |
Evaluation	A	B	C
Superior, excellent	8	3	14
Average or below	9	11	9
	17	14	23

Can it be assumed that the same proportion of superior and excellent ratings will be obtained from each supervisor if present conditions remain unchanged?

12.3 Data from realty firms in a certain city are arranged to show the number of days that elapse between first listing a used house and selling it. The following table is prepared:

| | Days from listing to sale | | |
Price	20 or less	Over 20	Total
Under $25,000	63	67	130
$25,000 and over	16	41	57

On the basis of this evidence is the time from listing to sale affected by price?   *Partial ans.* $\chi^2 = 5.96$.

12.4 In a supermarket during the past five months sales of the large-size package of the largest-selling brand of powdered laundry detergent have been growing steadily as a proportion of all packages of this product sold. The proportions for the series of months have been .21, .24, .28, .32, .33. Sales by type of package for a slower-selling competitor over the same period are shown below.

| | Month | | | | |
	1	2	3	4	5
Large-size package	58	84	106	95	126
Other sizes	185	285	328	277	180
Total	243	369	434	372	306

Could the proportions that apply to the first brand also apply to the slower-selling brand?   *Partial ans.* $\chi^2 = 19.60$, $m = 5$.

12.5 Instructions were given for selecting a simple random sample of 200 persons from a master list. The ages of the persons on the master list and in the sample are known. To check on how well the sample selection instructions were executed a conformance check is to be run. From tables published for the master list the quartiles for the age distribution are found. The sample is divided into five equal subsamples by a random process and the following table is prepared.

Population age group	Subsample				
	A	B	C	D	E
Above Q_4	9	14	12	6	14
Q_3 to Q_4	8	10	16	10	6
Q_2 to Q_3	7	6	8	11	14
Below Q_2	16	10	4	13	6
	40	40	40	40	40

Perform a contingency table test on these data and decide whether they constitute a suitable sample.

12.6 A gasoline service station manager wants to improve the scheduling of hours of work for his employees. He believes that the gasoline customer pattern by hour of the day is different for a weekday than for a Saturday. He has the following data immediately available on number of gasoline customers.

Hours	Wednesday	Saturday
6 A.M. to 9 A.M.	18	4
9 A.M. to 3 P.M.	10	8
3 P.M. to 7 P.M.	24	13
7 P.M. to 10 P.M.	12	19
	64	44

(a) Can he expect an equal number of customers, on the average, from each time class on Wednesdays?

(b) Can he expect an equal number of customers from each time class on Saturdays?

(c) Is the expected proportional pattern of customers on Wednesdays the same as it is on Saturdays?

12.7 A direct-mail firm is testing two different appeals that offer the same product. A random sample of 520 names and addresses is selected from a mailing list. Half of the sample is assigned to each of two subsamples by a random selection process. A month after mailing, 31 orders were received from those who received the first appeal and 49 were received from those who received the second. Test whether the population proportions of orders from the two appeals could be the same.   *Partial ans.* $\chi^2 = 4.28$.

12.8 In an effort to provide equitable appraisals on residential property, a municipality has had each of four appraisers use a proposed set of procedures on the same 20 properties. Five properties were chosen from each value class. Care was taken to insure that the appraisers were unfamiliar with the properties and that each appraiser worked independently of the others. Perform a test of the consistency of appraised values.

Appraised value class	Appraiser			
	A	B	C	D
a	8	4	6	3
b	5	6	4	3
c	4	6	3	8
d	3	4	7	6

12-4   Quantile Tests

As in the case of contingency table tests, the random variable for quantile tests must be a frequency count. It must represent a total number of frequencies allocated to cells or class groups defined by one or more descriptive variables. The appropriate situation for a quantile test differs from that for a contingency table test in that, for a quantile test, at least one descriptive variable must be quantitative and all descriptive variables may be quantitative. This contrasts with a contingency test in which at least one descriptive variable must be qualitative. Either term can be used to describe the situation when both a quantitative and a qualitative variable are present.

A quantile test is another test for association. As such, it is meant to determine whether a state of association exists, rather than to find what relationship best describes that association.

Medians test. At a certain university a battery of tests is used to select students for graduate study in business; the data for the medians test come from experience with one of the ability tests in this battery. A useful selection test is one that distinguishes between students who later prove to be successful in the graduate program and those who do not. In addition, a better prediction of whether or not a student will succeed can usually be had by combining several tests. Finding the proper combination of these tests to get the best prediction is the subject of Chapter 17 on discriminant analysis. The objective here is to establish whether or not a particular test is associated with success.

In Table 12–3, 55 students are classified by their performance in the first semester of the statistics course at the university and by their performance on the symbolic reasoning test given to them before they entered. Each student is assigned to one of the four cells in the table on the basis of where he stood relative to the medians of the two descriptive variables. Whenever the median of at least one descriptive variable is used to separate the random variable into classes, the data are in suitable form for a medians test.

Look at the marginal totals in the right column and in the bottom

Table 12-3

CLASSIFICATION OF GRADUATE BUSINESS STUDENTS BY STATISTICS
GRADE AND SYMBOLIC REASONING TEST SCORE*

First semester grade	Symbolic Reasoning Score		Total
	Below median	Above median	
Above median	11	15	26
Below median	17	12	29
Total	28	27	55

* Several cases that fell on one of the class divisions were omitted. As a result, marginal totals are not equal for each row and column.

row of Table 12–3. If no case fell exactly on the median value for either scale, then half of the grand total should be above the median and half below the median on each descriptive variable scale. This is very nearly true in the bottom row of Table 12–3, but there is a considerable difference from this situation in the right column. The reason is that several cases fell right on the median. A similar line of reasoning says that about 25 per cent of the grand total number of cases ought to fall in each of the four cells, on the assumption that there is no association between the two variables.

As in the case of contingency table tests, we can use marginal totals to compute frequencies that would be expected in each cell if there were no association between the two classification variables. For example, when we do this for the upper left-hand cell we get $g_{11} = (26/55)28 = 13.24$. After finding all the g_{ij}, we apply Eq. (12–3) to find chi-square. For Table 12–3 we get $\chi^2 = .88$ with one degree of freedom, which is between the 60th and 70th percentile of the chi-square distribution.

We have found no evidence of association between symbolic reasoning score and first semester statistics grade. We say that we have "found no evidence" because, as we shall see, the medians test is very crude. It is quick, but relatively insensitive.

Quartile-median test. Our example for this member of the quantile test family will be the same as for the medians test. In Table 12–4 we show the same data as in Table 12–3, arranged for a quartile-median test rather than for a simple medians test. Note that our grand number of cases is now reduced to 47 because an additional 8 cases have fallen on the boundaries dividing quartiles.

The expected frequency for the upper left corner cell in Table 12–4 ($g = 5.85$) is the result of multiplying (11/47) by 25. The other expected cell frequencies are computed by similar use of the marginal totals. The contribution to chi-square is shown for each cell. For example, $\chi^2 = (|2 - 5.85| - .5)^2/5.85 = 1.92$.

The restriction that the expected frequency in each cell equal or exceed 5 is slightly violated in two of the cells, which have expected frequen-

Table 12-4

CLASSIFICATION OF GRADUATE BUSINESS STUDENTS BY STATISTICS
GRADE AND SYMBOLIC REASONING TEST SCORE*

First semester	Symbolic Reasoning Score							
grade	Below median			Above median			Totals	
	f	g	χ^2	f	g	χ^2	f	χ^2
Above $X_{.75}$	2	5.85	1.92	9	5.15	2.18	11	4.10
$X_{.50}$ to $X_{.75}$	8	5.85	.47	3	5.15	.53	11	1.00
$X_{.25}$ to $X_{.50}$	4	4.79	.02	5	4.21	.02	9	.04
Below $X_{.25}$	11	8.51	.47	5	7.49	.53	16	1.00
	25		2.88	22		3.26	47	6.14

* Because cases falling on cell boundaries are omitted, marginal row totals and marginal column totals are not equal.

cies of 4.79 and 4.21. However, when we compute these cells' contributions to chi-square, results are .02 and .02—an immaterial amount. Consequently, we judge that the increase in degrees of freedom made possible by breaking down the semester statistics grade variable into quartiles is more valuable than the slight violation of the rule governing minimum expected values. We reach this conclusion after looking at the total chi-square value, 6.14. Three degrees of freedom apply to this quantity. The total is close to the 90th percentile of the applicable chi-square distribution.

Why does a more detailed classification of the statistics grade result in a change in the probability level for chi-square from less than the 70th percentile to very nearly the 90th percentile? Our conclusion when we used the medians test on the above data was that we had no evidence of association between symbolic reasoning scores and first semester statistics grades. By contrast, the result of the quartile-median test would allow us to make a conclusion of association at an alpha risk level of .15. Which result should we believe? Furthermore, we notice that it is possible in principle to extend the quantile tests even further. We can subdivide both variables into quartiles, or one into quintiles and the other into quartiles, or both into deciles, or on through a host of possible quantile tests. Where should we stop, and which test result should we believe? The answer is that we should subdivide the data into as many cells as possible without seriously violating the restriction on the lower limit for the g_{ij}. The change in the results here illustrates that an increase in the degrees of freedom increases the sensitivity of the chi-square test. It is very important to gain as many degrees of freedom as possible for the test without seriously violating the minimum restriction on the g_{ij}.

It is possible that several alternative classifications of the data may give rise to the same maximum number of degrees of freedom. There is a temptation to select from these alternatives the one that produces either the highest or lowest value of chi-square, depending upon one's objectives.

The danger in yielding to this temptation is that the particular result may have come about from a fortuitous sampling fluctuation rather than from a true underlying association or lack of association. To avoid the pitfall of mistakenly assuming a fortuitous sample result to be evidence of an underlying pattern in the population, we should proceed in one of two ways.

The first procedure forces us to choose which classification of the data we are going to use before we actually allocate the data to the cells. Knowing only the total number of items to be classified, we can get a very good estimate of the theoretical frequencies in all cells for any given quantile test. For example, in Table 12–4 we need only know that we are going to be dealing with approximately 50 frequencies and that we are going to run a quartile-median test in order to know that approximately one-eighth of the total number of frequencies will be the value of g_{ij} for each cell. Since 50/8 is somewhat more than 6, we can assume that we will not seriously violate the restriction on minimum g_{ij} by making a quartile-median test. Furthermore, we realize that we cannot subdivide the data into appreciably more classes without violating the restriction.

The second procedure to avoid the pitfall mentioned above consists in going ahead to find that alternative which yields the highest (lowest) value of chi-square. Having done this, we must select a second independent sample and subject this second set of data to the same sort of test.

The common principle in both procedures is that one cannot use the same set of data both to formulate and to test a hypothesis. In formulating a hypothesis one looks purposely for nonrandom patterns. If one is going to search the data for nonrandom patterns, then he cannot fairly select only the suspect elements for a formal test. For the alpha level to have any meaning, the hypothesis must be formulated in advance of any analysis of the data to be used in formally testing the hypothesis.

The second procedure seems preferable when it is feasible to take a further sample. By following it we have a chance of detecting situations in which peculiar patterns of association exist that may not be suspected in advance. The first procedure requires that we choose the test that we shall perform before we have examined any of the data. There are many instances imaginable in which this procedure would miss associations that the second procedure would detect. We shall have more to say on this point when we discuss the corner association test.

12-5 The Corner Association Test

To present the technique for making the corner association test we shall use the same example as was used for the quantile tests in Sec. 12–4. You will recall that this example dealt with the scores of graduate business students on a symbolic reasoning test and their first semester statistics grades.

The technique is best carried out by use of graphical procedures. The first step is to plot a scattergram of the data. This is shown in Fig. 12–1. The random variable is number of students, the criterion descriptive variable is first semester statistics grade, and the predictor variable is symbolic reasoning score. In accordance with custom the criterion variable is plotted on the vertical axis and the predictor variable is plotted on the horizontal axis. Each of the dots in the scattergram represents one student's results. For example, consider the point with coordinates (25, 82). This is the result for a student who scored 25 on the symbolic reasoning test and got a first semester statistics average of 82 out of a possible 100 points.

Once the raw data are plotted in the form of a scattergram, the next step is to plot the median test score and the median statistics grade as lines on the scattergram. The vertical line at 7 on the symbolic reasoning scale represents the median of the symbolic reasoning scores. Similarly, the horizontal line at 75 on the first semester statistics grade scale represents the median statistics grade. Note that the field is now divided into four quadrants.

Next, we give signs to the four quadrants. The lower left and upper right quadrants are each given a positive sign. The upper left and lower right quadrants are given negative signs.

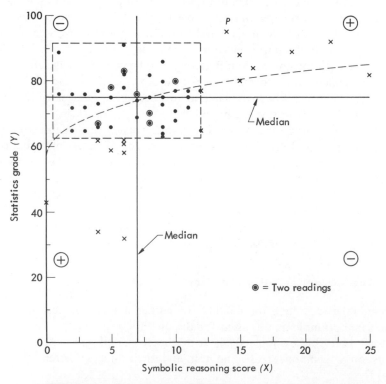

FIGURE 12-1 Scattergram of 64 graduate business students' scores

To begin our next step we select the extreme end of one of the two median lines arbitrarily. Suppose we select the far right end of the horizontal median line. Then we move toward the main pack of the data, counting the points as we go, until we find two consecutive points on opposite sides of the median line. We ignore any points that fall on either of the median lines. For example, the first point we encounter coming in from the right on the horizontal line of medians is the point (25, 82). The next point (22, 92) is also above the median, so we proceed on to the left. We continue in this manner until we come to the point (12, 77). All the points included so far are in a positive quadrant. This last point is above the median, but there is a point with the same X-value that lies below the median. This new point is (12, 65), which lies in a negative quadrant. We have encountered a "crossover tie" after passing 7 data points in a positive quadrant. The general rule on such ties is to give each tie point in the same quadrant as the cumulative count a value of $1/(1 +$ the number of tie points in the opposite quadrant). Tie points on the median line are not counted. For our example, the count is $+7 + (\frac{1}{2})$ $= +7.5$. Had there been two tie points below and one above the median, the count would have been $+7 + 1/(1 + 2) = +7.33$. Had there been two tie points above the median and one below, the count would have been $+7 + 2(\frac{1}{2}) = +8$.

We next move down the vertical median line from the top in the same manner. We encounter two points lying in the plus quadrant before we reach our first point lying in the negative quadrant. We therefore have $+2$ as our count for the upper portion of the vertical median. Note that the point P was counted here and also when we made our first count.

We proceed counterclockwise to the left end of the horizontal median and get a count of $+1$ in the same manner as before. The lower half of the vertical median gives us a count of $+8$.

The final step in the calculation of our test statistic is to find the absolute value of the algebraic sum of the four components. The test statistic is

$$T = |7.5 + 2 + 1 + 8| = 18.5.$$

Had the point (6, 32) been (9, 32), we would have had -1 as the count for the lower part of the vertical median instead of $+8$. In this case, T would have been only 9.5.

Let's stop for a moment to consider what should happen to our test statistic if there is no association between the two descriptive variables. By definition, half of the data lie respectively to the right and left of the vertical median line. Consider the half of the data lying to the right of the vertical median line. If there is no association between symbolic reasoning score and first semester statistics grade, then our knowing that a given data point lies to the right of the median on symbolic reasoning can give us no information about where it lies relative to the median statistics grade. It should be equally likely, granted no association, that the point lie either above or below the statistics median. As we move in from the right end of the horizontal median line, the probability is 1/2 that the first point we come to will lie above this median line. The probability is also 1/2 that the next point we come to will lie above the horizontal median line. So long as there is no association, the probability for each point stays at 1/2. Thus, a long sequence of points on the same side of the median would be unusual if there is no association. The expected value of T would be zero, and large positive or negative values of T are unlikely if there is no association.

The line of reasoning described above leads to a way for calculating the probabilities for various values of T on the assumption of no association between the variables. The result of these calculations is shown in Table 12–5. This table gives the probabilities in both tails of the sampling distribution of T given no association in the population.

For the example presented in Fig. 12–1, 8 points lie on one of the median lines. These are ignored in all counts for the test. We have a total of 64 less 8, or 56, points not on median lines. For use in Table 12–5 this gives us $n = 56$ and $2n = 112$. The value of our test statistic is $T = 18.5$. When we use these two values as arguments for entering Table 12–5, we find an alpha value from the body of the table of between .003 and .001. Less than

Table 12-5*

DISTRIBUTION OF QUADRANT SUM FOR CORNER TEST
OF ASSOCIATION FOR SAMPLES OF SIZE 2n†

T	2n				
	6	8	10	14	inf.
8	.111	.126	.133	.132	.122
9	.100	.084	.093	.092	.081
10	.100	.055	.064	.063	.053
11	.100	.038	.044	.043	.034
12	.100	.030	.029	.030	.022
13	.000	.029	.019	.020	.013
14		.029	.013	.014	.008
15		.029	.010	.010	.005
16		.029	.008	.007	.003
17		.000	.008	.005	.002
18			.008	.003	.001
19			.008	.002	.001
20			.008	.001	.000
21			.000	.001	.000
22				.001	.000
23				.001	.000

* Abridged and reproduced with permission from P. S. Olmstead, and J. W. Tukey, "A Corner Test for Association," *The Annals of Mathematical Statistics,* **XVIII:** 4 (1947), 502.

† The table gives α, the probability that the quadrant sum equals or exceeds T for an unassociated population.

3 times in 1000 can we expect to get as great an absolute T value as we got if there is no association between the two variables. It seems far more reasonable for us to assume strong association between symbolic reasoning scores and first semester statistics grades.

Recall our results with the same data when we made the quantile tests back in Sec. 12–4. Our medians test gave us no evidence of association between the two variables in question. The quartile-median test gave us only mild evidence of association. Yet the corner association test just concluded gives us strong evidence of association.

Perhaps we can find an answer to the apparent contradiction in association test results by trying to discover why the last test gave such conclusive results. Look at Fig. 12–1 again. Our quantile tests merely counted the number of points in each of the quadrants or octants of the scatter. They made no attempt to use information on how the individual points were spread within the quadrants. Yet when we examine the scatter more closely, certain patterns emerge. Very high symbolic reasoning scores are invariably associated with semester statistics grades above the median. Similarly, very low first semester statistics grades are associated invariably with symbolic reasoning scores below the median. Thus an association somewhat like that represented by the curve faired in through the intersection of the median lines in Fig. 12–1 seems to obtain. In other words, there seems to be a strongly *curvilinear* relationship between symbolic reasoning and statistics grade.

The curvilinear relationship between the two variables in Fig. 12–1 could be real in the actual population, and yet a sample from that population might have approximately one-quarter of the data in each of the quadrants. For instance, suppose that we had 100 cases in the population. Further suppose that 25 of these cases were located in each of the four quadrants. The 25 cases in the upper right quadrant are spread well to the right toward high symbolic reasoning scores. The 25 cases in the lower left quadrant are spread downward to the left toward very low statistics grade-symbolic reasoning score combinations. The 25 cases in each of the two remaining quadrants are located close to the intersection of the two median lines. A medians test on a sample would be expected to produce an insignificant value of chi-square, while the corner association test would be expected to detect the association.

It would seem that in many circumstances wherein both descriptive variables are quantitative, a corner association test is to be preferred to a quantile test. The quantile tests can very easily miss an underlying pattern of association unless the pattern is suspected in advance and allowed for in designing the classifications for the test. This superiority of the corner association test would appear to be more marked the smaller the sample size. It is an exact test for any sample size and can be used when the expected cell frequencies in a quantile test fall below the levels required for using the chi-square statistic.

12-6   Chi-Square Test for Goodness of Fit

In Chapter 5 we first encountered a situation in which we needed a test to tell us whether a model is a reasonable generalization of a particular empirical distribution. In the remainder of that chapter and in subsequent chapters we had to base our judgment on a visual comparison of the graphed cumulative distribution of actual data with that of the fitted model distribution. The time has come to present a more precise goodness-of-fit test.

Strictly speaking, the goodness-of-fit test that we shall now present is not a test for association. For example, we are not attempting to see whether positive differences in one variable are associated with either positive or negative differences in other variables. Yet, there is a sense in which we are searching for association. We make the assumption that a specified type of distribution with specified values for its parameters is an adequate model for a given set of data. We then calculate what the expected frequencies are for each of the classes in which our empirical data are arranged. Finally, we compare these expected frequencies with the frequencies actually observed by means of a chi-square test. If the observed data are closely enough associated with the "model" data, then a chi-square value somewhere near m (the mean and the number of degree of freedom for the relevant chi-square distribution) should result. Association in this case means agreement between actual and expected frequencies. In a cross-classified table, association usually means lack of agreement between actual frequencies and the frequencies expected.

To illustrate the goodness-of-fit test we shall use data on observed speeds on 365 passenger vehicles passing a highway check point. In Chapter 5 we fitted a normal distribution to these data. We found the *relative* frequencies to be expected in each class interval if the sample of 365 were drawn at random from a normally distributed population with mean and variance equal to the mean and variance estimated from the sample of 365. In Table 12–6 the actual and expected *absolute* frequencies are shown. (We get the expected frequencies by multiplying the four-digit normal probabilities in Table 5–3 by 365.) All that remains is to calculate the contribution of each class to chi-square, and sum the results. The three classes below 33 mph and five above 53 mph must be grouped to obtain expected frequencies of at least 5 for the resulting classes. Making use of the continuity correction, we find that the value of the chi-square statistic is 21.82 for the table.

We now need to determine the appropriate number of degrees of freedom. We subtract from the number of contributions to chi-square the number of independent ways in which the model is made to agree with the empirical data. The number to be subtracted is 3. In fitting the model we employed the mean and standard deviation estimated from the actual data. These parameters are independent, and each costs us a degree of freedom. In

Table 12-6

CHI-SQUARE GOODNESS-OF-FIT TEST FOR THE NORMAL
DISTRIBUTION OF AUTOMOBILE SPEEDS

Speed (mph)	f	g	f − g	χ^2
Below 29	− ⎤	.6 ⎤		
29—	4 ⎬10	1.5 ⎬6.6	3.4	1.27
31—	6 ⎦	4.5 ⎦		
33—	9	10.4	−1.4	.08
35—	21	20.9	.1	(a)
37—	19	35.3	−16.3	7.07
39—	59	49.9	9.1	1.48
41—	59	59.4	−.4	(a)
43—	66	59.4	6.6	.63
45—	62	49.9	12.1	2.70
47—	25	35.3	−10.3	2.72
49—	22	20.9	1.1	.02
51—	3	10.4	−7.4	4.58
53—	8 ⎤	4.5 ⎤		
55—	1	1.5		
57—	− ⎬10	.4 ⎬6.6	3.4	1.27
59—	1	.1		
61 and over	− ⎦	.1 ⎦		
	365	365.0	0.00	21.82

(a) Less than .005.

addition, we forced agreement in the sums of actual and expected frequencies, and this caused us to lose a third degree of freedom. The resultant applicable degrees of freedom are $12 - 3 = 9$.

The 99th percentile of the chi-square distribution with 9 degrees of freedom is 21.7. The discrepancy between the model and the actual distribution is too large for us to accept the hypothesis that the data were drawn from a normal population. We can reject the hypothesis that automobile speeds in this population are normally distributed with less than a .01 risk of having rejected a true hypothesis.

Automobile speeds in the original raw data were measured to the nearest 2 mph. In the goodness-of-fit test we have used the maximum number of classes possible. We have combined the 2-mph classes only where necessary to obtain expected frequencies in excess of 5. Further grouping of classes can mask the pattern in the observed distribution by balancing off one peculiarity against another. We leave it as an exercise to show that using class intervals of 4 mph results in an insignificant chi-square statistic in the automobile-speeds example. Once again, preservation of the maximum permissible number of degrees of freedom is the proper rule to follow.

The chi-square test for the goodness of fit of other model distributions to a set of empirical data is similar to that illustrated for the normal distribution. If necessary, the parameter(s) required for the model are estimated from the sample data. Employing these parameters, we find theoretical relative frequencies for the classes into which the data are grouped. We use the minimum amount of grouping possible to form these classes. Theoretical relative frequencies are converted to expected frequencies by multiplying them by n, the number of observations in the sample. After grouping adjacent classes where necessary to keep minimum expected frequencies of at least 5, we find the individual contributions to chi-square and sum them. The total is compared with the tabled chi-square for the appropriate degrees of freedom. The degrees of freedom will be the number of contributions to chi-square less the number of independent ways in which the model is made to agree with the data.

When we are fitting a Poisson or chi-square distribution, the only parameter we need to estimate from the data is the mean, because either of these distributions is completely specified by this single parameter. By forcing agreement between the model and the data with respect to the mean and the total number of observations, we lose only two degrees of freedom. Numerical examples wherein these two models as well as a binomial model are tested for goodness of fit are given in the exercises.

12-7   Kolmogorov-Smirnov Tests for Goodness of Fit

Kolmogorov-Smirnov tests are tests for the extent to which one cumulative frequency distribution differs from another. The two distributions may differ with respect to location, dispersion, or skewness. The cumulative distribution of one sample can be compared with that of a continuous population distribution. Comparisons also can be made between two samples, both of which are assumed to come from populations defined by continuous distributions. The procedures test whether the maximum observed differences are large enough to refute the hypothesis that identical population distributions are sources for both sets of data.

To illustrate the one-sample test, we shall use the sample data in Table 12-7. This is the information used in the corner association test: The distribution of symbolic reasoning scores of 64 graduate business students. The cumulative relative frequency distribution for this sample is plotted as the step function in Fig. 12-2. The sample mean score is 7.75 and the sample has marked skewness to the right. These considerations and the fact that we have chi-square tables for only integral degrees of freedom suggest comparison with a theoretical chi-square distribution with 8 degrees of freedom. The percentiles for this theoretical distribution come from the chi-square table in the appendices, and the smooth curve in Fig. 12-2 is passed through them. Although we chose a chi-square model with a mean nearly equal to that of our sample, the Kolmogorov-Smirnov one-sample test does not require us to do this.

Table 12-7

THE DISTRIBUTION OF SYMBOLIC REASONING SCORES

Scores (X)	Frequencies (f)	Cumulative frequencies (F)	Cumulative relative frequencies (F')
0	1	1	.0156
1	2	3	.0469
2	3	6	.0938
3	3	9	.1406
4	7	16	.2500
5	5	21	.3281
6	9	30	.4688
7	4	34	.5312
8	6	40	.6250
9	7	47	.7344
10	5	52	.8125
11	3	55	.8594
12	2	57	.8906
14	1	58	.9062
15	2	60	.9375
16	1	61	.9531
19	1	62	.9688
22	1	63	.9844
25	1	64	1.0000

Total   64

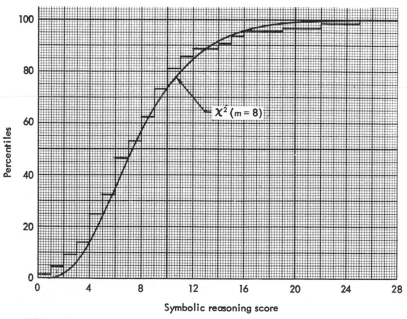

FIGURE 12-2 Cumulative distributions of 64 symbolic reasoning scores and of chi-square

The maximum vertical difference between the two cumulative relative frequency distributions must now be found. A visual examination of Fig. 12–2 suggests the maximum may be at either $X = 4$ or $X = 6$. We read 14 for the chi-square percentile at $X = 4$ and 35 at $X = 6$. Table 12–7 tells us the empirical distribution has percentiles of 25 and 47 at these two X values. Put in decimal form to correspond to tabled values for the Kolmogorov-Smirnov test, the maximum difference is .12 at $X = 6$. It makes no difference which distribution has the greater cumulative relative frequency at $X = 6$ for this form of the test. Appendix Table I, which is used to interpret the result, states probabilities for the greatest *absolute* difference.

Formally stated, the result for our example is

$$D(n) = \max | F'(n) - G' | = .12,$$

where $n = 64$, $F'(n) = .47$, and $G' = .35$. To enter Appendix Table I we use $n = 64$ and $c = n \cdot D(n) = 64(.12) = 7.68$. The table shows that the probability of observing a c value of 7.68 or less lies between .60057 and .75148 if the hypothesis is true. At an alpha risk of .05, we cannot deny that a chi-square distribution with 8 degrees of freedom could have been the source for our sample.

If the sample size, n, had been greater than 100, we could not have used Appendix Table I to test the difference between the distributions in our example. Appendix Table J would have been appropriate. This gives the limiting probability distribution for a statistic based on differences at two points:

$$D^+(n) = \max [F'(n) - G']$$

and

$$D^-(n) = \max [G' - F'(n)].$$

The first difference occurs where the empirical distribution has its greatest vertical distance *above* the theoretical curve. The second difference is the greatest distance that the empirical distribution falls *below* the theoretical distribution. The test statistic is

$$Z = \sqrt{n} [D^+(n) + D^-(n)].$$

The choice of a chi-square model to represent the symbolic reasoning score distribution was based on one more consideration than we mentioned above. Early in this chapter we noted that the square of a unit normal random variable will be distributed as chi-square. The converse is also true. We have shown that a chi-square model with its parameter approximately equal to the mean of the empirical distribution would not be an unreasonable model for symbolic reasoning scores. It would not be unreasonable, then, to expect the square roots of these scores to be distributed approximately normally.

As compared with the chi-square test for goodness of fit, Kolmogorov-Smirnov tests are better for small samples. The one-sample test described above applies to all sample sizes. A second advantage is that less calculation usually is needed for a Kolmogorov-Smirnov test than for a chi-square test. For neither test is it necessary to match the model parameters and sample estimates of these parameters. A priori criteria for the values of the parameters as well as for the form of the distribution can be used in selecting the model.

The chi-square goodness-of-fit test has two major advantages over the Kolmogorov-Smirnov alternative. The chi-square test is applicable to discrete variable models as well as continuous models, while the Kolmogorov-Smirnov tests assume only continuous models. The chi-square statistic is based on a number of comparisons along the distributions; there is a contribution to chi-square from each of the classes. The Kolmogorov-Smirnov tests are based on cumulative effects at one or, at most, two points of comparison.

Extensions of the Kolmogorov-Smirnov tests and tables for all members of this class of test are available. They appear in the first reference at the end of this chapter.

12-8 A Note on Grouping

A problem arises when one attempts to graph a frequency density distribution such as that in the first two columns of Table 12–7. Leaving the data as they are prevents a visual portrayal of the pattern. It also makes hand computation of point estimates difficult for larger samples. Alternatively, grouping of frequencies into symbolic score classes will help both the visual portrayal and the computational effort, but one can carry grouping so far that important detail is lost. The choice of the proper number of groups is arbitrary between these extremes. Nonetheless, in the past it was necessary to make the choice.

With the increasingly widespread availability of electronic data processing equipment it has become feasible to compute point estimates for even very large samples from the raw data. Most data processing installations have library programs already on hand to perform these tasks. Use of this alternative prevents biases in point estimates that may arise from unfortunate grouping.

There still remains the problem of visual comparison of the pattern in sample data with possible alternative models. The cumulative relative frequency distribution would seem to be superior to the frequency density distribution for this purpose. Unlike the density, the cumulative plot will reveal the pattern without grouping. It would seem reasonable to use a technique in which more detail produces more information rather than less.

EXERCISES

12.9 A finance company researcher wants to know whether contract length in months influences the default rate on loan contracts written on one type of major electrical appliance for the home. He has sorted data from several cooperating firms by length of contract. From each length-of-contract class he has selected a random sample of 50 loans. In each such group of 50 he has counted the number of loans that have at least one default notation on them. The counts are shown below.

Contract length	Defaults	Contract length	Defaults	Contract length	Defaults
1	1	17	0	33	0
2	2	18	2	34	4
3	1	19	1	35	2
4	2	20	3	36	3
5	3	21	1	37	2
6	4	22	0	38	1
7	4	23	0	39	4
8	3	24	2	40	3
9	4	25	1	41	5
10	0	26	0	42	2
11	2	27	1	43	2
12	1	28	4	44	2
13	4	29	0	45	0
14	0	30	1	46	3
15	3	31	1	47	1
16	3	32	1	48	4

(a) Plot a scattergram of the data with contract length on the horizontal axis and number of defaults on the vertical axis.
(b) Prepare a cross-classified table in which defaults are classified as "less than 2" and "2 or more" and in which contract lengths are classified as "1 through 16 months," "17 through 32 months," and "33 through 48 months."
(c) Perform a chi-square test where the risk of a type I error is .05 on the table in (b).
(d) Would a corner association test be appropriate for the data in this problem? Why or why not?

12.10 A random sample of 31 counties (or similar civil divisions) is selected from the population of about 3000 such geographical subdivisions in the United States. The resident civilian population and the ratio of general-practice physicians in private practice to resident population are determined for each county. Make a corner association test and a quantile test on the data (3-cycle semi-log paper is convenient for the scattergram). *Partial ans.* $T = |8|$.

Population	Ratio	Population	Ratio	Population	Ratio
2,200	.4545	12,300	.6504	30,100	.3987
3,400	.5882	13,400	.5224	34,000	.3824
4,000	.0000	14,600	.6164	38,100	.1837
5,600	.3571	16,000	.4375	43,900	.4556
6,500	.4615	17,200	.5232	50,200	.5976
7,400	.4054	18,600	.3763	60,100	.3494
8,200	.3659	20,300	.4433	73,800	.2846
9,100	.4396	22,100	.5430	96,400	.3320
10,100	.3960	24,000	.1667	145,000	.3299
11,000	.0909	26,600	.4135	254,000	.3845
				722,300	.3406

12.11 In Table 12–6, combine adjacent pairs of classes from 33 mph to 53 mph to form classes 4 mph in width. Perform a chi-square goodness-of-fit test for a normal model on the resulting distribution. Match the means, variances, and total frequency counts of the sample and the model. Show that the value of the resulting chi-square statistic is 4.46.

12.12 Use the information in Table 12–7 and in Fig. 12–2 to perform a chi-square goodness-of-fit test for a chi-square model with 8 degrees of freedom. To find expected frequencies for each symbolic reasoning score, (1) read the percentiles for the chi-square model at half-score points, (2) take first differences, and (3) multiply by 64, the total frequency count. For example, from Fig. 12–2 we read that .10 of the chi-square model distribution lies below $X = 3.5$ and that .19 lies below $X = 4.5$. The expected frequencies for $X \leq 3.5$ are .10(64) $= 6.4$. The expected frequencies for $3.5 < X < 4.5$ are 64(.19 − .10) $= 5.8$. These would be compared with the 9 and 7 frequencies observed in these two classes. Show that, with the continuity correction, the chi-square goodness-of-fit statistic is 2.89 with 8 degrees of freedom. If alpha were specified as .10 in advance of the test, what would you conclude?

12.13 In a light manufacturing plant, data are available on the number of final assemblies that have failed final inspection out of each set of 12 that have been inspected. Each set of 12 is inspected by a different person, but the observations have been consolidated and cannot be identified by inspector.

Number failing in set	Number of sets
0	70
1	63
2	38
3	20
4	6
5	2
6	0
7	1

Fit a binomial model to the data and test it for goodness of fit.

12.14 The main office of a large firm is considering changing its main telephone switchboard. Part of the planning is concerned with the volume and distribution of incoming calls. Data are collected on the number of calls received during 10-minute observation intervals in mid-morning hours:

Number of calls received	Number of observation intervals
0	23
1	19
2	14
3	10
4	2
5	2

To the nearest tenth, find the mean number of calls received per operation interval and test how well a Poisson distribution with parameter equal to the observed mean fits the observed distribution.

12.15 In a large suburb, newsboy weekly collections for a certain major metropolitan daily newspaper average $60 every two weeks. The standard deviation is $10 and the distribution is approximately normal. Data are available on collections by a random sample of 10 newsboys from a second suburb. They are:

$12	$50
18	65
21	79
39	105
41	129

Test the data with a Kolmogorov-Smirnov one-sample statistic to see whether the normal model applies to this suburb.

REFERENCES

Owen, D. B., *Handbook of Statistical Tables*. Reading, Mass.: Addison-Wesley Publishing Co., Inc., 1962.

Quenouille, M. H., *Associated Measurements*. New York: Academic Press, Inc., 1952.

Siegel, S., *Non-Parametric Statistics*. New York: McGraw-Hill Book Company, 1956.

Wilks, S. S., "Order Statistics." *Bulletin of the American Mathematical Society*, **54** (1948), 6–50.

13

Analysis
of
Variance

We have seen that two classes of technique are required in multivariate analysis. The first type is a set of search techniques to test whether a relationship among variables exists. If existence is established, a second class of techniques may be brought into play to describe the relationship. Our concern in Chapter 12 was with some of the search techniques that statisticians have developed. This chapter describes another class of search techniques.

13-1 Comparison of Search Techniques

The chi-square tests for association described in Chapter 12 compare observed frequencies in cells with frequencies to be expected in those cells. The cells are formed by dividing the variables being studied into classes, and the expected frequencies for the cells are those which are consistent with any hypothesis about the effects of the variables. A weakness of such tests appears to be a lack of sensitivity as compared with the corner association test. In the example in Chapter 12, the difference between the observed and expected patterns had to be marked, or we had to be fortunate in choosing classes, or both, before significant values of chi-square appeared. The corner association test detected association that the chi-square tests did not in a comparable situation. Furthermore, this ability of the corner association test did not depend upon a fortunate selection of class limits. The corner association test applies, however, only when frequencies can be cross-classified in accordance with just two variables, both of which must be quantitative. The technique can be generalized to more than two variables, but implementing it for more variables would be difficult.

Analysis of variance techniques provide another approach to discovering factors that produce systematic changes in some variable of interest. The proposed factors can be either quantitative variables or attributes. The dependent variable is quantitative and is observed within classes of the factors. This contrasts with chi-square and corner association techniques, in which the variable of interest as well as factor variables are used to classify frequencies. For instance, in Chapter 12 we used the variable of interest (semester statistics grade) as well as symbolic reasoning test scores to form four classes for frequencies in Table 12–3. An analysis of variance would use only symbolic reasoning test-score classes. Random samples of students in each test-score class would be selected, and the semester statistics grade for each student selected would be recorded in the proper test-score class. The first part of the analysis is a significance test to see whether it is better to consider the means for the statistics grade populations in the different test-score classes to be equal or unequal. The remainder of the analysis provides appropriate point and interval estimates of the population mean(s).

The analysis of variance is a logical extension of the t test for difference between two population means described in Sec. 7–6. The t test applies to only two populations, while analysis of variance is a more general technique which can be used to test for differences among means of two or more populations simultaneously. The t test for the difference between two population means can be regarded as a special case of the analysis of variance approach.

Analysis of variance techniques are powerful, versatile, and sensitive. They are considerably more useful than the search techniques we discussed earlier. Indeed, analysis of variance techniques play a major role in the branch of statistics known as *design of experiments*. Within the limits of a single chapter we can only suggest this versatility.

In spite of their versatility, analysis of variance techniques do not replace the tests for association discussed earlier. There are at least two situations in which the latter are more useful. If the variable of interest is an attribute, conventional analysis of variance will not apply. For example, we could be interested in the influence of sex of customer and geographic region of residence upon the model of a particular make of automobile that is purchased. The variable of interest is automobile model, an attribute. A second situation unsuitable for analysis of variance techniques is one in which the variable of interest does not or cannot be made to conform to the shape of the normal distribution within each classification cell established by the factor variables. For example, in Table 12–3 in Chapter 12 the 27 statistics grades in the "above median" symbolic reasoning test-score class might form a J-shaped distribution. If no way can be found to transform these grades into a distribution that is at least unimodal and nearly symmetrical, some distribution-free technique such as those we described in Chapter 12 would be required to test for association and isolate influencing factors.

13-2 One-Way Analysis of Variance

A systems and procedures specialist has spent some time studying the work flow for clerks all doing the same forms-processing job in one department of a large firm. In accordance with work-simplification principles, he has designed two work-flow layouts for a clerical work station as alternatives to the present layout. He wants to compare the three layouts with respect to their effects on clerical productivity. Nine clerks are available for the test. The layout each clerk will use is decided by random selection, subject only to the restriction that each type of layout must be used by three clerks.

In the parlance customarily used in analysis of variance we would refer to the nine clerks as experimental units. We are investigating the effects of only one factor (layout) on clerical productivity, the variable of interest. This is an example of a *one-way analysis*. The three layouts are the *treatments*, and these three treatments are the only *levels* of the layout factor in which we are interested. The treatments are assigned to the experimental units completely at random, subject only to the restriction that *balance* will be provided by having an equal number of units subjected to each treatment. With this arrangement we have a *one-way, balanced, completely randomized design*. For the time being we shall assume that the clerks in the department are a relatively homogeneous group with respect to the productivity effects of the three layouts.

The data for the analysis of variance are shown in Table 13–1. They consist of the mean number of units of output per hour for each clerk from a 5-day trial with the appropriate layout. To reduce possible influences from unfamiliarity with the two new layouts no data were collected until a training period was completed. More than one clerk was used for each layout, so that

Table 13-1

CLERICAL WEEKLY PRODUCTION RATES CLASSIFIED BY
LAYOUT OF WORK STATION

	Layout			
	a	b	c	
	90.8	85.5	65.9	
	100.0	83.0	77.1	
	81.1	73.7	68.5	
Sum	271.9	242.2	211.5	725.6
Mean	90.6	80.7	70.5	80.6

productivity differences among clerks would not be confused with differences attributable to changes in layout.

There are two reasons for using a 5-day mean rather than one hour's experience for each clerk. From other tests under essentially constant conditions, the specialist knows that the distribution of a clerk's hourly production data is skewed. He has found that 5-day totals (or means) of hourly production data are essentially normally distributed. This is to be expected when one recalls the central limit theorem. Since normality is a requirement for the variable of interest in analysis of variance, 5-day means are used. The second reason is that *means* of 5 days' hourly production data have much less inherent variability than do hourly data. As we shall see, this reduction in inherent variability increases the sensitivity of the analysis. With greater sensitivity we are more likely to detect true differences in output, if any, produced by varying the layout factor.

We have stressed the normality assumption in analysis of variance and we have described one way to meet it—at least approximately—in practice. There are situations in which the normality assumption cannot be met. Empirical investigations have shown that analysis of variance techniques are not highly sensitive to departures from normality. Nonetheless, where it is feasible to do so, one should bring the data into reasonable conformity with the normality assumption.

In Table 13–1 layout c is the present layout. From an examination of the means alone, layout a appears to be better than the other two with respect to influence on output. Layout c appears to be worse than the other two. Instead of being true population differences, however, these results could represent mere sampling fluctuations. Analysis of variance can be used to investigate this possibility by testing the hypothesis that $\mu_a = \mu_b = \mu_c$.

Before we conduct the analysis for Table 13–1, a final point must be mentioned. We should not conduct individual t tests at, say, the .05 level on the three possible pairs of means and expect to be controlling the entire experiment with an overall alpha risk of .05. In the first place, three *pairs* of independent random samples would be needed to make independent tests on all possible pairs of populations. In the second place, if the three population means are equal, using three t tests in the manner described would have a probability of $1 - (.95)^3 = .1426$, rather than .05, of showing at least one significant difference.

To conduct the analysis of variance upon Table 13–1, we first estimate the population variance by pooling the variances within the three samples shown in the three columns. By implication, this step assumes the population variances for all three layout populations are equal. We shall discuss a test of this assumption subsequently. In the second step, we estimate the population variance from the variance *among* the means of the three samples. In the third step, we form the ratio of the population variance estimate based on the variance *among means* to the population variance estimate based on pooled variances *within treatments*.

We learned in Sec. 7–5 that the ratio of two independent sample estimates of population variance from the same normal population will be distributed as F. If the three layouts have normally distributed output populations with identical parameters, the ratio formed in the third step of the analysis will conform to the F distribution. Alternatively, if the hypothesis that $\mu_a = \mu_b = \mu_c$ is violated while the assumptions of independent random samples and equal variances hold, we shall see that we can expect the numerator of the ratio to be larger than it would be if the population means were equal.

Testing equality of population means. An analysis of variance usually is performed by filling in a table with a rather standardized format. For a one-way analysis, we can use Table 13–2 to describe the entries symbolically.

Table 13-2

SYMBOLIC DESCRIPTION FOR ONE-WAY ANALYSIS OF VARIANCE

Source of variation	SS (sum of squares)	m (degrees of freedom)	MS (mean square)
Among means	$SS_A = \sum [n._j (\bar{X}._j - \bar{X}..)^2]$	$k - 1$	$SS_A/(k - 1)$
Within treatments	$SS_E = \sum \sum (X_{ij} - \bar{X}._j)^2$	$n.. - k$	$SS_E/(n.. - k)$
Total	$SS_T = SS_A + SS_E$	$n.. - 1$	

The symbols in Table 13–2 are defined as follows:

$n._j$ = the number of observations within the jth treatment ($n._1 = n._2 = n._3 = 3$ for our example);

$n..$ = $\sum n._j$, the total number of observations (9 for our example);

X_{ij} = the value of the ith observation within the jth treatment ($X_{32} = 73.7$ in Table 13–1);

$\bar{X}._j$ = the mean of the observations in the jth treatment ($\bar{X}._3 = 70.5$);

$\bar{X}..$ = the grand mean of all observations ($\bar{X}.. = 80.6$);

k = the number of treatments ($k = 3$).

In practice we do not calculate SS_A and SS_E from the formulas in Table 13–2. We use algebraically equivalent forms, which appear below. The correction term is found first:

$$C = \frac{(\sum_j \sum_i X_{ij})^2}{n..}. \tag{13–1a}$$

The sums of squares are then found:

$$SS_A = \sum_j \left[\frac{(\sum_i X_{ij})^2}{n._j} \right] - C, \tag{13–1b}$$

$$SS_E = \sum_j \sum_i (X_{ij}^2) - \sum_j \left[\frac{(\sum_i X_{ij})^2}{n_{.j}} \right], \tag{13-1c}$$

and

$$SS_T = \sum_j \sum_i (X_{ij}^2) - C. \tag{13-1d}$$

Note that $SS_T = SS_A + SS_E$. Also note that C, SS_A, SS_T, and SS_E can never be negative.

For the example in Table 13–1,

$$C = \frac{725.6^2}{9} = 58{,}499.48,$$

$$SS_A = \frac{1}{3}(271.9^2 + 242.2^2 + 211.5^2) - C$$

$$= 59{,}107.57 - 58{,}499.48 \qquad\qquad = 608.09$$

$$SS_E = (90.8^2 + \ldots + 68.5^2) - 59{,}107.57$$

$$= 59{,}432.26 - 59{,}107.57 \qquad\qquad = 324.69$$

$$SS_T = 59{,}432.26 - 58{,}499.48 \qquad\qquad = 932.78.$$

An alternative for finding SS_E that is often used in practice is to find SS_A and SS_T and then to find SS_E by subtracting SS_A from SS_T.

Our next step is to set up the standard analysis of variance table. This is done in Table 13–3. The F ratio is formed from the mean-square estimates of population variance. From Appendix G we find that, for 2 and 6 degrees of freedom, $F(.95) = 5.14$ and $F(.975) = 7.26$. The observed value of F is significant at the 5 per cent level, and we reject the hypothesis of equality among treatment means.

Table 13-3

ONE-WAY ANALYSIS OF VARIANCE FOR LAYOUT EXPERIMENT

Source	SS	m	MS	F
Among means	608.09	2	304.04	$F_{2,6} = \dfrac{304.04}{54.12} = 5.62^*$
Within treatments	324.69	6	54.12	
	932.78	8		

* Significant at $\alpha = .05$.

Point and interval estimates of means. Point estimates of the three treatment population means (μ_a, μ_b, and μ_c) can be obtained directly from Table 13–1. These estimates are the means of the sample observations within each treatment. The estimate of μ_a is $\bar{X}_{.1} = 90.6$, of μ_b is $\bar{X}_{.2} = 80.7$, and of μ_c is $\bar{X}_{.3} = 70.5$.

To determine the interval estimate for the mean of any given treatment population, we must have an estimate of the standard error for the point estimate of the sample mean. Our analysis of variance was based on the assumption that the three treatment populations have equal variances. If this assumption is true, then the most reliable estimate of the variance for any one treatment population can be had by pooling the three separate variance estimates obtained from the sample of each treatment. This pooled estimate of variance within a treatment population is

$$s_{..}^2 = \frac{SS_E}{n_{..} - k}. \tag{13-2}$$

For our example, we see from the information in Table 13–3 that

$$s_{..}^2 = \frac{324.69}{6} = 54.12,$$

the value shown in the mean-square column. Given the pooled estimate of the variance for each treatment population, the standard error of the sample mean within that treatment is

$$s_{\bar{x}_{.j}} = \sqrt{\frac{s_{..}^2}{n_{.j}}}. \tag{13-3}$$

In our example, the samples for all three treatments consist of three observations each. Consequently the standard error for each of the three sample means will be

$$s_{\bar{x}_{.j}} = \sqrt{\frac{54.12}{3}} = 4.247 \qquad \text{for} \quad j = 1, 2, 3.$$

The $(1 - \alpha)$ confidence interval and fiducial interval for the jth treatment mean is found by combining the sample mean from that treatment and its standard error:

$$L_{.j} = \bar{X}_{.j} - t_{1-(\alpha/2), m} s_{\bar{x}_{.j}}, \tag{13-4a}$$
$$U_{.j} = \bar{X}_{.j} - t_{\alpha/2, m} s_{\bar{x}_{.j}}, \tag{13-4b}$$

where

$$m = n_{..} - k.$$

For our example, $m = 6$ and $t(.975, 6) = 2.447$. Then

$$L_{.1} = 90.6 - (2.447)(4.247) = 80.2$$

and

$$U_{.1} = 90.6 - (-2.447)(4.247) = 101.0.$$

Multiple comparisons among means. Through analysis of variance we have concluded that the treatment means in our layout experiment are not the same. We have proceeded to make point and interval estimates of the separate population means. We might want to reach a further conclusion about which pair(s) of treatment means are different, or which one(s) are different from the remaining two. The systems and procedures specialist may want to know whether the mean productivity from layout a is significantly different from the mean productivity from layout b, for example. He might also want to compare the mean from layout a with the other two layouts, or make other possible comparisons. Earlier we made the point that such a series of tests could not be made piecemeal as a substitute for the analysis of variance test among multiple means.

The Duncan *multiple-range test* is one of many tests for multiple comparisons of this kind. It is restricted to means from a one-way analysis of variance in which the numbers of observations for all treatments are equal. Since in our example of a one-way analysis we have three observations for each treatment, this test applies. To make the test, we first rank the sample means. Then we find the *sample range* for any set of adjacent means and compare it with the proper *least significant range* for that set.

For the experiment with work-flow layouts, the sample means are arranged in decreasing order of magnitude.

Layout	a	b	c
Mean	90.6	80.7	70.5

The sample ranges for all possible sets of adjacent means are

for all three means: $90.6 - 70.5 = 20.1$;

for layouts a and b: $90.6 - 80.7 = 9.9$;

for layouts b and c: $80.7 - 70.5 = 10.2$.

The least significant range for comparison with a given sample range is found by multiplying the standard error for the treatment means by the appropriate value from Appendix K. The standard error for our example is found from Eq. (13–3) and is $s_{\bar{x}._j} = 4.25$. There are 6 degrees of freedom within the three treatment samples and we read from the table for $\alpha = .05$:

$r_p = 3.46$ for $p = 2$ and $m = 6$;

$r_p = 3.59$ for $p = 3$ and $m = 6$.

In this table p is the number of sample means from which a given sample range is obtained. Least significant ranges are found from the equation

$$R_p = s_{\bar{x}._j} \cdot r_p. \qquad (13\text{–}5)$$

For our example the values are as follows.

p	$s_{\bar{X}.j}$	r_p	R_p
2	4.25	3.46	14.70
3	4.25	3.59	15.26

The range for the set of all three sample means is 20.1. This exceeds $R_3 = 15.26$, the appropriate least significant range. This should not surprise us when we recall that the F test of means in Table 13–3 was significant at the .05 level. The sample ranges for both pairs of adjacent means (9.9 and 10.2) are less than $R_2 = 14.70$. Neither should this surprise us in view of the considerable overlap among the .95 confidence intervals. We conclude that, while the combined evidence from all three samples points to a significant difference among the means, there are not enough observations to single out any one mean as being significantly different from the other two in combination or to indicate that no two population means are equal.

There is a graphical procedure which makes it easier to form the conclusion from the multiple-range test. Lines are drawn under each set of means for which the range is not significant. For our samples we have:

90.6   80.7   70.5
‾‾‾‾‾‾‾‾‾‾‾‾‾‾‾‾‾‾‾‾‾‾‾‾‾‾‾‾
                        ‾‾‾‾‾‾‾‾‾‾‾‾‾‾‾‾‾‾‾‾‾‾‾‾‾‾‾‾‾

Suppose the means for layouts a, b, and c were 85, 80, and 70 but nothing else is changed. Then the procedure would yield only one line:

85   80   70
‾‾

Here nothing is significant. On the other hand, if the means for layouts a, b, and c were 100, 80, and 70, respectively, we would have

100   80   70
                      ‾‾‾‾‾‾‾‾‾‾‾‾‾‾‾‾‾‾‾‾‾‾‾‾‾‾‾‾

This would indicate that higher productivity is likely to result from layout a than from either of the other two layouts, but that layouts b and c might not produce appreciably different means in practice.

Before we go on, we must review and emphasize some important features of the results obtained in this section. Analysis of variance allowed us to do more than test for the existence of association between layout and production-rate variables; use of actual production-rate observations yielded two important additional benefits. First, we were able to get point and interval estimates of the mean production rate for each layout. Second, we were able to compare the three layouts to see whether any one of them is likely to be superior to the others with regard to mean production rate.

13-3 A Statistical Model for One-Way Analysis of Variance

In Sec. 13–2 we were concerned primarily with how to perform an analysis of variance on a given set of data and with what we could learn from such an analysis. We gave only secondary consideration to the underlying assumptions that justify the analysis. We now turn our attention to this latter topic.

Experiments and surveys to investigate possible influences of factors upon a dependent variable can be designed in a great many ways besides the one-way design illustrated previously. Versions of analysis of variance have been found to be applicable to many of these designs. A clear, concise description of the conditions assumed to prevail in generating the data to fulfill a particular design is often useful. Such a statement is termed a *statistical model*. Specification of the model is essential for understanding the form of analysis of variance to be employed, because the analysis stems directly from the assumptions of the model.

To illustrate the role of the statistical model, we return to the experiment with clerical production rates in Sec. 13–2. We mentioned there some important assumptions of one-way analysis of variance:

1. Each of the k samples is selected from a treatment population that has the same *variance* as does every other treatment population.
2. The treatment populations are each *normally distributed*.
3. Each sample is an *independent random* sample from its treatment population.

We can summarize assumptions equivalent to these three along with several additional assumptions in the following model for the one-way analysis of variance that we performed in Sec. 13–2:

$$X_{ij} = \mu + \tau_j + \epsilon_{ij}, \tag{13–6a}$$

wherein

$$\sum_j \tau_j = 0 \text{ or } \sum_j n_{.j} \tau_j = 0 \tag{13–6b}$$

and the ϵ_{ij} are independently and normally distributed with mean 0 and variance σ^2. In symbols,

$$\epsilon_{ij} \quad : \quad NID(0, \sigma^2). \tag{13–6c}$$

This model states that each observation (X_{ij}) is composed of three linear components, which are additive. The first is a true mean effect (μ), for which $\bar{X}.. = 80.6$ in Table 13–1 is a point estimate. The second is a true effect of the jth treatment (τ_j). $\bar{X}._1 - \bar{X}.. = 90.6 - 80.6 = +10.0$ is a point estimate of τ_1, the assumed true effect of layout a on clerical production rates. The point estimate of τ_3 is $70.5 - 80.6 = -10.1$. The third component is the experimental chance error of the ith experimental unit subjected to the jth treatment (ϵ_{ij}) and is often called the *residual error*.

The model also tells us that the ϵ_{ij} are assumed to be independently and normally distributed about a mean of 0. The point estimate for the variance of this distribution of the ϵ_{ij} for our example comes from Eq. (13–2) and is $s_{..}^2 = 54.12$.

Finally, the model states that the sum of the true effects of the j treatments (three for our example) is zero $(\sum \tau_j = 0)$. These treatment effects can be visualized as deviations from μ, the true mean effect. This assumption establishes that this is a *fixed-effects* model. An alternative *components-of-variance* model is also available. In this latter case, the three treatments in our example would be presumed to be a random sample from a population of layouts. We would not assume that $\sum \tau_j = 0$, but rather than the τ_j comprise a population that is normally and independently distributed with a mean of zero and a variance of σ_τ^2 not necessarily equal to σ^2 for the ϵ_{ij}. We will not discuss components-of-variance models in this book. The third and sixth references at the end of this chapter describe several of them in detail.

Given all assumptions from the above model, one can derive expected values for the mean squares in Table 13–2. If the design dictates that one observation is to be made on each experimental unit and that there are to be an equal number of observations within each treatment, the right column in Table 13–4 presents these expected values.

Table 13-4

ONE-WAY ANALYSIS OF VARIANCE: BALANCED, FIXED EFFECTS, COMPLETELY RANDOMIZED MODEL

Source of variation	Sum of squares	Degrees of freedom	Mean squares	Expected mean square
Among treatments	SS_A	$k - 1$	$\dfrac{SS_A}{k - 1}$	$\sigma^2 + \sum_j \left(\dfrac{\tau_j^2 n_{.j}}{k - 1} \right)$
Residual error	SS_E	$n_{..} - k$	$\dfrac{SS_E}{n_{..} - k}$	σ^2

We can now examine what would happen if we establish the hypothesis that the layout factor does not influence production rates. Under this hypothesis together with the foregoing assumptions not only is the *sum* of the true treatment effects presumed to be equal to zero but also *each* true treatment effect is presumed to be zero. In symbols, not only is $\sum \tau_j$ equal to zero but $\tau_1 = \tau_2 = \ldots = \tau_j = 0$. From Table 13–4 we see that under this hypothesis the expected mean square $SS_A/(k - 1)$ will be just σ^2, as will the expected mean square, $SS_E/(n_{..} - k)$. It follows that $SS_A/(k - 1)$ and $SS_E/(n_{..} - k)$ are independent estimates of σ^2 from equivalent normal populations and that their ratio will be distributed as F if the hypothesis is true.

This discussion of models illustrates the rather elaborate structure of assumptions that underlies analysis of variance. You may be skeptical about the utility of these techniques for business and economic applications because of the assumptions. Later we will discuss some tests that often can be applied to the data for an analysis of variance to gain reasonable assurance that they satisfy the more important assumptions.

13-4 Randomized Block Experiments

Compared with randomized block designs, one-way analysis of variance usually lacks sensitivity when extraneous environmental factors are present. In one-way analyses the residual variability within treatments reflects variation attributable to differences in extraneous factors among the experimental units within each treatment. An insignificant F ratio may result not because there are no treatment effects but because the denominator of the ratio is inflated by variability from extraneous factors.

If one suspects that a certain extraneous factor is important, he can select *blocks* of material each of which is essentially homogeneous with respect to the given extraneous factor. He can randomly assign the treatments being investigated to units within each block. The design makes it possible to separate the treatment effects and the extraneous factor effects from each other and from the residual error.

To compare a randomized block design with a one-way design, we will return to our example. Suppose the systems and procedures specialist does not assume that all clerks in the department comprise a homogeneous group with respect to the effects of the three work-flow layouts. He suspects that the type of supervision a clerk receives during the experiment is an extraneous factor that influences the clerk's production rate. The randomized complete block design will permit separation of supervisory effects from layout treatment effects and of both these effects from residual error.

A *randomized complete block design* has three characteristics:
1. There must be exactly as many experimental units within each block as there are treatments.
2. The treatments must be assigned at random to the units within each block.
3. The units within a block must be relatively homogeneous with respect to the extraneous factor being considered.

In our example all clerks within the department are assigned to one of seven sections. Each section is supervised by a section head. Only five of the sections can spare three clerks each for the experiment. Exactly three must be included in the experiment from each supervisory "block" because there are three layout treatments. Within each block the three layouts are assigned to the three clerks at random. Table 13–5 shows the 5-day mean hourly production rate for each of the 15 clerks during the experiment.

Table 13-5

CLERICAL PRODUCTION RATES CLASSIFIED BY WORK-STATION
LAYOUT AND SUPERVISOR

Supervisor	Layout			Total
	a	b	c	
A	91.0	88.6	81.6	261.2
B	91.8	80.0	73.6	245.4
C	90.5	89.7	85.1	265.3
D	89.0	83.2	73.7	245.9
E	91.0	90.1	85.0	266.1
Total	453.3	431.6	399.0	1283.9

The statistical model. The assumptions for this randomized complete block design with one observation for each experimental unit can be summarized as follows:

$$X_{ijk} = \mu + \varphi_i + \tau_j + \epsilon_{ijk}, \tag{13-7a}$$

wherein

$$\sum_i \varphi_i = 0, \qquad \sum_j \tau_j = 0, \tag{13-7b}$$

and

$$\epsilon_{ijk} \text{ is } NID(0, \sigma^2). \tag{13-7c}$$

Equations (13-7a) and (13-7c) state that each observation is assumed to be composed of a true mean effect (μ), an effect from supervision (φ_i), an effect from work layout (τ_j), and an experimental error term (ϵ_{ijk}) that is normally and independently distributed with a true mean of zero and variance σ^2. The components are assumed to be linearly additive. Equations (13-7b) identify this as a fixed-effects model rather than a components-of-variance model. Neither the work sections nor the layouts are samples from their respective populations. The five sections and three layouts constitute the limits within which conclusions from the experiment apply.

Formulas for sums of squares. Three of the formulas needed to get the sums of squares for this design are the same as those used in Eqs. (13-1a), (13-1b), and (13-1d). Two additional formulas are needed to find the sums of squares for blocks and for the residual error.

The correction term for our example in Table 13-5 is

$$C = \frac{(\sum_j \sum_i X_{ij})^2}{n_{..}} \tag{13-8a}$$

$$= \frac{1283.9^2}{15} = 109{,}893.28.$$

The sum of squares among layout treatments is

$$SS_A = \sum_j \left[\frac{(\sum_i X_{ij})^2}{n_{\cdot j}} \right] - C \tag{13-8b}$$

$$= \frac{453.3^2}{5} + \frac{431.6^2}{5} + \frac{399.0^2}{5} - C$$

$$= 110{,}192.09 - 109{,}893.28 = 298.81.$$

The sum of squares among supervisory blocks is

$$SS_B = \sum_i \left[\frac{(\sum_j X_{ij})^2}{n_{i\cdot}} \right] - C \tag{13-8c}$$

$$= \frac{261.2^2}{3} + \ldots + \frac{266.1^2}{3} - C$$

$$= 110{,}035.57 - 109{,}893.28 = 142.29.$$

The total sum of squares is

$$SS_T = \sum_j \sum_i (X_{ij}^2) - C \tag{13-8d}$$

$$= 91.0^2 + 91.8^2 + \ldots + 73.7^2 + 85.0^2 - C$$

$$= 110{,}411.01 - 109{,}893.28 = 517.73.$$

Finally, the sum of squares for residual error is

$$SS_E = SS_T - SS_A - SS_B \tag{13-8e}$$

$$= 517.73 - 298.81 - 142.29 = 76.63.$$

Expected values and tests for significance. Given the assumptions stated earlier for this design, the expected values for the mean squares are shown in the right column of Table 13–6. Recall that one observation is taken for each

Table 13-6

ANALYSIS OF VARIANCE: RANDOMIZED COMPLETE BLOCK DESIGN
WITH FIXED EFFECTS AND ONE OBSERVATION PER UNIT

Source of variation	Sum of squares	Degrees of freedom	Mean square	Expected mean square
Blocks	SS_B	$b - 1$	$\dfrac{SS_B}{b - 1}$	$\sigma^2 + \dfrac{k \sum \varphi_i^2}{b - 1}$
Treatments	SS_A	$k - 1$	$\dfrac{SS_A}{k - 1}$	$\sigma^2 + \dfrac{b \sum \tau_j^2}{k - 1}$
Residual error	SS_E	$(k - 1)(b - 1)$	$\dfrac{SS_E}{(k - 1)(b - 1)}$	σ^2

unit and the number of units in each block equals the number of treatments. The hypothesis that there are no treatment effects means that $\tau_j = 0$ for every j. In our example the hypothesis is that the three different work layouts have no effect on clerical production rates. Under this hypothesis and the model assumptions the mean square for treatments and the mean-square residual error are independent estimates of σ^2 as defined in Eq. (13–7c). Consequently, the ratio of the mean square for treatments to the mean-square residual error will be distributed as F.

The analysis of variance table for our example is Table 13–7. There are two important factors that were not present in similar tables from one-way

Table 13-7

RANDOMIZED BLOCK ANALYSIS FOR LAYOUT EXPERIMENT

Source	SS	m	MS	F
Blocks	142.29	4	35.57	3.71
Treatments	298.81	2	149.40	15.59*
Error	76.63	8	9.58	
	517.73	14		

* Significant at $\alpha = .01$.

analysis of variance. The first feature appears in the bottom row of Table 13–6. The degrees of freedom for residual error is the product of the number of treatments less one $(k - 1)$ and the number of blocks less one $(b - 1)$. The second feature is that an F test is performed upon both treatment effects and block effects in Table 13–7. $F(2, 8) = 15.59$ is significant at the 1 per cent level. We conclude that treatment effects are not zero. A variance-ratio test is also performed on blocks in Table 13–7. This test would be interpreted as F under an alternative hypothesis that supervisory blocking has no effect on production rates. Strictly speaking, it is not proper to test the significance of both blocking and treatment effects with the same set of data. Nevertheless, we form the variance ratio of blocking effects to residual error and find it is 3.71 with 4 and 8 degrees of freedom. As an approximate indication of the effectiveness of blocking we can compare this F value with $F(.95; 4, 8) = 3.84$. Without being able to make a precise statement concerning alpha, we can state that blocking probably did make our experiment somewhat more efficient than a comparable one-way design would have. Another rough indication of this increase in efficiency can be had by comparing the mean square for residual error in Table 13–3 with the mean-square residual error in Table 13–7. The reduction from 54.12 to 9.58 suggests a gain in efficiency. A measure of the efficiency of the randomized complete block design relative to a balanced one-way analysis is given in Exercise 13.5 at the end of this section.

Estimates. As in the case of one-way analysis of variance, point estimates of production rates from the three layouts can be made. Point estimates are the means of the three columns in Table 13–5. For layout a the estimate is $453.3/5 = 90.7$ units of output per hour. The estimate for the other new layout b is 86.3. For the present layout c the estimate is 79.8.

The estimate for σ^2 specified by the model in Eq. (13–7c) is the mean-square residual error in Tables 13–6 and 13–7. If we define $s^2_{..}$ as the estimate of σ^2, then

$$s^2_{..} = \frac{SS_E}{(b-1)(k-1)}. \tag{13–9}$$

For our layout example, $s^2_{..} = 9.58$. Since there are k observations within each treatment, the standard error of a treatment mean is,

$$s_{\bar{x}._j} = \sqrt{\frac{s^2_{..}}{k}}. \tag{13–10}$$

For our example,

$$s_{\bar{x}._j} = \sqrt{\frac{9.58}{5}} = 1.38.$$

As before, the $(1 - \alpha)$ confidence interval for a treatment mean is found by combining the sample mean for that treatment and its standard error multiplied by the appropriate t value. To illustrate, we will find the .95 confidence interval for a treatment mean in the layout experiment. The proper t value is $t(.975, 8)$, because 8 degrees of freedom apply to $s^2_{..}$ and to $s_{\bar{x}._j}$. This t value is 2.306. The confidence limits for layout a are $90.7 \pm 2.306(1.38)$ or $87.5 \leq \mu_a \leq 93.9$.

Other designs exist to permit isolation of the effects of more than one extraneous factor. Among these are Latin Square and Graeco-Latin Square designs. These designs are beyond the scope of this book, but descriptions of them are available in the last four references at the end of this chapter.

EXERCISES

13.1 Four women are conducting telephone interviews in conjunction with a survey. For properly completed interviews, the time from beginning to dial on one interview until beginning to dial on the next is recorded. Mean times per call for 10-call samples are calculated to eliminate skewness. Three such means for each interviewer are given below.

Mean Times per Call in Minutes

Interviewer

a	b	c	d
9.0	1.1	1.8	0.2
8.5	7.1	6.1	3.0
4.8	5.5	1.4	4.3

(a) Does this evidence support the hypothesis that all four interviewers take the same amount of time, on the average, to complete calls?

(b) Should the Duncan multiple-range test be performed on the four interviewer means? If yes, what conclusions does it yield? If not, why not?

13.2 A candy vending machine owner wants to eliminate the least popular candy bar. All his machines contain five types of candy bar and he stocks them all identically. He has daily total sales data for each bar in all machines for up to 25 days. Because one of his employees misunderstood instructions, he has 25 days of reliable sales data on only one candy bar and smaller amounts of reliable data for the other bars. The distribution of *daily* sales for each bar from past seasons is always skew right. He finds, however, that 5-day means of sales are approximately normally distributed. As a result he decides to analyze the following available mean sales data.

Five-Day Sales Means for Five Candy Bars

Bar

a	b	c	d	e
28	17	28	36	35
29	20	24	34	32
25	22	28	31	42
		33		32
				36

(a) Equations (13–1) apply to cases with the $n_{.j}$ unequal as well as equal. Use these formulas to test the class means for a significant difference by analysis of variance. *Partial ans.* $C = 15{,}723.56$; $SS_E = 141.96$.

(b) Perform a second analysis of variance on only the first three numbers for each bar in the table above. Is there any change in your conclusion? *Partial ans.* $C = 12{,}384.07$; $SS_A = 511.60$.

(c) Apply the Duncan multiple-range test to the means in part (b) of this problem to determine which, if any, candy bar can be eliminated. Let $\alpha = .01$.

(d) Place .99 confidence intervals around the mean sales of each bar in part (b).

(e) Repeat the Duncan multiple-range test with $\alpha = .05$.

13.3 A production analyst in a factory wants to study the influence of a number of factors on workers' production rates. Before introducing new factors he wants to know whether production rate varies by the time of day. He is convinced that differences in production rates among workers are likely to be large enough to overshadow effects from differences in time of day. He collects the following data on number of satisfactory units produced in 15-minute periods. What can he conclude about production rates at various times of day? Was his use of blocking effective?   *Partial ans.* $SS_A = 48.7$ with $m = 3$.

Production Rate by Time of Day

		Forenoon		Afternoon	
		Early	Late	Early	Late
	A	15	19	19	16
Worker	B	19	24	22	19
	C	17	22	21	17
	D	21	24	24	24

13.4 As part of a marketing study an auto manufacturing firm is investigating owners' maintenance expense on its basic model during the first five years of auto life. Fifteen owners have been selected from a large group of cooperating owners as sources for the data in the table below. The data are mean monthly maintenance expense on the previous 12 months' experience. Assume that the randomized complete block analysis presented in Sec. 13–4 applies.

Mean Monthly Maintenance Cost

Annual mileage	Age of Automobile		
	Less than 1 year	1 to 3 years	3 to 5 years
Less than 4000	$4.57	$4.61	$4.89
4000 to 7999	4.65	4.64	4.53
8000 to 11,999	4.01	4.53	5.18
12,000 to 15,999	4.87	4.42	6.26
16,000 to 20,000	4.99	5.33	6.82

(a) Test the means for the treatment (age) classes for equality.
                       Partial ans. $SS_E = 1.92$ with $m = 8$.

(b) Test the effectiveness of blocking by finding the proper F ratio.
                       Ans. $F = 3.02$.

(c) Place .95 confidence intervals on the first treatment mean.
                       Partial ans. Lower limit = $4.11.

13.5 The efficiency of a randomized complete block design with one observation per unit relative to a one-way design that would omit the blocking but retain all other features of the blocked design is often of interest. One means of measuring this relative efficiency is to compare the estimate of what the experimental error would have been within treatments under complete randomization to what it is with the randomized complete block design. The formula for this comparison is

$$R.\ E. = \frac{SS_B + b(k-1)MS_E}{(bk-1)MS_E},$$

where MS_E is the mean-square residual error in Table 13–6 and the other symbols are as defined for that table. Apply this measure to the situation described in Table 13–7. What is the estimated relative efficiency of blocking?   *Ans.* 1.78.

13-5 Factorial Experiments

In the one-way and randomized block experiments described previously, the systems and procedures specialist took the point of view that clerical work layout was an *effector*—a factor that can be controlled to produce changes in a variable of interest. In the one-way example no factor other than layout was considered. In the succeeding randomized block experiment an additional factor, supervision, was also considered. It was viewed as an *extraneous* factor—a factor in the general environment that influences the variable of interest and that can be identified but cannot easily be controlled.

In this section we will be concerned with an alternative way to deal with two factors. This technique can be applied to two factors one of which is an effector and the other an extraneous factor. It can also be applied to two effectors or to two extraneous factors. Looking toward application of results in operations, we usually are more interested in isolating two potential effectors for study.

For our example, we will continue with the clerical work-layout investigation. During the randomized block experiment the systems and procedures specialist noted a possibly useful difference in the way section heads A, C, and E supervised as compared with the supervision of section heads B and D. As you can see in Table 13–5, there seems to be a systematic difference between the total for any one of the first group of supervisors as compared with either one in the second group. The specialist noted that each supervisor in the group of three held formal work-planning sessions with her clerks while the two in the second group did not.

Based on the above observation, the specialist has decided to conduct an experiment that incorporates two levels of the planning factor. One set of clerks will have a brief daily planning session with the supervisor. The other set will have no planning sessions. The first set will lose production time that the second set will not. Only one supervisor will be used for all clerks in the experiment in order to eliminate other intersupervisor differences. To reduce the cost of this experiment, the specialist has elected to use only layouts *a* and *c* as levels for the second factor, even though neither of the two preceding experiments clearly established that *a* is superior to *b*.

A possible arrangement of treatments for the experiment would make use of two groups of clerks. One group would be subjected to a treatment composed of layout *a* and planning sessions. The second group would be subjected to a treatment composed of layout *c* and no planning sessions. This arrangement would make it impossible to separate planning effects from layout effects. In customary analysis-of-variance parlance, the effects of the two factors would be *confounded*.

Instead of the arrangement just described, treatments can be formed by combining each level of one factor with each level of the other factor. The four treatments would be: planning with layout *a*, no planning with layout *a*, planning with layout *c*, no planning with layout *c*. When all possible combinations of factor levels are used, we have what is called a *factorial treatment arrangement*. To illustrate, we would have a balanced, completely randomized design with a factorial arrangement of treatments if we selected 12 clerks for the four planning-layout combinations listed and assigned each clerk to a treatment at random, subject only to the restriction that three clerks must be assigned to each treatment. Three clerks rather than one are exposed to each treatment combination. When an equal number of experimental units are assigned to each combination and when that number is greater than one, we say that the experiment has been performed with *replication*. As we shall see in the example that follows, replication is desirable for a two-factor experiment. It is also desirable for experiments that include more than two factors.

For the work-layout, planning experiment we will assume the specialist has chosen a balanced, completely randomized design with a factorial arrangement of treatments. The production data from the experiment are shown in Table 13–8. Because of the factorial arrangement, we not only can get mean production rates for the three clerks in each treatment group. We

Table 13-8 (a)

FIVE-DAY MEAN PRODUCTION RATES FOR WORK-LAYOUT PLANNING EXPERIMENT

	Layout *a* with planning	Layout *a* without planning	Layout *c* with planning	Layout *c* without planning	Total	Mean
	89.9	89.6	82.5	76.4	338.4	84.6
	96.2	90.2	84.8	75.4	346.6	86.6
	92.5	89.2	90.5	73.9	346.1	86.5
Total	278.6	269.0	257.8	225.7	1031.1	
Mean	92.9	89.7	85.9	75.2	85.9	

Table 13-8 (b)

ADDITIONAL TOTALS AND MEANS FOR WORK-LAYOUT PLANNING EXPERIMENT

	Total	Mean
Layout a	547.6	91.3
Layout c	483.5	80.6
Planning	536.4	89.4
No planning	494.7	82.4

can also find mean production rates for each layout and for each level of planning. These are shown in the lower portion of the table.

The statistical model. The assumptions for this completely randomized design with a factorial arrangement of treatments for two factors, with one observation for each experimental unit, and with replication can be summarized as follows:

$$X_{ijk} = \mu + \varphi_i + \tau_j + (\varphi\tau)_{ij} + \rho_k + \epsilon_{ijk}, \quad (13\text{--}11a)$$

wherein

$$\sum_i \varphi_i = 0, \quad \sum_j \tau_j = 0, \quad \sum_k \rho_k = 0, \quad \sum_i (\varphi\tau)_{ij} = 0, \quad \sum_j (\varphi\tau)_{ij} = 0 \quad (13\text{--}11b)$$

and

$$\epsilon_{ijk} \text{ is } NID(0, \sigma^2). \quad (13\text{--}11c)$$

Equations (13–11a) and (13–11c) state that each observation (X_{ijk}) is assumed to be the sum of six linear components: a mean effect (μ), a main effect from planning (φ_i), a main effect from layout (τ_j), an effect from the *interaction* of each level of planning in combination with each level of layout ($\varphi\tau)_{ij}$, a replication effect (ρ_k) and an experimental error (ϵ_{ijk}) that is normally and independently distributed with a true mean of zero and variance σ^2. Equation (13–11b) identifies this as a fixed-effects model.

The interaction component of this model distinguishes it from the more general two-factor completely randomized model without factorial treatment arrangements. The concept of interaction will be explained more fully after computational formulas, tests of significance, expected values, and estimates have been described for this case.

Formulas for sums of squares. The general formulas for the sums of squares together with their application to the data in Table 13–8 are given below.

The correction term is found in the same manner as it was in the previous cases.

$$C = \frac{(\sum_i \sum_j \sum_k X_{ijk})^2}{n_{...}} \quad (13\text{--}12a)$$

$$= \frac{1031.1^2}{12} = 88{,}597.27.$$

The sum of squares for the main effect of the planning factor is

$$SS_P = \sum_i \left[\frac{(\sum_j \sum_k X_{ijk})^2}{n_{i..}} \right] - C \tag{13-12b}$$

$$= \frac{536.4^2}{6} + \frac{494.7^2}{6} - C$$

$$= 88,742.18 - 88,597.27 = 144.91.$$

The sum of squares for the main effect of the layout factor is

$$SS_L = \sum_j \left[\frac{(\sum_i \sum_k X_{ijk})^2}{n_{.j.}} \right] - C \tag{13-12c}$$

$$= \frac{547.6^2}{6} + \frac{483.5^2}{6} - C$$

$$= 88,939.67 - 88,597.27 = 342.40.$$

The sum of squares for the interaction effect is

$$SS_I = \sum_i \sum_j \left[\frac{(\sum_k X_{ijk})^2}{n_{ij.}} \right] - C - SS_P - SS_L \tag{13-12d}$$

$$= \frac{278.6^2}{3} + \frac{269.0^2}{3} + \frac{257.8^2}{3} + \frac{225.7^2}{3} - C - SS_P - SS_L$$

$$= 89,126.76 - 88,597.27 - 144.91 - 342.40 = 42.18.$$

The sum of squares for replication is

$$SS_R = \sum_k \left[\frac{(\sum_i \sum_j X_{ijk})^2}{n_{..k}} \right] - C \tag{13-12e}$$

$$= \frac{1}{4} (338.4^2 + 346.6^2 + 346.1^2) - C$$

$$= 88,607.83 - 88,597.27 = 10.56.$$

The total sum of squares is

$$SS_T = \sum_i \sum_j \sum_k (X_{ijk}^2) - C \tag{13-12f}$$

$$= 89,184.41 - 88,597.27 = 587.14.$$

Finally, the sum of squares for residual error is

$$SS_E = SS_T - SS_P - SS_L - SS_I - SS_R \tag{13-12g}$$

$$= 587.14 - 144.91 - 342.40 - 42.18 - 10.56 = 47.09.$$

Expected values and tests for significance. Given the assumptions stated earlier for this design with factorial treatments, the expected values for the mean squares are shown in the right column of Table 13–9.

Table 13-9

ANALYSIS OF VARIANCE: BALANCED COMPLETELY RANDOMIZED DESIGN WITH TWO-FACTOR FACTORIAL TREATMENTS, FIXED EFFECTS, AND ONE OBSERVATION PER UNIT

Source of variation	Sums of squares	Degrees of freedom	Mean squares	Expected mean squares
Main effects:				
Factor P	SS_P	$p-1$	$\dfrac{SS_P}{p-1}$	$\sigma^2 + \dfrac{rq}{p-1}\sum_i \varphi_i^2$
Factor L	SS_L	$q-1$	$\dfrac{SS_L}{q-1}$	$\sigma^2 + \dfrac{rp}{q-1}\sum_j \tau_j^2$
Replication (R)	SS_R	$r-1$	$\dfrac{SS_R}{r-1}$	$\sigma^2 + \dfrac{pq}{r-1}\sum_k \rho_k^2$
Interaction (LP)	SS_I	$(p-1)(q-1)$	$\dfrac{SS_I}{(p-1)(q-1)}$	$\sigma^2 + \dfrac{r}{(p-1)(q-1)}\sum_i \sum_j (\varphi\tau)_{ij}^2$
Residual error	SS_E	$(pq-1)(r-1)$	$\dfrac{SS_E}{(pq-1)(r-1)}$	σ^2

One of four hypotheses can be tested with the single set of data given in Table 13–8. The first hypothesis is that there are no layout main effects on production. The second is that there are no planning main effects on production. The third is that there are no replication effects on production. The fourth is that there are no interaction effects of layout and planning together on production. Since our primary interest has been in layout, we will choose the first hypothesis. If this hypothesis and the assumptions in the model are true, the mean square from layout main effects and the mean-square residual error will be independent estimates of σ^2 as defined in Eq. (13–11c). Consequently, the ratio of the mean square for layout main effect to mean-square residual error will be distributed as F with $(p-1)$ and $(pq-1)(r-1)$ degrees of freedom as these are described in Table 13–9.

The analysis of variance table for our example is Table 13–10. Because the layout factor was investigated at two levels, $q = 2$. Because the planning

Table 13-10

FACTORIAL ANALYSIS FOR LAYOUT-PLANNING EXPERIMENT

Source	SS	m	MS	F
Main effects:				
Planning	144.91	1	144.91	$144.91/7.85 = 18.46$
Layout	342.40	1	342.40	$342.40/7.85 = 43.62*$
Interaction	42.18	1	42.18	$42.18/7.85 = 5.37$
Replication	10.56	2	5.28	$5.28/7.85 = .67$
Residual error	47.09	6	7.85	
Total	587.14			

* Significant for $\alpha = .01$.

factor was investigated at two levels, $p = 2$. Because three units were included within each treatment combination, $r = 3$. The F test for our hypothesis of no main effect from layout gives us an F ratio that is significant at the .01 level. We conclude that the layout main effect influences output.

The variance ratios for the three alternative hypotheses stated above are also shown in Table 13–10. No precise alpha risk can be associated with these ratios because we have already tested the layout main effect. An indication of the results that might be obtained from experiments upon new data can be had by comparing these variance ratios with the F table:

$1 - \alpha$	$F(1,8)$
.95	5.32
.975	7.57
.99	11.26

These comparisons indicate that both planning main effects and interaction might very well prove significant in further independent experiments.

A procedural point should be mentioned in connection with Tables 13–8 and 13–10. You should note that replication is necessary. *It is necessary to have more than one observation per treatment combination in order to separate interaction effects from residual error.* Multiple observations per treatment combination are the source of an estimate of variance from within treatments here as they were in the completely randomized design in Sec. 13–2.

Special short-cut computational techniques have been developed for factorial experiments in which each factor is taken at only two levels. Furthermore, general techniques such as the one presented for the two-factor by two-level example above have been developed for more than two factors each taken at more than two levels. These extensions and other applications of analysis of variance are discussed in references listed at the end of this chapter.

Estimates. Point estimates of production rates to be expected from alternative layout and planning factor levels and combinations of them are provided by the means in Table 13–8. These means also provide estimates of the effects described in the statistical model, Eq. (13–11a). These estimates are shown in Table 13–11. No estimates of the replication effect should be made, because there is no indication that such an effect exists.

If replication effects are significant, the estimate of σ^2 in Eq. (13–11c) is the mean-square residual error in Tables 13–9 and 13–10. If we define $s_{..}^2$ as the estimate of σ^2, then

$$s_{..}^2 = \frac{SS_E}{(pq - 1)(r - 1)} = MS_E. \tag{13–13}$$

If replication effects are not significant, then we may pool the sums of squares

Table 13-11

ESTIMATES OF EFFECTS FOR FACTORIAL TREATMENTS

Effect		Estimate
Mean	(μ)	85.9
Planning	(φ_1)	$89.4 - 85.9 = +3.5$
	(φ_2)	$82.4 - 85.9 = -3.5$
Layout	(τ_1)	$91.3 - 85.9 = +5.4^*$
	(τ_2)	$80.6 - 85.9 = -5.3^*$
Interaction	$(\varphi\tau)_{11}$	$92.9 - 85.9 - 3.5 - 5.4 = -1.9\dagger$
	$(\varphi\tau)_{12}$	$85.9 - 85.9 - 3.5 + 5.3 = +1.8\dagger$
	$(\varphi\tau)_{21}$	$89.7 - 85.9 + 3.5 - 5.4 = +1.9$
	$(\varphi\tau)_{22}$	$75.2 - 85.9 + 3.5 + 5.3 = -1.9$

* The sum of these effects is not zero because of rounding.

† The sum of these effects is not zero because of rounding.

and degrees of freedom for replication and residual error to form the estimate. In this case the estimate is

$$s_{..}^2 = \frac{SS_R + SS_E}{pq(r-1)} \tag{13-14}$$
$$= \frac{10.56 + 47.09}{(2)(2)(2)}$$
$$= 7.21 \text{ (units per hour)}^2 \text{ for our example.}$$

Our primary interest centers in the treatment combination means in Table 13-8. We might want a confidence interval for the mean under the first treatment (layout *a* with planning). There are $r = 3$ observations in each mean. Hence, the standard error of a treatment mean is

$$s_{\bar{X}_{ij}.} = \sqrt{\frac{s_{..}^2}{r}} \tag{13-15}$$
$$= \sqrt{\frac{7.21}{3}} \text{ or } 1.55 \text{ for our example.}$$

Since there are 8 degrees of freedom associated with $s_{..}$, we must use $t(.975, 8) = 2.306$ for a .95 confidence interval. The limits are 92.9 ± 2.306 (1.55), or 89.3 and 96.5.

Response graphs. A device that often aids interpretation of results is the response graph for a factorial experiment. For our experiment, the data for such a graph come from Table 13-8. We find the mean production rate per clerk for each treatment combination and plot these means. The means are shown in Fig. 13-1. The rather marked departure of the two lines in Fig. 13-1 from parallelism suggests significant interaction between layout and planning factors.

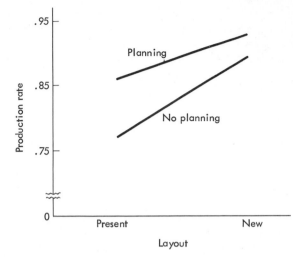

FIGURE 13-1 Production-rate response to variations in layout and planning

To gain more understanding of the influence of interaction as well as of the pure factors, we can make further use of Table 13–8. The grand mean over all levels of both factors is 85.9. In Fig. 13–2(a) we see what might happen if there were neither layout nor planning effects. If there were a layout effect but no planning effect, the sample result might be as in Fig. 13–2(b). Compare this with the corresponding means in Table 13–8(b). With both layout and planning effects but with no interaction effect, the result would be similar to that shown in Fig. 13–2(c). Finally, if interaction effects are present, the result is no longer a plane. Rather, when we compare Fig. 13–2(c) and (d), we see that the surface in (d) has been twisted slightly clockwise in the vertical *plan* plane and slightly counterclockwise in the vertical *no plan* plane. In Fig. 13–2(d) the straight lines from 75.2 to 89.7 and from 85.9 to 92.9 are the ones extracted for Fig. 13–1. Looking at this latter figure, we see there is a much greater improvement when we change to the new layout if we are not using planning sessions than if we are. Perhaps the present layout has less built-in work-flow procedure than does the new layout; hence, there is more room for planning to pay off. This could produce the interaction we have noted.

13-6 Testing Inputs to Analysis of Variance

In describing statistical models for analysis of variance, we pointed out the assumptions upon which the models are based. It would be helpful if a single test were available to check the data to be used in a given analysis of variance for conformance with the entire set of assumptions before the analysis is performed. Such a test would provide considerable assurance that conclusions based on the F tests in the subsequent analysis of variance are attributable to

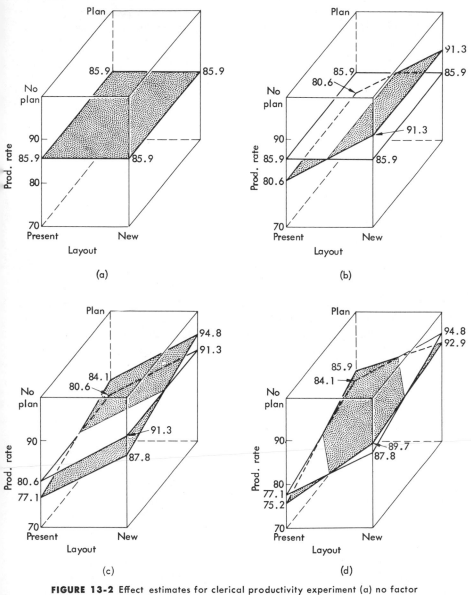

FIGURE 13-2 Effect estimates for clerical productivity experiment (a) no factor effects; (b) layout factor; (c) layout and planning—no interaction; and (d) layout and planning with interaction.

the truth or falsehood of the hypotheses being tested and not to a violation of some assumption(s) in the statistical model. So far as we know, no such composite test has been developed. Alternatively, there are tests that can be used to check on many of the assumptions individually. One can subject the given set of input data to each of the tests in turn. One difficulty with this procedure is that no way is known to combine the separate tests in order to determine the composite alpha risk for the entire battery of conformance tests.

Even though the tests for individual assumptions mentioned above leave something to be desired, it seems sensible to use them whenever it is important to avoid erroneous conclusions. Descriptions of these tests would occupy more space than can be made available here. The sixth reference at the end of this chapter discusses the individual assumptions and contains an extensive list of references to detailed descriptions of the techniques.

We may ask what should be done if the input variable for an analysis of variance is judged not to conform to assumptions. Skewness is often a problem. When the original variable has a markedly skewed distribution, we can sometimes substitute means of random sets of the original variable for that variable or transform the variable. The central limit theorem gives us reason to expect a more nearly normal distribution for the means than for the original variable; this was the technique used in Sec. 13–2. Tests of goodness of fit such as those discussed in Chapter 12 may then be applicable to give assurance that the sets from which the means were computed are large enough. In other instances there may be evidence of lack of homogeneity of variance among treatment combinations. In some cases, transformations of the original variable exist that can largely eliminate this shortcoming. The fourth and sixth references at the end of this chapter contain brief discussions of some of these transformations.

13-7 A Note on Research Methods

We wished to portray a typical research pattern by carrying the work-layout example through three stages of analysis. The purpose was to illustrate the manner in which an investigation typically suggests questions to be answered by subsequent investigations. If successful, these latter studies contribute enlarged understanding of the interdependencies among factors. In much research the objective is to find interdependencies between a set of factors we can control directly and a set of factors that affect us but that we cannot control directly.

An investigator can investigate interdependencies by means of a survey or an experiment. An experiment is being conducted when an investigator sets some of the qualitative or quantitative factors being considered at preselected values and observes the effects of differences in these settings upon values taken on by the remaining variables. This contrasts with survey procedure, in which no attempt is made to control the values of variables being studied. In a survey, individuals are selected from a population, and the values of all factors being studied that happen to be associated with each individual are recorded as one joint observation.

In many cases it is not feasible to do anything but apply survey techniques. In other cases surveys serve as valuable search techniques to discover associated factors. Whenever it is feasible, however, most investigators prefer to confirm tentative effects discovered in surveys or elsewhere by experiments. There is satisfaction and added safety in knowing that the direction and amount of change in value expected in one set of factors as a result of given changes in another set actually are produced when this latter set is purposely controlled at the designated values.

There are at least three major problems in attempting to establish and verify an association between a set of affected variables and a set of potential effectors by survey or experimentation. The first is to discover effectors—factors that when varied change the level of response in affected variables *significantly* relative to the variability in the affected variables. The second is to determine how to control or observe enough factors simultaneously to confine the remaining variability in affected variables within acceptable bounds. The third is to establish the ability of the effectors to produce predicted responses in the affected variables repeatedly within a variety of applicable operating environments.

Traditional laboratory experimentation is one approach for dealing with the above problems. This approach tends to emphasize the first problem —discovery of effectors. The laboratory is a purposefully constructed environment. Many factors that might affect the variables of interest are intentionally eliminated from that environment. Other factors are present but only at controlled constant values. All factors of these two types are called extraneous factors. By eliminating their variability, the variability in the set of affected variables is reduced. Potential effectors are then varied, and changes in the response levels of the affected variables are easier to detect and evaluate. Subsequently, variables previously treated as extraneous factors can be studied as potential effectors and vice versa.

Typically in the laboratory, it is feasible to deal only with a relatively small number of effectors at a time. Moral proscriptions, technical incapabilities, and expense limitations are other considerations that limit the usefulness of this approach in many subject-matter areas. Lastly, divergences between operating environments and feasible laboratory environments are sometimes so wide that effects found important in the laboratory are buried within the variability produced in the operating environment by factors held constant in the laboratory.

Designed experiments and surveys *within operating environments* constitute another major approach to dealing with the above three problems. As we mentioned earlier, analysis of variance techniques play a central role in this approach. The foregoing description of these techniques indicated that they are capable of dealing with all three of the problems mentioned, though perhaps they deal more effectively with the latter two—simultaneous observation of many factors and establishing ability to predict in the operating environment. If this type of investigation is successful, we can expect actual responses in practice to fall close to predicted values on the average. The associations were found in the actual operating environment and should be applicable to it in future instances. Whatever factors the statistical model and significance tests have not isolated for evaluation remain to exert their influence in the form of variability within the variable of interest. The typical result of failing to include important factors in the design will be to reduce the experiment's sensitivity. An important factor omitted in the design will tend to make residual error larger than it would otherwise be. This enlargement tends to reduce the experiment's ability to identify as significant those factors which are included in the design and which truly are effectors. On the other hand, this approach overcomes the principal weakness of the laboratory approach. The laboratory approach has a tendency to overestimate the effectiveness in the operating environment of a factor isolated in the laboratory. Protection in this respect from the operating-environment approach is at the expense of possibly not discovering the importance of a factor included in the design because an even more important factor has been overlooked. An unfortunate shortcoming of both approaches is that neither will automatically suggest the correct factors and the manner in which they should be combined to solve all three problems most efficiently.

EXERCISES

13.6 Verify the coordinates in Fig. 13–2 from the estimated effects in Table 13–11.

13.7 Treat the data in Table 13–8(a) as if they were suitable to analyze as a one-way, balanced, completely randomized design with fixed effects. Assume that there are just four treatments with three observations per treatment. Assume that no interaction terms are included in the model. Show that for these assumptions $SS_E = 57.65$ with 8 degrees of freedom and that $F = 24.48$ with 3 and 8 degrees of freedom for treatments. Compare the results with those given in Table 13–10.

13.8 A firm that does all its advertising and selling directly by mail is investigating alternative marketing programs for a new product. The product is a box of crystals which, when dissolved in water, forms a household metal-cleaning solution. The marketing programs consist of all combinations of three different advertising appeals and three different samples. The samples are 2-inch, 4-inch, and 9-inch squares of cloth moistened with the solution and sealed in plastic bags. Nine random samples of 100 names and addresses each are selected from a master mailing list. Each combination of a type of appeal and product sample is sent to one of the nine samples. The entire experiment has 3 replications—a total of 27 samples. Sales results are shown in the table below.

Advertising appeal	Product sample	Sales per Hundred		
		Replication		
		1	2	3
A	2"	4	7	8
A	4"	9	15	11
A	9"	4	4	3
B	2"	2	4	10
B	4"	9	8	7
B	9"	3	3	6
C	2"	10	8	10
C	4"	20	12	16
C	9"	13	12	12

(a) Analyze these data by means of a two-factor analysis of variance model with factorial treatment arrangement and fixed effects.
   Partial ans. SS (interaction) = 37.48 with 4 degrees of freedom.
(b) Construct a table of expected sales per 100 mailings for all possible marketing alternatives.
(c) Construct .95 confidence intervals for sales from marketing alternatives in part (b).
   Partial ans. $s_{..}$ = 2.427 with 18 degrees of freedom.
(d) Construct a response graph similar to that in Fig. 13–1 for the table of means in part (b).
(e) Which marketing alternative(s) would you recommend?

13.9 A major oil company is conducting a study to compare the miles per gallon delivered by each of five brands of gasoline. Fifteen current-year passenger automobiles have been selected from each of three automobile weight classes. Each automobile is run a month under varying conditions on a given brand of gasoline, after which the miles per gallon during the month are calculated. The data are given in the table below.
(a) Is gasoline brand a significant factor in accounting for differences in mileage?
   Ans. Yes; $F = 32.50$ with 4 and 28 degrees of freedom.
(b) Is automobile weight significant?
   Ans. Yes; $F = 119.02$ with 2 and 28 degrees of freedom.
(c) Is there evidence of interaction between gasoline brand and weight?
   Ans. Yes; $F = 21.83$ with 8 and 28 degrees of freedom.
(d) Construct a table of means and a response graph similar to Fig. 13–1 for these data.
(e) Construct .95 confidence intervals for the cell means in part (d).
(f) Interpret the response graph you constructed in part (d).
   Partial ans. The data for gasoline brand 1 are highly suspect.

Gasoline brand	Auto weight class	Miles per gallon		
		Rep. 1	Rep. 2	Rep. 3
1	1	21.3	20.7	19.2
1	2	12.7	13.2	13.2
1	3	16.6	17.5	18.1
2	1	15.5	16.4	16.1
2	2	14.3	14.5	15.2
2	3	11.2	11.3	10.6
3	1	19.3	18.6	19.0
3	2	16.0	15.1	14.8
3	3	16.0	15.1	15.4
4	1	16.8	15.3	16.6
4	2	15.5	14.9	15.1
4	3	11.6	11.9	12.5
5	1	15.6	18.0	16.8
5	2	16.4	17.6	16.3
5	3	13.3	12.8	14.4

REFERENCES

Bartlett, M. S., "Some Examples of Statistical Methods of Research in Agriculture and Applied Biology." *Suppl. J. Roy. Stat. Soc.*, 4 (1937), 137–183.

Bryant, E. C., *Statistical Analysis*, 2nd ed. New York: McGraw-Hill Book Company, 1966.

Cochran, W. G., and G. M. Cox, *Experimental Designs*, 2nd ed. New York: John Wiley & Sons, Inc., 1957.

Dixon, W. J., and F. J. Massey, Jr., *Introduction to Statistical Analysis*, 2nd ed. New York: McGraw-Hill Book Company, 1957.

Miller, I., and J. E. Freund, *Probability and Statistics for Engineers*. Englewood Cliffs, N.J.: Prentice-Hall, Inc., 1965.

Ostle, B., *Statistics in Research*, 2nd ed. Ames, Iowa: Iowa State University Press, 1963.

14

Linear
Regression

In Chapter 12 we considered techniques for detecting association between two variables. Those techniques usually make it possible also to state the direction of change in one variable in response to a given change in the other.

In Chapter 13 we considered analysis of variance techniques. We found that these techniques also can detect association and direction of change between two variables. In addition, they can yield benefits not gained from the tests of association in Chapter 12. If we find on the basis of an analysis of variance that two variables are associated, we can make a point estimate of the value of one variable given a value of the other. We shall call such estimates *point predictions*. We can go on to construct an interval estimate and to state a level of confidence or a fiducial probability that the true value of the variable lies within the interval. We shall call such an estimate an *interval prediction*.

As compared with the techniques in Chapter 12, the more powerful techniques of Chapter 13 place additional requirements upon statistical populations to qualify them for such analysis. Among these restrictions are normality within cells and equality of variance among cells. Though there is no way to guarantee conformance with these restrictions from samples, there are tests that can detect the more flagrant violations.

In this chapter we shall consider situations that involve only two variables. We shall introduce statistical models that place restrictions on these variables in addition to the restrictions required in Chapters 12 and 13. One of the major benefits will be that, for a given set of data, comparable interval predictions usually will be narrower than they would be with analysis of variance techniques.

14-1   Linear Regression

An example will help us understand linear regression. A cost analyst and a statistician in a certain plant are studying machine maintenance costs. Their eventual goal is to develop an optimal replacement policy for the type of machine under study. Their current task is to find an acceptable way to estimate maintenance cost per hour of running time.

One way to estimate the maintenance cost rate comes from our work in univariate analysis. The array from largest to smallest of mean hourly cost rates for a sample of twenty machines of the designated type is shown in Table 14–1. We can find the mean of the twenty observations (18.33 cents per hour) and use this as the estimate of maintenance cost rate, a point pre-

Table 14-1

MACHINE MAINTENANCE COST RATES

32.0	21.3	18.7	12.5
29.9	20.8	18.4	11.8
24.9	20.6	16.9	11.1
23.5	19.8	14.5	9.3
22.3	19.6	13.5	5.2

diction. We can go further by calculating s, the sample standard deviation, and by using this as a basis for an interval estimate. For the data in the table, s is 6.70 with 19 degrees of freedom. From the t table we find $t(.975, 19) = 2.093$. If we are willing to assume that the twenty numbers in Table 14–1 represent a random sample from a normal population, we can say the fiducial probability is .95 that the true mean cost rate lies in the interval

$$18.33 \pm (2.093)\left(\frac{6.70}{\sqrt{20}}\right) = 18.33 \pm 3.14.$$

Multivariate analysis may apply to the problem of estimating maintenance cost rate. The cost rate of each machine may be influenced by some characteristic of that machine. Perhaps the older a machine is, the higher its cost rate will be. Suppose the plant has put machines on the production line in batches. Suppose also that the statistician arbitrarily chose four machines at random from each of five age groups to constitute the sample shown in Table 14–1. To begin multivariate analysis of these data we rearrange them into age groups as shown in Table 14–2. Observing the mean cost for each age group, we see that our supposition may be useful. Cost does appear to increase with age.

The data are portrayed graphically in the form of a *scattergram* in Fig. 14–1. Here points are plotted at the intersection of each machine's age and cost coordinates. In addition to the scattergram of the twenty points,

Table 14-2

HOURLY MAINTENANCE COSTS CLASSIFIED BY
MACHINE AGE IN MONTHS

Age (X)	Cost (Y)	Mean cost ($\bar{Y}_X$)
6	5.2, 12.5, 9.3, 11.8	9.7
15	19.6, 13.5, 18.4, 14.5	16.5
24	11.1, 19.8, 21.3, 24.9	19.3
33	20.8, 18.7, 16.9, 20.6	19.2
42	32.0, 23.5, 22.3, 29.9	26.9

the figure shows the mean cost for each age group, and dashed line segments connect these means.

We may be willing to assume that maintenance costs in the five machine-age groups are normally distributed about the true mean cost in each group

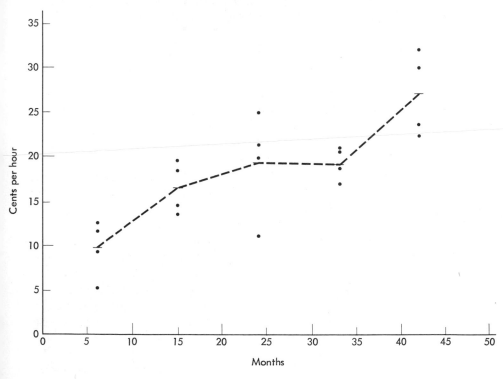

FIGURE 14-1 Machine maintenance costs and age

and that the variances are equal. If we do so, we can perform a one-way analysis of variance on the data. The results of such an analysis are given in Table 14–3. We see that the age-group means are significantly different, and we infer that machine age does have an appreciable effect on maintenance cost.

Table 14-3

ANALYSIS OF VARIANCE FOR MACHINE COST
AND AGE DATA

Source	SS	m	MS	F
Among means	613.93	4	153.48	9.62*
Residual error	239.33	15	15.96	
	853.26			

* Significant for $\alpha = .01$.

We learned in Chapter 13 that the mean-square residual error in Table 14–3 is an unbiased estimate of the variance within age groups ($s_{..}^2$). For our example, $s_{..} = \sqrt{15.96} = 4.0$. In turn, this estimate can be used as a basis for an interval prediction for the mean cost rate associated with a given machine age. The interval for machines 24 months old is

$$19.3 \pm (2.131)\frac{4.00}{\sqrt{4}} = 19.3 \pm 4.3,$$

where 2.131 is $t(.975, 15)$. This interval is wider than the one we found when we used univariate analysis. There, the half-width of the prediction interval was 3.1, which is less than the 4.3 we have just found from analysis of variance. Univariate analysis is estimating the *general* mean of 20 observations while analysis of variance is estimating the *conditional* means of four observations each. The condition is the age of the machine. Univariate analysis cannot tell us when a machine is so old that its future maintenance costs probably will exceed the pro-rata purchase and maintenance costs of replacing it with a new one.

Another form of analysis that we can consider for the data in Table 14–2 is linear regression. It may be reasonable for us to make some assumptions about the statistical populations in addition to those necessary for analysis of variance. One of these is that the population mean maintenance costs for all age groups of interest lie on a straight line. We shall state this and the other necessary assumptions in the form of a model. Before we do, it may be well to point out some advantages in changing from the analysis of variance model to a linear regression model.

In a one-way analysis of variance we require at least two observations of the dependent variable for at least some values of the independent variable. These are necessary to get an estimate of the variance within cells upon which we base the significance test and from which we get the estimates needed for an interval prediction. In linear regression it is not necessary to have multiple observations of the dependent variable for each value of the independent variable. In our example we have four cost observations for each machine age, but all twenty of the cost observations could have been made at different ages without ruling out linear regression.

As can be seen by examining Eq. (13–3) in Chapter 13, the width of the prediction interval for a cell mean in analysis of variance tends to decrease primarily as a result of an increase in the number of observations in that cell alone. For linear regression we shall find that the width of the prediction interval associated with a given value of the independent variable tends to decrease as the *total* number of observations increases. If observations are added anywhere along the scale of the independent variable, the prediction interval associated with any value of that variable will tend to decrease in width.

14-2 A Statistical Model for Linear Regression

The assumptions in the type of linear regression we shall consider can be described by means of a statistical model. The model is

$$Y_i = \beta_0 + \beta_1 X_i + \epsilon_i \qquad \text{with } \epsilon_i \colon NID(0, \sigma_{y \cdot x}). \tag{14–1}$$

The model states that the dependent variable (Y) is assumed to be composed (1) of a linear function ($\beta_0 + \beta_1 X$) of the variable (X) and (2) of a random variable that is normally distributed independently of X about a mean of zero with a standard deviation of $\sigma_{y \cdot x}$. Operationally, this means that values of X are assumed to be known exactly while Y is free to vary in accordance with the model. The parameter $\sigma_{y \cdot x}$ usually is called the *standard error of estimate*, although it is also called standard deviation from regression and conditional standard deviation.

To add clarity to the model we can shift our attention to the mean or expected value of Y associated with any particular value of X. We shall give this mean value of Y the symbol $\mu_{y \cdot x}$ to indicate that it is conditional upon the value of X. It is implicit in Eq. (14–1) that

$$\mu_{y \cdot x} = \beta_0 + \beta_1 X; \tag{14–2}$$

that is, the expected Y values form a straight line with Y intercept β_0 and a slope β_1. This line is called the *regression line*. Equation (14–1) then states, in effect, that the individual Y values for any given value of X are assumed to be distributed normally about $\mu_{y \cdot x}$ with standard deviation $\sigma_{y \cdot x}$.

The model can be illustrated graphically. To do so we shall return to our maintenance-cost example. The observations in Table 14–2 were actually

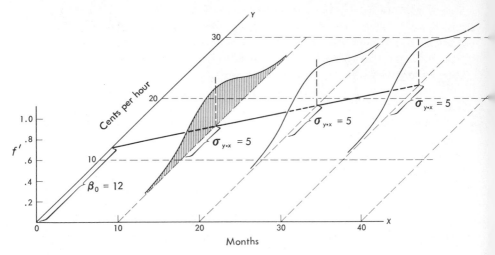

FIGURE 14-2 The linear regression model

randomly selected from a statistical population that conforms to the model
described in Eqs. (14–1) and (14–2). The Y variable is cost and the X variable
is age. The parameters chosen for the model were $\beta_0 = 12$ cents, $\beta_1 = \frac{1}{3}$
cent per hour, and $\sigma_{y \cdot x} = 5$ cents. In Fig. 14–2 we see the population regression line $\mu_{y \cdot x} = 12 + \frac{1}{3}X$. The Y intercept (β_0) and standard error of estimate $(\sigma_{y \cdot x})$ are indicated. The three cross sections illustrate that the individual
Y values are normally distributed about the population regression line with
a standard deviation of 5 cents at all X values.

14-3 Estimators and Estimates in Linear Regression

As was mentioned above, we deliberately selected the data in Table 14–2
by random sampling from a population, or model, in which the values of the
parameters β_0, β_1, and $\sigma_{y \cdot x}$ were known. Now, however, we place ourselves
in the position of the applied statistician who is faced with the problem of
estimating unknown parameters from sample data.

The data needed to estimate the parameters are random samples of Y
values at given levels of X. The values of X are assumed to be known exactly.
The X values may be selected arbitrarily. If we are willing to assume that the
linear model is appropriate, the most efficient procedure is to select an equal
number of X values at each extreme of the range of interest in the X variable.
Often we want to keep open the possibility of shifting to a curvilinear model.
In this case, we select X values at several points within the range of interest.
As we shall see, this procedure permits us to test the applicability of a linear
model.

For the machine-cost example, we have chosen to take a sample of four
Y values at each of five equally spaced X values within the range 6 months

$\leq X \leq 42$ months. These are the data in Table 14–2. Our problem is how to use the 20 randomly selected observations to estimate the numerical values of the three parameters in our model.

We begin by defining (x, y) to be an observation expressed in deviation units. In symbols,

$$x = X - \bar{X} \quad \text{and} \quad y = Y - \bar{Y}.$$

As an example consider the point $X = 6$ and $Y = 5.2$, or $(6, 5.2)$, in Table 14–2. We can find the mean of the 20 X values in that table. The result is $\bar{X} = 24$. It follows from the definition that $x = 6 - 24 = -18$. Similarly, the mean of the 20 Y values in Table 14–2 is $\bar{Y} = 18.3$, and $y = -13.1$. We would describe the point, in deviation units, as $(-18, -13.1)$.

Our immediate goal is to estimate the population regression line in Eq. (14–1) from a sample. The estimate will be a sample regression line of the form $\bar{Y}_x = b_0 + b_1 X$, together with an estimate, $s_{y \cdot x}$, of the standard error of estimate, $\sigma_{y \cdot x}$. It can be shown that the best* point estimators of the three parameters in the model described are, for $\sigma_{y \cdot x}^2$,

$$s_{y \cdot x}^2 = \frac{\sum x^2 \sum y^2 - (\sum xy)^2}{(n-2) \sum x^2}; \tag{14-3a}$$

for β_1,

$$b_1 = \frac{\sum xy}{\sum x^2}; \dagger \tag{14-3b}$$

for β_0,

$$b_0 = \frac{\sum Y}{n} - b_1 \frac{\sum X}{n} \dagger \tag{14-3c}$$

$$= \bar{Y} - b_1 \bar{X}.$$

In Eq. (14–3b) we have the sample estimate, b_1, for the slope of the regression line, β_1. If we divide both the numerator and the denominator of the right side of Eq. (14–3b) by $n - 2$, the degrees of freedom, we have

$$b_1 = \frac{\sum xy}{n-2} \bigg/ \frac{\sum x^2}{n-2}.$$

---

* Minimum-variance unbiased; consistent; asymptotically efficient; sufficient-complete, as is shown in Alexander M. Mood and Franklin A. Graybill, *Introduction to the Theory of Statistics*, 2nd ed. (New York: McGraw-Hill Book Company, 1963), pp. 328–333.

† These are also minimum-variance, unbiased point estimators for their respective parameters when the criterion is the minimization of the sum of the squared deviations (measured in the Y direction) of the Y values from the regression line. These "least-squares" estimates apply to a more general model than we discuss in this chapter. For a discussion of this point see Mood and Graybill, *Introduction to the Theory of Statistics*, pp. 340–343.

The quantity $(\sum xy/n - 2)$ is here defined to be the sample covariance and the quantity $(\sum x^2/n - 2)$ is here defined to be the sample variance for the variable X, although X is not a random variable by assumption. In Chapter 2 we learned that covariance is a measure of the degree of association between two variables.

In Eq. (14–3c) we have the sample estimate, b_0, for the Y-intercept of the population regression line, β_0. From this equation we can see that the sample regression line, $\bar{Y}_x = b_o + b_1 X$, must pass through the point $(\bar{X}, \bar{Y})$.

Useful insight also can be provided by manipulating Eq. (14–3a) algebraically. We begin by rewriting that equation as follows

$$s_{y\cdot x}^2 = \frac{\sum y^2}{n - 2} - \frac{(\sum xy)^2}{\sum x^2 (n - 2)}.$$

This can be rearranged to give

$$\frac{\sum y^2}{n - 2} = \frac{(\sum xy)^2}{(n - 2)\sum x^2} + s_{y\cdot x}^2. \tag{14–4}$$

We can restate the first term on the right of Eq. (14–4) and the result will be

$$\frac{\sum y^2}{n - 2} = \left[\left(\frac{\sum xy}{n - 2}\right)^2 \Big/ \left(\frac{\sum x^2}{n - 2}\right) \right] + s_{y\cdot x}^2.$$

The term on the left side is the sample Y-variance. The first term on the right is the ratio of the squared sample covariance to the sample X-variance and is often called the "Y-variance explained by regression." The second term on the right is the variance about the sample regression line. Hence, total Y-variance can be thought of as the sum of *variance explained by linear regression and unexplained variance about regression.*

Another useful concept and definition can be had from rearranging Eq. (14–4). If we divide through by $\sum y^2/(n - 2)$ we have

$$1 = \frac{(\sum xy)^2}{(\sum x^2)(\sum y^2)} + \frac{(n - 2)s_{y\cdot x}^2}{\sum y^2}.$$

Next, let's define the first term on the right to be the *sample coefficient of determination*, d. In symbols,

$$d = (\sum xy)^2/(\sum x^2)(\sum y^2). \tag{14–5}$$

The coefficient of determination is the *portion* of total Y-variance which is explained by linear regression with X.

The first step in calculating the point estimates from a sample is to process the observations to find $\sum X$, $\sum X^2$, $\sum Y$, $\sum Y^2$, $\sum XY$, and n, where n is the number of observations. An observation consists of an X value and an associated value of Y. In Table 14–2 there are 20 observations, of which $(6, 5.2)$ is one. A tabular form that shows how to find the five summations for our example is illustrated in Table 14–4.

Table 14-4

DATA AND SUMMATIONS FOR LINEAR REGRESSION

Age (X)	Cost (Y)	XY	X^2	Y^2
6	5.2	31.2	36	27.04
6	12.5	75.0	36	156.25
6	9.3	55.8	36	86.49
6	11.8	70.8	36	139.24
⋮	⋮	⋮	⋮	⋮
24	21.3	511.2	576	453.69
⋮	⋮	⋮	⋮	⋮
42	29.9	1255.8	1764	894.01
$\sum X = 480$	$\sum Y = 366.6$	$\sum XY = 10{,}137.6$	$\sum X^2 = 14{,}760$	$\sum Y^2 = 7573.04$

The summations found in Table 14–4 are needed to calculate intermediate values, the use of which is computationally efficient with relatively small rounding errors. These intermediate values are

$$S_{xx} = n \sum X^2 - (\sum X)^2, \qquad (14\text{–}6a)$$

which is the equivalent of $n \sum x^2$;

$$S_{yy} = n \sum Y^2 - (\sum Y)^2, \qquad (14\text{–}6b)$$

which is the equivalent of $n \sum y^2$; and

$$S_{xy} = n \sum XY - (\sum X)(\sum Y), \qquad (14\text{–}6c)$$

which is the equivalent of $n \sum xy$.

For our example,

$$S_{xx} = 20(14{,}760) - 480^2 = 64{,}800,$$

$$S_{yy} = 20(7573.04) - 366.6^2 = 17{,}065.24,$$

and

$$S_{xy} = 20(10{,}137.6) - (480)(366.6) = 26{,}784.$$

In terms of the computational notation in Eqs. (14–6), the calculation formulas for point estimates of two of the parameters are

$$s_{y \cdot x}^2 = \frac{S_{xx}S_{yy} - S_{xy}^2}{n(n-2)S_{xx}} \tag{14-7a}$$

and

$$b_1 = \frac{S_{xy}}{S_{xx}}. \tag{14-7b}$$

For our example,

$$s_{y \cdot x}^2 = \frac{64{,}800(17{,}065.24) - 26{,}784^2}{20(18)(64{,}800)} = 16.65$$

or

$$s_{y \cdot x} = 4.08 \text{ cents;}$$

$$b_1 = \frac{26{,}784}{64{,}800} = .4133 \text{ cents per hour.}$$

The remaining estimate is found from Eq. (14–3c):

$$b_0 = \frac{366.6}{20} - .4133\left(\frac{480}{20}\right) = 8.41 \text{ cents.}$$

The sample estimate of the coefficient of determination from Eq. (14–5) becomes

$$d = \frac{(S_{xy})^2}{S_{xx}S_{yy}}. \tag{14-8}$$

For our example,

$$d = \frac{26{,}784^2}{64{,}800(17{,}065.24)} = .6487;$$

about 65 per cent of the total Y-variance (cost) in the sample is accounted for by linear regression with X (age).

As we have said, a general algebraic form for a sample estimate of the population regression line given in Eq. (14–2) is

$$\bar{Y}_x = b_0 + b_1 X. \tag{14-9}$$

For the machine-cost example the population regression line is $\mu_{y \cdot x} = 12 + .33X$. Based on the random sample of 20 observations given in Table 14–2 our estimate of the regression line is $\bar{Y}_x = 8.41 + .4133X$. For the population, the standard error of estimate ($\sigma_{y \cdot x}$) is 5 cents. Our sample estimate ($s_{y \cdot x}$) is 4.08 cents.

The estimated regression line is shown graphically in Figs. 14–3 and

14–4. In Fig. 14–3 the estimate is shown in relation to the population regression line which we defined for our example in Sec. 14–2. The dashed lines will be discussed subsequently. In Fig. 14–4, the estimate is shown together with the 20 sample observations. The dashed line segments connect the cell means which were used in the analysis of variance described earlier in this chapter.

Interval estimators for the three parameters in Eq. (14–1) are obtainable from the sampling distributions of the point estimators in Eqs. (14–3). The interval estimator for β_1 is based upon the point estimator b_1 and the point estimator of its standard error, $s_{y \cdot x}\sqrt{n/S_{xx}}$. The interval estimator is

$$b_1 \pm t_{\alpha/2, m} s_{y \cdot x}\sqrt{\frac{n}{S_{xx}}}, \qquad (14\text{--}10)$$

where t has $n - 2$ degrees of freedom. For our example we have found that

$$b_1 = .4133, \qquad s_{y \cdot x} = 4.08, \quad \text{and} \quad S_{xx} = 64{,}800.$$

From the t table for $n - 2 = 18$ and an alpha risk of .05 we find $t(.025, 18) = -2.101$. When these are substituted in Eq. (14–10), we find that the .95 interval estimate is $.2627 < \beta_1 < .5639$. This interval contains the true value, $\beta_1 = .33$, given in Sec. 14–2.

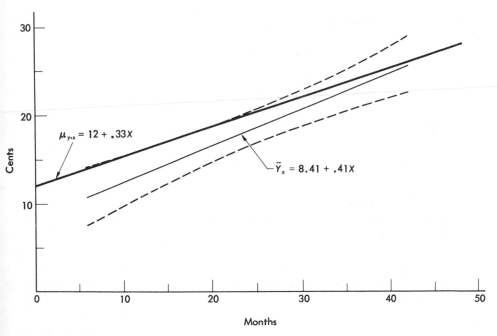

FIGURE 14-3 The population regression line and its sample estimate

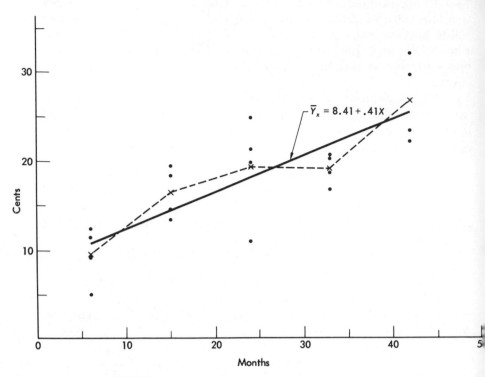

FIGURE 14-4 The regression-line estimate and the cell means

The interval estimator for β_0 is

$$b_0 \pm t_{\alpha/2,\,m} s_{y\cdot x} \sqrt{\frac{S_{xx} + (\sum X)^2}{n S_{xx}}}, \tag{14-11}$$

where $m = n - 2$. The estimator for our example is

$$8.41 \pm (-2.101)(4.08) \sqrt{\frac{64{,}800 + 480^2}{20(64{,}800)}}$$

or 8.41 ± 4.09, from which one who does not know β_0 can make the statement that $4.32 < \beta_0 < 12.50$ with .95 fiducial probability that it is correct. The interval happens to include the true value, $\beta_0 = 12$.

Given the assumptions in the model, Eq. (14–1), it can be shown that $(n - 2)s_{y\cdot x}^2/\sigma_{y\cdot x}^2$ is distributed as chi-square with $n - 2$ degrees of freedom. It follows that the $1 - \alpha$ interval estimate for $\sigma_{y\cdot x}^2$ has upper (U) and lower (L) limits of

$$U = \frac{(n - 2)s_{y\cdot x}^2}{\chi_{\alpha/2,\,m}^2} \tag{14-12a}$$

and

$$L = \frac{(n-2)s_{y \cdot x}^2}{\chi_{1-(\alpha/2),\, m}^2}, \qquad (14\text{–}12b)$$

where $m = n - 2$. For our example, for the .95 interval estimate for $\sigma_{y \cdot x}^2$,

$$U = \frac{18(16.65)}{8.23} = 36.42$$

and

$$L = \frac{18(16.65)}{31.5} = 9.51.$$

It follows that $6.03 > \sigma_{y \cdot x} > 3.08$ is the .95 interval estimate for the standard error of estimate. This interval also happens to include the true value from our model, $\sigma_{y \cdot x} = 5$ cents.

Expressions (14–10) and (14–11), the interval estimators for β_1 and β_0, can be converted for use in testing hypotheses about the values of these parameters. For example, we can state that

$$t = \frac{b_1 - \beta_1}{s_{y \cdot x}\sqrt{n/S_{xx}}} \qquad (14\text{–}13)$$

where t has $n - 2$ degrees of freedom. Equation (14–13) states that the difference between the true value of the parameter β_1 and its estimator b_1 divided by the standard error of b_1 will be distributed as t with $n - 2$ degrees of freedom. If we want to test the hypothesis that β_1 is equal to some value, $\hat{\beta}_1$, we substitute $\hat{\beta}_1$ for β_1 in Eq. (14–13), find the resulting value of t, and evaluate it with respect to a specified alpha risk.

EXERCISES

14.1 A life insurance company is studying its direct costs for a certain class of policy with $5000 face value. The net cost per premium dollar each year for the first six years of policy life can be calculated by computer at appreciable computing expense. Before a large sample of data is gathered, a small sample is calculated manually. The data give the net cost per premium dollar (Y) and the age of the policy in months (X).

X	Y	X	Y	X	Y	X	Y
8	$1.26	57	$.61	70	$.58	68	$.62
29	1.15	45	.88	40	.74	36	.91
47	.81	39	.99	66	.67	21	1.10
24	1.14	14	1.11	55	.70	38	.78

Estimate the linear regression relationship between these two variables.

Test the hypothesis that $\beta_1 = 0$. Does the sample give evidence of regression? ($\sum X = 657$, $\sum X^2 = 32{,}367$, $\sum Y = 14.05$, $\sum Y^2 = 13.0783$, $\sum XY = 517.96$.)   *Partial ans. $s_{y \cdot x} = .0825$.*

14.2 A hardware wholesale supply firm uses traveling salesmen to contact retail hardware stores throughout a twenty-state area. Alternative allocations of selling effort are being studied. As a portion of that study, a sample has been gathered that provides data on the number of sales calls made on a customer firm and the number of sales orders received last year. The data are:

X (Number of calls)	Y (Number of orders)
10	15, 10, 8
15	27, 25, 20
25	34, 27, 36
35	33, 32, 30

There are three salesmen in each "number of calls" class. On the assumption that a linear model is appropriate, find b_1, b_0, and $s_{y \cdot x}$.

14.3 For the machine-age (X) and maintenance-cost (Y) example in the text, suppose the analyst had assumed the regression to be linear and had selected the data below. These data came from the same model as the one used in the text. Find $s_{y \cdot x}$, b_1, and b_0 and state the regression equation.   *Partial ans. $b_1 = .4325$.*

X	Y		
6	5.1, 18.4, 5.5, 12.2, 19.2,	$\sum Y = 130.8$	
	15.0, 16.2, 11.9, 8.9, 18.4,	$\sum Y^2 = 1959.12$	
42	31.7, 28.6, 33.6, 25.8, 22.3,	$\sum Y = 286.5$	
	35.6, 25.4, 28.8, 28.2, 26.5,	$\sum Y^2 = 8354.19$	

14.4 What are the .95 interval estimates for β_0, β_1, and $\sigma_{y \cdot x}$ for the data in Exercise 14.3? Compare these results with those for the sample in the text. Does it appear that the sampling plan in Exercise 14.3 is superior to that used in the text?

14.5 Find the coefficient of determination for the sample in Exercise 14.3. How does this compare with the coefficient of determination for the sample given in the text ($d = .6487$). There are 20 observations in each sample. Is the result obtained for this exercise what we should expect? Why?

14-4 Variance Analysis in Linear Regression

Test for presence of regression. We can define the sum of squared deviations of the sample Y observations from $\bar{Y}$ as

$$SS_T = \frac{S_{yy}}{n} = \sum y^2.$$

Then the sample sum of squares can be partitioned into a portion attributable to regression with X, $SS_{R \cdot x}$, and a portion attributable to residual error, $SS_{W \cdot x}$. The relationship is

$$SS_T = SS_{R \cdot x} + SS_{W \cdot x}$$

where

$$SS_{R \cdot x} = \frac{(\sum xy)^2}{\sum x^2} = \frac{b_1^2 S_{xx}}{n} = \frac{(S_{xy})^2}{n S_{xx}}$$

and

$$SS_{W \cdot x} = (n - 2)s_{y \cdot x}^2 = SS_T - SS_{R \cdot x}.$$

Furthermore, it can be shown that the $(n - 1)$ degrees of freedom associated with SS_T can be partitioned into 1 degree of freedom associated with $SS_{R \cdot x}$ and $(n - 2)$ associated with $SS_{W \cdot x}$. Finally, given the hypothesis that $\beta_1 = 0$ in the population (which is equivalent to an hypothesis of no linear regression) and the assumptions in our linear regression model, $MS_{R \cdot x} / MS_{W \cdot x}$ will be distributed as F with 1 and $(n - 2)$ degrees of freedom. $MS_{R \cdot x}$ and $MS_{W \cdot x}$ are $SS_{R \cdot x}$ and $SS_{W \cdot x}$ divided by their respective degrees of freedom.

When we perform the analysis of variance test just described on our example, the results are:

Source	SS	m	MS	F
Regression	553.54	1	553.54	33.24*
Residual error	299.73	18	16.65	
	853.27	19		

* Significant at $\alpha = .01$.

We see that there is conclusive evidence of the presence of regression between X and Y in the population. Note that $MS_{W \cdot x}$ (16.65) is the value we obtained for $s_{y \cdot x}^2$ earlier.

Test for linearity of regression. A second use for analysis of variance in linear regression is to test the hypothesis that the regression is linear. The rationale of the test will be explained with reference to Fig. 14–4.

The figure shows estimates of the five cell means found by taking means of the four observations in each cell. These estimates are connected by dashed lines. There is no assumption in the analysis of variance model used in conjunction with Table 14–3 that the means of the five Y populations are *functionally* related to the X variable.

In Fig. 14–4 we have a second estimate for the mean of each cell. These estimates are the values of $\hat{Y}_x$ for $X = 6, 15, 24, 33, 42$. These second estimates come from a model that assumes the population means lie on a straight line.

In the test for the presence of linear regression we discussed the sum of squares attributable to residual error ($SS_{W \cdot x}$) and the related degrees of freedom $(n - 2)$. $SS_{w \cdot x}$ can be partitioned into the sum of a portion attributable to the dispersion of the cell *means* about the regression line $(SS_{M \cdot x})$ and a portion attributable to the variability within cells $(SS_{E \cdot x})$. $SS_{E \cdot x}$ is the residual error within cells found in the one-way analysis of variance conducted in Table 14–3. Eq. (13–1c) on page 302 is the formula for calculating this quantity. The 18 degrees of freedom can also be partitioned into the 15 within the five cells and the 3 associated with $SS_{M \cdot x}$, the residual error about regression.

Given the hypothesis that the regression is linear, the ratio of $SS_{M \cdot x}/3$ to $SS_{E \cdot x}/15$ will be distributed as F with 3 and 15 degrees of freedom. The analysis of variance is:

Source	SS	m	MS	F
Regression	553.54	1	553.54	
Residual of means about regression	60.39	3	20.13	1.26
Residual error within cells	239.33	15	15.96	
	853.26	19		

The analysis leads us to conclude that the linear regression model is suitable.

If the test for nonlinearity is to be performed, two special requirements must be met when collecting the data. First, the design must incorporate replication—that is, more than one observation on Y must be made for each value of X. Second, observations must be made at more than two values of X.

14-5   Linear Regression and Prediction

A major application for the regression equation from the sample, $\bar{Y}_x = b_0 + b_1 X$, is to estimate the value of $\mu_{y \cdot x}$ associated with a given value of X. The point estimate, or point prediction, is obtained directly from this equation. If we want to estimate the expected hourly maintenance cost for machines 33 months old, we substitute $X = 33$ in $\bar{Y}_x = 8.41 + .4133X$ and find $\bar{Y}_{33} = 22.05$ cents.

Seldom is one interested in an estimate from a sample without also being interested in how good that estimate is. The confidence interval provides a way to judge the quality of a point estimate. From the point estimate, $\bar{Y}_x$, we form the confidence interval

$$\bar{Y}_x \pm t_{\alpha/2, n-2} s_{y \cdot x} \sqrt{\frac{1}{n} + \frac{n(X - \bar{X})^2}{S_{xx}}}. \qquad (14\text{–}14)$$

The .95 confidence interval for expected maintenance cost of machines 33 months old is

$$22.05 \pm (2.101)(4.081)\sqrt{\frac{1}{20} + \frac{20(33 - 24)^2}{64,800}}$$

which is

$$22.05 \pm 2.348$$

or

$$19.70 < \mu_{y \cdot 33} < 24.40.$$

By repeated application of Eq. (14–14) we find the confidence intervals for the values of X in Table 14–5. These are the points that were used to plot the

Table 14-5

CONFIDENCE INTERVALS* FOR EXPECTED COSTS

X	$(X - \bar{X})^2$	$\bar{Y}_x$	Prediction interval
6	324	10.89	10.89 ± 3.321
15	81	14.61	14.61 ± 2.348
24	0	18.33	18.33 ± 1.917
33	81	22.05	22.05 ± 2.348
42	324	25.77	25.77 ± 3.321

* $1 - \alpha = .95$.

dashed curves in Fig. 14–3. In that figure we see that the line of population means, $\mu_{y \cdot x} = \beta_0 + \beta_1 X$, happens to fall within the .95 bounds of the various confidence intervals based upon $\bar{Y}_x = b_0 + b_1 X$. In Eq. (14–14),

$$s_{y \cdot x}\sqrt{\frac{1}{n} + \frac{n(X - \bar{X})^2}{S_{xx}}}$$

can be written

$$\sqrt{\frac{s_{y \cdot x}^2}{n} + \frac{n s_{y \cdot x}^2}{S_{xx}}(X - \bar{X})^2}.$$

The term $s_{y \cdot x}^2/n$ is the estimated sampling variance of the sample mean, $\bar{Y}_x$, which is normally distributed about $\mu_{y \cdot x}$ if the assumptions in the model apply. The first factor in the second term is $n s_{y \cdot x}^2/S_{xx}$. An examination of Eq. (14–10) shows this to be the estimated sampling variance of b_1, the sample estimate of the slope of the regression line. The further a given value of X is from $\bar{X}$, the greater the effect an error in b_1 will have in terms of units of Y. Hence, the second term under the radical allows for the total effect of an error in slope on the prediction interval, while the first term allows for $\bar{Y}$ variability about the population regression line.

To appreciate the predictive advantage of regression when it applies, we can compare the half-widths of the prediction intervals in Table 14–5 with the half-width obtained when we used analysis of variance early in this chapter. The half-width we found for the five cell means from the mean-square residual error in Table 14–3 was

$$- t_{\alpha/2,\, n-k-1} s_{..}/\sqrt{n_{.j}} = \frac{-t_{.025,\, 15}4.0}{\sqrt{4}} = 4.262.$$

This is larger than any of the half-widths in Table 14–5. For the same level of confidence (.95) we have been able to reduce the length of a given confidence interval through regression analysis.

In the maintenance-cost example we would want point estimates of expected maintenance costs ($\mu_{y.x}$) for various machine ages (X) to find expected costs for alternative replacement policies, for example. The values of $\bar{Y}_x$ would constitute these estimates. On other occasions we might need a point estimate or a prediction interval for a *single* Y value associated with a given X value. For instance, we might want a prediction of the maintenance cost of a given machine that is X months old. The point estimate is simply $Y_x = \bar{Y}_x$ from the sample regression equation. The prediction interval is

$$Y_x \pm t_{\alpha/2,\, n-2} s_{y.x} \sqrt{1 + \frac{1}{n} + \frac{n(X - \bar{X})^2}{S_{xx}}} \qquad (14\text{–}15)$$

which differs from Eq. (14–14) only in that *one* is added to the quantity under the radical. This reflects the estimated dispersion, $s_{y.x}$, of Y values about the true regression line.

There are two precautions that should be observed in applying linear regression analysis. The first is concerned with the intervals in Eqs. (14–14) and (14–15). If the alpha risk associated with such an interval is to apply, only *one* such interval should be found from a single set of sample data. Any number of point predictions can be made from a single sample, but only one interval prediction should be made. The second precaution is that one should be aware of the danger in making either type of prediction much beyond the extreme range of the sample data upon which the analysis is based. Typically, a two-variable curvilinear function can be satisfactorily approximated by a linear function within a sufficiently narrow range of the independent variable. But when one extrapolates by using values of the independent variable outside this range in the linear approximation, serious discrepancies between such predictions and true values of the dependent variable can arise. The important point is that these discrepancies are not considered in the adjustments for sampling error that are a part of prediction intervals.

EXERCISES

14.6 Perform an analysis of variance test for presence of linear regression on the sample in Exercise 14.3. If an analysis of variance test for linearity of regression can be performed on the sample in Exercise 14.3, do so. What conclusions can be drawn?

14.7 Test the hypothesis that the regression equation for Exercise 14.2 is linear. What would you recommend as a model for these data? A scattergram may help. ($SS_{M \cdot x} = 233.73$.)

REFERENCES

See the references listed at the end of Chapter 15.

15

Multiple
and
Curvilinear Regression

We continue our consideration of techniques for finding useful relationships among variables and the degree of confidence that can be placed in these relationships. Two techniques will be described: the first extends the linear regression techniques described in Chapter 14 to more than two variables; the second is concerned with finding curvilinear relationships.

As before, values of all but the dependent variable are assumed to be capable of selection without error. Selection may be done directly or indirectly. Direct selection was the approach in the machine-age and maintenance-cost example in Chapter 14; it is also used for both examples in this chapter. In the indirect approach the investigator may, for instance, have to select households at random and then determine the values of variables such as income and savings. When the indirect approach is used, regression analysis can be applied if all but the dependent variable can be assumed to be determined without error once the unit of association—a household—has been selected.

15-1 Multiple Regression

Our example is a hypothetical experiment in marketing a household cleaning product. We are conducting experiments in fifteen test markets to determine the effects of two variables upon sales. The first is the amount of television spot advertising with a particular fixed message, and the second is the price of the product. The levels of these two factors selected for each test market are held constant for eight weeks. At the end of this time a survey is conducted among 200 housewives in each market to find the proportion of housewives reporting purchases of the product during the preceding four weeks. The results for the fifteen test markets are presented in Table 15–1. Since the

Table 15-1

PROPORTION OF REPORTED PURCHASERS, CLASSIFIED BY ADVERTISING
EXPENSE (X_1) AND PRODUCT PRICE (X_2)

X_1	X_2	Sample proportions		
$2	$0.49	.255	.321	.319
2	.69	.158	.166	.141
12	.49	.449	.559	.426
12	.69	.349	.255	.332
7	.59	.342	.241	.284

markets are comparable in size of television audiences and TV spot rates, the advertising level has been expressed in monthly expenditures per thousand households.

Multiple regression assumes normal distributions and equal variances for the dependent variable *within each combination of levels* of the factor variables just as analysis of variance does. As we said earlier, conclusions resulting from these techniques usually are not seriously distorted by moderate violation of the normality assumption. On the other hand, the techniques are fairly sensitive to inequalities in intracell variances—that is, to violation of the assumption of equal variances for the dependent variable within each combination of levels of the factor variables. Difficulties on either score are usually relatively easy to avoid when proportions are involved. As we learned in Chapter 9, the transformation $Y = 2 \arcsin \sqrt{p'}$ will result in an approximately normal distribution of the Y's with variance $1/n$ regardless of the true p for samples in which $np'q' > 10$. Since the sample size is 200 in each test market, the values of p' in Table 15–1 meet these conditions, and the transformed Y-variances within cells are theoretically equal. Table 15–2 presents transformed data which will serve as input to our multiple regression analysis.

As we did with our first example in Chapter 14, we could perform a one-way analysis of variance on the data and find approximate point and interval predictions for a given cell mean. We shall not repeat that procedure here, however. Instead we shall assume linearity conditions apply in this three-variable case just as they did in the two-variable case discussed in Chapter 14. This assumption implies that all five population means lie on the same plane. For our example, this plane is illustrated in Fig. 15–1. The

Table 15-2

TRANSFORMED REPORTED PURCHASER PROPORTIONS (Y) CLASSIFIED
BY ADVERTISING (X_1) AND PRODUCT PRICE (X_2)

	$X_1 = \$2$ $X_2 = \$0.49$ Y	$X_1 = \$2$ $X_2 = \$0.69$ Y	$X_1 = \$12$ $X_2 = \$0.49$ Y	$X_1 = \$12$ $X_2 = \$0.69$ Y	$X_1 = \$7$ $X_2 = \$0.59$ Y
	1.058	.817	1.468	1.262	1.248
	1.205	.839	1.690	1.057	1.026
	1.200	.770	1.422	1.227	1.124
$\Sigma\, Y$:	3.463	2.426	4.580	3.546	3.398
$\Sigma\,(Y^2)$:	4.0114	1.9643	7.0332	4.2154	3.8736
		$\Sigma\Sigma\, Y = 17.413$		$\Sigma\Sigma\,(Y^2) = 21.097885$	

confidence interval from the multiple regression analysis is narrower than
it is for simple analysis of variance when this assumption is correct. There
is also an improvement over linear regression, which uses only one factor
variable.

Table 15–2 contains more than one observation for each combination
of levels of the factors. As in the case of linear regression, only one observation for each such combination is necessary to find the estimated regression
equation and to make point and interval estimates and predictions. On the
other hand, replication makes it possible to test for homogeneity of variance
within cells and to make a test for linearity of the multiple regression surface. We shall make this latter test subsequently.

15-2 A Statistical Model for Multiple Regression

We shall confine our model to only two factor variables. Extensions to more
than two such variables will be discussed in the latter part of this chapter.

For our model, one observation is composed of the triplet: Y_j, X_{1j},
X_{2j}. These values are assumed to be associated with each other in the following manner:

$$Y_j = \varphi_0 + \varphi_1 X_{1j} + \varphi_2 X_{2j} + \epsilon_j, \tag{15-1}$$

with ϵ: $NID(0, \sigma_{y \cdot 12})$.

The model states that the dependent variable is assumed to be a linear
function (1) of the factor variables ($\varphi_0 + \varphi_1 X_1 + \varphi_2 X_2$) and (2) of a random
variable which is normally distributed and independent of either X_1 or X_2.
The random variable has a mean of zero and a standard deviation of $\sigma_{y \cdot 12}$,
where the subscript indicates the number of factor variables. The constants
in Eq. (15–1) have been given the symbol φ to indicate that they come from a
different model than did the β's in Chapter 14.

The expected value of Y associated with given values of X_1 and X_2 is found to be

$$\mu_{y \cdot 12} = \varphi_0 + \varphi_1 X_1 + \varphi_2 X_2 \qquad (15\text{-}2)$$

from Eq. (15–1). This is called the *regression plane* instead of the regression line.

The data in Table 15–2 were obtained by random sampling from a model population of the type described in Eq. (15–1). To generate our marketing example, the following numerical values were assigned to the parameters:

$$\varphi_0 = 1.755, \qquad \varphi_1 = .04,$$
$$\varphi_2 = -1.5, \qquad \sigma_{y \cdot 12} = .1.$$

When we substitute in Eq. (15–2), we get

$$\mu_{y \cdot 12} = 1.755 + .04 X_1 - 1.5 X_2$$

as the equation of the regression plane.

A portion of this plane is illustrated in Fig. 15–1. The extended plane intercepts the $\mu_{y \cdot 12}$ axis at $\varphi_0 = 1.755$. The second constant, $\varphi_1 = +.04$, is the slope of the plane in the X_1 direction. For a fixed value of X_2 (say $X_2 = .49$), the value of $\mu_{y \cdot 12}$ is 1.1 at $X_1 = 2$ and is 1.5 at $X_1 = 12$. Hence, $\mu_{y \cdot 12}$ has increased by .4 while X_1 has increased by 10. The change per unit of X_1 is .4/10, which is φ_1. This tells us we can expect .04 units of increase in our transformed proportion for each dollar increase in advertising per thousand households.

As we would expect, the effect of an *increase* in price is a *decrease*

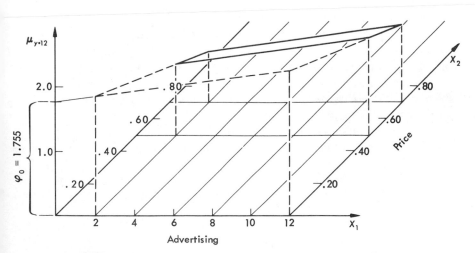

FIGURE 15-1 The regression plane $\mu_{y \cdot 12} = 1.755 + .04 X_1 - 1.5 X_2$

in transformed proportion reporting purchases. This is reflected in the fact that $\varphi_2 = -1.5$.

The populations from which the random observations in Table 15–2 came are normally distributed vertically above and below the regression plane with their means on the plane and with standard deviations of $\sigma_{y \cdot 12} = .1$.

15-3 Normal Equations and Point Estimators

From our sample of fifteen joint observations in Table 15–2 we must estimate the values of the four parameters in our model. For samples that satisfy the assumptions of our model, the maximum-likelihood estimates* for the three constants in Eq. (15–2) are contained in a set of so-called *normal equations*. The word "normal" in this expression has no connection with the normal distribution. If we let c_0, c_1, and c_2 be the sample estimates of φ_0, φ_1, and φ_2, respectively, then the normal equations for the general three-variable case are

$$c_0 n + c_1 \Sigma(X_1) + c_2 \Sigma(X_2) = \Sigma(Y), \qquad (15\text{–}3a)$$

$$c_0 \Sigma(X_1) + c_1 \Sigma(X_1^2) + c_2 \Sigma(X_1 X_2) = \Sigma(X_1 Y), \qquad (15\text{–}3b)$$

$$c_0 \Sigma(X_2) + c_1 \Sigma(X_1 X_2) + c_2 \Sigma(X_2^2) = \Sigma(X_2 Y). \qquad (15\text{–}3c)$$

We can use a procedure analogous to that used in Table 14–4 to find the necessary sums for the normal equations. With the sums inserted, we have a set of three simultaneous linear equations in three unknowns. We solve these equations for c_0, c_1, and c_2 and substitute their numerical values in

$$\bar{Y}_c = c_0 + c_1 X_1 + c_2 X_2 \qquad (15\text{–}4)$$

to form our sample estimate of the regression plane.

An important portion of a discussion of applied multiple regression techniques is usually devoted to efficient ways for solving normal equations or their equivalents. This poses no major problem when only three variables are involved, but it can be a formidable task when there are considerably more than three variables. We shall discuss this point in more detail in the latter portions of this chapter.

When we process the data in Table 15–2 to get the sums indicated in Eqs. (15–3), the result is the following set of normal equations:

$$15c_0 + 105c_1 + 8.85c_2 = 17.413,$$

$$105c_0 + 1035c_1 + 61.95c_2 = 133.076,$$

$$8.85c_0 + 61.95c_1 + 5.3415c_2 = 10.06657.$$

---

* These estimates are also minimum-variance unbiased, consistent, asymptotically efficient, and sufficient-complete.

When these are solved simultaneously, we get

$$c_0 = 1.918108, \qquad c_1 = .037283, \qquad c_2 = -1.725837.$$

The calculations are carried to six decimal places to minimize rounding errors in later applications of these constants. Given these constants, we can state the estimated regression relationship:

$$\bar{Y}_c = 1.918 + .037X_1 - 1.726X_2.$$

As a matter of interest, these values can be compared with the parameters given previously for the model.

We still must estimate the *standard error of estimate*, $\sigma_{y \cdot 12}$, from our sample. The minimum-variance, unbiased estimator of $\sigma_{y \cdot 12}^2$ is perhaps most easily understood in the following form:

$$s_{y \cdot 12}^2 = \frac{1}{n-3} \Sigma (Y - \bar{Y}_c)^2. \tag{15-5}$$

For each sample observation we can use the observed values of X_1 and X_2 in Eq. (15–4) to find the predicted value $\bar{Y}_c$. Then we can use the observed value of Y, together with the value of $\bar{Y}_c$ just found, to calculate the deviation of the observed value of Y from the predicted value. The sum of these squared deviations for all observations divided by $(n - 3)$ is the desired estimate, $s_{y \cdot 12}^2$. The divisor, $n - 3$, is the degrees of freedom present for estimating this variance. It is $n - 3$ because three parameters are being estimated in the regression equation. In general this quantity is n, the sample size, less the total number of variables in the regression analysis.

An algebraic equivalent to the expression given above is

$$s_{y \cdot 12} = \sqrt{\frac{\Sigma (Y^2) - c_0 \Sigma Y - c_1 \Sigma (X_1 Y) - c_2 \Sigma (X_2 Y)}{n-3}}. \tag{15-6}$$

This expression makes use of quantities already found and employed in normal equations (15–3) as well as the c_i obtained from solving those equations. The only additional quantity needed is $\Sigma (Y^2)$. We found this quantity for our example in Table 15–2. The entire substitution for our example is

$$
\begin{aligned}
s_{y \cdot 12}^2 &= \tfrac{1}{12}[21.097885 - 1.918108(17.413) \\
&\quad - .037283(133.076) - (-1.725837)(10.06657)] \\
&= \tfrac{1}{12}(.10928962) \\
&= .009107,
\end{aligned}
$$

from which $s_{y \cdot 12} = .0954$. Recall that $\sigma_{y \cdot 12}$ is .1.

15-4 Interval Estimators

Interval estimators for most of the parameters in multiple regression can be expressed succinctly as functions of sums of squared deviations and cross products. These latter types of quantities were presented in Eqs. (14–6) in Chapter 14. For three-variable regression the sums we shall need are expressed below both in terms of deviations ($x_1 = X_1 - \bar{X}_1$, $x_2 = X_2 - \bar{X}_2$, $y = Y - \bar{Y}$) and in terms of original variables. Numerical values for our example are also given.

$$S_{yy} = n\,\Sigma\,(y^2) = n\,\Sigma\,(Y^2) - (\Sigma\,Y)^2 = 13.255706, \qquad (15\text{–}7a)$$

$$S_{11} = n\,\Sigma\,(x_1^2) = n\,\Sigma\,(X_1^2) - (\Sigma\,X_1)^2 = 4500, \qquad (15\text{–}7b)$$

$$S_{22} = n\,\Sigma\,(x_2^2) = n\,\Sigma\,(X_2^2) - (\Sigma\,X_2)^2 = 1.8, \qquad (15\text{–}7c)$$

$$S_{1y} = n\,\Sigma\,(x_1 y) = n\,\Sigma\,(X_1 Y) - (\Sigma\,X_1)(\Sigma\,Y) = 167.775, \qquad (15\text{–}7d)$$

$$S_{2y} = n\,\Sigma\,(x_2 y) = n\,\Sigma\,(X_2 Y) - (\Sigma\,X_2)(\Sigma\,Y) = -3.1065, \qquad (15\text{–}7e)$$

$$S_{12} = n\,\Sigma\,(x_1 x_2) = n\,\Sigma\,(X_1 X_2) - (\Sigma\,X_1)(\Sigma\,X_2) = 0. \qquad (15\text{–}7f)$$

If we divide all six of these equations by $n(n-3)$, the first three become sample variances and the last three become the sample covariances for all possible pairs of variables.

Some of the quantities we need for our estimators are obtained from the S_{ij} found immediately above. These quantities are

$$S^{11} = \frac{S_{22}}{S_{11}S_{22} - S_{12}^2} = \frac{1}{4500}, \qquad (15\text{–}8a)$$

$$S^{22} = \frac{S_{11}}{S_{11}S_{22} - S_{12}^2} = \frac{1}{1.8}, \qquad (15\text{–}8b)$$

$$S^{12} = \frac{-S_{12}}{S_{11}S_{22} - S_{12}^2} = 0. \qquad (15\text{–}8c)$$

Although S_{12} and S^{12} are both zero for our numerical example, this is not true in general. The symbols on the left side of Eqs. (15–8) make use of *superscripts*. They are not to be interpreted as exponents but as elements of the inverse of a matrix. This will be explained later.

Typically, the parameters of chief interest in three-variable regression analysis are the coefficients φ_1 and φ_2. Interval estimators for these parameters come from the sampling distributions of c_1 and c_2. These interval estimators are, for φ_1,

$$c_1 \pm t_{\alpha/2,\,m} s_{y\cdot 12} \sqrt{nS^{11}}, \qquad (15\text{–}9a)$$

and for φ_2,

$$c_2 \pm t_{\alpha/2,\,m} s_{y\cdot 12} \sqrt{nS^{22}}, \qquad (15\text{–}9b)$$

where $m = n - 3$.

For an alpha risk of .05, the results for our example are, for φ_1,

$$.037283 \pm 2.179(.0954)\sqrt{15/4500}$$

or

$$.037283 \pm .011589$$

and for φ_2,

$$-1.725837 \pm 2.179(.0954)\sqrt{15/1.8}$$

or

$$-1.725837 \pm .600283.$$

Occasionally one needs an interval estimate for the parameter φ_0. Although we shall apply the general estimator to our numerical example, the sample data are far removed from $X_1 = X_2 = 0$ and such an estimate would not be appropriate in practice. The interval estimator for φ_0 is

$$c_0 \pm t_{\alpha/2,\,m} s_{y\cdot 12}\sqrt{\frac{1}{n} + n(S^{11}\bar{X}_1^2 + S^{22}\bar{X}_2^2 + 2S^{12}\bar{X}_1\bar{X}_2)}, \qquad (15\text{--}10)$$

where the $\bar{X}_i$ are sample means and $m = n - 3$. For our example the interval estimate is

$$1.918108 \pm 2.179(.0954)\sqrt{\frac{1}{15} + 15\left(\frac{49}{4500} + \frac{.3481}{1.8}\right)}$$

or

$$1.918108 \pm 0.367998.$$

The interval estimate for the last of the four parameters, $\sigma_{y\cdot 12}^2$, is based on the sampling distribution of $s_{y\cdot 12}^2$. It can be shown that $ms_{y\cdot 12}^2/\sigma_{y\cdot 12}^2$ is distributed as chi-square with $m = n - 3$ degrees of freedom. It follows that the interval estimate for a confidence level of $1 - \alpha$ is

$$\frac{ms_{y\cdot 12}^2}{\chi_{m,\,1-(\alpha/2)}^2} < \sigma_{y\cdot 12}^2 < \frac{ms_{y\cdot 12}^2}{\chi_{m,\,(\alpha/2)}^2}. \qquad (15\text{--}11)$$

For our example, with $\alpha = .05$,

$$\frac{12(.00911)}{23.34} < \sigma_{y\cdot 12}^2 < \frac{12(.00911)}{4.40},$$

or

$$.00468 < \sigma_{y\cdot 12}^2 < .02484.$$

Recall that, for our model, $\sigma_{y\cdot 12}^2 = (.1)^2 = .01$.

The sampling distribution of the point estimators can be used not only to find interval estimates of the parameters; they can also be used to test hypotheses about the values of these parameters. For instance, Eq. (15–9a) can be put in the following form:

$$t = \frac{c_1 - \varphi_1}{s_{y \cdot 12}\sqrt{nS^{11}}},$$
(15–12)

where t has $n - 3$ degrees of freedom. We can test the hypothesis that $\varphi_1 = 0$, for example, by setting $\varphi_1 = 0$ in Eq. (15–12). If we do so, $t = 3.22$ with 12 degrees of freedom—a highly significant difference.

15-5   Variance Analysis in Multiple Regression

For three-variable regression, an equivalent algebraic form for $s_{y \cdot 12}^2$ in Eq. (15–6) is

$$s_{y \cdot 12}^2 = \frac{\dfrac{S_{yy}}{n} - \dfrac{1}{n}(c_1 S_{1y} + c_2 S_{2y})}{n - 3}.$$
(15–13)

From Eqs. (15–7) we see that Eq. (15–13) in deviation units is

$$s_{y \cdot 12}^2 = \frac{\Sigma(y^2) - c_1 \Sigma(x_1 y) - c_2 \Sigma(x_2 y)}{n - 3}.$$
(15–14)

Eq. (15–14) can be written as follows:

$$s_{y \cdot 12}^2 = \frac{\Sigma y^2}{n - 3} - c_1 \frac{\Sigma(x_1 y)}{n - 3} - c_2 \frac{\Sigma(x_2 y)}{n - 3}.$$
(15–15)

The first term on the right is the Y-variance for the sample. The second and third terms on the right contain the sample covariances of Y with each of the X-variables. As in the case of two-variable regression, the square of the standard error of estimate can be viewed as the variance that remains in the sample of Y values after total Y variance is corrected for regression. The square of the standard error of estimate is called the *residual error variance*. It is the variance of the sample of Y values about the sample regression plane.

   Coefficient of multiple determination. We can rearrange Eq. (15–15),

$$\frac{\Sigma y^2}{n - 3} = c_1 \frac{\Sigma(x_1 y)}{n - 3} + c_2 \frac{\Sigma(x_2 y)}{n - 3} + s_{y \cdot 12}^2,$$
(15–16)

and divide it by $\dfrac{\Sigma y^2}{n - 3}$ to obtain

$$1 = \left(c_1 \frac{\Sigma(x_1 y)}{\Sigma y^2} + c_2 \frac{\Sigma(x_2 y)}{\Sigma y^2}\right) + \frac{(n - 3)s_{y \cdot 12}^2}{\Sigma y^2}.$$
(15–17)

Then we define the coefficient of multiple determination for the sample to be

$$d_{y \cdot 12} = c_1 \frac{\Sigma (x_1 y)}{\Sigma y^2} + c_2 \frac{\Sigma (x_2 y)}{\Sigma y^2}. \tag{15-18}$$

The coefficient of multiple determination is the portion of Y-variance in the sample which is accounted for by regression with X_1 and X_2. For calculation purposes it can be written as follows:

$$d_{y \cdot 12} = \frac{c_1 S_{1y} + c_2 S_{2y}}{S_{yy}}. \tag{15-19}$$

This coefficient is 0.876 for our example. Nearly 88 per cent of the variance in transformed proportions is accounted for by regression with advertising and price.

Test for regression. Given the hypothesis that $\varphi_1 = \varphi_2 = 0$, it can be shown that $s_{y \cdot 12}^2$ and $[c_1 \Sigma (x_1 y) + c_2 \Sigma (x_2 y)]/2$ are independent estimates of σ_y^2. Under sampling, the ratio formed by such independent estimates will follow an F distribution. As a consequence, we can use the F distribution to test the hypothesis that $\varphi_1 = \varphi_2 = 0$, which is equivalent to a hypothesis of no linear regression between Y and the variables X_1 and X_2.

We first calculate the sum of squares for regression:

$$SS_{R \cdot 12} = \frac{1}{n}(c_1 S_{1y} + c_2 S_{2y})$$

$$= .774430 \text{ for our example.}$$

We next calculate the total sum of squares.

$$SS_T = \frac{S_{yy}}{n} = .883714.$$

Finally, we find the sum of squares for residual error by subtraction:

$$SS_{W \cdot 12} = SS_T - SS_{R \cdot 12} = .109284.$$

The analysis-of-variance table is shown below.

Source	SS	m	MS	F
Regression	.774430	2	.387215	42.5
Residual error	.109284	12	.009107	
	.883714	14		

The value of F is highly significant. In the table, the degrees of freedom associated with regression are the number of factor variables.

Test for contribution from additional factor variables. We may wonder whether a particular factor variable or a subgroup of such variables can be expected to contribute anything to the prediction of the value of the dependent variable. In other words, we may want to know whether the residual sum of squares has been reduced significantly by using a model based on k factor variables in preference to one based on $k - a$ of these same variables. This is equivalent to a test of the hypothesis that the φ coefficients of the a factor variables in the subgroup are all zero. Analysis of variance provides an exact test for this hypothesis.

Suppose that for our marketing example we had chosen to consider only one factor variable, advertising (X_1), in our regression model. We find from Eqs. (14–3) that our sample estimates would have been $b_0 = .899886$, $b_1 = .037283$, and $s_{y \cdot x}^2 = .035900$. Note that when we used a model based on both X-variables earlier in this chapter we found that $c_0 = 1.918108$, $c_1 = .037283$, $c_2 = -1.725837$, and $s_{y \cdot 12}^2 = .009107$. Although $b_1 = c_1$ for our numerical example, this is true only because S_{12} happened to be zero. Usually all such sample estimates based on one model will differ from those based on another model that includes more factor variables. This is true even when the same data points are used to calculate both sets of estimates.

If we had chosen to work with advertising as the only factor, the sum of squares attributable to the regression equation

$$\bar{Y}_x = .8999 + .0373X$$

would have been

$$SS_{R \cdot 1} = \frac{S_{xy}^2}{n S_{xx}}$$

$$= \frac{(167.775)^2}{15(4500)} = .417014,$$

as we saw in Sec. 14–4. As we just found above, the sum of squares attributable to the regression equation

$$\bar{Y}_c = 1.9181 + .0373X_1 - 1.7258X_2$$

is

$$SS_{R \cdot 12} = \frac{1}{n} \Sigma (c_i S_{iy}) = .774430 \text{ for our example.}$$

And $SS_{W \cdot 12} = .109284$.

The analysis of variance to test the hypothesis that $\varphi_2 = 0$ is shown below.

Source	SS	m	MS	F
Regression with X_1	.417014	1		
Reduction in residual from regression with X_1 and X_2	.357416	1	.357416	39.25
Regression with X_1 and X_2	.774430	2		
Residual error	.109284	12	.009107	
	.883714	14		

The F ratio is highly significant, and we conclude that price as well as advertising is a producer of variation in reported purchases.

If there were a third factor variable, X_3, we would test the hypothesis that $\varphi_3 = 0$ by finding

$$SS_{R \cdot 123} = \frac{1}{n}(c_1 S_{1y} + c_2 S_{2y} + c_3 S_{3y})$$

and

$$SS_{W \cdot 123} = \frac{S_{yy}}{n} - SS_{R \cdot 123},$$

from which we would form the F ratio

$$F = \frac{(SS_{R \cdot 123} - SS_{R \cdot 12})/1}{SS_{W \cdot 123}/(n - 4)}.$$

As an alternative, we might want a *single* test of the hypothesis that $\varphi_2 = \varphi_3 = 0$. In this case the proper F ratio would be

$$F = \frac{(SS_{R \cdot 123} - SS_{R \cdot 1})/2}{SS_{W \cdot 123}/(n - 4)}.$$

Test for linearity of regression. We can partition the residual error sum of squares in multiple linear regression in the same way we did to test for linearity of regression in Chapter 14. We partition the residual error sum of squares into a portion that represents residual error of treatment means from regression and a portion that measures residual variability within treatments, wherein a given combination of levels of the factor variables represents a treatment. We return to Table 15–2 for the necessary inputs:

$$C = \frac{(\Sigma \Sigma Y)^2}{n_{..}} = \frac{(17.413)^2}{15} = 20.2142,$$

$$SS_A = \sum_j \left[\frac{(\sum_i Y_{ij})^2}{n_{.j}} \right] - C$$

$$= \frac{3.463^2 + \ldots + 3.398^2}{3} - C = .777417,$$

from which we find the residual error of treatment means:

$$SS_{M \cdot 12} = SS_A - SS_{R \cdot 12}$$
$$= .777417 - .774430 = .002987.$$

The analysis-of-variance table is shown below.

Source	SS	m	MS	F
Regression with X_1 and X_2	.774430	2		
Residual of means about regression	.002987	2	.001494	.14
Residual error	.106297	10	.010630	
Total	.883714	14		

The degrees of freedom for $SS_{M \cdot 12}$ are found by subtracting the degrees of freedom for regression (2) from the degrees of freedom among the five treatment means (4). The F ratio for residuals about regression is not significant at the .05 level, and the planar model is satisfactory as compared with any possible curvilinear model.

15-6 Point and Interval Predictions

The point prediction for the expected value of Y for a given combination of values of X_1 and X_2 is obtained from the sample estimate of the regression equation, Eq. (15–4). This is also the point prediction for a single Y value for the given values of X_1 and X_2.

We can best state interval predictions in terms of deviations of the given values of X_1 and X_2 from their sample means. In the following, $x_1 = X_1 - \bar{X}_1$ and $x_2 = X_2 - \bar{X}_2$. Then the interval prediction for the true mean Y, $\mu_{y \cdot 12}$, given specified levels of X_1 and X_2 is

$$\bar{Y}_c \pm t_{\alpha/2, m} s_{y \cdot 12} \sqrt{\frac{1}{n} + n(S^{11} x_1^2 + S^{22} x_2^2 + 2 S^{12} x_1 x_2)}, \qquad (15–20)$$

where $m = n - 3$.

The interval estimate for a single Y value for given values of X_1 and X_2 is formed by adding 1 to the quantity under the radical in Eq. (15–20).

EXERCISES

15.1 A firm that acts as sales agent for a number of manufacturers sells directly to retail shops. The firm is interested in the effect of calls by its salesmen on sales to the retail shops. For each shop, the firm knows its sales to that shop for the past year (Y), a salesman's estimate of the shop's total annual sales (X_1), and the number of sales calls made (X_2). Shops are classified by sales volume and number of calls. A small random sample is selected and the sample data are as follows.

Y (000 omitted)	X_1 (0000 omitted)	X_2
$16	$5	3
16	5	6
27	5	12
18	10	3
20	10	6
28	10	12
26	15	3
27	15	6
32	15	12

(a) Show that

$$\Sigma\, Y = 210, \qquad \Sigma\,(Y^2) = 5178, \qquad \Sigma\,(X_1 Y) = 2230,$$
$$\Sigma\, X_1 = 90, \qquad \Sigma\,(X_1^2) = 1050, \qquad \Sigma\,(X_2 Y) = 1602,$$
$$\Sigma\, X_2 = 63, \qquad \Sigma\,(X_2^2) = 567, \qquad \Sigma\,(X_1 X_2) = 630.$$

(b) Show that the sample estimate of the regression plane is

$$\bar{Y}_c = \tfrac{22}{3} + \tfrac{13}{15} X_1 + \tfrac{22}{21} X_2.$$

(c) Show that $s^2_{y \cdot 12} = 4.508$.

15.2 For the example in Exercise 15.1 conduct an analysis-of-variance test of the hypothesis that there is no regression.

15.3 For the example in Exercise 15.1 conduct an analysis-of-variance test of the hypothesis that X_2 does not contribute significantly more to linear regression than does X_1 alone.

  Ans. $F = 30.68$ with 1 and 6 degrees of freedom.

15.4 For the example in Exercise 15.1 find .95 interval estimates for φ_0, φ_1, φ_2, and $\sigma^2_{y \cdot 12}$.

15.5 Show that the coefficient of multiple determination for the example in Exercise 15.1 is .9027. Should a search be made for additional independent variables?

15.6 For the example in Exercise 15.1 perform a test of the hypothesis that regression is linear, if such a test can be carried out. If it cannot be carried out, what additional information is needed?

15.7 For the television-advertising example in the text show that the point and .95 interval estimates for Y when X_1 is 12 and X_2 is .49 are 1.5198 and $1.2889 < Y < 1.7508$.

15.8 For the television-advertising example in the text find the point and .95 interval estimates of $\mu_{y \cdot 12}$ when X_1 is 12 and X_2 is .49.

15-7 Curvilinear Regression

In Chapter 14 we considered a regression model that was linear in two variables. The first part of this chapter considered a regression model that was linear in three variables. Now we shall consider two extensions of regression theory. The first deals with only two variables but the relationship is curvilinear; the second considers linear models in more than three variables and efficient calculation techniques for finding the coefficients of the factor variables.

Our example for curvilinear regression is concerned with the relationship between production costs and operating rates in a factory. Economic theory leads us to expect that variable production costs per unit of output will be a U-shaped function of the plant's operating rate.

The data for our example are joint observations on two variables. The factor variable (X) is plant operating rate. Average hourly input rates of raw material corrected for in-process scrap losses are used as a proxy measure of this variable, because the plant uses the same raw material in a variety of products which are produced in essentially constant ratios. The dependent variable (Y) is variable production cost per unit of output. Careful cost allocation has isolated and measured costs directly influenced by the operating rate. Operating-rate stability was achieved before the appropriate costs were measured and attributed to the rate.

In Table 15-3 are five observations of cost rate for each of five different operating rates. Each set of five cost rates is a randomly selected sample from a large number of cost-rate observations in its operating-rate class. Operating rates are assumed to be measured with negligible error.

Table 15-3

VARIABLE UNIT PRODUCTION COSTS (Y) ASSOCIATED WITH
FIVE PLANT OPERATING RATES (X)

X (lb per minute)	Y (cents)	$\bar{Y}$
2	12.04, 10.12, 6.60, 6.77, 14.31	9.978
5	6.64, 7.78, 9.87, 10.19, 8.74	8.644
10	5.87, 12.86, 4.05, 6.75, 9.34	7.774
20	12.97, 15.55, 18.34, 16.66, 15.36	15.776
30	24.95, 29.79, 32.07, 26.32, 27.23	28.072

Since only two variables are involved, we can begin by plotting a scattergram of the data in Table 15-3. Not only have we plotted the twenty original observations from Table 15-3 in Fig. 15-2; we have also shown the mean of each set of five Y values. From the graph it appears that, as

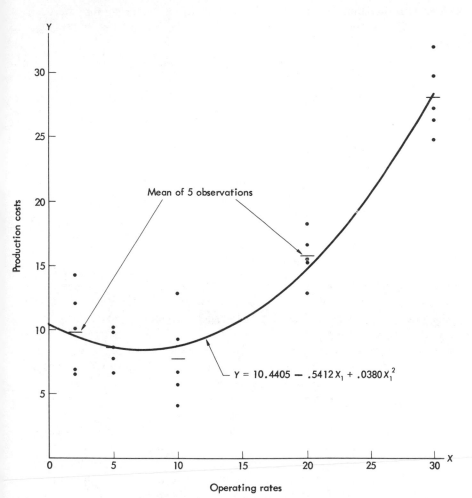

FIGURE 15-2 Relationship of production costs to operating rates

operating rate increases from zero, costs first decrease at a decreasing rate, reach a minimum, and then increase at an increasing rate.

For a mathematical regression model for our example we want a relationship between the two variables that is known to have the characteristics just described. Preferably, we would like this model to come from technological and economic theory as applied to the relevant properties of the particular production process. If we lack such theory, we can improvise by selecting the relationship based on knowledge of the behavior of mathematical functions. This procedure will permit making predictions until a deductive model is available. One relatively simple function that can be made to exhibit the desired characteristics is expressed algebraically as

$$Y = c_0 + c_1 X + c_2 X^2.$$

Geometrically, this function graphs as a parabola. The smooth curve in Fig. 15–2 is the parabola that has been found for our data in the analysis that follows.

One way we could develop the curvilinear regression analysis that we have decided our data require is to define a parabolic model for the population:

$$Y_j = \varphi_0 + \varphi_1 X_j + \varphi_2 X_j^2 + \epsilon_j, \qquad (15\text{–}21)$$

where ϵ_j is $NID(0, \sigma_{y \cdot x})$. Then maximum-likelihood techniques from mathematical statistics could be applied to find the necessary normal equations for determining sample estimates of the parameters.

If we proceeded as just described, the result would be equivalent to that from the procedure we shall now consider. We shall use the following model:

$$Y_j = \varphi_0 + \varphi_1 X_{1j} + \varphi_2 X_{2j} + \epsilon_j, \qquad (15\text{–}22)$$

where ϵ_j is $NID(0, \sigma_{y \cdot 12})$ and where $X_2 = X_1^2$. We define a new variable X_2 such that $X_2 = X_1^2$. Then we can use a linear model in three variables, and we can use the procedures developed for such a model in the earlier part of this chapter as a substitute for a curvilinear model in two variables. This same device can be used for additional terms in powers of X_1 or for any function that can be transformed into a sum of terms each of which consists of a coefficient and a variable. For example, we can use Eq. (15–22) and techniques associated with it as a working model for a relationship of the form $Y = aX^c$ by taking the logarithm of both sides, $\log Y = \log a + c \log X$, and by defining new variables and constants: $Y' = \log Y, a' = \log a,$ and $X' = \log X$. Hence, if we have techniques to handle a linear model such as that in Eq. (15–22) for any number of variables, we will also have techniques for any curvilinear relationship that can be transformed to linear form. This is the only type of curvilinear relationship we shall discuss.

15-8   Normal and Reduced Normal Equations

In Eqs. (15–3) we presented the general normal equations for three-variable linear regression. These can be generalized to any number of variables. The result is

$$c_0 n \quad\quad + c_1 \Sigma(X_1) \quad + \ldots + c_k \Sigma(X_k) \quad = \Sigma(Y), \qquad (15\text{–}23\text{a})$$

$$c_0 \Sigma(X_1) + c_1 \Sigma(X_1^2) \quad + \ldots + c_k \Sigma(X_1 X_k) = \Sigma(X_1 Y), \qquad (15\text{–}23\text{b})$$

$$\vdots$$

$$c_0 \Sigma(X_k) + c_1 \Sigma(X_1 X_k) + \ldots + c_k \Sigma(X_k^2) \quad = \Sigma(X_k Y). \qquad (15\text{–}23\text{k})$$

An easy way to remember these normal equations is to remember the initial equation $c_0 + c_1 X_1 + \ldots + c_k X_k = Y$. Then Eq. (15–23a) is the sum of n such equations. Equation (15–23b) is formed by multiplying the initial equation by X_1 and summing. The third equation is formed by using X_2 as the multiplier and then summing, and so on.

We can restate the system of Eqs. (15–23) in terms of the S_{ij} that we defined in Eqs. (15–7). To do so, we solve for c_0 in Eq. (15–23a) in terms of the other coefficients and sums. Then we substitute this result for c_0 in the remaining equations. Finally we replace the summations by their equivalent S_{ij}'s. The final result is a set of k equations in k unknowns in place of $(k + 1)$ equations in $(k + 1)$ unknowns. The restated system is the set of *reduced normal equations:*

$$c_1 S_{11} + c_2 S_{12} + \ldots + c_k S_{1k} = S_{1y}, \tag{15–24a}$$

$$c_1 S_{21} + c_2 S_{22} + \ldots + c_k S_{2k} = S_{2y}, \tag{15–24b}$$

$$\begin{matrix} \cdot & & \cdot & & \cdot & & \cdot & & & \cdot \\ \cdot & & \cdot & & \cdot & & \cdot & & & \cdot \\ \cdot & & \cdot & & \cdot & & \cdot & & & \cdot \end{matrix}$$

$$c_1 S_{k1} + c_2 S_{k2} + \ldots + c_k S_{kk} = S_{ky}. \tag{15–24k}$$

We can then solve these equations for $c_1, \ldots, c_k$. The value of c_0 can be had from

$$c_0 = \bar{Y} - \Sigma (c_i \bar{X}_i). \tag{15–25}$$

From the data for our production-cost example in Table 15–3 we find that

$$\bar{X}_1 = 13.40, \qquad \bar{X}_2 = 285.80, \qquad \bar{Y} = 14.05,$$

$$S_{11} = 66,400, \qquad S_{12} = 2,123,050, \qquad S_{1y} = 44,665.80,$$

$$S_{21} = 2,123,050, \qquad S_{22} = 71,529,100, \qquad S_{2y} = 1,566,608.10,$$

$$S_{yy} = 39,308.47, \qquad n = 25.$$

The specific set of equations we must solve is

$$66,400 c_1 + 2,123,050 c_2 = 44,665.80, \tag{15–26a}$$

$$2,123,050 c_1 + 71,529,100 c_2 = 1,566,608.10. \tag{15–26b}$$

After doing so, we can find c_0 from

$$c_0 = 14.05 - 13.40 c_1 - 285.80 c_2. \tag{15–27}$$

The coefficients in Eqs. (15–24) have an important characteristic. Notice that S_{12} in Eq. (15–26a) equals S_{21} in Eq. (15–26b). From the definitions of the S_{ij} it can be seen that $S_{12} = S_{21}$, $S_{13} = S_{31}, \ldots, S_{45} = S_{54}$, or, in general,

$S_{ij} = S_{ji}$. Hence, the numerical values of the S_{ij} are *symmetrical* with respect to the *main diagonal*, which passes straight from $c_1 S_{11}$ to $c_k S_{kk}$ in Eqs. (15–24).

15-9   Algebraic Treatment of Reduced Normal Equations

A number of techniques can be employed to solve for the c_i in a specific set of equations of the form of Eqs. (15–24). For several reasons, a matrix technique usually is most convenient for this purpose and for related purposes in multivariate analysis. It is relatively efficient when the model includes many variables. It will provide quantities needed for certain interval estimates. It is often the basis for computer programs designed for multivariate analysis and for short-cut techniques that make use of desk calculators.

A complete and rigorous treatment of multivariate analysis using matrix techniques is beyond the scope of this book. We must, however, realize some of the benefits of matrix analysis. The *elimination* technique will provide what we need. In order to describe this technique conveniently we require some of the basic definitions and concepts from matrix algebra, particularly as these relate to systems of linear equations such as Eqs. (15–24).

Concepts from matrix algebra.* A matrix is a rectangular array of *elements*, which may be numbers. A matrix is formed by listing the elements in the array and enclosing it in parentheses or brackets. For example,

$$\begin{bmatrix} 5 & -7 & 10 \\ 0 & 20 & 3 \\ 4 & 9 & 6 \end{bmatrix}, \qquad \begin{bmatrix} f_1 & f_2 & f_3 \\ f_4 & f_5 & f_6 \end{bmatrix},$$

$$\begin{bmatrix} 1 \\ 12 \\ -4 \end{bmatrix}, \qquad \text{and} \qquad \begin{bmatrix} a & b & c \end{bmatrix}$$

are matrices. A matrix may have one or more rows and one or more columns. A matrix with r rows and c columns is called a *matrix of order* (r, c) or *an $r \times c$ (r by c) matrix*. When $r = c$, the matrix is a *square matrix of order r*. The first matrix above is a square matrix of order 3. The second is a 2×3 matrix.

Often it is convenient to represent a matrix by means of a capital letter. We also need a general notation to describe the elements in a matrix. One such notation is:

---

* For a more complete and rigorous, yet lucid, discussion of basic matrix definitions and operations see Franz E. Hohn, *Elementary Matrix Algebra*, 2nd ed. (New York: The Macmillan Company, 1964).

$$A = \begin{bmatrix} a_{11} & a_{12} & \cdots & a_{1c} \\ a_{21} & a_{22} & \cdots & a_{2c} \\ \cdot & \cdot & & \cdot \\ \cdot & \cdot & & \cdot \\ \cdot & \cdot & & \cdot \\ a_{r1} & a_{r2} & \cdots & a_{rc} \end{bmatrix},$$

in which the first subscript on an element identifies its row and the second identifies its column. When A is a square matrix, the elements $a_{11}, a_{22}, \ldots, a_{rr}$ constitute the *main diagonal*. If, in such a matrix, $a_{21} = a_{12}$, $a_{31} = a_{13}$, and, in general, $a_{ij} = a_{ji}$ for all i, j, the matrix is said to be *symmetrical about its main diagonal*. Many matrices in multivariate analysis are of this type. The matrix

$$\begin{bmatrix} 3 & 6 & 12 \\ 6 & 8 & 16 \\ 12 & 16 & 4 \end{bmatrix}$$

is an example.

Two matrices are equal if each element of one matrix is identical to the corresponding element in the other matrix. One matrix may be added to or subtracted from another only if both matrices are of the same order. The result will be a matrix of this same order. An element of the matrix of sums (differences) is found by adding (subtracting) the two elements located in corresponding positions in the original matrices. If

$$A = \begin{bmatrix} -3 & 2 & 4 \\ 7 & -8 & 3 \end{bmatrix} \quad \text{and} \quad B = \begin{bmatrix} 0 & 6 & -11 \\ -4 & 13 & 2 \end{bmatrix}$$

and if $C = A + B$, then

$$C = \begin{bmatrix} (-3+0) & (2+6) & (4-11) \\ (7-4) & (-8+13) & (3+2) \end{bmatrix} = \begin{bmatrix} -3 & 8 & -7 \\ 3 & 5 & 5 \end{bmatrix}.$$

If $D = A - B$, then

$$D = \begin{bmatrix} -3 & -4 & 15 \\ 11 & -21 & 1 \end{bmatrix}.$$

To multiply a matrix by a constant, multiply every element in the matrix by the constant. Thus,

$$3 \cdot \begin{bmatrix} 1 & -2 \\ 0 & 3 \end{bmatrix} = \begin{bmatrix} 3 & -6 \\ 0 & 9 \end{bmatrix}.$$

Let the symbols AB represent multiplication of matrix B by matrix A

in the designated order. Then multiplication of the matrix B by the matrix A is defined *only if B has the same number of rows as A has columns.*

Suppose that

$$A = \begin{bmatrix} a & b & c \\ d & e & f \end{bmatrix}, \qquad B = \begin{bmatrix} g & m \\ h & n \\ k & p \end{bmatrix},$$

and $C = A \cdot B = AB$. Then

$$C = \begin{bmatrix} t & u \\ v & w \end{bmatrix},$$

where

$$t = ag + bh + ck,$$
$$u = am + bn + cp,$$
$$v = dg + eh + fk,$$
$$w = dm + en + fp.$$

For example,

$$\begin{bmatrix} 2 & 5 & -1 & 8 \\ 3 & 6 & 9 & 11 \\ -4 & 7 & 10 & 3 \end{bmatrix} \cdot \begin{bmatrix} 3 & 8 \\ 5 & -4 \\ 2 & 3 \\ -1 & 7 \end{bmatrix} = \begin{bmatrix} 21 & 49 \\ 46 & 104 \\ 40 & -9 \end{bmatrix}.$$

It is *not necessarily true* that, if AB is defined, BA is also defined. For instance, the two matrices in the numerical example just given cannot have their roles reversed. Even if A and B are square matrices of the same order so that AB and BA are defined, the two product matrices are not equal, in general. Since the order of multiplication is important, we usually say that, if $AB = C$ is defined, B can be *premultiplied* by A.

A square matrix of order r that has *ones* along its main diagonal and *zeros* elsewhere is called an *identity matrix of order r*. Thus,

$$I_3 = \begin{bmatrix} 1 & 0 & 0 \\ 0 & 1 & 0 \\ 0 & 0 & 1 \end{bmatrix}$$

is a third-order identity matrix. The role of the identity matrix in multiplication arises from the fact that, for an $r \times c$ matrix A_{rc}

$$I_r A_{rc} = A_{rc} I_c = A_{rc}.$$

For a square matrix,

$$I_r A_r = A_r I_r = A_r.$$

The role of the identity matrix in matrix multiplication is similar to that of the number *one* in ordinary multiplication.

Suppose we are given a square matrix A of order r. If there is a matrix B of the same order such that

$$AB = BA = I,$$

then B is the *inverse* of A. The notation A^{-1} is often used to designate the inverse of A.

Matrices and systems of linear equations. Suppose we have the following system of linear equations:

$$3x + 6y + 12z = -6, \qquad (15\text{--}28a)$$

$$6x + 8y + 16z = 0, \qquad (15\text{--}28b)$$

$$12x + 16y - 4z = 180. \qquad (15\text{--}28c)$$

If we let

$$A = \begin{bmatrix} 3 & 6 & 12 \\ 6 & 8 & 16 \\ 12 & 16 & -4 \end{bmatrix}, \quad U = \begin{bmatrix} x \\ y \\ z \end{bmatrix}, \quad C = \begin{bmatrix} -6 \\ 0 \\ 180 \end{bmatrix},$$

then we can state Eqs. (15–28) in matrix notation:

$$AU = C. \qquad (15\text{--}29)$$

A is called the *matrix of coefficients*.

We can also indicate how to solve for x, y, and z in matrix notation. If we premultiply both sides of Eq. (15–29) by the inverse of A, we have

$$A^{-1}(AU) = A^{-1}C.$$

But this is the same as

$$(A^{-1}A)U = IU = A^{-1}C \quad \text{or simply} \quad U = A^{-1}C.$$

As yet, of course, we do not know how to find A^{-1}, when it exists, by matrix algebra.

The elimination technique. As an alternative to carrying out the matrix procedure, we can satisfy our immediate needs for multivariate analysis by means of the elimination technique.

We begin by reviewing the use of the elimination technique to solve systems of linear equations in ordinary algebra. The technique is based upon two fundamental operations:

1. We can multiply each term in an equation by a constant without affecting the (unknown) solution values of the variables.

2. We can add the expressions on the two sides of one equation to the corresponding expressions on the two sides of another equation without changing the solution values.

Applying these rules we can solve Eqs. (15–28).

Equation number	Equation	Operation
I:	$3x + 6y + 12z = -6$	
II:	$6x + 8y + 16z = 0$	
III:	$12x + 16y - 4z = 180$	
IV:	$6x + 12y + 24z = -12$	(I) × 2
V:	$- 4y - 8z = 12$	(II) − (IV)
VI:	$12x + 24y + 48z = -24$	(I) × 4
VII:	$- 8y - 52z = 204$	(III) − (VI)
VIII:	$- 8y - 16z = 24$	(V) × 2
IX:	$- 36z = 180$	(VII) − (VIII)
	$z = -5$	
From VIII:	$y = 7$	
From VI:	$x = 4$	

Other sequences of the two fundamental operations will produce the same solution.

We can express the above result in matrix notation as follows:

$$IU = D$$

where

$$I = \begin{bmatrix} 1 & 0 & 0 \\ 0 & 1 & 0 \\ 0 & 0 & 1 \end{bmatrix}, \qquad U = \begin{bmatrix} x \\ y \\ z \end{bmatrix}, \quad \text{and} \quad D = \begin{bmatrix} 4 \\ 7 \\ -5 \end{bmatrix}.$$

This can be simplified to $U = D$ by performing the indicated matrix multiplication.

In matrix algebra there are three *row operations* which are similar to the fundamental operations described in connection with solving systems of linear equations. These are:

1. Any row in a given matrix can be replaced with a new row formed by multiplying each element in the original row by the same number different from zero.
2. Any row can be replaced with a row formed by adding to its elements the corresponding elements of one or more other rows of the same matrix.

3. The above operations can be combined to replace any row in the matrix with a new row the elements of which are the sums of nonzero multiples of its elements and nonzero multiples of corresponding elements of any other row or rows in the matrix.

Returning to our discussion of Eqs. (15–28), we now form the matrix

$$[A \mid C \mid I],$$

where A is the matrix of coefficients, C is composed of the constant terms, and I is an identity matrix of the same order as A. With row operations we are going to transform $[A \mid C \mid I]$ to $[I \mid D \mid A^{-1}]$. Transforming A and C to I and D, respectively, is equivalent to a solution of the original equations by algebraic elimination. The same operations also yield the inverse, A^{-1}. Elements of this inverse are used in the next section of this chapter on interval estimates.

For Eqs. (15–28), the proper procedure is illustrated in Table 15-4. In the top three rows we simply record the elements of the matrix $[A \mid C \mid I]$.

Table 15-4

THE ELIMINATION TECHNIQUE

Row	Matrix							Operation
(a1)	3	6	12	−6	1	0	0	
(b1)	6	8	16	0	0	1	0	
(c1)	12	16	−4	180	0	0	1	
(a2)	1	2	4	−2	1/3	0	0	(a1)/3
(b2)	0	−4	−8	12	−2	1	0	(b1) − 6(a2)
(c2)	0	−8	−52	204	−4	0	1	(c1) − 12(a2)
(b3)	0	1	2	−3	1/2	−1/4	0	(b2)/−4
(a3)	1	0	0	4	−2/3	1/2	0	(a2) − 2(b3)
(c3)	0	0	−36	180	0	−2	1	(c2) + 8(b3)
(c4)	0	0	1	−5	0	1/18	−1/36	(c3)/−36
(b4)	0	1	0	7	1/2	−13/36	1/18	(b3) − 2(c4)
(a3)	1	0	0	4	−2/3	1/2	0	
(b4)	0	1	0	7	1/2	−13/36	1/18	
(c4)	0	0	1	−5	0	1/18	−1/36	

In the first stage of the solution, the results of which appear in rows (a2), (b2), and (c2), our goal is to replace the 3, 6, and 12 in the first column of the beginning matrix with 1, 0, and 0, respectively. We must accomplish this only by using the fundamental addition and multiplication rules, given earlier, alternatively on every number in one of the first three rows. To get the 1 we desire in the upper left, we simply divide all seven numbers in row (a1) by 3 and record the result as row (a2). To replace the 6 that is the first number in row (b1) with a zero, we multiply row (a2) through by −6 and add the result, term by term, to row (b1). We record these sums as row (b2). To replace the 12 that is the first number in row (c1) by 0, we multiply row (a2) through by −12 and add the result, term by term, to row (c1). We record these sums in row (c2). We have now produced the first column of our identity matrix for coefficients.

In the second phase of our solution, we want to replace the 2, −4, and −8 in the second column of rows (a2), (b2), and (c2) with 0, 1, and 0, respectively. We begin by dividing row (b2) by −4, term by term, and recording the result in row (b3). We next change the 2 in column 2 of row (a2) to 0 by multiplying row (b3) by −2, adding the result to row (a2), and recording the sums in row (a3). Row (c2) added to +8 times row (b3) gives us row (c3). If we were to interchange rows (a3) and (b3), we would have the first two columns of the identity matrix we desire. But we can go on to the third phase directly and then rearrange as necessary in the final step.

In the final phase of our solution, we want to replace the +2 and −36 in the third column of rows (b3) and (c3) with 0 and 1, respectively. Since there is already a 0 in the third column of row (a3), we don't need to do anything further to this row. We begin by dividing row (c3) by −36 and recording the result in row (c4). Then we add −2 times row (c4) to row (b3) to get row (b4). In the final three rows we simply record the solution rows in their proper order.

We have already explained how to interpret the first four columns of the final matrix. The last three columns stated as a matrix,

$$\begin{bmatrix} -2/3 & 1/2 & 0 \\ 1/2 & -13/36 & 1/18 \\ 0 & 1/18 & -1/36 \end{bmatrix},$$

constitute the inverse of the original matrix of coefficients.

The procedure just described can be applied to any system of linear equations. If the system has a unique solution, results corresponding to those obtained above will be realized. If not, it will be impossible to complete the procedure.

We next apply the matrix solution procedure just described to

Table 15-5

ELIMINATION APPLIED TO NORMAL EQUATIONS*

66,400	2,123,050	44,666	1	0
2,123,050	71,529,100	1,566,608	0	1
1	31.9736	.6727	$.0^4 1506$	0
0	3,647,457	138,473	−31.9736	1
0	1	.0380	$-.0^5 8766$	$.0^6 2742$
1	0	−.5412	$.0^3 2953$	$-.0^5 8766$
0	1	.0380	$-.0^5 8766$	$.0^6 2742$

* Calculations were carried out to more figures than are shown.

regression Eqs. (15–26) for our production-cost, operating-rate example. The result appears in Table 15–5. From the final phase we see that $c_1 = -.5412$ and $c_2 = .0380$. We substitute these in Eq. (15–27) and find $c_0 = 10.4405$. Now, if we replace X_2 by its equivalent, X_1^2, our estimated regression equation is

$$Y_{X_1} = 10.4405 - .5412X_1 + .0380X_1^2.$$

This is the equation of the parabola plotted in Fig. 15–2.

Modifications of this elimination technique are used in computer programs for multiple regression analysis. Other modifications are used in a variety of short-cut routines for solving regression equations by hand with the aid of only a desk calculator. Several of these procedures are presented in the second, third, and fourth references at the end of this chapter.

15-10 More General Interval Estimates and Prediction Intervals

In Eqs. (15–9), (15–10), and (15–20) in the earlier part of this chapter we gave formulas for interval estimates for regression coefficients, φ_i, and for mean Y, given levels of the factor variables. These formulas all involved the quantities identified by superscripts and defined in Eqs. (15–8) for linear regression in which only two factor variables are used. The definitions in Eqs. (15–8) are, in fact, elements of the inverse matrix when only two factor variables are involved. To illustrate, if Eqs. (15–28) were reduced normal equations, then $S_{11} = 3$, $S_{12} = 6$, $S_{13} = 12, \ldots$, and $S_{33} = -4$. To find S^{11} we would go to the inverse and find the element in the first row and column. Hence, $S^{11} = -2/3$, $S^{12} = 1/2$, $S^{13} = 0, \ldots$, $S^{33} = -1/36$.

We can now generalize the formulas for interval estimates. Definition (15–9) becomes

$$c_i \pm t_{\alpha/2,\,m} s_{y \cdot 12 \ldots k} \sqrt{nS^{ii}} \tag{15–31}$$

for i running from 1 to k. The interval estimates for the coefficients are found as before except that the S^{ii} are the successive elements of the main diagonal of the inverse of the matrix of coefficients. The quantity *under the radical* in definition (15–10) generalizes to

$$\frac{1}{n} + n(S^{11}\bar{X}_1^2 + \ldots + S^{kk}\bar{X}_k^2 + 2S^{12}\bar{X}_1\bar{X}_2 + \ldots + 2S^{(k-1)k}\bar{X}_k\bar{X}_{k-1}). \tag{15–32}$$

In formula (15–20), the quantity under the radical generalizes to the same as that just presented in Eq. (15–32) except that the $\bar{X}_i$ are replaced by deviations, x_i. In both of the latter instances all possible cross products must appear in the sum of terms of the form $2S^{ij}\bar{X}_i\bar{X}_j$ or $2S^{ij}x_ix_j$.

EXERCISES

15.9 You are given the following matrices:

$$\begin{bmatrix} 3 & 1 & 3 \\ 1 & 4 & 2 \\ 0 & 5 & 2 \end{bmatrix} \quad \text{and} \quad \begin{bmatrix} 4 & 0 & 5 \\ 0 & 1 & -6 \\ 3 & 0 & 4 \end{bmatrix}.$$

(a) Use the elimination technique to show that the inverses of these matrices are

$$\frac{1}{7} \cdot \begin{bmatrix} -2 & 13 & -10 \\ -2 & 6 & -3 \\ 5 & -15 & 11 \end{bmatrix} \quad \text{and} \quad \begin{bmatrix} 4 & 0 & -5 \\ -18 & 1 & 24 \\ -3 & 0 & 4 \end{bmatrix}.$$

(b) Multiply each matrix above by its inverse to prove the inverse is correct.

15.10 The personnel director of an organization with a large number of clerical personnel is studying the effect of factors the organization can control upon clerical performance. The variables are mean performance rating during the employee's first year with the firm (Y), the number of days the employee spent in the formal induction training program (X_1), the job level of the employee's first position in the organization (X_2), and the number of formal performance-evaluation interviews conducted by the employee's supervisor during the first year of employment (X_3). A random sample of 20 clerks' records is selected. Data from the first five clerks' records are as follows:

Y	X_1	X_2	X_3
33	2	2	4
46	4	2	5
68	8	4	6
50	4	2	7
86	8	4	10

Show that

$$\Sigma\, Y = 283, \quad \Sigma\, Y^2 = 17{,}725, \quad \Sigma\, X_1 Y = 1682, \quad \Sigma\, X_1 X_2 = 84,$$
$$\Sigma\, X_1 = 26, \quad \Sigma\, X_1^2 = 164, \quad \Sigma\, X_2 Y = 874, \quad \Sigma\, X_1 X_3 = 184,$$
$$\Sigma\, X_2 = 14, \quad \Sigma\, X_2^2 = 44, \quad \Sigma\, X_3 Y = 1980, \quad \Sigma\, X_2 X_3 = 96.$$
$$\Sigma\, X_3 = 32, \quad \Sigma\, X_3^2 = 226,$$

15.11 For all 20 observations in Exercise 15.10,

$$S_{yy} = 147,860, \qquad S_{1y} = 14,720, \qquad S_{12} = 832,$$
$$S_{11} = 2704, \qquad S_{2y} = 5320, \qquad S_{13} = 408,$$
$$S_{22} = 416, \qquad S_{3y} = 14,740, \qquad S_{23} = 144,$$
$$S_{33} = 2696, \qquad \bar{Y} = 55.5, \qquad \bar{X}_1 = 5.8,$$
$$\bar{X}_2 = 3.4, \qquad \bar{X}_3 = 5.6.$$

(a) Use the elimination technique to find (1) the coefficients of the four-variable linear regression relationship for the entire sample and (2) the inverse of the matrix of coefficients. Carry all calculations to six decimals to reduce rounding errors.

   Partial ans. $c_0 = 5.4832$, $c_1 = 3.3783$, $c_2 = 4.3976$, $c_3 = 4.7212$.

(b) Check the correctness of the inverse by multiplying the coefficient matrix by this inverse.

(c) Find the standard error of estimate and the coefficient of determination.

15.12 For the example in Exercise 15.11, find .99 interval estimates of φ_1, φ_2, and φ_3.

15.13 Perform an analysis-of-variance test of the hypothesis that there is no regression in the population from which the sample in Exercise 15.11 comes.

   Partial ans. The residual error sum of squares is 257.547.

15.14 For the sample described in Exercise 15.11 test the hypothesis that variable X_3 makes no contribution to multiple linear regression.

15.15 Explain why we cannot make a test for the linearity of regression in Exercise 15.11.

15.16 Given the matrix

$$\begin{bmatrix} S_{11} & S_{12} \\ S_{21} & S_{22} \end{bmatrix},$$

where $S_{12} = S_{21}$, show that the elements of the inverse are Eqs. (15-8) in this chapter.

15.17 The statistician who gathered the data in Table 15–3 also gathered a similar set of data for another plant. Again, five production-cost observations (Y) were picked for each of five operating rates (X). The raw data and the means are as follows:

X_j:	5	10	15	20	25
Y_{1j}	5.92	4.26	5.50	9.98	15.22
Y_{2j}	5.94	7.91	7.95	13.20	15.30
Y_{3j}	3.35	7.56	10.96	10.16	17.88
Y_{4j}	5.08	6.44	7.13	15.20	16.91
Y_{5j}	4.94	5.58	7.74	12.13	18.08
$\bar{Y}_j$	5.046	6.350	7.856	12.134	16.678

If $X_2 = X_1^2$ and if the linear model $\bar{Y}_c = c_0 + c_1 X_1 + c_2 X_2$ is used, the necessary inputs to a multiple linear regression analysis are

$$S_{11} = 31{,}250, \qquad S_{12} = 937{,}500, \qquad S_{1Y} = 18{,}155,$$
$$S_{21} = 937{,}500, \qquad S_{22} = 29{,}238{,}750, \qquad S_{2Y} = 573{,}562.50,$$
$$n = 25, \qquad S_{YY} = 12{,}748.0626.$$

(a) Process the data to check the correctness of the S_{ij}.
(b) Use the elimination technique to show that $c_1 = -.1978$, $c_2 = .0260$, and that

$$[S^{ij}] = \begin{bmatrix} .0008401 & -.0000269 \\ -.0000269 & .0000009 \end{bmatrix}.$$

Check your work by matrix multiplication.

15.18 Assume that a linear model of the form $\mu_{y \cdot x} = \beta_0 + \beta_1 X_1$ applies to the situation described in Exercise 15.17.
(a) Show that the estimated regression equation is $\bar{Y}_x = .8978 + .5810 X_1$.
(b) Perform an analysis-of-variance test of the hypothesis that the two-variable linear model applies.

REFERENCES

Anderson, R. L., and T. A. Bancroft, *Statistical Theory in Research*. New York: McGraw-Hill Book Company, 1952.

Bryant, E. C., *Statistical Analysis*, 2nd ed. New York: McGraw-Hill Book Company, 1966.

Dwyer, P. S., *Linear Computations*. New York: John Wiley & Sons, Inc., 1951.

Ezekiel, M., and K. A. Fox, *Methods of Correlation and Regression Analysis*, 3rd ed. New York: John Wiley & Sons, Inc., 1959.

16

Correlation

In this chapter we shall discuss correlation techniques for analyzing relationships among two or more variables. Like regression analysis, correlation analysis may seek first to determine the nature of the relationship and second to measure the degree of association among the variables; however, in correlation the emphasis often is reversed, and in some instances the sole interest lies in measuring the degree of association.

16-1 Linear Correlation

Chapters 14 and 15 pointed out that factor variables in regression analysis are not assumed to be random variables. In correlation analysis all variables are assumed to be random variables.

Let us consider an example of a situation to which correlation analysis can be applied. The personnel department of a large firm is working on a management development program. For a large number of managers, records are available that contain each person's total score on the present management training course and his composite rating on job performance by his supervisors during the same period of his career with the firm.

The course score and performance rating are both considered to be approximate measures of managerial ability. The more closely associated they are, the more likely to be true is the assumption that they are both measuring the same trait.

To measure the association between the two sets of scores, we begin by selecting 50 managers' personnel files at random. For each manager we observe the training-course score and the performance rating. We arbitrarily designate the first score as the variable, X. The rating becomes the variable, Y. Note that both X and Y are free to vary. The 50 observations of two measurements each are shown in Table 16–1.

A scattergram of the 50 points is shown in Fig. 16–1. The dashed vertical and horizontal lines are drawn through the means of the 50 X values and the 50 Y values, respectively. There is an apparent tendency for high values of X to be associated with high values of Y and for low values of X to be associated with low values of Y. The analysis will determine whether it is likely that this could be the result of sampling fluctuation within a popula-

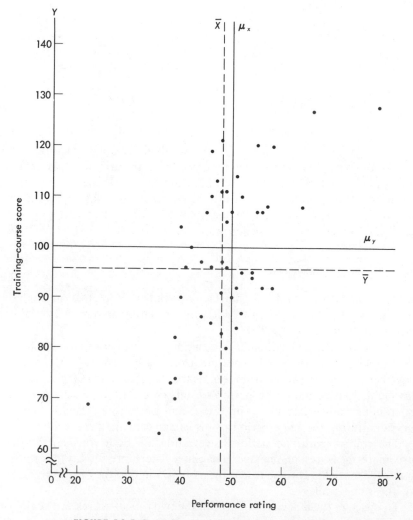

FIGURE 16-1 Scattergram of 50 observations in Table 16-1

Table 16-1

FIFTY OBSERVATIONS OF PERFORMANCE
RATING (X) AND TRAINING-COURSE SCORE (Y)

X	Y	X	Y	X	Y	X	Y	X	Y
48	83	50	90	36	63	39	74	45	107
41	96	56	92	54	94	40	90	52	95
46	119	55	120	54	95	30	65	79	128
39	82	58	100	49	80	44	75	39	70
50	107	48	97	58	92	49	96	38	73
44	86	40	62	55	107	51	92	49	111
56	107	46	96	44	97	22	69	46	110
42	100	48	111	49	105	57	108	48	121
48	91	40	104	51	114	52	110	66	127
51	84	64	108	46	85	52	87	47	113

tion in which there is no association. The solid vertical and horizontal lines in the figure will be explained when we discuss the statistical model.

16-2 A Statistical Model for Linear Correlation

For two-variable linear correlation, we shall assume that items are selected at random from a population of such items. For each item selected, an observation is made. The observation consists of measurements of two characteristics (X_i, Y_i). Thus X_i and Y_i are values of random variables. Each pair of values constitutes a data point, and the entire set of such points is assumed to be distributed in accordance with the *bivariate normal distribution*.

To describe the bivariate normal distribution, we shall begin by recalling Fig. 14–2. For each value of X in that figure there is a normal statistical population with mean $\mu_{y \cdot x}$ and standard deviation $\sigma_{y \cdot x}$. As we learned in the case of two-variable linear regression, $\mu_{y \cdot x} = \beta_0 + \beta_1 X$, or the value of $\mu_{y \cdot x}$ depends upon the value of X. Hence, the statistical populations referred to are *conditional distributions*.

In the bivariate normal distribution we also assume conditional distributions of Y values. These distributions are normal with means

$$\mu_{y \cdot x} = \beta_0 + \beta_1 X \qquad (16\text{--}1)$$

and variances $\sigma_{y \cdot x}^2$.

In two-variable linear regression the X variable is assumed not to be a random variable. In two-variable linear correlation, values of X are assumed to form a *marginal distribution* that is normal with mean μ_X and variance σ_X^2.

The bivariate normal distribution* is a *joint distribution* that is the

---

* For a more rigorous development of this distribution see I. Miller and J. E. Freund, *Probability and Statistics for Engineers* (Englewood Cliffs, N.J.: Prentice-Hall, Inc., 1965), pp. 254–256.

product of the marginal distribution of X and the conditional distribution of Y given X as these two are described above. The parameters of this joint distribution are μ_x, σ_x, β_0, β_1, and $\sigma_{y\cdot x}$.

In two-variable correlation, interest often centers upon the degree of association between the variables. For this reason and others to be described shortly the bivariate normal distribution customarily is defined in terms of parameters, one of which is ρ, the *correlation coefficient*. For discrete distributions this coefficient was defined in Sec. 2–6. As we learned there, the value of ρ can range from -1 for complete negative dependence through 0, for independence, to $+1$ for complete positive dependence. The definition of ρ for continuous distributions is analogous. It is

$$\rho = \frac{\sigma_{xy}}{\sigma_x \sigma_y}, \tag{16-2}$$

where σ_{xy} is population covariance* and σ_x and σ_y are standard deviations of the marginal distributions of X and Y values in the bivariate normal population.

On page 335 we saw that the slope of a sample regression line is a function of the sample covariance. Analogously, for the population in linear correlation,

$$\beta_1 = \frac{\sigma_{xy}}{\sigma_x^2}, \tag{16-3a}$$

and, from Eq. (16–2), we see that

$$\beta_1 = \rho \frac{\sigma_y}{\sigma_x}. \tag{16-3b}$$

It can be shown that the line defined in Eq. (16–1) includes the point (μ_x, μ_y). With the use of this fact and Eq. (16–3b), it follows that Eq. (16–1) can be restated as

$$\mu_{y\cdot x} = \left(\mu_y - \rho \frac{\sigma_y}{\sigma_x}\mu_x\right) + \rho \frac{\sigma_y}{\sigma_x}X,$$

which simplifies to

$$\mu_{y\cdot x} = \mu_y + \rho \frac{\sigma_y}{\sigma_x}(X - \mu_x). \tag{16-4}$$

The parameters of the revised model are the two means, μ_x and μ_y; the two standard deviations, σ_x and σ_y; and the correlation coefficient, ρ.

To become more familiar with the model we shall assign numbers to the

_____

* The expected value of $[(X - \mu_x)(Y - \mu_y)]$ in the population is the general definition of population covariance, σ_{xy}.

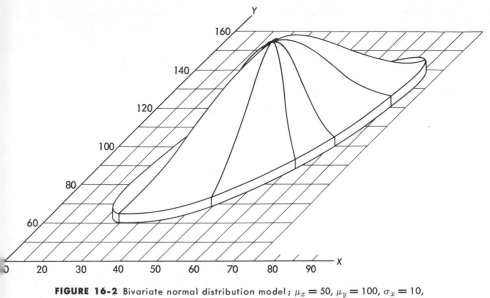

FIGURE 16-2 Bivariate normal distribution model; $\mu_x = 50$, $\mu_y = 100$, $\sigma_x = 10$, $\sigma_y = 20$, $\rho = +.7$

parameters and illustrate the result. We shall let

$$\mu_x = 50, \qquad \sigma_x = 10,$$
$$\mu_y = 100, \qquad \sigma_y = 20,$$
$$\rho = +.7.$$

An illustration of a bivariate normal distribution with these parameters appears in Fig. 16–2.

16-3 Estimators and Tests of Significance

We have established that ρ is a measure of association between two variables. Now we need an estimator of the population correlation coefficient. Suppose that we have selected a random sample of n items from a population and that we have made an observation of two characteristics (X_i, Y_i) on each item selected. The customary point estimator of ρ is called the *sample correlation coefficient* and is given the symbol r. The definition of r is

$$r = \frac{S_{xy}}{\sqrt{S_{xx}S_{yy}}}, \tag{16-5}$$

where

$$S_{xy} = n\,\Sigma\,(XY) - (\Sigma\,X)(\Sigma\,Y),$$
$$S_{xx} = n\,\Sigma\,(X^2) - (\Sigma\,X)^2,$$
$$S_{yy} = n\,\Sigma\,(Y^2) - (\Sigma\,Y)^2.$$

This estimator is biased but is generally used because of its relative simplicity and because the bias is negligible for large samples. Note also that $r^2 = d$, the sample coefficient of determination as defined in Eq. (14–8).

To illustrate calculation of r, we shall return to the sample data in Table 16–1. The Monte Carlo technique was used to select this sample of 50 observations from the bivariate normal population illustrated in Fig. 16–2. Recall that the parameters for this population have the values $\mu_x = 50$, $\mu_y = 100$, $\sigma_x = 10$, $\sigma_y = 20$, and $\rho = +.7$. The sample from this population is shown in Fig. 16–1. The solid horizontal and vertical lines in that figure pass through μ_y and μ_x.

The calculations for the data in Table 16–1 are

$$\Sigma X = 2411, \qquad \Sigma X^2 = 120{,}301, \qquad \Sigma XY = 235{,}747,$$

$$\Sigma Y = 4788, \qquad \Sigma Y^2 = 471{,}900, \qquad n = 50,$$

from which

$$S_{xx} = 202{,}129, \qquad S_{xy} = 243{,}482, \qquad S_{yy} = 670{,}056,$$

and

$$r = \frac{243{,}482}{368{,}018} = +.662.$$

Recall that $\rho = .70$ for the model.

To describe an interval estimator for r we must begin with some observations about the sampling distribution of r. Only when ρ is zero is the sampling distribution of r symmetrical and bell-shaped. Even then it is not normal. There is a transformation, however, the values of which are distributed as t with $(n - 2)$ degrees of freedom. This is

$$t = \frac{r\sqrt{n - 2}}{\sqrt{1 - r^2}}. \qquad (16\text{–}6)$$

Since this transformation applies only when $\rho = 0$, it is not suitable for a general interval estimator. On the other hand, we use it later for a test of significance.

When ρ is not zero, the sampling distribution of r is skewed. The sampling distribution becomes increasingly skewed as ρ approaches either $+1$ or -1. Furthermore, the mathematical function that describes the distribution is very complicated.

Fortunately, Sir Ronald Fisher found a transformation that yields a variable that is distributed very nearly normally for all values of ρ and for all but very small sample sizes ($n \leq 10$). Furthermore, the variance of the transformed variable is not dependent on ρ. We shall designate the transformation function with the symbol $w(r)$ and the value of the transformed variable with the symbol w. The definition of $w(r)$ is

$$w(r) = 1.1513 \log \left(\frac{1 + r}{1 - r}\right), \qquad (16\text{-}7a)$$

where the logarithm is to the base 10.* The variable w is very nearly normally distributed with mean

$$\mu_w = 1.1513 \log \left(\frac{1 + \rho}{1 - \rho}\right) \qquad (16\text{-}7b)$$

and variance

$$\sigma_w^2 = \frac{1}{n - 3}, \qquad (16\text{--}7c)$$

where n is the sample size.

From Eq. (16–7) we can form an interval estimator for ρ. The $1 - \alpha$ confidence interval for $w(r)$ is

$$w(r) \pm z_{\alpha/2}(\sigma_w), \qquad (16\text{--}8)$$

where z is the standard normal deviate.

For our example we want the .95 interval estimate of ρ. For $r = .662$ we find that

$$w(.662) = 1.1513 \log\left(\frac{1.662}{.338}\right)$$
$$= 1.1513[(10.2206 - 10) - (9.5289 - 10)]$$
$$= 1.1513(.6917) = .7964,$$

$$1.96\sigma_u = \frac{1.96}{\sqrt{47}} = .2859,$$

and the interval estimate is

$$.5105 \le w(\rho) \le 1.0823.$$

Values of w for various values of r or ρ have been tabled; this table is given in Appendix O. We can estimate the value of $w(.662)$ directly from the table and avoid the computation given above. We can also use the table to convert values of w to their r equivalents. The conversion for the interval estimate of ρ for our example is

$$.47 \le \rho \le .79.$$

This interval includes .70, the value assigned to ρ in the model.

---

* An alternative definition is $w(r) = \frac{1}{2} \ln \left(\frac{1 + r}{1 - r}\right)$ where $\ln$ designates the natural logarithm.

   A significance test that is often required in correlation analysis tests the hypothesis that ρ is zero. We learned earlier that the transformation in Eq. (16–6) produces a random variable distributed exactly as t with $(n - 2)$ degrees of freedom when ρ is zero. Suppose we test the hypothesis that $\rho = 0$ when $r = .662$ and $n = 50$. We find that

$$t = \frac{r\sqrt{n - 2}}{\sqrt{1 - r^2}}$$

$$= \frac{.662\sqrt{48}}{\sqrt{1 - .4377}}$$

$$= 6.11 \text{ with 48 degrees of freedom.}$$

We conclude that the sample did not come from a popuation with $\rho = 0$.
   We may want to test a hypothesis that ρ is some value other than zero. To do so we substitute the hypothesized value of ρ in Eq. (16–7b), find the value of w for our sample value of r from Eq. (16–7a), and calculate

$$z = \frac{w - \mu_w}{\sigma_w},$$

where z is interpreted as a standard normal deviate.
   Suppose we want to test the hypothesis that $\rho = +.7$ when $n = 50$ and $r = +.662$. From Eq. (16–7b)

$$\mu_w = 1.1513 \log \left(\frac{1 + .7}{1 - .7}\right) = .8673$$

from Appendix O. From Eq. (16–7a)

$$w = 1.1513 \log \left(\frac{1 + .662}{1 - .662}\right) = .7964.$$

From Eq. (16–7c)

$$\sigma_w = \frac{1}{\sqrt{47}} = .14586.$$

Thus

$$z = \frac{.7964 - .8673}{.14586} = -.49,$$

and we cannot reject the hypothesis at the .05 level of significance.
   To test a hypothesis that $\rho_1 = \rho_2$ when we have independent sample values r_1 and r_2, we first find $w(r_1)$, $w(r_2)$, $\sigma_w^2(r_1)$, and $\sigma_w^2(r_2)$. Then we find

$$z = \frac{w(r_1) - w(r_2)}{\sqrt{\sigma_w^2(r_1) + \sigma_w^2(r_2)}}$$

and interpret it as a standard normal deviate. For example, if $r_1 = -.4$, $r_2 = +.2$, $n_1 = 67$, and $n_2 = 39$, we find that

$$w(r_1) = -.4236, \qquad w(r_2) = +.2027,$$
$$\sigma_w^2(r_1) = \tfrac{1}{64}, \qquad \sigma_w^2(r_2) = \tfrac{1}{36}.$$

It follows that

$$z = \frac{-.4236 - .2027}{\sqrt{\tfrac{1}{64} + \tfrac{1}{36}}} = -3.01,$$

a highly significant value.

EXERCISES

16.1 A reasoning test was given to 64 students shortly before they enrolled in a statistics class. Their scores on this test are to be compared with their semester statistics grade. For this purpose both variables must be transformed to achieve essentially normal distributions. Data for the transformed test score (X) and statistics grade (Y) are

$$\Sigma X = 168.9, \qquad \Sigma X^2 = 493.53, \qquad n = 64,$$
$$\Sigma Y = 327.0, \qquad \Sigma Y^2 = 1747.88, \qquad \Sigma XY = 836.64.$$

Find the sample correlation coefficient. *Ans. $r = -.4338$.*

16.2 The reasoning test described in the previous exercise has been given to a very large number of statistics students throughout the nation. The composite result has been a correlation statistic of $-.6$. Assume this is the population parameter and test the hypothesis that our sample came from this population. Does the negative sign necessarily mean that raw scores in the reasoning test are negatively related to statistics grades?

16.3 For the sample in Exercise 16.1 use the exact sampling distribution to test the hypothesis that there is no correlation in the population.
Ans. $t = -3.79$ with $n - 2 = 62$ degrees of freedom.

16.4 A second group of 38 students taught by a different instructor were given the same reasoning test as that described in Exercise 16.1. The correlation of this group's transformed test scores and statistics grades was $-.8300$. Test the hypothesis that this sample and the sample in Exercise 16.1 came from the same population.
Partial ans. $z = 3.41$.

16.5 In a certain city under controlled pricing, distribution, and display conditions, a consumer survey has produced information on the number of television spot ads for a certain product seen by housewives in a two-week period (X) and the amount spent, in cents, for the product during the same period (Y). Assume the distributions are suitable for correlation analysis. The required sums are $\Sigma\,X = 496$, $\Sigma\,X^2 = 5272$, $n = 64$, $\Sigma\,Y = 4651$, $\Sigma\,Y^2 = 346{,}665$, $\Sigma\,XY = 37{,}537$.

(a) Find r, and, using Eqs. (14–3), b_1, and b_0. *Partial ans. r = .4240.*

(b) Make a .95 interval estimate of the amount a housewife will spend if she sees five spot ads during such a period.

Ans. $66.7 \leq \mu_{y\cdot5} \leq 72.9$.

16.6 If you had only the information given in Exercise 16.5, what would be your estimate of the expected expenditure on the product by housewives who saw two spot ads? If there are ten thousand housewives in this market, how much of an increase in sales can one additional spot ad be expected to produce?

16.7 A sample of 18 observations yields a correlation coefficient of $+.468$. Perform an exact test of the hypothesis that $\rho = 0$. Then transform r to w and perform an approximate test of the same hypothesis. Do both tests produce the same probability of a type I error?

Partial ans. $t = 2.12$; $z = 1.966$.

16.8 For our machine maintenance-cost example in Chapter 14 we found that $b_1 = .4133$, $s_{y\cdot x} = 4.08$, $S_{xy} = 26{,}784$, $S_{xx} = 64{,}800$, $S_{yy} = 17{,}065.24$.

(a) Compute the sample correlation coefficient. *Ans. r = .8054.*

(b) Perform a t test of the hypothesis of no correlation.

(c) Perform a t test using Eq. (14–13) to test the hypothesis that the slope, β_1, is zero. Compare your answer with (b).

(d) Square the values of t found in parts (b) and (c) of this question. Compare these results with the value of F found in the test for the presence of regression on page 343 of Chapter 14.

16-4 Multiple Linear Correlation

For linear correlation involving more than two variables, we shall assume that objects are selected at random from a population of such objects. For each object selected an observation is made that consists of measurements of $k + 1$ characteristics ($Y_i, X_{1i}, \ldots, X_{ki}$). Each measurement is the value of a random variable, and one such variable is designated the dependent variable, Y. Each observation constitutes a data point, and the entire set of such points is distributed in accordance with the *multivariate normal distribution*, a generalization of the bivariate normal distribution.

As in the case of two-variable linear correlation we assume conditional distributions of Y values. These distributions are normal with means

$$\mu_{y(1\ldots k)} = \varphi_0 + \varphi_1 X_1 + \ldots + \varphi_k X_k \tag{16-9}$$

and variances $\sigma^2_{y(1\ldots k)}$.

In multiple linear correlation each of the random variables $X_1, \ldots, X_k$ is assumed to have a marginal distribution that is normal with mean μ_i and variance σ_i^2 with i running from 1 through k. Note that the σ_i^2 are not necessarily equal in value.

In multiple linear correlation, as in the two-variable case, we often need a measure of the degree of association among the variables. One such measure is provided by the *coefficient of multiple determination* (δ_m), which is

$$\delta_m = \frac{\varphi_1 \sigma_{1y} + \varphi_2 \sigma_{2y} + \ldots + \varphi_k \sigma_{ky}}{\sigma_y^2}. \qquad (16\text{-}10)$$

The φ_i are the coefficients given in Eq. (16–9) and the σ_{iy} are the covariances of the X_i with Y.

The coefficient of multiple determination represents the portion of Y variance (σ_y^2) attributable to association with the X variables. Thus

$$\delta_m = 1 - \frac{\sigma_{y(1 \ldots k)}^2}{\sigma_y^2}, \qquad (16\text{-}11)$$

where σ_y^2 is the variance of the marginal distribution of Y.

The *multiple correlation coefficient* (ρ_m) is defined as follows:

$$\rho_m = \sqrt{\delta_m}. \qquad (16\text{-}12)$$

Both are measures of association. *The range for both measures is from zero to one.* In the two-variable case, ρ ranges from -1 to $+1$.

As a consequence of Eqs. (16–11) and (16–12) we can express the standard error of estimate, $\sigma_{y(1 \ldots k)}$, defined in Eq. (16–9), in terms of ρ_m. The expression is

$$\sigma_{y(1 \ldots k)} = \sigma_y \sqrt{1 - \rho_m^2}. \qquad (16\text{-}13)$$

16-5 Reduced Normal Equations and Estimators

A sample estimator of the coefficient of multiple determination is

$$d_m = \frac{c_1 S_{1y} + c_2 S_{2y} + \ldots + c_k S_{ky}}{S_{yy}}, \qquad (16\text{-}14)$$

where the S_{ij} are functions of the deviations defined as in Eqs. (15–7). Given the value of d_m, an estimate of ρ_m is

$$r_m = \sqrt{d_m}. \qquad (16\text{-}15)$$

From our work in multiple regression we already know how to evaluate all quantities on the right side of Eq. (16–14) for a given random sample. Hence, we can readily obtain the point estimate, r_m, of the principal measure of association used in multiple linear correlation.

Often the two-variable sample correlation coefficients, r_{ij}, defined in Eq. (16–5), are available for all possible pairs of variables in a multivariate correlation analysis. In such cases it is more efficient to work with the set of reduced normal equations expressed in terms of these sample correlation coefficients. Recall that the reduced normal equations as applied to sample data are

$$c_1 S_{11} + c_2 S_{12} + \ldots + c_k S_{1k} = S_{1y},$$
$$c_1 S_{21} + c_2 S_{22} + \ldots + c_k S_{2k} = S_{2y},$$
$$\vdots \qquad \vdots \qquad \qquad \vdots \qquad \vdots$$
$$c_1 S_{k1} + c_2 S_{k2} + \ldots + c_k S_{kk} = S_{ky}.$$

We can see from Eq. (16–5) that, in general,

$$r_{ij} = \frac{S_{ij}}{\sqrt{S_{ii} S_{jj}}}$$

or

$$S_{ij} = r_{ij} \sqrt{S_{ii} S_{jj}}. \tag{16-16}$$

If we substitute the right side of the latter expression for the S_{ij} in the reduced normal equations, we shall have equations involving the r_{ij}. These will be of the form

$$c_1 r_{i1} \sqrt{S_{ii} S_{11}} + \ldots + c_k r_{ik} \sqrt{S_{ii} S_{kk}} = r_{iy} \sqrt{S_{ii} S_{yy}} \text{ for } i = 1, \ldots, k,$$

which, upon dividing through by $\sqrt{S_{ii} S_{yy}}$, become

$$c_1 r_{i1} \sqrt{\frac{S_{11}}{S_{yy}}} + \ldots + c_k r_{ik} \sqrt{\frac{S_{kk}}{S_{yy}}} = r_{iy}, \text{ for } i = 1, \ldots, k.$$

For convenience, let's define new coefficients, h_i, such that

$$h_i = c_i \sqrt{\frac{S_{ii}}{S_{yy}}}. \tag{16-17}$$

When we make this substitution, the reduced normal equations become

$$h_1(1) + h_2 r_{12} + \ldots + h_k r_{1k} = r_{1y}, \tag{16-18a}$$
$$h_1 r_{21} + h_2(1) + \ldots + h_k r_{2k} = r_{2y}, \tag{16-18b}$$
$$\vdots \qquad \vdots \qquad \qquad \vdots \qquad \vdots$$
$$h_1 r_{k1} + h_2 r_{k2} + \ldots + h_k(1) = r_{ky}, \tag{16-18k}$$

which accomplishes the objective of stating the reduced normal equations in terms of sample two-variable correlation coefficients.

Another way to derive Eqs. (16–18) from the original set of reduced normal equations is to transform the original variables to standard normal deviates. When this is done, the h_i are seen to be coefficients in a regression relationship expressed in standard normal variables. These are often called "beta" coefficients. The contributions of the X variables to variance explained by linear regression is often taken to be roughly proportional to the squares of their "beta" weights.

We can also express the sample coefficient of multiple determination defined in Eq. (16–14) in terms of the h_i and the r_{ij}. When we make the substitutions given in Eqs. (16–16) and (16–17) in the right side of Eq. (16–14), we can express the result as

$$r_m^2 = h_1 r_{1y} + h_2 r_{2y} + \ldots + h_k r_{ky}. \tag{16-19}$$

We now want to illustrate what has been said with a numerical example. An example to which multiple linear correlation can be applied is found in a hypothetical airline that employs women to furnish in-flight services to customers. Over a period of time the organization has collected customer rating scores on these employees. The median of such scores for a given employee is defined to be the dependent variable (Y). For each employee three other scores are available from post-training procedures; these are scores from an apperception test, an arithmetic reasoning test, and a vocabulary test. The employee is the unit of association, and data on all four variables are available for each of 64 women. Our variables are

$Y =$ median customer rating score,
$X_1 =$ arithmetic reasoning test score,
$X_2 =$ apperception test score,
$X_3 =$ vocabulary test score.

The raw data have been used to calculate the two-variable correlation coefficients. The results are

$$r_{12} = r_{21} = +.22, \quad r_{13} = r_{31} = +.30, \quad r_{23} = r_{32} = +.61,$$
$$r_{1y} = +.57, \quad r_{2y} = +.09, \quad r_{3y} = +.39.$$

From these we find that the initial matrix for solution of reduced normal Eqs. (16–18) is

$$\begin{bmatrix} 1.00 & .22 & .30 & .57 \\ .22 & 1.00 & .61 & .09 \\ .30 & .61 & 1.00 & .39 \end{bmatrix}.$$

When we apply the techniques presented in Sec. 15–9 to this matrix the results are $h_1 = +.5086$, $h_2 = -.2655$, and $h_3 = +.3994$.

The values we have just found for the h_i can be employed in Eq. (16–19) to find the sample multiple correlation coefficient. The calculations are

$$r_m^2 = .5086(.57) - .2655(.09) + .3994(.39) = .4218,$$

from which

$$r_m = +.6495.$$

Slightly more than 42 per cent of the Y variance in the sample is the result of association of Y with the other three variables.

In a case such as this there may be some interest in predicting values of Y from a candidate's test scores. We can make use of the relationships we have already learned to determine the sample regression relationship and standard error of estimate and all the other estimates we discussed in conjunction with multiple regression. These procedures are discussed in the next two paragraphs.

We know from Eq. (16–17) that $c_i = h_i\sqrt{S_{yy}/S_{ii}}$. For our example we find from the raw data that

$$\Sigma Y = 327.0, \qquad \Sigma(Y^2) = 1747.88, \qquad n = 64,$$
$$\Sigma X_3 = 168.9, \qquad \text{and} \qquad \Sigma(X_3^2) = 493.53.$$

From these we determine that

$$S_{yy} = 64(1747.88) - 327^2 = 4935.32$$

and

$$S_{33} = 64(493.53) - 168.9^2 = 3058.71.$$

Then we find c_3 as follows:

$$c_3 = h_3\sqrt{\frac{S_{yy}}{S_{33}}}$$
$$= .3994\sqrt{\frac{4935.32}{3058.71}} = .5073.$$

The remaining coefficients would be obtained in a similar fashion.

Equation (16–13) stated that

$$\sigma_{y(1\ldots k)} = \sigma_y\sqrt{1 - \rho_m^2}.$$

A sample estimate of $\sigma_{y(1\ldots k)}$ is

$$s_m = \sqrt{\frac{S_{yy}(1 - r_m^2)}{n(n - k - 1)}}.$$

For our example

$$s_m = \sqrt{\frac{4935.32(1 - .4218)}{64(60)}} = \sqrt{.7431}.$$

We have seen a number of parallels between two-variable linear correlation analysis and the general linear multivariate case. Another parallel occurs when we come to the interval estimator for the population multiple correlation coefficient. In the two-variable case we found that an approximate interval estimator was obtainable if we would first transform r to w in Eq. (16–7a) and substitute this result in expression (16–8).

If we substitute r_m for r in Eq. (16–7a), we shall have an estimator $[w(r_m)]$ that is very nearly normally distributed about $w(\rho_m)$. The variance of $w(r_m)$ is *not* obtained directly from Eq. (16–7c), however. In general, the variance of w is

$$\sigma_w^2 = \frac{1}{n - k - 1}.$$

With this generalization, the same procedures used at the end of Sec. 16–3 can be applied to set interval estimates for and test hypotheses about ρ_m.

An exact test of the hypothesis that ρ_m is zero is available. It will be presented when we discuss the uses of analysis of variance in connection with multiple correlation.

16-6 Partial Correlation

The partial correlation between two variables is the degree of association that exists between them after the effect of other variables has been removed from each of them. A simple example should help clarify the concept. Consider a population of five observations on three associated variables as follows:

Observation	X_1	X_2	X_3
1	10	25	10
2	20	5	30
3	30	15	25
4	40	25	20
5	50	5	40

For these observations we find that $N = 5$, $\sigma_1^2 = 1000$, $\sigma_2^2 = 400$, $\sigma_3^2 = 500$, $\sigma_{12} = -200$, $\sigma_{13} = 500$, $\sigma_{23} = -400$. We next find the two-variable regression lines:

$$\beta_{1(12)} = \frac{\sigma_{12}}{\sigma_2^2} = -\frac{1}{2}; \qquad \beta_{0(12)} = \mu_1 - \beta_{1(12)}\mu_2 = 37.5;$$

so

$$\mu_{1 \cdot 2} = 37.5 - .5X_2.$$

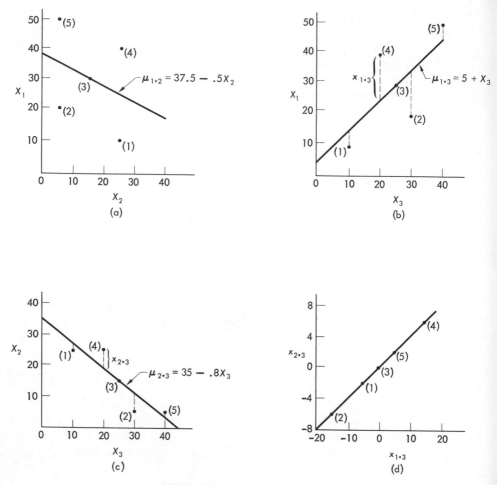

FIGURE 16-3 A partial correlation example

Similarly,

$$\mu_{1 \cdot 3} = 5.0 + 1.0X_3$$

and

$$\mu_{2 \cdot 3} = 35.0 - .8X_3.$$

The two-variable scattergrams, the data, and the regression lines above appear in Fig. 16–3.

It is apparent from the scattergram for X_1 and X_2 in Fig. 16–3 that the uncorrected correlation between X_1 and X_2 is negative and is not perfect. In fact, $\rho_{12} = -200/\sqrt{400,000} = -1/\sqrt{10}$. We want the correlation between

X_1 and X_2 corrected for the effect of X_3. The symbol we shall use for this *partial correlation coefficient* is $\rho_{12\cdot3}$.

We can adjust for the effect of X_3 upon X_1 by finding $\mu_{1\cdot3}$ for each of the five observations and subtracting $\mu_{1\cdot3}$ from X_1 for that observation. We shall call this difference $x_{1\cdot3}$. The calculations are shown in the first five columns below.

X_3	$\beta_{1(13)}X_3$	$\mu_{1\cdot3}$	X_1	$x_{1\cdot3}$	$x_{2\cdot3}$
10	10	15	10	-5	-2
30	30	35	20	-15	-6
25	25	30	30	0	0
20	20	25	40	15	6
40	40	45	50	5	2

The values of $x_{2\cdot3} = X_2 - \mu_{2\cdot3}$ are found in an analogous manner and appear in the right column above.

To find $\rho_{12\cdot3}$ we must find the correlation between $x_{1\cdot3}$ and $x_{2\cdot3}$. This can be done algebraically by finding the variances of these two variables ($\sigma^2_{1\cdot3}$ and $\sigma^2_{2\cdot3}$), finding their covariance ($\sigma_{12\cdot3}$), and then substituting in the relationship:

$$\rho_{12\cdot3} = \frac{\sigma_{12\cdot3}}{\sqrt{\sigma^2_{1\cdot3}\sigma^2_{2\cdot3}}}.$$

As an alternative to the expression just given, it can be shown that

$$\rho_{12\cdot3} = \frac{\rho_{12} - \rho_{13}\rho_{23}}{\sqrt{(1 - \rho^2_{13})(1 - \rho^2_{23})}}.$$

For our example we find that

$$\rho_{12} = \frac{-1}{\sqrt{10}}, \quad \rho_{13} = \frac{+5}{\sqrt{50}}, \quad \text{and} \quad \rho_{23} = \frac{-2}{\sqrt{5}}.$$

Hence,

$$\rho_{12\cdot3} = \frac{(-1/\sqrt{10}) - (-10/\sqrt{250})}{\sqrt{(1/2)(1/5)}} = \frac{1/\sqrt{10}}{1/\sqrt{10}} = 1.$$

A scattergram of the observations expressed in terms of variables $x_{1\cdot3}$ and $x_{2\cdot3}$ shows five points in a straight line. This is another way to conclude that $\rho_{12\cdot3}$ is one.

In general, sample estimates of $\rho_{12\cdot3}$ and $\rho_{12\cdot34}$ are

$$r_{12\cdot3} = \frac{r_{12} - r_{13}r_{23}}{\sqrt{(1 - r^2_{13})(1 - r^2_{23})}}$$

and

$$r_{12 \cdot 34} = \frac{r_{12 \cdot 4} - r_{13 \cdot 4} r_{23 \cdot 4}}{\sqrt{(1 - r_{13 \cdot 4}^2)(1 - r_{23 \cdot 4}^2)}}.$$

The pattern when additional variables are involved should now be apparent. Let's return to our airline example to find $r_{2y \cdot 3}$. The formula is

$$r_{2y \cdot 3} = \frac{r_{2y} - r_{23} r_{3y}}{\sqrt{(1 - r_{23}^2)(1 - r_{3y}^2)}}.$$

We substitute the two-variable correlation coefficients from the matrix as follows:

$$r_{2y \cdot 3} = \frac{.09 - (.61)(.39)}{\sqrt{(1 - .61^2)(1 - .39^2)}} = -.2027.$$

When X_2 is corrected for the effect of X_3, it appears to have a much stronger relationship with Y in the *opposite* direction. We shall have more to say on this point in the next section.

Interval estimators and tests of hypotheses. As we did in the case of two-variable and multiple correlation coefficients, we can get an interval estimator of a population partial correlation coefficient by making a w transformation of the corresponding partial coefficient from the sample. The only difference is that the variance of w will no longer be $1/(n - 3)$, where n is the number of observations. Instead, we must subtract from the denominator, $(n - 3)$, the number of variables held constant. For example, if we are transforming $r_{12 \cdot 3}$, the variance for w will be $1/(n - 4)$. If we are transforming $r_{12 \cdot 34}$, the variance for w will be $1/(n - 5)$. The w transformation can also be used to test hypotheses about the value of a partial correlation coefficient or to test for a significant difference between two partial correlation coefficients.

Although the w transformation provides a very good test for hypotheses about a partial correlation coefficient, that transformation is an approximation. An exact test for the hypothesis that a population partial correlation coefficient is zero can be had from the fact that

$$t = \frac{r_{12(3 \ldots k)} \sqrt{n - k}}{\sqrt{1 - r_{12(3 \ldots k)}^2}}$$

with $(n - k)$ degrees of freedom. Earlier in this section we found that $r_{2y \cdot 3} = -.20$ for $n = 64$. If we hypothesize that $\rho_{2y \cdot 3} = 0$,

$$t = \frac{-.20 \sqrt{61}}{\sqrt{(1 - .04)}} = -1.59$$

with 61 degrees of freedom. We cannot deny that $\rho_{2y \cdot 3} = 0$ at the .05 level of significance.

16-7 Variance Analysis in Multiple Correlation

In our discussion of a statistical model for multiple correlation we said that

$$\rho_m^2 = \delta_m = \frac{\Sigma\,(\varphi_i \sigma_{iy})}{\sigma_y^2}.$$

We also defined the standard error of estimate, $\sigma_{y(1\ldots k)}$ such that

$$\sigma_{y(1\ldots k)}^2 = \sigma_y^2(1 - \rho_m^2).$$

When we substitute the first expression for ρ_m^2 in the second and rearrange it, the result is

$$\sigma_y^2 = \sigma_{y(1\ldots k)}^2 + \Sigma\,(\varphi_i \sigma_{iy})$$

or

$$\sigma_y^2 = \sigma_y^2(1 - \rho_m^2) + \sigma_y^2 \rho_m^2.$$

Both of the last two expressions show that the Y variance is composed of a portion accounted for by the linear relationship among the variables and a portion that is residual variance about the relationship.

The statistic $s_{y(1\ldots k)}^2 = s_y^2(1 - r_m^2)$ is an estimate of $\sigma_{y(1\ldots k)}^2$, and $s_y^2 r_m^2$ is an estimate of the portion of Y variance accounted for by multiple correlation. When there is no correlation, these two estimates are independent estimates of σ_y^2. Consequently, their ratio will be distributed as F. We can use this fact to perform an analysis of variance on sample results to test the hypothesis that there is no correlation.

To perform the test, we begin by finding the sum of squares attributable to multiple correlation:

$$SS_{R(1\ldots k)} = \frac{S_{yy}}{n}(r_m^2).$$

For our airline example,

$$SS_{R\cdot 123} = \frac{4935.32}{64}(.4218) = 32.52.$$

This has three degrees of freedom associated with it, one for each X-variable. We next find the residual error sum of squares:

$$SS_{W(1\ldots k)} = \frac{S_{yy}}{n}(1 - r_m^2) = \frac{4935.32}{64}(.5782),$$

$$SS_{W\cdot 123} = 44.59$$

with 60 degrees of freedom, the number of observations less the *total* number of variables.

The analysis of variance can now be performed to test the hypothesis of no correlation among the four variables in our airline example:

Source	SS	m	MS	F
Correlation	32.52	3	10.84	14.59
Residual error	44.59	60	.7432	
	77.11	63		

Since $F(.99; 3, 60)$ is only 4.13, we conclude that multiple correlation is present in the population.

In multiple regression we tested linear models based upon one factor variable and upon two factor variables to see whether the latter model could be expected to reduce residual error significantly as compared with the former. We can employ the same type of test in multiple linear correlation.

Suppose that, given the variance analysis just completed above, we want to test whether putting X_2 and X_3 together with X_1 in a four-variable model is likely to reduce residual error significantly below that which would result from using only X_1 in a two-variable model. The hypothesis is that addition of X_2 and X_3 to the model will not reduce residual error. From our matrix of sample correlation coefficients we know that $r_{1y} = +.57$. Then

$$SS_{R\cdot 1} = \frac{S_{yy}}{n}(r_{1y}^2)$$

$$= 77.11(.3249) = 25.05$$

with one degree of freedom for the single X-variable.

Were X_1 the only variable, $77.11 - 25.05 = 52.06$ would be the residual error sum of squares with 62 degrees of freedom. From our previous analysis we know that the residual error when we use a four-variable model is only 44.59. The difference, 7.47, is the reduction in residual error. Two degrees of freedom, one for each variable, are associated with it. The remaining residual error is 44.59 with 60 degrees of freedom, as before. If the hypothesis is true, the ratio of the two related mean squares will be distributed as F. The analysis-of-variance table is as follows:

Source	SS	m	MS	F
Y correlation with X_1	25.05	1		
Reduction in residual from Y correlation with X_1, X_2, and X_3	7.47	2	3.735	5.03
	32.52			
Residual error	44.59	60	.7432	
	77.11	63		

From the table, $F(.99; 2, 60) = 4.98$ and we conclude that X_2 and X_3 should be included in the model.

The suppressant variable. Our last F test solved the problem as to whether we should include both X_2 and X_3 or neither one. We still need to know whether only one of the two should be included.

In the correlation matrix, $r_{2y} = .09$ and $r_{3y} = .39$. Separate tests of hypotheses that $\rho_{2y} = 0$ and $\rho_{3y} = 0$ yield t values of .71 and 3.34. Even $r_{2y \cdot 3} = -.20$ produced a t value of only -1.59. We might be led to believe that the significance in our last F test was produced primarily by a three-variable relationship among Y, X_1, and X_3.

To test whether the four-variable model is significantly better than the three-variable model with X_1 and X_3, we must first find h_1' and h_3' from the 2×3 matrix of correlation coefficients formed by cutting out the second row and second column of the 3×4 matrix with which we began. When we do so, we find that $h_1' = .4978$ and $h_3' = .2407$. From these we obtain $r_{y \cdot 13}^2 = .3776$ by use of Eq. (16–19). Finally, we find

$$SS_{R \cdot 13} = 77.11(.3776) = 29.12.$$

The analysis-of-variance table is given below.

Source	SS	m	MS	F
Y correlation with X_1 and X_3	29.12	2		
Reduction in residual from Y correlation with X_1, X_2, and X_3	3.40	1	3.40	4.57
	32.52			
Residual error	44.59	60	.7432	
	77.11	63		

From the table, $F(.95; 1, 60) = 4.00$. Apparently X_2 is contributing appreciably in spite of our earlier suppositions.

Apperception test score, X_2, is an example of a *suppressant variable*. To understand what this means we can begin by noting that, at the outset, we might reasonably expect the arithmetic, apperception, and vocabulary scores all to be positively related to customer rating in two senses. First, it would seem plausible to expect each to correlate positively with rating in two-variable correlations. We see that the sample r_{iy} are all positive, even though r_{2y} is so small that doubt is cast upon its significance. Second, in the regression equation we might expect such factor variables to have positive coefficients. The rationale under which the factor variables were selected could very well have been the expectation that they were each highly correlated with customer rating and virtually uncorrelated with each other. Under these conditions, each would be measuring a different aspect of potential for performance with customers, and the optimally weighted sum of all three could prove to have a significantly higher association than any combination of less than three.

At first glance, the situation we have encountered appears strange. All correlations in the original matrix were positive, yet h_2 came out negative.

We must *subtract* weighted values of X_2 from the weighted sum of X_1 and X_3 to get the best sample association.

When we examine r_{23}, (.61), we see it is the highest coefficient in the matrix except for the trivial cases of the correlations of the variables with themselves. Furthermore, r_{2y} is the lowest coefficient in the matrix. Variable X_2 seems to be associated with some factor in variable X_3 that is not present in Y. By subtracting weighted X_2 values we seem to be *suppressing* this extraneous factor, or correcting for it, so that the relevant component in X_3 can exert its full effect in accounting for Y variance.

We can now summarize the properties of desirable variables for multiple correlation analysis. One desirable type is highly correlated with the criterion variable (Y) but has relatively low intercorrelations with noncriterion variables which are themselves highly correlated with the criterion. It tends to be measuring some relatively independent factor which accounts for variability in the criterion. A second desirable type is highly correlated with a noncriterion variable and has very low correlation with the criterion. This latter type is the suppressant variable mentioned above.

In variance analysis for multiple correlation it usually is not possible to test for linearity of the regression surface as was done in multiple regression. To do so requires multiple observations on the dependent variable for several fixed combinations of levels of the factor variables. In correlation, the necessity to select items and then measure all variables will almost always preclude such replication.

A final point must be brought out. All techniques in this book assume the data are gathered under conditions of statistical stability. This means that the parameters in the various models are assumed to remain constant through time. Hence, the models cannot be used to make inferences about populations in which the parameters cannot be assumed to be fixed. The assumptions of statistical stability also usually are violated in time-series data. Correlations and regression relationships in which time is treated as either an explicit or implicit variable require special models beyond the scope of this book in almost all instances. The first three references at the end of this chapter are relevant for this purpose.

EXERCISES

16.9 Decide whether each of the following situations satisfies the necessary conditions for regression analysis, correlation analysis, or neither:
   (a) In a major corporation salesmen are selected for a study by means of a table of random numbers. Data on total dollar sales for the first half of the year and on number of calls made upon customers are collected for each salesman.
   (b) All salesmen of the above corporation are first put into classes by

number of calls made during the first half of the year. Three salesmen are selected randomly from each such class. Then total dollar
sales for the same period for each salesman selected are also collected.

(c) The situation is as described in (b) except that only one salesman is
selected at random from each "number-of-calls" class.

(d) The situation is as in (b) except that proportion of calls on which
a sale was made is collected in place of dollar sales.

(e) The situation is the same as in (b) except that each salesman's arbitrarily assigned payroll number is collected in place of dollar sales.

16.10 In a test battery designed to predict a student's final grade in statistics
(Y), the following results were obtained from the raw-score data:

$n = 40$;

$S_{yy} = 43,875.20$, $S_{11} = 17,136.00$, $S_{22} = 23,471.20$,

$S_{33} = 1059.60$, $S_{1y} = 10,250.04$, $S_{12} = 7616.00$,

$S_{23} = 1860.40$, $S_{2y} = 8372.00$, $S_{13} = 548.80$,

$S_{3y} = 156.40$.

(a) Make use of the elimination technique described in Chapter 15
to show that $c_1 = .511747$, $c_2 = .232274$, and $c_3 = -.525271$.

(b) Find the coefficient of multiple determination by using Eq. (16–14).

(c) Test for the presence of a linear relationship by means of an analysis of variance.

16.11 For the data given in Exercise 16.10:

(a) Show that

$r_{1y} = .3738$, $r_{12} = .3798$, $r_{23} = .3731$,

$r_{2y} = .2609$, $r_{13} = .1288$,

$r_{3y} = .0229$.

(b) Apply the elimination technique to show that

$h_1 = .3198$, $h_2 = .1698$,   and $h_3 = -.0816$.

(c) Find the coefficient of multiple correlation and square it. Compare
the result to your answer in Exercise 16.10(b).

(d) Change the h_i just found in part (b) to c_i by using Eq. (16–17)
and compare your results with Exercise 16.10(a).

(e) Test for the presence of multiple linear correlation by an analysis
of variance. Compare this test to the one you performed in Exercise
16.10(c).

16.12 Three sets of test scores on 100 clerks give the following two-variable correlations:

$$r_{1y} = .20, \qquad r_{12} = .90, \qquad r_{2y} = .01,$$

where Y is the dependent variable. Show that the second factor variable acts as a suppressant on the first factor variable by finding h_1, h_2, and r_m. *Partial ans.* $r_m = .44$.

16.13 For the airline-hostess example in this chapter we are given that $r_{12} = +.22$, $r_{13} = +.30$, $r_{23} = +.61$, $r_{1y} = +.57$, $r_{2y} = +.09$, and $r_{3y} = +.39$. From this information show that $r_{1y \cdot 3} = +.5157$, $r_{2y \cdot 3} = -.2027$, and $r_{21 \cdot 3} = +.0489$. Then use these results to show that $r_{2y \cdot 13} = -.2663$.

16.14 For the airline-hostess example in this chapter we found that $h_2 = -.266$. We can show that this coefficient can be expressed in terms of partial correlation coefficients.

(a) For the example in the text we found that the coefficient of multiple determination between customer rating and variables X_1 and X_3 was .3776. We shall give this the symbol $r_{y \cdot 13}^2 = .3776$. Recall that $r_{13} = .30$, $r_{12} = .22$, $r_{32} = .61$, and show that $r_{2 \cdot 13}^2 = .3736$.

(b) Use the results from part (a) and from Exercise 16.13 to show that

$$h_2 = r_{2y \cdot 13} \frac{\sqrt{1 - r_{y \cdot 13}^2}}{\sqrt{1 - r_{2 \cdot 13}^2}}.$$

REFERENCES

Brown, R. G., *Smoothing, Forecasting, and Prediction of Discrete Time Series.* Englewood Cliffs, N.J.: Prentice-Hall, Inc., 1963.

Ezekiel, M., and K. Fox, *Methods of Correlation and Regression Analysis.* New York: John Wiley & Sons, Inc., 1959.

Goldberger, A. S., *Econometric Theory.* New York: John Wiley & Sons, Inc., 1964.

Mood, A., and F. Graybill, *Introduction to the Theory of Statistics,* 2nd ed. New York: McGraw-Hill Book Company, 1963.

Ostle, B., *Statistics in Research,* 2nd ed. Ames, Iowa: Iowa State University Press, 1963.

Richmond, S., *Statistical Analysis,* 2nd ed. New York: The Ronald Press Company, 1964.

17

Discriminant
Analysis

The example we considered in the chapter on analysis of variance was concerned with the influence of three work-flow layouts on clerical productivity. The dependent factor was a continuous variable, mean output per unit time. The independent factor was categorical, or qualitative.

Sometimes the situation just described is reversed. For instance, suppose a major oil company has separated its present and past gasoline service station managers into two groups: (1) those whose performance has been highly satisfactory, (2) all the other managers. Suppose the company currently has a class of prospective managers in training. On the basis of some of the present characteristics of these prospective managers it may be possible to predict with considerable accuracy whether they will join the highly satisfactory group or the other group.

In the work-layout example we observed performance and assigned the clerks to potentially different performance populations. The object of our analysis was to determine whether the populations were, in fact, different. In the service-station example we know each of the trainees belongs to one of two statistical populations, but we do not know to which population he belongs. The object of our analysis is to find a way to assign him to the proper population. Usually we cannot do so with absolute accuracy; we must settle for a procedure that minimizes the probability of misclassification or the expected cost of misclassification or some other criterion based upon the expected accuracy of the procedure.

Discriminant analysis is designed to establish a procedure for assigning items to predetermined populations. At the same time, this type of analysis assesses the potential adequacy of the procedure in a particular application. Later in this chapter we shall describe how to carry out such an analysis, but first we shall show what can be done with the results of a simplified discriminant analysis in a typical business context.

17-1   An Illustration

Credit managers in retail stores need a way to predict whether a credit applicant will prove to be a good credit risk. We shall assume that the manager of a small loan company has begun a search for such a procedure by classifying all his past borrowers as either satisfactory or unsatisfactory. For each borrower the original loan application gives his household's total fixed payments per month and his household's total monthly income. The manager calculates the logarithm of the ratio of income to payments for each borrower as a crude index of ability to pay.

Now suppose the manager takes the group of satisfactory borrowers and prepares a frequency distribution of the proportion of such good borrowers that fall within successive classes along the ability-to-pay scale. Then he passes a smooth curve through these points. Next he makes a similar plot for the unsatisfactory group on the same graph. The result is shown in Fig. 17–1.

For the sake of simplicity we shall assume that the two distributions in

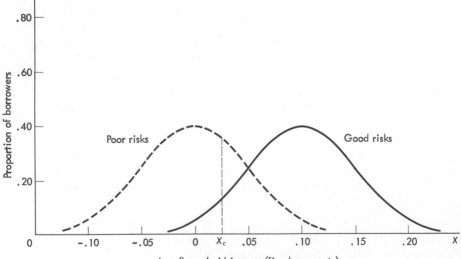

FIGURE 17-1 Distributions of good and poor credit risks

Fig. 17–1 constitute the entire populations of good and poor risks. The distributions are normal and they have the same standard deviation ($\sigma_x = .05$ on the ability-to-pay scale). They differ only with respect to their means. The good-risk group has a mean of .10 ($\mu_1 = .10$) and the bad-risk group has a mean of 0 ($\mu_2 = 0$).

The probability of misclassification. We now want to find a way to use the information in Fig. 17–1 to assign a given loan applicant to one of the two risk groups. We begin by arbitrarily selecting a tentative *cutting score* of $X_c = +.025$. If a loan applicant scores above .025 on ability to pay, we shall conclude he is a good risk and give him the loan. If he scores .025 or less, we shall conclude he is a poor risk and refuse him the loan.

One way that we can evaluate the expected performance of the procedure just described is to find the probabilities that it will misclassify an individual from each population. For the poor-risk group, we can find how many standard deviations X_c is above the mean and then find the portion of the poor-risk population below X_c from a table of areas under the normal curve. We find that

$$z_2 = \frac{X_c - \mu_2}{\sigma_2} = \frac{.025 - 0}{.05} = +.5.$$

From the table of areas under the normal curve we see that 69.15 per cent of the poor-risk group lies below X_c. We can expect to misclassify 30.85 per cent of this group, or we can say the probability is .3085 that we shall misclassify a poor-risk applicant. By a similar line of reasoning we find for the good-risk group that $z_1 = -1.5$ standard deviations and the probability of misclassification for an applicant from this group is .0668.

We may consider the probabilities of the two possible types of misclassification to be equally important. We see that the area under the dashed curve to the right of X_c in Fig. 17–1 represents the probability of misclassifying a poor risk, while the area to the left of X_c under the solid curve represents the probability of misclassifying a good risk. By increasing X_c we reduce the probability of misclassifying a poor risk and increase the probability of misclassifying a good risk. By increasing X_c to the value at which these curves intersect we can equalize these two probabilities. Algebraically, we can find this value of X (which we shall call X_p) from the fact that $z_1 = -z_2$ when $X = X_p$. In general, if $z_1 = -z_2$, then

$$\frac{X_p - \mu_1}{\sigma_1} = \frac{-(X_p - \mu_2)}{\sigma_2}$$

or

$$X_p = \frac{\sigma_1 \mu_2 + \sigma_2 \mu_1}{\sigma_1 + \sigma_2}. \tag{17-1}$$

For our example

$$X_p = \frac{.05(0) + .05(.10)}{2(.05)} = .05,$$

as we can see by inspection.

Given the value of X_p, we can find the probability of misclassifying either type of risk. We see that

$$z_1 = \frac{X_p - \mu_1}{\sigma_1} = \frac{.05 - .10}{.05} = -1.$$

From the table of areas under the normal curve we find there is .1587 of the good-risk population below X_p. It follows that there is .1587 of the poor-risk population above X_p and that the probability of misclassification is .1587 for a random loan applicant who is to be assigned to one of the populations on the basis of this ability-to-pay score.

The proportionate yield. Up to this point we have ignored any differences there might be in the number of persons in the two populations of loan applicants. Suppose that the good-risk population that applies for loans from our illustrative firm is twice as large as the poor-risk population. On a relative basis, the two populations can be represented by the distributions in Fig. 17–2.

Now, if we set our cut-off score at $X_p = .05$, the probability of misclassification will still be .1587 for each population. This is so because this probability is the ratio of the expected number misclassified in one of the

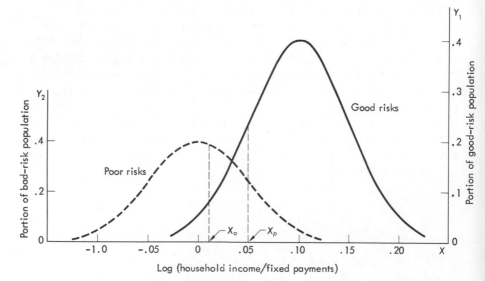

FIGURE 17-2 Risk populations plotted to reflect their relative sizes

populations to the total number *in that population*. But what will the expected proportion of good risks to bad be in the group of persons whose loans are approved because their ability to pay is greater than $X_p = .05$? In a group of 300 applicants we can expect 200 good risks and 100 poor risks. Of the 200 good risks, we can expect to approve loans for $100 - 15.87 = 84.13$ per cent, or 168.26. Of the 100 bad risks we can expect to approve loans for 15.87 per cent, or 15.87. The proportionate yield from this approval procedure will be $100(168.26)/(168.26 + 15.87)$, or 91.38 per cent good risks in the accepted group.

We can generalize this result. To do so we shall need the following definitions:

$p_1 =$ proportion of population 1 in the group to be classified,
$1 - p_1 =$ proportion of population 2 in the group to be classified,
$v_1 =$ proportion of population 1 correctly classified,
$v_2 =$ proportion of population 2 correctly classified,
$P_{11} =$ proportion of population 1 in group classified as population 1.

Then

$$P_{11} = \frac{p_1 v_1}{p_1 v_1 + (1 - v_2)(1 - p_1)}. \qquad (17\text{--}2)$$

For our example, two-thirds of those applying for loans are good risks ($p_1 = 2/3$) and, with a cutting score of $X_p = .05$, we can expect 84.13 per cent of each population to be correctly classified ($v_1 = v_2 = .8413$). Hence

$$P_{11} = \frac{(.6667)(.8413)}{(.6667)(.8413) + (.1587)(.3333)} = .9138,$$

the same result we had earlier.

From an examination of Fig. 17–2 and of Eq. (17–2) we can see that the higher we set the cutting score, the higher the proportion of good risks there will be in the group whose applications we approve. But the higher we set the cutting score, the higher the proportion of good risks there will be in the group whose application we refuse, too. We might be able to find a cutting score that equates the marginal return from raising the cutting score to that point with the marginal cost of raising it.

The optimal cutting score. Suppose that our loan company has found from a study of past borrowers that it makes $70 on the average from a good credit risk and loses $30 on the average on a poor risk. We have said that, out of every 300 loan applicants, we can expect 200 good risks and 100 poor risks. Of the 200 good risks we can expect to select 168.26 on the average with a cutting score of $X_p = .05$. Since we earn an average of $70 from each, we can expect to earn $11,778.20 from these 168.26. We can also expect to accept $100(1 - .8413)$ poor risks who will cost us $30(100)(.1587) = \$476.10$. Our net earnings will be $11,302.10, or $37.67 per applicant.

With two additional definitions we can generalize the calculation of expected return from an assignment procedure such as the one we have been discussing. The definitions are

m_1 = the expected gain from assigning a single member of population 1 to that population,

m_2 = the expected gain from assigning a single member of population 2 to population 1.

Given these two definitions, the expected net gain from setting a cutting score of X_c will be given the symbol $G(X_c)$. Then

$$G(X_c) = m_1 p_1 v_1 + m_2(1 - p_1)(1 - v_2),\qquad(17\text{--}3)$$

where v_1 and v_2 are a function of X_c.

For our example, $X_c = X_p = .05$ and, for this cutting score, $z_1 = -z_2 = -1$, as before. From the table of areas under the normal curve, $v_1 = .8413 = v_2$, so $1 - v_2 = .1587$. We also know that $p_1 = 200/300$, $m_1 = \$70$, and $m_2 = -\$30$. When we substitute these values in Eq. (17--3), we have

$$G(.05) = \$70(.6667)(.8413) - \$30(.3333)(.1587)$$
$$= \$39.26 - \$1.59 = \$37.67,$$

which is the same result we got before.

By a trial-and-error technique we can find the cutting score that will maximize our expected gain. In Table 17--1 we begin with $X_c = .05$ and

Table 17-1

CALCULATION OF OPTIMAL CUTTING SCORE

X_c	z_1	v_1	z_2	$1 - v_2$	$m_1 p_1 v_1$	$m_2(1 - p_1)(1 - v_2)$	$G(X_c)$
.05	−1.00	.8413	1.00	.1587	$39.26	−$1.59	$37.67
.04	−1.20	.8849	.80	.2119	41.30	−2.12	40.08
.03	−1.40	.9192	.60	.2743	42.90	−2.74	40.16
.02	−1.60	.9452	.40	.3446	44.11	−3.45	40.66
.01	−1.80	.9641	.20	.4207	44.994	−4.207	40.787
.00	−2.00	.9772	.00	.5000	45.60	−5.00	40.60
.012	−1.76	.9608	.24	.4052	44.840	−4.052	40.788
.013	−1.74	.9591	.26	.3974	44.760	−3.974	40.786
.011	−1.78	.9625	.22	.4129	44.919	−4.129	40.790

decrease it by increments of .01 until expected net gain, $G(X_c)$, fails to increase as a result of the decrease in X_c. Then we repeat the process using smaller increments until we locate a maximum for $G(X_c)$ at $X_c = X_o = .011$ where X_o symbolizes the optimal cutting score. This optimal cutting score will lead the loan manager to approve 96.25 per cent of the good risks and 41.29 per cent of the bad risks. As we can see from applying Eq. (17–2), in the group of approved borrowers there will be $100P_{11} = 82.34$ per cent good risks. The optimal cutting score, X_o, is shown on Fig. 17–2.

EXERCISES

17.1 An electronics-component manufacturing firm has a test battery from which it gets a composite score on applicants for boardwiring jobs. For the group of those hired who have satisfactorily completed training the mean test score was 120 with a standard deviation of 30. For the group of those hired who have not proven satisfactory the mean score was 90 with a standard deviation of 30. Use these values as point estimates of their respective parameters and find the probability that a potentially satisfactory employee will be rejected by a cutting score of 100.   *Ans.* 0.2514.

17.2 For the situation described in Exercise 17.1 find X_p, the estimated cutting score that will equalize the probabilities of correct classification for the two types of job applicants hired.

17.3 The electronics firm discussed in Exercise 17.1 estimates that, in the absence of the test, only 40 per cent of the applicants for boardwiring jobs can successfully complete the training program and become regular employees.

(a) Show that a cutting score of 100 on the composite test-battery score can be expected to produce 57.38 per cent successes out of those applicants who are hired.

(b) Find the per cent of potential successes in the applicants who are not hired.

17.4 For the situation described in Exercises 17.1 and 17.3 find the probability that an applicant who scores 110 on the test battery will complete training successfully.

17.5 For the situation described in Exercises 17.1 and 17.3 it costs $800 to hire and train a successful trainee and $600 on the average to hire, train, and terminate an unsuccessful trainee.

(a) On the assumption that marginal testing costs are negligible, show that the expected cost *per applicant* is $373.00 if the cutting score is 100.

(b) Show that the expected cost *per successful trainee* is $1245.67.

17.6 For the situation described in Exercise 17.5, assume the company estimates that, for each successful employee, the average first-year gain, net of hiring and training costs, is $1200, and $-$600 for an unsuccessful one. Find the optimal cutting score.   *Ans.* $X_o = 97$.

17-2   The Linear Discriminant Function

In our illustration in the previous section we arbitrarily developed the crude index of ability-to-pay in order to concentrate on the applications aspects of such a measure. For the remainder of the chapter we shall concentrate on development of a suitable measure to use as a basis for assigning items to two predetermined populations.

When we examine Fig. 17–1, we can discern some desirable properties a measure should have if it is to help us distinguish items in one population from those in another. We would like the measure to do two things: (1) separate the means of the two populations and (2) concentrate the items in each population about their respective means in order to make the probability of correct classification as large as possible.

The composition of the measure we seek is also worth considering. For the ability-to-pay index the loan manager mentioned earlier could well have combined the separate components of each household's fixed payments by simple addition of the dollar amounts. Might there not be an alternative weighted total of these amounts that would produce a better measure? For that matter, might there not be other variables, not measured in dollars, that could be combined with those already considered to produce an even better scoring system? For instance, it is at least plausible that the number of delinquencies reported on members of the household by local merchants to the local credit bureau during the six months prior to the loan application would constitute a desirable component.

It appears that we need a measure that will combine a set of variables in such manner that the difference between the two population means per unit of dispersion about those means is a maximum. A *discriminant function* of the variables is such a measure. Furthermore, if the two multivariate populations that serve as inputs for determining the function satisfy some assumptions, we realize additional benefits. On the basis of sample information we can test whether the function is likely to discriminate effectively in practice. We can also test whether the inclusion of additional variables in the function is likely to improve its power to discriminate.

We have indicated that we shall consider discriminant functions designed to distinguish between members of only two populations, although the technique can be extended to more than two populations. We shall also restrict our discussion to *linear* discriminant functions of the input variables.

To illustrate the determination and testing of a linear discriminant function we need a new example. For some types of life insurance policies the cumulative premium income will be less than cumulative expenses accrued by the insuring company unless a newly issued policy remains in force for two years. We want to construct a discriminant function based on information available in the application that will distinguish prospective policyholders who will allow their policy to lapse during the first two years from those who will not. The variables we shall use are

X_1 = an ability-to-pay index constructed from several items on the application,

X_2 = annual income as a per cent of life insurance currently owned,

X_3 = the number of dependents supported by the applicant.

Our goal is to find numerical values for the a_i in a function of the form

$$Y = a_1 X_1 + a_2 X_2 + a_3 X_3$$

that will distinguish between the two populations. We shall use a sample from the company's records of policies of the type being studied that have lapsed in less than two years and another sample of those which remained in force at least two years.

17-3   A Statistical Model for Linear Discrimination

We assume that individual units from two populations appear in intermingled random order for assignment to one of the two populations. Prior to assignment it is not possible to tell to which population a unit belongs. We observe measures of k characteristics $(X_1, \ldots, X_k)$ of each unit. These two populations of measurements are *multivariate normal* in the k variables. The multivariate normal distribution was described in Sec. 16–5.

We shall let $\sigma_{ii \cdot 1}$ be the *variance* of the ith variable in the first population and $\sigma_{ij \cdot 1}$ be the covariance of the ith and jth variables in the first population. Counterparts for the second population are $\sigma_{ii \cdot 2}$ and $\sigma_{ij \cdot 2}$. It is assumed that the variance-covariance matrix of the first population equals, component by component, the variance-covariance matrix of the second population, or

$$[\sigma_{ij \cdot 1}] = [\sigma_{ij \cdot 2}]$$

for all pairs of i, j formed from the numbers $1, \ldots, k$.

Because the variance-covariance matrices are equal, we can abandon the notation of the previous paragraph in favor of one that is simpler and more familiar. Since it makes no difference to which population we have reference when we are considering variances and covariances, we will not distinguish between them. The symbol σ_i^2 will be the variance of the ith variable in either population and σ_{ij} will be the covariance of the ith and jth variables.

We further assume that the two populations differ with respect to their means. In other words, we assume that the point $(\mu_{11}, \ldots, \mu_{k1})$ does not coincide with the point $(\mu_{12}, \ldots, \mu_{k2})$ where μ_{ij} designates the mean of the ith variable $(i = 1, \ldots, k)$ in the jth population $(j = 1, 2)$. In view of the assumption of equal variance-covariance matrices, we see that the two populations are assumed to be identical in every respect except their means.

Given the foregoing assumptions, we can form two *univariate normal* populations by subjecting each possible k-variate observation in the two populations to the single linear transformation

$$Y = \alpha_1 X_1 + \ldots + \alpha_k X_k. \tag{17-4}$$

When we do so, the resulting populations will have identical variances—that is,

$$\sigma_{y \cdot 1}^2 = \sigma_{y \cdot 2}^2 = \sigma_y^2,$$

but their means, μ_{y1} and μ_{y2}, will differ.

Suppose we find numerical values for the α_i by solving the set of simultaneous linear equations

$$\alpha_1 \sigma_1^2 + \alpha_2 \sigma_{12} + \ldots + \alpha_k \sigma_{1k} = \mu_{11} - \mu_{12}, \tag{17-5a}$$

$$\vdots \qquad \vdots \qquad \qquad \vdots \qquad \qquad \vdots \qquad \qquad \vdots$$

$$\alpha_1 \sigma_{k1} + \alpha_2 \sigma_{k2} + \ldots + \alpha_k \sigma_k^2 = \mu_{k1} - \mu_{k2}. \tag{17-5k}$$

Then it can be shown* that these values of the α_i will maximize the expression

$$\frac{(\mu_{y1} - \mu_{y2})^2}{\sigma_y^2}. \tag{17-6}$$

In other words, solving for the α_i in this manner will maximize the square of the difference between the means of the transformed observations per unit of their variance. If the *square* of the difference is a maximum, so will the *difference* be a maximum per unit of dispersion.

When the alpha coefficients in Eqs. (17-5) are determined as described, we shall call that equation a *linear discriminant function*. It may be well to emphasize that Eqs. (17-5), used in finding the coefficients for such a function, are different than the normal equations used in multiple regression and correlation. The right sides of Eqs. (17-5) are differences in means, not covariances of each independent variable with the dependent variable.

17-4 Estimators and Estimates

To illustrate how a sample estimate of the linear discriminant function is found, we shall return to our insurance company example. We left it after

---

* M. G. Kendall, *A Course in Multivariate Analysis* (New York: Hafner Publishing Company, 1957), p. 147. An alternative criterion and proof are given in Paul G. Hoel, *Introduction to Mathematical Statistics* (New York: John Wiley & Sons, Inc., 1947), pp. 121–125.

pointing out that a random sample of policyholders who had lapsed in less than two years was selected and an entirely independent random sample of those who had retained their policies at least two years was also selected. We shall refer to these as samples from the *lapsing* and *retaining* populations.

Our first task is to estimate the variance-covariance matrix for the populations. The necessary data appear in Table 17-2. The bottom row of that table shows the sample sizes for the lapsing and retaining groups and for the two groups combined. In the first two columns the remaining rows show for the three X variables the sums of squares and cross products of deviations for each sample with respect to the *means of that sample*. For instance, the sum of the 124 values of X_1 in the retaining group is 4943.012 and the sum of these squared X_1 values is 213,583.96. Hence, for the retaining group,

$$S_{11} = n \sum x_1^2 = n \sum (X_1^2) - (\sum X_1)^2$$
$$= 124(213, 583.96) - (4943.01)^2$$

and

$$\sum x_1^2 = \frac{S_{11}}{n} = 16,540.67, \qquad \text{the value shown.}$$

Table 17-2

SUMS OF SQUARED DEVIATIONS, SUMS OF CROSS-PRODUCTS,
AND SAMPLE SIZES

	Retaining group	Lapsing group	Combined
$\sum x_1^2$	16,540.67	3,551.90	20,092.57
$\sum x_2^2$	3,740.43	1,041.81	4,782.24
$\sum x_3^2$	95.71	28.97	124.68
$\sum (x_1 x_2)$	664.97	313.34	978.31
$\sum (x_1 x_3)$	158.78	78.19	236.97
$\sum (x_2 x_3)$	432.52	185.36	617.88
n	124	40	164

As we learned in Sec. 7–6, Eq. (7–4), we can pool estimates of the same population variance to get a more dependable single estimate. Of course, before we do so, we should perform F tests on the separate sample estimates to see whether we can assume they came from populations with the same variance. We shall assume that it is legitimate to pool the data in this example. The right column is the result: it is the sums of the other two columns. If we were to divide this column by the degrees of freedom, 162, we would have unbiased estimates of the components of the variance-covariance matrix. As we shall see shortly, we can work with the sums directly and avoid this step.

The remaining data we shall need are shown in Table 17–3. They are the means for the three X variables within each of the two samples and the differences between these means.

Table 17-3

MEANS AND DIFFERENCES BETWEEN MEANS

	Retaining group	Lapsing group	Differences
$\bar{X}_1$	39.863	35.550	4.313
$\bar{X}_2$	34.123	31.377	2.746
$\bar{X}_3$	2.694	2.616	.078

We now have sample estimates of all quantities required in Eqs. (17–5). In general, the set of equations from which we obtain the sample estimates, a_i, of the alpha coefficients is as follows:

$$a_1 \sum x_1^2 + a_2 \sum (x_1 x_2) + \ldots + a_k \sum (x_1 x_k) = \Delta \bar{X}_1, \quad (17\text{–}7a)$$

$$a_1 \sum (x_1 x_2) + \quad a_2 \sum x_2^2 \quad + \ldots + a_k \sum (x_2 x_k) = \Delta \bar{X}_2, \quad (17\text{–}7b)$$

$$\begin{array}{ccccc} \cdot & \cdot & \cdot & \cdot & \cdot \\ \cdot & \cdot & \cdot & \cdot & \cdot \\ \cdot & \cdot & \cdot & \cdot & \cdot \end{array}$$

$$a_1 \sum (x_1 x_k) + a_2 \sum (x_2 x_k) + \ldots + \quad a_k \sum x_k^2 \quad = \Delta \bar{X}_k, \quad (17\text{–}7k)$$

where $\Delta \bar{X}_i = \bar{X}_{i1} - \bar{X}_{i2}$, the difference in means of the ith variable for the two groups.

For our example we can construct the necessary equations to solve for the a_i from the data in Tables 17–2 and 17–3. The equations are

$$20{,}092.57a_1 + \quad 978.31a_2 + 236.97a_3 = 4.313,$$

$$978.31a_1 + 4782.24a_2 + 617.88a_3 = 2.746,$$

$$236.97a_1 + \quad 617.88a_2 + 124.68a_3 = \quad .078.$$

We can use the elimination technique discussed in Chapter 15 to solve these equations. When we do so the results are

$$a_1 = \quad .00022598,$$

$$a_2 = \quad .00139741,$$

$$a_3 = -.00672922,$$

and the sample estimate of the discriminant function is

$$Y = .000226X_1 + .001397X_2 - .006729X_3. \quad (17\text{–}8)$$

From Eq. (17–8) we can find estimates of the means of the retaining and lapsing populations of Y values. In general,

$$\bar{Y}_j = a_1 \bar{X}_{1j} + a_2 \bar{X}_{2j} + a_3 \bar{X}_{3j}; \tag{17-9}$$

we find the estimate of the mean of the discriminant function for the jth population by finding the discriminant of the means of the X_i for the sample from that group. We have the $\bar{X}_i$ in Table 17–3. Hence

$$\bar{Y}_1 = .000226(39.863) + .001397(34.123) - .006729(2.694)$$
$$= .038585$$

and

$$\bar{Y}_2 = .034296.$$

In addition to the $\bar{Y}_i$, we need an estimate of the standard deviation of the two populations in order to find estimates of probabilities of correct classification for cutting scores we might use in analyses similar to those in Sec. 17–1. We could get such an estimate by substituting the two sample sets of X values into Eq. (17–8), computing s_{y1}^2 and s_{y2}^2 for the two sets, and pooling these variance estimates. This estimate, however, would not be unbiased. All this labor can be avoided because, for a sample discriminant function determined as Eq. (17–8) was,

$$s_y^2 = \frac{\bar{Y}_1 - \bar{Y}_2}{n_1 + n_2 - 4}, \tag{17-10}$$

where s_y^2 is the unbiased estimator of σ_y^2. Hence, for our example,

$$s_y^2 = \frac{.038585 - .034296}{160} = .000026806.$$

Therefore

$$s_y = .005177$$

and the sample means are an estimated

$$\frac{\bar{Y}_1 - \bar{Y}_2}{s_y} = \frac{.004289}{.005177} = .828$$

standard deviations apart.

17-5 Variance Analysis in Discrimination

Usually we shall want to test the hypothesis that the population discriminant function does not discriminate. This is equivalent to a test that the α_i are all equal to zero. An analysis-of-variance test can be used, and the analysis-of-variance table is Table 17–4. In this table

$$k = \frac{n_1 n_2}{n_1 + n_2}, \qquad D = \bar{Y}_1 - \bar{Y}_2,$$

p is the number of X variables in the discriminant function, and $n = n_1 + n_2$. The quantity kD^2 is equal to the sum of squares between the means of the two samples, and D is the sum of squares within the samples.

Table 17-4

ANALYSIS OF VARIANCE FOR THE DISCRIMINANT FUNCTION

Source	SS	m	MS
Discriminant	kD^2	p	kD^2/p
Residual error	D	$n - p - 1$	$D/(n - p - 1)$

For our example

$$k = \frac{40(124)}{164} = 30.2439,$$

$$D = .038585 - .034296 = .004289,$$

$$p = 3,$$

$$n = 164.$$

The analysis-of-variance table is as follows:

Source	SS	m	MS	F
Discriminant	.000556	3	.000185	6.85
Residual error	.004289	160	.000027	

Since $F(.9995; 3,120) = 6.34$, we conclude that the population discriminant function will discriminate.

In addition to an overall test for discrimination, we may want to know whether this three-variable discriminant is significantly better than a two-variable discriminant. To make such a test we must first find the sample two-variable discriminant by repeating the procedure given in Sec. 17–4 using only two X variables. Then we repeat the procedure given in Sec. 17–5 up to the point at which we have found $(kD^2)_2$, the discriminant sum of squares for the two-variable model. Next we find $(kD^2)_3 - (kD^2)_2$, the decrease in the discriminant sum of squares when we go from three variables to two. There will be one degree of freedom associated with this difference. Finally, we form an F ratio with this difference in the numerator and the residual error mean square from our three-variable analysis (.000027) in the denominator and compare it with the F-table values for 1 and $n - 3 - 1$ degrees of freedom. If the result is not significant, we can assume a two-variable model is appropriate.

EXERCISES

17.7 Find the sample discriminant function of X_1 and X_2 for the insurance example discussed in Sec. 17–4 of the text.

Ans. $a_1 = .00018858$, $a_2 = .00053563$.

17.8 Find the sample discriminant function of X_2 and X_3 for the insurance example discussed in Sec. 17–4 of the text.

17.9 Perform an analysis of variance to test whether the three-variable discriminant function discussed in the text has significantly greater ability to discriminate than does the two-variable discriminant function in Exercise 17.7. *Partial ans.* $(k D^2)_2 = .0001578.$

17.10 Repeat Exercise 17.9 for the two-variable discriminant function based upon X_2 and X_3.

17.11 From the information given in Tables 17–2 and 17–3:

(a) Run three t tests on the differences among the three sets of means in Table 17–3.

(b) Find the 3×3 matrix of correlation coefficients (r_{ij}) from the pooled matrix in Table 17–2.

(c) From the results of parts (a) and (b) of this exercise can you tell why a_3 is negative in Eq. (17–8)? If not, refer to pages 395 through 398 in Chapter 16.

REFERENCES

Bryant, E. C., *Statistical Analysis*, 2nd ed. New York: McGraw-Hill Book Company, 1966.

Hoel, P. G., *Introduction to Mathematical Statistics*. New York: John Wiley & Sons, Inc., 1947.

Kendall, M. G., *A Course in Multivariate Analysis*. New York: Hafner Publishing Company, Inc., 1957.

Williams, E. J., *Regression Analysis*. New York: John Wiley & Sons, Inc., 1959.

Glossary
of
Major Symbols

* First page on which the symbol appears.

417

Symbol	Description	Page
λ	A general symbol for any parameter	147
μ	The mean, or expected value of a random variable	30
μ	The true mean effect over all treatment populations in analysis of variance	306
$\hat{\mu}$	The estimated mean of a random variable (see also $\bar{X}$)	181
$\hat{\mu}$	The mean of the probability distribution of the population mean	181
μ_b	A break-even value of μ	229
$\mu_{\bar{X}}$	The expectation of the sample mean of X	48
$\mu_{y \cdot x}$	The mean value of Y associated with a given value of X in the population linear regression model	333
$\mu_{y \cdot 1 \ldots k}$ or $\mu_{y(1 \ldots k)}$	The population mean value of Y associated with a given set of the X values in multiple regression or multiple correlation	386
π	The constant $3.1416 \ldots$	83
ρ	The population correlation coefficient between two random variables	41
ρ_k	The true effect of the kth replication for factorial design in analysis of variance	317
ρ_m	The multiple correlation coefficient	387
$\rho_{12 \cdot 3 \ldots k}$	The population partial correlation coefficient for the first and second variables with the third through the kth variables held constant	393
$\sigma_{\bar{X}}$	The standard error of the sample mean	123
σ_μ	The standard deviation of the probability distribution of the population mean	181
σ_V	The standard deviation of the probability distribution of economic value, V	235
$\sigma_{V'}$	The standard deviation of the probability distribution of value anticipated (preposterior) from a sample of size n'	244
$\sigma_{y \cdot x}$	The population standard error of estimate in two-variable linear regression	333
$\sigma_{y \cdot 12 \ldots k}$ or $\sigma_{y(1 \ldots k)}$	The population standard error of estimate in multiple linear regression and multiple correlation models	350
σ^2	The variance of a random variable	30
$\sigma_{p'}^2$	The variance of a sample proportion	191

Symbol	Description	Page
$\sigma_{\bar{X}}^2$	The variance of the probability distribution of sample means	121
$\hat{\sigma}^2$	The estimated variance of a random variable (see also s^2)	236
$\sigma_{X_1 X_2}$	The covariance of X_1 and X_2	39
$\sigma_{12 \cdot 3}$	In partial correlation analysis, the population covariance between the first and second variables with the third variable held constant	393
τ_j	The mean effect of the jth treatment population in analysis of variance	306
φ_i	The mean effect of the ith block in randomized block experiments	309
$\varphi_0, \varphi_1, \ldots, \varphi_k$	Population coefficients in the multiple linear regression model	350
$(\varphi\tau)_{ij}$	The true interaction effect of the ith block and jth treatment for factorial design in analysis of variance	317
χ^2	A variable distributed as chi-square	107

ROMAN SYMBOLS

Symbol	Description	Page*
a	A fixed cost, or maximum value of a linear opportunity loss function	229
a_i	A coefficient in the sample linear discriminant function	412
b	Unit variable return, or slope of linear opportunity loss function	229
b_u	Cost per unit of underestimate	258
b_o	Cost per unit of overestimate	258
b_0	A sample estimate of the regression line intercept in two-variable linear regression	335
b_1	A sample estimate of the slope of the regression line in two-variable linear regression	335
$c_0, c_1, \ldots, c_k$	Sample estimates of the regression coefficients in multiple linear regression	352

* First page on which the symbol appears.

Symbol	Description	Page
C	The correction term for finding certain sums of squares in analysis of variance	301
C_s	Cost of further sample information	245
C_o	Total cost of an overestimate	258
C_u	Total cost of an underestimate	258
$C.V.$	The coefficient of variation	103
$_KC_n$	The combination of K elements taken n at a time	19
d	A value of a random variable formed by differences in paired observations	153
d	The sample coefficient of determination in two-variable regression analysis	336
d_m	The sample coefficient of multiple determination	387
D	The difference between the sample means of the linear discriminant function	414
$D(n)$ $D^+(n)$ $D^-(n)$	Kolmogorov-Smirnov statistics used in measuring goodness of fit	292
e	The constant 2.7183	75
f	The frequency of a specified value or range of values of X in a population or in a sample	47
F	A cumulative "less than" frequency	115
F	Fisher's variance statistic	149
$F'(n)$	The observed cumulative relative "less than" frequency	292
g	Expected frequencies in a chi-square test for association	271
G'	The expected cumulative relative "less than" frequency	292
$G(X_c)$	The expected net gain associated with a cutting score of X_c in linear discriminant analysis	406
h	The variable, $2 \arcsin \sqrt{p'}$	205
h_i	Standardized coefficients for the reduced normal equations in multiple correlation analysis	388
H	The variable, $2 \arcsin \sqrt{p}$	205
H_0	A null hypothesis	147
i	An interval of time or distance, or a unit of area, volume, etc.	192

Symbol	Description	Page
k	Variable cost per sample observation	245
Ku	A coefficient of kurtosis	102
l	A statistic	147
L	Lower limit of a confidence interval	169
L	Economic opportunity loss	221
$\mathscr{L}$	The standard normal loss integral	232
$\mathscr{L}'$	The normal loss integral anticipated (preposterior) from a sample of size n'	244
$\bar{L}_{opt}$	Expected economic opportunity loss under an optimal strategy	221
$L(\mu)$	A loss function of μ	229
m	Degrees of freedom	106
M	Sample size multiple, n'/n	247
M_{opt}	Optimal sample size multiple	248
n	The number of elements in a sample	48
n'	A contemplated (preposterior) total sample size	244
n'_{opt}	Optimal total sample size	245
$n._{j}$	The number of observations in the jth column of an analysis-of-variance table	301
$n_{..}$	The total number of observations in an analysis-of-variance table	301
N	The number of elements in a finite population	47
p	The probability of success in a binomial process	67
p	The number of means for a Duncan multiple range test in one-way analysis of variance	304
p'	A sample proportion	191
$\bar{p}$	A pooled estimate of p from two or more samples	210
$\hat{p}$	Mean of the probability distribution of the population proportion, p. See also p'	255
$P(E)$	The probability of an event	2
$P(S)$	The probability of a state	52
$P(X)$	The probability of a value of a random variable	30
$P(AB)$	The joint probability of the events A and B	10
$P(B|A)$	The probability of event B conditional on the occurrence of the event A	10

Symbol	Description	Page
$_KP_n$	The permutation of K elements taken n at a time	20
P_c	The percentile of X at which the total expected cost of errors of estimation is minimized	259
q	The probability of failure in a binomial probability process	67
r	The number of successes in n trials of a binomial probability process	67
r	Number of occurrences of a Poisson-distributed phenomenon	75
r	The sample correlation coefficient for the two-variable case	381
r_c	A decision limit, or critical value of r in a binomial or Poisson process	197
$r_{12 \cdot 3 \ldots k}$	In partial correlation analysis, the sample correlation between the first and second variables with the third through the kth variables held constant	394
r_m	The sample multiple correlation coefficient	387
r_p	The multiple-range statistic for Duncan's test in one-way analysis of variance	304
R_p	The least significant range for Duncan's test in one-way analysis of variance	304
s^2	The best unbiased estimate of σ^2 (population variance) obtained from a set of sample values	50
$s_{\bar{X}}^2$	The estimated variance of the sample mean	134
$\bar{s}^2$	A pooled estimate of the population variance from two or more samples	151
s_m	The sample estimate of the standard error of estimate in multiple correlation analysis	390
$s_{..}^2$	An estimate of the variance within treatment populations for an analysis of variance	303
$s_{\bar{X} \cdot j}$	The standard error of the jth treatment mean in analysis of variance	303
$s_{y \cdot 12 \ldots k}$	The sample estimate of the standard error of estimate in multiple linear regression	353
$s_{y \cdot x}$	A sample estimate of the standard error of estimate in two-variable linear regression	335
Sk	A coefficient of skewness	103
SS_A	Sum of squared deviations among means in a one-way analysis of variance	301

Symbol	Description	Page
SS_B	Sum of squared deviations among blocks in analysis of variance	310
SS_E	In analysis of variance, the sum of squared deviations associated with residual error within cells	301
$SS_{E \cdot X}$ or $SS_{E \cdot 1 \ldots k}$	The sum of squares attributable to residual error about cell means in linear regression	344
SS_I	Sum of squared deviations for the interaction effect in factorial designed analysis of variance	318
S_{ij}	An element of the matrix of weighted sums of squares and cross products of deviations	354
S^{ij}	An element of the inverse of the matrix of weighted sums of squares and cross products of deviations	354
$SS_{M \cdot X}$	The sum of squares attributable to dispersion of cell means about the sample regression line in two-variable linear regression of Y with X	344
SS_R	Sum of squared deviations for the replication effect in analysis of variance with factorial treatment arrangement	318
$SS_{R \cdot X}$	The sum of squared deviations attributable to the relationship of Y with X in two-variable linear regression	343
$SS_{R(1 \ldots k)}$ or $SS_{R \cdot 1 \ldots k}$	The sum of squares attributable to regression in multiple linear regression and multiple correlation	357
SS_T	Total sum of squared deviations about the grand mean in analysis of variance	301
$SS_{W \cdot X}$	The sum of squares attributable to dispersion of X values about values of $\bar{Y}_x$ in two-variable linear regression of Y with X	343
$SS_{W(1 \ldots k)}$ or $SS_{W \cdot 1 \ldots k}$	The sum of squares attributable to residual error about the regression plane in multiple linear regression and multiple correlation	357
S_{xx}	$n \sum (X^2) - (\sum X)^2$	337
S_{yy}	$n \sum (Y^2) - (\sum Y)^2$	337
S_{xy}	$n \sum (XY) - (\sum X)(\sum Y)$	337
t	Student's t statistic	135

Symbol	Description	Page
$\hat{t}$	Student's t statistic for the probability distribution of the population mean given the sample mean	181
T	The absolute value of the sum of the four components in the corner association test (see Table 12–5 in Sec. 12–5)	285
U	Upper limit of a confidence interval	169
V	The value associated with an outcome, X	60
$\bar{V}$	The expected economic value of the outcome of a random variable	60
$\bar{V}_c$	The expected economic value of perfect, or complete, information	221
$\bar{V}'_c$	The expected value of perfect information anticipated (preposterior) on the basis of a sample of size n'	245
$\bar{V}_m$	The expected economic value under certainty	220
$\bar{V}_{opt}$	The expected economic value of an optimal strategy	220
$\bar{V}_s$	The expected value of further sample information	245
$w(r)$	Fisher's transformation of the correlation coefficient	383
x	The deviation of a value of a random variable from the mean of the random variable, i.e., $X-\mu$	39
X	A value of a random variable	30
$\hat{X}$	An estimate of a value of a random variable, X	257
X_P	A percentile of a random variable, X (with P expressed as a decimal fraction)	92
$\hat{X}_P$	An estimated percentile of a random variable, X (with P expressed as a decimal fraction)	100
X_c	The cutting score in linear discriminant analysis	403
$\hat{X}_{opt}$	The optimal (economic) estimate of X	259
$\bar{X}$	The sample mean of X	48
$\bar{X}_c$	A decision limit, or critical value of $\bar{X}$	158
$\bar{X}'$	The anticipated (preposterior) sample mean from a sample of n'	263
$\bar{X}_{..}$	The grand mean of all observations in analysis of variance	301

Appendix
Tables

CUMULATIVE BINOMIAL DISTRIBUTION

$$P(r \geq r \mid n, p)$$

$n = 1$

p	01	02	03	04	05	06	07	08	09	10
r 1	0100	0200	0300	0400	0500	0600	0700	0800	0900	1000
p	11	12	13	14	15	16	17	18	19	20
r 1	1100	1200	1300	1400	1500	1600	1700	1800	1900	2000
p	21	22	23	24	25	26	27	28	29	30
r 1	2100	2200	2300	2400	2500	2600	2700	2800	2900	3000
p	31	32	33	34	35	36	37	38	39	40
r 1	3100	3200	3300	3400	3500	3600	3700	3800	3900	4000
p	41	42	43	44	45	46	47	48	49	50
r 1	4100	4200	4300	4400	4500	4600	4700	4800	4900	5000

$n = 2$

p	01	02	03	04	05	06	07	08	09	10
r 1	0199	0396	0591	0784	0975	1164	1351	1536	1719	1900
2	0001	0004	0009	0016	0025	0036	0049	0064	0081	0100
p	11	12	13	14	15	16	17	18	19	20
r 1	2079	2256	2431	2604	2775	2944	3111	3276	3439	3600
2	0121	0144	0169	0196	0225	0256	0289	0324	0361	0400
p	21	22	23	24	25	26	27	28	29	30
r 1	3759	3916	4071	4224	4375	4524	4671	4816	4959	5100
2	0441	0484	0529	0576	0625	0676	0729	0784	0841	0900
p	31	32	33	34	35	36	37	38	39	40
r 1	5239	5376	5511	5644	5775	5904	6031	6156	6279	6400
2	0961	1024	1089	1156	1225	1296	1369	1444	1521	1600
p	41	42	43	44	45	46	47	48	49	50
r 1	6519	6636	6751	6864	6975	7084	7191	7296	7399	7500
2	1681	1764	1849	1936	2025	2116	2209	2304	2401	2500

$n = 3$

p	01	02	03	04	05	06	07	08	09	10
r 1	0297	0588	0873	1153	1426	1694	1956	2213	2464	2710
2	0003	0012	0026	0047	0073	0104	0140	0182	0228	0280
3				0001	0001	0002	0003	0005	0007	0010
p	11	12	13	14	15	16	17	18	19	20
r 1	2950	3185	3415	3639	3859	4073	4282	4486	4686	4880
2	0336	0397	0463	0533	0608	0686	0769	0855	0946	1040
3	0013	0017	0022	0027	0034	0041	0049	0058	0069	0080
p	21	22	23	24	25	26	27	28	29	30
r 1	5070	5254	5435	5610	5781	5948	6110	6268	6421	6570
2	1138	1239	1344	1452	1563	1676	1793	1913	2035	2160
3	0093	0106	0122	0138	0156	0176	0197	0220	0244	0270
p	31	32	33	34	35	36	37	38	39	40
r 1	6715	6856	6992	7125	7254	7379	7500	7617	7730	7840
2	2287	2417	2548	2682	2818	2955	3094	3235	3377	3520
3	0298	0328	0359	0393	0429	0467	0507	0549	0593	0640

Appendix A *(cont.)*

n = 3   CUMULATIVE BINOMIAL DISTRIBUTION

p	41	42	43	44	45	46	47	48	49	50
r 1	7946	8049	8148	8244	8336	8425	8511	8594	8673	8750
2	3665	3810	3957	4104	4253	4401	4551	4700	4850	5000
3	0689	0741	0795	0852	0911	0973	1038	1106	1176	1250

n = 4

p	01	02	03	04	05	06	07	08	09	10
r 1	0394	0776	1147	1507	1855	2193	2519	2836	3143	3439
2	0006	0023	0052	0091	0140	0199	0267	0344	0430	0523
3			0001	0002	0005	0008	0013	0019	0027	0037
4									0001	0001

p	11	12	13	14	15	16	17	18	19	20
r 1	3726	4003	4271	4530	4780	5021	5254	5479	5695	5904
2	0624	0732	0847	0968	1095	1228	1366	1509	1656	1808
3	0049	0063	0079	0098	0120	0144	0171	0202	0235	0272
4	0001	0002	0003	0004	0005	0007	0008	0010	0013	0016

p	21	22	23	24	25	26	27	28	29	30
r 1	6105	6298	6485	6664	6836	7001	7160	7313	7459	7599
2	1963	2122	2285	2450	2617	2787	2959	3132	3307	3483
3	0312	0356	0403	0453	0508	0566	0628	0694	0763	0837
4	0019	0023	0028	0033	0039	0046	0053	0061	0071	0081

p	31	32	33	34	35	36	37	38	39	40
r 1	7733	7862	7985	8103	8215	8322	8425	8522	8615	8704
2	3660	3837	4015	4193	4370	4547	4724	4900	5075	5248
3	0915	0996	1082	1171	1265	1362	1464	1569	1679	1792
4	0092	0105	0119	0134	0150	0168	0187	0209	0231	0256

p	41	42	43	44	45	46	47	48	49	50
r 1	8788	8868	8944	9017	9085	9150	9211	9269	9323	9375
2	5420	5590	5759	5926	6090	6252	6412	6569	6724	6875
3	1909	2030	2155	2283	2415	2550	2689	2831	2977	3125
4	0283	0311	0342	0375	0410	0448	0488	0531	0576	0625

n = 5

p	01	02	03	04	05	06	07	08	09	10
r 1	0490	0961	1413	1846	2262	2661	3043	3409	3760	4095
2	0010	0038	0085	0148	0226	0319	0425	0544	0674	0815
3		0001	0003	0006	0012	0020	0031	0045	0063	0086
4						0001	0001	0002	0003	0005

p	11	12	13	14	15	16	17	18	19	20
r 1	4416	4723	5016	5296	5563	5818	6061	6293	6513	6723
2	0965	1125	1292	1467	1648	1835	2027	2224	2424	2627
3	0112	0143	0179	0220	0266	0318	0375	0437	0505	0579
4	0007	0009	0013	0017	0022	0029	0036	0045	0055	0067
5				0001	0001	0001	0001	0002	0002	0003

p	21	22	23	24	25	26	27	28	29	30
r 1	6923	7113	7293	7464	7627	7781	7927	8065	8196	8319
2	2833	3041	3251	3461	3672	3883	4093	4303	4511	4718
3	0659	0744	0836	0933	1035	1143	1257	1376	1501	1631
4	0081	0097	0114	0134	0156	0181	0208	0238	0272	0308
5	0004	0005	0006	0008	0010	0012	0014	0017	0021	0024

Appendix A (*cont.*)

CUMULATIVE BINOMIAL DISTRIBUTION $n = 5$

p	31	32	33	34	35	36	37	38	39	40
r 1	8436	8546	8650	8748	8840	8926	9008	9084	9155	9222
2	4923	5125	5325	5522	5716	5906	6093	6276	6455	6630
3	1766	1905	2050	2199	2352	2509	2670	2835	3003	3174
4	0347	0390	0436	0486	0540	0598	0660	0726	0796	0870
5	0029	0034	0039	0045	0053	0060	0069	0079	0090	0102

p	41	42	43	44	45	46	47	48	49	50
r 1	9285	9344	9398	9449	9497	9541	9582	9620	9655	9688
2	6801	6967	7129	7286	7438	7585	7728	7865	7998	8125
3	3349	3525	3705	3886	4069	4253	4439	4625	4813	5000
4	0949	1033	1121	1214	1312	1415	1522	1635	1753	1875
5	0116	0131	0147	0165	0185	0206	0229	0255	0282	0313

$$n = 6$$

p	01	02	03	04	05	06	07	08	09	10
r 1	0585	1142	1670	2172	2649	3101	3530	3936	4321	4686
2	0015	0057	0125	0216	0328	0459	0608	0773	0952	1143
3		0002	0005	0012	0022	0038	0058	0085	0118	0159
4					0001	0002	0003	0005	0008	0013
5										0001

p	11	12	13	14	15	16	17	18	19	20
r 1	5030	5356	5664	5954	6229	6487	6731	6960	7176	7379
2	1345	1556	1776	2003	2235	2472	2713	2956	3201	3446
3	0206	0261	0324	0395	0473	0560	0655	0759	0870	0989
4	0018	0025	0034	0045	0059	0075	0094	0116	0141	0170
5	0001	0001	0002	0003	0004	0005	0007	0010	0013	0016
6										0001

p	21	22	23	24	25	26	27	28	29	30
r 1	7569	7748	7916	8073	8220	8358	8487	8607	8719	8824
2	3692	3937	4180	4422	4661	4896	5128	5356	5580	5798
3	1115	1250	1391	1539	1694	1856	2023	2196	2374	2557
4	0202	0239	0280	0326	0376	0431	0492	0557	0628	0705
5	0020	0025	0031	0038	0046	0056	0067	0079	0093	0109
6	0001	0001	0001	0002	0002	0003	0004	0005	0006	0007

p	31	32	33	34	35	36	37	38	39	40
r 1	8921	9011	9095	9173	9246	9313	9375	9432	9485	9533
2	6012	6220	6422	6619	6809	6994	7172	7343	7508	7667
3	2744	2936	3130	3328	3529	3732	3937	4143	4350	4557
4	0787	0875	0969	1069	1174	1286	1404	1527	1657	1792
5	0127	0148	0170	0195	0223	0254	0288	0325	0365	0410
6	0009	0011	0013	0015	0018	0022	0026	0030	0035	0041

p	41	42	43	44	45	46	47	48	49	50
r 1	9578	9619	9657	9692	9723	9752	9778	9802	9824	9844
2	7819	7965	8105	8238	8364	8485	8599	8707	8810	8906
3	4764	4971	5177	5382	5585	5786	5985	6180	6373	6563
4	1933	2080	2232	2390	2553	2721	2893	3070	3252	3438
5	0458	0510	0566	0627	0692	0762	0837	0917	1003	1094
6	0048	0055	0063	0073	0083	0095	0108	0122	0138	0156

Appendix A (*cont.*)

$n = 7$

CUMULATIVE BINOMIAL DISTRIBUTION

$n = 7$

p	01	02	03	04	05	06	07	08	09	10
r 1	0679	1319	1920	2486	3017	3515	3983	4422	4832	5217
2	0020	0079	0171	0294	0444	0618	0813	1026	1255	1497
3		0003	0009	0020	0038	0063	0097	0140	0193	0257
4				0001	0002	0004	0007	0012	0018	0027
5								0001	0001	0002

p	11	12	13	14	15	16	17	18	19	20
r 1	5577	5913	6227	6521	6794	7049	7286	7507	7712	7903
2	1750	2012	2281	2556	2834	3115	3396	3677	3956	4233
3	0331	0416	0513	0620	0738	0866	1005	1154	1313	1480
4	0039	0054	0072	0094	0121	0153	0189	0231	0279	0333
5	0003	0004	0006	0009	0012	0017	0022	0029	0037	0047
6					0001	0001	0001	0002	0003	0004

p	21	22	23	24	25	26	27	28	29	30
r 1	8080	8243	8395	8535	8665	8785	8895	8997	9090	9176
2	4506	4775	5040	5298	5551	5796	6035	6266	6490	6706
3	1657	1841	2033	2231	2436	2646	2861	3081	3304	3529
4	0394	0461	0536	0617	0706	0802	0905	1016	1134	1260
5	0058	0072	0088	0107	0129	0153	0181	0213	0248	0288
6	0005	0006	0008	0011	0013	0017	0021	0026	0031	0038
7					0001	0001	0001	0001	0002	0002

p	31	32	33	34	35	36	37	38	39	40
r 1	9255	9328	9394	9454	9510	9560	9606	9648	9686	9720
2	6914	7113	7304	7487	7662	7828	7987	8137	8279	8414
3	3757	3987	4217	4447	4677	4906	5134	5359	5581	5801
4	1394	1534	1682	1837	1998	2167	2341	2521	2707	2898
5	0332	0380	0434	0492	0556	0625	0701	0782	0869	0963
6	0046	0055	0065	0077	0090	0105	0123	0142	0164	0188
7	0003	0003	0004	0005	0006	0008	0009	0011	0014	0016

p	41	42	43	44	45	46	47	48	49	50
r 1	9751	9779	9805	9827	9848	9866	9883	9897	9910	9922
2	8541	8660	8772	8877	8976	9068	9153	9233	9307	9375
3	6017	6229	6436	6638	6836	7027	7213	7393	7567	7734
4	3094	3294	3498	3706	3917	4131	4346	4563	4781	5000
5	1063	1169	1282	1402	1529	1663	1803	1951	2105	2266
6	0216	0246	0279	0316	0357	0402	0451	0504	0562	0625
7	0019	0023	0027	0032	0037	0044	0051	0059	0068	0078

$n = 8$

p	01	02	03	04	05	06	07	08	09	10
r 1	0773	1492	2163	2786	3366	3904	4404	4868	5297	5695
2	0027	0103	0223	0381	0572	0792	1035	1298	1577	1869
3	0001	0004	0013	0031	0058	0096	0147	0211	0289	0381
4			0001	0002	0004	0007	0013	0022	0034	0050
5							0001	0001	0003	0004

Appendix A (cont.)

CUMULATIVE BINOMIAL DISTRIBUTION $n = 8$

r	p	11	12	13	14	15	16	17	18	19	20
	1	6063	6404	6718	7008	7275	7521	7748	7956	8147	8322
	2	2171	2480	2794	3111	3428	3744	4057	4366	4670	4967
	3	0487	0608	0743	0891	1052	1226	1412	1608	1815	2031
	4	0071	0097	0129	0168	0214	0267	0328	0397	0476	0563
	5	0007	0010	0015	0021	0029	0038	0050	0065	0083	0104
	6		0001	0001	0002	0002	0003	0005	0007	0009	0012
	7									0001	0001

r	p	21	22	23	24	25	26	27	28	29	30
	1	8483	8630	8764	8887	8999	9101	9194	9278	9354	9424
	2	5257	5538	5811	6075	6329	6573	6807	7031	7244	7447
	3	2255	2486	2724	2967	3215	3465	3718	3973	4228	4482
	4	0659	0765	0880	1004	1138	1281	1433	1594	1763	1941
	5	0129	0158	0191	0230	0273	0322	0377	0438	0505	0580
	6	0016	0021	0027	0034	0042	0052	0064	0078	0094	0113
	7	0001	0002	0002	0003	0004	0005	0006	0008	0010	0013
	8									0001	0001

r	p	31	32	33	34	35	36	37	38	39	40
	1	9486	9543	9594	9640	9681	9719	9752	9782	9808	9832
	2	7640	7822	7994	8156	8309	8452	8586	8711	8828	8936
	3	4736	4987	5236	5481	5722	5958	6189	6415	6634	6846
	4	2126	2319	2519	2724	2936	3153	3374	3599	3828	4059
	5	0661	0750	0846	0949	1061	1180	1307	1443	1586	1737
	6	0134	0159	0187	0218	0253	0293	0336	0385	0439	0498
	7	0016	0020	0024	0030	0036	0043	0051	0061	0072	0085
	8	0001	0001	0001	0002	0002	0003	0004	0004	0005	0007

r	p	41	42	43	44	45	46	47	48	49	50
	1	9853	9872	9889	9903	9916	9928	9938	9947	9954	9961
	2	9037	9130	9216	9295	9368	9435	9496	9552	9602	9648
	3	7052	7250	7440	7624	7799	7966	8125	8276	8419	8555
	4	4292	4527	4762	4996	5230	5463	5694	5922	6146	6367
	5	1895	2062	2235	2416	2604	2798	2999	3205	3416	3633
	6	0563	0634	0711	0794	0885	0982	1086	1198	1318	1445
	7	0100	0117	0136	0157	0181	0208	0239	0272	0310	0352
	8	0008	0010	0012	0014	0017	0020	0024	0028	0033	0039

$n = 9$

r	p	01	02	03	04	05	06	07	08	09	10
	1	0865	1663	2398	3075	3698	4270	4796	5278	5721	6126
	2	0034	0131	0282	0478	0712	0978	1271	1583	1912	2252
	3	0001	0006	0020	0045	0084	0138	0209	0298	0405	0530
	4			0001	0003	0006	0013	0023	0037	0057	0083
	5						0001	0002	0003	0005	0009
	6										0001

Appendix A (cont.)

n = 9   CUMULATIVE BINOMIAL DISTRIBUTION

p	11	12	13	14	15	16	17	18	19	20
r 1	6496	6835	7145	7427	7684	7918	8131	8324	8499	8658
2	2599	2951	3304	3657	4005	4348	4685	5012	5330	5638
3	0672	0833	1009	1202	1409	1629	1861	2105	2357	2618
4	0117	0158	0209	0269	0339	0420	0512	0615	0730	0856
5	0014	0021	0030	0041	0056	0075	0098	0125	0158	0196
6	0001	0002	0003	0004	0006	0009	0013	0017	0023	0031
7						0001	0001	0002	0002	0003

p	21	22	23	24	25	26	27	28	29	30
r 1	8801	8931	9048	9154	9249	9335	9411	9480	9542	9596
2	5934	6218	6491	6750	6997	7230	7452	7660	7856	8040
3	2885	3158	3434	3713	3993	4273	4552	4829	5102	5372
4	0994	1144	1304	1475	1657	1849	2050	2260	2478	2703
5	0240	0291	0350	0416	0489	0571	0662	0762	0870	0988
6	0040	0051	0065	0081	0100	0122	0149	0179	0213	0253
7	0004	0006	0008	0010	0013	0017	0022	0028	0035	0043
8			0001	0001	0001	0001	0002	0003	0003	0004

p	31	32	33	34	35	36	37	38	39	40
r 1	9645	9689	9728	9762	9793	9820	9844	9865	9883	9899
2	8212	8372	8522	8661	8789	8908	9017	9118	9210	9295
3	5636	5894	6146	6390	6627	6856	7076	7287	7489	7682
4	2935	3173	3415	3662	3911	4163	4416	4669	4922	5174
5	1115	1252	1398	1553	1717	1890	2072	2262	2460	2666
6	0298	0348	0404	0467	0536	0612	0696	0787	0886	0994
7	0053	0064	0078	0094	0112	0133	0157	0184	0215	0250
8	0006	0007	0009	0011	0014	0017	0021	0026	0031	0038
9				0001	0001	0001	0001	0002	0002	0003

p	41	42	43	44	45	46	47	48	49	50
r 1	9913	9926	9936	9946	9954	9961	9967	9972	9977	9980
2	9372	9442	9505	9563	9615	9662	9704	9741	9775	9805
3	7866	8039	8204	8359	8505	8642	8769	8889	8999	9102
4	5424	5670	5913	6152	6386	6614	6836	7052	7260	7461
5	2878	3097	3322	3551	3786	4024	4265	4509	4754	5000
6	1109	1233	1366	1508	1658	1817	1985	2161	2346	2539
7	0290	0334	0383	0437	0498	0564	0637	0717	0804	0898
8	0046	0055	0065	0077	0091	0107	0125	0145	0169	0195
9	0003	0004	0005	0006	0008	0009	0011	0014	0016	0020

n = 10

p	01	02	03	04	05	06	07	08	09	10
r 1	0956	1829	2626	3352	4013	4614	5160	5656	6106	6513
2	0043	0162	0345	0582	0861	1176	1517	1879	2254	2639
3	0001	0009	0028	0062	0115	0188	0283	0401	0540	0702
4			0001	0004	0010	0020	0036	0058	0088	0128
5					0001	0002	0003	0006	0010	0016
6									0001	0001

Appendix A (cont.)

CUMULATIVE BINOMIAL DISTRIBUTION $n = 10$

p r	11	12	13	14	15	16	17	18	19	20
1	6882	7215	7516	7787	8031	8251	8448	8626	8784	8926
2	3028	3417	3804	4184	4557	4920	5270	5608	5932	6242
3	0884	1087	1308	1545	1798	2064	2341	2628	2922	3222
4	0178	0239	0313	0400	0500	0614	0741	0883	1039	1209
5	0025	0037	0053	0073	0099	0130	0168	0213	0266	0328
6	0003	0004	0006	0010	0014	0020	0027	0037	0049	0064
7			0001	0001	0001	0002	0003	0004	0006	0009
8									0001	0001

p r	21	22	23	24	25	26	27	28	29	30
1	9053	9166	9267	9357	9437	9508	9570	9626	9674	9718
2	6536	6815	7079	7327	7560	7778	7981	8170	8345	8507
3	3526	3831	4137	4442	4744	5042	5335	5622	5901	6172
4	1391	1587	1794	2012	2241	2479	2726	2979	3239	3504
5	0399	0479	0569	0670	0781	0904	1037	1181	1337	1503
6	0082	0104	0130	0161	0197	0239	0287	0342	0404	0473
7	0012	0016	0021	0027	0035	0045	0056	0070	0087	0106
8	0001	0002	0002	0003	0004	0006	0007	0010	0012	0016
9							0001	0001	0001	0001

p r	31	32	33	34	35	36	37	38	39	40
1	9755	9789	9818	9843	9865	9885	9902	9916	9929	9940
2	8656	8794	8920	9035	9140	9236	9323	9402	9473	9536
3	6434	6687	6930	7162	7384	7595	7794	7983	8160	8327
4	3772	4044	4316	4589	4862	5132	5400	5664	5923	6177
5	1679	1867	2064	2270	2485	2708	2939	3177	3420	3669
6	0551	0637	0732	0836	0949	1072	1205	1348	1500	1662
7	0129	0155	0185	0220	0260	0305	0356	0413	0477	0548
8	0020	0025	0032	0039	0048	0059	0071	0086	0103	0123
9	0002	0003	0003	0004	0005	0007	0009	0011	0014	0017
10								0001	0001	0001

p r	41	42	43	44	45	46	47	48	49	50
1	9949	9957	9964	9970	9975	9979	9983	9986	9988	9990
2	9594	9645	9691	9731	9767	9799	9827	9852	9874	9893
3	8483	8628	8764	8889	9004	9111	9209	9298	9379	9453
4	6425	6665	6898	7123	7340	7547	7745	7933	8112	8281
5	3922	4178	4436	4696	4956	5216	5474	5730	5982	6230
6	1834	2016	2207	2407	2616	2832	3057	3288	3526	3770
7	0626	0712	0806	0908	1020	1141	1271	1410	1560	1719
8	0146	0172	0202	0236	0274	0317	0366	0420	0480	0547
9	0021	0025	0031	0037	0045	0054	0065	0077	0091	0107
10	0001	0002	0002	0003	0003	0004	0005	0006	0008	0010

Appendix A (cont.)

n = 11   CUMULATIVE BINOMIAL DISTRIBUTION

$n = 11$

p	01	02	03	04	05	06	07	08	09	10
r 1	1047	1993	2847	3618	4312	4937	5499	6004	6456	6862
2	0052	0195	0413	0692	1019	1382	1772	2181	2601	3026
3	0002	0012	0037	0083	0152	0248	0370	0519	0695	0896
4			0002	0007	0016	0030	0053	0085	0129	0185
5					0001	0003	0005	0010	0017	0028
6								0001	0002	0003

p	11	12	13	14	15	16	17	18	19	20
r 1	7225	7549	7839	8097	8327	8531	8712	8873	9015	9141
2	3452	3873	4286	4689	5078	5453	5811	6151	6474	6779
3	1120	1366	1632	1915	2212	2521	2839	3164	3494	3826
4	0256	0341	0442	0560	0694	0846	1013	1197	1397	1611
5	0042	0061	0087	0119	0159	0207	0266	0334	0413	0504
6	0005	0008	0012	0018	0027	0037	0051	0068	0090	0117
7		0001	0001	0002	0003	0005	0007	0010	0014	0020
8							0001	0001	0002	0002

p	21	22	23	24	25	26	27	28	29	30
r 1	9252	9350	9436	9511	9578	9636	9686	9730	9769	9802
2	7065	7333	7582	7814	8029	8227	8410	8577	8730	8870
3	4158	4488	4814	5134	5448	5753	6049	6335	6610	6873
4	1840	2081	2333	2596	2867	3146	3430	3719	4011	4304
5	0607	0723	0851	0992	1146	1313	1493	1685	1888	2103
6	0148	0186	0231	0283	0343	0412	0490	0577	0674	0782
7	0027	0035	0046	0059	0076	0095	0119	0146	0179	0216
8	0003	0005	0007	0009	0012	0016	0021	0027	0034	0043
9			0001	0001	0001	0002	0002	0003	0004	0006

p	31	32	33	34	35	36	37	38	39	40
r 1	9831	9856	9878	9896	9912	9926	9938	9948	9956	9964
2	8997	9112	9216	9310	9394	9470	9537	9597	9650	9698
3	7123	7361	7587	7799	7999	8186	8360	8522	8672	8811
4	4598	4890	5179	5464	5744	6019	6286	6545	6796	7037
5	2328	2563	2807	3059	3317	3581	3850	4122	4397	4672
6	0901	1031	1171	1324	1487	1661	1847	2043	2249	2465
7	0260	0309	0366	0430	0501	0581	0670	0768	0876	0994
8	0054	0067	0082	0101	0122	0148	0177	0210	0249	0293
9	0008	0010	0013	0016	0020	0026	0032	0039	0048	0059
10	0001	0001	0001	0002	0002	0003	0004	0005	0006	0007

Appendix A (cont.)

CUMULATIVE BINOMIAL DISTRIBUTION　　　　$n = 11$

p / r	41	42	43	44	45	46	47	48	49	50
1	9970	9975	9979	9983	9986	9989	9991	9992	9994	9995
2	9739	9776	9808	9836	9861	9882	9900	9916	9930	9941
3	8938	9055	9162	9260	9348	9428	9499	9564	9622	9673
4	7269	7490	7700	7900	8089	8266	8433	8588	8733	8867
5	4948	5223	5495	5764	6029	6288	6541	6787	7026	7256
6	2690	2924	3166	3414	3669	3929	4193	4460	4729	5000
7	1121	1260	1408	1568	1738	1919	2110	2312	2523	2744
8	0343	0399	0461	0532	0610	0696	0791	0895	1009	1133
9	0072	0087	0104	0125	0148	0175	0206	0241	0282	0327
10	0009	0012	0014	0018	0022	0027	0033	0040	0049	0059
11	0001	0001	0001	0001	0002	0002	0002	0003	0004	0005

$n = 12$

p / r	01	02	03	04	05	06	07	08	09	10
1	1136	2153	3062	3873	4596	5241	5814	6323	6775	7176
2	0062	0231	0486	0809	1184	1595	2033	2487	2948	3410
3	0002	0015	0048	0107	0196	0316	0468	0652	0866	1109
4		0001	0003	0010	0022	0043	0075	0120	0180	0256
5				0001	0002	0004	0009	0016	0027	0043
6							0001	0002	0003	0005
7										0001

p / r	11	12	13	14	15	16	17	18	19	20
1	7530	7843	8120	8363	8578	8766	8931	9076	9202	9313
2	3867	4314	4748	5166	5565	5945	6304	6641	6957	7251
3	1377	1667	1977	2303	2642	2990	3344	3702	4060	4417
4	0351	0464	0597	0750	0922	1114	1324	1552	1795	2054
5	0065	0095	0133	0181	0239	0310	0393	0489	0600	0726
6	0009	0014	0022	0033	0046	0065	0088	0116	0151	0194
7	0001	0002	0003	0004	0007	0010	0015	0021	0029	0039
8					0001	0001	0002	0003	0004	0006
9										0001

p / r	21	22	23	24	25	26	27	28	29	30
1	9409	9493	9566	9629	9683	9730	9771	9806	9836	9862
2	7524	7776	8009	8222	8416	8594	8755	8900	9032	9150
3	4768	5114	5450	5778	6093	6397	6687	6963	7225	7472
4	2326	2610	2904	3205	3512	3824	4137	4452	4765	5075
5	0866	1021	1192	1377	1576	1790	2016	2254	2504	2763
6	0245	0304	0374	0453	0544	0646	0760	0887	1026	1178
7	0052	0068	0089	0113	0143	0178	0219	0267	0322	0386
8	0008	0011	0016	0021	0028	0036	0047	0060	0076	0095
9	0001	0001	0002	0003	0004	0005	0007	0010	0013	0017
10						0001	0001	0001	0002	0002

Appendix A (cont.)

$n = 12$ CUMULATIVE BINOMIAL DISTRIBUTION

p	31	32	33	34	35	36	37	38	39	40
r 1	9884	9902	9918	9932	9943	9953	9961	9968	9973	9978
2	9256	9350	9435	9509	9576	9634	9685	9730	9770	9804
3	7704	7922	8124	8313	8487	8648	8795	8931	9054	9166
4	5381	5681	5973	6258	6533	6799	7053	7296	7528	7747
5	3032	3308	3590	3876	4167	4459	4751	5043	5332	5618
6	1343	1521	1711	1913	2127	2352	2588	2833	3087	3348
7	0458	0540	0632	0734	0846	0970	1106	1253	1411	1582
8	0118	0144	0176	0213	0255	0304	0359	0422	0493	0573
9	0022	0028	0036	0045	0056	0070	0086	0104	0127	0153
10	0003	0004	0005	0007	0008	0011	0014	0018	0022	0028
11				0001	0001	0001	0001	0002	0002	0003

p	41	42	43	44	45	46	47	48	49	50
r 1	9982	9986	9988	9990	9992	9994	9995	9996	9997	9998
2	9834	9860	9882	9901	9917	9931	9943	9953	9961	9968
3	9267	9358	9440	9513	9579	9637	9688	9733	9773	9807
4	7953	8147	8329	8498	8655	8801	8934	9057	9168	9270
5	5899	6175	6443	6704	6956	7198	7430	7652	7862	8062
6	3616	3889	4167	4448	4731	5014	5297	5577	5855	6128
7	1765	1959	2164	2380	2607	2843	3089	3343	3604	3872
8	0662	0760	0869	0988	1117	1258	1411	1575	1751	1938
9	0183	0218	0258	0304	0356	0415	0481	0555	0638	0730
10	0035	0043	0053	0065	0079	0095	0114	0137	0163	0193
11	0004	0005	0007	0009	0011	0014	0017	0021	0026	0032
12				0001	0001	0001	0001	0001	0002	0002

$n = 13$

p	01	02	03	04	05	06	07	08	09	10
r 1	1225	2310	3270	4118	4867	5526	6107	6617	7065	7458
2	0072	0270	0564	0932	1354	1814	2298	2794	3293	3787
3	0003	0020	0062	0135	0245	0392	0578	0799	1054	1339
4		0001	0005	0014	0031	0060	0103	0163	0242	0342
5				0001	0003	0007	0013	0024	0041	0065
6						0001	0001	0003	0005	0009
7									0001	0001

p	11	12	13	14	15	16	17	18	19	20
r 1	7802	8102	8364	8592	8791	8963	9113	9242	9354	9450
2	4270	4738	5186	5614	6017	6396	6751	7080	7384	7664
3	1651	1985	2337	2704	3080	3463	3848	4231	4611	4983
4	0464	0609	0776	0967	1180	1414	1667	1939	2226	2527
5	0097	0139	0193	0260	0342	0438	0551	0681	0827	0991
6	0015	0024	0036	0053	0075	0104	0139	0183	0237	0300
7	0002	0003	0005	0008	0013	0019	0027	0038	0052	0070
8			0001	0001	0002	0003	0004	0006	0009	0012
9								0001	0001	0002

Appendix A (cont.)

CUMULATIVE BINOMIAL DISTRIBUTION $n = 13$

p	21	22	23	24	25	26	27	28	29	30
r 1	9533	9604	9666	9718	9762	9800	9833	9860	9883	9903
2	7920	8154	8367	8559	8733	8889	9029	9154	9265	9363
3	5347	5699	6039	6364	6674	6968	7245	7505	7749	7975
4	2839	3161	3489	3822	4157	4493	4826	5155	5478	5794
5	1173	1371	1585	1816	2060	2319	2589	2870	3160	3457
6	0375	0462	0562	0675	0802	0944	1099	1270	1455	1654
7	0093	0120	0154	0195	0243	0299	0365	0440	0527	0624
8	0017	0024	0032	0043	0056	0073	0093	0118	0147	0182
9	0002	0004	0005	0007	0010	0013	0018	0024	0031	0040
10			0001	0001	0001	0002	0003	0004	0005	0007
11									0001	0001

p	31	32	33	34	35	36	37	38	39	40
r 1	9920	9934	9945	9955	9963	9970	9975	9980	9984	9987
2	9450	9527	9594	9653	9704	9749	9787	9821	9849	9874
3	8185	8379	8557	8720	8868	9003	9125	9235	9333	9421
4	6101	6398	6683	6957	7217	7464	7698	7917	8123	8314
5	3760	4067	4376	4686	4995	5301	5603	5899	6188	6470
6	1867	2093	2331	2581	2841	3111	3388	3673	3962	4256
7	0733	0854	0988	1135	1295	1468	1654	1853	2065	2288
8	0223	0271	0326	0390	0462	0544	0635	0738	0851	0977
9	0052	0065	0082	0102	0126	0154	0187	0225	0270	0321
10	0009	0012	0015	0020	0025	0032	0040	0051	0063	0078
11	0001	0001	0002	0003	0003	0005	0006	0008	0010	0013
12							0001	0001	0001	0001

p	41	42	43	44	45	46	47	48	49	50
r 1	9990	9992	9993	9995	9996	9997	9997	9998	9998	9999
2	9895	9912	9928	9940	9951	9960	9967	9974	9979	9983
3	9499	9569	9630	9684	9731	9772	9808	9838	9865	9888
4	8492	8656	8807	8945	9071	9185	9288	9381	9464	9539
5	6742	7003	7254	7493	7721	7935	8137	8326	8502	8666
6	4552	4849	5146	5441	5732	6019	6299	6573	6838	7095
7	2524	2770	3025	3290	3563	3842	4127	4415	4707	5000
8	1114	1264	1426	1600	1788	1988	2200	2424	2659	2905
9	0379	0446	0520	0605	0698	0803	0918	1045	1183	1334
10	0096	0117	0141	0170	0203	0242	0287	0338	0396	0461
11	0017	0021	0027	0033	0041	0051	0063	0077	0093	0112
12	0002	0002	0003	0004	0005	0007	0009	0011	0014	0017
13							0001	0001	0001	0001

$$n = 14$$

p	01	02	03	04	05	06	07	08	09	10
r 1	1313	2464	3472	4353	5123	5795	6380	6888	7330	7712
2	0084	0310	0645	1059	1530	2037	2564	3100	3632	4154
3	0003	0025	0077	0167	0301	0478	0698	0958	1255	1584
4		0001	0006	0019	0042	0080	0136	0214	0315	0441
5				0002	0004	0010	0020	0035	0059	0092
6						0001	0002	0004	0008	0015
7									0001	0002

Appendix A (cont.)

n = 14   CUMULATIVE BINOMIAL DISTRIBUTION

p	11	12	13	14	15	16	17	18	19	20
r 1	8044	8330	8577	8789	8972	9129	9264	9379	9477	9560
2	4658	5141	5599	6031	6433	6807	7152	7469	7758	8021
3	1939	2315	2708	3111	3521	3932	4341	4744	5138	5519
4	0594	0774	0979	1210	1465	1742	2038	2351	2679	3018
5	0137	0196	0269	0359	0467	0594	0741	0907	1093	1298
6	0024	0038	0057	0082	0115	0157	0209	0273	0349	0439
7	0003	0006	0009	0015	0022	0032	0046	0064	0087	0116
8		0001	0001	0002	0003	0005	0008	0012	0017	0024
9						0001	0001	0002	0003	0004

p	21	22	23	24	25	26	27	28	29	30
r 1	9631	9691	9742	9786	9822	9852	9878	9899	9917	9932
2	8259	8473	8665	8837	8990	9126	9246	9352	9444	9525
3	5887	6239	6574	6891	7189	7467	7727	7967	8188	8392
4	3366	3719	4076	4432	4787	5136	5479	5813	6137	6448
5	1523	1765	2023	2297	2585	2884	3193	3509	3832	4158
6	0543	0662	0797	0949	1117	1301	1502	1718	1949	2195
7	0152	0196	0248	0310	0383	0467	0563	0673	0796	0933
8	0033	0045	0060	0079	0103	0132	0167	0208	0257	0315
9	0006	0008	0011	0016	0022	0029	0038	0050	0065	0083
10	0001	0001	0002	0002	0003	0005	0007	0009	0012	0017
11						0001	0001	0001	0002	0002

p	31	32	33	34	35	36	37	38	39	40
r 1	9945	9955	9963	9970	9976	9981	9984	9988	9990	9992
2	9596	9657	9710	9756	9795	9828	9857	9881	9902	9919
3	8577	8746	8899	9037	9161	9271	9370	9457	9534	9602
4	6747	7032	7301	7556	7795	8018	8226	8418	8595	8757
5	4486	4813	5138	5458	5773	6080	6378	6666	6943	7207
6	2454	2724	3006	3297	3595	3899	4208	4519	4831	5141
7	1084	1250	1431	1626	1836	2059	2296	2545	2805	3075
8	0381	0458	0545	0643	0753	0876	1012	1162	1325	1501
9	0105	0131	0163	0200	0243	0294	0353	0420	0497	0583
10	0022	0029	0037	0048	0060	0076	0095	0117	0144	0175
11	0003	0005	0006	0008	0011	0014	0019	0024	0031	0039
12		0001	0001	0001	0001	0002	0003	0003	0005	0006
13										0001

p	41	42	43	44	45	46	47	48	49	50
r 1	9994	9995	9996	9997	9998	9998	9999	9999	9999	9999
2	9934	9946	9956	9964	9971	9977	9981	9985	9988	9991
3	9661	9713	9758	9797	9830	9858	9883	9903	9921	9935
4	8905	9039	9161	9270	9368	9455	9532	9601	9661	9713
5	7459	7697	7922	8132	8328	8510	8678	8833	8974	9102
6	5450	5754	6052	6344	6627	6900	7163	7415	7654	7880
7	3355	3643	3937	4236	4539	4843	5148	5451	5751	6047
8	1692	1896	2113	2344	2586	2840	3105	3380	3663	3953
9	0680	0789	0910	1043	1189	1348	1520	1707	1906	2120
10	0212	0255	0304	0361	0426	0500	0583	0677	0782	0898
11	0049	0061	0076	0093	0114	0139	0168	0202	0241	0287
12	0008	0010	0013	0017	0022	0027	0034	0042	0053	0065
13	0001	0001	0001	0002	0003	0003	0004	0006	0007	0009
14										0001

Appendix A (cont.)

CUMULATIVE BINOMIAL DISTRIBUTION $n = 15$

$n = 15$

p	01	02	03	04	05	06	07	08	09	10
r 1	1399	2614	3667	4579	5367	6047	6633	7137	7570	7941
2	0096	0353	0730	1191	1710	2262	2832	3403	3965	4510
3	0004	0030	0094	0203	0362	0571	0829	1130	1469	1841
4		0002	0008	0024	0055	0104	0175	0273	0399	0556
5			0001	0002	0006	0014	0028	0050	0082	0127
6					0001	0001	0003	0007	0013	0022
7								0001	0002	0003

p	11	12	13	14	15	16	17	18	19	20
r 1	8259	8530	8762	8959	9126	9269	9389	9490	9576	9648
2	5031	5524	5987	6417	6814	7179	7511	7813	8085	8329
3	2238	2654	3084	3520	3958	4392	4819	5234	5635	6020
4	0742	0959	1204	1476	1773	2092	2429	2782	3146	3518
5	0187	0265	0361	0478	0617	0778	0961	1167	1394	1642
6	0037	0057	0084	0121	0168	0227	0300	0387	0490	0611
7	0006	0010	0015	0024	0036	0052	0074	0102	0137	0181
8	0001	0001	0002	0004	0006	0010	0014	0021	0030	0042
9					0001	0001	0002	0003	0005	0008
10									0001	0001

p	21	22	23	24	25	26	27	28	29	30
r 1	9709	9759	9802	9837	9866	9891	9911	9928	9941	9953
2	8547	8741	8913	9065	9198	9315	9417	9505	9581	9647
3	6385	6731	7055	7358	7639	7899	8137	8355	8553	8732
4	3895	4274	4650	5022	5387	5742	6086	6416	6732	7031
5	1910	2195	2495	2810	3135	3469	3810	4154	4500	4845
6	0748	0905	1079	1272	1484	1713	1958	2220	2495	2784
7	0234	0298	0374	0463	0566	0684	0817	0965	1130	1311
8	0058	0078	0104	0135	0173	0219	0274	0338	0413	0500
9	0011	0016	0023	0031	0042	0056	0073	0094	0121	0152
10	0002	0003	0004	0006	0008	0011	0015	0021	0028	0037
11			0001	0001	0001	0002	0002	0003	0005	0007
12									0001	0001

p	31	32	33	34	35	36	37	38	39	40
r 1	9962	9969	9975	9980	9984	9988	9990	9992	9994	9995
2	9704	9752	9794	9829	9858	9883	9904	9922	9936	9948
3	8893	9038	9167	9281	9383	9472	9550	9618	9678	9729
4	7314	7580	7829	8060	8273	8469	8649	8813	8961	9095
5	5187	5523	5852	6171	6481	6778	7062	7332	7587	7827
6	3084	3393	3709	4032	4357	4684	5011	5335	5654	5968
7	1509	1722	1951	2194	2452	2722	3003	3295	3595	3902
8	0599	0711	0837	0977	1132	1302	1487	1687	1902	2131
9	0190	0236	0289	0351	0422	0504	0597	0702	0820	0950
10	0048	0062	0079	0099	0124	0154	0190	0232	0281	0338
11	0009	0012	0016	0022	0028	0037	0047	0059	0075	0093
12	0001	0002	0003	0004	0005	0006	0009	0011	0015	0019
13					0001	0001	0001	0002	0002	0003

Appendix A *(cont.)*

$n = 15$ CUMULATIVE BINOMIAL DISTRIBUTION

p	41	42	43	44	45	46	47	48	49	50
r 1	9996	9997	9998	9998	9999	9999	9999	9999	10000	10000
2	9958	9966	9973	9979	9983	9987	9990	9992	9994	9995
3	9773	9811	9843	9870	9893	9913	9929	9943	9954	9963
4	9215	9322	9417	9502	9576	9641	9697	9746	9788	9824
5	8052	8261	8454	8633	8796	8945	9080	9201	9310	9408
6	6274	6570	6856	7131	7392	7641	7875	8095	8301	8491
7	4214	4530	4847	5164	5478	5789	6095	6394	6684	6964
8	2374	2630	2898	3176	3465	3762	4065	4374	4686	5000
9	1095	1254	1427	1615	1818	2034	2265	2510	2767	3036
10	0404	0479	0565	0661	0769	0890	1024	1171	1333	1509
11	0116	0143	0174	0211	0255	0305	0363	0430	0506	0592
12	0025	0032	0040	0051	0063	0079	0097	0119	0145	0176
13	0004	0005	0007	0009	0011	0014	0018	0023	0029	0037
14			0001	0001	0001	0002	0002	0003	0004	0005

$n = 16$

p	01	02	03	04	05	06	07	08	09	10
r 1	1485	2762	3857	4796	5599	6284	6869	7366	7789	8147
2	0109	0399	0818	1327	1892	2489	3098	3701	4289	4853
3	0005	0037	0113	0242	0429	0673	0969	1311	1694	2108
4		0002	0011	0032	0070	0132	0221	0342	0496	0684
5			0001	0003	0009	0019	0038	0068	0111	0170
6					0001	0002	0005	0010	0019	0033
7							0001	0001	0003	0005
8										0001

p	11	12	13	14	15	16	17	18	19	20
r 1	8450	8707	8923	9105	9257	9386	9493	9582	9657	9719
2	5386	5885	6347	6773	7161	7513	7830	8115	8368	8593
3	2545	2999	3461	3926	4386	4838	5277	5698	6101	6482
4	0907	1162	1448	1763	2101	2460	2836	3223	3619	4019
5	0248	0348	0471	0618	0791	0988	1211	1458	1727	2018
6	0053	0082	0120	0171	0235	0315	0412	0527	0662	0817
7	0009	0015	0024	0038	0056	0080	0112	0153	0204	0267
8	0001	0002	0004	0007	0011	0016	0024	0036	0051	0070
9			0001	0001	0002	0003	0004	0007	0010	0015
10							0001	0001	0002	0002

p	21	22	23	24	25	26	27	28	29	30
r 1	9770	9812	9847	9876	9900	9919	9935	9948	9958	9967
2	8791	8965	9117	9250	9365	9465	9550	9623	9686	9739
3	6839	7173	7483	7768	8029	8267	8482	8677	8851	9006
4	4418	4814	5203	5583	5950	6303	6640	6959	7260	7541
5	2327	2652	2991	3341	3698	4060	4425	4788	5147	5501
6	0992	1188	1405	1641	1897	2169	2458	2761	3077	3402
7	0342	0432	0536	0657	0796	0951	1125	1317	1526	1753
8	0095	0127	0166	0214	0271	0340	0420	0514	0621	0744
9	0021	0030	0041	0056	0075	0098	0127	0163	0206	0257
10	0004	0006	0008	0012	0016	0023	0031	0041	0055	0071
11	0001	0001	0001	0002	0003	0004	0006	0008	0011	0016
12						0001	0001	0001	0002	0003

Appendix A (cont.)

CUMULATIVE BINOMIAL DISTRIBUTION $n = 16$

p	31	32	33	34	35	36	37	38	39	40
r 1	9974	9979	9984	9987	9990	9992	9994	9995	9996	9997
2	9784	9822	9854	9880	9902	9921	9936	9948	9959	9967
3	9144	9266	9374	9467	9549	9620	9681	9734	9778	9817
4	7804	8047	8270	8475	8661	8830	8982	9119	9241	9349
5	5846	6181	6504	6813	7108	7387	7649	7895	8123	8334
6	3736	4074	4416	4759	5100	5438	5770	6094	6408	6712
7	1997	2257	2531	2819	3119	3428	3746	4070	4398	4728
8	0881	1035	1205	1391	1594	1813	2048	2298	2562	2839
9	0317	0388	0470	0564	0671	0791	0926	1076	1242	1423
10	0092	0117	0148	0185	0229	0280	0341	0411	0491	0583
11	0021	0028	0037	0048	0062	0079	0100	0125	0155	0191
12	0004	0005	0007	0010	0013	0017	0023	0030	0038	0049
13		0001	0001	0001	0002	0003	0004	0005	0007	0009
14								0001	0001	0001

p	41	42	43	44	45	46	47	48	49	50
r 1	9998	9998	9999	9999	9999	9999	10000	10000	10000	10000
2	9974	9979	9984	9987	9990	9992	9994	9995	9997	9997
3	9849	9876	9899	9918	9934	9947	9958	9966	9973	9979
4	9444	9527	9600	9664	9719	9766	9806	9840	9869	9894
5	8529	8707	8869	9015	9147	9265	9370	9463	9544	9616
6	7003	7280	7543	7792	8024	8241	8441	8626	8795	8949
7	5058	5387	5711	6029	6340	6641	6932	7210	7476	7728
8	3128	3428	3736	4051	4371	4694	5019	5343	5665	5982
9	1619	1832	2060	2302	2559	2829	3111	3405	3707	4018
10	0687	0805	0936	1081	1241	1416	1607	1814	2036	2272
11	0234	0284	0342	0409	0486	0574	0674	0786	0911	1051
12	0062	0078	0098	0121	0149	0183	0222	0268	0322	0384
13	0012	0016	0021	0027	0035	0044	0055	0069	0086	0106
14	0002	0002	0003	0004	0006	0007	0010	0013	0016	0021
15					0001	0001	0001	0001	0002	0003

$n = 17$

p	01	02	03	04	05	06	07	08	09	10
r 1	1571	2907	4042	5004	5819	6507	7088	7577	7988	8332
2	0123	0446	0909	1465	2078	2717	3362	3995	4604	5182
3	0006	0044	0134	0286	0503	0782	1118	1503	1927	2382
4		0003	0014	0040	0088	0164	0273	0419	0603	0826
5			0001	0004	0012	0026	0051	0089	0145	0221
6					0001	0003	0007	0015	0027	0047
7							0001	0002	0004	0008
8										0001

p	11	12	13	14	15	16	17	18	19	20
r 1	8621	8862	9063	9230	9369	9484	9579	9657	9722	9775
2	5723	6223	6682	7099	7475	7813	8113	8379	8613	8818
3	2858	3345	3836	4324	4802	5266	5711	6133	6532	6904
4	1087	1383	1710	2065	2444	2841	3251	3669	4091	4511
5	0321	0446	0598	0778	0987	1224	1487	1775	2087	2418

Appendix A (cont.)

n = 17   CUMULATIVE BINOMIAL DISTRIBUTION

p	11	12	13	14	15	16	17	18	19	20
r 6	0075	0114	0166	0234	0319	0423	0548	0695	0864	1057
7	0014	0023	0037	0056	0083	0118	0163	0220	0291	0377
8	0002	0004	0007	0011	0017	0027	0039	0057	0080	0109
9		0001	0001	0002	0003	0005	0008	0012	0018	0026
10						0001	0001	0002	0003	0005
11										0001

p	21	22	23	24	25	26	27	28	29	30
r 1	9818	9854	9882	9906	9925	9940	9953	9962	9970	9977
2	8996	9152	9285	9400	9499	9583	9654	9714	9765	9807
3	7249	7567	7859	8123	8363	8578	8771	8942	9093	9226
4	4927	5333	5728	6107	6470	6814	7137	7440	7721	7981
5	2766	3128	3500	3879	4261	4643	5023	5396	5760	6113
6	1273	1510	1770	2049	2347	2661	2989	3329	3677	4032
7	0479	0598	0736	0894	1071	1268	1485	1721	1976	2248
8	0147	0194	0251	0320	0402	0499	0611	0739	0884	1046
9	0037	0051	0070	0094	0124	0161	0206	0261	0326	0403
10	0007	0011	0016	0022	0031	0042	0057	0075	0098	0127
11	0001	0002	0003	0004	0006	0009	0013	0018	0024	0032
12				0001	0001	0002	0002	0003	0005	0007
13									0001	0001

p	31	32	33	34	35	36	37	38	39	40
r 1	9982	9986	9989	9991	9993	9995	9996	9997	9998	9998
2	9843	9872	9896	9917	9933	9946	9957	9966	9973	9979
3	9343	9444	9532	9608	9673	9728	9775	9815	9849	9877
4	8219	8437	8634	8812	8972	9115	9241	9353	9450	9536
5	6453	6778	7087	7378	7652	7906	8142	8360	8559	8740
6	4390	4749	5105	5458	5803	6139	6465	6778	7077	7361
7	2536	2838	3153	3479	3812	4152	4495	4839	5182	5522
8	1227	1426	1642	1877	2128	2395	2676	2971	3278	3595
9	0492	0595	0712	0845	0994	1159	1341	1541	1757	1989
10	0162	0204	0254	0314	0383	0464	0557	0664	0784	0919
11	0043	0057	0074	0095	0120	0151	0189	0234	0286	0348
12	0009	0013	0017	0023	0030	0040	0051	0066	0084	0106
13	0002	0002	0003	0004	0006	0008	0011	0015	0019	0025
14				0001	0001	0001	0002	0002	0003	0005
15										0001

p	41	42	43	44	45	46	47	48	49	50
r 1	9999	9999	9999	9999	10000	10000	10000	10000	10000	10000
2	9984	9987	9990	9992	9994	9996	9997	9998	9998	9999
3	9900	9920	9935	9948	9959	9968	9975	9980	9985	9988
4	9610	9674	9729	9776	9816	9849	9877	9901	9920	9936
5	8904	9051	9183	9301	9404	9495	9575	9644	9704	9755
6	7628	7879	8113	8330	8529	8712	8878	9028	9162	9283
7	5856	6182	6499	6805	7098	7377	7641	7890	8122	8338
8	3920	4250	4585	4921	5257	5590	5918	6239	6552	6855

Appendix A (cont.)

CUMULATIVE BINOMIAL DISTRIBUTION $n = 17$

p	41	42	43	44	45	46	47	48	49	50
r 9	2238	2502	2780	3072	3374	3687	4008	4335	4667	5000
10	1070	1236	1419	1618	1834	2066	2314	2577	2855	3145
11	0420	0503	0597	0705	0826	0962	1112	1279	1462	1662
12	0133	0165	0203	0248	0301	0363	0434	0517	0611	0717
13	0033	0042	0054	0069	0086	0108	0134	0165	0202	0245
14	0006	0008	0011	0014	0019	0024	0031	0040	0050	0064
15	0001	0001	0002	0002	0003	0004	0005	0007	0009	0012
16							0001	0001	0001	0001

$n = 18$

p	01	02	03	04	05	06	07	08	09	10
r 1	1655	3049	4220	5204	6028	6717	7292	7771	8169	8499
2	0138	0495	1003	1607	2265	2945	3622	4281	4909	5497
3	0007	0052	0157	0333	0581	0898	1275	1702	2168	2662
4		0004	0018	0050	0109	0201	0333	0506	0723	0982
5			0002	0006	0015	0034	0067	0116	0186	0282
6				0001	0002	0005	0010	0021	0038	0064
7							0001	0003	0006	0012
8									0001	0002

p	11	12	13	14	15	16	17	18	19	20
r 1	8773	8998	9185	9338	9464	9566	9651	9719	9775	9820
2	6042	6540	6992	7398	7759	8080	8362	8609	8824	9009
3	3173	3690	4206	4713	5203	5673	6119	6538	6927	7287
4	1282	1618	1986	2382	2798	3229	3669	4112	4554	4990
5	0405	0558	0743	0959	1206	1482	1787	2116	2467	2836
6	0102	0154	0222	0310	0419	0551	0708	0889	1097	1329
7	0021	0034	0054	0081	0118	0167	0229	0306	0400	0513
8	0003	0006	0011	0017	0027	0041	0060	0086	0120	0163
9		0001	0002	0003	0005	0008	0013	0020	0029	0043
10					0001	0001	0002	0004	0006	0009
11								0001	0001	0002

p	21	22	23	24	25	26	27	28	29	30
r 1	9856	9886	9909	9928	9944	9956	9965	9973	9979	9984
2	9169	9306	9423	9522	9605	9676	9735	9784	9824	9858
3	7616	7916	8187	8430	8647	8839	9009	9158	9288	9400
4	5414	5825	6218	6591	6943	7272	7578	7860	8119	8354
5	3220	3613	4012	4414	4813	5208	5594	5968	6329	6673
6	1586	1866	2168	2488	2825	3176	3538	3907	4281	4656
7	0645	0799	0974	1171	1390	1630	1891	2171	2469	2783
8	0217	0283	0363	0458	0569	0699	0847	1014	1200	1407
9	0060	0083	0112	0148	0193	0249	0316	0395	0488	0596
10	0014	0020	0028	0039	0054	0073	0097	0127	0164	0210
11	0003	0004	0006	0009	0012	0018	0025	0034	0046	0061
12		0001	0001	0002	0002	0003	0005	0007	0010	0014
13						0001	0001	0001	0002	0003

Appendix A (cont.)

$n = 18$ CUMULATIVE BINOMIAL DISTRIBUTION

p	31	32	33	34	35	36	37	38	39	40
r 1	9987	9990	9993	9994	9996	9997	9998	9998	9999	9999
2	9886	9908	9927	9942	9954	9964	9972	9978	9983	9987
3	9498	9581	9652	9713	9764	9807	9843	9873	9897	9918
4	8568	8759	8931	9083	9217	9335	9439	9528	9606	9672
5	7001	7309	7598	7866	8114	8341	8549	8737	8907	9058
6	5029	5398	5759	6111	6450	6776	7086	7379	7655	7912
7	3111	3450	3797	4151	4509	4867	5224	5576	5921	6257
8	1633	1878	2141	2421	2717	3027	3349	3681	4021	4366
9	0720	0861	1019	1196	1391	1604	1835	2084	2350	2632
10	0264	0329	0405	0494	0597	0714	0847	0997	1163	1347
11	0080	0104	0133	0169	0212	0264	0325	0397	0480	0576
12	0020	0027	0036	0047	0062	0080	0102	0130	0163	0203
13	0004	0005	0008	0011	0014	0019	0026	0034	0044	0058
14	0001	0001	0001	0002	0003	0004	0005	0007	0010	0013
15						0001	0001	0001	0002	0002

p	41	42	43	44	45	46	47	48	49	50
r 1	9999	9999	10000	10000	10000	10000	10000	10000	10000	10000
2	9990	9992	9994	9996	9997	9998	9998	9999	9999	9999
3	9934	9948	9959	9968	9975	9981	9985	9989	9991	9993
4	9729	9777	9818	9852	9880	9904	9923	9939	9952	9962
5	9193	9313	9418	9510	9589	9658	9717	9767	9810	9846
6	8151	8372	8573	8757	8923	9072	9205	9324	9428	9519
7	6582	6895	7193	7476	7742	7991	8222	8436	8632	8811
8	4713	5062	5408	5750	6085	6412	6728	7032	7322	7597
9	2928	3236	3556	3885	4222	4562	4906	5249	5591	5927
10	1549	1768	2004	2258	2527	2812	3110	3421	3742	4073
11	0686	0811	0951	1107	1280	1470	1677	1902	2144	2403
12	0250	0307	0372	0449	0537	0638	0753	0883	1028	1189
13	0074	0094	0118	0147	0183	0225	0275	0334	0402	0481
14	0017	0022	0029	0038	0049	0063	0079	0100	0125	0154
15	0003	0004	0006	0007	0010	0013	0017	0023	0029	0038
16		0001	0001	0001	0001	0002	0003	0004	0005	0007
17									0001	0001

$n = 19$

p	01	02	03	04	05	06	07	08	09	10
r 1	1738	3188	4394	5396	6226	6914	7481	7949	8334	8649
2	0153	0546	1100	1751	2453	3171	3879	4560	5202	5797
3	0009	0061	0183	0384	0665	1021	1439	1908	2415	2946
4		0005	0022	0061	0132	0243	0398	0602	0853	1150
5			0002	0007	0020	0044	0085	0147	0235	0352
6				0001	0002	0006	0014	0029	0051	0086
7						0001	0002	0004	0009	0017
8								0001	0001	0003

Appendix A (*cont.*)

CUMULATIVE BINOMIAL DISTRIBUTION $n = 19$

p	11	12	13	14	15	16	17	18	19	20
r 1	8908	9119	9291	9431	9544	9636	9710	9770	9818	9856
2	6342	6835	7277	7669	8015	8318	8581	8809	9004	9171
3	3488	4032	4568	5089	5587	6059	6500	6910	7287	7631
4	1490	1867	2275	2708	3159	3620	4085	4549	5005	5449
5	0502	0685	0904	1158	1444	1762	2107	2476	2864	3267
6	0135	0202	0290	0401	0537	0700	0891	1110	1357	1631
7	0030	0048	0076	0113	0163	0228	0310	0411	0532	0676
8	0005	0009	0016	0026	0041	0061	0089	0126	0173	0233
9	0001	0002	0003	0005	0008	0014	0021	0032	0047	0067
10				0001	0001	0002	0004	0007	0010	0016
11							0001	0001	0002	0003

p	21	22	23	24	25	26	27	28	29	30
r 1	9887	9911	9930	9946	9958	9967	9975	9981	9985	9989
2	9313	9434	9535	9619	9690	9749	9797	9837	9869	9896
3	7942	8222	8471	8692	8887	9057	9205	9333	9443	9538
4	5877	6285	6671	7032	7369	7680	7965	8224	8458	8668
5	3681	4100	4520	4936	5346	5744	6129	6498	6848	7178
6	1929	2251	2592	2950	3322	3705	4093	4484	4875	5261
7	0843	1034	1248	1487	1749	2032	2336	2657	2995	3345
8	0307	0396	0503	0629	0775	0941	1129	1338	1568	1820
9	0093	0127	0169	0222	0287	0366	0459	0568	0694	0839
10	0023	0034	0047	0066	0089	0119	0156	0202	0258	0326
11	0005	0007	0011	0016	0023	0032	0044	0060	0080	0105
12	0001	0001	0002	0003	0005	0007	0010	0015	0021	0028
13				0001	0001	0001	0002	0003	0004	0006
14									0001	0001

p	31	32	33	34	35	36	37	38	39	40
r 1	9991	9993	9995	9996	9997	9998	9998	9999	9999	9999
2	9917	9935	9949	9960	9969	9976	9981	9986	9989	9992
3	9618	9686	9743	9791	9830	9863	9890	9913	9931	9945
4	8856	9022	9169	9297	9409	9505	9588	9659	9719	9770
5	7486	7773	8037	8280	8500	8699	8878	9038	9179	9304
6	5641	6010	6366	6707	7032	7339	7627	7895	8143	8371
7	3705	4073	4445	4818	5188	5554	5913	6261	6597	6919
8	2091	2381	2688	3010	3344	3690	4043	4401	4762	5122
9	1003	1186	1389	1612	1855	2116	2395	2691	3002	3325
10	0405	0499	0608	0733	0875	1035	1213	1410	1626	1861
11	0137	0176	0223	0280	0347	0426	0518	0625	0747	0885
12	0038	0051	0068	0089	0114	0146	0185	0231	0287	0352
13	0009	0012	0017	0023	0031	0041	0054	0070	0091	0116
14	0002	0002	0003	0005	0007	0009	0013	0017	0023	0031
15			0001	0001	0001	0002	0002	0003	0005	0006
16									0001	0001

$n = 19$ CUMULATIVE BINOMIAL DISTRIBUTION

p	41	42	43	44	45	46	47	48	49	50
r 1	10000	10000	10000	10000	10000	10000	10000	10000	10000	10000
2	9994	9995	9996	9997	9998	9999	9999	9999	9999	10000
3	9957	9967	9974	9980	9985	9988	9991	9993	9995	9996
4	9813	9849	9878	9903	9923	9939	9952	9963	9971	9978
5	9413	9508	9590	9660	9720	9771	9814	9850	9879	9904
6	8579	8767	8937	9088	9223	9342	9446	9537	9615	9682
7	7226	7515	7787	8039	8273	8488	8684	8862	9022	9165
8	5480	5832	6176	6509	6831	7138	7430	7706	7964	8204
9	3660	4003	4353	4706	5060	5413	5762	6105	6439	6762
10	2114	2385	2672	2974	3290	3617	3954	4299	4648	5000
11	1040	1213	1404	1613	1841	2087	2351	2631	2928	3238
12	0429	0518	0621	0738	0871	1021	1187	1372	1575	1796
13	0146	0183	0227	0280	0342	0415	0500	0597	0709	0835
14	0040	0052	0067	0086	0109	0137	0171	0212	0261	0318
15	0009	0012	0016	0021	0028	0036	0046	0060	0076	0096
16	0001	0002	0003	0004	0005	0007	0010	0013	0017	0022
17				0001	0001	0001	0001	0002	0003	0004

$n = 20$

p	01	02	03	04	05	06	07	08	09	10
r 1	1821	3324	4562	5580	6415	7099	7658	8113	8484	8784
2	0169	0599	1198	1897	2642	3395	4131	4831	5484	6083
3	0010	0071	0210	0439	0755	1150	1610	2121	2666	3231
4		0006	0027	0074	0159	0290	0471	0706	0993	1330
5			0003	0010	0026	0056	0107	0183	0290	0432
6				0001	0003	0009	0019	0038	0068	0113
7						0001	0003	0006	0013	0024
8								0001	0002	0004
9										0001

p	11	12	13	14	15	16	17	18	19	20
r 1	9028	9224	9383	9510	9612	9694	9759	9811	9852	9885
2	6624	7109	7539	7916	8244	8529	8773	8982	9159	9308
3	3802	4369	4920	5450	5951	6420	6854	7252	7614	7939
4	1710	2127	2573	3041	3523	4010	4496	4974	5439	5886
5	0610	0827	1083	1375	1702	2059	2443	2849	3271	3704
6	0175	0260	0370	0507	0673	0870	1098	1356	1643	1958
7	0041	0067	0103	0153	0219	0304	0409	0537	0689	0867
8	0008	0014	0024	0038	0059	0088	0127	0177	0241	0321
9	0001	0002	0005	0008	0013	0021	0033	0049	0071	0100
10			0001	0001	0002	0004	0007	0011	0017	0026
11						0001	0001	0002	0004	0006
12									0001	0001

p	21	22	23	24	25	26	27	28	29	30
r 1	9910	9931	9946	9959	9968	9976	9982	9986	9989	9992
2	9434	9539	9626	9698	9757	9805	9845	9877	9903	9924
3	8230	8488	8716	8915	9087	9237	9365	9474	9567	9645
4	6310	6711	7085	7431	7748	8038	8300	8534	8744	8929
5	4142	4580	5014	5439	5852	6248	6625	6981	7315	7625

Appendix A (cont.)

CUMULATIVE BINOMIAL DISTRIBUTION $n = 20$

p	21	22	23	24	25	26	27	28	29	30
r 6	2297	2657	3035	3427	3828	4235	4643	5048	5447	5836
7	1071	1301	1557	1838	2142	2467	2810	3169	3540	3920
8	0419	0536	0675	0835	1018	1225	1455	1707	1982	2277
9	0138	0186	0246	0320	0409	0515	0640	0784	0948	1133
10	0038	0054	0075	0103	0139	0183	0238	0305	0385	0480
11	0009	0013	0019	0028	0039	0055	0074	0100	0132	0171
12	0002	0003	0004	0006	0009	0014	0019	0027	0038	0051
13			0001	0001	0002	0003	0004	0006	0009	0013
14							0001	0001	0002	0003

p	31	32	33	34	35	36	37	38	39	40
r 1	9994	9996	9997	9998	9998	9999	9999	9999	9999	10000
2	9940	9953	9964	9972	9979	9984	9988	9991	9993	9995
3	9711	9765	9811	9848	9879	9904	9924	9940	9953	9964
4	9092	9235	9358	9465	9556	9634	9700	9755	9802	9840
5	7911	8173	8411	8626	8818	8989	9141	9274	9390	9490
6	6213	6574	6917	7242	7546	7829	8090	8329	8547	8744
7	4305	4693	5079	5460	5834	6197	6547	6882	7200	7500
8	2591	2922	3268	3624	3990	4361	4735	5108	5478	5841
9	1340	1568	1818	2087	2376	2683	3005	3341	3688	4044
10	0591	0719	0866	1032	1218	1424	1650	1897	2163	2447
11	0220	0279	0350	0434	0532	0645	0775	0923	1090	1275
12	0069	0091	0119	0154	0196	0247	0308	0381	0466	0565
13	0018	0025	0034	0045	0060	0079	0102	0132	0167	0210
14	0004	0006	0008	0011	0015	0021	0028	0037	0049	0065
15	0001	0001	0001	0002	0003	0004	0006	0009	0012	0016
16						0001	0001	0002	0002	0003

p	41	42	43	44	45	46	47	48	49	50
r 1	10000	10000	10000	10000	10000	10000	10000	10000	10000	10000
2	9996	9997	9998	9998	9999	9999	9999	10000	10000	10000
3	9972	9979	9984	9988	9991	9993	9995	9996	9997	9998
4	9872	9898	9920	9937	9951	9962	9971	9977	9983	9987
5	9577	9651	9714	9767	9811	9848	9879	9904	9924	9941
6	8921	9078	9217	9340	9447	9539	9619	9687	9745	9793
7	7780	8041	8281	8501	8701	8881	9042	9186	9312	9423
8	6196	6539	6868	7183	7480	7759	8020	8261	8482	8684
9	4406	4771	5136	5499	5857	6207	6546	6873	7186	7483
10	2748	3064	3394	3736	4086	4443	4804	5166	5525	5881
11	1480	1705	1949	2212	2493	2791	3104	3432	3771	4119
12	0679	0810	0958	1123	1308	1511	1734	1977	2238	2517
13	0262	0324	0397	0482	0580	0694	0823	0969	1133	1316
14	0084	0107	0136	0172	0214	0265	0326	0397	0480	0577
15	0022	0029	0038	0050	0064	0083	0105	0133	0166	0207
16	0004	0006	0008	0011	0015	0020	0027	0035	0046	0059
17	0001	0001	0001	0002	0003	0004	0005	0007	0010	0013
18						0001	0001	0001	0001	0002

Appendix A (cont.)

n = 50   CUMULATIVE BINOMIAL DISTRIBUTION

n = 50

p \ r	01	02	03	04	05	06	07	08	09	10
1	3950	6358	7819	8701	9231	9547	9734	9845	9910	9948
2	0894	2642	4447	5995	7206	8100	8735	9173	9468	9662
3	0138	0784	1892	3233	4595	5838	6892	7740	8395	8883
4	0016	0178	0628	1391	2396	3527	4673	5747	6697	7497
5	0001	0032	0168	0490	1036	1794	2710	3710	4723	5688
6		0005	0037	0144	0378	0776	1350	2081	2928	3839
7		0001	0007	0036	0118	0289	0583	1019	1596	2298
8			0001	0008	0032	0094	0220	0438	0768	1221
9				0001	0008	0027	0073	0167	0328	0579
10					0002	0007	0022	0056	0125	0245
11						0002	0006	0017	0043	0094
12							0001	0005	0013	0032
13								0001	0004	0010
14									0001	0003
15										0001

p \ r	11	12	13	14	15	16	17	18	19	20
1	9971	9983	9991	9995	9997	9998	9999	10000	10000	10000
2	9788	9869	9920	9951	9971	9983	9990	9994	9997	9998
3	9237	9487	9661	9779	9858	9910	9944	9965	9979	9987
4	8146	8655	9042	9330	9540	9688	9792	9863	9912	9943
5	6562	7320	7956	8472	8879	9192	9428	9601	9726	9815
6	4760	5647	6463	7186	7806	8323	8741	9071	9327	9520
7	3091	3935	4789	5616	6387	7081	7686	8199	8624	8966
8	1793	2467	3217	4010	4812	5594	6328	6996	7587	8096
9	0932	1392	1955	2605	3319	4071	4832	5576	6280	6927
10	0435	0708	1074	1537	2089	2718	3403	4122	4849	5563
11	0183	0325	0535	0824	1199	1661	2203	2813	3473	4164
12	0069	0135	0242	0402	0628	0929	1309	1768	2300	2893
13	0024	0051	0100	0179	0301	0475	0714	1022	1405	1861
14	0008	0018	0037	0073	0132	0223	0357	0544	0791	1106
15	0002	0006	0013	0027	0053	0096	0164	0266	0411	0607
16	0001	0002	0004	0009	0019	0038	0070	0120	0197	0308
17			0001	0003	0007	0014	0027	0050	0087	0144
18				0001	0002	0005	0010	0019	0036	0063
19					0001	0001	0003	0007	0013	0025
20							0001	0002	0005	0009
21								0001	0002	0003
22										0001

p \ r	21	22	23	24	25	26	27	28	29	30
1	10000	10000	10000	10000	10000	10000	10000	10000	10000	10000
2	9999	9999	10000	10000	10000	10000	10000	10000	10000	10000
3	9992	9995	9997	9998	9999	10000	10000	10000	10000	10000
4	9964	9978	9986	9992	9995	9997	9998	9999	9999	10000
5	9877	9919	9948	9967	9979	9987	9992	9995	9997	9998

Appendix A (cont.)

CUMULATIVE BINOMIAL DISTRIBUTION $n = 50$

p	21	22	23	24	25	26	27	28	29	30
r 6	9663	9767	9841	9893	9930	9954	9970	9981	9988	9993
7	9236	9445	9603	9720	9806	9868	9911	9941	9961	9975
8	8523	8874	9156	9377	9547	9676	9772	9842	9892	9927
9	7505	8009	8437	8794	9084	9316	9497	9635	9740	9817
10	6241	6870	7436	7934	8363	8724	9021	9260	9450	9598
11	4864	5552	6210	6822	7378	7871	8299	8663	8965	9211
12	3533	4201	4878	5544	6184	6782	7329	7817	8244	8610
13	2383	2963	3585	4233	4890	5539	6163	6749	7287	7771
14	1490	1942	2456	3023	3630	4261	4901	5534	6145	6721
15	0862	1181	1565	2013	2519	3075	3669	4286	4912	5532
16	0462	0665	0926	1247	1631	2075	2575	3121	3703	4308
17	0229	0347	0508	0718	0983	1306	1689	2130	2623	3161
18	0105	0168	0259	0384	0551	0766	1034	1359	1741	2178
19	0045	0075	0122	0191	0287	0418	0590	0809	1080	1406
20	0018	0031	0054	0088	0139	0212	0314	0449	0626	0848
21	0006	0012	0022	0038	0063	0100	0155	0232	0338	0478
22	0002	0004	0008	0015	0026	0044	0071	0112	0170	0251
23	0001	0001	0003	0006	0010	0018	0031	0050	0080	0123
24			0001	0002	0004	0007	0012	0021	0035	0056
25				0001	0001	0002	0004	0008	0014	0024
26						0001	0002	0003	0005	0009
27								0001	0002	0003
28									0001	0001

p	31	32	33	34	35	36	37	38	39	40
r 1	10000	10000	10000	10000	10000	10000	10000	10000	10000	10000
2	10000	10000	10000	10000	10000	10000	10000	10000	10000	10000
3	10000	10000	10000	10000	10000	10000	10000	10000	10000	10000
4	10000	10000	10000	10000	10000	10000	10000	10000	10000	10000
5	9999	9999	10000	10000	10000	10000	10000	10000	10000	10000
6	9996	9997	9998	9999	9999	10000	10000	10000	10000	10000
7	9984	9990	9994	9996	9998	9999	9999	10000	10000	10000
8	9952	9969	9980	9987	9992	9995	9997	9998	9999	9999
9	9874	9914	9942	9962	9975	9984	9990	9994	9996	9998
10	9710	9794	9856	9901	9933	9955	9971	9981	9988	9992
11	9409	9563	9683	9773	9840	9889	9924	9949	9966	9978
12	8916	9168	9371	9533	9658	9753	9825	9878	9916	9943
13	8197	8564	8873	9130	9339	9505	9635	9736	9811	9867
14	7253	7732	8157	8524	8837	9097	9310	9481	9616	9720
15	6131	6698	7223	7699	8122	8491	8805	9069	9286	9460
16	4922	5530	6120	6679	7199	7672	8094	8462	8779	9045
17	3734	4328	4931	5530	6111	6664	7179	7649	8070	8439
18	2666	3197	3760	4346	4940	5531	6105	6653	7164	7631
19	1786	2220	2703	3227	3784	4362	4949	5533	6101	6644
20	1121	1447	1826	2257	2736	3255	3805	4376	4957	5535
21	0657	0882	1156	1482	1861	2289	2764	3278	3824	4390
22	0360	0503	0685	0912	1187	1513	1890	2317	2788	3299
23	0184	0267	0379	0525	0710	0938	1214	1540	1916	2340
24	0087	0133	0196	0282	0396	0544	0730	0960	1236	1562

Appendix A (*cont.*)

$n = 50$ CUMULATIVE BINOMIAL DISTRIBUTION

p	31	32	33	34	35	36	37	38	39	40
r 25	0039	0061	0094	0141	0207	0295	0411	0560	0748	0978
26	0016	0026	0042	0066	0100	0149	0216	0305	0423	0573
27	0006	0011	0018	0029	0045	0070	0106	0155	0223	0314
28	0002	0004	0007	0012	0019	0031	0048	0074	0110	0160
29	0001	0001	0002	0004	0007	0012	0020	0032	0050	0076
30			0001	0002	0003	0005	0008	0013	0021	0034
31					0001	0002	0003	0005	0008	0014
32						0001	0001	0002	0003	0005
33								0001	0001	0002
34										0001

p	41	42	43	44	45	46	47	48	49	50
r 1	10000	10000	10000	10000	10000	10000	10000	10000	10000	10000
2	10000	10000	10000	10000	10000	10000	10000	10000	10000	10000
3	10000	10000	10000	10000	10000	10000	10000	10000	10000	10000
4	10000	10000	10000	10000	10000	10000	10000	10000	10000	10000
5	10000	10000	10000	10000	10000	10000	10000	10000	10000	10000
6	10000	10000	10000	10000	10000	10000	10000	10000	10000	10000
7	10000	10000	10000	10000	10000	10000	10000	10000	10000	10000
8	10000	10000	10000	10000	10000	10000	10000	10000	10000	10000
9	9999	9999	10000	10000	10000	10000	10000	10000	10000	10000
10	9995	9997	9998	9999	9999	10000	10000	10000	10000	10000
11	9986	9991	9994	9997	9998	9999	9999	10000	10000	10000
12	9962	9975	9984	9990	9994	9996	9998	9999	9999	10000
13	9908	9938	9958	9973	9982	9989	9993	9996	9997	9998
14	9799	9858	9902	9933	9955	9970	9981	9988	9992	9995
15	9599	9707	9789	9851	9896	9929	9952	9968	9980	9987
16	9265	9443	9585	9696	9780	9844	9892	9926	9950	9967
17	8757	9025	9248	9429	9573	9687	9774	9839	9888	9923
18	8051	8421	8740	9010	9235	9418	9565	9680	9769	9836
19	7152	7617	8037	8406	8727	8998	9225	9410	9559	9675
20	6099	6638	7143	7608	8026	8396	8718	8991	9219	9405
21	4965	5539	6099	6635	7138	7602	8020	8391	8713	8987
22	3840	4402	4973	5543	6100	6634	7137	7599	8018	8389
23	2809	3316	3854	4412	4981	5548	6104	6636	7138	7601
24	1936	2359	2826	3331	3866	4422	4989	5554	6109	6641
25	1255	1580	1953	2375	2840	3343	3876	4431	4996	5561
26	0762	0992	1269	1593	1966	2386	2850	3352	3885	4439
27	0432	0584	0772	1003	1279	1603	1975	2395	2858	3359
28	0229	0320	0439	0591	0780	1010	1286	1609	1981	2399
29	0113	0164	0233	0325	0444	0595	0784	1013	1289	1611
30	0052	0078	0115	0166	0235	0327	0446	0596	0784	1013
31	0022	0034	0053	0079	0116	0167	0236	0327	0445	0595
32	0009	0014	0022	0035	0053	0079	0116	0166	0234	0325
33	0003	0005	0009	0014	0022	0035	0053	0078	0114	0164
34	0001	0002	0003	0005	0009	0014	0022	0034	0052	0077
35		0001	0001	0002	0003	0005	0008	0014	0021	0033
36				0001	0001	0002	0003	0005	0008	0013

Appendix A (cont.)

CUMULATIVE BINOMIAL DISTRIBUTION $n = 50$

p	41	42	43	44	45	46	47	48	49	50
r 37						0001	0001	0002	0003	0005
38								0001	0001	0002

$n = 100$

p	01	02	03	04	05	06	07	08	09	10
r 1	6340	8674	9524	9831	9941	9979	9993	9998	9999	10000
2	2642	5967	8054	9128	9629	9848	9940	9977	9991	9997
3	0794	3233	5802	7679	8817	9434	9742	9887	9952	9981
4	0184	1410	3528	5705	7422	8570	9256	9633	9827	9922
5	0034	0508	1821	3711	5640	7232	8368	9097	9526	9763
6	0005	0155	0808	2116	3840	5593	7086	8201	8955	9424
7	0001	0041	0312	1064	2340	3936	5557	6968	8060	8828
8		0009	0106	0475	1280	2517	4012	5529	6872	7939
9		0002	0032	0190	0631	1463	2660	4074	5506	6791
10			0009	0068	0282	0775	1620	2780	4125	5487
11			0002	0022	0115	0376	0908	1757	2882	4168
12				0007	0043	0168	0469	1028	1876	2970
13				0002	0015	0069	0224	0559	1138	1982
14					0005	0026	0099	0282	0645	1239
15					0001	0009	0041	0133	0341	0726
16						0003	0016	0058	0169	0399
17						0001	0006	0024	0078	0206
18							0002	0009	0034	0100
19							0001	0003	0014	0046
20								0001	0005	0020
21									0002	0008
22									0001	0003
23										0001

p	11	12	13	14	15	16	17	18	19	20
r 1	10000	10000	10000	10000	10000	10000	10000	10000	10000	10000
2	9999	10000	10000	10000	10000	10000	10000	10000	10000	10000
3	9992	9997	9999	10000	10000	10000	10000	10000	10000	10000
4	9966	9985	9994	9998	9999	10000	10000	10000	10000	10000
5	9886	9947	9977	9990	9996	9998	9999	10000	10000	10000
6	9698	9848	9926	9966	9984	9993	9997	9999	10000	10000
7	9328	9633	9808	9903	9953	9978	9990	9996	9998	9999
8	8715	9239	9569	9766	9878	9939	9970	9986	9994	9997
9	7835	8614	9155	9508	9725	9853	9924	9962	9982	9991
10	6722	7743	8523	9078	9449	9684	9826	9908	9953	9977
11	5471	6663	7663	8440	9006	9393	9644	9800	9891	9943
12	4206	5458	6611	7591	8365	8939	9340	9605	9773	9874
13	3046	4239	5446	6566	7527	8297	8876	9289	9567	9747
14	2076	3114	4268	5436	6526	7469	8234	8819	9241	9531
15	1330	2160	3173	4294	5428	6490	7417	8177	8765	9196
16	0802	1414	2236	3227	4317	5420	6458	7370	8125	8715
17	0456	0874	1492	2305	3275	4338	5414	6429	7327	8077
18	0244	0511	0942	1563	2367	3319	4357	5408	6403	7288

Appendix A (cont.)

$n = 100$ CUMULATIVE BINOMIAL DISTRIBUTION

p	11	12	13	14	15	16	17	18	19	20
r 19	0123	0282	0564	1006	1628	2424	3359	4374	5403	6379
20	0059	0147	0319	0614	1065	1689	2477	3395	4391	5398
21	0026	0073	0172	0356	0663	1121	1745	2525	3429	4405
22	0011	0034	0088	0196	0393	0710	1174	1797	2570	3460
23	0005	0015	0042	0103	0221	0428	0754	1223	1846	2611
24	0002	0006	0020	0051	0119	0246	0462	0796	1270	1891
25	0001	0003	0009	0024	0061	0135	0271	0496	0837	1314
26		0001	0004	0011	0030	0071	0151	0295	0528	0875
27			0001	0005	0014	0035	0081	0168	0318	0558
28			0001	0002	0006	0017	0041	0091	0184	0342
29				0001	0003	0008	0020	0048	0102	0200
30					0001	0003	0009	0024	0054	0112
31						0001	0004	0011	0027	0061
32						0001	0002	0005	0013	0031
33							0001	0002	0006	0016
34								0001	0003	0007
35									0001	0003
36										0001
37										0001

p	21	22	23	24	25	26	27	28	29	30
r 1	10000	10000	10000	10000	10000	10000	10000	10000	10000	10000
2	10000	10000	10000	10000	10000	10000	10000	10000	10000	10000
3	10000	10000	10000	10000	10000	10000	10000	10000	10000	10000
4	10000	10000	10000	10000	10000	10000	10000	10000	10000	10000
5	10000	10000	10000	10000	10000	10000	10000	10000	10000	10000
6	10000	10000	10000	10000	10000	10000	10000	10000	10000	10000
7	10000	10000	10000	10000	10000	10000	10000	10000	10000	10000
8	9999	10000	10000	10000	10000	10000	10000	10000	10000	10000
9	9996	9998	9999	10000	10000	10000	10000	10000	10000	10000
10	9989	9995	9998	9999	10000	10000	10000	10000	10000	10000
11	9971	9986	9993	9997	9999	9999	10000	10000	10000	10000
12	9933	9965	9983	9992	9996	9998	9999	10000	10000	10000
13	9857	9922	9959	9979	9990	9995	9998	9999	10000	10000
14	9721	9840	9911	9953	9975	9988	9994	9997	9999	9999
15	9496	9695	9823	9900	9946	9972	9986	9993	9997	9998
16	9153	9462	9671	9806	9889	9939	9967	9983	9992	9996
17	8668	9112	9430	9647	9789	9878	9932	9963	9981	9990
18	8032	8625	9074	9399	9624	9773	9867	9925	9959	9978
19	7252	7991	8585	9038	9370	9601	9757	9856	9918	9955
20	6358	7220	7953	8547	9005	9342	9580	9741	9846	9911
21	5394	6338	7189	7918	8512	8973	9316	9560	9726	9835
22	4419	5391	6320	7162	7886	8479	8943	9291	9540	9712
23	3488	4432	5388	6304	7136	7856	8448	8915	9267	9521
24	2649	3514	4444	5386	6289	7113	7828	8420	8889	9245
25	1933	2684	3539	4455	5383	6276	7091	7802	8393	8864
26	1355	1972	2717	3561	4465	5381	6263	7071	7778	8369
27	0911	1393	2009	2748	3583	4475	5380	6252	7053	7756
28	0588	0945	1429	2043	2776	3602	4484	5378	6242	7036

Appendix A (cont.)

CUMULATIVE BINOMIAL DISTRIBUTION $n = 100$

p / r	21	22	23	24	25	26	27	28	29	30
29	0364	0616	0978	1463	2075	2803	3621	4493	5377	6232
30	0216	0386	0643	1009	1495	2105	2828	3638	4501	5377
31	0123	0232	0406	0669	1038	1526	2134	2851	3654	4509
32	0067	0134	0247	0427	0693	1065	1554	2160	2873	3669
33	0035	0074	0144	0262	0446	0717	1091	1580	2184	2893
34	0018	0039	0081	0154	0276	0465	0739	1116	1605	2207
35	0009	0020	0044	0087	0164	0290	0482	0760	1139	1629
36	0004	0010	0023	0048	0094	0174	0303	0499	0780	1161
37	0002	0005	0011	0025	0052	0101	0183	0316	0515	0799
38	0001	0002	0005	0013	0027	0056	0107	0193	0328	0530
39		0001	0002	0006	0014	0030	0060	0113	0201	0340
40			0001	0003	0007	0015	0032	0064	0119	0210
41				0001	0003	0008	0017	0035	0068	0125
42				0001	0001	0004	0008	0018	0037	0072
43					0001	0002	0004	0009	0020	0040
44						0001	0002	0005	0010	0021
45							0001	0002	0005	0011
46								0001	0002	0005
47									0001	0003
48										0001
49										0001

p / r	31	32	33	34	35	36	37	38	39	40
1	10000	10000	10000	10000	10000	10000	10000	10000	10000	10000
2	10000	10000	10000	10000	10000	10000	10000	10000	10000	10000
3	10000	10000	10000	10000	10000	10000	10000	10000	10000	10000
4	10000	10000	10000	10000	10000	10000	10000	10000	10000	10000
5	10000	10000	10000	10000	10000	10000	10000	10000	10000	10000
6	10000	10000	10000	10000	10000	10000	10000	10000	10000	10000
7	10000	10000	10000	10000	10000	10000	10000	10000	10000	10000
8	10000	10000	10000	10000	10000	10000	10000	10000	10000	10000
9	10000	10000	10000	10000	10000	10000	10000	10000	10000	10000
10	10000	10000	10000	10000	10000	10000	10000	10000	10000	10000
11	10000	10000	10000	10000	10000	10000	10000	10000	10000	10000
12	10000	10000	10000	10000	10000	10000	10000	10000	10000	10000
13	10000	10000	10000	10000	10000	10000	10000	10000	10000	10000
14	10000	10000	10000	10000	10000	10000	10000	10000	10000	10000
15	9999	10000	10000	10000	10000	10000	10000	10000	10000	10000
16	9998	9999	10000	10000	10000	10000	10000	10000	10000	10000
17	9995	9998	9999	10000	10000	10000	10000	10000	10000	10000
18	9989	9995	9997	9999	9999	10000	10000	10000	10000	10000
19	9976	9988	9994	9997	9999	9999	10000	10000	10000	10000
20	9950	9973	9986	9993	9997	9998	9999	10000	10000	10000
21	9904	9946	9971	9985	9992	9996	9998	9999	10000	10000
22	9825	9898	9942	9968	9983	9991	9996	9998	9999	10000
23	9698	9816	9891	9938	9966	9982	9991	9995	9998	9999
24	9504	9685	9806	9885	9934	9963	9980	9990	9995	9997
25	9224	9487	9672	9797	9879	9930	9961	9979	9989	9994
26	8841	9204	9471	9660	9789	9873	9926	9958	9977	9988

Appendix A (cont.)

$n = 100$ CUMULATIVE BINOMIAL DISTRIBUTION

p	31	32	33	34	35	36	37	38	39	40
r 27	8346	8820	9185	9456	9649	9780	9867	9922	9956	9976
28	7736	8325	8800	9168	9442	9638	9773	9862	9919	9954
29	7021	7717	8305	8781	9152	9429	9628	9765	9857	9916
30	6224	7007	7699	8287	8764	9137	9417	9618	9759	9852
31	5376	6216	6994	7684	8270	8748	9123	9405	9610	9752
32	4516	5376	6209	6982	7669	8254	8733	9110	9395	9602
33	3683	4523	5375	6203	6971	7656	8240	8720	9098	9385
34	2912	3696	4530	5375	6197	6961	7643	8227	8708	9087
35	2229	2929	3708	4536	5376	6192	6953	7632	8216	8697
36	1650	2249	2946	3720	4542	5376	6188	6945	7623	8205
37	1181	1671	2268	2961	3731	4547	5377	6184	6938	7614
38	0816	1200	1690	2285	2976	3741	4553	5377	6181	6932
39	0545	0833	1218	1708	2301	2989	3750	4558	5378	6178
40	0351	0558	0849	1235	1724	2316	3001	3759	4562	5379
41	0218	0361	0571	0863	1250	1739	2330	3012	3767	4567
42	0131	0226	0371	0583	0877	1265	1753	2343	3023	3755
43	0075	0136	0233	0380	0594	0889	1278	1766	2355	3033
44	0042	0079	0141	0240	0389	0605	0901	1290	1778	2365
45	0023	0044	0082	0146	0246	0397	0614	0911	1301	1789
46	0012	0024	0046	0085	0150	0252	0405	0623	0921	1311
47	0006	0012	0025	0048	0088	0154	0257	0411	0631	0930
48	0003	0006	0013	0026	0050	0091	0158	0262	0417	0638
49	0001	0003	0007	0014	0027	0052	0094	0162	0267	0423
50	0001	0001	0003	0007	0015	0029	0054	0096	0165	0271
51		0001	0002	0003	0007	0015	0030	0055	0098	0168
52			0001	0002	0004	0008	0016	0030	0056	0100
53				0001	0002	0004	0008	0016	0031	0058
54					0001	0002	0004	0008	0017	0032
55						0001	0002	0004	0009	0017
56							0001	0002	0004	0009
57								0002	0004	0004
58									0001	0002
59										0001

p	41	42	43	44	45	46	47	48	49	50
r 1	10000	10000	10000	10000	10000	10000	10000	10000	10000	10000
2	10000	10000	10000	10000	10000	10000	10000	10000	10000	10000
3	10000	10000	10000	10000	10000	10000	10000	10000	10000	10000
4	10000	10000	10000	10000	10000	10000	10000	10000	10000	10000
5	10000	10000	10000	10000	10000	10000	10000	10000	10000	10000
6	10000	10000	10000	10000	10000	10000	10000	10000	10000	10000
7	10000	10000	10000	10000	10000	10000	10000	10000	10000	10000
8	10000	10000	10000	10000	10000	10000	10000	10000	10000	10000
9	10000	10000	10000	10000	10000	10000	10000	10000	10000	10000
10	10000	10000	10000	10000	10000	10000	10000	10000	10000	10000
11	10000	10000	10000	10000	10000	10000	10000	10000	10000	10000
12	10000	10000	10000	10000	10000	10000	10000	10000	10000	10000
13	10000	10000	10000	10000	10000	10000	10000	10000	10000	10000
14	10000	10000	10000	10000	10000	10000	10000	10000	10000	10000

Appendix A (cont.)

CUMULATIVE BINOMIAL DISTRIBUTION $n = 100$

r \ p	41	42	43	44	45	46	47	48	49	50
15	10000	10000	10000	10000	10000	10000	10000	10000	10000	10000
16	10000	10000	10000	10000	10000	10000	10000	10000	10000	10000
17	10000	10000	10000	10000	10000	10000	10000	10000	10000	10000
18	10000	10000	10000	10000	10000	10000	10000	10000	10000	10000
19	10000	10000	10000	10000	10000	10000	10000	10000	10000	10000
20	10000	10000	10000	10000	10000	10000	10000	10000	10000	10000
21	10000	10000	10000	10000	10000	10000	10000	10000	10000	10000
22	10000	10000	10000	10000	10000	10000	10000	10000	10000	10000
23	10000	10000	10000	10000	10000	10000	10000	10000	10000	10000
24	9999	9999	10000	10000	10000	10000	10000	10000	10000	10000
25	9997	9999	9999	10000	10000	10000	10000	10000	10000	10000
26	9994	9997	9999	9999	10000	10000	10000	10000	10000	10000
27	9987	9994	9997	9998	9999	10000	10000	10000	10000	10000
28	9975	9987	9993	9997	9998	9999	10000	10000	10000	10000
29	9952	9974	9986	9993	9996	9998	9999	10000	10000	10000
30	9913	9950	9972	9985	9992	9996	9998	9999	10000	10000
31	9848	9910	9948	9971	9985	9992	9996	9998	9999	10000
32	9746	9844	9907	9947	9970	9984	9992	9996	9998	9999
33	9594	9741	9840	9905	9945	9969	9984	9991	9996	9998
34	9376	9587	9736	9837	9902	9944	9969	9983	9991	9996
35	9078	9368	9581	9732	9834	9900	9942	9968	9983	9991
36	8687	9069	9361	9576	9728	9831	9899	9941	9967	9982
37	8196	8678	9061	9355	9571	9724	9829	9897	9941	9967
38	7606	8188	8670	9054	9349	9567	9721	9827	9896	9940
39	6927	7599	8181	8663	9049	9345	9563	9719	9825	9895
40	6176	6922	7594	8174	8657	9044	9341	9561	9717	9824
41	5380	6174	6919	7589	8169	8653	9040	9338	9558	9716
42	4571	5382	6173	6916	7585	8165	8649	9037	9335	9557
43	3782	4576	5383	6173	6913	7582	8162	8646	9035	9334
44	3041	3788	4580	5385	6172	6912	7580	8160	8645	9033
45	2375	3049	3794	4583	5387	6173	6911	7579	8159	8644
46	1799	2384	3057	3799	4587	5389	6173	6911	7579	8159
47	1320	1807	2391	3063	3804	4590	5391	6174	6912	7579
48	0938	1328	1815	2398	3069	3809	4593	5393	6176	6914
49	0644	0944	1335	1822	2404	3074	3813	4596	5395	6178
50	0428	0650	0950	1341	1827	2409	3078	3816	4599	5398
51	0275	0432	0655	0955	1346	1832	2413	3082	3819	4602
52	0170	0278	0436	0659	0960	1350	1836	2417	3084	3822
53	0102	0172	0280	0439	0662	0963	1353	1838	2419	3086
54	0059	0103	0174	0282	0441	0664	0965	1355	1840	2421
55	0033	0059	0104	0175	0284	0443	0666	0967	1356	1841
56	0017	0033	0060	0105	0176	0285	0444	0667	0967	1356
57	0009	0018	0034	0061	0106	0177	0286	0444	0667	0967
58	0004	0009	0018	0034	0061	0106	0177	0286	0444	0666
59	0002	0005	0009	0018	0034	0061	0106	0177	0285	0443
60	0001	0002	0005	0009	0018	0034	0061	0106	0177	0284
61		0001	0002	0005	0009	0018	0034	0061	0106	0176
62			0001	0002	0005	0009	0018	0034	0061	0105
63				0001	0002	0005	0009	0018	0034	0060

Appendix A (cont.)

$n = 100$ CUMULATIVE BINOMIAL DISTRIBUTION

p	41	42	43	44	45	46	47	48	49	50
r 64					0001	0002	0005	0009	0018	0033
65						0001	0002	0005	0009	0018
66							0001	0002	0004	0009
67								0001	0002	0004
68									0001	0002
69										0001

Appendix B

CUMULATIVE POISSON DISTRIBUTION

$$P(r \le r_0 \mid \mu)$$

μ \ r_0	0	1	2	3	4	5	6	7	8	9
0.02	980	1000								
0.04	961	999	1000							
0.06	942	998	1000							
0.08	923	997	1000							
0.10	905	995	1000							
0.15	861	990	999	1000						
0.20	819	982	999	1000						
0.25	779	974	998	1000						
0.30	741	963	996	1000						
0.35	705	951	994	1000						
0.40	670	938	992	999	1000					
0.45	638	925	989	999	1000					
0.50	607	910	986	998	1000					
0.55	577	894	982	998	1000					
0.60	549	878	977	997	1000					
0.65	522	861	972	996	999	1000				
0.70	497	844	966	994	999	1000				
0.75	472	827	959	993	999	1000				
0.80	449	809	953	991	999	1000				
0.85	427	791	945	989	998	1000				
0.90	407	772	937	987	998	1000				
0.95	387	754	929	984	997	1000				
1.00	368	736	920	981	996	999	1000			
1.1	333	699	900	974	995	999	1000			
1.2	301	663	879	966	992	998	1000			
1.3	273	627	857	957	989	998	1000			
1.4	247	592	833	946	986	997	999	1000		
1.5	223	558	809	934	981	996	999	1000		
1.6	202	525	783	921	976	994	999	1000		
1.7	183	493	757	907	970	992	998	1000		
1.8	165	463	731	891	964	990	997	999	1000	
1.9	150	434	704	875	956	987	997	999	1000	
2.0	135	406	677	857	947	983	995	999	1000	
2.2	111	355	623	819	928	975	993	998	1000	
2.4	091	308	570	779	904	964	988	997	999	1000
2.6	074	267	518	736	877	951	983	995	999	1000
2.8	061	231	469	692	848	935	976	992	998	999
3.0	050	199	423	647	815	916	966	988	996	999

μ	10
2.8	1000
3.0	1000

459

Appendix B (*cont.*)

CUMULATIVE POISSON DISTRIBUTION

r_0 / μ	0	1	2	3	4	5	6	7	8	9
3.2	041	171	380	603	781	895	955	983	994	998
3.4	033	147	340	558	744	871	942	977	992	997
3.6	027	126	303	515	706	844	927	969	988	996
3.8	022	107	269	473	668	816	909	960	984	994
4.0	018	092	238	433	629	785	889	949	979	992
4.2	015	078	210	395	590	753	867	936	972	989
4.4	012	066	185	359	551	720	844	921	964	985
4.6	010	056	163	326	513	686	818	905	955	980
4.8	008	048	143	294	476	651	791	887	944	975
5.0	007	040	125	265	440	616	762	867	932	968
5.2	006	034	109	238	406	581	732	845	918	960
5.4	005	029	095	213	373	546	702	822	903	951
5.6	004	024	082	191	342	512	670	797	886	941
5.8	003	021	072	170	313	478	638	771	867	929
6.0	002	017	062	151	285	446	606	744	847	916
6.2	002	015	054	134	259	414	574	716	826	902
6.4	002	012	046	119	235	384	542	687	803	886
6.6	001	010	040	105	213	355	511	658	780	869
6.8	001	009	034	093	192	327	480	628	755	850
7.0	001	007	030	082	173	301	450	599	729	830

μ	10	11	12	13	14	15	16	17
3.2	1000							
3.4	999	1000						
3.6	999	1000						
3.8	998	999	1000					
4.0	997	999	1000					
4.2	996	999	1000					
4.4	994	998	999	1000				
4.6	992	997	999	1000				
4.8	990	996	999	1000				
5.0	986	995	998	999	1000			
5.2	982	993	997	999	1000			
5.4	977	990	996	999	1000			
5.6	972	988	995	998	999	1000		
5.8	965	984	993	997	999	1000		
6.0	957	980	991	996	999	999	1000	
6.2	949	975	989	995	998	999	1000	
6.4	939	969	986	994	997	999	1000	
6.6	927	963	982	992	997	999	999	1000
6.8	915	955	978	990	996	998	999	1000
7.0	901	947	973	987	994	998	999	1000

Appendix B (cont.)

CUMULATIVE POISSON DISTRIBUTION

μ \ r_0	0	1	2	3	4	5	6	7	8	9
7.2	001	006	025	072	156	276	420	569	703	810
7.4	001	005	022	063	140	253	392	539	676	788
7.6	001	004	019	055	125	231	365	510	648	765
7.8	000	004	016	048	112	210	338	481	620	741
8.0	000	003	014	042	100	191	313	453	593	717
8.5	000	002	009	030	074	150	256	386	523	653
9.0	000	001	006	021	055	116	207	324	456	587
9.5	000	001	004	015	040	089	165	269	392	522
10.0	000	000	003	010	029	067	130	220	333	458
10.5	000	000	002	007	021	050	102	179	279	397
11.0	000	000	001	005	015	038	079	143	232	341
11.5	000	000	001	003	011	028	060	114	191	289
12.0	000	000	001	002	008	020	046	090	155	242
12.5	000	000	000	002	005	015	035	070	125	201

μ	10	11	12	13	14	15	16	17	18	19
7.2	887	937	967	984	993	997	999	999	1000	
7.4	871	926	961	980	991	996	998	999	1000	
7.6	854	915	954	976	989	995	998	999	1000	
7.8	835	902	945	971	986	993	997	999	1000	
8.0	816	888	936	966	983	992	996	998	999	1000
8.5	763	849	909	949	973	986	993	997	999	999
9.0	706	803	876	926	959	978	989	995	998	999
9.5	645	752	836	898	940	967	982	991	996	998
10.0	583	697	792	864	917	951	973	986	993	997
10.5	521	639	742	825	888	932	960	978	988	994
11.0	460	579	689	781	854	907	944	968	982	991
11.5	402	520	633	733	815	878	924	954	974	986
12.0	347	462	576	682	772	844	899	937	963	979
12.5	297	406	519	628	725	806	869	916	948	969

μ	20	21	22	23	24	25	26
8.5	1000						
9.0	1000						
9.5	999	1000					
10.0	998	999	1000				
10.5	997	999	999	1000			
11.0	995	998	999	1000			
11.5	992	996	998	999	1000		
12.0	988	994	997	999	999	1000	
12.5	983	991	995	998	999	999	1000

Appendix B (cont.)

CUMULATIVE POISSON DISTRIBUTION

μ \ r_0	0	1	2	3	4	5	6	7	8	9
13.0	000	000	000	001	004	011	026	054	100	166
13.5	000	000	000	001	003	008	019	041	079	135
14.0	000	000	000	000	002	006	014	032	062	109
14.5	000	000	000	000	001	004	010	024	048	088
15.0	000	000	000	000	001	003	008	018	037	070

	10	11	12	13	14	15	16	17	18	19
13.0	252	353	463	573	675	764	835	890	930	957
13.5	211	304	409	518	623	718	798	861	908	942
14.0	176	260	358	464	570	669	756	827	883	923
14.5	145	220	311	413	518	619	711	790	853	901
15.0	118	185	268	363	466	568	664	749	819	875

	20	21	22	23	24	25	26	27	28	29
13.0	975	986	992	996	998	999	1000			
13.5	965	980	989	994	997	998	999	1000		
14.0	952	971	983	991	995	997	999	999	1000	
14.5	936	960	976	986	992	996	998	999	999	1000
15.0	917	947	967	981	989	994	997	998	999	1000

Appendix B (cont.)

CUMULATIVE POISSON DISTRIBUTION

r_0 / μ	4	5	6	7	8	9	10	11	12	13
16	000	001	004	010	022	043	077	127	193	275
17	000	001	002	005	013	026	049	085	135	201
18	000	000	001	003	007	015	030	055	092	143
19	000	000	001	002	004	009	018	035	061	098
20	000	000	000	001	002	005	011	021	039	066
21	000	000	000	000	001	003	006	013	025	043
22	000	000	000	000	001	002	004	008	015	028
23	000	000	000	000	000	001	002	004	009	017
24	000	000	000	000	000	000	001	003	005	011
25	000	000	000	000	000	000	001	001	003	006

	14	15	16	17	18	19	20	21	22	23
16	368	467	566	659	742	812	868	911	942	963
17	281	371	468	564	655	736	805	861	905	937
18	208	287	375	469	562	651	731	799	855	899
19	150	215	292	378	469	561	647	725	793	849
20	105	157	221	297	381	470	559	644	721	787
21	072	111	163	227	302	384	471	558	640	716
22	048	077	117	169	232	306	387	472	556	637
23	031	052	082	123	175	238	310	389	472	555
24	020	034	056	087	128	180	243	314	392	473
25	012	022	038	060	092	134	185	247	318	394

	24	25	26	27	28	29	30	31	32	33
16	978	987	993	996	998	999	999	1000		
17	959	975	985	991	995	997	999	999	1000	
18	932	955	972	983	990	994	997	998	999	1000
19	893	927	951	969	980	988	993	996	998	999
20	843	888	922	948	966	978	987	992	995	997
21	782	838	883	917	944	963	976	985	991	994
22	712	777	832	877	913	940	959	973	983	989
23	635	708	772	827	873	908	936	956	971	981
24	554	632	704	768	823	868	904	932	953	969
25	473	553	629	700	763	818	863	900	929	950

	34	35	36	37	38	39	40	41	42	43
19	999	1000								
20	999	999	1000							
21	997	998	999	999	1000					
22	994	996	998	999	999	1000				
23	988	993	996	997	999	999	1000			
24	979	987	992	995	997	998	999	999	1000	
25	966	978	985	991	994	997	998	999	999	1000

Appendix C

ORDINATES OF THE NORMAL DISTRIBUTION FUNCTION

z	.00	.01	.02	.03	.04	.05	.06	.07	.08	.09
.0	.3989	.3989	.3989	.3988	.3986	.3984	.3982	.3980	.3977	.3973
.1	.3970	.3965	.3961	.3956	.3951	.3945	.3939	.3932	.3925	.3918
.2	.3910	.3902	.3894	.3885	.3876	.3867	.3857	.3847	.3836	.3825
.3	.3814	.3802	.3790	.3778	.3765	.3752	.3739	.3725	.3712	.3697
.4	.3683	.3668	.3653	.3637	.3621	.3605	.3589	.3572	.3555	.3538
.5	.3521	.3503	.3485	.3467	.3448	.3429	.3410	.3391	.3372	.3352
.6	.3332	.3312	.3292	.3271	.3251	.3230	.3209	.3187	.3166	.3144
.7	.3123	.3101	.3079	.3056	.3034	.3011	.2989	.2966	.2943	.2920
.8	.2897	.2874	.2850	.2827	.2803	.2780	.2756	.2732	.2709	.2685
.9	.2661	.2637	.2613	.2589	.2565	.2541	.2516	.2492	.2468	.2444
1.0	.2420	.2396	.2371	.2347	.2323	.2299	.2275	.2251	.2227	.2203
1.1	.2179	.2155	.2131	.2107	.2083	.2059	.2036	.2012	.1989	.1965
1.2	.1942	.1919	.1895	.1872	.1849	.1826	.1804	.1781	.1758	.1736
1.3	.1714	.1691	.1669	.1647	.1626	.1604	.1582	.1561	.1539	.1518
1.4	.1497	.1476	.1456	.1435	.1415	.1394	.1374	.1354	.1334	.1315
1.5	.1295	.1276	.1257	.1238	.1219	.1200	.1182	.1163	.1145	.1127
1.6	.1109	.1092	.1074	.1057	.1040	.1023	.1006	.09893	.09728	.09566
1.7	.09405	.09246	.09089	.08933	.08780	.08628	.08478	.08329	.08183	.08038
1.8	.07895	.07754	.07614	.07477	.07341	.07206	.07074	.06943	.06814	.06687
1.9	.06562	.06438	.06316	.06195	.06077	.05959	.05844	.05730	.05618	.05508
2.0	.05399	.05292	.05186	.05082	.04980	.04879	.04780	.04682	.04586	.04491
2.1	.04398	.04307	.04217	.04128	.04041	.03955	.03871	.03788	.03706	.03626
2.2	.03547	.03470	.03394	.03319	.03246	.03174	.03103	.03034	.02965	.02898
2.3	.02833	.02768	.02705	.02643	.02582	.02522	.02463	.02406	.02349	.02294
2.4	.02239	.02186	.02134	.02083	.02033	.01984	.01936	.01888	.01842	.01797
2.5	.01753	.01709	.01667	.01625	.01585	.01545	.01506	.01468	.01431	.01394
2.6	.01358	.01323	.01289	.01256	.01223	.01191	.01160	.01130	.01100	.01071
2.7	.01042	.01014	$.0^29871$	$.0^29606$	$.0^29347$	$.0^29094$	$.0^28846$	$.0^28605$	$.0^28370$	$.0^28140$

Appendix C (cont.)

ORDINATES OF THE NORMAL DISTRIBUTION FUNCTION

z	.00	.01	.02	.03	.04	.05	.06	.07	.08	.09
2.8	$.0^27915$	$.0^27697$	$.0^27483$	$.0^27274$	$.0^27071$	$.0^26873$	$.0^26679$	$.0^26491$	$.0^26307$	$.0^26127$
2.9	$.0^25953$	$.0^25782$	$.0^25616$	$.0^25454$	$.0^25296$	$.0^25143$	$.0^24993$	$.0^24847$	$.0^24705$	$.0^24567$
3.0	$.0^24432$	$.0^24301$	$.0^24173$	$.0^24049$	$.0^23928$	$.0^23810$	$.0^23695$	$.0^23584$	$.0^23475$	$.0^23370$
3.1	$.0^23267$	$.0^23167$	$.0^23070$	$.0^22975$	$.0^22884$	$.0^22794$	$.0^22707$	$.0^22623$	$.0^22541$	$.0^22461$
3.2	$.0^22384$	$.0^22309$	$.0^22236$	$.0^22165$	$.0^22096$	$.0^22029$	$.0^21964$	$.0^21901$	$.0^21840$	$.0^21780$
3.3	$.0^21723$	$.0^21667$	$.0^21612$	$.0^21560$	$.0^21508$	$.0^21459$	$.0^21411$	$.0^21364$	$.0^21319$	$.0^21275$
3.4	$.0^21232$	$.0^21191$	$.0^21151$	$.0^21112$	$.0^21075$	$.0^21038$	$.0^21003$	$.0^39689$	$.0^39358$	$.0^39037$
3.5	$.0^38727$	$.0^38426$	$.0^38135$	$.0^37853$	$.0^37581$	$.0^37317$	$.0^37061$	$.0^36814$	$.0^36575$	$.0^36343$
3.6	$.0^36119$	$.0^35902$	$.0^35693$	$.0^35490$	$.0^35294$	$.0^35105$	$.0^34921$	$.0^34744$	$.0^34573$	$.0^34408$
3.7	$.0^34248$	$.0^34093$	$.0^33944$	$.0^33800$	$.0^33661$	$.0^33526$	$.0^33396$	$.0^33271$	$.0^33149$	$.0^33032$
3.8	$.0^32919$	$.0^32810$	$.0^32705$	$.0^32604$	$.0^32506$	$.0^32411$	$.0^32320$	$.0^32232$	$.0^32147$	$.0^32065$
3.9	$.0^31987$	$.0^31910$	$.0^31837$	$.0^31766$	$.0^31698$	$.0^31633$	$.0^31569$	$.0^31508$	$.0^31449$	$.0^31393$
4.0	$.0^31338$	$.0^31286$	$.0^31235$	$.0^31186$	$.0^31140$	$.0^31094$	$.0^31051$	$.0^31009$	$.0^49687$	$.0^49299$
4.1	$.0^48926$	$.0^48567$	$.0^48222$	$.0^47890$	$.0^47570$	$.0^47263$	$.0^46967$	$.0^46683$	$.0^46410$	$.0^46147$
4.2	$.0^45894$	$.0^45652$	$.0^45418$	$.0^45194$	$.0^44979$	$.0^44772$	$.0^44573$	$.0^44382$	$.0^44199$	$.0^44023$
4.3	$.0^43854$	$.0^43691$	$.0^43535$	$.0^43386$	$.0^43242$	$.0^43104$	$.0^42972$	$.0^42845$	$.0^42723$	$.0^42606$
4.4	$.0^42494$	$.0^42387$	$.0^42284$	$.0^42185$	$.0^42090$	$.0^41999$	$.0^41912$	$.0^41829$	$.0^41749$	$.0^41672$
4.5	$.0^41598$	$.0^41528$	$.0^41461$	$.0^41396$	$.0^41334$	$.0^41275$	$.0^41218$	$.0^41164$	$.0^41112$	$.0^41062$
4.6	$.0^41014$	$.0^59684$	$.0^59248$	$.0^58830$	$.0^58430$	$.0^58047$	$.0^57681$	$.0^57331$	$.0^56996$	$.0^56676$
4.7	$.0^56370$	$.0^56077$	$.0^55797$	$.0^55530$	$.0^55274$	$.0^55030$	$.0^54796$	$.0^54560$	$.0^54360$	$.0^54156$
4.8	$.0^53961$	$.0^53775$	$.0^53598$	$.0^53428$	$.0^53267$	$.0^53112$	$.0^52965$	$.0^52824$	$.0^52690$	$.0^52561$
4.9	$.0^52439$	$.0^52322$	$.0^52211$	$.0^52105$	$.0^52003$	$.0^51907$	$.0^51814$	$.0^51727$	$.0^51643$	$.0^51563$

Appendix D

CUMULATIVE (LOWER TAIL) AREAS OF THE NORMAL DISTRIBUTION FUNCTION

z	.00	.01	.02	.03	.04	.05	.06	.07	.08	.09
−.0	.5000	.4960	.4920	.4880	.4840	.4801	.4761	.4721	.4681	.4641
−.1	.4602	.4562	.4522	.4483	.4443	.4404	.4364	.4325	.4286	.4247
−.2	.4207	.4168	.4129	.4090	.4052	.4013	.3974	.3936	.3897	.3859
−.3	.3821	.3783	.3745	.3707	.3669	.3632	.3594	.3557	.3520	.3483
−.4	.3446	.3409	.3372	.3336	.3300	.3264	.3228	.3192	.3156	.3121
−.5	.3085	.3050	.3015	.2981	.2946	.2912	.2877	.2843	.2810	.2776
−.6	.2743	.2709	.2676	.2643	.2611	.2578	.2546	.2514	.2483	.2451
−.7	.2420	.2389	.2358	.2327	.2297	.2266	.2236	.2206	.2177	.2148
−.8	.2119	.2090	.2061	.2033	.2005	.1977	.1949	.1922	.1894	.1867
−.9	.1841	.1814	.1788	.1762	.1736	.1711	.1685	.1660	.1635	.1611
−1.0	.1587	.1562	.1539	.1515	.1492	.1469	.1446	.1423	.1401	.1379
−1.1	.1357	.1335	.1314	.1292	.1271	.1251	.1230	.1210	.1190	.1170
−1.2	.1151	.1131	.1112	.1093	.1075	.1056	.1038	.1020	.1003	.09853
−1.3	.09680	.09510	.09342	.09176	.09012	.08851	.08691	.08534	.08379	.08226
−1.4	.08076	.07927	.07780	.07636	.07493	.07353	.07215	.07078	.06944	.06811
−1.5	.06681	.06552	.06426	.06301	.06178	.06057	.05938	.05821	.05705	.05592
−1.6	.05480	.05370	.05262	.05155	.05050	.04947	.04846	.04746	.04648	.04551
−1.7	.04457	.04363	.04272	.04182	.04093	.04006	.03920	.03836	.03754	.03673
−1.8	.03593	.03515	.03438	.03362	.03288	.03216	.03144	.03074	.03005	.02938
−1.9	.02872	.02807	.02743	.02680	.02619	.02559	.02500	.02442	.02385	.02330
−2.0	.02275	.02222	.02169	.02118	.02068	.02018	.01970	.01923	.01876	.01831
−2.1	.01786	.01743	.01700	.01659	.01618	.01578	.01539	.01500	.01463	.01426
−2.2	.01390	.01355	.01321	.01287	.01255	.01222	.01191	.01160	.01130	.01101
−2.3	.01072	.01044	.01017	$.0^{2}9903$	$.0^{2}9642$	$.0^{2}9387$	$.0^{2}9137$	$.0^{2}8894$	$.0^{2}8656$	$.0^{2}8424$
−2.4	$.0^{2}8198$	$.0^{2}7976$	$.0^{2}7760$	$.0^{2}7549$	$.0^{2}7344$	$.0^{2}7143$	$.0^{2}6947$	$.0^{2}6756$	$.0^{2}6569$	$.0^{2}6387$
−2.5	$.0^{2}6210$	$.0^{2}6037$	$.0^{2}5868$	$.0^{2}5703$	$.0^{2}5543$	$.0^{2}5386$	$.0^{2}5234$	$.0^{2}5085$	$.0^{2}4940$	$.0^{2}4799$
−2.6	$.0^{2}4661$	$.0^{2}4527$	$.0^{2}4396$	$.0^{2}4269$	$.0^{2}4145$	$.0^{2}4025$	$.0^{2}3907$	$.0^{2}3793$	$.0^{2}3681$	$.0^{2}3573$
−2.7	$.0^{2}3467$	$.0^{2}3364$	$.0^{2}3264$	$.0^{2}3167$	$.0^{2}3072$	$.0^{2}2980$	$.0^{2}2890$	$.0^{2}2803$	$.0^{2}2718$	$.0^{2}2635$

Appendix D (cont.)

CUMULATIVE (LOWER TAIL) AREAS OF THE NORMAL DISTRIBUTION FUNCTION

z	.00	.01	.02	.03	.04	.05	.06	.07	.08	.09
−2.8	$.0^{2}2555$	$.0^{2}2477$	$.0^{2}2401$	$.0^{2}2327$	$.0^{2}2256$	$.0^{2}2186$	$.0^{2}2118$	$.0^{2}2052$	$.0^{2}1988$	$.0^{2}1926$
−2.9	$.0^{2}1866$	$.0^{2}1807$	$.0^{2}1750$	$.0^{2}1695$	$.0^{2}1641$	$.0^{2}1589$	$.0^{2}1538$	$.0^{2}1489$	$.0^{2}1441$	$.0^{2}1395$
−3.0	$.0^{2}1350$	$.0^{2}1306$	$.0^{2}1264$	$.0^{2}1223$	$.0^{2}1183$	$.0^{2}1144$	$.0^{2}1107$	$.0^{2}1070$	$.0^{2}1035$	$.0^{2}1001$
−3.1	$.0^{3}9676$	$.0^{3}9354$	$.0^{3}9043$	$.0^{3}8740$	$.0^{3}8447$	$.0^{3}8164$	$.0^{3}7888$	$.0^{3}7622$	$.0^{3}7364$	$.0^{3}7114$
−3.2	$.0^{3}6871$	$.0^{3}6637$	$.0^{3}6410$	$.0^{3}6190$	$.0^{3}5976$	$.0^{3}5770$	$.0^{3}5571$	$.0^{3}5377$	$.0^{3}5190$	$.0^{3}5009$
−3.3	$.0^{3}4834$	$.0^{3}4665$	$.0^{3}4501$	$.0^{3}4342$	$.0^{3}4189$	$.0^{3}4041$	$.0^{3}3897$	$.0^{3}3758$	$.0^{3}3624$	$.0^{3}3495$
−3.4	$.0^{3}3369$	$.0^{3}3248$	$.0^{3}3131$	$.0^{3}3018$	$.0^{3}2909$	$.0^{3}2803$	$.0^{3}2701$	$.0^{3}2602$	$.0^{3}2507$	$.0^{3}2415$
−3.5	$.0^{3}2326$	$.0^{3}2241$	$.0^{3}2158$	$.0^{3}2078$	$.0^{3}2001$	$.0^{3}1926$	$.0^{3}1854$	$.0^{3}1785$	$.0^{3}1718$	$.0^{3}1653$
−3.6	$.0^{3}1591$	$.0^{3}1531$	$.0^{3}1473$	$.0^{3}1417$	$.0^{3}1363$	$.0^{3}1311$	$.0^{3}1261$	$.0^{3}1213$	$.0^{3}1166$	$.0^{3}1121$
−3.7	$.0^{3}1078$	$.0^{3}1036$	$.0^{4}9961$	$.0^{4}9574$	$.0^{4}9201$	$.0^{4}8842$	$.0^{4}8496$	$.0^{4}8162$	$.0^{4}7841$	$.0^{4}7532$
−3.8	$.0^{4}7235$	$.0^{4}6948$	$.0^{4}6673$	$.0^{4}6407$	$.0^{4}6152$	$.0^{4}5906$	$.0^{4}5669$	$.0^{4}5442$	$.0^{4}5223$	$.0^{4}5012$
−3.9	$.0^{4}4810$	$.0^{4}4615$	$.0^{4}4427$	$.0^{4}4247$	$.0^{4}4074$	$.0^{4}3908$	$.0^{4}3747$	$.0^{4}3594$	$.0^{4}3446$	$.0^{4}3304$
−4.0	$.0^{4}3167$	$.0^{4}3036$	$.0^{4}2910$	$.0^{4}2789$	$.0^{4}2673$	$.0^{4}2561$	$.0^{4}2454$	$.0^{4}2351$	$.0^{4}2252$	$.0^{4}2157$
−4.1	$.0^{4}2066$	$.0^{4}1978$	$.0^{4}1894$	$.0^{4}1814$	$.0^{4}1737$	$.0^{4}1662$	$.0^{4}1591$	$.0^{4}1523$	$.0^{4}1458$	$.0^{4}1395$
−4.2	$.0^{4}1335$	$.0^{4}1277$	$.0^{4}1222$	$.0^{4}1168$	$.0^{4}1118$	$.0^{4}1069$	$.0^{4}1022$	$.0^{5}9774$	$.0^{5}9345$	$.0^{5}8934$
−4.3	$.0^{5}8540$	$.0^{5}8163$	$.0^{5}7801$	$.0^{5}7455$	$.0^{5}7124$	$.0^{5}6807$	$.0^{5}6503$	$.0^{5}6212$	$.0^{5}5934$	$.0^{5}5668$
−4.4	$.0^{5}5413$	$.0^{5}5169$	$.0^{5}4935$	$.0^{5}4712$	$.0^{5}4498$	$.0^{5}4294$	$.0^{5}4098$	$.0^{5}3911$	$.0^{5}3732$	$.0^{5}3561$
−4.5	$.0^{5}3398$	$.0^{5}3241$	$.0^{5}3092$	$.0^{5}2949$	$.0^{5}2813$	$.0^{5}2682$	$.0^{5}2558$	$.0^{5}2439$	$.0^{5}2325$	$.0^{5}2216$
−4.6	$.0^{5}2112$	$.0^{5}2013$	$.0^{5}1919$	$.0^{5}1828$	$.0^{5}1742$	$.0^{5}1660$	$.0^{5}1581$	$.0^{5}1506$	$.0^{5}1434$	$.0^{5}1366$
−4.7	$.0^{5}1301$	$.0^{5}1239$	$.0^{5}1179$	$.0^{5}1123$	$.0^{5}1069$	$.0^{5}1017$	$.0^{6}9680$	$.0^{6}9211$	$.0^{6}8765$	$.0^{6}8339$
−4.8	$.0^{6}7933$	$.0^{6}7547$	$.0^{6}7178$	$.0^{6}6827$	$.0^{6}6492$	$.0^{6}6173$	$.0^{6}5869$	$.0^{6}5580$	$.0^{6}5304$	$.0^{6}5042$
−4.9	$.0^{6}4792$	$.0^{6}4554$	$.0^{6}4327$	$.0^{6}4111$	$.0^{6}3906$	$.0^{6}3711$	$.0^{6}3525$	$.0^{6}3348$	$.0^{6}3179$	$.0^{6}3019$

Appendix D (cont.)

CUMULATIVE (LOWER TAIL) AREAS OF THE NORMAL DISTRIBUTION FUNCTION

z	.00	.01	.02	.03	.04	.05	.06	.07	.08	.09
.0	.5000	.5040	.5080	.5120	.5160	.5199	.5239	.5279	.5319	.5359
.1	.5398	.5438	.5478	.5517	.5557	.5596	.5636	.5675	.5714	.5753
.2	.5793	.5832	.5871	.5910	.5948	.5987	.6026	.6064	.6103	.6141
.3	.6179	.6217	.6255	.6293	.6331	.6368	.6406	.6443	.6480	.6517
.4	.6554	.6591	.6628	.6664	.6700	.6736	.6772	.6808	.6844	.6879
.5	.6915	.6950	.6985	.7019	.7054	.7088	.7123	.7157	.7190	.7224
.6	.7257	.7291	.7324	.7357	.7389	.7422	.7454	.7486	.7517	.7549
.7	.7580	.7611	.7642	.7673	.7703	.7734	.7764	.7794	.7823	.7852
.8	.7881	.7910	.7939	.7967	.7995	.8023	.8051	.8078	.8106	.8133
.9	.8159	.8186	.8212	.8238	.8264	.8289	.8315	.8340	.8365	.8389
1.0	.8413	.8438	.8461	.8485	.8508	.8531	.8554	.8577	.8599	.8621
1.1	.8643	.8665	.8686	.8708	.8729	.8749	.8770	.8790	.8810	.8830
1.2	.8849	.8869	.8888	.8907	.8925	.8944	.8962	.8980	.8997	.90147
1.3	.90320	.90490	.90658	.90824	.90988	.91149	.91309	.91466	.91621	.91774
1.4	.91924	.92073	.92220	.92364	.92507	.92647	.92785	.92922	.93056	.93189
1.5	.93319	.93448	.93574	.93699	.93822	.93943	.94062	.94179	.94295	.94408
1.6	.94520	.94630	.94738	.94845	.94950	.95053	.95154	.95254	.95352	.95449
1.7	.95543	.95637	.95728	.95818	.95907	.95994	.96080	.96164	.96246	.96327
1.8	.96407	.96485	.96562	.96638	.96712	.96784	.96856	.96926	.96995	.97062
1.9	.97128	.97193	.97257	.97320	.97381	.97441	.97500	.97558	.97615	.97670
2.0	.97725	.97778	.97831	.97882	.97932	.97982	.98030	.98077	.98124	.98169
2.1	.98214	.98257	.98300	.98341	.98382	.98422	.98461	.98500	.98537	.98574
2.2	.98610	.98645	.98679	.98713	.98745	.98778	.98809	.98840	.98870	.98899
2.3	.98928	.98956	.98983	$.9^{2}0097$	$.9^{2}0358$	$.9^{2}0613$	$.9^{2}0863$	$.9^{2}1106$	$.9^{2}1344$	$.9^{2}1576$
2.4	$.9^{2}1802$	$.9^{2}2024$	$.9^{2}2240$	$.9^{2}2451$	$.9^{2}2656$	$.9^{2}2857$	$.9^{2}3053$	$.9^{2}3244$	$.9^{2}3431$	$.9^{2}3613$
2.5	$.9^{2}3790$	$.9^{2}3963$	$.9^{2}4132$	$.9^{2}4297$	$.9^{2}4457$	$.9^{2}4614$	$.9^{2}4766$	$.9^{2}4915$	$.9^{2}5060$	$.9^{2}5201$
2.6	$.9^{2}5339$	$.9^{2}5473$	$.9^{2}5604$	$.9^{2}5731$	$.9^{2}5855$	$.9^{2}5975$	$.9^{2}6093$	$.9^{2}6207$	$.9^{2}6319$	$.9^{2}6427$
2.7	$.9^{2}6533$	$.9^{2}6636$	$.9^{2}6736$	$.9^{2}6833$	$.9^{2}6928$	$.9^{2}7020$	$.9^{2}7110$	$.9^{2}7197$	$.9^{2}7282$	$.9^{2}7365$

Appendix D (cont.)

CUMULATIVE (LOWER TAIL) AREAS OF THE NORMAL DISTRIBUTION FUNCTION

z	.00	.01	.02	.03	.04	.05	.06	.07	.08	.09
2.8	$.9^{2}7445$	$.9^{2}7523$	$.9^{2}7599$	$.9^{2}7673$	$.9^{2}7744$	$.9^{2}7814$	$.9^{2}7882$	$.9^{2}7948$	$.9^{2}8012$	$.9^{2}8074$
2.9	$.9^{2}8134$	$.9^{2}8193$	$.9^{2}8250$	$.9^{2}8305$	$.9^{2}8359$	$.9^{2}8411$	$.9^{2}8462$	$.9^{2}8511$	$.9^{2}8559$	$.9^{2}8605$
3.0	$.9^{2}8650$	$.9^{2}8694$	$.9^{2}8736$	$.9^{2}8777$	$.9^{2}8817$	$.9^{2}8856$	$.9^{2}8893$	$.9^{2}8930$	$.9^{2}8965$	$.9^{2}8999$
3.1	$.9^{3}0324$	$.9^{3}0646$	$.9^{3}0957$	$.9^{3}1260$	$.9^{3}1553$	$.9^{3}1836$	$.9^{3}2112$	$.9^{3}2378$	$.9^{3}2636$	$.9^{3}2886$
3.2	$.9^{3}3129$	$.9^{3}3363$	$.9^{3}3590$	$.9^{3}3810$	$.9^{3}4024$	$.9^{3}4230$	$.9^{3}4429$	$.9^{3}4623$	$.9^{3}4810$	$.9^{3}4991$
3.3	$.9^{3}5166$	$.9^{3}5335$	$.9^{3}5499$	$.9^{3}5658$	$.9^{3}5811$	$.9^{3}5959$	$.9^{3}6103$	$.9^{3}6242$	$.9^{3}6376$	$.9^{3}6505$
3.4	$.9^{3}6631$	$.9^{3}6752$	$.9^{3}6869$	$.9^{3}6982$	$.9^{3}7091$	$.9^{3}7197$	$.9^{3}7299$	$.9^{3}7398$	$.9^{3}7493$	$.9^{3}7585$
3.5	$.9^{3}7674$	$.9^{3}7759$	$.9^{3}7842$	$.9^{3}7922$	$.9^{3}7999$	$.9^{3}8074$	$.9^{3}8146$	$.9^{3}8215$	$.9^{3}8282$	$.9^{3}8347$
3.6	$.9^{3}8409$	$.9^{3}8469$	$.9^{3}8527$	$.9^{3}8583$	$.9^{3}8637$	$.9^{3}8689$	$.9^{3}8739$	$.9^{3}8787$	$.9^{3}8834$	$.9^{3}8879$
3.7	$.9^{3}8922$	$.9^{3}8964$	$.9^{4}0039$	$.9^{4}0426$	$.9^{4}0799$	$.9^{4}1158$	$.9^{4}1504$	$.9^{4}1838$	$.9^{4}2159$	$.9^{4}2468$
3.8	$.9^{4}2765$	$.9^{4}3052$	$.9^{4}3327$	$.9^{4}3593$	$.9^{4}3848$	$.9^{4}4094$	$.9^{4}4331$	$.9^{4}4558$	$.9^{4}4777$	$.9^{4}4988$
3.9	$.9^{4}5190$	$.9^{4}5385$	$.9^{4}5573$	$.9^{4}5753$	$.9^{4}5926$	$.9^{4}6092$	$.9^{4}6253$	$.9^{4}6406$	$.9^{4}6554$	$.9^{4}6696$
4.0	$.9^{4}6833$	$.9^{4}6964$	$.9^{4}7090$	$.9^{4}7211$	$.9^{4}7327$	$.9^{4}7439$	$.9^{4}7546$	$.9^{4}7649$	$.9^{4}7748$	$.9^{4}7843$
4.1	$.9^{4}7934$	$.9^{4}8022$	$.9^{4}8106$	$.9^{4}8186$	$.9^{4}8263$	$.9^{4}8338$	$.9^{4}8409$	$.9^{4}8477$	$.9^{4}8542$	$.9^{4}8605$
4.2	$.9^{4}8665$	$.9^{4}8723$	$.9^{4}8778$	$.9^{4}8832$	$.9^{4}8882$	$.9^{4}8931$	$.9^{4}8978$	$.9^{5}0226$	$.9^{5}0655$	$.9^{5}1066$
4.3	$.9^{5}1460$	$.9^{5}1837$	$.9^{5}2199$	$.9^{5}2545$	$.9^{5}2876$	$.9^{5}3193$	$.9^{5}3497$	$.9^{5}3788$	$.9^{5}4066$	$.9^{5}4332$
4.4	$.9^{5}4587$	$.9^{5}4831$	$.9^{5}5065$	$.9^{5}5288$	$.9^{5}5502$	$.9^{5}5706$	$.9^{5}5902$	$.9^{5}6089$	$.9^{5}6268$	$.9^{5}6439$
4.5	$.9^{5}6602$	$.9^{5}6759$	$.9^{5}6908$	$.9^{5}7051$	$.9^{5}7187$	$.9^{5}7318$	$.9^{5}7442$	$.9^{5}7561$	$.9^{5}7675$	$.9^{5}7784$
4.6	$.9^{5}7888$	$.9^{5}7987$	$.9^{5}8081$	$.9^{5}8172$	$.9^{5}8258$	$.9^{5}8340$	$.9^{5}8419$	$.9^{5}8494$	$.9^{5}8566$	$.9^{5}8634$
4.7	$.9^{5}8699$	$.9^{5}8761$	$.9^{5}8821$	$.9^{5}8877$	$.9^{5}8931$	$.9^{5}8983$	$.9^{6}0320$	$.9^{6}0789$	$.9^{6}1235$	$.9^{6}1661$
4.8	$.9^{6}2067$	$.9^{6}2453$	$.9^{6}2822$	$.9^{6}3173$	$.9^{6}3508$	$.9^{6}3827$	$.9^{6}4131$	$.9^{6}4420$	$.9^{6}4696$	$.9^{6}4958$
4.9	$.9^{6}5208$	$.9^{6}5446$	$.9^{6}5673$	$.9^{6}5889$	$.9^{6}6094$	$.9^{6}6289$	$.9^{6}6475$	$.9^{6}6652$	$.9^{6}6821$	$.9^{6}6981$

Appendix E

PERCENTILES OF THE CHI-SQUARE DISTRIBUTION

m	\\ P	0.05	0.1	0.5	1.0	2.5	5.0	10.0	20.0	30.0	40.0
						Probability in Per Cent					
1		$.0^3393$	$.0^5157$	$.0^4393$	$.0^3157$	$.0^3982$	$.0^2393$	.0158	.0642	.148	.275
2		$.0^2100$	$.0^2200$	.0100	.0201	.0506	.103	.211	.446	.713	1.02
3		.0153	.0243	.0717	.115	.216	.352	.584	1.00	1.42	1.87
4		.0639	.908	.207	.297	.484	.711	1.06	1.65	2.19	2.75
5		.158	.210	.412	.554	.831	1.15	1.61	2.34	3.00	3.66
6		.299	.381	.676	.872	1.24	1.64	2.20	3.07	3.83	4.57
7		.485	.598	.989	1.24	1.69	2.17	2.83	3.82	4.67	5.49
8		.710	.857	1.34	1.65	2.18	2.73	3.49	4.59	5.53	6.42
9		.972	1.15	1.73	2.09	2.70	3.33	4.17	5.38	6.39	7.36
10		1.26	1.48	2.16	2.56	3.25	3.94	4.87	6.18	7.27	8.30
11		1.59	1.83	2.60	3.05	3.82	4.57	5.58	6.99	8.15	9.24
12		1.93	2.21	3.07	3.57	4.40	5.23	6.30	7.81	9.03	10.2
13		2.31	2.62	3.57	4.11	5.01	5.89	7.04	8.63	9.93	11.1
14		2.70	3.04	4.07	4.66	5.63	6.57	7.79	9.47	10.8	12.1
15		3.11	3.48	4.60	5.23	6.26	7.26	8.55	10.3	11.7	13.0
16		3.54	3.94	5.14	5.81	6.91	7.96	9.31	11.2	12.6	14.0
17		3.98	4.42	5.70	6.41	7.56	8.67	10.1	12.0	13.5	14.9
18		4.44	4.90	6.26	7.01	8.23	9.39	10.9	12.9	14.4	15.9
19		4.91	5.41	6.84	7.63	8.91	10.1	11.7	13.7	15.4	16.9
20		5.40	5.92	7.43	8.26	9.59	10.9	12.4	14.6	16.3	17.8
21		5.90	6.45	8.03	8.90	10.3	11.6	13.2	15.4	17.2	18.8
22		6.40	6.98	8.64	9.54	11.0	12.3	14.0	16.3	18.1	19.7
23		6.92	7.53	9.26	10.2	11.7	13.1	14.8	17.2	19.0	20.7
24		7.45	8.08	9.89	10.9	12.4	13.8	15.7	18.1	19.9	21.7
25		7.99	8.65	10.5	11.5	13.1	14.6	16.5	18.9	20.9	22.6

Appendix E (cont.)

PERCENTILES OF THE CHI-SQUARE DISTRIBUTION

P / m	Probability in Per Cent									
	0.05	0.1	0.5	1.0	2.5	5.0	10.0	20.0	30.0	40.0
26	8.54	9.22	11.2	12.2	13.8	15.4	17.3	19.8	21.8	23.6
27	9.09	9.80	11.8	12.9	14.6	16.2	18.1	20.7	22.7	24.5
28	9.66	10.4	12.5	13.6	15.3	16.9	18.9	21.6	23.6	25.5
29	10.2	11.0	13.1	14.3	16.0	17.7	19.8	22.5	24.6	26.5
30	10.8	11.6	13.8	15.0	16.8	18.5	20.6	23.4	25.5	27.4
40	16.9	17.9	20.7	22.2	24.4	26.5	29.1	32.3	34.9	37.1
50	23.5	24.7	28.0	29.7	32.4	34.8	37.7	41.4	44.3	46.9
60	30.3	31.7	35.5	37.5	40.5	43.2	46.5	50.6	53.8	56.6
70	37.5	39.0	43.3	45.4	48.8	51.7	55.3	59.9	63.3	66.4
80	44.8	46.5	51.2	53.5	57.2	60.4	64.3	69.2	72.9	76.2
90	52.3	54.2	59.2	61.8	65.6	69.1	73.3	78.6	82.5	86.0
100	59.9	61.9	67.3	70.1	74.2	77.9	82.4	87.1	92.1	95.8

Appendix E (cont.)

PERCENTILES OF THE CHI-SQUARE DISTRIBUTION

m	Probability in Per Cent										
	50.0	60.0	70.0	80.0	90.0	95.0	97.5	99.0	99.5	99.9	99.95
1	.455	.708	1.07	1.64	2.71	3.84	5.02	6.63	7.88	10.8	12.1
2	1.39	1.83	2.41	3.22	4.61	5.99	7.38	9.21	10.6	13.8	15.2
3	2.37	2.95	3.67	4.64	6.25	7.81	9.35	11.3	12.8	16.3	17.7
4	3.36	4.04	4.88	5.99	7.78	9.49	11.1	13.3	14.9	18.5	20.0
5	4.35	5.13	6.06	7.29	9.24	11.1	12.8	15.1	16.7	20.5	22.1
6	5.35	6.21	7.23	8.56	10.6	12.6	14.4	16.8	18.5	22.5	24.1
7	6.35	7.28	8.38	9.80	12.0	14.1	16.0	18.5	20.3	24.3	26.0
8	7.34	8.35	9.52	11.0	13.4	15.5	17.5	20.1	22.0	26.1	27.9
9	8.34	9.41	10.7	12.2	14.7	16.9	19.0	21.7	23.6	27.9	29.7
10	9.34	10.5	11.8	13.4	16.0	18.3	20.5	23.2	25.2	29.6	31.4
11	10.3	11.5	12.9	14.6	17.3	19.7	21.9	24.7	26.8	31.3	33.1
12	11.3	12.6	14.0	15.8	18.5	21.0	23.3	26.2	28.3	32.9	34.8
13	12.3	13.6	15.1	17.0	19.8	22.4	24.7	27.7	29.8	34.5	36.5
14	13.3	14.7	16.2	18.2	21.1	23.7	26.1	29.1	31.3	36.1	38.1
15	14.3	15.7	17.3	19.3	22.3	25.0	27.5	30.6	32.8	37.7	39.7
16	15.3	16.8	18.4	20.5	23.5	26.3	28.8	32.0	34.3	39.3	41.3
17	16.3	17.8	19.5	21.6	24.8	27.6	30.2	33.4	35.7	40.8	42.9
18	17.3	18.9	20.6	22.8	26.0	28.9	31.5	34.8	37.2	42.3	44.4
19	18.3	19.9	21.7	23.9	27.2	30.1	32.9	36.2	38.6	43.8	46.0
20	19.3	21.0	22.8	25.0	28.4	31.4	34.2	37.6	40.0	45.3	47.5
21	20.3	22.0	23.9	26.2	29.6	32.7	35.5	38.9	41.4	46.8	49.0
22	21.3	23.0	24.9	27.3	30.8	33.9	36.8	40.3	42.8	48.3	50.5
23	22.3	24.1	26.0	28.4	32.0	35.2	38.1	41.6	44.2	49.7	52.0
24	23.3	25.1	27.1	29.6	33.2	36.4	39.4	43.0	45.6	51.2	53.5
25	24.3	26.1	28.2	30.7	34.4	37.7	40.6	44.3	46.9	52.6	54.9

Appendix E (cont.)

PERCENTILES OF THE CHI-SQUARE DISTRIBUTION

m \ P	Probability in Per Cent										
	50.0	60.0	70.0	80.0	90.0	95.0	97.5	99.0	99.5	99.9	99.95
26	25.3	27.2	29.2	31.8	35.6	38.9	41.9	45.6	48.3	54.1	56.4
27	26.3	28.2	30.3	32.9	36.7	40.1	43.2	47.0	49.6	55.5	57.9
28	27.3	29.2	31.4	34.0	37.9	41.3	44.5	48.3	51.0	56.9	59.3
29	28.3	30.3	32.5	35.1	39.1	42.6	45.7	49.6	52.3	58.3	60.7
30	29.3	31.3	33.5	36.3	40.3	43.8	47.0	50.9	53.7	59.7	62.2
40	39.3	41.6	44.2	47.3	51.8	55.8	59.3	63.7	66.8	73.4	76.1
50	49.3	51.9	54.7	58.2	63.2	67.5	71.4	76.2	79.5	86.7	89.6
60	59.3	62.1	65.2	69.0	74.4	79.1	83.3	84.4	92.0	99.6	102.7
70	69.3	72.4	75.7	79.7	85.5	90.5	95.0	100.4	104.2	112.3	115.6
80	79.3	82.6	86.1	90.4	96.6	101.9	106.6	112.3	116.3	124.8	128.3
90	89.3	92.8	96.5	101.1	107.6	113.1	118.1	124.1	128.3	137.2	140.8
100	99.3	102.9	106.9	111.7	118.5	124.3	129.6	135.8	140.2	149.4	153.2

Appendix F

PERCENTILES OF THE t DISTRIBUTION*

m	$t_{.60}$	$t_{.70}$	$t_{.80}$	$t_{.90}$	$t_{.95}$	$t_{.975}$	$t_{.99}$	$t_{.995}$
1	.325	.727	1.376	3.078	6.314	12.706	31.821	63.657
2	.289	.617	1.061	1.886	2.920	4.303	6.965	9.925
3	.277	.584	.978	1.638	2.353	3.182	4.541	5.841
4	.271	.569	.941	1.533	2.132	2.776	3.747	4.604
5	.267	.559	.920	1.476	2.015	2.571	3.365	4.032
6	.265	.553	.906	1.440	1.943	2.447	3.143	3.707
7	.263	.549	.896	1.415	1.895	2.365	2.998	3.499
8	.262	.546	.889	1.397	1.860	2.306	2.896	3.355
9	.261	.543	.883	1.383	1.833	2.262	2.821	3.250
10	.260	.542	.879	1.372	1.812	2.228	2.764	3.169
11	.260	.540	.876	1.363	1.796	2.201	2.718	3.106
12	.259	.539	.873	1.356	1.782	2.179	2.681	3.055
13	.259	.538	.870	1.350	1.771	2.160	2.650	3.012
14	.258	.537	.868	1.345	1.761	2.145	2.624	2.977
15	.258	.536	.866	1.341	1.753	2.131	2.602	2.947
16	.258	.535	.865	1.337	1.746	2.120	2.583	2.921
17	.257	.534	.863	1.333	1.740	2.110	2.567	2.898
18	.257	.534	.862	1.330	1.734	2.101	2.552	2.878
19	.257	.533	.861	1.328	1.729	2.093	2.539	2.861
20	.257	.533	.860	1.325	1.725	2.086	2.528	2.845
21	.257	.532	.859	1.323	1.721	2.080	2.518	2.831
22	.256	.532	.858	1.321	1.717	2.074	2.508	2.819
23	.256	.532	.858	1.319	1.714	2.069	2.500	2.807
24	.256	.531	.857	1.318	1.711	2.064	2.492	2.797
25	.256	.531	.856	1.316	1.708	2.060	2.485	2.787

Appendix F (cont.)

PERCENTILES OF THE t DISTRIBUTION*

m	$t_{.60}$	$t_{.70}$	$t_{.80}$	$t_{.90}$	$t_{.95}$	$t_{.975}$	$t_{.99}$	$t_{.995}$
26	.256	.531	.856	1.315	1.706	2.056	2.479	2.779
27	.256	.531	.855	1.314	1.703	2.052	2.473	2.771
28	.256	.530	.855	1.313	1.701	2.048	2.467	2.763
29	.256	.530	.854	1.311	1.699	2.045	2.462	2.756
30	.256	.530	.854	1.310	1.697	2.042	2.457	2.750
40	.255	.529	.851	1.303	1.684	2.021	2.423	2.704
60	.254	.527	.848	1.296	1.671	2.000	2.390	2.660
120	.254	.526	.845	1.289	1.658	1.980	2.358	2.617
∞	.253	.524	.842	1.282	1.645	1.960	2.326	2.576
m	$t_{.40}$	$t_{.30}$	$t_{.20}$	$t_{.10}$	$t_{.05}$	$t_{.025}$	$t_{.01}$	$t_{.005}$

* When the table is read from the foot, the tabled values are to be prefixed with a negative sign.

Appendix G

PERCENTLIES OF THE F DISTRIBUTION

$F_{.90}\,(m_1 m_2)$

$\alpha = 0.1$

m_1 = degrees of freedom for numerator

freedom for denominator

m_1 \ m_2	1	2	3	4	5	6	7	8	9	10	12	15	20	24	30	40	60	120	∞
1	39.86	49.50	53.59	55.83	57.24	58.20	58.91	59.44	59.86	60.19	60.71	61.22	61.74	62.00	62.26	62.53	62.79	63.06	63.33
2	8.53	9.00	9.16	9.24	9.29	9.33	9.35	9.37	9.38	9.39	9.41	9.42	9.44	9.45	9.46	9.47	9.47	9.48	9.49
3	5.54	5.46	5.39	5.34	5.31	5.28	5.27	5.25	5.24	5.23	5.22	5.20	5.18	5.18	5.17	5.16	5.15	5.14	5.13
4	4.54	4.32	4.19	4.11	4.05	4.01	3.98	3.95	3.94	3.92	3.90	3.87	3.84	3.83	3.82	3.80	3.79	3.78	3.76
5	4.06	3.78	3.62	3.52	3.45	3.40	3.37	3.34	3.32	3.30	3.27	3.24	3.21	3.19	3.17	3.16	3.14	3.12	3.10
6	3.78	3.46	3.29	3.18	3.11	3.05	3.01	2.98	2.96	2.94	2.90	2.87	2.84	2.82	2.80	2.78	2.76	2.74	2.72
7	3.59	3.26	3.07	2.96	2.88	2.83	2.78	2.75	2.72	2.70	2.67	2.63	2.59	2.58	2.56	2.54	2.51	2.49	2.47
8	3.46	3.11	2.92	2.81	2.73	2.67	2.62	2.59	2.56	2.50	2.50	2.46	2.42	2.40	2.38	2.36	2.34	2.32	2.29
9	3.36	3.01	2.81	2.69	2.61	2.55	2.51	2.47	2.44	2.42	2.38	2.34	2.30	2.28	2.25	2.23	2.21	2.18	2.16
10	3.29	2.92	2.73	2.61	2.52	2.46	2.41	2.38	2.35	2.32	2.28	2.24	2.20	2.18	2.16	2.13	2.11	2.08	2.06
11	3.23	2.86	2.66	2.54	2.45	2.39	2.34	2.30	2.27	2.25	2.21	2.17	2.12	2.10	2.08	2.05	2.03	2.00	1.97
12	3.18	2.81	2.61	2.48	2.39	2.33	2.28	2.24	2.21	2.19	2.15	2.10	2.06	2.04	2.01	1.99	1.96	1.93	1.90
13	3.14	2.76	2.56	2.43	2.35	2.28	2.23	2.20	2.16	2.14	2.10	2.05	2.01	1.98	1.96	1.93	1.90	1.88	1.85
14	3.10	2.73	2.52	2.39	2.31	2.24	2.19	2.15	2.12	2.10	2.05	2.01	1.96	1.94	1.91	1.89	1.86	1.83	1.80
15	3.07	2.70	2.49	2.36	2.27	2.21	2.16	2.12	2.09	2.06	2.02	1.97	1.92	1.90	1.87	1.85	1.82	1.79	1.76
16	3.05	2.67	2.46	2.33	2.24	2.18	2.13	2.09	2.06	2.03	1.99	1.94	1.89	1.87	1.84	1.81	1.78	1.75	1.72
17	3.03	2.64	2.44	2.31	2.22	2.15	2.10	2.06	2.03	2.00	1.96	1.91	1.86	1.84	1.81	1.78	1.75	1.72	1.69
18	3.01	2.62	2.42	2.29	2.20	2.13	2.08	2.04	2.00	1.98	1.93	1.89	1.84	1.81	1.78	1.75	1.72	1.69	1.66
19	2.99	2.61	2.40	2.27	2.18	2.11	2.06	2.02	1.98	1.96	1.91	1.86	1.81	1.79	1.76	1.73	1.70	1.67	1.63

$\alpha = .01$

Appendix G (cont.)

PERCENTILES OF THE F DISTRIBUTION

$\alpha = 0.1$

$F_{.90}(m_1 m_2)$

m_1 = degrees of freedom for numerator

m_2 \ m_1	1	2	3	4	5	6	7	8	9	10	12	15	20	24	30	40	60	120	∞
20	2.97	2.59	2.38	2.25	2.16	2.09	2.04	2.00	1.96	1.94	1.89	1.84	1.79	1.77	1.74	1.71	1.68	1.64	1.61
21	2.96	2.57	2.36	2.23	2.14	2.08	2.02	1.98	1.95	1.92	1.87	1.83	1.78	1.75	1.72	1.69	1.66	1.62	1.59
22	2.95	2.56	2.35	2.22	2.13	2.06	2.01	1.97	1.93	1.90	1.86	1.81	1.76	1.73	1.70	1.67	1.64	1.60	1.57
23	2.94	2.55	2.34	2.21	2.11	2.05	1.99	1.95	1.92	1.89	1.84	1.80	1.74	1.72	1.69	1.66	1.62	1.59	1.55
24	2.93	2.54	2.33	2.19	2.10	2.04	1.98	1.94	1.91	1.88	1.83	1.78	1.73	1.70	1.67	1.64	1.61	1.57	1.53
25	2.92	2.53	2.32	2.18	2.09	2.02	1.97	1.93	1.89	1.87	1.82	1.77	1.72	1.69	1.66	1.63	1.59	1.56	1.52
26	2.91	2.52	2.31	2.17	2.08	2.01	1.96	1.92	1.88	1.86	1.81	1.76	1.71	1.68	1.65	1.61	1.58	1.54	1.50
27	2.90	2.51	2.30	2.17	2.07	2.00	1.95	1.91	1.87	1.85	1.80	1.75	1.70	1.67	1.64	1.60	1.57	1.53	1.49
28	2.89	2.50	2.29	2.16	2.06	2.00	1.94	1.90	1.87	1.84	1.79	1.74	1.69	1.66	1.63	1.59	1.56	1.52	1.48
29	2.89	2.50	2.28	2.15	2.06	1.99	1.93	1.89	1.86	1.83	1.78	1.73	1.68	1.65	1.62	1.58	1.55	1.51	1.47
30	2.88	2.49	2.28	2.14	2.05	1.98	1.93	1.88	1.85	1.82	1.77	1.72	1.67	1.64	1.61	1.57	1.54	1.50	1.46
40	2.84	2.44	2.23	2.09	2.00	1.93	1.87	1.83	1.79	1.76	1.71	1.66	1.61	1.57	1.54	1.51	1.47	1.42	1.38
60	2.79	2.39	2.18	2.04	1.95	1.87	1.82	1.77	1.74	1.71	1.66	1.60	1.54	1.51	1.48	1.44	1.40	1.35	1.29
120	2.75	2.35	2.13	1.99	1.90	1.82	1.77	1.72	1.68	1.65	1.60	1.55	1.48	1.45	1.41	1.37	1.32	1.26	1.19
∞	2.71	2.30	2.08	1.94	1.85	1.77	1.72	1.67	1.63	1.60	1.55	1.49	1.42	1.38	1.34	1.30	1.24	1.17	1.00

m_2 = degrees of freedom

Note: This table does not give lower tail percentage points of F. To find a lower percentile of F, take the reciprocal of the complementary upper percentile of F with the numerator and denominator degrees of freedom reversed. For example, $F_{.05}$, $m_1 = 6$, $m_2 = 12 = 1/F_{.95}$, $m_1 = 12$, $m_2 = 6 = 1/4.00 = 0.25$. In testing quality of variances, one may routinely treat the larger estimated variance as the numerator variance. In so doing $F_{.90}$ corresponds to an alpha level of .20, $F_{.95}$ to an alpha level of .10, $F_{.975}$ to an alpha level of .05, and $F_{.99}$ to an alpha level of .02. However, in analysis of variance tests where the denominator variance is pre-assigned, the alpha levels indicated in the table hold.

Appendix G *(cont.)*

PERCENTILES OF THE F DISTRIBUTION

$F_{.95}(m_1 m_2)$

$a = 0.05$

m_1 = degrees of freedom for numerator

m_2 \ m_1	1	2	3	4	5	6	7	8	9	10	12	15	20	24	30	40	60	120	∞
1	161.4	199.5	215.7	224.6	230.2	234.0	236.8	238.9	240.5	241.9	243.9	245.9	248.0	249.1	250.1	251.1	252.2	253.3	254.3
2	18.51	19.00	19.16	19.25	19.30	19.33	19.35	19.37	19.38	19.40	19.41	19.43	19.45	19.45	19.46	19.47	19.48	19.49	19.50
3	10.13	9.55	9.28	9.12	9.01	8.94	8.89	8.85	8.81	8.79	8.74	8.70	8.66	8.64	8.62	8.59	8.57	8.55	8.53
4	7.71	6.94	6.59	6.39	6.26	6.16	6.09	6.04	6.00	5.96	5.91	5.86	5.80	5.77	5.75	5.72	5.69	5.66	5.63
5	6.61	5.79	5.41	5.19	5.05	4.95	4.88	4.82	4.77	4.74	4.68	4.62	4.56	4.53	4.50	4.46	4.43	4.40	4.36
6	5.99	5.14	4.76	4.53	4.39	4.28	4.21	4.15	4.10	4.06	4.00	3.94	3.87	3.84	3.81	3.77	3.74	3.70	3.67
7	5.59	4.74	4.35	4.12	3.97	3.87	3.79	3.73	3.68	3.64	3.57	3.51	3.44	3.41	3.38	3.34	3.30	3.27	3.23
8	5.32	4.46	4.07	3.84	3.69	3.58	3.50	3.44	3.39	3.35	3.28	3.22	3.15	3.12	3.08	3.04	3.01	2.97	2.93
9	5.12	4.26	3.86	3.63	3.48	3.37	3.29	3.23	3.18	3.14	3.07	3.01	2.94	2.90	2.86	2.83	2.79	2.75	2.71
10	4.96	4.10	3.71	3.48	3.33	3.22	3.14	3.07	3.02	2.98	2.91	2.85	2.77	2.74	2.70	2.66	2.62	2.58	2.54
11	4.84	3.98	3.59	3.36	3.20	3.09	3.01	2.95	2.90	2.85	2.79	2.72	2.65	2.61	2.57	2.53	2.49	2.45	2.40
12	4.75	3.89	3.49	3.26	3.11	3.00	2.91	2.85	2.80	2.75	2.69	2.62	2.54	2.51	2.47	2.43	2.38	2.34	2.30
13	4.67	3.81	3.41	3.18	3.03	2.92	2.83	2.77	2.71	2.67	2.60	2.53	2.46	2.42	2.38	2.34	2.30	2.25	2.21
14	4.60	3.74	3.34	3.11	2.96	2.85	2.76	2.70	2.65	2.60	2.53	2.46	2.39	2.35	2.31	2.27	2.22	2.18	2.13
15	4.54	3.68	3.29	3.06	2.90	2.79	2.71	2.64	2.59	2.54	2.48	2.40	2.33	2.29	2.25	2.20	2.16	2.11	2.07
16	4.49	3.63	3.24	3.01	2.85	2.74	2.66	2.59	2.54	2.49	2.42	2.35	2.28	2.24	2.19	2.15	2.11	2.06	2.01
17	4.45	3.59	3.20	2.96	2.81	2.70	2.61	2.55	2.49	2.45	2.38	2.31	2.23	2.19	2.15	2.10	2.06	2.01	1.96
18	4.41	3.55	3.16	2.93	2.77	2.66	2.58	2.51	2.46	2.41	2.34	2.27	2.19	2.15	2.11	2.06	2.02	1.97	1.92
19	4.38	3.52	3.13	2.90	2.74	2.63	2.54	2.48	2.42	2.38	2.31	2.23	2.16	2.11	2.07	2.03	1.98	1.93	1.88

m_2 = degrees of freedom for denominator

Appendix G (cont.)

PERCENTILES OF THE F DISTRIBUTION

$F_{.95}(m_1 m_2)$

$a = 0.05$

m_1 = degrees of freedom for numerator

m_2 = degrees of freedom

m_2 \ m_1	1	2	3	4	5	6	7	8	9	10	12	15	20	24	30	40	60	120	∞
20	4.35	3.49	3.10	2.87	2.71	2.60	2.51	2.45	2.39	2.35	2.28	2.20	2.12	2.08	2.04	1.99	1.95	1.90	1.84
21	4.32	3.47	3.07	2.84	2.68	2.57	2.49	2.42	2.37	2.32	2.25	2.18	2.10	2.05	2.01	1.96	1.92	1.87	1.81
22	4.30	3.44	3.05	2.82	2.66	2.55	2.46	2.40	2.34	2.30	2.23	2.15	2.07	2.03	1.98	1.94	1.89	1.84	1.78
23	4.28	3.42	3.03	2.80	2.64	2.53	2.44	2.37	2.32	2.27	2.20	2.13	2.05	2.01	1.96	1.91	1.86	1.81	1.76
24	4.26	3.40	3.01	2.78	2.62	2.51	2.42	2.36	2.30	2.25	2.18	2.11	2.03	1.98	1.94	1.89	1.84	1.79	1.73
25	4.24	3.39	2.99	2.76	2.60	2.49	2.40	2.34	2.28	2.24	2.16	2.09	2.01	1.96	1.92	1.87	1.82	1.77	1.71
26	4.23	3.37	2.98	2.74	2.59	2.47	2.39	2.32	2.27	2.22	2.15	2.07	1.99	1.95	1.90	1.85	1.80	1.75	1.69
27	4.21	3.35	2.96	2.73	2.57	2.46	2.37	2.31	2.25	2.20	2.13	2.06	1.97	1.93	1.88	1.84	1.79	1.73	1.67
28	4.20	3.34	2.95	2.71	2.56	2.45	2.36	2.29	2.24	2.19	2.12	2.04	1.96	1.91	1.87	1.82	1.77	1.71	1.65
29	4.18	3.33	2.93	2.70	2.55	2.43	2.35	2.28	2.22	2.18	2.10	2.03	1.94	1.90	1.85	1.81	1.75	1.70	1.64
30	4.17	3.32	2.92	2.69	2.53	2.42	2.33	2.27	2.21	2.16	2.09	2.01	1.93	1.89	1.84	1.79	1.74	1.68	1.62
40	4.08	3.23	2.84	2.61	2.45	2.34	2.25	2.18	2.12	2.08	2.00	1.92	1.84	1.79	1.74	1.69	1.64	1.58	1.51
60	4.00	3.15	2.76	2.53	2.37	2.25	2.17	2.10	2.04	1.99	1.92	1.84	1.75	1.70	1.65	1.59	1.53	1.47	1.39
120	3.92	3.07	2.68	2.45	2.29	2.17	2.09	2.02	1.96	1.91	1.83	1.75	1.66	1.61	1.55	1.50	1.43	1.35	1.25
∞	3.84	3.00	2.60	2.37	2.21	2.10	2.01	1.94	1.88	1.83	1.75	1.67	1.57	1.52	1.46	1.39	1.32	1.22	1.00

Appendix G (cont.)

PERCENTILES OF THE F DISTRIBUTION

$F_{.975}(m_1 m_2)$

$a = 0.025$

m_1 = degrees of freedom for numerator

$m_2 \backslash m_1$	1	2	3	4	5	6	7	8	9	10	12	15	20	24	30	40	60	120	∞
1	647.8	799.5	864.2	899.6	921.8	937.1	948.2	956.7	963.3	968.6	976.7	984.9	993.1	997.2	1001	1006	1010	1014	1018
2	38.51	39.00	39.17	39.25	39.30	39.33	39.36	39.37	39.39	39.40	39.41	39.43	39.45	39.46	39.46	39.47	39.48	39.49	39.50
3	17.44	16.04	15.44	15.10	14.88	14.73	14.62	14.54	14.47	14.42	14.34	14.25	14.17	14.12	14.08	14.04	13.99	13.95	13.90
4	12.22	10.65	9.98	9.60	9.36	9.20	9.07	8.98	8.90	8.84	8.75	8.66	8.56	8.51	8.46	8.41	8.36	8.31	8.26
5	10.01	8.43	7.76	7.39	7.15	6.98	6.85	6.76	6.68	6.62	6.52	6.43	6.33	6.28	6.23	6.18	6.12	6.07	6.02
6	8.81	7.26	6.60	6.23	5.99	5.82	5.70	5.60	5.52	5.46	5.37	5.27	5.17	5.12	5.07	5.01	4.96	4.90	4.85
7	8.07	6.54	5.89	5.52	5.29	5.12	4.99	4.90	4.82	4.76	4.67	4.57	4.47	4.42	4.36	4.31	4.25	4.20	4.14
8	7.57	6.06	5.42	5.05	4.82	4.65	4.53	4.43	4.36	4.30	4.20	4.10	4.00	3.95	3.89	3.84	3.78	3.73	3.67
9	7.21	5.71	5.08	4.72	4.48	4.32	4.20	4.10	4.03	3.96	3.87	3.77	3.67	3.61	3.56	3.51	3.45	3.39	3.33
10	6.94	5.46	4.83	4.47	4.24	4.07	3.95	3.85	3.78	3.72	3.62	3.52	3.42	3.37	3.31	3.26	3.20	3.14	3.08
11	6.72	5.26	4.63	4.28	4.04	3.88	3.76	3.66	3.59	3.53	3.43	3.33	3.23	3.17	3.12	3.06	3.00	2.94	2.88
12	6.55	5.10	4.47	4.12	3.89	3.73	3.61	3.51	3.44	3.37	3.28	3.18	3.07	3.02	2.96	2.91	2.85	2.79	2.72
13	6.41	4.97	4.35	4.00	3.77	3.60	3.48	3.39	3.31	3.25	3.15	3.05	2.95	2.89	2.84	2.78	2.72	2.66	2.60
14	6.30	4.86	4.24	3.89	3.66	3.50	3.38	3.29	3.21	3.15	3.05	2.95	2.84	2.79	2.73	2.67	2.61	2.55	2.49
15	6.20	4.77	4.15	3.80	3.58	3.41	3.29	3.20	3.12	3.06	2.96	2.86	2.76	2.70	2.64	2.59	2.52	2.46	2.40
16	6.12	4.69	4.08	3.73	3.50	3.34	3.22	3.12	3.05	2.99	2.89	2.79	2.68	2.63	2.57	2.51	2.45	2.38	2.32
17	6.04	4.62	4.01	3.66	3.44	3.28	3.16	3.06	2.98	2.92	2.82	2.72	2.62	2.56	2.50	2.44	2.38	2.32	2.25
18	5.98	4.56	3.95	3.61	3.38	3.22	3.10	3.01	2.93	2.87	2.77	2.67	2.56	2.50	2.44	2.38	2.32	2.26	2.19
19	5.92	4.51	3.90	3.56	3.33	3.17	3.05	2.96	2.88	2.82	2.72	2.62	2.51	2.45	2.39	2.33	2.27	2.20	2.13

m_2 = degrees of freedom for denominator

Appendix G (cont.)

PERCENTILES OF THE F DISTRIBUTION

$\alpha = 0.025$

$F_{.975}\,(m_1 m_2)$

m_1 = degrees of freedom for numerator

m_2 \ m_1	1	2	3	4	5	6	7	8	9	10	12	15	20	24	30	40	60	120	∞
20	5.87	4.46	3.86	3.51	3.29	3.13	3.01	2.91	2.84	2.77	2.68	2.57	2.46	2.41	2.35	2.29	2.22	2.16	2.09
21	5.83	4.42	3.82	3.48	3.25	3.09	2.97	2.87	2.80	2.73	2.64	2.53	2.42	2.37	2.31	2.25	2.18	2.11	2.04
22	5.79	4.38	3.78	3.44	3.22	3.05	2.93	2.84	2.76	2.70	2.60	2.50	2.39	2.33	2.27	2.21	2.14	2.08	2.00
23	5.75	4.35	3.75	3.41	3.18	3.02	2.90	2.81	2.73	2.67	2.57	2.47	2.36	2.30	2.24	2.18	2.11	2.04	1.97
24	5.72	4.32	3.72	3.38	3.15	2.99	2.87	2.78	2.70	2.64	2.54	2.44	2.33	2.27	2.21	2.15	2.08	2.01	1.94
25	5.69	4.29	3.69	3.35	3.13	2.97	2.85	2.75	2.68	2.61	2.51	2.41	2.30	2.24	2.18	2.12	2.05	1.98	1.91
26	5.66	4.27	3.67	3.33	3.10	2.94	2.82	2.73	2.65	2.59	2.49	2.39	2.28	2.22	2.16	2.09	2.03	1.95	1.88
27	5.63	4.24	3.65	3.31	3.08	2.92	2.80	2.71	2.63	2.57	2.47	2.36	2.25	2.19	2.13	2.07	2.00	1.93	1.85
28	5.61	4.22	3.63	3.29	3.06	2.90	2.78	2.69	2.61	2.55	2.45	2.34	2.23	2.17	2.11	2.05	1.98	1.91	1.83
29	5.59	4.20	3.61	3.27	3.04	2.88	2.76	2.67	2.59	2.53	2.43	2.32	2.21	2.15	2.09	2.03	1.96	1.89	1.81
30	5.57	4.18	3.59	3.25	3.03	2.87	2.75	2.65	2.57	2.51	2.41	2.31	2.20	2.14	2.07	2.01	1.94	1.87	1.79
40	5.42	4.05	3.46	3.13	2.90	2.74	2.62	2.53	2.45	2.39	2.29	2.18	2.07	2.01	1.94	1.88	1.80	1.72	1.64
60	5.29	3.93	3.34	3.01	2.79	2.63	2.51	2.41	2.33	2.27	2.17	2.06	1.94	1.88	1.82	1.74	1.67	1.58	1.48
120	5.15	3.80	3.23	2.89	2.67	2.52	2.39	2.30	2.22	2.16	2.05	1.94	1.82	1.76	1.69	1.61	1.53	1.43	1.31
∞	5.02	3.69	3.12	2.79	2.57	2.41	2.29	2.19	2.11	2.05	1.94	1.83	1.71	1.64	1.57	1.48	1.39	1.27	1.00

m_2 = degrees of

Appendix G (cont.)

PERCENTILES OF THE F DISTRIBUTION

$a = 0.01$

$F_{.99}\ (m_1, m_2)$

m_1 = degrees of freedom for numerator

m_2 \ m_1	1	2	3	4	5	6	7	8	9	10	12	15	20	24	30	40	60	120	∞
1	4052	4999.5	5403	5625	5764	5859	5928	5982	6022	6056	6106	6157	6209	6235	6261	6287	6313	6339	6366
2	98.50	99.00	99.17	99.25	99.30	99.33	99.36	99.37	99.39	99.40	99.42	99.43	99.45	99.46	99.47	99.47	99.48	99.49	99.50
3	34.12	30.82	29.46	28.71	28.24	27.91	27.67	27.49	27.35	27.23	27.05	26.87	26.69	26.60	26.50	26.41	26.32	26.22	26.13
4	21.20	18.00	16.69	15.98	15.52	15.21	14.98	14.80	14.66	14.55	14.37	14.20	14.02	13.93	13.84	13.75	13.65	13.56	13.46
5	16.26	13.27	12.06	11.39	10.97	10.67	10.46	10.29	10.16	10.05	9.89	9.72	9.55	9.47	9.38	9.29	9.20	9.11	9.02
6	13.75	10.92	9.78	9.15	8.75	8.47	8.26	8.10	7.98	7.87	7.72	7.56	7.40	7.31	7.23	7.14	7.06	6.97	6.88
7	12.25	9.55	8.45	7.85	7.46	7.19	6.99	6.84	6.72	6.62	6.47	6.31	6.16	6.07	5.99	5.91	5.82	5.74	5.65
8	11.26	8.65	7.59	7.01	6.63	6.37	6.18	6.03	5.91	5.81	5.67	5.52	5.36	5.28	5.20	5.12	5.03	4.95	4.86
9	10.56	8.02	6.99	6.42	6.06	5.80	5.61	5.47	5.35	5.26	5.11	4.96	4.81	4.73	4.65	4.57	4.48	4.40	4.31
10	10.04	7.56	6.55	5.99	5.64	5.39	5.20	5.06	4.94	4.85	4.71	4.56	4.41	4.33	4.25	4.17	4.08	4.00	3.91
11	9.65	7.21	6.22	5.67	5.32	5.07	4.89	4.74	4.63	4.54	4.40	4.25	4.10	4.02	3.94	3.86	3.78	3.69	3.60
12	9.33	6.93	5.95	5.41	5.06	4.82	4.64	4.50	4.39	4.30	4.16	4.01	3.86	3.78	3.70	3.62	3.54	3.45	3.36
13	9.07	6.70	5.74	5.21	4.86	4.62	4.44	4.30	4.19	4.10	3.96	3.82	3.66	3.59	3.51	3.43	3.34	3.25	3.17
14	8.86	6.51	5.56	5.04	4.69	4.46	4.28	4.14	4.03	3.94	3.80	3.66	3.51	3.43	3.35	3.27	3.18	3.09	3.00
15	8.68	6.36	5.42	4.89	4.56	4.32	4.14	4.00	3.89	3.80	3.67	3.52	3.37	3.29	3.21	3.13	3.05	2.96	2.87
16	8.53	6.23	5.29	4.77	4.44	4.20	4.03	3.89	3.78	3.69	3.55	3.41	3.26	3.18	3.10	3.02	2.93	2.84	2.75
17	8.40	6.11	5.18	4.67	4.34	4.10	3.93	3.79	3.68	3.59	3.46	3.31	3.16	3.08	3.00	2.92	2.83	2.75	2.65
18	8.29	6.01	5.09	4.58	4.25	4.01	3.84	3.71	3.60	3.51	3.37	3.23	3.08	3.00	2.92	2.84	2.75	2.66	2.57
19	8.18	5.93	5.01	4.50	4.17	3.94	3.77	3.63	3.52	3.43	3.30	3.15	3.00	2.92	2.84	2.76	2.67	2.58	2.49

m_2 = degrees of freedom for denominator

Appendix G (cont.)

PERCENTILES OF THE F DISTRIBUTION

$$F_{.99}\ (m_1 m_2)$$

$a = 0.01$

m_1 = degrees of freedom for numerator

m_2 \ m_1	1	2	3	4	5	6	7	8	9	10	12	15	20	24	30	40	60	120	∞
20	8.10	5.85	4.94	4.43	4.10	3.87	3.70	3.56	3.46	3.37	3.23	3.09	2.94	2.86	2.78	2.69	2.61	2.52	2.42
21	8.02	5.78	4.87	4.37	4.04	3.81	3.64	3.51	3.40	3.31	3.17	3.03	2.88	2.80	2.72	2.64	2.55	2.46	2.36
22	7.95	5.72	4.82	4.31	3.99	3.76	3.59	3.45	3.35	3.26	3.12	2.98	2.83	2.75	2.67	2.58	2.50	2.40	2.31
23	7.88	5.66	4.76	4.26	3.94	3.71	3.54	3.41	3.30	3.21	3.07	2.93	2.78	2.70	2.62	2.54	2.45	2.35	2.26
24	7.82	5.61	4.72	4.22	3.90	3.67	3.50	3.36	3.26	3.17	3.03	2.89	2.74	2.66	2.58	2.49	2.40	2.31	2.21
25	7.77	5.57	4.68	4.18	3.85	3.63	3.46	3.32	3.22	3.13	2.99	2.85	2.70	2.62	2.54	2.45	2.36	2.27	2.17
26	7.72	5.53	4.64	4.14	3.82	3.59	3.42	3.29	3.18	3.09	2.96	2.81	2.66	2.58	2.50	2.42	2.33	2.23	2.13
27	7.68	5.49	4.60	4.11	3.78	3.56	3.39	3.26	3.15	3.06	2.93	2.78	2.63	2.55	2.47	2.38	2.29	2.20	2.10
28	7.64	5.45	4.57	4.07	3.75	3.53	3.36	3.23	3.12	3.03	2.90	2.75	2.60	2.52	2.44	2.35	2.26	2.17	2.06
29	7.60	5.42	4.54	4.04	3.73	3.50	3.33	3.20	3.09	3.00	2.87	2.73	2.57	2.49	2.41	2.33	2.23	2.14	2.03
30	7.56	5.39	4.51	4.02	3.70	3.47	3.30	3.17	3.07	2.98	2.84	2.70	2.55	2.47	2.39	2.30	2.21	2.11	2.01
40	7.31	5.18	4.31	3.83	3.51	3.29	3.12	2.99	2.89	2.80	2.66	2.52	2.37	2.29	2.20	2.11	2.02	1.92	1.80
60	7.08	4.98	4.13	3.65	3.34	3.12	2.95	2.82	2.72	2.63	2.50	2.35	2.20	2.12	2.03	1.94	1.84	1.73	1.60
120	6.85	4.79	3.95	3.48	3.17	2.96	2.79	2.66	2.56	2.47	2.34	2.19	2.03	1.95	1.86	1.76	1.66	1.53	1.38
∞	6.63	4.61	3.78	3.32	3.02	2.80	2.64	2.51	2.41	2.32	2.18	2.04	1.88	1.79	1.70	1.59	1.47	1.32	1.00

m_2 = degrees of

Appendix H

UNIT NORMAL LOSS INTEGRAL

z	.00	.01	.02	.03	.04	.05	.06	.07	.08	.09
.0	.3989	.3940	.3890	.3841	.3793	.3744	.3697	.3649	.3602	.3556
.1	.3509	.3464	.3418	.3373	.3328	.3284	.3240	.3197	.3154	.3111
.2	.3069	.3027	.2986	.2944	.2904	.2863	.2824	.2784	.2745	.2706
.3	.2668	.2530	.2592	.2555	.2518	.2481	.2445	.2409	.2374	.2339
.4	.2304	.2270	.2236	.2203	.2169	.2137	.2104	.2072	.2040	.2009
.5	.1978	.1947	.1917	.1887	.1857	.1828	.1799	.1771	.1742	.1714
.6	.1687	.1659	.1633	.1606	.1580	.1554	.1528	.1503	.1478	.1453
.7	.1429	.1405	.1381	.1358	.1334	.1312	.1289	.1267	.1245	.1223
.8	.1202	.1181	.1160	.1140	.1120	.1100	.1080	.1061	.1042	.1023
.9	.1004	.09860	.09680	.09503	.09328	.09156	.08986	.08819	.08654	.08491
1.0	.08332	.08174	.08019	.07866	.07716	.07568	.07422	.07279	.07138	.06999
1.1	.06862	.06727	.06595	.06465	.06336	.06210	.06086	.05964	.05844	.05726
1.2	.05610	.05496	.05384	.05274	.05165	.05059	.04954	.04851	.04750	.04650
1.3	.04553	.04457	.04363	.04270	.04179	.04090	.04002	.03916	.03831	.03748
1.4	.03667	.03587	.03508	.03431	.03356	.03281	.03208	.03137	.03067	.02998
1.5	.02931	.02865	.02800	.02736	.02674	.02612	.02552	.02494	.02436	.02380
1.6	.02324	.02270	.02217	.02165	.02114	.02064	.02015	.01967	.01920	.01874
1.7	.01829	.01785	.01742	.01699	.01658	.01617	.01578	.01539	.01501	.01464
1.8	.01428	.01392	.01357	.01323	.01290	.01257	.01226	.01195	.01164	.01134
1.9	.01105	.01077	.01049	.01022	$.0^{2}9957$	$.0^{2}9698$	$.0^{2}9445$	$.0^{2}9198$	$.0^{2}8957$	$.0^{2}8721$
2.0	$.0^{2}8491$	$.0^{2}8266$	$.0^{2}8046$	$.0^{2}7832$	$.0^{2}7623$	$.0^{2}7418$	$.0^{2}7219$	$.0^{2}7024$	$.0^{2}6835$	$.0^{2}6649$
2.1	$.0^{2}6468$	$.0^{2}6292$	$.0^{2}6120$	$.0^{2}5952$	$.0^{2}5788$	$.0^{2}5628$	$.0^{2}5472$	$.0^{2}5320$	$.0^{2}5172$	$.0^{2}5028$
2.2	$.0^{2}4887$	$.0^{2}4750$	$.0^{2}4616$	$.0^{2}4486$	$.0^{2}4358$	$.0^{2}4235$	$.0^{2}4114$	$.0^{2}3996$	$.0^{2}3882$	$.0^{2}3770$
2.3	$.0^{2}3662$	$.0^{2}3556$	$.0^{2}3453$	$.0^{2}3352$	$.0^{2}3255$	$.0^{2}3159$	$.0^{2}3067$	$.0^{2}2977$	$.0^{2}2889$	$.0^{2}2804$
2.4	$.0^{2}2720$	$.0^{2}2640$	$.0^{2}2561$	$.0^{2}2484$	$.0^{2}2410$	$.0^{2}2337$	$.0^{2}2267$	$.0^{2}2199$	$.0^{2}2132$	$.0^{2}2067$

Appendix H (cont.)

UNIT NORMAL LOSS INTEGRAL

z	.00	.01	.02	.03	.04	.05	.06	.07	.08	.09
2.5	$.0^{2}2004$	$.0^{2}1943$	$.0^{2}1883$	$.0^{2}1826$	$.0^{2}1769$	$.0^{2}1715$	$.0^{2}1662$	$.0^{2}1610$	$.0^{2}1560$	$.0^{2}1511$
2.6	$.0^{2}1464$	$.0^{2}1418$	$.0^{2}1373$	$.0^{2}1330$	$.0^{2}1288$	$.0^{2}1247$	$.0^{2}1207$	$.0^{2}1169$	$.0^{2}1132$	$.0^{2}1095$
2.7	$.0^{2}1060$	$.0^{2}1026$	$.0^{3}9928$	$.0^{3}9607$	$.0^{3}9295$	$.0^{3}8992$	$.0^{3}8699$	$.0^{3}8414$	$.0^{3}8138$	$.0^{3}7870$
2.8	$.0^{3}7611$	$.0^{3}7359$	$.0^{3}7115$	$.0^{3}6879$	$.0^{3}6650$	$.0^{3}6428$	$.0^{3}6213$	$.0^{3}6004$	$.0^{3}5802$	$.0^{3}5606$
2.9	$.0^{3}5417$	$.0^{3}5233$	$.0^{3}5055$	$.0^{3}4883$	$.0^{3}4716$	$.0^{3}4555$	$.0^{3}4398$	$.0^{3}4247$	$.0^{3}4101$	$.0^{3}3959$
3.0	$.0^{3}3822$	$.0^{3}3689$	$.0^{3}3560$	$.0^{3}3436$	$.0^{3}3316$	$.0^{3}3199$	$.0^{3}3087$	$.0^{3}2978$	$.0^{3}2873$	$.0^{3}2771$
3.1	$.0^{3}2673$	$.0^{3}2577$	$.0^{3}2485$	$.0^{3}2396$	$.0^{3}2311$	$.0^{3}2227$	$.0^{3}2147$	$.0^{3}2070$	$.0^{3}1995$	$.0^{3}1922$
3.2	$.0^{3}1852$	$.0^{3}1785$	$.0^{3}1720$	$.0^{3}1657$	$.0^{3}1596$	$.0^{3}1537$	$.0^{3}1480$	$.0^{3}1426$	$.0^{3}1373$	$.0^{3}1322$
3.3	$.0^{3}1273$	$.0^{3}1225$	$.0^{3}1179$	$.0^{3}1135$	$.0^{3}1093$	$.0^{3}1051$	$.0^{3}1012$	$.0^{4}9734$	$.0^{4}9365$	$.0^{4}9009$
3.4	$.0^{4}8666$	$.0^{4}8335$	$.0^{4}8016$	$.0^{4}7709$	$.0^{4}7413$	$.0^{4}7127$	$.0^{4}6852$	$.0^{4}6587$	$.0^{4}6331$	$.0^{4}6085$
3.5	$.0^{4}5848$	$.0^{4}5620$	$.0^{4}5400$	$.0^{4}5188$	$.0^{4}4984$	$.0^{4}4788$	$.0^{4}4599$	$.0^{4}4417$	$.0^{4}4242$	$.0^{4}4073$
3.6	$.0^{4}3911$	$.0^{4}3755$	$.0^{4}3605$	$.0^{4}3460$	$.0^{4}3321$	$.0^{4}3188$	$.0^{4}3059$	$.0^{4}2935$	$.0^{4}2816$	$.0^{4}2702$
3.7	$.0^{4}2592$	$.0^{4}2486$	$.0^{4}2385$	$.0^{4}2287$	$.0^{4}2193$	$.0^{4}2103$	$.0^{4}2016$	$.0^{4}1933$	$.0^{4}1853$	$.0^{4}1776$
3.8	$.0^{4}1702$	$.0^{4}1632$	$.0^{4}1563$	$.0^{4}1498$	$.0^{4}1435$	$.0^{4}1375$	$.0^{4}1317$	$.0^{4}1262$	$.0^{4}1208$	$.0^{4}1157$
3.9	$.0^{4}1108$	$.0^{4}1061$	$.0^{4}1016$	$.0^{5}9723$	$.0^{5}9307$	$.0^{5}8908$	$.0^{5}8525$	$.0^{5}8158$	$.0^{5}7806$	$.0^{5}7469$
4.0	$.0^{5}7145$	$.0^{5}6835$	$.0^{5}6538$	$.0^{5}6253$	$.0^{5}5980$	$.0^{5}5718$	$.0^{5}5468$	$.0^{5}5227$	$.0^{5}4997$	$.0^{5}4777$
4.1	$.0^{5}4566$	$.0^{5}4364$	$.0^{5}4170$	$.0^{5}3985$	$.0^{5}3807$	$.0^{5}3637$	$.0^{5}3475$	$.0^{5}3319$	$.0^{5}3170$	$.0^{5}3027$
4.2	$.0^{5}2891$	$.0^{5}2760$	$.0^{5}2635$	$.0^{5}2516$	$.0^{5}2402$	$.0^{5}2292$	$.0^{5}2188$	$.0^{5}2088$	$.0^{5}1992$	$.0^{5}1901$
4.3	$.0^{5}1814$	$.0^{5}1730$	$.0^{5}1650$	$.0^{5}1574$	$.0^{5}1501$	$.0^{5}1431$	$.0^{5}1365$	$.0^{5}1301$	$.0^{5}1241$	$.0^{5}1183$
4.4	$.0^{5}1127$	$.0^{5}1074$	$.0^{5}1024$	$.0^{6}9756$	$.0^{6}9296$	$.0^{6}8857$	$.0^{6}8437$	$.0^{6}8037$	$.0^{6}7655$	$.0^{6}7290$
4.5	$.0^{6}6942$	$.0^{6}6610$	$.0^{6}6294$	$.0^{6}5992$	$.0^{6}5704$	$.0^{6}5429$	$.0^{6}5167$	$.0^{6}4917$	$.0^{6}4679$	$.0^{6}4452$
4.6	$.0^{6}4236$	$.0^{6}4029$	$.0^{6}3833$	$.0^{6}3645$	$.0^{6}3467$	$.0^{6}3297$	$.0^{6}3135$	$.0^{6}2981$	$.0^{6}2834$	$.0^{6}2694$
4.7	$.0^{6}2560$	$.0^{6}2433$	$.0^{6}2313$	$.0^{6}2197$	$.0^{6}2088$	$.0^{6}1984$	$.0^{6}1884$	$.0^{6}1790$	$.0^{6}1700$	$.0^{6}1615$
4.8	$.0^{6}1533$	$.0^{6}1456$	$.0^{6}1382$	$.0^{6}1312$	$.0^{6}1246$	$.0^{6}1182$	$.0^{6}1122$	$.0^{6}1065$	$.0^{6}1011$	$.0^{7}9588$
4.9	$.0^{7}9096$	$.0^{7}8629$	$.0^{7}8185$	$.0^{7}7763$	$.0^{7}7362$	$.0^{7}6982$	$.0^{7}6620$	$.0^{7}6276$	$.0^{7}5950$	$.0^{7}5640$

Appendix I

PROBABILITY DISTRIBUTION OF THE KOLMOGOROV-SMIRNOV ONE-SAMPLE STATISTIC

$$Pr\,[D(n) \leq c/n]$$

n \ c	1	2	3	4	5	6	7	8
1	1.00000							
2	.50000	1.00000						
3	.22222	.92593	1.00000					
4	.09375	.81250	.99219	1.00000				
5	.03840	.69120	.96992	.99936	1.00000			
6	.01543	.57656	.93441	.99623	.99996	1.00000		
7	.00612	.47446	.88937	.98911	.99960	1.00000		
8	.00240	.38659	.83842	.97741	.99849	.99996	1.00000	
9	.00094	.31261	.78442	.96121	.99615	.99982	1.00000	
10	.00036	.25128	.72946	.94101	.99222	.99943	.99998	1.00000

n \ c	11	12	13	14	15	16	17	18	19	20
1	.00014	.00005	.00002	.00001	.00000	.00000	.00000	.00000	.00000	.00000
2	.20100	.16014	.12715	.10066	.07950	.06265	.04927	.03869	.03033	.02374
3	.67502	.62209	.57136	.52323	.47795	.43564	.39630	.35991	.32636	.29553
4	.91747	.89126	.86935	.83337	.80275	.77158	.74019	.70887	.67784	.64728
5	.98648	.97885	.96935	.95807	.94517	.93081	.91517	.89844	.88079	.86237
6	.99865	.99732	.99530	.99250	.98882	.98425	.97875	.97235	.96506	.95693
7	.99993	.99979	.99953	.99908	.99837	.99736	.99598	.99419	.99195	.98924
8	1.00000	.99999	.99997	.99993	.99984	.99968	.99944	.99907	.99856	.99788
9		1.00000	1.00000	1.00000	.99999	.99997	.99994	.99989	.99980	.99968
10					1.00000	1.00000	1.00000	.99999	.99998	.99996
11								1.00000	1.00000	1.00000

Appendix I (cont.)

PROBABILITY DISTRIBUTION OF THE KOLMOGOROV-SMIRNOV ONE-SAMPLE STATISTIC

n c	21	22	23	24	25	26	27	28	29	30
1	.00000	.00000	.00000	.00000	.00000	.00000	.00000	.00000	.00000	.00000
2	.01857	.01450	.01132	.00882	.00687	.00535	.00416	.00323	.00251	.00195
3	.26729	.24147	.21793	.19650	.17702	.15935	.14334	.12885	.11575	.10392
4	.61733	.58811	.55970	.53216	.50554	.47987	.45517	.43145	.40870	.38693
5	.84335	.82386	.80401	.78392	.76368	.74338	.72309	.70288	.68280	.66290
6	.94802	.93837	.92805	.91712	.90565	.89368	.88128	.86851	.85541	.84203
7	.98605	.98236	.97817	.97349	.96832	.96269	.95661	.95010	.94318	.93588
8	.99700	.99590	.99456	.99296	.99110	.98895	.98651	.98378	.98076	.97745
9	.99949	.99924	.99890	.99846	.99792	.99725	.99645	.99551	.99441	.99315
10	.99993	.99989	.99982	.99973	.99960	.99943	.99921	.99894	.99861	.99821
11	.99999	.99999	.99998	.99996	.99994	.99990	.99985	.99979	.99971	.99960
12	1.00000	1.00000	1.00000	1.00000	.99999	.99999	.99998	.99997	.99995	.99992
13					1.00000	1.00000	1.00000	1.00000	.99999	.99999
14									1.00000	1.00000

n c	31	32	33	34	35	36	37	38	39	40
1	.00000	.00000	.00000	.00000	.00000	.00000	.00000	.00000	.00000	.00000
2	.00151	.00117	.00091	.00070	.00054	.00042	.00033	.00025	.00020	.00015
3	.09325	.08363	.07497	.06717	.06016	.05386	.04820	.04312	.03856	.03448
4	.36612	.34624	.32729	.30923	.29205	.27570	.26018	.24544	.23145	.21819
5	.64323	.62382	.60470	.58590	.56744	.54934	.53161	.51427	.49733	.48078
6	.82843	.81463	.80069	.78663	.77250	.75831	.74410	.72990	.71572	.70159
7	.92822	.92022	.91192	.90332	.89447	.88538	.87608	.86658	.85690	.84707

Appendix I (cont.)

PROBABILITY DISTRIBUTION OF THE KOLMOGOROV-SMIRNOV ONE-SAMPLE STATISTIC

n \ c	31	32	33	34	35	36	37	38	39	40
8	.97384	.96995	.96578	.96134	.95664	.95168	.94648	.94104	.93539	.92952
9	.99172	.99012	.98834	.98638	.98423	.98191	.97939	.97670	.97382	.97077
10	.99773	.99717	.99652	.99578	.99494	.99399	.99294	.99178	.99050	.98910
11	.99946	.99930	.99910	.99886	.99857	.99824	.99785	.99741	.99692	.99636
12	.99989	.99985	.99980	.99973	.99965	.99954	.99942	.99928	.99911	.99891
13	.99998	.99997	.99996	.99994	.99992	.99990	.99986	.99982	.99977	.99971
14	1.00000	.99997	.99996	.99994	.99999	.99998	.99997	.99996	.99995	.99993
15		1.00000	1.00000	1.00000	1.00000	1.00000	.99999	.99999	.99999	.99999

n \ c	41	42	43	44	45	46	47	48	49	50
1	.00000	.00000	.00000	.00000	.00000	.00000	.00000	.00000	.00000	.00000
2	.00012	.00009	.00007	.00005	.00004	.00003	.00002	.00002	.00001	.00001
3	.03081	.02753	.02459	.02196	.01960	.01750	.01561	.01393	.01242	.01108
4	.20562	.19373	.18247	.17181	.16174	.15222	.14323	.13474	.12672	.11916
5	.46464	.44891	.43359	.41868	.40418	.39008	.37639	.36310	.35020	.33769
6	.68752	.67354	.65965	.64588	.63223	.61872	.60536	.59215	.57911	.56623
7	.83711	.82702	.81684	.80657	.79623	.78583	.77539	.76492	.75442	.74392
8	.92345	.91719	.91075	.90415	.89739	.89048	.88344	.87628	.86899	.86160
9	.96754	.96413	.96056	.95682	.95293	.94888	.94467	.94033	.93584	.93122
10	.98759	.98596	.98421	.98233	.98033	.97822	.97598	.97363	.97115	.96856
11	.99573	.99504	.99428	.99344	.99253	.99154	.99047	.98933	.98810	.98679
12	.99868	.99842	.99813	.99779	.99742	.99701	.99655	.99605	.99550	.99490
13	.99963	.99955	.99945	.99933	.99919	.99904	.99886	.99866	.99844	.99820

Appendix I (cont.)

PROBABILITY DISTRIBUTION OF THE KOLMOGOROV-SMIRNOV ONE-SAMPLE STATISTIC

n	41	42	43	44	45	46	47	48	49	50
c										
14	.99991	.99988	.99985	.99982	.99977	.99972	.99966	.99959	.99951	.99941
15	.99998	.99997	.99996	.99995	.99994	.99993	.99991	.99988	.99986	.99983

n	51	52	53	54	55	56	57	58	59	60
c										
1	.00000	.00000	.00000	.00000	.00000	.00000	.00000	.00000	.00000	.00000
2	.00001	.00001	.00001	.00000	.00000	.00000	.00000	.00000	.00000	.00000
3	.00988	.00880	.00785	.00699	.00623	.00555	.00494	.00440	.00392	.00349
4	.11203	.10530	.09896	.09298	.08735	.08205	.07706	.07236	.06793	.06377
5	.32556	.31381	.30242	.29140	.28073	.27041	.26042	.25077	.24144	.23242
6	.55353	.54101	.52868	.51654	.50459	.49283	.48128	.46992	.45876	.44780
7	.73342	.72294	.71247	.70203	.69162	.68126	.67094	.66068	.65049	.64035
8	.85412	.84654	.83889	.83116	.82337	.81552	.80762	.79968	.79171	.78370
9	.92648	.92161	.91662	.91152	.90632	.90102	.89562	.89013	.88455	.87889
10	.96586	.96304	.96011	.95708	.95393	.95069	.94734	.94390	.94036	.93674
11	.98540	.98392	.98237	.98073	.97900	.97720	.97531	.97334	.97129	.96916
12	.99425	.99356	.99280	.99200	.99113	.99022	.98924	.98821	.98712	.98598
13	.99792	.99762	.99729	.99693	.99654	.99611	.99565	.99515	.99462	.99406
14	.99931	.99919	.99906	.99891	.99875	.99857	.99837	.99815	.99791	.99765
15	.99979	.99975	.99970	.99964	.99958	.99951	.99943	.99934	.99925	.99914

n	61	62	63	64	65	66	67	68	69	70
c										
1	.00000	.00000	.00000	.00000	.00000	.00000	.00000	.00000	.00000	.00000
2	.00000	.00000	.00000	.00000	.00000	.00000	.00000	.00000	.00000	.00000

Appendix I (cont.)

PROBABILITY DISTRIBUTION OF THE KOLMOGOROV-SMIRNOV ONE-SAMPLE STATISTIC

n / c	61	62	63	64	65	66	67	68	69	70
3	.00310	.00276	.00246	.00219	.00195	.00173	.00154	.00137	.00122	.00108
4	.05986	.05617	.05271	.04946	.04640	.04352	.04082	.03828	.03589	.03365
5	.22371	.21529	.20717	.19933	.19176	.18445	.17741	.17061	.16406	.15774
6	.43705	.42649	.41614	.40599	.39603	.38628	.37672	.36736	.35819	.34921
7	.63029	.62030	.61040	.60057	.59083	.58119	.57163	.56217	.55280	.54354
8	.77567	.76761	.75955	.75148	.74340	.73533	.72726	.71919	.71115	.70311
9	.87316	.86736	.86150	.85557	.84953	.84355	.83746	.83133	.82516	.81895
10	.93302	.92921	.92533	.92136	.91731	.91320	.90901	.90475	.90042	.89604
11	.96695	.96466	.96230	.95986	.95735	.95476	.95211	.94938	.94659	.94373
12	.98477	.98351	.98218	.98080	.97936	.97786	.97630	.97469	.97301	.97128
13	.99345	.99281	.99212	.99140	.99063	.98983	.98898	.98809	.98716	.98619
14	.99737	.99707	.99674	.99639	.99602	.99562	.99519	.99474	.99425	.99374
15	.99902	.99889	.99874	.99858	.99841	.99823	.99803	.99781	.99758	.99733

n / c	71	72	73	74	75	76	77	78	79	80
1	.00000	.00000	.00000	.00000	.00000	.00000	.00000	.00000	.00000	.00000
2	.00000	.00000	.00000	.00000	.00000	.00000	.00000	.00000	.00000	.00000
3	.00096	.00086	.00076	.00068	.00060	.00053	.00047	.00042	.00037	.00033
4	.03155	.02958	.02772	.02598	.02435	.02282	.02138	.02003	.01877	.01758
5	.15165	.14578	.14013	.13468	.12943	.12438	.11951	.11482	.11031	.10597
6	.34043	.33183	.32342	.31519	.30714	.29928	.29159	.28407	.27672	.26955
7	.53437	.52531	.51635	.50750	.49875	.49011	.48158	.47316	.46485	.45664
8	.69510	.68712	.67916	.67123	.66333	.65546	.64764	.63985	.63211	.62441

Appendix I (cont.)

PROBABILITY DISTRIBUTION OF THE KOLMOGOROV-SMIRNOV ONE-SAMPLE STATISTIC

n \ c	71	72	73	74	75	76	77	78	79	80
9	.81271	.80644	.80014	.79382	.78748	.78112	.77475	.76836	.76197	.75557
10	.89159	.88709	.88253	.87792	.87326	.86856	.86381	.85902	.85419	.84932
11	.94080	.93781	.93476	.93165	.92848	.92525	.92197	.91864	.91525	.91182
12	.96950	.96765	.96576	.96380	.96180	.95974	.95762	.95546	.95324	.95098
13	.98518	.98412	.98302	.98187	.98069	.97946	.97819	.97687	.97552	.97412
14	.99321	.99264	.99204	.99142	.99076	.99008	.98936	.98861	.98783	.98702
15	.99707	.99678	.99648	.99616	.99582	.99546	.99508	.99468	.99426	.99382

n \ c	81	82	83	84	85	86	87	88	89	90
1	.00000	.00000	.00000	.00000	.00000	.00000	.00000	.00000	.00000	.00000
2	.00000	.00000	.00000	.00000	.00000	.00000	.00000	.00000	.00000	.00000
3	.00030	.00026	.00023	.00021	.00018	.00016	.00015	.00013	.00011	.00010
4	.01647	.01542	.01444	.01353	.01267	.01186	.01110	.01040	.00973	.00911
5	.10178	.09776	.09389	.09017	.08659	.08314	.07983	.07664	.07357	.07063
6	.26253	.25569	.24900	.24247	.23609	.22986	.22379	.21786	.21207	.20643
7	.44855	.44056	.43269	.42493	.41727	.40973	.40229	.39497	.38775	.38064
8	.61675	.60914	.60159	.59408	.58662	.57922	.57188	.56459	.55735	.55018
9	.74917	.74276	.73636	.72996	.72356	.71717	.71079	.70442	.69806	.69172
10	.84442	.83949	.83452	.82953	.82451	.81947	.81440	.80932	.80421	.79909
11	.90833	.90480	.90123	.89761	.89395	.89025	.88651	.88273	.87892	.87507
12	.94867	.94630	.94390	.94144	.93894	.93640	.93381	.93118	.92851	.92580
13	.97268	.97119	.96967	.96811	.96650	.96486	.96317	.96145	.95969	.95789
14	.98618	.98531	.98440	.98346	.98249	.98149	.98046	.97939	.97830	.97717
15	.99336	.99287	.99237	.99184	.99129	.99071	.99011	.98949	.98884	.98818

Appendix I (cont.)

PROBABILITY DISTRIBUTION OF THE KOLMOGOROV-SMIRNOV ONE-SAMPLE STATISTIC

c	91	92	93	94	95	96	97	98	99	100
1	.00000	.00000	.00000	.00000	.00000	.00000	.00000	.00000	.00000	.00000
2	.00000	.00000	.00000	.00000	.00000	.00000	.00000	.00000	.00000	.00000
3	.00009	.00008	.00007	.00006	.00006	.00005	.00004	.00004	.00003	.00003
4	.00853	.00798	.00747	.00699	.00654	.00612	.00573	.00536	.00502	.00469
5	.06779	.0650,	.06245	.05994	.05752	.05520	.05297	.05082	.04876	.04678
6	.20092	.19555	.19031	.18520	.18022	.17536	.17062	.16600	.16150	.15712
7	.37364	.36674	.35995	.35327	.34669	.34021	.33384	.32757	.32140	.31533
8	.54306	.53600	.52901	.52207	.51520	.50839	.50164	.49496	.48834	.48178
9	.68539	.679C8	.67279	.66651	.66026	.65403	.64783	.64165	.63549	.62937
10	.79395	.78880	.78364	.77847	.77329	.76810	.76291	.75771	.75251	.74731
11	.87119	.86728	.86334	.85937	.85538	.85136	.84731	.84324	.83915	.83504
12	.92305	.92026	.91743	.91457	.91167	.90874	.90578	.90278	.89975	.89670
13	.95605	.95418	.95226	.95032	.94833	.94632	.94426	.94218	.94006	.93791
14	.97601	.97482	.97359	.97234	.97105	.96974	.96839	.96702	.96561	.96417
15	.98748	.98677	.98602	.98526	.98447	.98366	.98282	.98196	.98107	.98016

Appendix J

LIMITING DISTRIBUTION OF THE STATISTIC $\sqrt{n}\,[D^+(n) + D^-(n)] = Z$

Z	P	Z	P	Z	P	Z	P
0.50	0.000001	1.05	0.243174	1.50	0.822255	1.95	0.985848
0.52	0.000003	1.06	0.257083	1.51	0.830121	1.96	0.986769
0.54	0.000007	1.07	0.271223	1.52	0.837724	1.97	0.987635
0.56	0.000021	1.08	0.285570	1.53	0.845067	1.98	0.988450
0.58	0.000054	1.09	0.300099	1.54	0.852155	1.99	0.989216
0.60	0.000128	1.10	0.314786	1.55	0.858991	2.00	0.989936
0.62	0.000276	1.11	0.329607	1.56	0.865580	2.01	0.990612
0.64	0.000553	1.12	0.344538	1.57	0.871927	2.02	0.991247
0.66	0.001035	1.13	0.359554	1.58	0.878036	2.03	0.991843
0.68	0.001824	1.14	0.374632	1.59	0.883913	2.04	0.992402
0.70	0.003050	1.15	0.389749	1.60	0.889563	2.05	0.992925
0.71	0.003874	1.16	0.404883	1.61	0.894991	2.06	0.993416
0.72	0.004867	1.17	0.420012	1.62	0.900203	2.07	0.993875
0.73	0.006050	1.18	0.435114	1.63	0.905203	2.08	0.994305
0.74	0.007447	1.19	0.450170	1.64	0.909998	2.09	0.994707
0.75	0.009082	1.20	0.465160	1.65	0.914593	2.10	0.995083
0.76	0.010978	1.21	0.480064	1.66	0.918994	2.12	0.995762
0.77	0.013159	1.22	0.494865	1.67	0.923206	2.14	0.996355
0.78	0.015650	1.23	0.509546	1.68	0.927235	2.16	0.996870
0.79	0.018472	1.24	0.524090	1.69	0.931087	2.18	0.997317
0.80	0.021649	1.25	0.538483	1.70	0.934766	2.20	0.997704
0.81	0.025202	1.26	0.552710	1.71	0.938280	2.22	0.998039
0.82	0.029149	1.27	0.566758	1.72	0.941633	2.24	0.998328
0.83	0.033510	1.28	0.580614	1.73	0.944830	2.26	0.998577
0.84	0.038300	1.29	0.594266	1.74	0.947878	2.28	0.998791
0.85	0.043534	1.30	0.607703	1.75	0.950781	2.30	0.998975
0.86	0.049223	1.31	0.620917	1.76	0.953546	2.32	0.999132
0.87	0.055378	1.32	0.633898	1.77	0.956175	2.34	0.999267
0.88	0.062006	1.33	0.646638	1.78	0.958676	2.36	0.999382
0.89	0.069112	1.34	0.659129	1.79	0.961053	2.40	0.999562
0.90	0.076699	1.35	0.671366	1.80	0.963311	2.44	0.999692
0.91	0.084767	1.36	0.683343	1.81	0.965455	2.48	0.999785
0.92	0.093313	1.37	0.695055	1.82	0.967488	2.52	0.999851
0.93	0.102333	1.38	0.706498	1.83	0.969417	2.56	0.999898
0.94	0.111821	1.39	0.717669	1.84	0.971245	2.60	0.999930
0.95	0.121767	1.40	0.728565	1.85	0.972976	2.64	0.999953
0.96	0.132161	1.41	0.739183	1.86	0.974615	2.68	0.999968
0.97	0.142989	1.42	0.749524	1.87	0.976166	2.72	0.999979
0.98	0.154236	1.43	0.759585	1.88	0.977633	2.76	0.999986
0.99	0.165887	1.44	0.769367	1.89	0.979020	2.80	0.999991
1.00	0.177924	1.45	0.778871	1.90	0.980329	2.84	0.999994
1.01	0.190326	1.46	0.788097	1.91	0.981566	2.88	0.999996
1.02	0.203075	1.47	0.797046	1.92	0.982733	2.92	0.999997
1.03	0.216147	1.48	0.805720	1.93	0.983833	2.96	0.999998
1.04	0.229521	1.49	0.814122	1.94	0.984871	3.04	1.000000

Appendix K

CRITICAL VALUES FOR DUNCAN'S MULTIPLE RANGE TEST

Significance Level $\alpha = .10$

d.f.	2	3	4	5	6	7	8	9	10	11	12	13	14	15
								p						
1	8.929	8.929	8.929	8.929	8.929	8.929	8.929	8.929	8.929	8.929	8.929	8.929	8.929	8.929
2	4.130	4.130	4.130	4.130	4.130	4.130	4.130	4.130	4.130	4.130	4.130	4.130	4.130	4.130
3	3.328	3.330	3.330	3.330	3.330	3.330	3.330	3.330	3.330	3.330	3.330	3.330	3.330	3.330
4	3.015	3.074	3.081	3.081	3.081	3.081	3.081	3.081	3.081	3.081	3.081	3.081	3.081	3.081
5	2.850	2.934	2.964	2.970	2.970	2.970	2.970	2.970	2.970	2.970	2.970	2.970	2.970	2.970
6	2.748	2.846	2.890	2.908	2.911	2.911	2.911	2.911	2.911	2.911	2.911	2.911	2.911	2.911
7	2.680	2.785	2.838	2.864	2.876	2.878	2.878	2.878	2.878	2.878	2.878	2.878	2.878	2.878
8	2.630	2.742	2.800	2.832	2.849	2.857	2.858	2.858	2.858	2.858	2.858	2.858	2.858	2.858
9	2.592	2.708	2.771	2.808	2.829	2.840	2.845	2.847	2.847	2.847	2.847	2.847	2.847	2.847
10	2.563	2.682	2.748	2.788	2.813	2.827	2.835	2.839	2.839	2.839	2.839	2.839	2.839	2.839
11	2.540	2.660	2.730	2.772	2.799	2.817	2.827	2.833	2.835	2.835	2.835	2.835	2.835	2.835
12	2.521	2.643	2.714	2.759	2.789	2.808	2.821	2.828	2.832	2.833	2.833	2.833	2.833	2.833
13	2.505	2.628	2.701	2.748	2.779	2.800	2.815	2.824	2.829	2.832	2.832	2.832	2.832	2.832
14	2.491	2.616	2.690	2.739	2.771	2.704	2.810	2.820	2.827	2.831	2.832	2.833	2.833	2.833
15	2.479	2.605	2.681	2.731	2.765	2.789	2.805	2.817	2.825	2.830	2.833	2.834	2.834	2.834
16	2.469	2.596	2.673	2.723	2.759	2.784	2.802	2.815	2.824	2.829	2.833	2.835	2.836	2.836
17	2.460	2.588	2.665	2.717	2.753	2.780	2.798	2.812	2.822	2.829	2.834	2.836	2.838	2.838
18	2.452	2.580	2.659	2.712	2.749	2.776	2.796	2.810	2.821	2.828	2.834	2.838	2.840	2.840
19	2.445	2.574	2.653	2.707	2.745	2.773	2.793	2.808	2.820	2.828	2.834	2.839	2.841	2.842
20	2.439	2.568	2.648	2.702	2.741	2.770	2.791	2.807	2.819	2.828	2.834	2.839	2.843	2.845
24	2.420	2.550	2.632	2.688	2.729	2.760	2.783	2.801	2.816	2.827	2.835	2.842	2.848	2.851
30	2.400	2.532	2.615	2.674	2.717	2.750	2.776	2.796	2.813	2.826	2.837	2.846	2.853	2.859
40	2.381	2.514	2.600	2.660	2.705	2.741	2.769	2.791	2.810	2.825	2.838	2.849	2.858	2.866
60	2.363	2.497	2.584	2.646	2.694	2.731	2.761	2.786	2.807	2.825	2.839	2.853	2.864	2.874
120	2.344	2.479	2.568	2.632	2.682	2.722	2.754	2.781	2.804	2.824	2.842	2.857	2.871	2.883
∞	2.326	2.462	2.552	2.619	2.670	2.712	2.746	2.776	2.801	2.824	2.844	2.861	2.877	2.892

Appendix K (cont.)

CRITICAL VALUES FOR DUNCAN'S MULTIPLE RANGE TEST

Significance Level $\alpha = .05$

d.f.	2	3	4	5	6	7	8	9	10	11	12	13	14	15
1	17.97	17.97	17.97	17.97	17.97	17.97	17.97	17.97	17.97	17.97	17.97	17.97	17.97	17.97
2	6.085	6.085	6.085	6.085	6.085	6.085	6.085	6.085	6.085	6.085	6.085	6.085	6.085	6.085
3	4.501	4.516	4.516	4.516	4.516	4.516	4.516	4.516	4.516	4.516	4.516	4.516	4.516	4.516
4	3.927	4.013	4.033	4.033	4.033	4.033	4.033	4.033	4.033	4.033	4.033	4.033	4.033	4.033
5	3.635	3.749	3.797	3.814	3.814	3.814	3.814	3.814	3.814	3.814	3.814	3.814	3.814	3.814
6	3.461	3.587	3.649	3.680	3.694	3.697	3.697	3.697	3.697	3.697	3.697	3.697	3.697	3.697
7	3.344	3.477	3.548	3.588	3.611	3.622	3.626	3.626	3.626	3.626	3.626	3.626	3.626	3.626
8	3.261	3.399	3.475	3.521	3.549	3.566	3.575	3.579	3.579	3.579	3.579	3.579	3.579	3.579
9	3.199	3.339	3.420	3.470	3.502	3.523	3.536	3.544	3.547	3.547	3.547	3.547	3.547	3.547
10	3.151	3.293	3.376	3.430	3.465	3.489	3.505	3.516	3.522	3.525	3.526	3.526	3.526	3.526
11	3.113	3.256	3.342	3.397	3.435	3.462	3.480	3.493	3.501	3.506	3.509	3.510	3.510	3.510
12	3.082	3.225	3.313	3.370	3.410	3.439	3.459	3.474	3.484	3.491	3.496	3.498	3.499	3.499
13	3.055	3.200	3.289	3.348	3.389	3.419	3.442	3.458	3.470	3.478	3.484	3.488	3.490	3.490
14	3.033	3.178	3.268	3.329	3.372	3.403	3.426	3.444	3.457	3.467	3.474	3.479	3.482	3.484
15	3.014	3.160	3.250	3.312	3.356	3.389	3.413	3.432	3.446	3.457	3.465	3.471	3.476	3.478
16	2.998	3.144	3.235	3.298	3.343	3.376	3.402	3.422	3.437	3.449	3.458	3.465	3.470	3.473
17	2.984	3.130	3.222	3.285	3.331	3.366	3.392	3.412	3.429	3.441	3.451	3.459	3.465	3.469
18	2.971	3.118	3.210	3.274	3.321	3.356	3.383	3.405	3.421	3.435	3.445	3.454	3.460	3.465
19	2.960	3.107	3.199	3.264	3.311	3.347	3.375	3.397	3.415	3.429	3.440	3.449	3.456	3.462
20	2.950	3.097	3.190	3.255	3.303	3.339	3.368	3.391	3.409	3.424	3.436	3.445	3.453	3.459
24	2.919	3.066	3.160	3.226	3.276	3.315	3.345	3.370	3.390	3.406	3.420	3.432	3.441	3.449
30	2.888	3.035	3.131	3.199	3.250	3.290	3.322	3.349	3.371	3.389	3.405	3.418	3.430	3.439
40	2.858	3.006	3.102	3.171	3.224	3.266	3.300	3.328	3.352	3.373	3.390	3.405	3.418	3.429
60	2.829	2.976	3.073	3.143	3.198	3.241	3.277	3.307	3.333	3.355	3.374	3.391	3.406	3.419
120	2.800	2.947	3.045	3.116	3.172	3.217	3.254	3.287	3.314	3.337	3.359	3.377	3.394	3.409
∞	2.772	2.918	3.017	3.089	3.146	3.193	3.232	3.265	3.294	3.320	3.343	3.363	3.382	3.399

Appendix K (cont.)

CRITICAL VALUES FOR DUNCAN'S MULTIPLE RANGE TEST

Significance Level $\alpha = .01$

d.f.	p = 2	3	4	5	6	7	8	9	10	11	12	13	14	15
1	90.03	90.03	90.03	90.03	90.03	90.03	90.03	90.03	90.03	90.03	90.03	90.03	90.03	90.03
2	14.04	14.04	14.04	14.04	14.04	14.04	14.04	14.04	14.04	14.04	14.04	14.04	14.04	14.04
3	8.261	8.321	8.321	8.321	8.321	8.321	8.321	8.321	8.321	8.321	8.321	8.321	8.321	8.321
4	6.512	6.677	6.740	6.756	6.756	6.756	6.756	6.756	6.756	6.756	6.756	6.756	6.756	6.756
5	5.702	5.893	5.989	6.040	6.065	6.074	6.074	6.074	6.074	6.074	6.074	6.074	6.074	6.074
6	5.243	5.439	5.549	5.614	5.655	5.680	5.694	5.701	5.703	5.703	5.703	5.703	5.703	5.703
7	4.949	5.145	5.260	5.334	5.383	5.416	5.439	5.454	5.464	5.470	5.472	5.472	5.472	5.472
8	4.746	4.939	5.057	5.135	5.189	5.227	5.256	5.276	5.291	5.302	5.309	5.314	5.316	5.317
9	4.596	4.787	4.906	4.986	5.043	5.086	5.118	5.142	5.160	5.174	5.185	5.193	5.199	5.203
10	4.482	4.671	4.790	4.871	4.931	4.975	5.010	5.037	5.058	5.074	5.088	5.098	5.106	5.112
11	4.392	4.579	4.697	4.780	4.841	4.887	4.924	4.952	4.975	4.994	5.009	5.021	5.031	5.039
12	4.320	4.504	4.622	4.706	4.767	4.815	4.852	4.883	4.907	4.927	4.944	4.958	4.969	4.978
13	4.260	4.442	4.560	4.644	4.706	4.755	4.793	4.824	4.850	4.872	4.889	4.904	4.917	4.928
14	4.210	4.391	4.508	4.591	4.654	4.704	4.743	4.775	4.802	4.824	4.843	4.859	4.872	4.884
15	4.168	4.347	4.463	4.547	4.610	4.660	4.700	4.733	4.760	4.783	4.803	4.820	4.834	4.846
16	4.131	4.309	4.425	4.509	4.572	4.622	4.663	4.696	4.724	4.748	4.768	4.786	4.800	4.813
17	4.099	4.275	4.391	4.475	4.539	4.589	4.630	4.664	4.693	4.717	4.738	4.756	4.771	4.785
18	4.071	4.246	4.362	4.445	4.509	4.560	4.601	4.635	4.664	4.689	4.711	4.729	4.745	4.759
19	4.046	4.220	4.335	4.419	4.483	4.534	4.575	4.610	4.639	4.665	4.686	4.705	4.722	4.736
20	4.024	4.197	4.312	4.395	4.459	4.510	4.552	4.587	4.617	4.642	4.664	4.684	4.701	4.716
24	3.956	4.126	4.239	4.322	4.386	4.437	4.480	4.516	4.546	4.573	4.596	4.616	4.634	4.651
30	3.889	4.056	4.168	4.250	4.314	4.366	4.409	4.445	4.477	4.504	4.528	4.550	4.569	4.586
40	3.825	3.988	4.098	4.180	4.244	4.296	4.339	4.376	4.408	4.436	4.461	4.483	4.503	4.521
60	3.762	3.922	4.031	4.111	4.174	4.226	4.270	4.307	4.340	4.368	4.394	4.417	4.438	4.456
120	3.702	3.858	3.965	4.044	4.107	4.158	4.202	4.239	4.272	4.301	4.327	4.351	4.372	4.392
∞	3.643	3.796	3.900	3.978	4.040	4.091	4.135	4.172	4.205	4.235	4.261	4.285	4.307	4.327

Appendix K (cont.)

CRITICAL VALUES FOR DUNCAN'S MULTIPLE RANGE TEST

Significance Level α = .005

d.f.	2	3	4	5	6	7	8	9	10	11	12	13	14	15
1	180.1	180.1	180.1	180.1	180.1	180.1	180.1	180.1	180.1	180.1	180.1	180.1	180.1	180.1
2	19.93	19.93	19.93	19.93	19.93	19.93	19.93	19.93	19.93	19.93	19.93	19.93	19.93	19.93
3	10.55	10.63	10.63	10.63	10.63	10.63	10.63	10.63	10.63	10.63	10.63	10.63	10.63	10.63
4	7.916	8.126	8.210	8.238	8.238	8.238	8.238	8.238	8.238	8.238	8.238	8.238	8.238	8.238
5	6.751	6.980	7.100	7.167	7.204	7.222	7.228	7.228	7.228	7.228	7.228	7.228	7.228	7.228
6	6.105	6.334	6.466	6.547	6.600	6.635	6.658	6.672	6.679	6.682	6.682	6.682	6.682	6.682
7	5.699	5.922	6.057	6.145	6.207	6.250	6.281	6.304	6.320	6.331	6.339	6.343	6.345	6.345
8	5.420	5.638	5.773	5.864	5.930	5.978	6.014	6.042	6.064	6.080	6.092	6.101	6.108	6.113
9	5.218	5.430	5.565	5.657	5.725	5.776	5.815	5.846	5.871	5.891	5.907	5.920	5.930	5.938
10	5.065	5.273	5.405	5.498	5.567	5.620	5.662	5.695	5.722	5.744	5.762	5.777	5.790	5.800
11	4.945	5.149	5.280	5.372	5.442	5.496	5.539	5.574	5.603	5.626	5.646	5.663	5.678	5.690
12	4.849	5.048	5.178	5.270	5.341	5.396	5.439	5.475	5.505	5.531	5.552	5.570	5.585	5.599
13	4.770	4.966	5.094	5.186	5.256	5.312	5.356	5.393	5.424	5.450	5.472	5.492	5.508	5.523
14	4.704	4.897	5.023	5.116	5.185	5.241	5.286	5.324	5.355	5.382	5.405	5.425	5.442	5.458
15	4.647	4.838	4.964	5.055	5.125	5.181	5.226	5.264	5.297	5.324	5.348	5.368	5.386	5.402
16	4.599	4.787	4.912	5.003	5.073	5.129	5.175	5.213	5.245	5.273	5.298	5.319	5.338	5.354
17	4.557	4.744	4.867	4.958	5.027	5.084	5.130	5.168	5.201	5.229	5.254	5.275	5.295	5.311
18	4.521	4.705	4.828	4.918	4.987	5.043	5.090	5.129	5.162	5.190	5.215	5.237	5.256	5.274
19	4.488	4.671	4.793	4.883	4.952	5.008	5.054	5.093	5.127	5.156	5.181	5.203	5.222	5.240
20	4.460	4.641	4.762	4.851	4.920	4.976	5.022	5.061	5.095	5.124	5.150	5.172	5.193	5.210
24	4.371	4.547	4.666	4.753	4.822	4.877	4.924	4.963	4.997	5.027	5.053	5.076	5.097	5.116
30	4.285	4.456	4.572	4.658	4.726	4.781	4.827	4.867	4.901	4.931	4.958	4.981	5.003	5.022
40	4.202	4.369	4.482	4.566	4.632	4.687	4.733	4.772	4.806	4.837	4.864	4.888	4.910	4.930
60	4.122	4.284	4.394	4.476	4.541	4.595	4.640	4.679	4.713	4.744	4.771	4.796	4.818	4.838
120	4.045	4.201	4.308	4.388	4.452	4.505	4.550	4.588	4.622	4.652	4.679	4.704	4.726	4.747
∞	3.970	4.121	4.225	4.303	4.365	4.417	4.461	4.499	4.532	4.562	4.589	4.614	4.636	4.657

Appendix L

VALUES OF $\sqrt{pq}$ WHEN $p + q = 1$

p	.000	.001	.002	.003	.004	.005	.006	.007	.008	.009	p
.000	.0000	.0316	.0447	.0547	.0631	.0705	.0772	.0834	.0891	.0944	.990
.010	.0995	.1043	.1089	.1133	.1175	.1216	.1255	.1293	.1330	.1365	.980
.020	.1400	.1434	.1467	.1499	.1530	.1561	.1591	.1621	.1650	.1678	.970
.030	.1706	.1733	.1760	.1786	.1812	.1838	.1863	.1888	.1912	.1936	.960
.040	.1960	.1983	.2006	.2029	.2051	.2073	.2095	.2116	.2138	.2159	.950
.050	.2179	.2200	.2220	.2240	.2260	.2280	.2299	.2318	.2337	.2356	.940
.060	.2375	.2393	.2412	.2430	.2448	.2465	.2483	.2500	.2517	.2535	.930
.070	.2551	.2568	.2585	.2601	.2618	.2634	.2650	.2666	.2682	.2697	.920
.080	.2713	.2728	.2744	.2759	.2774	.2789	.2804	.2818	.2833	.2847	.910
.090	.2862	.2876	.2890	.2904	.2918	.2932	.2946	.2960	.2973	.2987	.900
.100	.3000	.3013	.3026	.3040	.3053	.3066	.3078	.3091	.3104	.3116	.890
.110	.3129	.3141	.3154	.3166	.3178	.3190	.3202	.3214	.3226	.3238	.880
.120	.3250	.3261	.3273	.3284	.3296	.3307	.3318	.3330	.3341	.3352	.870
.130	.3363	.3374	.3385	.3396	.3407	.3417	.3428	.3438	.3449	.3459	.860
.140	.3470	.3480	.3491	.3501	.3511	.3521	.3531	.3541	.3551	.3561	.850
.150	.3571	.3580	.3590	.3600	.3609	.3619	.3628	.3638	.3647	.3657	.840
.160	.3666	.3675	.3685	.3694	.3703	.3712	.3721	.3730	.3739	.3748	.830
.170	.3756	.3765	.3774	.3782	.3791	.3800	.3808	.3817	.3825	.3834	.820
.180	.3842	.3850	.3858	.3867	.3875	.3883	.3891	.3899	.3907	.3915	.810
.190	.3923	.3931	.3939	.3947	.3954	.3962	.3970	.3977	.3985	.3993	.800
.200	.4000	.4007	.4015	.4022	.4030	.4037	.4044	.4052	.4059	.4066	.790
.210	.4073	.4080	.4087	.4094	.4101	.4108	.4115	.4122	.4129	.4136	.780
.220	.4142	.4149	.4156	.4163	.4169	.4176	.4182	.4189	.4195	.4202	.770
.230	.4208	.4215	.4221	.4227	.4234	.4240	.4246	.4252	.4259	.4265	.760
.240	.4271	.4277	.4283	.4289	.4295	.4301	.4307	.4313	.4319	.4324	.750

Appendix L (cont.)

VALUES OF $\sqrt{pq}$ WHEN $p + q = 1$

p	.000	.001	.002	.003	.004	.005	.006	.007	.008	.009	p
.250	.4330	.4336	.4342	.4347	.4353	.4359	.4364	.4370	.4375	.4381	.740
.250	.4386	.4392	.4397	.4404	.4408	.4413	.4419	.4424	.4429	.4434	.730
.270	.4440	.4445	.4450	.4455	.4460	.4465	.4470	.4475	.4480	.4485	.720
.280	.4490	.4495	.4500	.4505	.4509	.4514	.4519	.4524	.4528	.4533	.710
.290	.4538	.4542	.4547	.4551	.4556	.4560	.4565	.4569	.4574	.4578	.700
.300	.4583	.4587	.4591	.4596	.4600	.4604	.4608	.4612	.4617	.4621	.690
.310	.4625	.4629	.4633	.4637	.4641	.4645	.4649	.4653	.4657	.4661	.680
.320	.4665	.4669	.4672	.4676	.4680	.4684	.4687	.4691	.4695	.4698	.670
.330	.4702	.4706	.4709	.4713	.4716	.4720	.4723	.4727	.4730	.4734	.660
.340	.4737	.4740	.4744	.4747	.4750	.4754	.4757	.4760	.4763	.4767	.650
.350	.4770	.4773	.4776	.4779	.4782	.4785	.4788	.4791	.4794	.4797	.640
.360	.4800	.4803	.4806	.4809	.4811	.4814	.4817	.4820	.4823	.4825	.630
.370	.4828	.4831	.4833	.4836	.4839	.4841	.4844	.4846	.4849	.4851	.620
.380	.4854	.4856	.4859	.4861	.4864	.4866	.4868	.4871	.4873	.4875	.610
.390	.4877	.4880	.4882	.4884	.4886	.4889	.4891	.4893	.4895	.4897	.600
.400	.4899	.4901	.4903	.4905	.4907	.4909	.4911	.4913	.4915	.4916	.590
.410	.4918	.4920	.4922	.4924	.4925	.4927	.4929	.4931	.4932	.4934	.580
.420	.4936	.4937	.4939	.4940	.4942	.4943	.4945	.4946	.4948	.4949	.570
.430	.4951	.4952	.4954	.4955	.4956	.4958	.4959	.4960	.4961	.4963	.560
.440	.4964	.4965	.4966	.4967	.4969	.4970	.4971	.4972	.4973	.4974	.550
.450	.4975	.4976	.4977	.4978	.4979	.4980	.4981	.4981	.4982	.4983	.540
.460	.4984	.4985	.4986	.4986	.4987	.4988	.4988	.4989	.4990	.4990	.530
.470	.4991	.4992	.4992	.4993	.4993	.4994	.4994	.4995	.4995	.4996	.520
.480	.4996	.4996	.4997	.4997	.4997	.4998	.4998	.4998	.4999	.4999	.510
.490	.4999	.4999	.4999	.5000	.5000	.5000	.5000	.5000	.5000	.5000	.500
p	.010	.009	.008	.007	.006	.005	.004	.003	.002	.001	p

Appendix M

ARCSIN TRANSFORMATION FOR PROPORTIONS

$$h = 2 \arcsin \sqrt{p}$$

p	.000	.001	.002	.003	.004	.005	.006	.007	.008	.009
.00	0.0000	0.0633	0.0895	0.1096	0.1266	0.1415	0.1551	0.1675	0.1791	0.1900
.01	0.2003	0.2101	0.2195	0.2285	0.2372	0.2456	0.2537	0.2615	0.2691	0.2766
.02	0.2838	0.2909	0.2977	0.3045	0.3111	0.3176	0.3239	0.3301	0.3362	0.3423
.03	0.3482	0.3540	0.3597	0.3653	0.3709	0.3764	0.3818	0.3871	0.3924	0.3976
.04	0.4027	0.4078	0.4128	0.4178	0.4227	0.4275	0.4323	0.4371	0.4418	0.4464
.05	0.4510	0.4556	0.4601	0.4646	0.4690	0.4734	0.4778	0.4822	0.4864	0.4907
.06	0.4949	0.4991	0.5033	0.5074	0.5115	0.5156	0.5196	0.5236	0.5276	0.5316
.07	0.5355	0.5394	0.5433	0.5472	0.5510	0.5548	0.5586	0.5624	0.5661	0.5698
.08	0.5735	0.5772	0.5808	0.5845	0.5881	0.5917	0.5953	0.5988	0.6024	0.6059
.09	0.6094	0.6129	0.6163	0.6198	0.6232	0.6266	0.6300	0.6334	0.6368	0.6402
.10	0.6435	0.6468	0.6501	0.6534	0.6567	0.6600	0.6632	0.6665	0.6697	0.6729
.11	0.6761	0.6793	0.6825	0.6857	0.6888	0.6920	0.6951	0.6982	0.7013	0.7044
.12	0.7075	0.7106	0.7136	0.7167	0.7197	0.7227	0.7258	0.7288	0.7318	0.7347
.13	0.7377	0.7407	0.7437	0.7466	0.7495	0.7525	0.7554	0.7583	0.7612	0.7641
.14	0.7670	0.7699	0.7727	0.7756	0.7785	0.7813	0.7841	0.7870	0.7898	0.7926
.15	0.7954	0.7982	0.8010	0.8038	0.8065	0.8093	0.8121	0.8148	0.8176	0.8203
.16	0.8230	0.8258	0.8285	0.8312	0.8339	0.8366	0.8393	0.8420	0.8446	0.8473
.17	0.8500	0.8526	0.8553	0.8579	0.8606	0.8632	0.8658	0.8685	0.8711	0.8737
.18	0.8763	0.8789	0.8815	0.8841	0.8867	0.8892	0.8918	0.8944	0.8969	0.8995
.19	0.9021	0.9046	0.9071	0.9097	0.9122	0.9147	0.9173	0.9198	0.9223	0.9248
.20	0.9273	0.9298	0.9323	0.9348	0.9373	0.9397	0.9422	0.9447	0.9471	0.9496
.21	0.9521	0.9545	0.9570	0.9594	0.9619	0.9643	0.9667	0.9692	0.9716	0.9740
.22	0.9764	0.9788	0.9812	0.9836	0.9860	0.9884	0.9908	0.9932	0.9956	0.9980
.23	1.0004	1.0027	1.0051	1.0075	1.0098	1.0122	1.0146	1.0169	1.0193	1.0216
.24	1.0239	1.0263	1.0286	1.0310	1.0333	1.0356	1.0379	1.0403	1.0426	1.0449

Appendix M (cont.)

ARCSIN TRANSFORMATION FOR PROPORTIONS

p	.000	.001	.002	.003	.004	.005	.006	.007	.008	.009
.25	1.0472	1.0495	1.0518	1.0541	1.0564	1.0587	1.0610	1.0633	1.0656	1.0679
.26	1.0701	1.0724	1.0747	1.0770	1.0792	1.0815	1.0838	1.0860	1.0883	1.0905
.27	1.0928	1.0951	1.0973	1.0995	1.1018	1.1040	1.1063	1.1085	1.1107	1.1130
.28	1.1152	1.1174	1.1196	1.1219	1.1241	1.1263	1.1285	1.1307	1.1329	1.1351
.29	1.1373	1.1396	1.1418	1.1440	1.1461	1.1483	1.1505	1.1527	1.1549	1.1571
.30	1.1593	1.1615	1.1636	1.1658	1.1680	1.1702	1.1723	1.1745	1.1767	1.1788
.31	1.1810	1.1832	1.1853	1.1875	1.1896	1.1918	1.1939	1.1961	1.1982	1.2004
.32	1.2025	1.2047	1.2068	1.2090	1.2111	1.2132	1.2154	1.2175	1.2196	1.2217
.33	1.2239	1.2260	1.2281	1.2303	1.2324	1.2345	1.2366	1.2387	1.2408	1.2430
.34	1.2451	1.2472	1.2493	1.2514	1.2535	1.2556	1.2577	1.2598	1.2619	1.2640
.35	1.2661	1.2682	1.2703	1.2724	1.2745	1.2766	1.2787	1.2807	1.2828	1.2849
.36	1.2870	1.2891	1.2912	1.2932	1.2953	1.2974	1.2995	1.3016	1.3036	1.3057
.37	1.3078	1.3098	1.3119	1.3140	1.3161	1.3181	1.3202	1.3222	1.3243	1.3264
.38	1.3284	1.3305	1.3325	1.3346	1.3367	1.3387	1.3408	1.3428	1.3449	1.3469
.39	1.3490	1.3510	1.3531	1.3551	1.3572	1.3592	1.3613	1.3633	1.3654	1.3674
.40	1.3694	1.3715	1.3735	1.3756	1.3776	1.3796	1.3817	1.3837	1.3857	1.3878
.41	1.3898	1.3918	1.3939	1.3959	1.3979	1.4000	1.4020	1.4040	1.4061	1.4081
.42	1.4101	1.4121	1.4142	1.4162	1.4182	1.4202	1.4222	1.4243	1.4263	1.4283
.43	1.4303	1.4324	1.4344	1.4364	1.4384	1.4404	1.4424	1.4445	1.4465	1.4485
.44	1.4505	1.4525	1.4545	1.4565	1.4586	1.4606	1.4626	1.4646	1.4666	1.4686
.45	1.4706	1.4726	1.4746	1.4767	1.4787	1.4807	1.4827	1.4847	1.4867	1.4887
.46	1.4907	1.4927	1.4947	1.4967	1.4987	1.5007	1.5027	1.5048	1.5068	1.5088
.47	1.5108	1.5128	1.4158	1.5168	1.5188	1.5208	1.5228	1.5248	1.5268	1.5288
.48	1.5308	1.5328	1.5348	1.5368	1.5388	1.5408	1.5428	1.5448	1.5468	1.5488
.49	1.5508	1.5528	1.5548	1.5568	1.5588	1.5608	1.5628	1.5648	1.5668	1.5688

Example: $2 \arcsin \sqrt{0.296} = 1.1505$.

Appendix M (cont.)

ARCSIN TRANSFORMATION FOR PROPORTIONS

$$h = 2 \arcsin \sqrt{p}$$

p	.000	.001	.002	.003	.004	.005	.006	.007	.008	.009
.50	1.5708	1.5728	1.5748	1.5768	1.5788	1.5808	1.5828	1.5848	1.5868	1.5888
.51	1.5908	1.5928	1.5948	1.5968	1.5988	1.6008	1.6028	1.6048	1.6068	1.6088
.52	1.6108	1.6128	1.6148	1.6168	1.6188	1.6208	1.6228	1.6248	1.6268	1.6288
.53	1.6308	1.6328	1.6348	1.6368	1.6388	1.6409	1.6429	1.6449	1.6469	1.6489
.54	1.6509	1.6529	1.6549	1.6569	1.6589	1.6609	1.6629	1.6649	1.6669	1.6690
.55	1.6710	1.6730	1.6750	1.6770	1.6790	1.6810	1.6830	1.6850	1.6871	1.6891
.56	1.6911	1.6931	1.6951	1.6971	1.6992	1.7012	1.7032	1.7052	1.7072	1.7092
.57	1.7113	1.7133	1.7153	1.7173	1.7193	1.7214	1.7234	1.7254	1.7274	1.7295
.58	1.7315	1.7335	1.7355	1.7376	1.7396	1.7416	1.7437	1.7457	1.7477	1.7498
.59	1.7518	1.7538	1.7559	1.7579	1.7599	1.7620	1.7640	1.7660	1.7681	1.7701
.60	1.7722	1.7742	1.7762	1.7783	1.7803	1.7824	1.7844	1.7865	1.7885	1.7906
.61	1.7926	1.7947	1.7967	1.7988	1.8008	1.8029	1.8049	1.8070	1.8090	1.8111
.62	1.8132	1.8152	1.8173	1.8193	1.8214	1.8235	1.8255	1.8276	1.8297	1.8317
.63	1.8338	1.8359	1.8380	1.8400	1.8421	1.8442	1.8463	1.8483	1.8504	1.8525
.64	1.8546	1.8567	1.8588	1.8608	1.8629	1.8650	1.8671	1.8692	1.8713	1.8734
.65	1.8755	1.8776	1.8797	1.8818	1.8839	1.8860	1.8881	1.8902	1.8923	1.8944
.66	1.8965	1.8986	1.9008	1.9029	1.9050	1.9071	1.9092	1.9113	1.9135	1.9156
.67	1.9177	1.9198	1.9220	1.9241	1.9262	1.9284	1.9305	1.9326	1.9348	1.9369
.68	1.9391	1.9412	1.9434	1.9455	1.9477	1.9498	1.9520	1.9541	1.9563	1.9584
.69	1.9606	1.9628	1.9649	1.9671	1.9693	1.9714	1.9736	1.9758	1.9780	1.9801
.70	1.9823	1.9845	1.9867	1.9889	1.9911	1.9932	1.9954	1.9976	1.9998	2.0020
.71	2.0042	2.0064	2.0087	2.0109	2.0131	2.0153	2.0175	2.0197	2.0219	2.0242
.72	2.0264	2.0286	2.0309	2.0331	2.0353	2.0376	2.0398	2.0420	2.0443	2.0465
.73	2.0488	2.0510	2.0533	2.0556	2.0578	2.0601	2.0624	2.0646	2.0669	2.0692
.74	2.0714	2.0737	2.0760	2.0783	2.0806	2.0829	2.0852	2.0875	2.0898	2.0921

Appendix M (cont.)

ARCSIN TRANSFORMATION FOR PROPORTIONS

p	.000	.001	.002	.003	.004	.005	.006	.007	.008	.009
.75	2.0944	2.0967	2.0990	2.1013	2.1037	2.1060	2.1083	2.1106	2.1130	2.1153
.76	2.1176	2.1200	2.1223	2.1247	2.1270	2.1294	2.1318	2.1341	2.1365	2.1389
.77	2.1412	2.1436	2.1460	2.1484	2.1508	2.1532	2.1556	2.1580	2.1604	2.1628
.78	2.1652	2.1676	2.1700	2.1724	2.1749	2.1773	2.1797	2.1822	2.1846	2.1871
.79	2.1895	2.1920	2.1944	2.1969	2.1994	2.2019	2.2043	2.2068	2.2093	2.2118
.80	2.2143	2.2168	2.2193	2.2218	2.2243	2.2269	2.2294	2.2319	2.2345	2.2370
.81	2.2395	2.2421	2.2446	2.2472	2.2498	2.2523	2.2549	2.2575	2.2601	2.2627
.82	2.2653	2.2679	2.2705	2.2731	2.2758	2.2784	2.2810	2.2837	2.2863	2.2890
.83	2.2916	2.2943	2.2970	2.2996	2.3023	2.3050	2.3077	2.3104	2.3131	2.3158
.84	2.3186	2.3213	2.3240	2.3268	2.3295	2.3323	2.3351	2.3378	2.3406	2.3434
.85	2.3462	2.3490	2.3518	2.3546	2.3575	2.3603	2.3631	2.3660	2.3689	2.3717
.86	2.3746	2.3775	2.3804	2.3833	2.3862	2.3891	2.3921	2.3950	2.3979	2.4009
.87	2.4039	2.4068	2.4098	2.4128	2.4158	2.4189	2.4219	2.4249	2.4280	2.4310
.88	2.4341	2.4372	2.4403	2.4434	2.4465	2.4496	2.4528	2.4559	2.4591	2.4623
.89	2.4655	2.4687	2.4719	2.4751	2.4783	2.4816	2.4849	2.4882	2.4915	2.4948
.90	2.4981	2.5014	2.5048	2.5082	2.5115	2.5149	2.5184	2.5218	2.5253	2.5287
.91	2.5322	2.5357	2.5392	2.5428	2.5463	2.5499	2.5535	2.5571	2.5607	2.5644
.92	2.5681	2.5718	2.5755	2.5792	2.5830	2.5868	2.5906	2.5944	2.5983	2.6022
.93	2.6061	2.6100	2.6140	2.6179	2.6220	2.6260	2.6301	2.6342	2.6383	2.6425
.94	2.6467	2.6509	2.6551	2.6594	2.6638	2.6681	2.6725	2.6770	2.6815	2.6860
.95	2.6906	2.6952	2.6998	2.7045	2.7093	2.7141	2.7189	2.7238	2.7288	2.7338
.96	2.7389	2.7440	2.7492	2.7545	2.7598	2.7652	2.7707	2.7762	2.7819	2.7876
.97	2.7934	2.7993	2.8053	2.8115	2.8177	2.8240	2.8305	2.8371	2.8438	2.8507
.98	2.8578	2.8650	2.8725	2.8801	2.8879	2.8960	2.9044	2.9131	2.9221	2.9314
.99	2.9413	2.9516	2.9625	2.9741	2.9865	3.0001	3.0150	3.0320	3.0521	3.0783
1.00	3.1416									

Example: $2 \arcsin \sqrt{0.724} = 2.0353$.

Appendix N

RANDOM DIGITS

45 65 06 59 33	70 32 79 24 35	98 51 17 62 13	44 63 55 18 98	48 41 13 15 90
49 16 36 76 68	91 97 85 56 84	39 78 78 10 41	65 37 26 64 45	00 23 64 58 17
27 29 03 62 17	92 30 38 12 38	07 56 17 91 83	81 55 60 05 21	92 08 20 72 73
29 82 08 43 17	19 40 62 49 27	50 77 71 60 47	21 38 28 40 38	08 05 22 70 20
39 00 35 04 12	11 23 18 83 35	50 52 68 29 23	40 14 96 94 54	37 42 22 28 07
17 02 64 97 77	85 39 47 09 44	33 01 10 93 68	86 53 37 90 22	23 40 81 39 82
91 04 47 43 68	98 74 52 87 03	34 42 06 64 13	71 82 42 39 88	99 33 08 94 70
90 61 33 67 11	33 90 38 82 52	09 52 54 47 56	95 57 16 11 77	08 03 04 48 17
95 63 95 67 95	81 79 05 46 93	97 40 47 36 78	03 11 52 62 29	75 14 60 64 65
80 20 15 88 98	65 86 73 28 60	60 29 18 90 93	73 21 45 76 96	94 53 57 96 43
76 37 60 65 53	70 14 18 48 82	58 48 78 51 28	74 74 10 03 88	54 35 75 97 63
48 40 25 11 66	61 26 48 75 42	05 82 00 79 89	69 23 02 72 67	35 41 65 46 25
35 52 90 13 23	73 34 57 35 83	94 56 67 66 60	77 82 60 68 75	28 73 92 07 95
67 80 20 31 03	69 30 66 55 80	10 72 74 76 82	04 31 23 93 42	16 29 97 86 21
34 24 23 38 64	36 35 68 90 35	22 50 13 36 91	58 45 43 36 46	46 70 32 12 40
86 96 03 15 47	50 06 92 48 78	07 32 83 01 69	50 15 14 48 14	86 58 54 40 84
35 42 93 07 61	68 24 56 70 47	86 77 80 84 49	09 80 72 91 85	76 68 79 20 44
01 47 50 67 73	27 18 16 54 96	56 82 89 75 76	85 70 27 22 56	92 03 74 00 53
52 89 64 37 15	07 57 05 32 52	90 80 28 50 51	46 72 40 25 22	47 94 15 10 50
76 64 19 09 80	34 45 02 05 03	14 39 06 86 87	17 17 77 66 14	68 26 85 11 16
33 05 53 29 70	17 05 02 35 53	67 31 34 00 48	74 35 17 03 05	23 98 49 42 29
25 48 89 25 99	46 08 76 21 57	77 54 96 02 73	76 56 98 68 05	45 45 19 37 93
73 20 26 90 79	57 01 97 33 64	01 50 29 54 46	11 43 09 62 32	91 69 48 07 64
09 54 42 01 80	06 06 26 57 79	52 80 45 68 59	48 12 35 91 89	49 33 10 55 60
10 37 08 99 12	66 31 85 63 73	98 11 83 88 99	65 80 74 69 09	91 80 44 12 63

Appendix N (cont.)

RANDOM DIGITS

```
27 05 26 58 42   93 95 45 39 65   29 37 43 92 51   74 77 74 45 26   46 04 69 19 61
66 94 15 21 33   18 01 61 39 82   48 38 78 36 59   53 99 07 27 95   66 52 44 47 15
73 59 74 92 92   92 25 04 19 91   31 44 24 62 54   87 43 75 89 67   73 85 72 55 94
70 66 14 70 25   59 20 11 07 03   67 87 84 86 16   21 87 40 34 97   13 62 11 48 42
62 25 28 52 05   63 96 22 25 26   16 14 59 93 68   37 98 88 20 73   17 83 37 52 23

72 24 71 33 65   35 93 27 96 61   25 10 70 86 45   24 38 63 92 75   94 24 35 49 04
29 95 72 28 23   91 23 28 69 54   96 38 66 11 96   59 81 18 74 64   54 76 99 54 00
33 93 33 10 90   24 00 45 97 77   62 54 92 35 33   54 93 80 87 26   07 53 31 96 35
06 01 52 56 78   92 48 12 02 13   00 97 79 60 83   42 68 72 60 45   91 83 80 15 59
41 29 74 61 70   47 36 08 91 93   77 40 88 28 34   86 22 09 81 01   36 52 88 80 46

38 18 41 39 85   57 71 31 74 86   07 70 70 56 05   41 52 92 37 87   97 05 90 17 32
38 63 89 11 97   23 24 39 74 18   00 00 66 95 15   04 52 74 11 20   06 14 46 23 69
07 52 28 96 84   06 68 43 67 66   85 15 92 41 40   79 53 87 75 01   30 14 54 56 19
41 95 66 82 20   33 00 79 04 59   43 45 79 66 43   46 72 60 47 19   38 49 51 15 45
76 11 45 01 05   56 54 03 54 01   53 15 88 88 34   51 08 81 16 36   94 19 43 86 94

80 18 13 44 35   07 34 47 09 39   19 71 90 99 44   04 84 02 24 45   26 48 62 08 98
43 30 87 54 37   94 19 54 69 88   69 29 54 43 89   49 09 15 94 41   32 62 51 18 33
71 11 46 62 94   98 52 62 01 25   39 15 12 15 20   74 07 27 38 96   06 04 10 95 80
79 95 75 38 00   39 05 22 85 74   70 68 10 86 69   96 82 12 96 71   40 91 24 75 79
36 19 89 93 77   27 14 56 45 05   01 44 02 01 31   71 65 50 14 98   37 25 33 63 18

48 17 45 81 80   21 80 75 52 52   19 71 01 79 97   70 22 73 55 77   02 39 94 02 74
24 03 09 04 36   55 92 71 12 56   69 29 51 33 05   43 71 33 99 80   11 56 84 17 54
56 33 12 46 88   40 34 33 97 09   39 15 17 38 59   27 48 98 07 52   83 98 44 66 11
94 99 00 02 15   46 75 75 32 32   70 68 53 29 02   10 47 96 24 31   28 79 47 32 48
38 69 87 84 01   15 16 82 30 10   01 44 40 58 35   76 19 79 63 87   38 41 49 07 69
```

Appendix O

THE w TRANSFORMATION OF THE CORRELATION COEFFICIENT, $w = \tanh^{-1} r$

r	.000	.002	.004	.006	.008	1	2	3	4	5	6	7	8	9	10	.000	.002	.004	.006	.008	r
.00	.0000	.0020	.0040	.0060	.0080	1	3	4	5	7	8	9	11	12	13	.5493	.5520	.5547	.5573	.5600	.50
1	.0100	.0120	.0140	.0160	.0180	1	3	4	5	7	8	10	11	12	14	.5627	.5654	.5682	.5709	.5736	1
2	.0200	.0220	.0240	.0260	.0280	1	3	4	6	7	8	10	11	13	14	.5763	.5791	.5818	.5846	.5874	2
3	.0300	.0320	.0340	.0360	.0380	1	3	4	6	7	8	10	11	13	14	.5901	.5929	.5957	.5985	.6013	3
4	.0400	.0420	.0440	.0460	.0480	1	3	4	6	7	9	10	11	13	14	.6042	.6070	.6098	.6127	.6155	4
.05	.0500	.0520	.0541	.0561	.0581	1	3	4	6	7	9	10	12	13	14	.6184	.6213	.6241	.6270	.6299	.55
6	.0601	.0621	.0641	.0661	.0681	1	3	4	6	7	9	10	12	13	15	.6328	.6358	.6387	.6416	.6446	6
7	.0701	.0721	.0741	.0761	.0782	1	3	4	6	7	9	10	12	14	15	.6475	.6505	.6535	.6565	.6595	7
8	.0802	.0822	.0842	.0862	.0882	2	3	5	6	8	9	11	12	14	15	.6625	.6655	.6685	.6716	.6746	8
9	.0902	.0923	.0943	.0963	.0983	2	3	5	6	8	9	11	12	14	15	.6777	.6807	.6838	.6869	.6900	9
.10	.1003	.1024	.1044	.1064	.1084	2	3	5	6	8	9	11	13	14	16	.6931	.6963	.6994	.7026	.7057	.60
1	.1104	.1125	.1145	.1165	.1186	2	3	5	6	8	10	11	13	14	16	.7089	.7121	.7153	.7185	.7218	1
2	.1206	.1226	.1246	.1267	.1287	2	3	5	7	8	10	11	13	15	16	.7250	.7283	.7315	.7348	.7381	2
3	.1307	.1328	.1348	.1368	.1389	2	3	5	7	8	10	12	13	15	17	.7414	.7447	.7481	.7514	.7548	3
4	.1409	.1430	.1450	.1471	.1491	2	3	5	7	9	10	12	14	15	17	.7582	.7616	.7650	.7684	.7718	4
.15	.1511	.1532	.1552	.1573	.1593	2	4	5	7	9	11	12	14	16	18	.7753	.7788	.7823	.7858	.7893	.65
6	.1614	.1634	.1655	.1676	.1696	2	4	5	7	9	11	13	14	16	18	.7928	.7964	.7999	.8035	.8071	6
7	.1717	.1737	.1758	.1779	.1799	2	4	6	7	9	11	13	15	17	18	.8107	.8144	.8180	.8217	.8254	7
8	.1820	.1841	.1861	.1882	.1903	2	4	6	8	9	11	13	15	17	19	.8291	.8328	.8366	.8404	.8441	8
9	.1923	.1944	.1965	.1986	.2007	2	4	6	8	10	12	14	15	17	19	.8480	.8518	.8556	.8595	.8634	9
.20	.2027	.2048	.2069	.2090	.2111	2	4	6	8	10	12	14	16	18	20	.8673	.8712	.8752	.8792	.8832	.70
1	.2132	.2153	.2174	.2195	.2216	2	4	6	8	10	12	15	16	18	20	.8872	.8912	.8953	.8994	.9035	1
2	.2237	.2258	.2279	.2300	.2321	2	4	6	8	11	13	15	17	19	21	.9076	.9118	.9160	.9202	.9245	2
3	.2342	.2363	.2384	.2405	.2427	2	4	7	9	11	13	15	17	20	22	.9287	.9330	.9373	.9417	.9461	3
4	.2448	.2469	.2490	.2512	.2533	2	4	7	9	11	13	16	18	20	22	.9505	.9549	.9594	.9639	.9684	4
.25	.2554	.2575	.2597	.2618	.2640	1	2	3	4	5	6	7	9	10	11	0.973	0.978	0.982	0.987	0.991	.75
6	.2661	.2683	.2704	.2726	.2747	1	2	3	4	5	6	8	9	10	11	0.996	1.001	1.006	1.011	1.015	6
7	.2769	.2790	.2812	.2833	.2855	1	2	3	4	5	6	8	9	10	11	1.020	1.025	1.030	1.035	1.040	7
8	.2877	.2899	.2920	.2942	.2964	1	2	3	4	5	7	8	9	10	11	1.045	1.050	1.056	1.061	1.066	8

THE w TRANSFORMATION OF THE CORRELATION COEFFICIENT, $w = \tanh^{-1} r$

r	r (3rd decimal) .000	.002	.004	.006	.008	← Proportional parts, for left side 1	2	3	4	5	6	7	8	9	10	r (3rd decimal) .000	.002	.004	.006	.008	r
9	.2986	.3008	.3029	.3051	.3073	1	2	3	4	5	7	8	9	10	11	1.071	1.077	1.082	1.088	1.093	9
.30	.3095	.3117	.3139	.3161	.3183	1	2	3	4	6	7	8	9	10	11	1.099	1.104	1.110	1.116	1.121	.80
1	.3205	.3228	.3250	.3272	.3294	1	2	3	4	6	7	8	9	10	11	1.127	1.133	1.139	1.145	1.151	1
2	.3316	.3339	.3361	.3383	.3406	1	2	3	4	6	7	8	9	10	11	1.157	1.163	1.169	1.175	1.182	2
3	.3428	.3451	.3473	.3496	.3518	1	2	3	5	6	7	8	9	10	11	1.188	1.195	1.201	1.208	1.214	3
4	.3541	.3564	.3586	.3609	.3632	1	2	3	5	6	7	8	9	10	11	1.221	1.228	1.235	1.242	1.249	4
.35	.3654	.3677	.3700	.3723	.3746	1	2	3	5	6	7	8	9	10	11	1.256	1.263	1.271	1.278	1.286	.85
6	.3769	.3792	.3815	.3838	.3861	1	2	3	5	6	7	8	9	10	12	1.293	1.301	1.309	1.317	1.325	6
7	.3884	.3907	.3931	.3954	.3977	1	2	3	5	6	7	8	9	10	12	1.333	1.341	1.350	1.358	1.367	7
8	.4001	.4024	.4047	.4071	.4094	1	2	4	5	6	7	8	9	11	12	1.376	1.385	1.394	1.403	1.412	8
9	.4118	.4142	.4165	.4189	.4213	1	2	4	5	6	7	8	9	11	12	1·422	1.432	1.442	1.452	1.462	9
.40	.4236	.4260	.4284	.4308	.4332	1	2	4	5	6	7	8	10	11	12	1.472	1.483	1.494	1.505	1.516	.90
1	.4356	.4380	.4404	.4428	.4453	1	2	4	5	6	7	8	10	11	12	1.528	1.539	1.551	1.564	1.576	1
2	.4477	.4501	.4526	.4550	.4574	1	2	4	5	6	7	9	10	11	12	1.589	1.602	1.616	1.630	1.644	2
3	.4599	.4624	.4648	.4673	.4698	1	2	4	5	6	7	9	10	11	12	1.658	1.673	1.689	1.705	1.721	3
4	.4722	.4747	.4772	.4797	.4822	1	2	4	5	6	7	9	10	11	12	1.738	1.756	1.774	1.792	1.812	4
.45	.4847	.4872	.4897	.4922	.4948	1	3	4	5	6	8	9	10	11	13	1.832	1.853	1.874	1.897	1.921	.95
6	.4973	.4999	.5024	.5049	.5075	1	3	4	5	6	8	9	10	11	13	1.946	1.972	2.000	2.029	2.060	6
7	.5101	.5126	.5152	.5178	.5204	1	3	4	5	6	8	9	10	12	13	2.092	2.127	2.165	2.205	2.249	7
8	.5230	·5256	.5282	.5308	.5334	1	3	4	5	7	8	9	10	12	13	2.298	2.351	2.410	2.477	2.555	8
9	.5361	.5387	.5413	.5440	.5466	1	3	4	5	7	8	9	11	12	13	2.647	2.759	2.903	3.106	3.453	9

Interpolation

(1) $0 \leqslant r \leqslant 0.25$: find argument r_0 nearest to r and form $w = w(r_0) + \Delta r$ (where $\Delta r = r - r_0$), e.g. for $r = 0.2042$, $w = 0.2069 + 0.0002 = 0.2071$.

(2) $0.25 \leqslant r \leqslant 0.75$: find argument r_0 nearest to r and form $w = w(r_0) \pm P$, where P is the proportional part for $\Delta r = r - r_0$, e.g. for $r = 0.5682 + 0.0008 = 0.5690$; for $r = 0.5372$, $w = 0.6013 - 0.0011 = 0.6002$.

(3) $0.75 \leqslant r \leqslant 0.98$: use linear interpolation to get 3-decimal place accuracy.

(4) $0.98 \leqslant r < 1$: form $w = -\frac{1}{2}\log_e(1 - r) + 0.097 + \frac{1}{4}r$.

Appendix P
FOUR-PLACE COMMON LOGARITHMS

N	0	1	2	3	4	5	6	7	8	9	PP1	PP2	PP3	PP4	PP5
10	0000	0043	0086	0128	0170	0212	0253	0294	0334	0374	4	8	12	17	21
11	0414	0453	0492	0531	0569	0607	0645	0682	0719	0755	4	8	11	15	19
12	0792	0828	0864	0899	0934	0969	1004	1038	1072	1106	3	7	10	14	17
13	1139	1173	1206	1239	1271	1303	1335	1367	1399	1430	3	6	10	13	16
14	1461	1492	1523	1553	1584	1614	1644	1673	1703	1732	3	6	9	12	15
15	1761	1790	1818	1847	1875	1903	1931	1959	1987	2014	3	6	8	11	14
16	2041	2068	2095	2122	2148	2175	2201	2227	2253	2279	3	5	8	11	13
17	2304	2330	2355	2380	2405	2430	2455	2480	2504	2529	2	5	7	10	12
18	2553	2577	2601	2625	2648	2672	2695	2718	2742	2765	2	5	7	9	12
19	2788	2810	2833	2856	2878	2900	2923	2945	2967	2989	2	4	7	9	11
20	3010	3032	3054	3075	3096	3118	3139	3160	3181	3201	2	4	6	8	11
21	3222	3243	3263	3284	3304	3324	3345	3365	3385	3404	2	4	6	8	10
22	3424	3444	3464	3483	3502	3522	3541	3560	3579	3598	2	4	6	8	10
23	3617	3636	3655	3674	3692	3711	3729	3747	3766	3784	2	4	6	7	9
24	3802	3820	3838	3856	3874	3892	3909	3927	3945	3962	2	4	5	7	9
25	3979	3997	4014	4031	4048	4065	4082	4099	4116	4133	2	4	5	7	9
26	4150	4166	4183	4200	4216	4232	4249	4265	4281	4298	2	3	5	7	8
27	4314	4330	4346	4362	4378	4393	4409	4425	4440	4456	2	3	5	6	8
28	4472	4487	4502	4518	4533	4548	4564	4579	4594	4609	2	3	5	6	8
29	4624	4639	4654	4669	4683	4698	4713	4728	4742	4757	1	3	4	6	7
30	4771	4786	4800	4814	4829	4843	4857	4871	4886	4900	1	3	4	6	7
31	4914	4928	4942	4955	4969	4983	4997	5011	5024	5038	1	3	4	5	7
32	5051	5065	5079	5092	5105	5119	5132	5145	5159	5172	1	3	4	5	7

(PP1–PP5 = Proportional Parts 1 through 5)

Appendix P (cont.)

FOUR-PLACE COMMON LOGARITHMS

N	0	1	2	3	4	5	6	7	8	9	Proportional Parts				
											1	2	3	4	5
33	5185	5198	5211	5224	5237	5250	5263	5276	5289	5302	1	3	4	5	7
34	5315	5328	5340	5353	5366	5378	5391	5403	5416	5428	1	2	4	5	6
35	5441	5453	5465	5478	5490	5502	5514	5527	5539	5551	1	2	4	5	6
36	5563	5575	5587	5599	5611	5623	5635	5647	5658	5670	1	2	4	5	6
37	5682	5694	5705	5717	5729	5740	5752	5763	5775	5786	1	2	4	5	6
38	5798	5809	5821	5832	5843	5855	5866	5877	5888	5899	1	2	3	5	6
39	5911	5922	5933	5944	5955	5966	5977	5988	5999	6010	1	2	3	4	5
40	6021	6031	6042	6053	6064	6075	6085	6096	6107	6117	1	2	3	4	5
41	6128	6138	6149	6160	6170	6180	6191	6201	6212	6222	1	2	3	4	5
42	6232	6243	6253	6263	6274	6284	6294	6304	6314	6325	1	2	3	4	5
43	6335	6345	6355	6365	6375	6385	6395	6405	6415	6425	1	2	3	4	5
44	6435	6444	6454	6464	6474	6484	6493	6503	6513	6522	1	2	3	4	5
45	6532	6542	6551	6561	6571	6580	6590	6599	6609	6618	1	2	3	4	5
46	6628	6637	6646	6656	6665	6675	6684	6693	6702	6712	1	2	3	4	5
47	6721	6730	6739	6749	6758	6767	6776	6785	6794	6803	1	2	3	4	5
48	6812	6821	6830	6839	6848	6857	6866	6875	6884	6893	1	2	3	4	5
49	6902	6911	6920	6928	6937	6946	6955	6964	6972	6981	1	2	3	4	4
50	6990	6998	7007	7016	7024	7033	7042	7050	7059	7067	1	2	3	3	4
51	7076	7084	7093	7101	7110	7118	7126	7135	7143	7152	1	2	3	3	4
52	7160	7168	7177	7185	7193	7202	7210	7218	7226	7235	1	2	3	3	4
53	7243	7251	7259	7267	7275	7284	7292	7300	7308	7316	1	2	2	3	4
54	7324	7332	7340	7348	7356	7364	7372	7380	7388	7396	1	2	2	3	4

Appendix P (cont.)

FOUR-PLACE COMMON LOGARITHMS

N	0	1	2	3	4	5	6	7	8	9	Proportional Parts 1	2	3	4	5
55	7404	7412	7419	7427	7435	7443	7451	7459	7466	7474	1	2	2	3	4
56	7482	7490	7497	7505	7513	7520	7528	7536	7543	7551	1	2	2	3	4
57	7559	7566	7574	7582	7589	7597	7604	7612	7619	7627	1	1	2	3	4
58	7634	7642	7649	7657	7664	7672	7679	7686	7694	7701	1	1	2	3	4
59	7709	7716	7723	7731	7738	7745	7752	7760	7767	7774	1	1	2	3	4
60	7782	7789	7796	7803	7810	7818	7825	7832	7839	7846	1	1	2	3	4
61	7853	7860	7868	7875	7882	7889	7896	7903	7910	7917	1	1	2	3	3
62	7924	7931	7938	7945	7952	7959	7966	7973	7980	7987	1	1	2	3	3
63	7993	8000	8007	8014	8021	8028	8035	8041	8048	8055	1	1	2	3	3
64	8062	8069	8075	8082	8089	8096	8102	8109	8116	8122	1	1	2	3	3
65	8129	8136	8142	8149	8156	8162	8169	8176	8182	8189	1	1	2	3	3
66	8195	8202	8209	8215	8222	8228	8235	8241	8248	8254	1	1	2	3	3
67	8261	8267	8274	8280	8287	8293	8299	8306	8312	8319	1	1	2	3	3
68	8325	8331	8338	8344	8351	8357	8363	8370	8376	8382	1	1	2	3	3
69	8388	8395	8401	8407	8414	8420	8426	8432	8439	8445	1	1	2	3	3
70	8451	8457	8463	8470	8476	8482	8488	8494	8500	8506	1	1	2	3	3
71	8513	8519	8525	8531	8537	8543	8549	8555	8561	8567	1	1	2	3	3
72	8573	8579	8585	8591	8597	8603	8609	8615	8621	8627	1	1	2	3	3
73	8633	8639	8645	8651	8657	8663	8669	8675	8681	8686	1	1	2	2	3
74	8692	8698	8704	8710	8716	8722	8727	8733	8739	8745	1	1	2	2	3
75	8751	8756	8762	8768	8774	8779	8785	8791	8797	8802	1	1	2	2	3
76	8808	8814	8820	8825	8831	8837	8842	8848	8854	8859	1	1	2	2	3
77	8865	8871	8876	8882	8887	8893	8899	8904	8910	8915	1	1	2	2	3

Appendix P (cont.)

FOUR-PLACE COMMON LOGARITHMS

N	0	1	2	3	4	5	6	7	8	9	PP 1	PP 2	PP 3	PP 4	PP 5
78	8921	8927	8932	8938	8943	8949	8954	8960	8965	8971	1	1	2	2	3
79	8976	8982	8987	8993	8998	9004	9009	9015	9020	9025	1	1	2	2	3
80	9031	9036	9042	9047	9053	9058	9063	9069	9074	9079	1	1	2	2	3
81	9085	9090	9096	9101	9106	9112	9117	9122	9128	9133	1	1	2	2	3
82	9138	9143	9149	9154	9159	9165	9170	9175	9180	9186	1	1	2	2	3
83	9191	9196	9201	9206	9212	9217	9222	9227	9232	9238	1	1	2	2	3
84	9243	9248	9253	9258	9263	9269	9274	9279	9284	9289	1	1	2	2	3
85	9294	9299	9304	9309	9315	9320	9325	9330	9335	9340	1	1	2	2	3
86	9345	9350	9355	9360	9365	9370	9375	9380	9385	9390	1	1	2	2	3
87	9395	9400	9405	9410	9415	9420	9425	9430	9435	9440	1	1	2	2	3
88	9445	9450	9455	9460	9465	9469	9474	9479	9484	9489	0	1	1	2	2
89	9494	9499	9504	9509	9513	9518	9523	9528	9533	9538	0	1	1	2	2
90	9542	9547	9552	9557	9562	9566	9571	9576	9581	9586	0	1	1	2	2
91	9590	9595	9600	9605	9609	9614	9619	9624	9628	9633	0	1	1	2	2
92	9638	9643	9647	9652	9657	9661	9666	9671	9675	9680	0	1	1	2	2
93	9685	9689	9694	9699	9703	9708	9713	9717	9722	9727	0	1	1	2	2
94	9731	9736	9741	9745	9750	9754	9759	9763	9768	9773	0	1	1	2	2
95	9777	9782	9786	9791	9795	9800	9805	9809	9814	9818	0	1	1	2	2
96	9823	9827	9832	9836	9841	9845	9850	9854	9859	9863	0	1	1	2	2
97	9868	9872	9877	9881	9886	9890	9894	9899	9903	9908	0	1	1	2	2
98	9912	9917	9921	9926	9930	9934	9939	9943	9948	9952	0	1	1	2	2
99	9956	9961	9965	9969	9974	9978	9983	9987	9991	9996	0	1	1	2	2

(Columns PP 1–5 = Proportional Parts)

Appendix Q

SQUARES, SQUARE ROOTS, AND RECIPROCALS 1–1000

N	N^2	$\sqrt{N}$	$\sqrt{10N}$	$1/N$
1	1	1.000 000	3.162 278	1.0000000
2	4	1.414 214	4.472 136	.5000000
3	9	1.732 051	5.477 226	.3333333
4	16	2.000 000	6.324 555	.2500000
5	25	2.236 068	7.071 068	.2000000
6	36	2.449 490	7.745 967	.1666667
7	49	2.645 751	8.366 600	.1428571
8	64	2.828 427	8.944 272	.1250000
9	81	3.000 000	9.486 833	.1111111
10	100	3.162 278	10.00000	.1000000
11	121	3.316 625	10.48809	.09090909
12	144	3.464 102	10.95445	.08333333
13	169	3.605 551	11.40175	.07692308
14	196	3.741 657	11.83216	.07142857
15	225	3.872 983	12.24745	.06666667
16	256	4.000 000	12.64911	.06250000
17	289	4.123 106	13.03840	.05882353
18	324	4.242 641	13.41641	.05555556
19	361	4.358 899	13.78405	.05263158
20	400	4.472 136	14.14214	.05000000
21	441	4.582 576	14.49138	.04761905
22	484	4.690 416	14.83240	.04545455
23	529	4.795 832	15.16575	.04347826
24	576	4.898 979	15.49193	.04166667
25	625	5.000 000	15.81139	.04000000
26	676	5.099 020	16.12452	.03846154
27	729	5.196 152	16.43168	.03703704
28	784	5.291 503	16.73320	.03571429
29	841	5.385 165	17.02939	.03448276
30	900	5.477 226	17.32051	.03333333
31	961	5.567 764	17.60682	.03225806
32	1 024	5.656 854	17.88854	.03125000
33	1 089	5.744 563	18.16590	.03030303
34	1 156	5.830 952	18.43909	.02941176
35	1 225	5.916 080	18.70829	.02857143
36	1 296	6.000 000	18.97367	.02777778
37	1 369	6.082 763	19.23538	.02702703
38	1 444	6.164 414	19.49359	.02631579
39	1 521	6.244 998	19.74842	.02564103
40	1 600	6.324 555	20.00000	.02500000
41	1 681	6.403 124	20.24846	.02439024
42	1 764	6.480 741	20.49390	.02380952
43	1 849	6.557 439	20.73644	.02325581
44	1 936	6.633 250	20.97618	.02272727
45	2 025	6.708 204	21.21320	.02222222
46	2 116	6.782 330	21.44761	.02173913
47	2 209	6.855 655	21.67948	.02127660
48	2 304	6.928 203	21.90890	.02083333
49	2 401	7.000 000	22.13594	.02040816
50	2 500	7.071 068	22.36068	.02000000

Appendix Q (cont.)

SQUARES, SQUARE ROOTS, AND RECIPROCALS 1–1000

N	N^2	$\sqrt{N}$	$\sqrt{10N}$	1/N .0
50	2 500	7.071 068	22.36068	2000000
51	2 601	7.141 428	22.58318	1960784
52	2 704	7.211 103	22.80351	1923077
53	2 809	7.280 110	23.02173	1886792
54	2 916	7.348 469	23.23790	1851852
55	3 025	7.416 198	23.45208	1818182
56	3 136	7.483 315	23.66432	1785714
57	3 249	7.549 834	23.87467	1754386
58	3 364	7.615 773	24.08319	1724138
59	3 481	7.681 146	24.28992	1694915
60	3 600	7.745 967	24.49490	1666667
61	3 721	7.810 250	24.69818	1639344
62	3 844	7.874 008	24.89980	1612903
63	3 969	7.937 254	25.09980	1587302
64	4 096	8.000 000	25.29822	1562500
65	4 225	8.062 258	25.49510	1538462
66	4 356	8.124 038	25.69047	1515152
67	4 489	8.185 353	25.88436	1492537
68	4 624	8.246 211	26.07681	1470588
69	4 761	8.306 624	26.26785	1449275
70	4 900	8.366 600	26.45751	1428571
71	5 041	8.426 150	26.64583	1408451
72	5 184	8.485 281	26.83282	1388889
73	5 329	8.544 004	27.01851	1369863
74	5 476	8.602 325	27.20294	1351351
75	5 625	8.660 254	27.38613	1333333
76	5 776	8.717 798	27.56810	1315789
77	5 929	8.774 964	27.74887	1298701
78	6 084	8.831 761	27.92848	1282051
79	6 241	8.888 194	28.10694	1265823
80	6 400	8.944 272	28.28427	1250000
81	6 561	9.000 000	28.46050	1234568
82	6 724	9.055 385	28.63564	1219512
83	6 889	9.110 434	28.80972	1204819
84	7 056	9.165 151	28.98275	1190476
85	7 225	9.219 544	29.15476	1176471
86	7 396	9.273 618	29.32576	1162791
87	7 569	9.327 379	29.49576	1149425
88	7 744	9.380 832	29.66479	1136364
89	7 921	9.433 981	29.83287	1123596
90	8 100	9.486 833	30.00000	1111111
91	8 281	9.539 392	30.16621	1098901
92	8 464	9.591 663	30.33150	1086957
93	8 649	9.643 651	30.49590	1075269
94	8 836	9.695 360	30.65942	1063830
95	9 025	9.746 794	30.82207	1052632
96	9 216	9.797 959	30.98387	1041667
97	9 409	9.848 858	31.14482	1030928
98	9 604	9.899 495	31.30495	1020408
99	9 801	9.949 874	31.46427	1010101
100	10 000	10.00000	31.62278	1000000

Appendix Q *(cont.)*

SQUARES, SQUARE ROOTS, AND RECIPROCALS 1–1000

N	N^2	$\sqrt{N}$	$\sqrt{10N}$	$1/N$ .0
100	10 000	10.00000	31.62278	10000000
101	10 201	10.04988	31.78050	09900990
102	10 404	10.09950	31.93744	09803922
103	10 609	10.14889	32.09361	09708738
104	10 816	10.19804	32.24903	09615385
105	11 025	10.24695	32.40370	09523810
106	11 236	10.29563	32.55764	09433962
107	11 449	10.34408	32.71085	09345794
108	11 664	10.39230	32.86335	09259259
109	11 881	10.44031	33.01515	09174312
110	12 100	10.48809	33.16625	09090909
111	12 321	10.53565	33.31666	09009009
112	12 544	10.58301	33.46640	08928571
113	12 769	10.63015	33.61547	08849558
114	12 996	10.67708	33.76389	08771930
115	13 225	10.72381	33.91165	08695652
116	13 456	10.77033	34.05877	08620690
117	13 689	10.81665	34.20526	08547009
118	13 924	10.86278	34.35113	08474576
119	14 161	10.90871	34.49638	08403361
120	14 400	10.95445	34.64102	08333333
121	14 641	11.00000	34.78505	08264463
122	14 884	11.04536	34.92850	08196721
123	15 129	11.09054	35.07136	08130081
124	15 376	11.13553	35.21363	08064516
125	15 625	11.18034	35.35534	08000000
126	15 876	11.22497	35.49648	07936508
127	16 129	11.26943	35.63706	07874016
128	16 384	11.31371	35.77709	07812500
129	16 641	11.35782	35.91657	07751938
130	16 900	11.40175	36.05551	07692308
131	17 161	11.44552	36.19392	07633588
132	17 424	11.48913	36.33180	07575758
133	17 689	11.53256	36.46917	07518797
134	17 956	11.57584	36.60601	07462687
135	18 225	11.61895	36.74235	07407407
136	18 496	11.66190	36.87818	07352941
137	18 769	11.70470	37.01351	07299270
138	19 044	11.74734	37.14835	07246377
139	19 321	11.78983	37.28270	07194245
140	19 600	11.83216	37.41657	07142857
141	19 881	11.87434	37.54997	07092199
142	20 164	11.91638	37.68289	07042254
143	20 449	11.95826	37.81534	06993007
144	20 736	12.00000	37.94733	06944444
145	21 025	12.04159	38.07887	06896552
146	21 316	12.08305	38.20995	06849315
147	21 609	12.12436	38.34058	06802721
148	21 904	12.16553	38.47077	06756757
149	22 201	12.20656	38.60052	06711409
150	22 500	12.24745	38.72983	06666667

Appendix Q (cont.)

SQUARES, SQUARE ROOTS, AND RECIPROCALS 1-1000

N	N²	√N	√10N	1/N .00
150	22 500	12.24745	38.72983	6666667
151	22 801	12.28821	38.85872	6622517
152	23 104	12.32883	38.98718	6578947
153	23 409	12.36932	39.11521	6535948
154	23 716	12.40967	39.24283	6493506
155	24 025	12.44990	39.37004	6451613
156	24 336	12.49000	39.49684	6410256
157	24 649	12.52996	39.62323	6369427
158	24 964	12.56981	39.74921	6329114
159	25 281	12.60952	39.87480	6289308
160	25 600	12.64911	40.00000	6250000
161	25 921	12.68858	40.12481	6211180
162	26 244	12.72792	40.24922	6172840
163	26 569	12.76715	40.37326	6134969
164	26 896	12.80625	40.49691	6097561
165	27 225	12.84523	40.62019	6060606
166	27 556	12.88410	40.74310	6024096
167	27 889	12.92285	40.86563	5988024
168	28 224	12.96148	40.98780	5952381
169	28 561	13.00000	41.10961	5917160
170	28 900	13.03840	41.23106	5882353
171	29 241	13.07670	41.35215	5847953
172	29 584	13.11488	41.47288	5813953
173	29 929	13.15295	41.59327	5780347
174	30 276	13.19091	41.71331	5747126
175	30 625	13.22876	41.83300	5714286
176	30 976	13.26650	41.95235	5681818
177	31 329	13.30413	42.07137	5649718
178	31 684	13.34166	42.19005	5617978
179	32 041	13.37909	42.30839	5586592
180	32 400	13.41641	42.42641	5555556
181	32 761	13.45362	42.54409	5524862
182	33 124	13.49074	42.66146	5494505
183	33 489	13.52775	42.77850	5464481
184	33 856	13.56466	42.89522	5434783
185	34 225	13.60147	43.01163	5405405
186	34 596	13.63818	43.12772	5376344
187	34 969	13.67479	43.24350	5347594
188	35 344	13.71131	43.35897	5319149
189	35 721	13.74773	43.47413	5291005
190	36 100	13.78405	43.58899	5263158
191	36 481	13.82027	43.70355	5235602
192	36 864	13.85641	43.81780	5208333
193	37 249	13.89244	43.93177	5181347
194	37 636	13.92839	44.04543	5154639
195	38 025	13.96424	44.15880	5128205
196	38 416	14.00000	44.27189	5102041
197	38 809	14.03567	44.38468	5076142
198	39 204	14.07125	44.49719	5050505
199	39 601	14.10674	44.60942	5025126
200	40 000	14.14214	44.72136	5000000

Appendix Q *(cont.)*

SQUARES, SQUARE ROOTS, AND RECIPROCALS 1-1000

N	N^2	$\sqrt{N}$	$\sqrt{10N}$	1/N .00
200	40 000	14.14214	44.72136	5000000
201	40 401	14.17745	44.83302	4975124
202	40 804	14.21267	44.94441	4950495
203	41 209	14.24781	45.05552	4926108
204	41 616	14.28286	45.16636	4901961
205	42 025	14.31782	45.27693	4878049
206	42 436	14.35270	45.38722	4854369
207	42 849	14.38749	45.49725	4830918
208	43 264	14.42221	45.60702	4807692
209	43 681	14.45683	45.71652	4784689
210	44 100	14.49138	45.82576	4761905
211	44 521	14.52584	45.93474	4739336
212	44 944	14.56022	46.04346	4716981
213	45 369	14.59452	46.15192	4694836
214	45 796	14.62874	46.26013	4672897
215	46 225	14.66288	46.36809	4651163
216	46 656	14.69694	46.47580	4629630
217	47 089	14.73092	46.58326	4608295
218	47 524	14.76482	46.69047	4587156
219	47 961	14.79865	46.79744	4566210
220	48 400	14.83240	46.90416	4545455
221	48 841	14.86607	47.01064	4524887
222	49 284	14.89966	47.11688	4504505
223	49 729	14.93318	47.22288	4484305
224	50 176	14.96663	47.32864	4464286
225	50 625	15.00000	47.43416	4444444
226	51 076	15.03330	47.53946	4424779
227	51 529	15.06652	47.64452	4405286
228	51 984	15.09967	47.74935	4385965
229	52 441	15.13275	47.85394	4366812
230	52 900	15.16575	47.95832	4347826
231	53 361	15.19868	48.06246	4329004
232	53 824	15.23155	48.16638	4310345
233	54 289	15.26434	48.27007	4291845
234	54 756	15.29706	48.37355	4273504
235	55 225	15.32971	48.47680	4255319
236	55 696	15.36229	48.57983	4237288
237	56 169	15.39480	48.68265	4219409
238	56 644	15.42725	48.78524	4201681
239	57 121	15.45962	48.88763	4184100
240	57 600	15.49193	48.98979	4166667
241	58 081	15.52417	49.09175	4149378
242	58 564	15.55635	49.19350	4132231
243	59 049	15.58846	49.29503	4115226
244	59 536	15.62050	49.39636	4098361
245	60 025	15.65248	49.49747	4081633
246	60 516	15.68439	49.59839	4065041
247	61 009	15.71623	49.69909	4048583
248	61 504	15.74802	49.79960	4032258
249	62 001	15.77973	49.89990	4016064
250	62 500	15.81139	50.00000	4000000

Appendix Q (cont.)

SQUARES, SQUARE ROOTS, AND RECIPROCALS 1–1000

N	N²	√N	√10N	1/N .00
250	62 500	15.81139	50.00000	4000000
251	63 001	15.84298	50.09990	3984064
252	63 504	15.87451	50.19960	3968254
253	64 009	15.90597	50.29911	3952569
254	64 516	15.93738	50.39841	3937008
255	65 025	15.96872	50.49752	3921569
256	65 536	16.00000	50.59644	3906250
257	66 049	16.03122	50.69517	3891051
258	66 564	16.06238	50.79370	3875969
259	67 081	16.09348	50.89204	3861004
260	67 600	16.12452	50.99020	3846154
261	68 121	16.15549	51.08816	3831418
262	68 644	16.18641	51.18594	3816794
263	69 169	16.21727	51.28353	3802281
264	69 696	16.24808	51.38093	3787879
265	70 225	16.27882	51.47815	3773585
266	70 756	16.30951	51.57519	3759398
267	71 289	16.34013	51.67204	3745318
268	71 824	16.37071	51.76872	3731343
269	72 361	16.40122	51.86521	3717472
270	72 900	16.43168	51.96152	3703704
271	73 441	16.46208	52.05766	3690037
272	73 984	16.49242	52.15362	3676471
273	74 529	16.52271	52.24940	3663004
274	75 076	16.55295	52.34501	3649635
275	75 625	16.58312	52.44044	3636364
276	76 176	16.61325	52.53570	3623188
277	76 729	16.64332	52.63079	3610108
278	77 284	16.67333	52.72571	3597122
279	77 841	16.70329	52.82045	3584229
280	78 400	16.73320	52.91503	3571429
281	78 961	16.76305	53.00943	3558719
282	79 524	16.79286	53.10367	3546099
283	80 089	16.82260	53.19774	3533569
284	80 656	16.85230	53.29165	3521127
285	81 225	16.88194	53.38539	3508772
286	81 796	16.91153	53.47897	3496503
287	82 369	16.94107	53.57238	3484321
288	82 944	16.97056	53.66563	3472222
289	83 521	17.00000	53.75872	3460208
290	84 100	17.02939	53.85165	3448276
291	84 681	17.05872	53.94442	3436426
292	85 264	17.08801	54.03702	3424658
293	85 849	17.11724	54.12947	3412969
294	86 436	17.14643	54.22177	3401361
295	87 025	17.17556	54.31390	3389831
296	87 616	17.20465	54.40588	3378378
297	88 209	17.23369	54.49771	3367003
298	88 804	17.26268	54.58938	3355705
299	89 401	17.29162	54.68089	3344482
300	90 000	17.32051	54.77226	3333333

SQUARES, SQUARE ROOTS, AND RECIPROCALS 1–1000

N	N^2	$\sqrt{N}$	$\sqrt{10N}$	1/N .00
300	90 000	17.32051	54.77226	3333333
301	90 601	17.34935	54.86347	3322259
302	91 204	17.37815	54.95453	3311258
303	91 809	17.40690	55.04544	3300330
304	92 416	17.43560	55.13620	3289474
305	93 025	17.46425	55.22681	3278689
306	93 636	17.49286	55.31727	3267974
307	94 249	17.52142	55.40758	3257329
308	94 864	17.54993	55.49775	3246753
309	95 481	17.57840	55.58777	3236246
310	96 100	17.60682	55.67764	3225806
311	96 721	17.63519	55.76737	3215434
312	97 344	17.66352	55.85696	3205128
313	97 969	17.69181	55.94640	3194888
314	98 596	17.72005	56.03570	3184713
315	99 225	17.74824	56.12486	3174603
316	99 856	17.77639	56.21388	3164557
317	100 489	17.80449	56.30275	3154574
318	101 124	17.83255	56.39149	3144654
319	101 761	17.86057	56.48008	3134796
320	102 400	17.88854	56.56854	3125000
321	103 041	17.91647	56.65686	3115265
322	103 684	17.94436	56.74504	3105590
323	104 329	17.97220	56.83309	3095975
324	104 976	18.00000	56.92100	3086420
325	105 625	18.02776	57.00877	3076923
326	106 276	18.05547	57.09641	3067485
327	106 929	18.08314	57.18391	3058104
328	107 584	18.11077	57.27128	3048780
329	108 241	18.13836	57.35852	3039514
330	108 900	18.16590	57.44563	3030303
331	109 561	18.19341	57.53260	3021148
332	110 224	18.22087	57.61944	3012048
333	110 889	18.24829	57.70615	3003003
334	111 556	18.27567	57.79273	2994012
335	112 225	18.30301	57.87918	2985075
336	112 896	18.33030	57.96551	2976190
337	113 569	18.35756	58.05170	2967359
338	114 244	18.38478	58.13777	2958580
339	114 921	18.41195	58.22371	2949853
340	115 600	18.43909	58.30952	2941176
341	116 281	18.46619	58.39521	2932551
342	116 964	18.49324	58.48077	2923977
343	117 649	18.52026	58.56620	2915452
344	118 336	18.54724	58.65151	2906977
345	119 025	18.57418	58.73670	2898551
346	119 716	18.60108	58.82176	2890173
347	120 409	18.62794	58.90671	2881844
348	121 104	18.65476	58.99152	2873563
349	121 801	18.68154	59.07622	2865330
350	122 500	18.70829	59.16080	2857143

Appendix Q *(cont.)*

SQUARES, SQUARE ROOTS, AND RECIPROCALS 1–1000

N	N^2	$\sqrt{N}$	$\sqrt{10N}$	1/N .00
350	122 500	18.70829	59.16080	2857143
351	123 201	18.73499	59.24525	2849003
352	123 904	18.76166	59.32959	2840909
353	124 609	18.78829	59.41380	2832861
354	125 316	18.81489	59.49790	2824859
355	126 025	18.84144	59.58188	2816901
356	126 736	18.86796	59.66574	2808989
357	127 449	18.89444	59.74948	2801120
358	128 164	18.92089	59.83310	2793296
359	128 881	18.94730	59.91661	2785515
360	129 600	18.97367	60.00000	2777778
361	130 321	19.00000	60.08328	2770083
362	131 044	19.02630	60.16644	2762431
363	131 769	19.05256	60.24948	2754821
364	132 496	19.07878	60.33241	2747253
365	133 225	19.10497	60.41523	2739726
366	133 956	19.13113	60.49793	2732240
367	134 689	19.15724	60.58052	2724796
368	135 424	19.18333	60.66300	2717391
369	136 161	19.20937	60.74537	2710027
370	136 900	19.23538	60.82763	2702703
371	137 641	19.26136	60.90977	2695418
372	138 384	19.28730	60.99180	2688172
373	139 129	19.31321	61.07373	2680965
374	139 876	19.33908	61.15554	2673797
375	140 625	19.36492	61.23724	2666667
376	141 376	19.39072	61.31884	2659574
377	142 129	19.41649	61.40033	2652520
378	142 884	19.44222	61.48170	2645503
379	143 641	19.46792	61.56298	2638522
380	144 400	19.49359	61.64414	2631579
381	145 161	19.51922	61.72520	2624672
382	145 924	19.54483	61.80615	2617801
383	146 689	19.57039	61.88699	2610966
384	147 456	19.59592	61.96773	2604167
385	148 225	19.62142	62.04837	2597403
386	148 996	19.64688	62.12890	2590674
387	149 769	19.67232	62.20932	2583979
388	150 544	19.69772	62.28965	2577320
389	151 321	19.72308	62.36986	2570694
390	152 100	19.74842	62.44998	2564103
391	152 881	19.77372	62.52999	2557545
392	153 664	19.79899	62.60990	2551020
393	154 449	19.82423	62.68971	2544529
394	155 236	19.84943	62.76942	2538071
395	156 025	19.87461	62.84903	2531646
396	156 816	19.89975	62.92853	2525253
397	157 609	19.92486	63.00794	2518892
398	158 404	19.94994	63.08724	2512563
399	159 201	19.97498	63.16645	2506266
400	160 000	20.00000	63.24555	2500000

SQUARES, SQUARE ROOTS, AND RECIPROCALS 1–1000

N	N^2	$\sqrt{N}$	$\sqrt{10N}$	1/N .00
400	160 000	20.00000	63.24555	2500000
401	160 801	20.02498	63.32456	2493766
402	161 604	20.04994	63.40347	2487562
403	162 409	20.07486	63.48228	2481390
404	163 216	20.09975	63.56099	2475248
405	164 025	20.12461	63.63961	2469136
406	164 836	20.14944	63.71813	2463054
407	165 649	20.17424	63.79655	2457002
408	166 464	20.19901	63.87488	2450980
409	167 281	20.22375	63.95311	2444988
410	168 100	20.24846	64.03124	2439024
411	168 921	20.27313	64.10928	2433090
412	169 744	20.29778	64.18723	2427184
413	170 569	20.32240	64.26508	2421308
414	171 396	20.34699	64.34283	2415459
415	172 225	20.37155	64.42049	2409639
416	173 056	20.39608	64.49806	2403846
417	173 889	20.42058	64.57554	2398082
418	174 724	20.44505	64.65292	2392344
419	175 561	20.46949	64.73021	2386635
420	176 400	20.49390	64.80741	2380952
421	177 241	20.51828	64.88451	2375297
422	178 084	20.54264	64.96153	2369668
423	178 929	20.56696	65.03845	2364066
424	179 776	20.59126	65.11528	2358491
425	180 625	20.61553	65.19202	2352941
426	181 476	20.63977	65.26868	2347418
427	182 329	20.66398	65.34524	2341920
428	183 184	20.68816	65.42171	2336449
429	184 041	20.71232	65.49809	2331002
430	184 900	20.73644	65.57439	2325581
431	185 761	20.76054	65.65059	2320186
432	186 624	20.78461	65.72671	2314815
433	187 489	20.80865	65.80274	2309469
434	188 356	20.83267	65.87868	2304147
435	189 225	20.85665	65.95453	2298851
436	190 096	20.88061	66.03030	2293578
437	190 969	20.90454	66.10598	2288330
438	191 844	20.92845	66.18157	2283105
439	192 721	20.95233	66.25708	2277904
440	193 600	20.97618	66.33250	2272727
441	194 481	21.00000	66.40783	2267574
442	195 364	21.02380	66.48308	2262443
443	196 249	21.04757	66.55825	2257336
444	197 136	21.07131	66.63332	2252252
445	198 025	21.09502	66.70832	2247191
446	198 916	21.11871	66.78323	2242152
447	199 809	21.14237	66.85806	2237136
448	200 704	21.16601	66.93280	2232143
449	201 601	21.18962	67.00746	2227171
450	202 500	21.21320	67.08204	2222222

Appendix Q (cont.)

SQUARES, SQUARE ROOTS, AND RECIPROCALS 1-1000

N	N²	√N	√10N	1/N .00
450	202 500	21.21320	67.08204	2222222
451	203 401	21.23676	67.15653	2217295
452	204 304	21.26029	67.23095	2212389
453	205 209	21.28380	67.30527	2207506
454	206 116	21.30728	67.37952	2202643
455	207 025	21.33073	67.45369	2197802
456	207 936	21.35416	67.52777	2192982
457	208 849	21.37756	67.60178	2188184
458	209 764	21.40093	67.67570	2183406
459	210 681	21.42429	67.74954	2178649
460	211 600	21.44761	67.82330	2173913
461	212 521	21.47091	67.89698	2169197
462	213 444	21.49419	67.97058	2164502
463	214 369	21.51743	68.04410	2159827
464	215 296	21.54066	68.11755	2155172
465	216 225	21.56386	68.19091	2150538
466	217 156	21.58703	68.26419	2145923
467	218 089	21.61018	68.33740	2141328
468	219 024	21.63331	68.41053	2136752
469	219 961	21.65641	68.48357	2132196
470	220 900	21.67948	68.55655	2127660
471	221 841	21.70253	68.62944	2123142
472	222 784	21.72556	68.70226	2118644
473	223 729	21.74856	68.77500	2114165
474	224 676	21.77154	68.84766	2109705
475	225 625	21.79449	68.92024	2105263
476	226 576	21.81742	68.99275	2100840
477	227 529	21.84033	69.06519	2096436
478	228 484	21.86321	69.13754	2092050
479	229 441	21.88607	69.20983	2087683
480	230 400	21.90890	69.28203	2083333
481	231 361	21.93171	69.35416	2079002
482	232 324	21.95450	69.42622	2074689
483	233 289	21.97726	69.49820	2070393
484	234 256	22.00000	69.57011	2066116
485	235 225	22.02272	69.64194	2061856
486	236 196	22.04541	69.71370	2057613
487	237 169	22.06808	69.78539	2053388
488	238 144	22.09072	69.85700	2049180
489	239 121	22.11334	69.92853	2044990
490	240 100	22.13594	70.00000	2040816
491	241 081	22.15852	70.07139	2036660
492	242 064	22.18107	70.14271	2032520
493	243 049	22.20360	70.21396	2028398
494	244 036	22.22611	70.28513	2024291
495	245 025	22.24860	70.35624	2020202
496	246 016	22.27106	70.42727	2016129
497	247 009	22.29350	70.49823	2012072
498	248 004	22.31591	70.56912	2008032
499	249 001	22.33831	70.63993	2004008
500	250 000	22.36068	70.71068	2000000

Appendix Q (cont.)

SQUARES, SQUARE ROOTS, AND RECIPROCALS 1–1000

N	N^2	$\sqrt{N}$	$\sqrt{10N}$	1/N .00
500	250 000	22.36068	70.71068	2000000
501	251 001	22.38303	70.78135	1996008
502	252 004	22.40536	70.85196	1992032
503	253 009	22.42766	70.92249	1988072
504	254 016	22.44994	70.99296	1984127
505	255 025	22.47221	71.06335	1980198
506	256 036	22.49444	71.13368	1976285
507	257 049	22.51666	71.20393	1972387
508	258 064	22.53886	71.27412	1968504
509	259 081	22.56103	71.34424	1964637
510	260 100	22.58318	71.41428	1960784
511	261 121	22.60531	71.48426	1956947
512	262 144	22.62742	71.55418	1953125
513	263 169	22.64950	71.62402	1949318
514	264 196	22.67157	71.69379	1945525
515	265 225	22.69361	71.76350	1941748
516	266 256	22.71563	71.83314	1937984
517	267 289	22.73763	71.90271	1934236
518	268 324	22.75961	71.97222	1930502
519	269 361	22.78157	72.04165	1926782
520	270 400	22.80351	72.11103	1923077
521	271 441	22.82542	72.18033	1919386
522	272 484	22.84732	72.24957	1915709
523	273 529	22.86919	72.31874	1912046
524	274 576	22.89105	72.38784	1908397
525	275 625	22.91288	72.45688	1904762
526	276 676	22.93469	72.52586	1901141
527	277 729	22.95648	72.59477	1897533
528	278 784	22.97825	72.66361	1893939
529	279 841	23.00000	72.73239	1890359
530	280 900	23.02173	72.80110	1886792
531	281 961	23.04344	72.86975	1883239
532	283 024	23.06513	72.93833	1879699
533	284 089	23.08679	73.00685	1876173
534	285 156	23.10844	73.07530	1872659
535	286 225	23.13007	73.14369	1869159
536	287 296	23.15167	73.21202	1865672
537	288 369	23.17326	73.28028	1862197
538	289 444	23.19483	73.34848	1858736
539	290 521	23.21637	73.41662	1855288
540	291 600	23.23790	73.48469	1851852
541	292 681	23.25941	73.55270	1848429
542	293 764	23.28089	73.62065	1845018
543	294 849	23.30236	73.68853	1841621
544	295 936	23.32381	73.75636	1838235
545	297 025	23.34524	73.82412	1834862
546	298 116	23.36664	73.89181	1831502
547	299 209	23.38803	73.95945	1828154
548	300 304	23.40940	74.02702	1824818
549	301 401	23.43075	74.09453	1821494
550	302 500	23.45208	74.16198	1818182

Appendix Q *(cont.)*

SQUARES, SQUARE ROOTS, AND RECIPROCALS 1–1000

N	N^2	$\sqrt{N}$	$\sqrt{10N}$	1/N .00
550	302 500	23.45208	74.16198	1818182
551	303 601	23.47339	74.22937	1814882
552	304 704	23.49468	74.29670	1811594
553	305 809	23.51595	74.36397	1808318
554	306 916	23.53720	74.43118	1805054
555	308 025	23.55844	74.49832	1801802
556	309 136	23.57965	74.56541	1798561
557	310 249	23.60085	74.63243	1795332
558	311 364	23.62202	74.69940	1792115
559	312 481	23.64318	74.76630	1788909
560	313 600	23.66432	74.83315	1785714
561	314 721	23.68544	74.89993	1782531
562	315 844	23.70654	74.96666	1779359
563	316 969	23.72762	75.03333	1776199
564	318 096	23.74868	75.09993	1773050
565	319 225	23.76973	75.16648	1769912
566	320 356	23.79075	75.23297	1766784
567	321 489	23.81176	75.29940	1763668
568	322 624	23.83275	75.36577	1760563
569	323 761	23.85372	75.43209	1757469
570	324 900	23.87467	75.49834	1754386
571	326 041	23.89561	75.56454	1751313
572	327 184	23.91652	75.63068	1748252
573	328 329	23.93742	75.69676	1745201
574	329 476	23.95830	75.76279	1742160
575	330 625	23.97916	75.82875	1739130
576	331 776	24.00000	75.89466	1736111
577	332 929	24.02082	75.96052	1733102
578	334 084	24.04163	76.02631	1730104
579	335 241	24.06242	76.09205	1727116
580	336 400	24.08319	76.15773	1724138
581	337 561	24.10394	76.22336	1721170
582	338 724	24.12468	76.28892	1718213
583	339 889	24.14539	76.35444	1715266
584	341 056	24.16609	76.41989	1712329
585	342 225	24.18677	76.48529	1709402
586	343 396	24.20744	76.55064	1706485
587	344 569	24.22808	76.61593	1703578
588	345 744	24.24871	76.68116	1700680
589	346 921	24.26932	76.74634	1697793
590	348 100	24.28992	76.81146	1694915
591	349 281	24.31049	76.87652	1692047
592	350 464	24.33105	76.94154	1689189
593	351 649	24.35159	77.00649	1686341
594	352 836	24.37212	77.07140	1683502
595	354 025	24.39262	77.13624	1680672
596	355 216	24.41311	77.20104	1677852
597	356 409	24.43358	77.26578	1675042
598	357 604	24.45404	77.33046	1672241
599	358 801	24.47448	77.39509	1669449
600	360 000	24.49490	77.45967	1666667

Appendix Q (*cont.*)

SQUARES, SQUARE ROOTS, AND RECIPROCALS 1–1000

N	N^2	$\sqrt{N}$	$\sqrt{10N}$	1/N .00
600	360 000	24.49490	77.45967	1666667
601	361 201	24.51530	77.52419	1663894
602	362 404	24.53569	77.58866	1661130
603	363 609	24.55606	77.65307	1658375
604	364 816	24.57641	77.71744	1655629
605	366 025	24.59675	77.78175	1652893
606	367 236	24.61707	77.84600	1650165
607	368 449	24.63737	77.91020	1647446
608	369 664	24.65766	77.97435	1644737
609	370 881	24.67793	78.03845	1642036
610	372 100	24.69818	78.10250	1639344
611	373 321	24.71841	78.16649	1636661
612	374 544	24.73863	78.23043	1633987
613	375 769	24.75884	78.29432	1631321
614	376 996	24.77902	78.35815	1628664
615	378 225	24.79919	78.42194	1626016
616	379 456	24.81935	78.48567	1623377
617	380 689	24.83948	78.54935	1620746
618	381 924	24.85961	78.61298	1618123
619	383 161	24.87971	78.67655	1615509
620	384 400	24.89980	78.74008	1612903
621	385 641	24.91987	78.80355	1610306
622	386 884	24.93993	78.86698	1607717
623	388 129	24.95997	78.93035	1605136
624	389 376	24.97999	78.99367	1602564
625	390 625	25.00000	79.05694	1600000
626	391 876	25.01999	79.12016	1597444
627	393 129	25.03997	79.18333	1594896
628	394 384	25.05993	79.24645	1592357
629	395 641	25.07987	79.30952	1589825
630	396 900	25.09980	79.37254	1587302
631	398 161	25.11971	79.43551	1584786
632	399 424	25.13961	79.49843	1582278
633	400 689	25.15949	79.56130	1579779
634	401 956	25.17936	79.62412	1577287
635	403 225	25.19921	79.68689	1574803
636	404 496	25.21904	79.74961	1572327
637	405 769	25.23886	79.81228	1569859
638	407 044	25.25866	79.87490	1567398
639	408 321	25.27845	79.93748	1564945
640	409 600	25.29822	80.00000	1562500
641	410 881	25.31798	80.06248	1560062
642	412 164	25.33772	80.12490	1557632
643	413 449	25.35744	80.18728	1555210
644	414 736	25.37716	80.24961	1552795
645	416 025	25.39685	80.31189	1550388
646	417 316	25.41653	80.37413	1547988
647	418 609	25.43619	80.43631	1545595
648	419 904	25.45584	80.49845	1543210
649	421 201	25.47548	80.56054	1540832
650	422 500	25.49510	80.62258	1538462

SQUARES, SQUARE ROOTS, AND RECIPROCALS 1–1000

N	N²	√N	√10N	1/N .00
650	422 500	25.49510	80.62258	1538462
651	423 801	25.51470	80.68457	1536098
652	425 104	25.53429	80.74652	1533742
653	426 409	25.55386	80.80842	1531394
654	427 716	25.57342	80.87027	1529052
655	429 025	25.59297	80.93207	1526718
656	430 336	25.61250	80.99383	1524390
657	431 649	25.63201	81.05554	1522070
658	432 964	25.65151	81.11720	1519757
659	434 281	25.67100	81.17881	1517451
660	435 600	25.69047	81.24038	1515152
661	436 921	25.70992	81.30191	1512859
662	438 244	25.72936	81.36338	1510574
663	439 569	25.74879	81.42481	1508296
664	440 896	25.76820	81.48620	1506024
665	442 225	25.78759	81.54753	1503759
666	443 556	25.80698	81.60882	1501502
667	444 889	25.82634	81.67007	1499250
668	446 224	25.84570	81.73127	1497006
669	447 561	25.86503	81.79242	1494768
670	448 900	25.88436	81.85353	1492537
671	450 241	25.90367	81.91459	1490313
672	451 584	25.92296	81.97561	1488095
673	452 929	25.94224	82.03658	1485884
674	454 276	25.96151	82.09750	1483680
675	455 625	25.98076	82.15838	1481481
676	456 976	26.00000	82.21922	1479290
677	458 329	26.01922	82.28001	1477105
678	459 684	26.03843	82.34076	1474926
679	461 041	26.05763	82.40146	1472754
680	462 400	26.07681	82.46211	1470588
681	463 761	26.09598	82.42272	1468429
682	465 124	26.11513	82.58329	1466276
683	466 489	26.13427	82.64381	1464129
684	467 856	26.15339	82.70429	1461988
685	469 225	26.17250	82.76473	1459854
686	470 596	26.19160	82.82512	1457726
687	471 969	26.21068	82.88546	1455604
688	473 344	26.22975	82.94577	1453488
689	474 721	26.24881	83.00602	1451379
690	476 100	26.26785	83.06624	1449275
691	477 481	26.28688	83.12641	1447178
692	478 864	26.30589	83.18654	1445087
693	480 249	26.32489	83.24662	1443001
694	481 636	26.34388	83.30666	1440922
695	483 025	26.36285	83.36666	1438849
696	484 416	26.38181	83.42661	1436782
697	485 809	26.40076	83.48653	1434720
698	487 204	26.41969	83.54639	1432665
699	488 601	26.43861	83.60622	1430615
700	490 000	26.45751	83.66600	1428571

Appendix Q (*cont.*)

SQUARES, SQUARE ROOTS, AND RECIPROCALS 1–1000

N	N^2	$\sqrt{N}$	$\sqrt{10N}$	1/N .00
700	490 000	26.45751	83.66600	1428571
701	491 401	26.47640	83.72574	1426534
702	492 804	26.49528	83.78544	1424501
703	494 209	26.51415	83.84510	1422475
704	495 616	26.53300	83.90471	1420455
705	497 025	26.55184	83.96428	1418440
706	498 436	26.57066	84.02381	1416431
707	499 849	26.58947	84.08329	1414427
708	501 264	26.60827	84.14274	1412429
709	502 681	26.62705	84.20214	1410437
710	504 100	26.64583	84.26150	1408451
711	505 521	26.66458	84.32082	1406470
712	506 944	26.68333	84.38009	1404494
713	508 369	26.70206	84.43933	1402525
714	509 796	26.72078	84.49852	1400560
715	511 225	26.73948	84.55767	1398601
716	512 656	26.75818	84.61678	1396648
717	514 089	26.77686	84.67585	1394700
718	515 524	26.79552	84.73488	1392758
719	516 961	26.81418	84.79387	1390821
720	518 400	26.83282	84.85281	1388889
721	519 841	26.85144	84.91172	1386963
722	521 284	26.87006	84.97058	1385042
723	522 729	26.88866	85.02941	1383126
724	524 176	26.90725	85.08819	1381215
725	525 625	26.92582	85.14693	1379310
726	527 076	26.94439	85.20563	1377410
727	528 529	26.96294	85.26429	1375516
728	529 984	26.98148	85.32292	1373626
729	531 441	27.00000	85.38150	1371742
730	532 900	27.01851	85.44004	1369863
731	534 361	27.03701	85.49854	1367989
732	535 824	27.05550	85.55700	1366120
733	537 289	27.07397	85.61542	1364256
734	538 756	27.09243	85.67380	1362398
735	540 225	27.11088	85.73214	1360544
736	541 696	27.12932	85.79044	1358696
737	543 169	27.14774	85.84870	1356852
738	544 644	27.16616	85.90693	1355014
739	546 121	27.18455	85.96511	1353180
740	547 600	27.20294	86.02325	1351351
741	549 081	27.22132	86.08136	1349528
742	550 564	27.23968	86.13942	1347709
743	552 049	27.25803	86.19745	1345895
744	553 536	27.27636	86.25543	1344086
745	555 025	27.29469	86.31338	1342282
746	556 516	27.31300	86.37129	1340483
747	558 009	27.33130	86.42916	1338688
748	559 504	27.34959	86.48699	1336898
749	561 001	27.36786	86.54479	1335113
750	562 500	27.38613	86.60254	1333333

Appendix Q (cont.)

SQUARES, SQUARE ROOTS, AND RECIPROCALS 1–1000

N	N^2	$\sqrt{N}$	$\sqrt{10N}$	1/N .00
750	562 500	27.38613	86.60254	1333333
751	564 001	27.40438	86.66026	1331558
752	565 504	27.42262	86.71793	1329787
753	567 009	27.44085	86.77557	1328021
754	568 516	27.45906	86.83317	1326260
755	570 025	27.47726	86.89074	1324503
756	571 536	27.49545	86.94826	1322751
757	573 049	27.51363	87.00575	1321004
758	574 564	27.53180	87.06320	1319261
759	576 081	27.54995	87.12061	1317523
760	577 600	27.56810	87.17798	1315789
761	579 121	27.58623	87.23531	1314060
762	580 644	27.60435	87.29261	1312336
763	582 169	27.62245	87.34987	1310616
764	583 696	27.64055	87.40709	1308901
765	585 225	27.65863	87.46428	1307190
766	586 756	27.67671	87.52143	1305483
767	588 289	27.69476	87.57854	1303781
768	589 824	27.71281	87.63561	1302083
769	591 361	27.73085	87.69265	1300390
770	592 900	27.74887	87.74964	1298710
771	594 441	27.76689	87.80661	1297017
772	595 984	27.78489	87.86353	1295337
773	597 529	27.80288	87.92042	1293661
774	599 076	27.82086	87.97727	1291990
775	600 625	27.83882	88.03408	1290323
776	602 176	27.85678	88.09086	1288660
777	603 729	27.87472	88.14760	1287001
778	605 284	27.89265	88.20431	1285347
779	606 841	27.90157	88.26098	1283697
780	608 400	27.92848	88.31761	1282051
781	609 961	27.94638	88.37420	1280410
782	611 524	27.96426	88.43076	1278772
783	613 089	27.98214	88.48729	1277139
784	614 656	28.00000	88.54377	1275510
785	616 225	28.01785	88.60023	1273885
786	617 796	28.03569	88.65664	1272265
787	619 369	28.05352	88.71302	1270648
788	620 944	28.07134	88.76936	1269036
789	622 521	28.08914	88.82567	1267427
790	624 100	28.10694	88.88194	1265823
791	625 681	28.12472	88.93818	1264223
792	627 264	28.14249	88.99438	1262626
793	628 849	28.16026	89.05055	1261034
794	630 436	28.17801	89.10668	1259446
795	632 025	28.19574	89.16277	1257862
796	633 616	28.21347	89.21883	1256281
797	635 209	28.23119	89.27486	1254705
798	636 804	28.24889	89.33085	1253133
799	638 401	28.26659	89.38680	1251564
800	640 000	28.28427	89.44272	1250000

Appendix Q (cont.)

SQUARES, SQUARE ROOTS, AND RECIPROCALS 1-1000

N	N^2	$\sqrt{N}$	$\sqrt{10N}$	1/N .00
800	640 000	28.28427	89.44272	1250000
801	641 601	28.30194	89.49860	1248439
802	643 204	28.31960	89.55445	1246883
803	644 809	28.33725	89.61027	1245330
804	646 416	28.35489	89.66605	1243781
805	648 025	28.37252	89.72179	1242236
806	649 636	28.39014	89.77750	1240695
807	651 249	28.40775	89.83318	1239157
808	652 864	28.42534	89.88882	1237624
809	654 481	28.44293	89.94443	1236094
810	656 100	28.46050	90.00000	1234568
811	657 721	28.47806	90.05554	1233046
812	659 344	28.49561	90.11104	1231527
813	660 969	28.51315	90.16651	1230012
814	662 596	28.53069	90.22195	1228501
815	664 225	28.54820	90.27735	1226994
816	665 856	28.56571	90.33272	1225490
817	667 489	28.58321	90.38805	1223990
818	669 124	28.60070	90.44335	1222494
819	670 761	28.61818	90.49862	1221001
820	672 400	28.63564	90.55385	1219512
821	674 041	28.65310	90.60905	1218027
822	675 684	28.67054	90.66422	1216545
823	677 329	28.68798	90.71935	1215067
824	678 976	28.70540	90.77445	1213592
825	680 625	28.72281	90.82951	1212121
826	682 276	28.74022	90.88454	1210654
827	683 929	28.75761	90.93954	1209190
828	685 584	28.77499	90.99451	1207729
829	687 241	28.79236	91.04944	1206273
830	688 900	28.80972	91.10434	1204819
831	690 561	28.82707	91.15920	1203369
832	692 224	28.84441	91.21403	1201923
833	693 889	28.86174	91.26883	1200480
834	695 556	28.87906	91.32360	1199041
835	697 225	28.89637	91.37833	1197605
836	698 896	28.91366	91.43304	1196172
837	700 569	28.93095	91.48770	1194743
838	702 244	28.94823	91.54234	1193317
839	703 921	28.96550	91.59694	1191895
840	705 600	28.98275	91.65151	1190476
841	707 281	29.00000	91.70605	1189061
842	708 964	29.01724	91.76056	1187648
843	710 649	29.03446	91.81503	1186240
844	712 336	29.05168	91.86947	1184834
845	714 025	29.06888	91.92388	1183432
846	715 716	29.08608	91.97826	1182033
847	717 409	29.10326	92.03260	1180638
848	719 104	29.12044	92.08692	1179245
849	720 801	29.13760	92.14120	1177856
850	722 500	29.15476	92.19544	1176471

Appendix Q (cont.)

SQUARES, SQUARE ROOTS, AND RECIPROCALS 1–1000

N	N²	√N	√10N	1/N .00
850	722 500	29.15476	92.19544	1176471
851	724 201	29.17190	92.24966	1175088
852	725 904	29.18904	92.30385	1173709
853	727 609	29.20616	92.35800	1172333
854	729 316	29.22328	92.41212	1170960
855	731 025	29.24038	92.46621	1169591
856	732 736	29.25748	92.52027	1168224
857	734 449	29.27456	92.57429	1166861
858	736 164	29.29164	92.62829	1165501
859	737 881	29.30870	92.68225	1164144
860	739 600	29.32576	92.73618	1162791
861	741 321	29.34280	92.79009	1161440
862	743 044	29.35984	92.84396	1160093
863	744 769	29.37686	92.89779	1158749
864	746 496	29.39388	92.95160	1157407
865	748 225	29.41088	93.00538	1156069
866	749 956	29.42788	93.05912	1154734
867	751 689	29.44486	93.11283	1153403
868	753 424	29.46184	93.16652	1152074
869	755 161	29.47881	93.22017	1150748
870	756 900	29.49576	93.27379	1149425
871	758 641	29.51271	93.32738	1148106
872	760 384	29.52965	93.38094	1146789
873	762 129	29.54657	93.43447	1145475
874	763 876	29.56349	93.48797	1144165
875	765 625	29.58040	93.54143	1142857
876	767 376	29.59730	93.59487	1141553
877	769 129	29.61419	93.64828	1140251
878	770 884	29.63106	93.70165	1138952
879	772 641	29.64793	93.75500	1137656
880	774 400	29.66479	93.80832	1136364
881	776 161	29.68164	93.86160	1135074
882	777 924	29.69848	93.91486	1133787
883	779 689	29.71532	93.96808	1132503
884	781 456	29.73214	94.02127	1131222
885	783 225	29.74895	94.07444	1129944
886	784 996	29.76575	94.12757	1128668
887	786 769	29.78255	94.18068	1127396
888	788 544	29.79933	94.23375	1126126
889	790 321	29.81610	94.28680	1124859
890	792 100	29.83287	94.33981	1123596
891	793 881	29.84962	94.39280	1122334
892	795 664	29.86637	94.44575	1121076
893	797 449	29.88311	94.49868	1119821
894	799 236	29.89983	94.55157	1118568
895	801 025	29.91655	94.60444	1117318
896	802 816	29.93326	94.65728	1116071
897	804 609	29.94996	94.71008	1114827
898	806 404	29.96665	94.76286	1113586
899	808 201	29.98333	94.81561	1112347
900	810 000	30.00000	94.86833	1111111

Appendix Q (*cont.*)

SQUARES, SQUARE ROOTS, AND RECIPROCALS 1–1000

N	N^2	$\sqrt{N}$	$\sqrt{10N}$	1/N .00
900	810 000	30.00000	94.86833	1111111
901	811 801	30.01666	94.92102	1109878
902	813 604	30.03331	94.97368	1108647
903	815 409	30.04996	95.02631	1107420
904	817 216	30.06659	95.07891	1106195
905	819 025	30.08322	95.13149	1104972
906	820 836	30.09983	95.18403	1103753
907	822 649	30.11644	95.23655	1102536
908	824 464	30.13304	95.28903	1101322
909	826 281	30.14963	95.34149	1100110
910	828 100	30.16621	95.39392	1098901
911	829 921	30.18278	95.44632	1097695
912	831 744	30.19934	95.49869	1096491
913	833 569	30.21589	95.55103	1095290
914	835 396	30.23243	95.60335	1094092
915	837 225	30.24897	95.65563	1092896
916	839 056	30.26549	95.70789	1091703
917	840 889	30.28201	95.76012	1090513
918	842 724	30.29851	95.81232	1089325
919	844 561	30.31501	95.86449	1088139
920	846 400	30.33150	95.91663	1086957
921	848 241	30.34798	95.96874	1085776
922	850 084	30.36445	96.02083	1084599
923	851 929	30.38092	96.07289	1083424
924	853 776	30.39737	96.12492	1082251
925	855 625	30.41381	96.17692	1081081
926	857 476	30.43025	96.22889	1079914
927	859 329	30.44667	96.28084	1078749
928	861 184	30.46309	96.33276	1077586
929	863 041	30.47950	96.38465	1076426
930	864 900	30.49590	96.43651	1075269
931	866 761	30.51229	96.48834	1074114
932	868 624	30.52868	96.54015	1072961
933	870 489	30.54505	96.59193	1071811
934	872 356	30.56141	96.64368	1070664
935	874 225	30.57777	96.69540	1069519
936	876 096	30.59412	96.74709	1068376
937	877 969	30.61046	96.79876	1067236
938	879 844	30.62679	96.85040	1066098
939	881 721	30.64311	96.90201	1064963
940	883 600	30.65942	96.95360	1063830
941	885 481	30.67572	97.00515	1062699
942	887 364	30.69202	97.05668	1061571
943	889 249	30.70831	97.10819	1060445
944	891 136	30.72458	97.15966	1059322
945	893 025	30.74085	97.21111	1058201
946	894 916	30.75711	97.26253	1057082
947	896 809	30.77337	97.31393	1055966
948	898 704	30.78961	97.36529	1054852
949	900 601	30.80584	97.41663	1053741
950	902 500	30.82207	97.46794	1052632

Appendix Q (cont.)

SQUARES, SQUARE ROOTS, AND RECIPROCALS 1–1000

N	N²	√N	√10N	1/N .00
950	902 500	30.82207	97.46794	1052632
951	904 401	30.83829	97.51923	1051525
952	906 304	30.85450	97.57049	1050420
953	908 209	30.87070	97.62172	1049318
954	910 116	30.88689	97.67292	1048218
955	912 025	30.90307	97.72410	1047120
956	913 936	30.91925	97.77525	1046025
957	915 849	30.93542	97.82638	1044932
958	917 764	30.95158	97.87747	1043841
959	919 681	30.96773	97.92855	1042753
960	921 600	30.98387	97.97959	1041667
961	923 521	31.00000	98.03061	1040583
962	925 444	31.01612	98.08160	1039501
963	927 369	31.03224	98.13256	1038422
964	929 296	31.04835	98.18350	1037344
965	931 225	31.06445	98.23441	1036269
966	933 156	31.08054	89.28530	1035197
967	935 089	31.09662	98.33616	1034126
968	937 024	31.11270	98.38699	1033058
969	938 961	31.12876	98.43780	1031992
970	940 900	31.14482	98.48858	1030928
971	942 841	31.16087	98.53933	1029866
972	944 784	31.17691	98.59006	1028807
973	946 729	31.19295	98.64076	1027749
974	948 676	31.20897	98.69144	1026694
975	950 625	31.22499	98.74209	1025641
976	952 576	31.24100	98.79271	1024590
977	954 529	31.25700	98.84331	1023541
978	956 484	31.27299	98.89388	1022495
979	958 441	31.28898	98.94443	1021450
980	960 400	31.30495	98.99495	1020408
981	962 361	31.32092	99.04544	1019368
982	964 324	31.33688	99.09591	1018330
983	966 289	31.35283	99.14636	1017294
984	968 256	31.36877	99.19677	1016260
985	970 225	31.38471	99.24717	1015228
986	972 196	31.40064	99.29753	1014199
987	974 169	31.41656	99.34787	1013171
988	976 144	31.43247	99.39819	1012146
989	978 121	31.44837	99.44848	1011122
990	980 100	31.46427	99.49874	1010101
991	982 081	31.48015	99.54898	1009082
992	984 064	31.49603	99.59920	1008065
993	986 049	31.51190	99.64939	1007049
994	988 036	31.52777	99.69955	1006036
995	990 025	31.54362	99.74969	1005025
996	992 016	31.55947	99.79980	1004016
997	994 009	31.57531	99.84989	1003009
998	996 004	31.59114	99.89995	1002004
999	998 001	31.60696	99.94999	1001001
1000	1 000 000	31.62278	100.00000	1000000

Index

A

Addition theorem:
  for mutually exclusive events, 14
  for probabilities, 13
Alpha and beta errors, 141
Analysis of variance, 297–327
  assumptions, 298–300
  compared with chi square association
    test, 297
  compared with discriminant analysis, 401,
    402
  components-of-variance model, 307
  in correlation, multiple, 395–398
  design of experiments, 298
  in discriminant analysis, 413
  expected mean squares, 307, 310, 319
  factorial experiments, 315
    alternative significance tests, 319
    computation formulas for sums of
      squares, 317
    confounding, 316
    degrees of freedom, 319
    estimators for parameters, 320
    expected mean squares, 319
    factorial treatment arrangement, 316
    interaction, 317, 321
    replication, 316, 320
    response graphs, 321
    significance tests, 319
    statistical model, 317

M